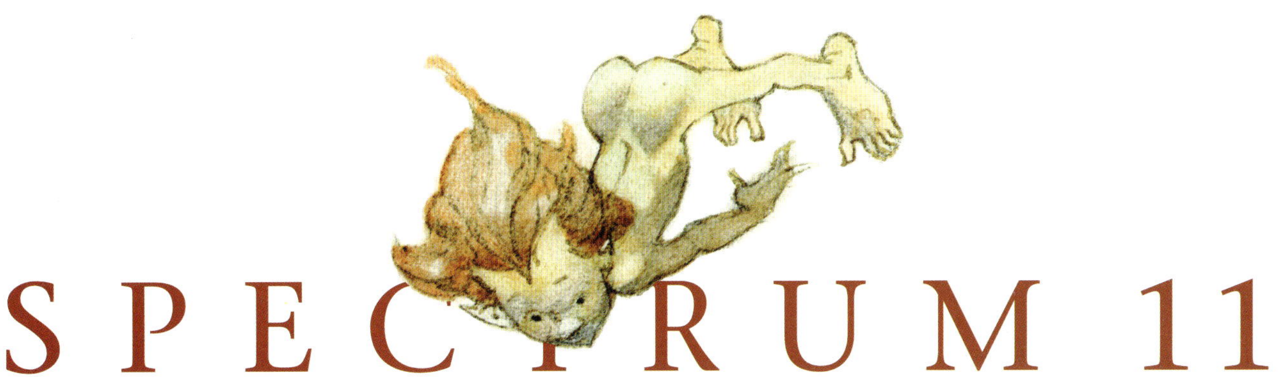

SPECTRUM 11

The Best In Contemporary Fantastic Art

Edited by Cathy Fenner & Arnie Fenner

UNDERWOOD BOOKS
Nevada City, CA • 2004

Chairman's Message

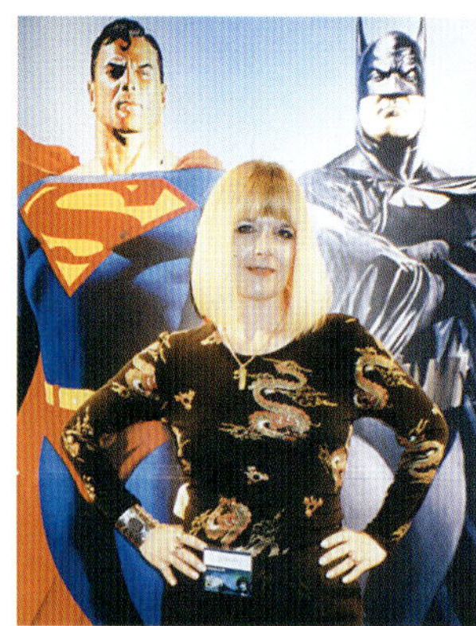

How time flies!

It's hard for us to comprehend, but with the publication of *Spectrum 11* we begin our second decade of the competition. It seems like only yesterday that we were wandering around the artists' alleys and art shows at conventions, shaking hands with the illustrators while they looked at us with raised eyebrows and tried to decide if we and our ideas for *Spectrum* were worth taking a chance on. We were ten years younger then and had a lot more energy (and more hair and a few less pounds), but our love for the idea for an annual "best of the year" collection has not diminished with time and experience at all—in fact it's only become stronger.

As long-time readers and participants will notice, with this volume we have moved to a slightly larger format. At 9"X12" and a few more pages our intent is to provide a better showcase for the artists. Hopefully there will be fewer cramped pages and a little more "creative white space" to give the eye some respite without compromising on the size of the art. It is our goal to always keep trying to improve and freshen the book: the field of fantastic art is exciting and constantly changing and we want *Spectrum* to reflect that energy and evolution. In an effort to more readily make information and news available and to help make contacting us much faster and easier, we finally created an official *Spectrum* website [www.spectrumfantasticart.com] late last year. (It took so long for us to go online because, hey! in case you haven't noticed, we've been busy!) We are always ready to listen to suggestions and concerns from readers and artists alike.

The 2004 judging event took place as usual over the final weekend in February. The weather gods smiled on us this year and none of the jurors had any problems flying into Kansas City or departing. We moved the competition to the Hyatt Regency Crown Center for the first time and were very pleased with the service and results. Set up in a ballroom containing sixty tables, the jurors moved around the room all day, dropping a bean in an inverted cup for art they thought exceptional: they had to evaluate just shy of 4000 works. Each judge surveyed the entries independently and discussions of the work during that phase of the voting was discouraged. When votes had been cast in the final category, art that had been singled out for award consideration (by a juror dropping a paperclip in the cup along with their voting bean) was brought back out. There were a number of lively discussions this year concerning the virtues (or lack of same) of each piece, but a consensus was reached and awards were presented in each category.

Assisting Arnie and I this year in tabulating votes, setting the room, and keeping the proceedings moving along were Armen Davis, Gillian Titus, Terry Lee, Lucy Moreno and her daughter Lucy Moreno. Without the help of the people who give up their Saturday each year *Spectrum* would not be possible—there is no way Arnie and myself could possibly do it all.

As with every previous volume of *Spectrum,* this book is only made possible by the active participation of the artists (both those selected for the book and of those that disappointingly were not) and to the readers that purchase each edition. This book, this project, belongs to all of you. To everyone we again humbly extend our warmest thanks for allowing us to be a part of this community.

—Cathy Fenner/Show Co-Chairman

Corrections: The back cover to *Spectrum 10* was wrongly credited to Michael Swanland. The correct credit should have read ***Raymond* Swanland**. The contact information in *Spectrum 10's* artist index for **Mick Wood** was incorrect. The artist may be contacted at: Mick Wood, c/o Michael F. Heintzelman, Pelennor Fields, 802 Rising Star Dr., Henderson, NV 89014. 702-451-7282 e-mail: pelennorfields@earthlink.net.

Trade Softcover Edition ISBN 1-887424-82-2
Hardcover Edition ISBN 1-887424-81-4
10 9 8 7 6 5 4 3 2 1

Artists, art directors, and publishers interested in receiving entry information for the next Spectrum competition should send their name and address to:

Spectrum Design, P.O. Box 4422, Overland Park, KS 66204

Or visit the official website for information & printable PDF entry forms: **www.spectrumfantasticart.com**

Call For Entries posters (which contain complete rules, list of fees, and forms for participation) are mailed out in October each year.

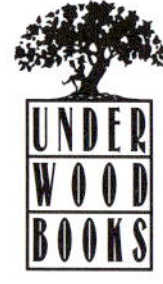

Published by **UNDERWOOD BOOKS**, P.O. BOX 1919, NEVADA CITY, CA 95959
www.underwoodbooks.com
Tim Underwood/Publisher

The Jury

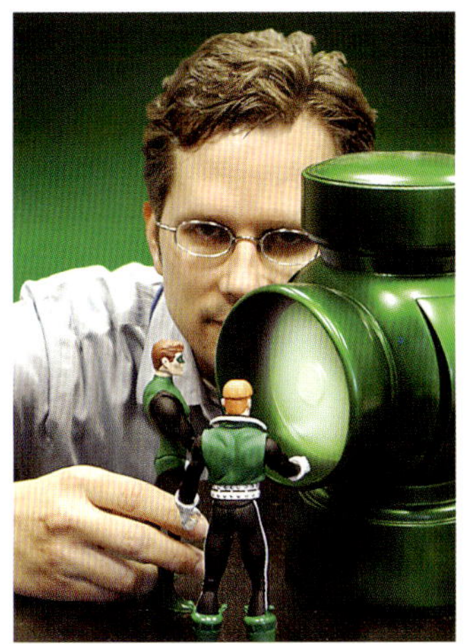

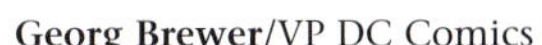

Georg Brewer/VP DC Comics

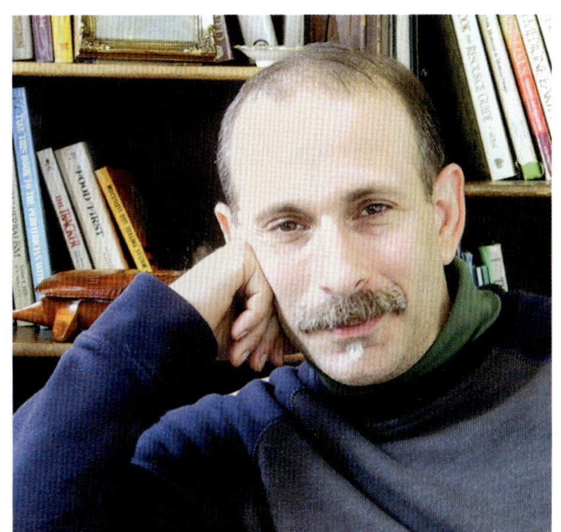

Joseph DeVito/Artist

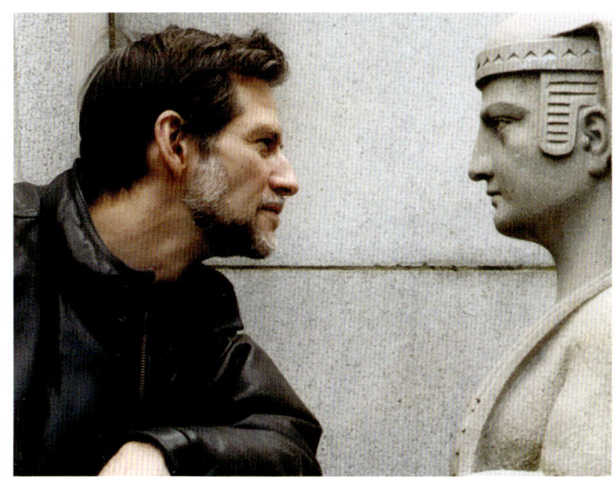

Gary Gianni/Artist

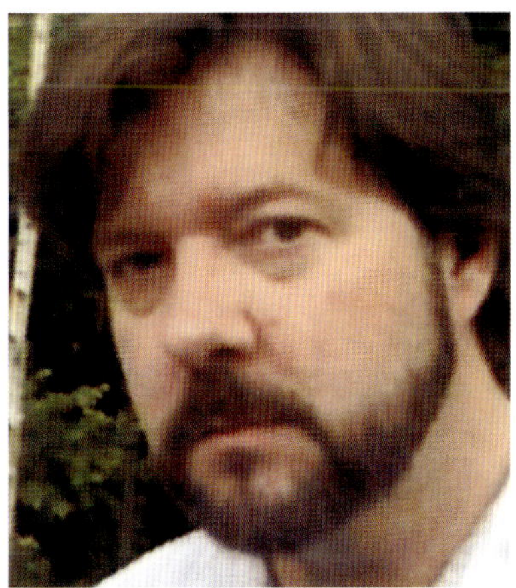

John Jude Palencar/Artist

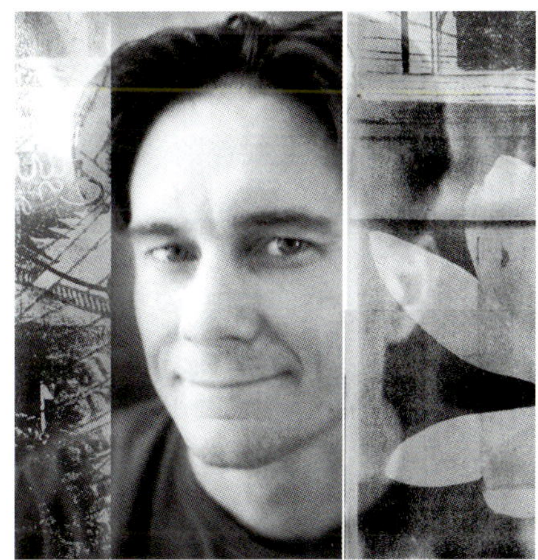

Greg Spalenka/Artist

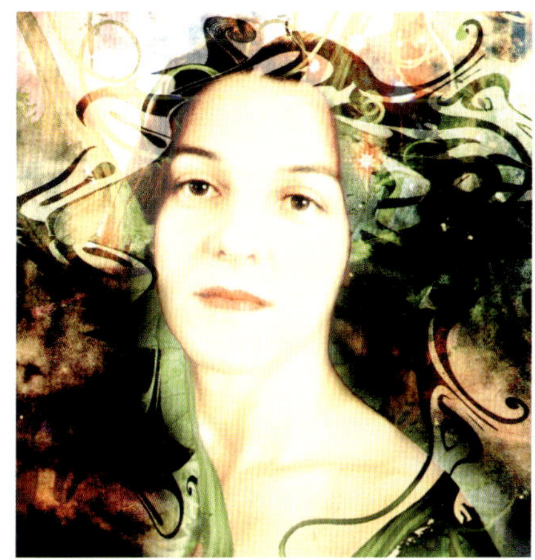

Roxana Villa/Artist

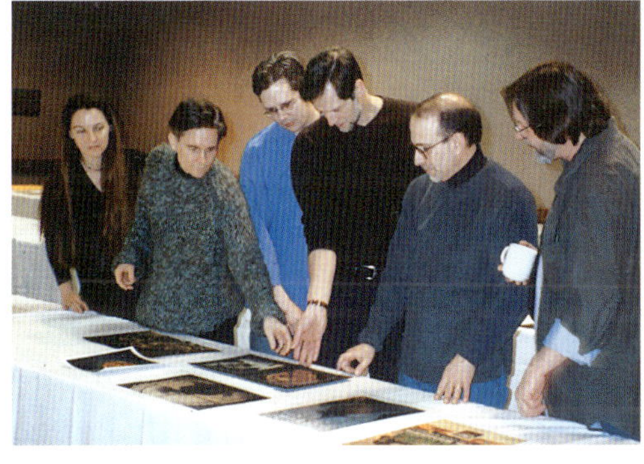

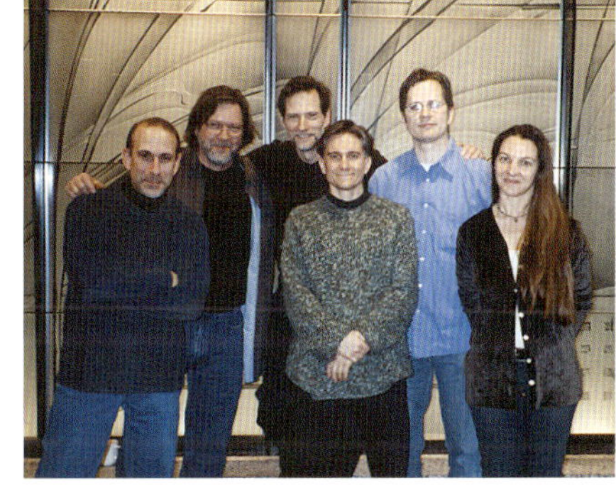

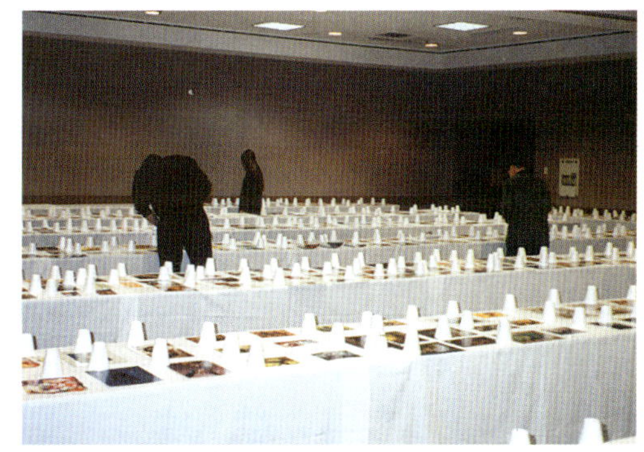

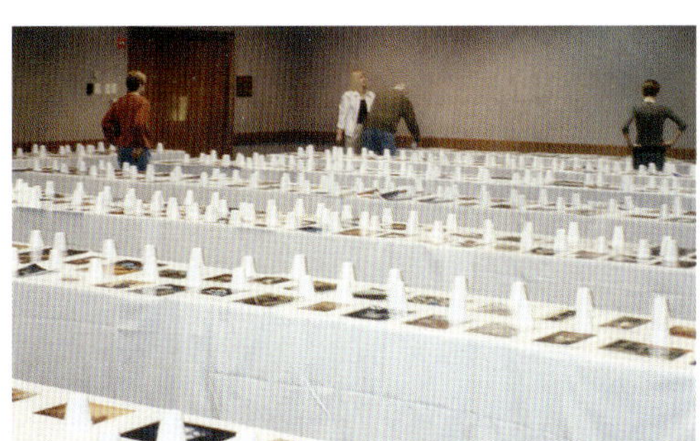

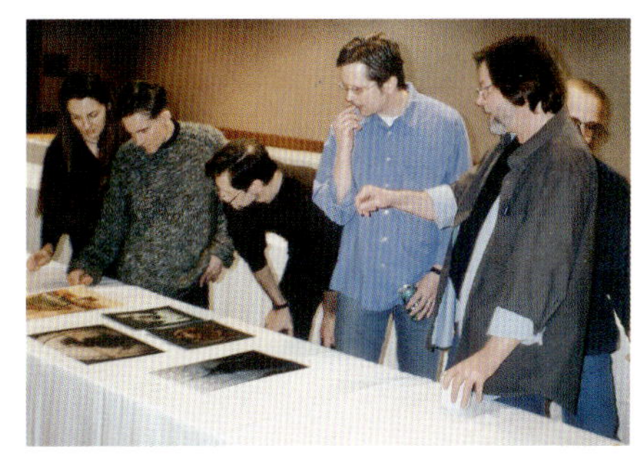

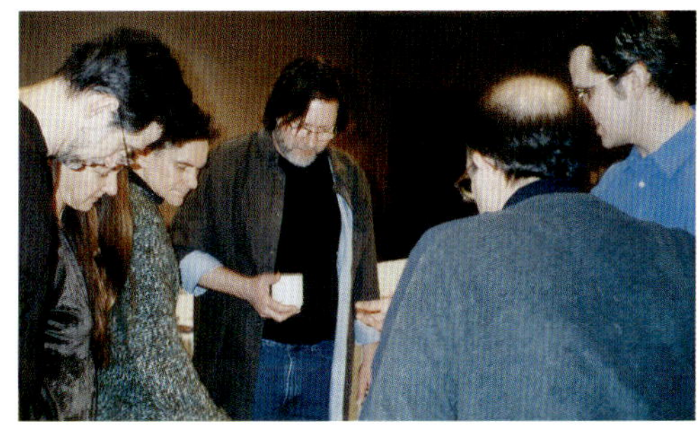

GRAND MASTER
Michael R. Whelan

born 1950/Culver City, CA

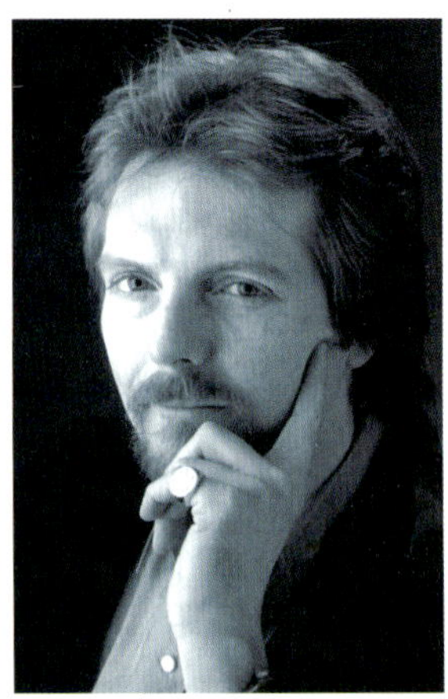

There was a time—not too terribly long ago, actually—when fantasy and science fiction were relatively tiny parts of the publishers' lines. Just as it was simple to buy and read every book the field had to offer (and have money left over), you could just as easily count the number of artists regularly painting genre covers on your fingers. And, if you wanted to consider only those who were any good...well, there were really only a handful who could not only draw and paint well, but who would create work that transcended the confines of its subject matter.

Suddenly in the mid-1970s there was a buzz in the F&SF field: DAW books was making serious noises as a genre-specific publishing company and others were energetically creating imprints (like Random House's Del Rey) and ramping up their lines. Ian and Betty Ballantine created the Peacock Press for Bantam books and began packaging a stunning selection of art books (including first titles by Frank Frazetta and James Bama). Hollywood started to pay attention to science fiction again after many years of benign neglect and there were rumors about a new movie—something called *Star Wars*—which had a heretofore unheard of budget of $8 million! And there was a pack of new artists, weaned on comics and B-movies and anxious to shake off the confines of art school, eager to prove themselves, ready to burst on the scene and take the field by storm.

Michael Whelan led the charge.

Born in Culver City, California, in 1950, Michael ("Mike" just doesn't seem to fit) grew up in a varicty of locations. The son of an aerospace engineer, the family relocated frequently throughout his youth. Bouncing between Colorado and California the one constant was his imagination and interest in drawing. "When I was eight," Whelan recalls, "our family was packing up to move and my father overturned the coffeetable to discover the control panel for a spaceship drawn on the underside, complete with a viewscreen featuring a lunar landscape! You see, in all the space movies I'd seen, the astronauts were reclining when they took off...I'll bet my parents wondered why I spent so much time lying under the furniture and talking to myself. There's no doubt in my mind that my parents were the first to become cognizant of my interest in drawing. Whether they thought it was worth anything is another story."

During high school he attended summer classes at the Rocky Mountain School of Art in Denver; while attending San Jose State University he studied biology and art with the intention of eventually taking pre-med and becoming a doctor. But his interest in art and his natural abilities inevitably led him to change his major. After graduating Whelan continued his formal education at the Art Center College of Design in Los Angeles in 1974. Always drawing, always painting, always learning, Michael would entertain himself by sketching remembered scenes from films like *The Mysterians* and *The War of the Worlds* or by illustrating his favorite books. "The tuition at the Art Center were enormous," he remembers. "As the summer of '74 wound on, I was doing more work for myself and one by one dropping out of my classes, wondering what my next move should be. Then it happened. I was absentmindedly walking down a corridor at the Art Center when I happened to see a notice for the San Diego Comic Con, inviting submissions to the convention's art show. I spent a week or so matting up some of my better pieces and went down to San Diego to put up the work. I couldn't afford to stay for the convention, but when I went back to pick up my work I found—to my utter astonishment—that everything had sold. (Having everything priced under fifteen dollars might have had something to do with it.) Nevertheless, it was a vote of confidence that buoyed my spirits immensely. I also met someone there who offered to take some of my work to the World SF Convention in Washington the following month."

Michael was just as flabbergasted when his new friend returned from WorldCon with a first place award for his painting of a spaceship passing an asteroid, "Outbound." He was also immediately contacted by Thomas Schluck, a German agent who had seen his work in the art show, offering to represent him in Europe. "Those two events gave me enough confidence to send slides to two New York publishers. Donald Wollheim of DAW Books wrote back expressing an interest in my work. And the rest, as they say..."

Is history. Cramming most of his possessions into his Volkswagen (including a selection of new pieces for his portfolio), Michael headed cross-country to New York. Quickly landing assignments from DAW and Ace Books (as well as selling publication rights to several sample pieces to Marvel Comics), Whelan's professional career was off and running at warp speed.

Thirty years later he is undoubtedly the most popular, most honored creator of fantastic art. Hugos, World Fantasy Awards, medals from the Society of Illustrators and Spectrum: his list of honors is as long as your arm. The subject of three bestselling books (the first, *Wonderworks*, appeared in 1979, slightly less than five years after his art first began to show up in print), acknowledged as the "go-to" guy when publishers wanted that special jacket art to help push an author onto the bestseller lists, popular as a lecturer and as a visiting teacher, Michael Whelan helped change the face of fantasy, horror, and science fiction for a new generation of readers and artists. Switching easily between oils and acrylics (with an occasional excursion into the digital realm just because he can), adept with pencil, brush, and airbrush, Michael helped to bring literal, narrative covers back into vogue. Art featuring accurate depictions of characters, beautifully designed and impeccably painted in a fresh, contemporary style are the trademarks of a Whelan. He raised the bar of excellence for his fellow artists at the same time he inspired them to simply be better illustrators for the pure joy of doing good work. His love of the field—and camaraderie with fellow painters—led him to join with Wayne Barlowe to organize the first major show of F&SF art in the U.S. at the Society of Illustrators Gallery in 1984 (it was that show and our subsequent conversations with Michael over a number of years which helped lead to the creation of *Spectrum*).

His artistic restlessness and personal interests have led him to periodically take time from his commercial assignments to paint Fine Art (unofficially referred to as his "Passages" works). And he has achieved admirable success in the gallery art market (hardly a surprise). As thoughtful, mysterious, and evocative as these canvases are, it would be a mistake to interpret them as the "real" Whelan, as an indication of his desire to put his illustration career behind him. That's not the way he thinks.

Michael Whelan simply loves to create, sometimes for a client, sometimes only for himself. It's not *what* the art is for or how others will categorize it that matters; what matters is the joy he feels while standing in front a blank canvas, brush in hand, and the inspiration magically *comes*.

Michael is a storyteller, a craftsman, an innovator, and a leader. On this tenth anniversary of the first Grand Master Award, we can think of no one more deserving of this recognition. †

Spectrum Grand Masters

1995	1996	1997	1998	1999	2000	2001	2002	2003	2004
Frank Frazetta b. 1928	Don Ivan Punchatz b. 1936	Leo & Diane Dillon b. 1933	James Bama b. 1926	John Berkey b. 1932	Alan Lee b. 1947	Jean Giraud b. 1938	Kinuko Y. Craft b. 1940	Michael Wm. Kaluta b. 1947	Michael Whelan b. 1950

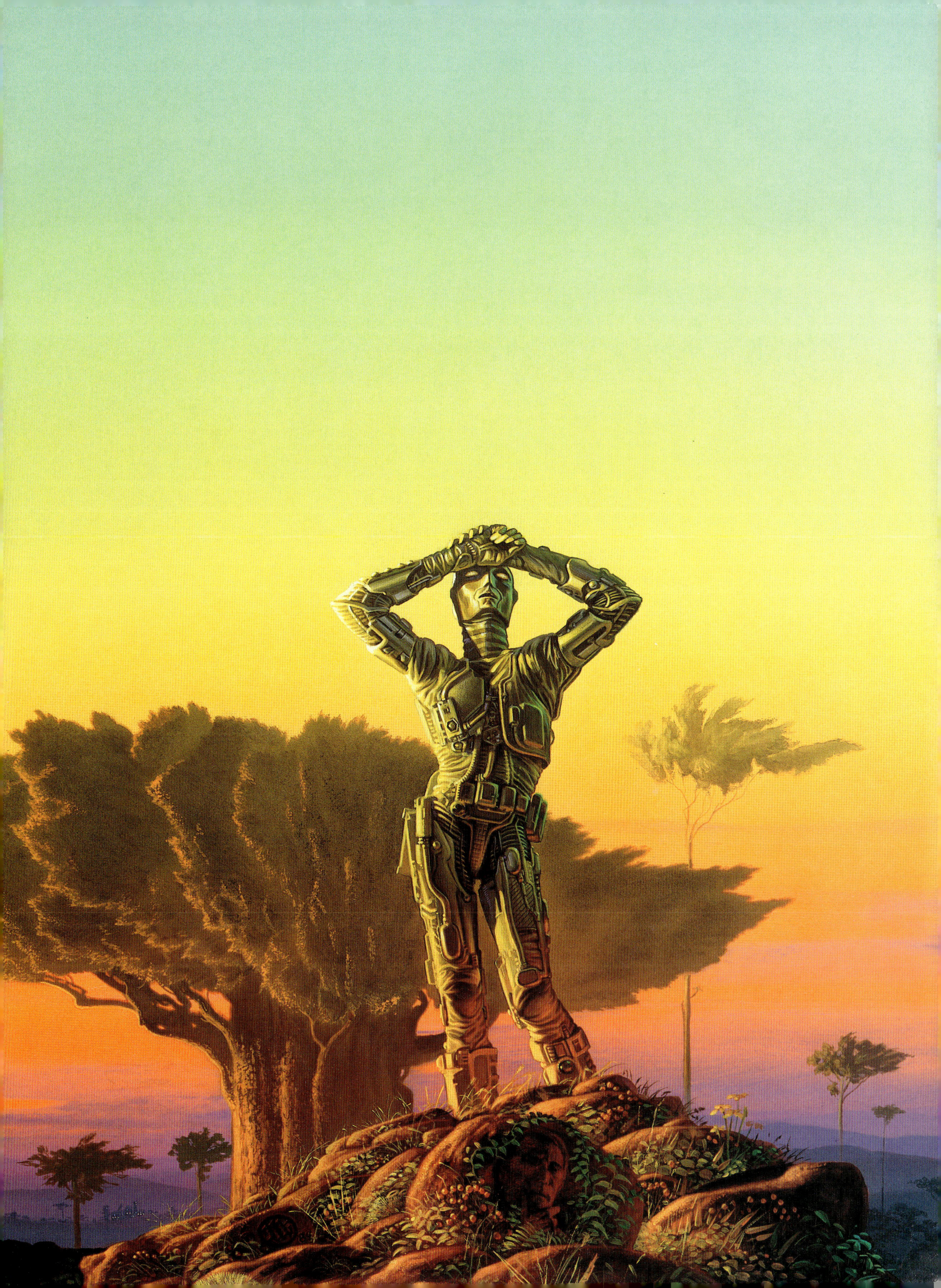

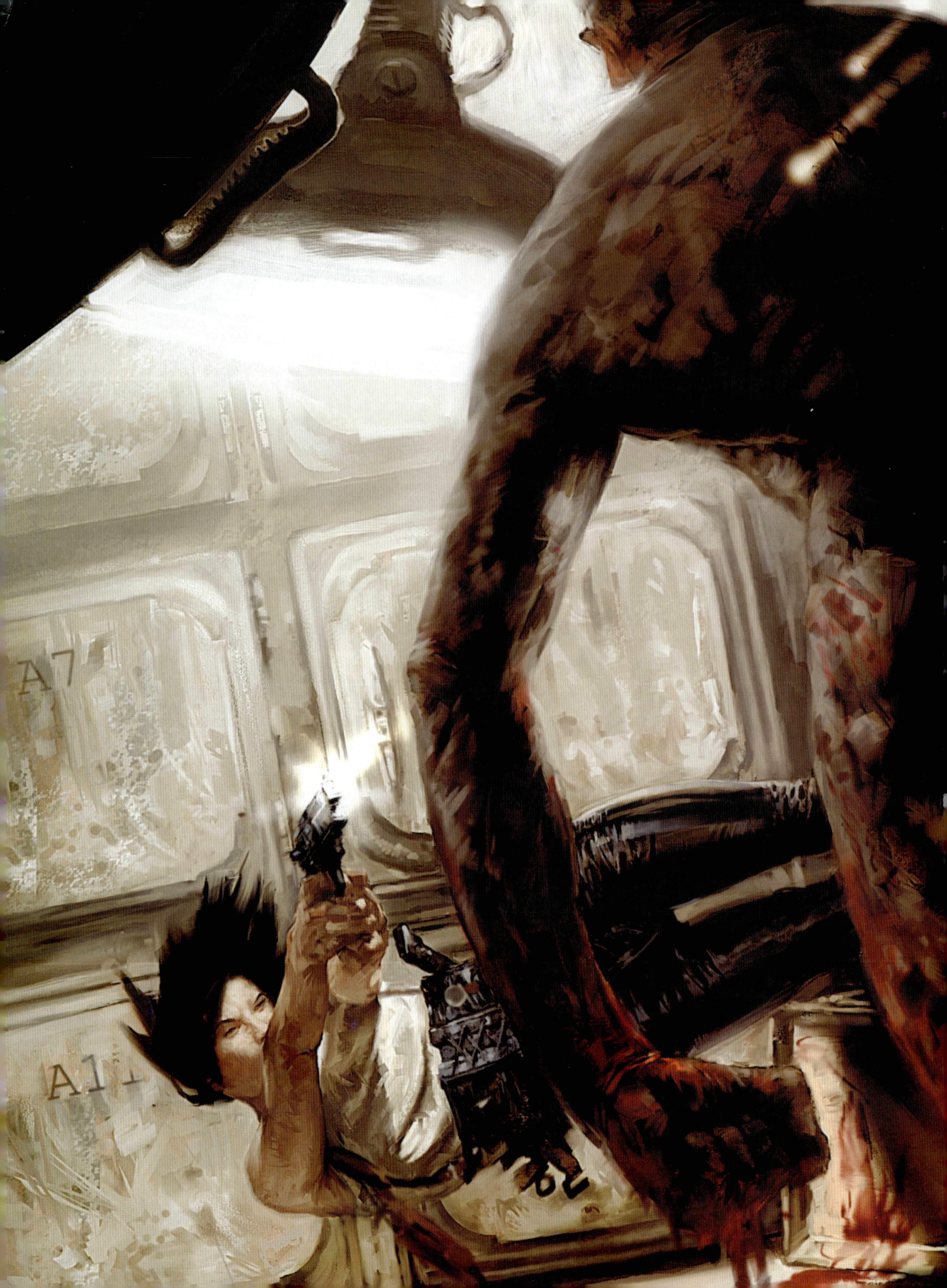
A7
A11

2003 The Year In Review

BY ARNIE FENNER

"We're the baddest-assed sons of bitches that ever jogged in Reeboks. We're three-quarters grizzly bear and two-thirds car wreck and descended from a stock market crash on our mother's side. You take your Germany, France, Spain, roll them together and it wouldn't give us room to park our cars. We're the big boys, Jack, the original, giant, economy-sized, new and improved butt kickers of all time. When we snort coke in Houston, people lose their hats in Cap d'Antibes. And we've got an American Express Card credit limit higher than your piss-ant metric numbers go."

—*P.J. O'Rourke* **Holidays In Hell**

After months of finger pointing, accusations, speeches, and ultimatums; after a year of posturing and denials, rhetoric, protests, and rallys, the Yanks, Brits, Aussies, and Poles in unison cried "Havoc!" and unleashed the dogs of war on Saddam Hussein's Iraq. The Abrams and Bradleys rolled, the B-2s and Apaches took to the air, and the battle [a] against terrorism, [b] for Iraqi freedom, [c] for oil, [d] of Christian conquest, or [e] _________ (fill in the blank). . .was on. (The "correct" answer to the "why" question about Gulf War 2 probably depends upon your political point of view.)

Certainly, the outcome was inevitable.

Though there were criticisms voiced by the instant-gratification pack of armchair generals (who simply couldn't understand "what's taking so long" and interpreted the Iraqi army actually putting up a sporadic defense as being a failure of the coalition's troops and planning) and those with anti-war sentiments expressed their outrage, there were two things everyone had to agree on when Baghdad fell on April 7 (two weeks after the war's start):

First, no one's going to miss Saddam or his sadistic sons, Uday and Quasay.

Second, Iraq is going to be a mess for many years to come. (Anyone who thinks otherwise should explain how the Clinton administration's one-year deployment of troops to Bosnia and Kosovo in 1995 has lasted for the better part of a decade...and counting.)

That's not to say the war should or shouldn't have been waged—I'm not weighing in on one side or the other—but only restating the obvious. Winning the war can be the easy part: winning the *peace* is what's usually hard (as the occupying soldiers have found).

Right or wrong, justified or not, the war in Iraq was just one more divisive event that widened the political fissure in America, contributed to international tensions, and negatively impacted global economies. Bush detractors in this country and abroad had more reasons and opportunities to express their anger, while the President's supporters...were usually on the defensive. But the harsh reality is that regardless of which side of the political fence you found yourself on, what's done is done. And given that truth, there is no moral alternative other than to stick it out and rebuild the country, no matter what it costs, no matter how long it takes. Like it or lump it, we—the U.S., it's allies, and the people of Iraq—are "stuck."

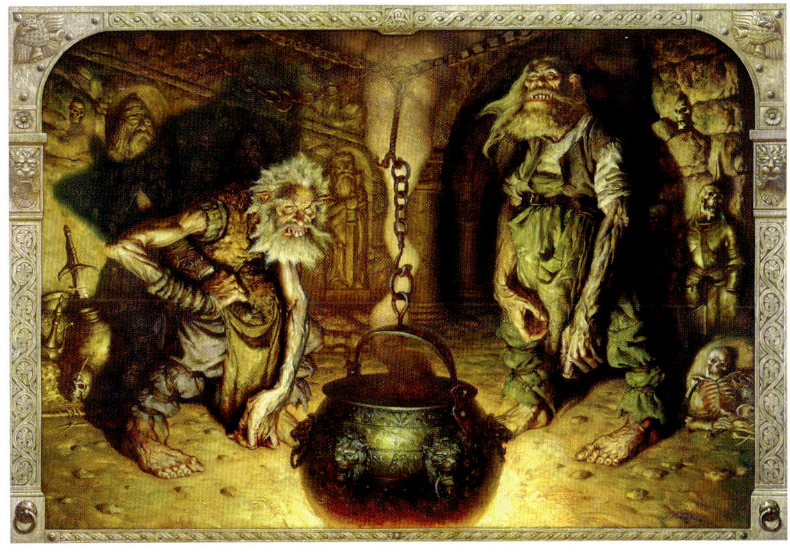

Facing page: Jon Foster collaborated with Dave Dorman on this exciting illustration for *The Uninvited* by Del Stone Jr. [6 3/4"x 10 1/4", digital.] *Above:* Petar Meseldžija created this stunning painting for a retelling of the classic folk tale, *A Lengend Called Steel-Bashow.* [39 1/2"x 27 1/2", oils.]

Naturally, numerous questions have been raised regarding the intelligence that was presented to help legitimize military action in the first place; queries about the hampering of U.N. weapons inspectors by both sides and the subsequent failure of occupying forces to find the weapons of mass-destruction that Saddam Hussein (at one point, at least) and President Bush both insisted were hiding some place in the desert, ready to be used. (Ha-ha. Joke's on us!) But the *one* question no one seemed to be asking—except me, anyway—as A.P. photos were posted on news websites, printed in magazines, and shown on television was this:

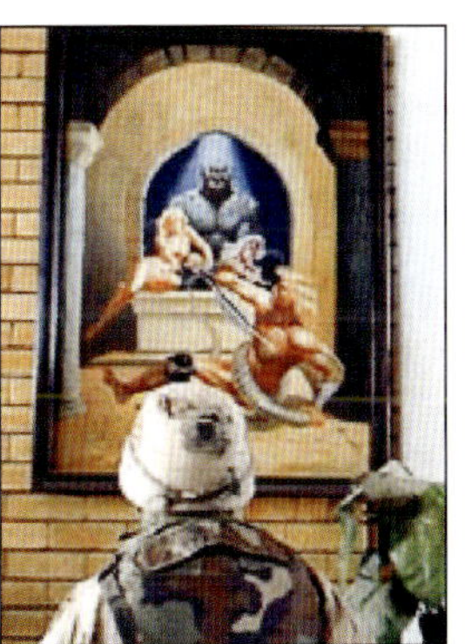

A U.S. Marine "admires" the Hussein Bros. art collection in Baghdad. A.P.

Why oh why did Uday and Quasay Hussein have to decorate their swingers apartments with fantasy art?

Shag carpets. Black-light fixtures. Fur-covered sofas. Rowena Morrell art (either originals or forgeries) hanging on the walls. (Other pictures weren't identifiable.)

Awww crap.

Even the *frames* were tacky, for chrissakes. Why couldn't they have been like other thugs and stuck up posters of girls in wet tee-shirts sitting on Corvettes? You work and work to try to get people to take fantasy art seriously only to have these clowns give the world something to make fun of. Yeesh. It'll be just the luck if it's revealed that executors found Kelly Freas paintings while cataloging the late tin-pot dictator Idi Amin's estate...

Though the war in—and occupation of—Iraq dominated the news in 2003, there were a host of other unfortunate events that could, when looked at with a jaundiced eye, form the basis of the next Lemony Snicket novel. The break-up of the Columbia as it reentered the atmosphere over Texas on February 1 and deaths of her seven astronauts shut down the shuttle program and left NASA scrambling for ways to support the construction of the space station while insuring the safety of future missions. An unusual summer heat wave throughout Europe (where air conditioning isn't especially common or usually necessary and ice in their drinks is an American affectation) caused a horrifying number of weather-related fatalities, including 15,000 in France alone! A massive power failure in August blacked out parts of Canada and eight states from the midwest to the eastern seaboard—and left politicians on both sides of the border pointing accusatory fingers at each other. Unemployment in the U.S. reached a nine-year high, the Chinese government finally warned the world of the SARS epidemic and restricted travel, civil war raged in Liberia, the Taliban started to pop their heads up in Afghanistan, predatory business practices drove some retailers out of business and left others barely hanging on (thank Wal-Mart and Target for driving K-B Toys and FAO Schwarz under last Christmas), the music industry started suing individuals for downloading songs to and from the Internet and... movie star Arnold Schwarzenegger became governor of California?!? Wow. The first few years of the new millennium have turned out to be even odder than any of the psychics predicted! With a sure-to-be contentious presidential election slated for November 2004, it's bound to get even *more* interesting.

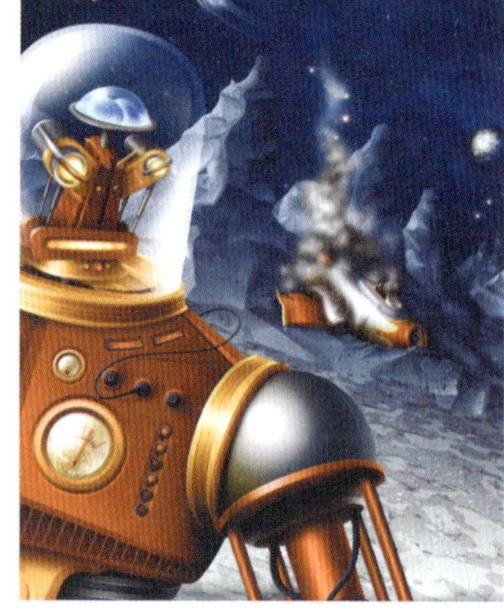

This dandy robot was created by Tyson Mangelsdorf as a promotion for American Showcase.

Of course, good things happened in 2003. That's a given. It's just that there was a lot going on in the U.S. and in the world that made things difficult for everyone, including artists, their employers, and their fans. When the power goes out, you can't paint in the dark or burn a disc or print your book or track your order. When you're worried about the safety of your friends or family, when you're concerned about your livelihood and the bills that need to be paid, it's hard to do anything *but* worry. We're all in this together. I keep saying each year that things run in cycles, that everything is bound to get better sooner or late—and I still believe that.

I sure hope I'm right.

ADVERTISING

Given the fact that we're inundated with pitches for gee-gaws and doohickies and all kinds of crap every time we fire up the computer, switch on the TV or radio, go to the movies, drive down the street, or flip through a magazine or newspaper, it's hard to believe that the advertising industry was still in something of a slump throughout '03. Despite low inflation and record-low interest rates, the economy was stuck in the doldrums (unless you were a realtor). The music industry continued to suffer from disappointing sales—which meant there was less promotional and collateral material produced to promote the bands. Airlines were still suffering from a down-turn, partially because of residual post-9/11 fears, partially because of the slow economy; rental car companies, restaurants, and hotels were similarly affected. The tobacco industry was limited as to how and where it could advertise cigarettes (tobacco has been so demonized over the last decade that I'm sure the only thing keeping it from being outlawed are the tax revenues it generates) and other "big-time" advertising clients (like movie companies) relied on PhotoShopped photos for their campaigns. The age-old ripple effect kicked in as limited job growth and modest (if any) wage increases put a cap on disposable incomes. Less spending meant fewer sales which translated into smaller profit margins which ultimately put the squeeze on budgets. Ad venues, for the most part, stubbornly refused to reduce rates in an effort to protect their own profitability and were alarmed to discover that long-term accounts found ways to market without them. Magazine revenues dropped at the same time that Internet advertising shot upwards. The most common—and annoying—form of cheap advertising in 2003 was in the form of "spam": unsolicited e-mail come-ons (and scams) that increasingly clogged computer servers. The e-mail issue became such an overwhelming problem that Congress eventually passed an anti-spam law—time will tell whether the legislation has any teeth. As it is, I'm *still* receiving stacks of offers for Viagra, cheap mortgages, and porn every day despite all the blocking filters the Techies claim they're using.

I'm always fussing about how hard it is to track down credits for various advertising illustrations—and it hasn't gotten any better. Some of the pieces by artists I *was* able to identify included Shag's oh-so-hip ads for the Ameristar Casinos, Michael Koelsch's devil-with-people-suits painting for the Minnesota Department of Health, Lisa's Eng's dragon poster for the alternative Stereophonics Concert, and a minotaur for a Nike ad by Simon Bisley. Other works by Bill Mayer, David Lance Goines, and Gary Baseman also caught my attention. But I was especially intrigued by James Bland's photographic recreations of lurid pulp covers, which he used as direct-mail advertising. They were such nostalgic fun that I'm hoping he'll think about turning them into posters or a calendar.

BOOKS

Though growth was slow and sales slumped slightly, 2003 saw an industry-wide jump of 19% of new books published in the U.S.—something like 175,000 new titles hit the stands last year (up from 135,000 in '01).

Civil libertarians, booksellers, and librarians increased their opposition to the clause in the Patriot Act that allows law enforcement to examine sales records and library transactions of suspects and "persons of interest." The Supreme Court will undoubtedly be called upon to decide on the Act's constitutionality, probably sooner rather than latter.

Time Warner opted not to sell its very-profitable book division after entertaining offers for several months, but they *did* decide to drop the AOL moniker from their corporate identity. Print-on-demand publishing had negligible increases in sales (POD still smacks of cheap, unedited vanity press stuff to me), Barnes & Noble produced more low-priced illustrated titles exclusively for their stores (prompting complaints from publishers that B&N was unfairly competing with them with similar editions), while Borders lobbied the companies *not* to print the prices on books, believing they should be able to set their own prices (much like grocery stores) and insisting that, "...publishers don't know what their books are worth."

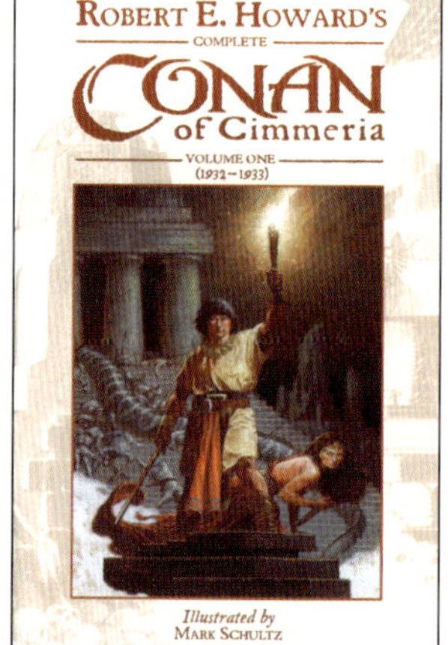

Mark Schultz's art beautifully complimented Wandering Star's new Conan edition

But unquestionably the BIG event of the year (no, it wasn't Al Franken and Bill O'Reilly yelling at each other at the BEA) was the release of the fifth Harry Potter novel, *Harry Potter and the Order of the Phoenix* by J.K. Rowling [Scholastic]. With five million copies sold on the *first day alone* it's safe to say that the HP phenomenon (and the popularity of the series' illustrator, Mary GrandPré) is going to continue for several more years ahead.

As discussed in past reviews, narrative art isn't as common as it once was as solutions for book covers—which is probably the reason good examples stand out so readily when displayed beside titles that feature strictly type or stock illustration. Douglas Smith provided an appropriately intriguing cover for *Mirror, Mirror* by Gregory Maguire [Regan], Chris Moore's painting for *Roma Eterna* by Robert Silverberg [Eos] captured my attention by combining a 1950s-style rocket and ancient Egyptians, and I was thoroughly charmed by Lisa Desimini's art for *Club Dead* by Charlaine Harris [Ace]. Michael Whelan was in top form with his cover for Wild *Magic: Fool's Gold Book 2* by Jude Fisher [DAW], Gary Ruddell moodily captured the world of Dan Simmons' *Ilium* [Eos], the Dillons created a typically stunning jacket for *Abhorsen* by Garth Nix [Eos], and David Bowers provided a knock-out painting for *Paladin of Souls* by Mary Gentle [Eos]. And I can't forget to mention Kinuko Y. Craft's cover for *Wolfskin* by Juliet Marillier [Tor] or John Jude Palencar's dragon for the bestselling *Eragon* by home-schooled wünderkind writer, Christopher Paolini [Knof]. Also filtered throughout the bookracks were notable paintings by Greg Spalenka, Tom Canty, Stephen Youll, Judy York, Stephan "Cricket" Martiniere, Gregory Bridges, John Bolton, Christophe Vacher, Tom Kidd, and Rick Berry to name only a very few.

Gary Larson got the star treatment with the two-volume slip-cased collection, *The Complete Far Side.* A deluxe leather-bound signed edition was available in the gallery market for $750.

In the illustrated books category, Mark Schultz was a winner with his art for Wandering Star's *Conan of Cimmeria* Vol. 1 by Robert E. Howard. Likewise, erstwhile *Star Wars* design director Doug Chiang wowed audiences with his wonderfully mythic *Robota* (written in collaboration with Orson Scott Card) [Chronicle]—with the only disappointment being that there's no film to go along with the eye-popping CGI-animated "trailer" Doug created and had posted on the Internet as promotion in advance of the book's release. And how could you top the winning combination of Dave McKean and Neil Gaiman as displayed in their latest collaboration, *Wolves In the Walls* [HarperCollins]? Also of merit were Gennady Spririn's illustrations for *Simeon's Gift* by Julie Andrews and Emma Walton Hamilton [Harper Collins], Art Spiegelman's and Françoise Mouly's latest *Comic Lit* compilation *It Was a Dark and Silly Night...* [Joanna Cotler] with contributions by Richard Sala, William Joyce, Gahan Wilson, and, Kaz (among other notables), Scott Gustafson's drop-dead-gorgeous *Classic Fairy Tales* [Greenwich Workshop Press], Karl Kofoed's *Galactic Geographic* [Paper Tiger], Brian Froud's *Runes of Elfland* (text by Ari Berk) [Abrams], and Berkeley Breathed's endearingly off-the-wall *Flawed Dogs: The Year End Leftovers at the Piddleton "last Chance" Dog Pound* [Little Brown].

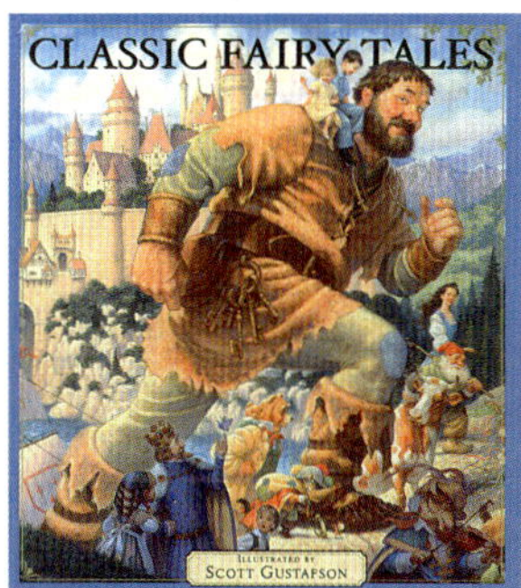

Classic Fairy Tales featured a nice mix of Scott Gustafson's best work from the past decade along with many exceptional new paintings.

The year saw a nice selection of single artist collections. At the top of my list of favorites was *The Art of John Berkey* by Jane Frank [Paper Tiger], a great combination of dazzling art and interesting text. I was also quite taken with *Lowlife Paradise* by Glenn Barr [Last Gasp] (a fabulous collection of sexy and subversive paintings), the self titled *Joe Chiodo* [Hermes Press] (which included a welcome array of all-new nudes and gallery art), *Narcolepsy* by Dave Mckean [Allen Spiegel Fine Art], *Mythology: The DC Comics Art of Alex Ross* by Chip Kidd [Pantheon], *The Art of Maurice Sendak: 1980 to Present* by Tony Kushner [Abrams], and the absolutely breathtaking *Dreamlands,* a knock-out gathering of the most recent canvases by Todd Schorr [Last Gasp]. While not fantasy art by any stretch (though some of the landscapes are suitably abstract), *Mark English* by Jill Bossert [Madison Square Press] was a radiant retrospective of one of the major illustrators of the later 20th Century (I just wish it had included even more examples of his commercial work). I was happy to see John Fleskes' follow-up his invaluable Franklin Booth book with *Joseph Clement Coll: The Art of Adventure* [Flesk Publications], a sumptuous edition every fan of fine drawing should own. And, of course, it'll be no surprise to readers of previous Year End Summaries that I ran like a greyhound to snap up *The Art of Hellboy* by Mike Mignola [Dark Horse] when it appeared in March of '03. Even though Mike said with tongue-in-cheek that he was afraid people would see the collection as "my epitaph," it proved to be a striking showcase for his moody illustrations.

Other art books worthy of attention were *Illumina: The Art of Jean Pierre Targete* [Paper Tiger], *Witching Hour: The Art of Larry MacDougall* [Cartouche], *Mythos: A Collection of Fantastical Drawings and Paintings* by Peter Clarke [Enigmyth], *Transistions: The Art of Todd Lockwood* [Paper Tiger], *The Art of Lorenzo Sperlonga* and *The Daniel Horne Sketchbook* [both from SQP], and *Doesn't* by Yasushi Nirasawa [WamPix]. I'll only mention in passing that Cathy and I revised and greatly expanded *Icon* by Frank Frazetta [Underwood Books] for it's 2003 softcover release—I think it made for a *much* better book. (And who ever *doesn't* want *more* Frazetta?)

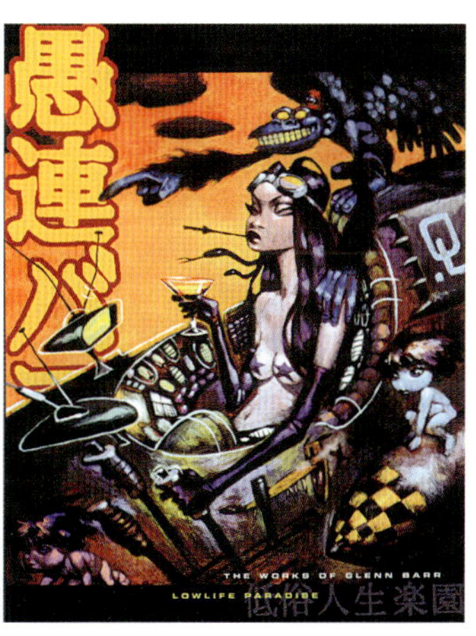

Detroit artist Glenn Barr's first book included some startling paintings that might prevent viewers from ever seeing Judy Jetson and Betty Ruble in quite the same innocent way ever again. *Whoopee!*

Artists also began to aggressively publish their own sketchbooks to sell at the conventions they were appearing at. Limited to relatively modest press runs of 1000—2000 copies, these rapidly sold for ridiculous prices on eBay and might well turn into *the* hot collectible in before you know it. Production values and actual content were all over the place, but some of the nicest booklets included those by Dave Stevens, Adam Hughes, Steranko, Frank Cho, and the ambitious *Sign of Four* by Dave Dorman, Scott Hampton, Ray Lago, and Christopher Moeller (check out Chris' self-portrait!) which was released by Rolling Thunder.

Some of the multiple-artist "anthologies" of merit included Mark Evanier's fun and breezy *Mad Art* [Watson Guptill], the perennial must-have *Illustrators 44* (edited by Jill Bossert) [Harper Design International], *American Illustration 22* (edited by Gary Baseman) [Amilua], and *The Chesley Awards* (edited by John Grant, Elizabeth Humphrey, and Pamela Scoville) [Artist & Photographers Press].

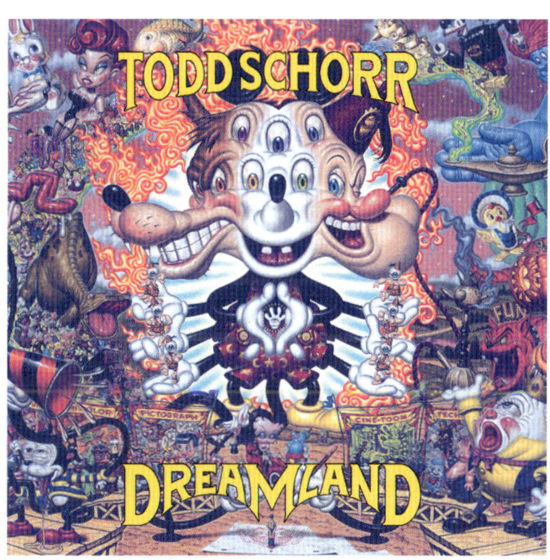

Todd Schorr's follow-up to 1998's *Secret Mystic Rites* is a splendid pop-culture spectacle, featuring art that is both hilariously entertaining *and* emotionally challenging.

Almost a decade after his retirement, Andrews McMeel produced *The Complete Far Side* (an "18-pound hernia giver," as Gary called it), a massive two-volume $135 collection of every "Far Side" cartoon—and were pleased when it immediately sold out its first edition and turned up on the bestseller lists. (Count on a similar frenzy in 2005 when they release *The Complete Calvin and Hobbes*!) I was glad to see Bhob Stewart's *Against the Grain: Mad Artist Wally Wood* [TwoMorrows] finally appear after several false starts with other publishers over the years: bittersweet and absorbing, the book was worth the wait. *Mutts: The Comic Art of Patrick McDonnell* [Abrams] was an enjoyable overview of a gifted creator's oeuvre while I thought *The Art of Marvel* [Marvel], though featuring some great pieces by Alex Ross, Joe Quesada, and Tim Bradstreet, was rather small and skimpy for the price. And my immediate reaction to *Steranko: Arte Noir* by Angel de la Calle and Dave Spurlock [Semana Negra]? "It's about time!" It was nice to see some of the color work I grew up with (like the cover for the old Hans Stefan Santesson-edited anthology *The Mighty Barbarians*) finally reproduced properly. (And who out there has Steranko's original cover for *Master of the Dark Gate* by John Jakes? I'd like to see a nice repro of *that* one, too!)

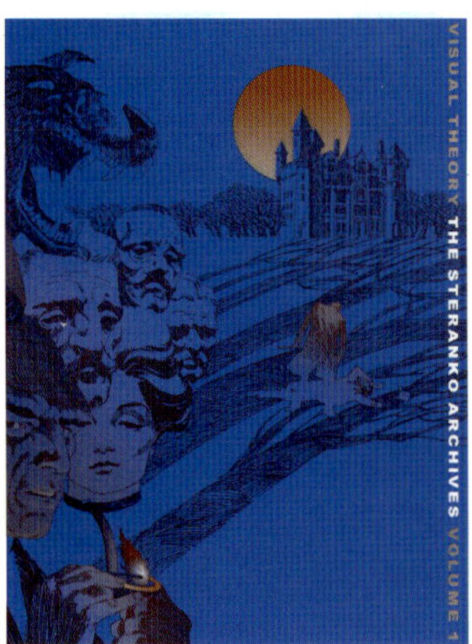

Jim Steranko was one of the many artists who by-passed traditional publishers and printed their own sketchbooks to sell to fans during the year.

There's always a certain amount of concern each year about the unending battle for customers between small independent booksellers and the big chains with their superstores. But when I take a moment to consider it, I'm not terribly worried. The big stores are a great resource for general titles and bestsellers, but when you want something special, something esoteric, or something that's simply not a part of the mainstream, the independent and specialty retailers are the way to go. Every year I recommend Bud Plant Comic Art (which is something of a misnomer since Bud doesn't stock monthly comics) as a one-stop shopping destination for all sorts of art and photography books (and magazines, posters, statues, etc.). This year is no exception: call up one of Bud's friendly salesfolk at 800-242-6642 to receive an illustrated catalog or visit their on-line store at www.budplant.com. I'd also like to steer readers to Greg Ketter at www.dreamhavenbooks.com and to Mark Ziesing at www.ziesing.rockin.net for an eclectic and off-beat selection of rare and new titles.

C O M I C S

"Manga makes the world go around
"the world go around
"the world go around
"Manga makes the world go around
"It makes a lovely sound..."

(Sing it to the tune of "Money, Money" from *Cabaret*.)

Well, maybe. Much as I love the funnybooks themselves, the comics industry confuses the hell out of me. For the last decade (or more)—certainly since the big speculators' boom and bust in the mid-'90s—the market always has seemed to be looking for a metaphorical superhero to fly in and save the day (meaning something, some event or strategy that would reverse declining sales and dwindling, aging readerships).

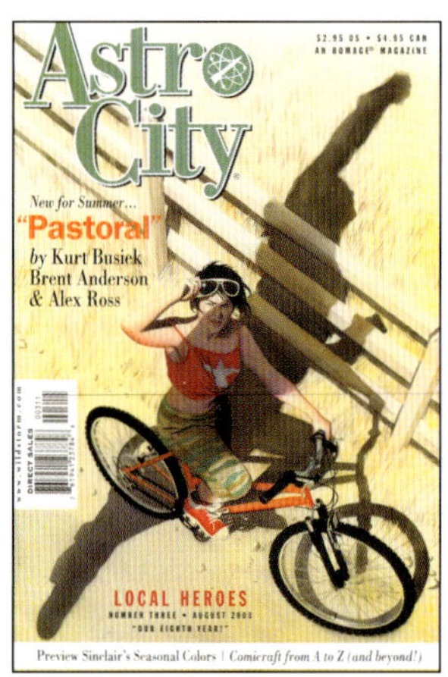

Alex Ross' cover for *Astro City: Local Heroes* #3 proved once again why he's so damn popular.

The first marketing strategy (that quickly turned around and bit the industry in the butt) was when publishers virtually abandoned younger readers (always the core audience for comics and other low-priced entertainments) to pursue the collectors market. Envious of the "investors" who were obsessively spending their paychecks on Beany Babies and trading cards, they pumped product into the market, offering "limited editions" and variant covers and special "events"—all at a jacked-up price, naturally. When people found that there was simply no way to make a profit on their Image and Tundra Comics or their pre-bagged, absolute mint "Death of This Month's Superhero" collector's item, they dumped their "investments" and never looked back.

It took quite awhile for the industry to recover—there were a lot of casualties among publishers, comic shops, and creators alike.

The next bit of conventional wisdom was that successful film adaptations would create new readers for the monthly pamphlets and the companies began to purposefully license their characters to Hollywood. But as popular as the first *Batman* and *Superman* films proved to be, as wildly successful as *Spider-Man 1* was, the comics themselves seemed to be the only "tie-in" or "spin-off" products that didn't especially benefit from the adaptations at the cash register. The general public didn't know (or really care, in the long run) where the inspiration for *Men In Black, The Mask*, or *Ghost World* came from. (Lesson: people who go to comics-based movies aren't necessarily interested in actual comics.)

Charles Vess reinvisioned *Peter Pan* for this new illustrated edition from Tor.

Beginning in 2002 and carrying on into '03 the buzz was about how selling comics and graphic novels through traditional bookstores would be the salvation of the art form. Comic shop owners expressed some alarm at having to contend with an 800-pound-gorilla as a new competitor.

The mass-market turned out to be all for it, of course. With the deeper discounts major retailers are able to negotiate and the right to return unsold product (unlike the smaller comics specialty stores), why *not* take a chance?

And it actually seemed to be successful. Sales of graphic novels and other comics-related books exceeded not only the expectations of the chains, but of the publishers themselves. (The impact on the direct market is yet to be seen.) Strong sales generally didn't help everyone: CrossGen Comics, despite some good titles and heavy promotion, began to experience financial problems (all thoroughly reported on the Internet fan and news sites, much to CrossGen's consternation) and their future looked rocky (they filed bankruptcy in 2004).

The truly hot comics, though, weren't produced by "the Big 2" or any of their smaller American competitors, however: Japanese manga, translated and released by Viz and TokyoPop and a host of other importers, dominated the bestseller charts. Selling equally well to guys and gals (and face it, boys: comic shops aren't especially female-friendly shopping establishments), Japanese comics were such a financial windfall to the bookstores that by year's end several major New York publishers had announced formation of manga divisions.

Is it a fad or will it last? Time will tell.

Me? Boy. Artistically, it all seems to be pretty similar so I have a hard time getting worked up about manga. Talk to our son, Rob: he's the expert.

But I *will* talk about good old fashioned red white and blue *Amurican* comics, dagnabit!

I always like DC, if for no other reason than they're not afraid to either experiment with their characters or to take a chance on different art styles. Some of the highlights included Neil Gaiman's *New York Times* bestseller *The Sandman: Endless Nights* with art by Dave McKean, Milo Manara, Craig Russell, and Barron Story, among many others; the alternate WWII history *Life Eaters* by SF writer David Brin with art by Scott Hampton; *JLA: Liberty & Justice* by Paul Dini with art

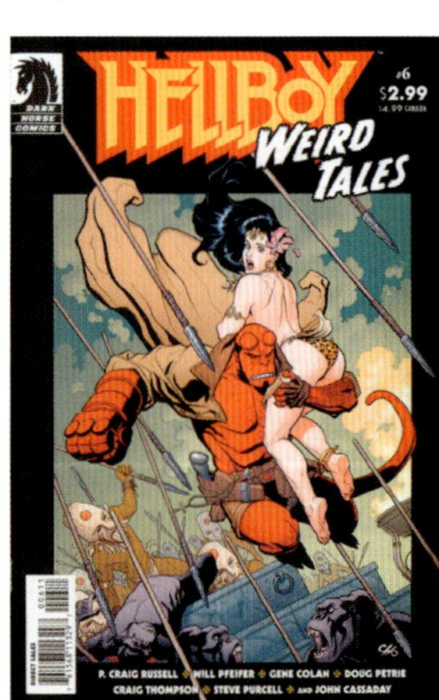

Mike Mignola's *Hellboy* was kept in the spotlight with some great spin-off titles while Mike himself was off working on the film adaptation of his character. Frank Cho drew this fun cover for *Hellboy: Weird Tales* #6

by the ever-popular Alex Ross; *Batman: Child of Dreams*, written and illustrated by Kia Asamiya; the *Batman: Hush* series by Jim Lee, written by Jeph Loeb; and unquestionably *The League of Extraordinary Gentleman Book 2* (in which the League takes on H.G. Wells' Martians) by Alan Moore and artist Kevin O'Neill (too bad the movie-version of the first book was so awful—the filmmakers should've followed Moore's story instead of making up a bad one of their own). I was quite impressed by James Jean's covers for the *Fables* series (released under DC's Vertigo imprint), as I was with Brian Bolland's for *Zatanna: Everyday Magic* and *Batman: Gotham Knights* #39 and #46. Adam Hughes' covers for *Wonder Woman* were as stunning as always and Tim Bradstreet's *Hellblazer* pieces were all attitude and mood. Other excellent covers appeared by Christopher Moeller, Chris Bachalo, Jo Chen, Phil Noto, Glenn Orbik, Bruce Timm, Bill Wray, and Sean Phillips.

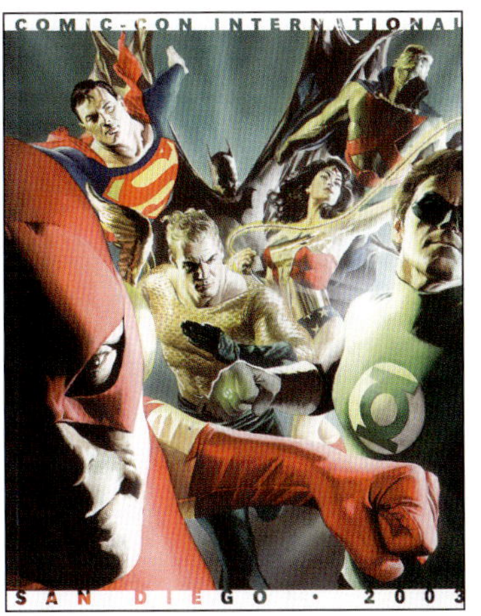

Alex Ross painted this exquisite cover for the San Diego Comic Con International souvenir book.

If the film-version of *The Hulk* failed to elicit the same acclaim and boxoffice revenues of Sam Rami's *Spider-Man* adaptation, Marvel execs still had a jaunty bounce in their steps through the better part of '03. Sales were up, licensing revenues were healthy, and they even felt confident enough to vary their men-in-tights routine...a little. The only hiccups seemed to result from some occasionally belligerent posturing by CEO Bill Jemas as directed at staff, fans, and online journalists—which reportedly led to his ouster. Marvel's fondness for mainstream publicity blew up in its face when they trumpeted an issue of *X-Statix* featuring Princess Diana as a superhero, "Di Another Day." Complaints about their crassness were loud and intense. (I'm guessing there are many who saw the departure of Marvel's controversial CEO as the proverbial silver lining to his storm cloud).

Some of their most interesting titles that turned up on the racks within the last twelve months included *Spider-Man: Blue*, written by Jeph Loeb with art by Tim Sale; *1602*, written by Neil Gaiman with art by Andy Kubert and Richard Isanove (and great covers by Scott McKowen); and *Wolverine: Snikt* featuring story and art by Tsutomu Nihei. Kaare Andrews did an amusing take-off on Maurice Sendak's *Where the Wild Things Are* for his cover to *The Incredible Hulk* #49. I also liked various covers by Bill Sienkiewicz, Paolo Rivera, Alex Maleev, Wieslaw Walkuski, Darwyn Cooke, Sam Kieth, and Tim Bradstreet.

Dark Horse perked along nicely with their mix of licensed and creator-owned titles. They vigorously marketed newly repackaged *Hellboy* graphic novels and Mignola-less spin-off comics as a warm-up to the 2004 release of the film adaptation—all were worth checking out. I was entertained by Eric Powell's manic *The Goon*, Masamune Shirow's *Ghost In the Shell 2*, and *Criminal Macabre* as written by Steve Stiles and illustrated by Ben Templesmith. DH also released a nice anthology, *The Dark Horse Book of Hauntings*, which featured a great Gary Gianni cover (and illustrations for a William Hope Hodgson prose ghost story) and a—yowza!—quirky new "Hellboy" story by Mignola.

Fantagraphics found themselves in the uncomfortable position of being overstocked with inventory and understocked with ready cash, despite publishing some of the best comics-related books in the field. They put out a plea on the Internet for retailers and fans to "buy their stuff" and were rapidly inundated with orders and revenue. Besides producing the always interesting and often controversial *Comics Journal*, they also released the invaluable retrospective *Will Elder: The Mad Playboy of Art* and *Weasel #6: Overbite* by Dave Cooper, as well as their ongoing Chris Ware-designed series of reprints of George Herriman's classic *Krazy Kat*.

"I'm ready for my close-up, Mr. De Mille!" *The Sandman's* Neil Gaiman went Hollywood for a day and shed his trademark shades and leather jacket for the photo accompanying this glowing article that ran in *Entertainment Weekly*.

Ambling along the "other guys" aisle a few of the items that caught my interest included *Liberty Meadows* by Frank Cho [Image], *Al Williamson Adventures* [Insight Studios], *Barefoot Serpent* by Scott Morse [Top Shelf], and *Bone* by Jeff Smith [Cartoon Books]. I liked several *Vampirella* covers by Jason Alexander and Joe Chiodo while Glenn Barr's piece for *Graphic Classics* #7 stopped me in my tracks.

There are still a host of magazines that cater to the comics reader: *Alter Ego, Sketch*, the previously mentioned *Comics Journal, Wizard, Comics Buyers Guide*, and *The Comic Book Marketplace*. Jon Cooke's entertaining *Comic Book Artist* seemed to have encountered some roadblocks to getting back on a regular schedule after switching publishers; hopefully '04 will find it back on track.

Most cities host some sort of comics convention at least once a year, but those in the know save their money for a pilgrimage to Comic Con International in San Diego every summer. Last year a whopping 75,000 people attended the convention over five days who not only had the opportunity to buy all manner of comics, books, and original art, but had the opportunity to meet everyone from Dave McKean and Travis Charest to Halle Berry and Elija Wood. Each year gets bigger and better: start planning now for next year! (Information can be found at www.comic-con.org)

DIMENSIONAL

Every year I say "no more" to new statues and toys: our shelves are crammed full, the display cases and curios are filled to the brim. "No more of this dust gathering crap!" I'll insist. And then I'll see something new at the comic shop or at Sun Coast Video or in the Diamond Previews catalog...and another chatchkie will find a place in our house.

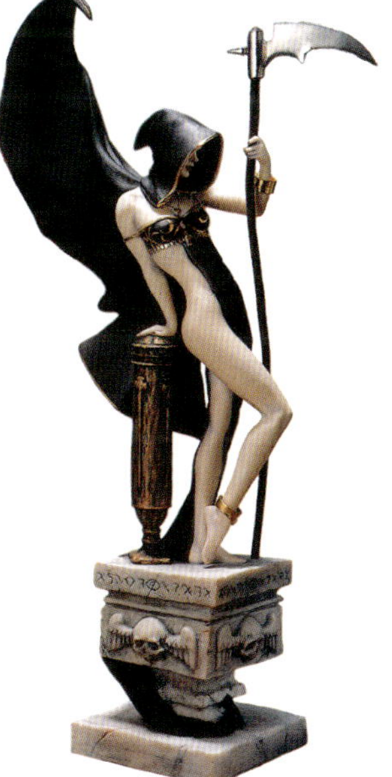

This seductive Grim Reaper was part of the Franklin Mint's line of Brom-designed statuettes.

It was a lot easier when I was a kid and did away with older stuff on the Fourth of July with a coffee can full of Black Cats and bottle rockets.

Since the Warner Bros. Studio stores went to that shopping mall in the sky, DC Direct has done a good job of filling the void with some very nice collectibles. Favorites included Tim Bruckner's "Batman" statue (based on Jim Lee's design), along with his Alex Ross-inspired *Kingdom Come* action figures; Jonathan Matthews' "The Sandman Manga Statue" (based on a design by Jill Thompson; a "Desire" mini-bust by Barsom; and William Paquet's "Batgirl" statue (based on a design by Damion Scott).

Dark Horse released a variety of *Star Wars* busts and statues from the Gentle Giant Studio—who were able to achieve remarkable likenesses through their digital scanning of the actual actors and props. (More and more 3D companies are utilizing this technology).

Sideshow Productions, in collaboration with Peter Jackson's WETA special effects studio, produced an astonishing selection of *Lord of the Rings* busts, statues, swords, and jewelry for the third year running: their success was the envy of other collectibles companies and the quality of their merchandise was top-notch. Their new offerings based on Brian Froud's faeries and Wayne Barlowe's vision of Hell's denizens weren't anything to sneeze at, either.

Tony McVey created a fun statue based on Arthur Adams' comic duo, "Monkey Man & O'Brien" for Menagerie Productions while Diamond marketed some exclusive items directly to the comic shops, including Gabriel Marquez's 3D version of the *Army of Darkness* movie poster and several *Vampire Hunter D*-inspired busts by Susumu Sugita.

Todd McFarlane's toy division offered some nice additions to their *Matrix* line as well as a new batch of their "Movie Maniacs" figures—their "Alien Queen" diorama was a gloriously ghastly hunk of plastic!

Palisades Toys also did some worthwhile *Alien* vinyl statuettes, including the "Alien Space Jockey" from the first film. Kotobukiya offered some incredibly detailed *Final Fantasy X-2* figures and X-Plus continued to release new toys based on Ray Harryhausen's creatures.

I haven't been terribly impressed for the last few years with the normally-excellent sculpts by Randy Bowen—it's probably just me. But his new line of Robert Crumb figures likewise left me cold—*except* for his "Fritz the Cat," which was a pert-near perfect interpretation that made it a "gotta have" item.

The Franklin Mint produced a variety of items (statues, knives, chess sets, etc.) based on designs by Michael Whelan, Brom, Boris, and Julie Bell. Now, whether mainstream American collectors were ready for some of these dragons and wizards and barbarian women remains to be seen—the Mint apparently experienced some financial difficulties in '03—but I must admit to being impressed.

2003 saw plenty of garage model kits, wall plaques, action figures, and busts, something for everyone and more than I could possibly list. The best resource to track these dimensional beasts is the bimonthly magazine *Amazing Figure Modeler.* (www.amazingmodeler.com).

EDITORIAL

My pal Jane Frank and I argue all the time as to whether this is a "golden age" for F&SF art or not. (I chant "is so," Jane sneers "is not" back—we don't accomplish a lot, but we have a good time—*I* do, anyway.) But if we were basing the argument on the amount of *new* art featured in the genre magazines, I'm afraid I might lose.

But the thing of it is, '03 was tough for *all* magazines, really: the industry saw unusually poor sales through the year with many major publishers missing their advertising rate bases. Subscriptions dipped generally and newsstand circulations on average dropped for virtually everyone, some by as much as 7%.

Magazines were still a viable market for illustrators, of course, and marvelous art could be found in all of the normal places: *Playboy,* the *New Yorker, Texas Monthly, National Geographic, Entertainment Weekly, Cricket,* etc. Art directors were encouraged by "the suits" to watch the bottom line, though, and it will be interesting to see what happens in 2004.

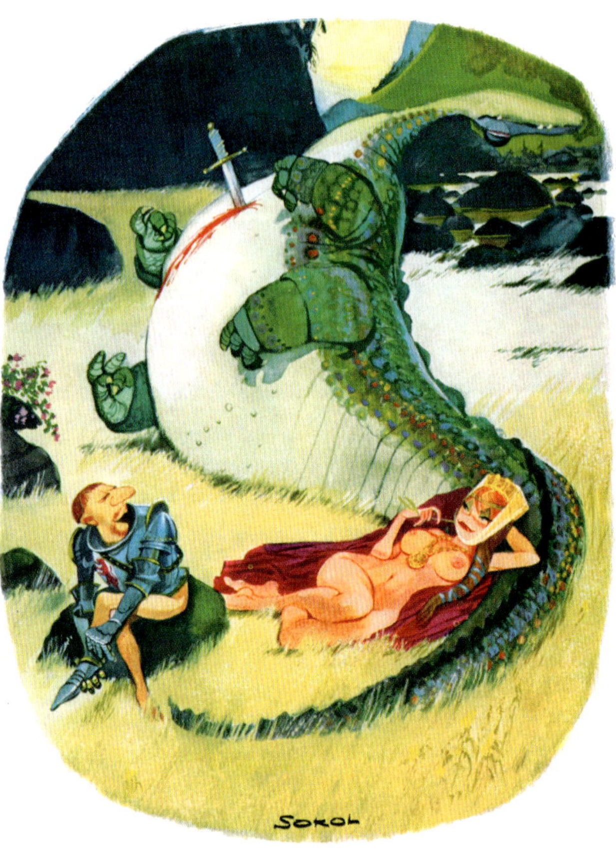

"This wasn't the first time you were saved from a dragon, was it?"

Czech-born Erich Sokol was best known in this country for his *Playboy* cartoons (like the one above), but in Europe he was highly regarded for his biting political cartoons and social commentary.

On a positive note, none of the magazines catering specifically to the SF field disappeared last year, though most relied on stock art for their covers. *Asimov's SF did* have a nice piece by Michael Koelsch and *Analog* sported an effective cover by Vincent Di Fate. I was also happy to see *many* fine illustrations in *Realms of Fantasy*

Juxtapoz kept happily thumbing its nose at the traditional art establishment with its showcase of great "outsider" art, *AirBrush Action* kept abreast of who-was-who and what-was-what in their specific area of art interest, and *Communication Arts* and *Print* both admirably covered the contemporary advertising and illustration markets. For publications with a focus on classic art, you couldn't ask for better than Dan Zimmer's *Illustration* and *Comic Art,* and Jim Vadeboncoeur's *ImageS.*

I admit to being a little perplexed at the relaunch of Coppervale's *International Studio* (one issue appeared in '03) and the premiere of their fiction digest, *Argosy*. The production values for both can't be beat: design and content were delightful. But...with print runs that *had* to be at best modest, I have to ask how the hell were they able to convince A-list companies like Victoria's Secret, Altoids, Apple—and more!—to advertise in their pages? They've *gotta* have a sales pitch that would make P.T. Barnum blush!

Still the best way to track the doings of the F&SF field-proper is to subscribe to the trade journal, *Locus.* Information can be found at www.locusmag.com.

INSTITUTIONAL

Not a tremendous amount of room left, so I'll quickly wrap by mentioning that there were some attractive calendars featuring the work of Michael Whelan, Brom, Barry Moser, Boris & Julie Bell, Kinuko Y. Craft, Royo, and Simon Bisley.

Dark Horse produced a variety of items geared toward the alternative gift and stationary market, including products by Tim Biskup, Shag, Coop, and Kirsten Ulve. For art-oriented tee-shirts Gaphitti Designs released a dazzling selection. I wish I knew more about who was doing what for RPGs and the film industry—I'm going to have to recruit some informants!

If you yearn to own original art but can't make it to a gallery with a decent selection, may I suggest:
Worlds of Wonder: wow-art.com
Heritage Comics: heritagecomics.com

REQUIEM

In 2003 we said "rest in peace" to these talented creators:

Leo Bachle (b. 1926) comic artist
Zeke Barlow (b. 1915) artist
Wah Ming Chang (b. 1917) spfx artist
Guido Crepax (b. 1933) comic artist
Tom Feelings (b. 1933) artist
Rudy O. Florese (b. 1946) comic artist
Bob Gregory (b. 1921) comic artist
Al Hartley (b. 1922) comic artist
Mike Hinge (b. 1931) illustrator
Al Hirschfeld (b. 1903) "characterist"
Don Lawrence (b. 1928) comic artist
Bill Mauldin (b. 1921) cartoonist
Robert McClosky (b. 1915) writer/artist
Jack McLeod (b. 1931) cartoonist
Pete Millar (b. 1928) comic artist
Pete Morisi (b. 1928) comic artist
Terence Parkes (b. 1927) cartoonist
George Pichard (b. 1920) comic artist
Pierce Rice (b. 1917) comic artist/educator
Dave Schreiner (b. 1946) art editor
Erich Sokol (b. 1934) cartoonist
William Steig (b. 1908) cartoonist
Gordon Stowell (b. 1928) illustrator
John Tartaglione (b. 1921) comic artist
Art Wetherell (b. 1956) comic artist †

SPECTRUM 11

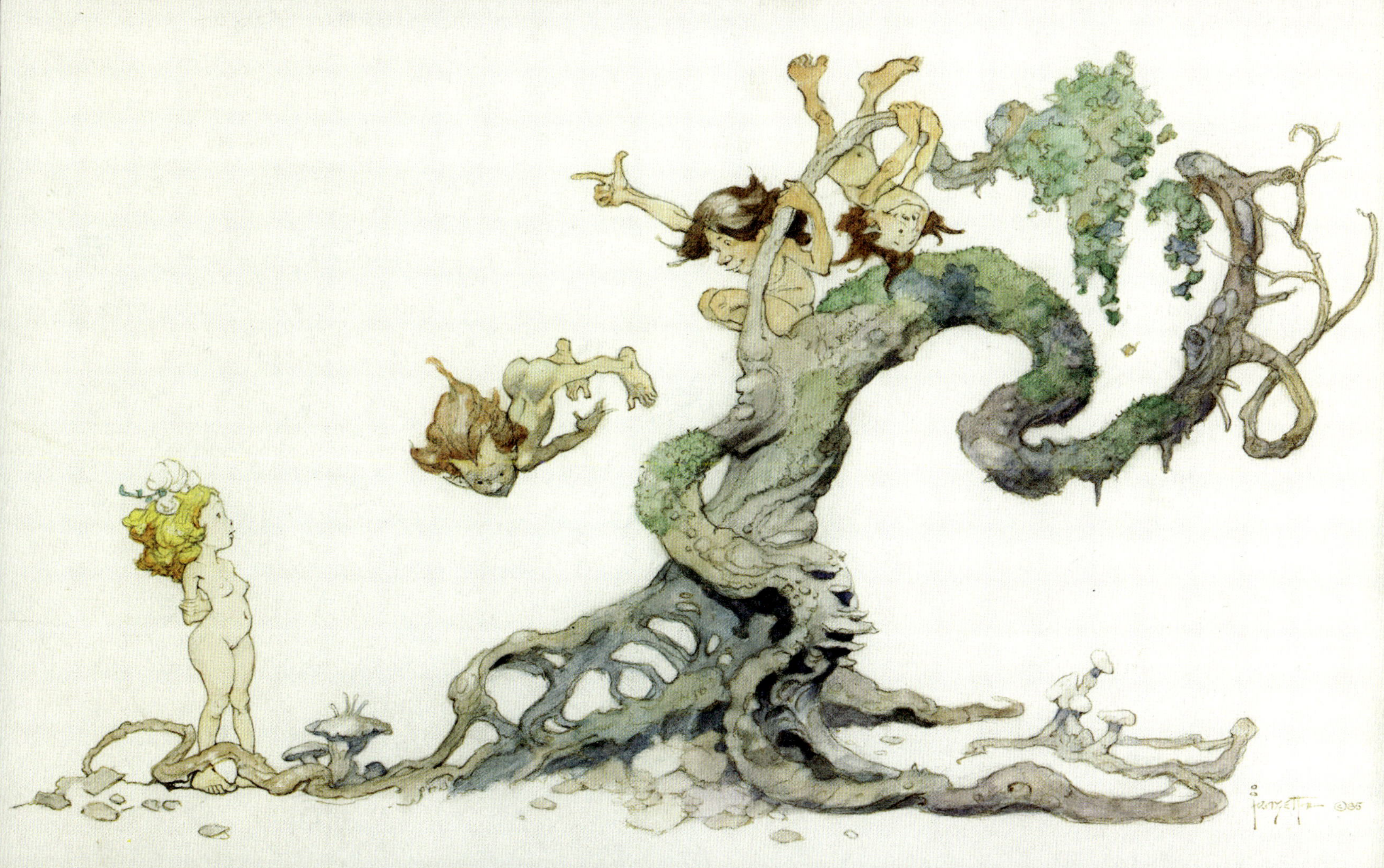

The Show

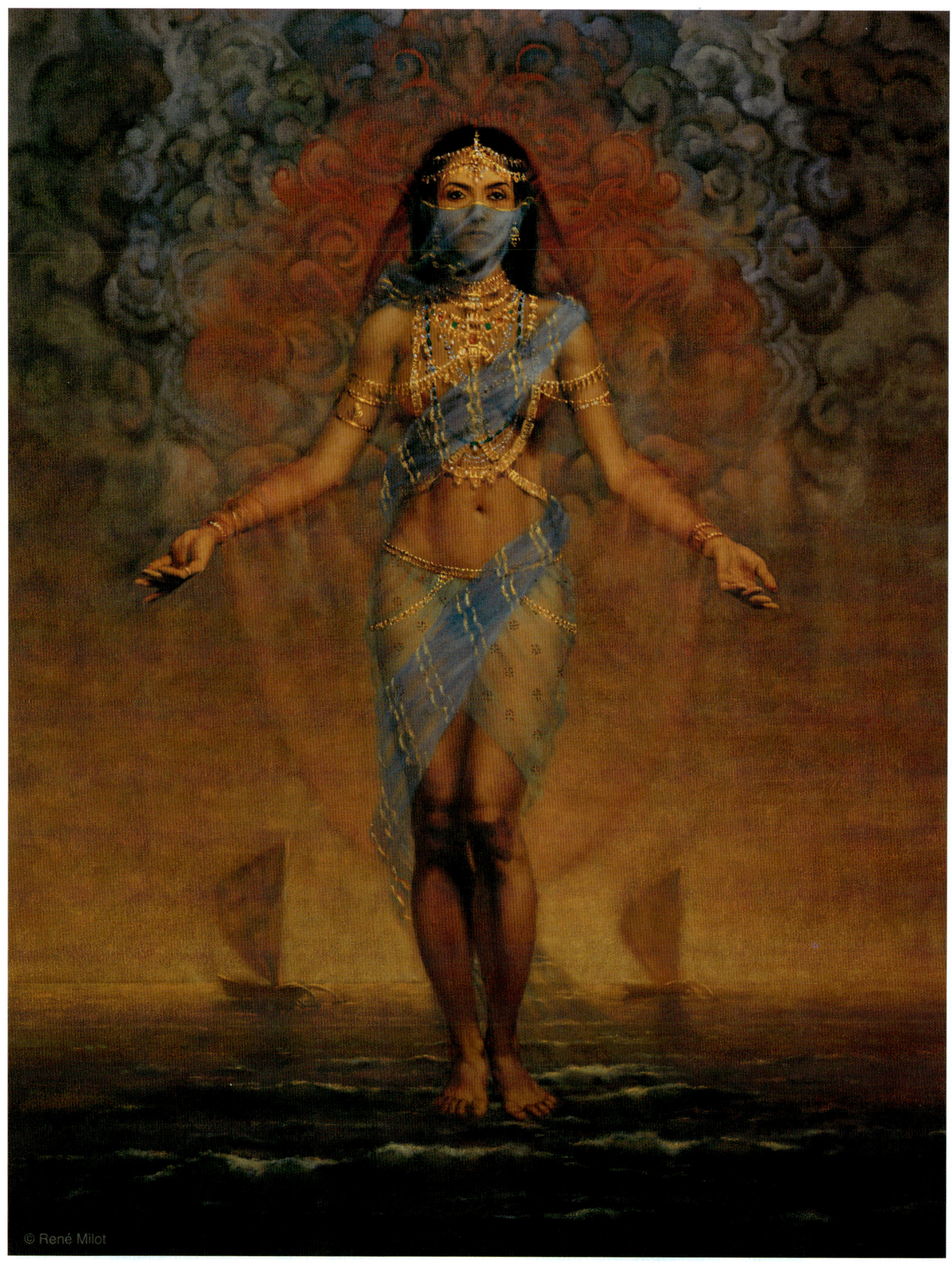

artist: **René Milot**
art director: Randall Jones *client:* Philadelphia Opera *title:* The Pearl Fishers *medium:* Oil on canvas
size: 21″x28″

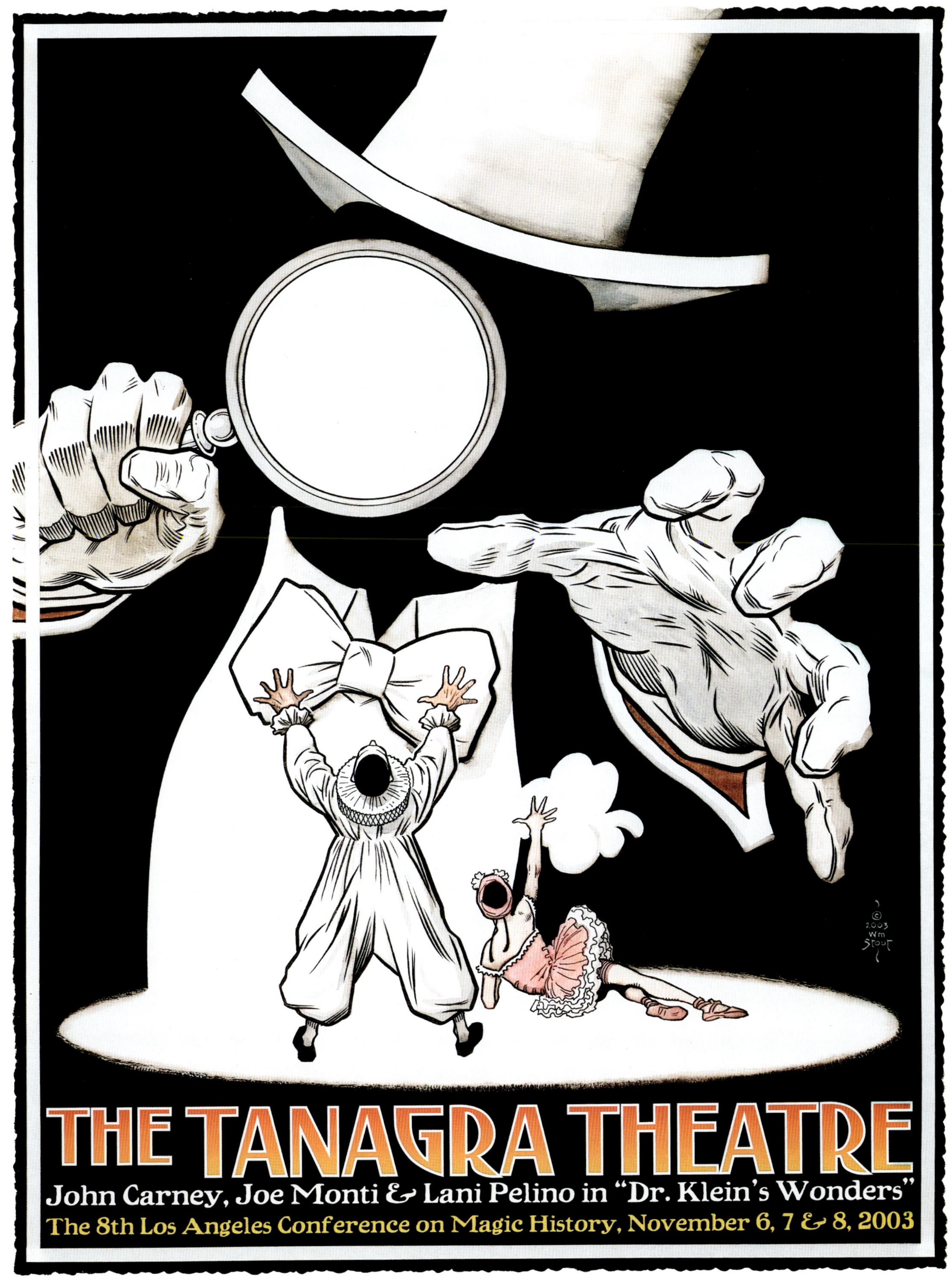

artist: **William Stout**
art director: Jim Steinmeyer/William Stout *client:* Eighth Los Angeles Conference on Magic History
title: The Tanagra Theater *medium:* Ink & watercolor *size:* 18"x24"

1
artist: **Wes Benscoter**
client: Relapse Records
title: Darkest Day of Horror
medium: Mixed
size: $12^1/_2$"x$12^1/_2$"

2
artist: **Rainer Kalwitz**
client: Spirit Web
title: Fanal Fatal
medium: Acrylics on canvas
size: $15^1/_2$"x$19^1/_2$"

3
artist: **Greg Horn**
client: Wizard
title: Spider Eye
medium: Digital

4
artist: **Glen Orbik**
art director: Peter Bickford
designer: Glen Orbik & Laurel Blechman
client: Human Computing
title: Comic Base #8
medium: Oil
size: 15"x21"

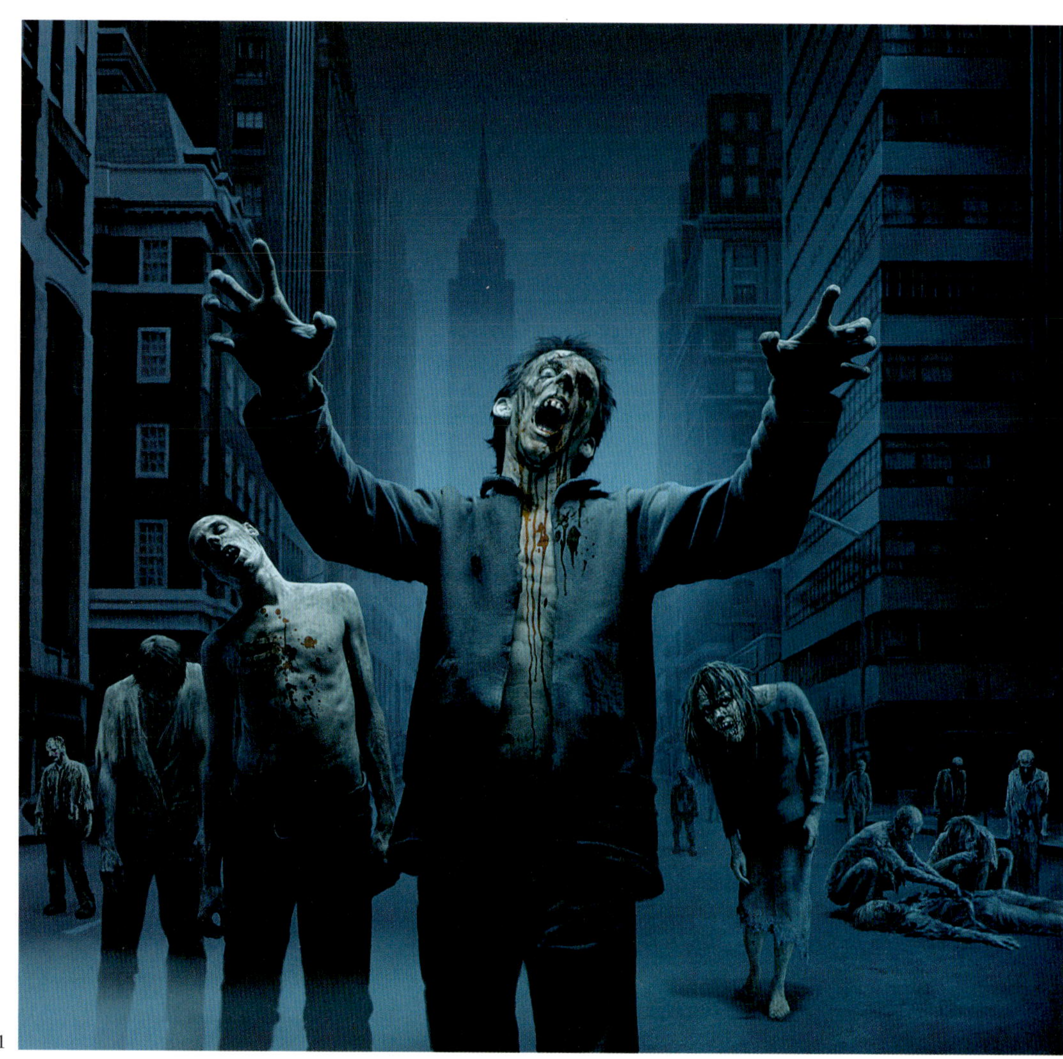
1

2
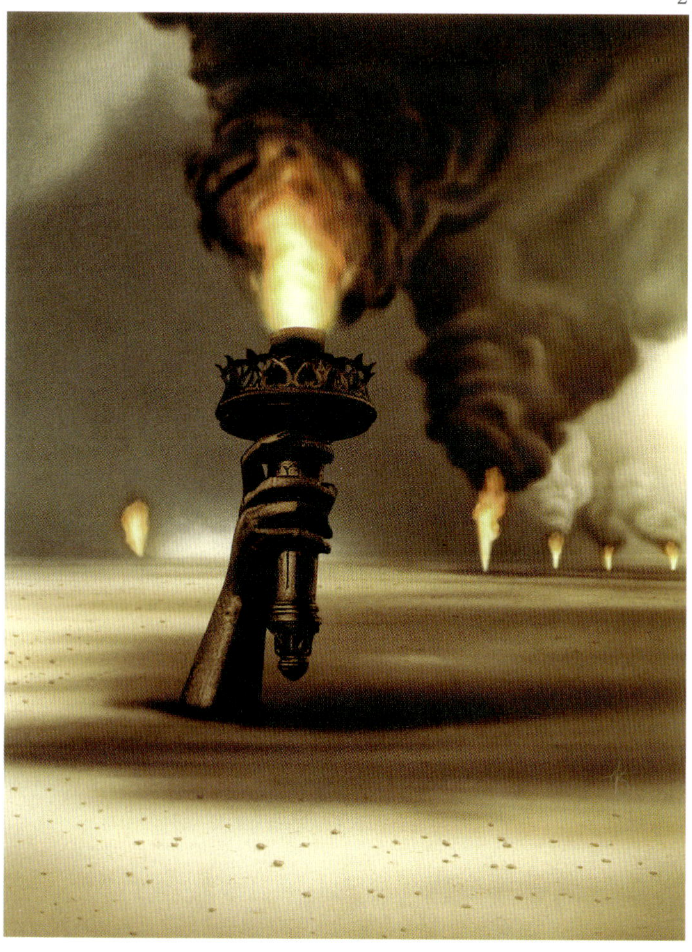

3
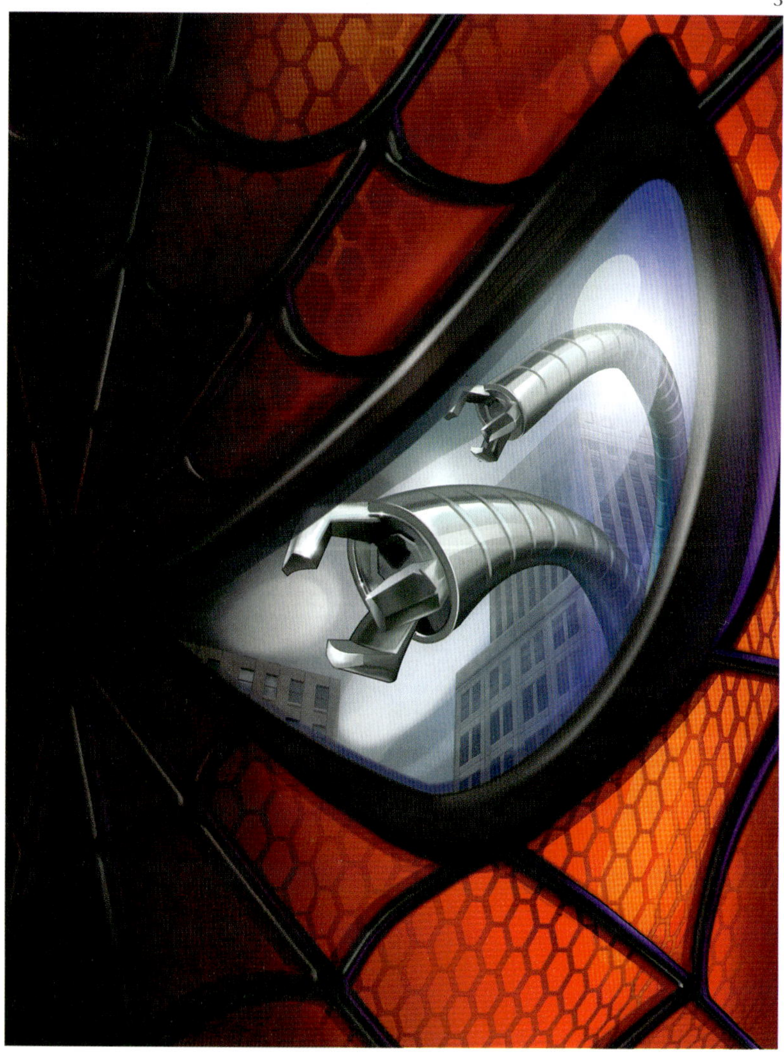

4

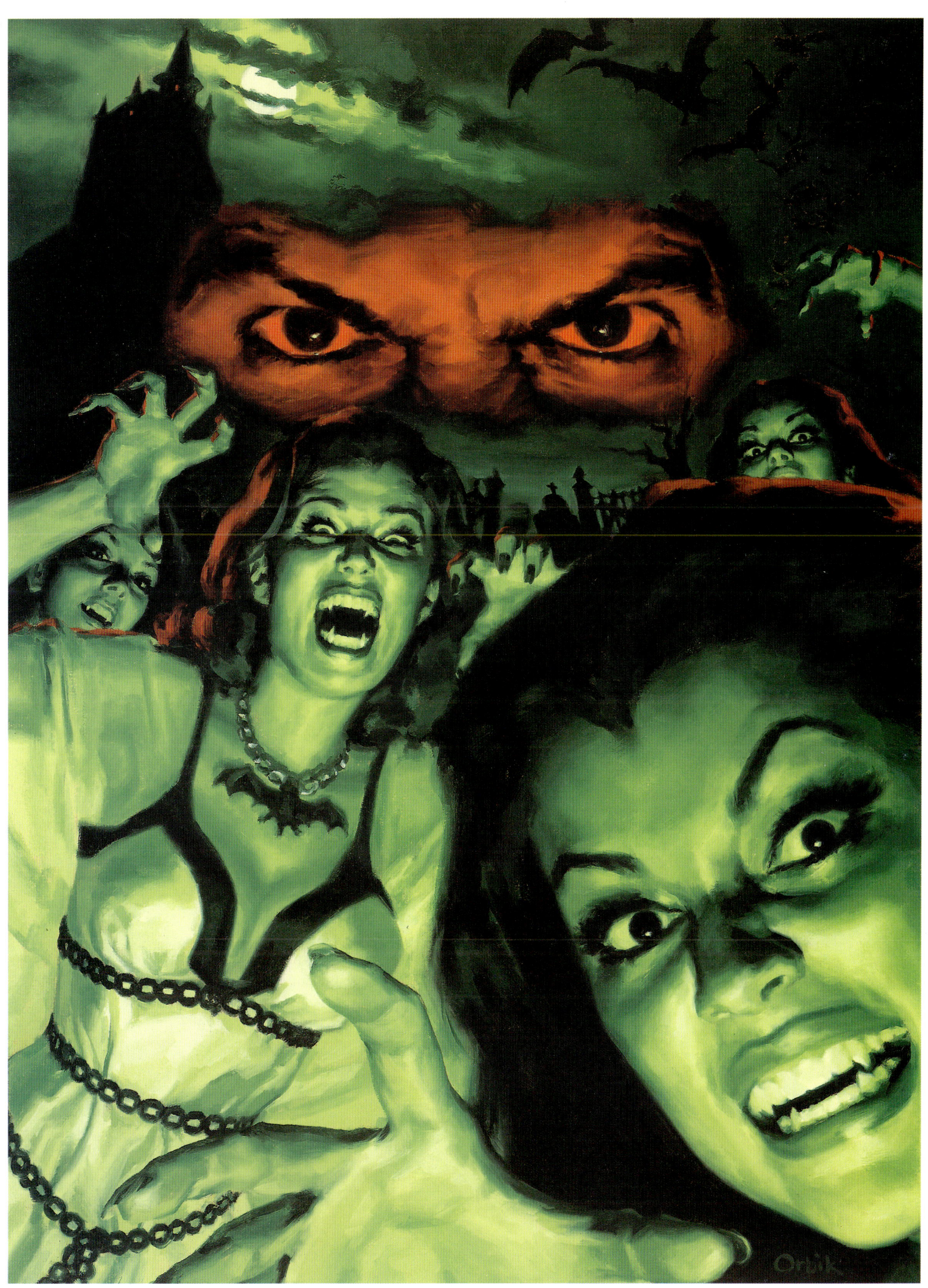

1
artist: **Rainer Kalwitz**
client: Resistance
title: Lies in Black
medium: Acrylics on canvas
size: 26"x26"

2
artist: **Dan Seagrave**
designer: Dan Seagrave
client: Karmageddon Media
title: Where Iron Crosses Grow
medium: Acrylic on board
size: 17"x17"

3
artist: **Vince Evans**
client: Kino International
title: The Man Who Laughs
medium: Oil
size: 11"x17"

4
artist: **Glenn Rane**
art director: Ron Walters
client: VU Games
title: Lord of the Realms III
medium: Digital
size: 8 1/2"x11"

5
artist: **Gary L. Freeman**
designer: Gary L. Freeman
client: Westwood Studios
title: Cabal
medium: Digital
size: 5 1/2"x8 1/2"

6
artist: **John Dickenson**
art director: Jon Hales
designer: John Dickenson
client: Interplay Productions
title: The City
medium: Digital
size: 6 1/2"x7 1/2"

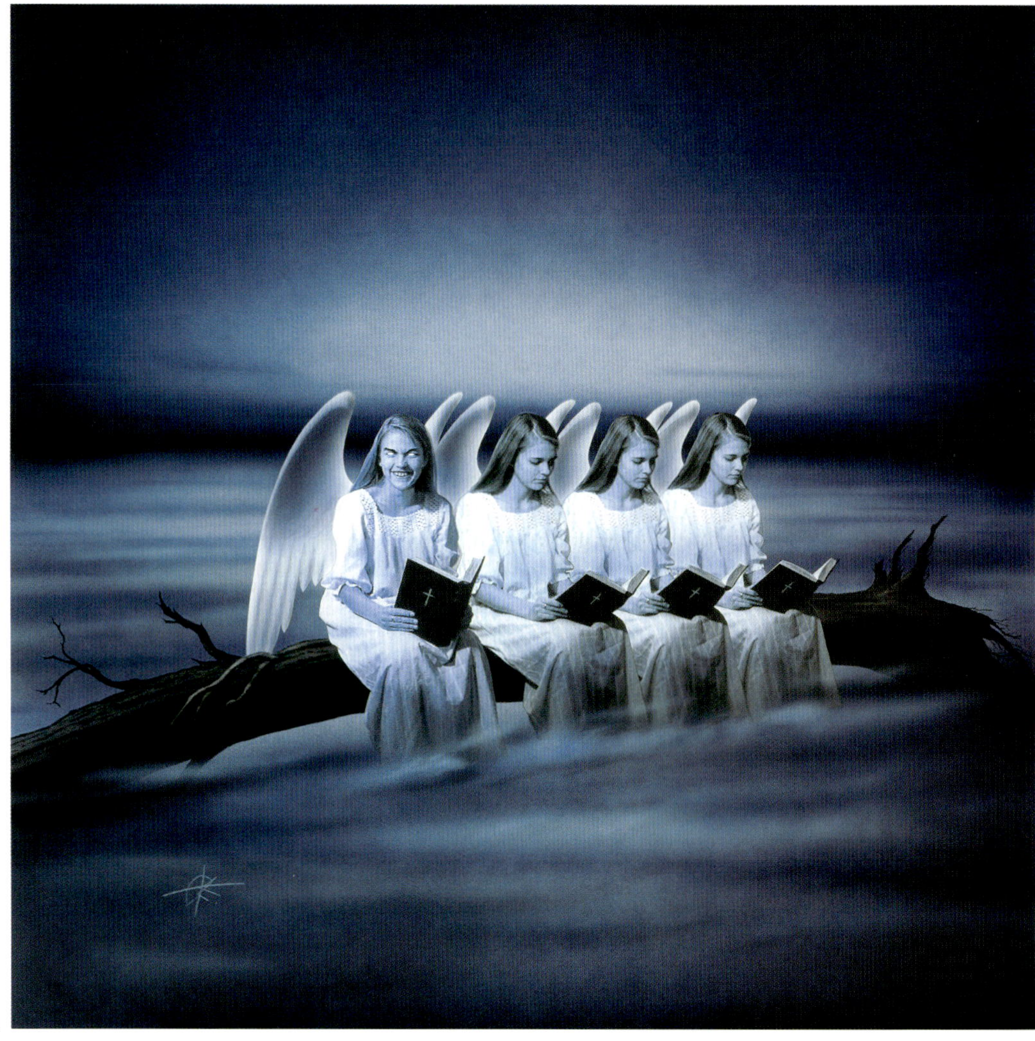

1

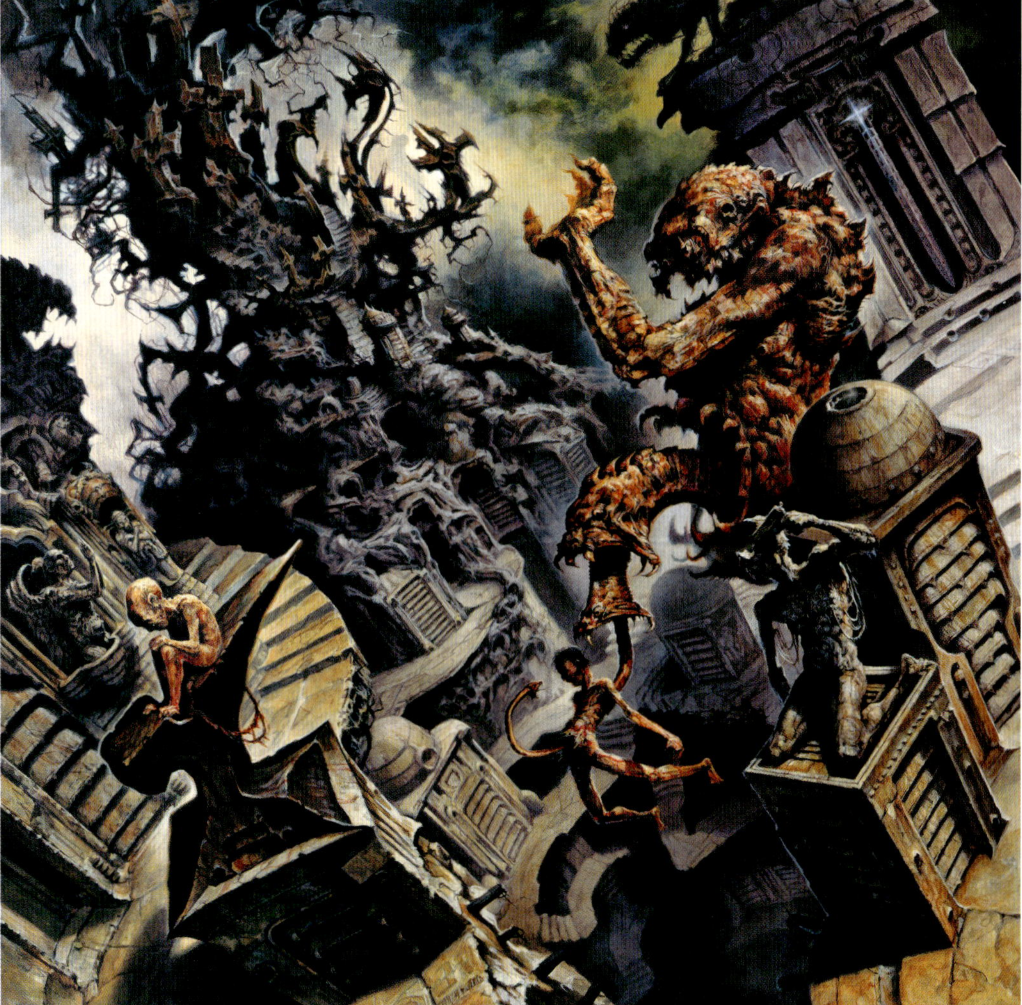

2

3

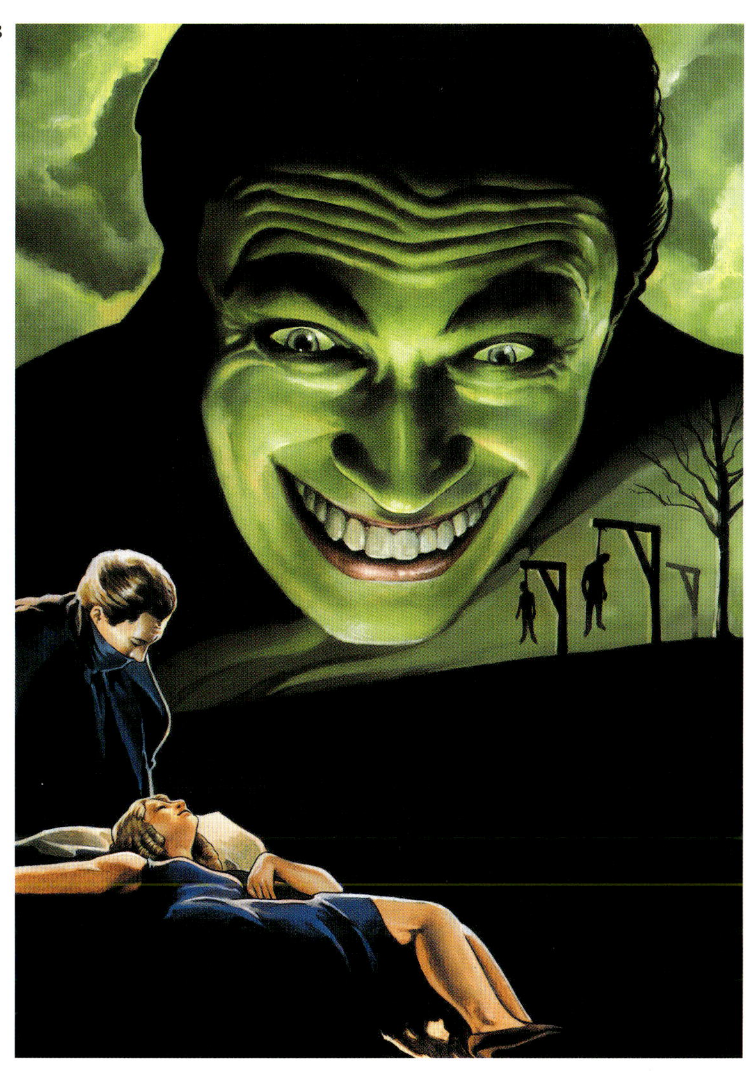

4

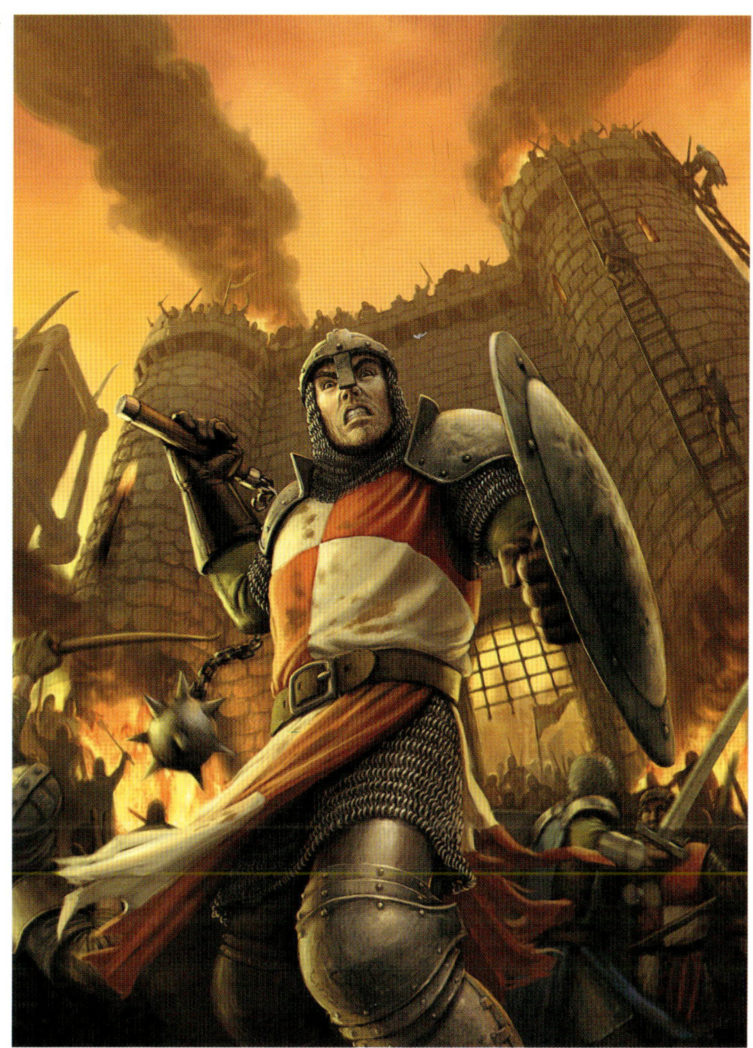

5

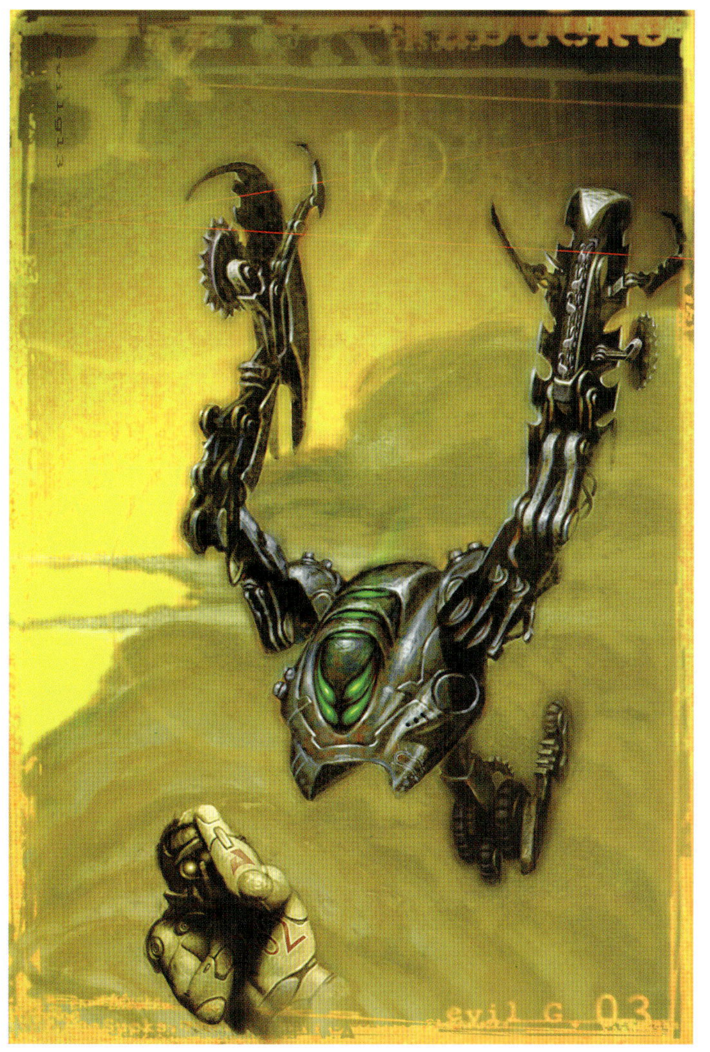

6

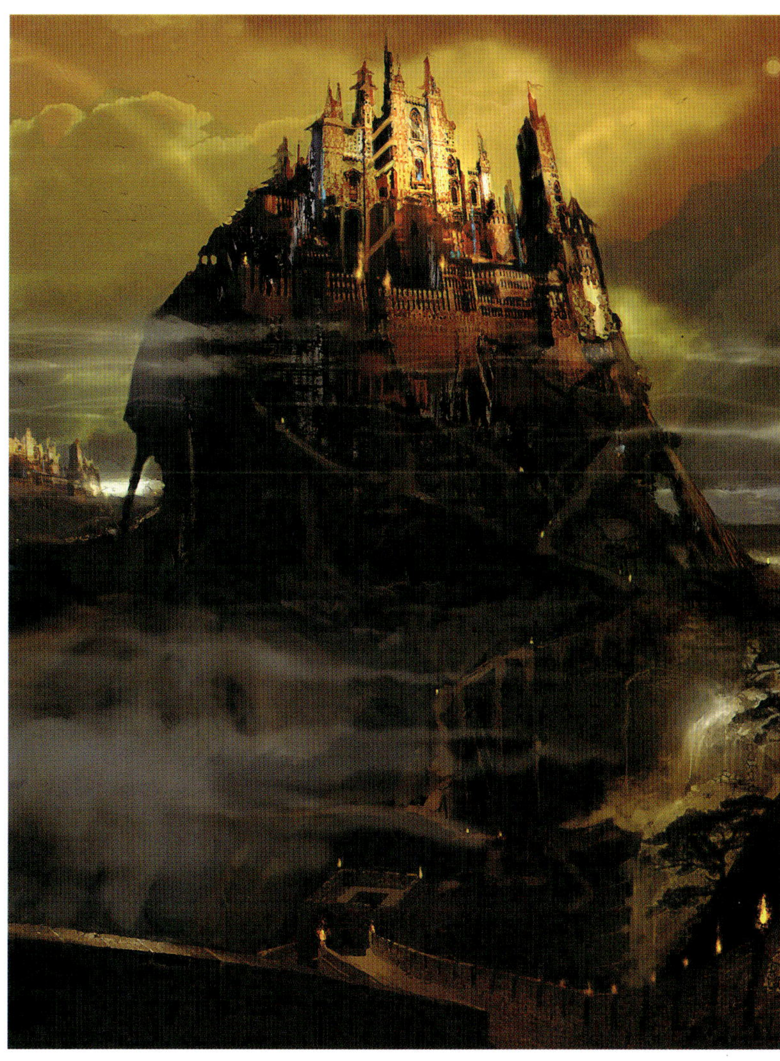

Advertising

1
artist: **John Dunivant**
art director: Dan Walker
client: Theater Bizarre
title: Zombo the Clown
medium: Acrylics *size:* 84″x96″

2
artist: **John Dunivant**
art director: Scott Kodrik
client: Thrall/Alternative Tentacles
title: Lifer
medium: Acrylics *size:* 23″x24″

3
artist: **Sam Wood**
art director: Corey Dangel
designer: Ossenm Entertainment
client: Microsoft Game Studios
title: Jormungand
medium: Digital *size:* 8″x20″

4
artist: **Rafal Olbinski**
client: Alegro, Inc.
title: Otello
medium: Acrylics *size:* 16″x20″

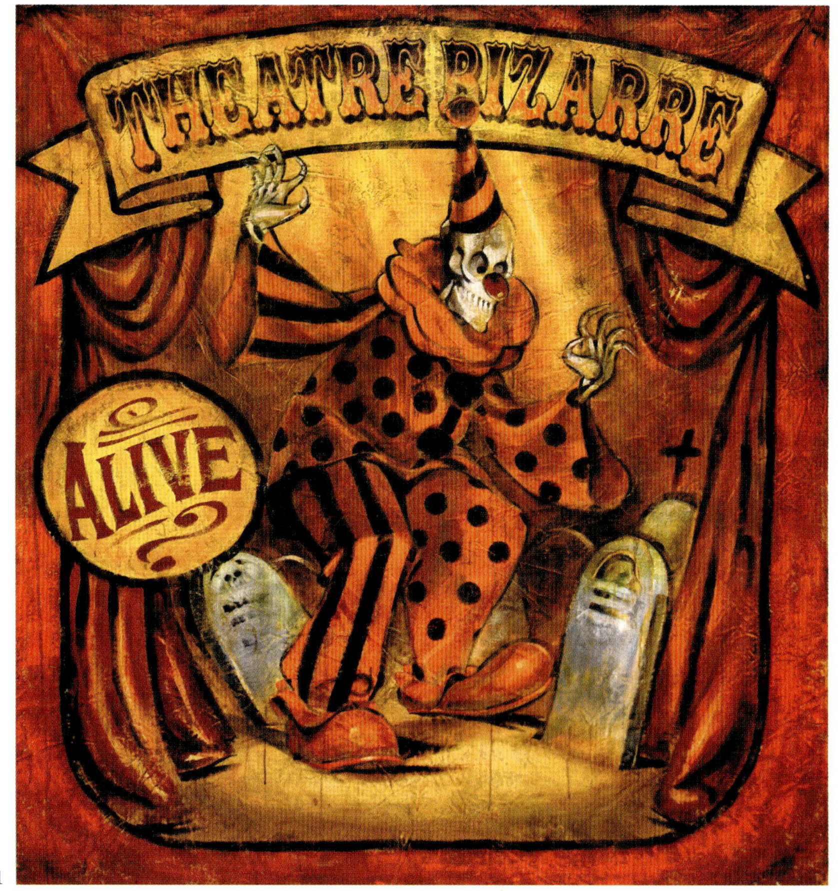

1

2

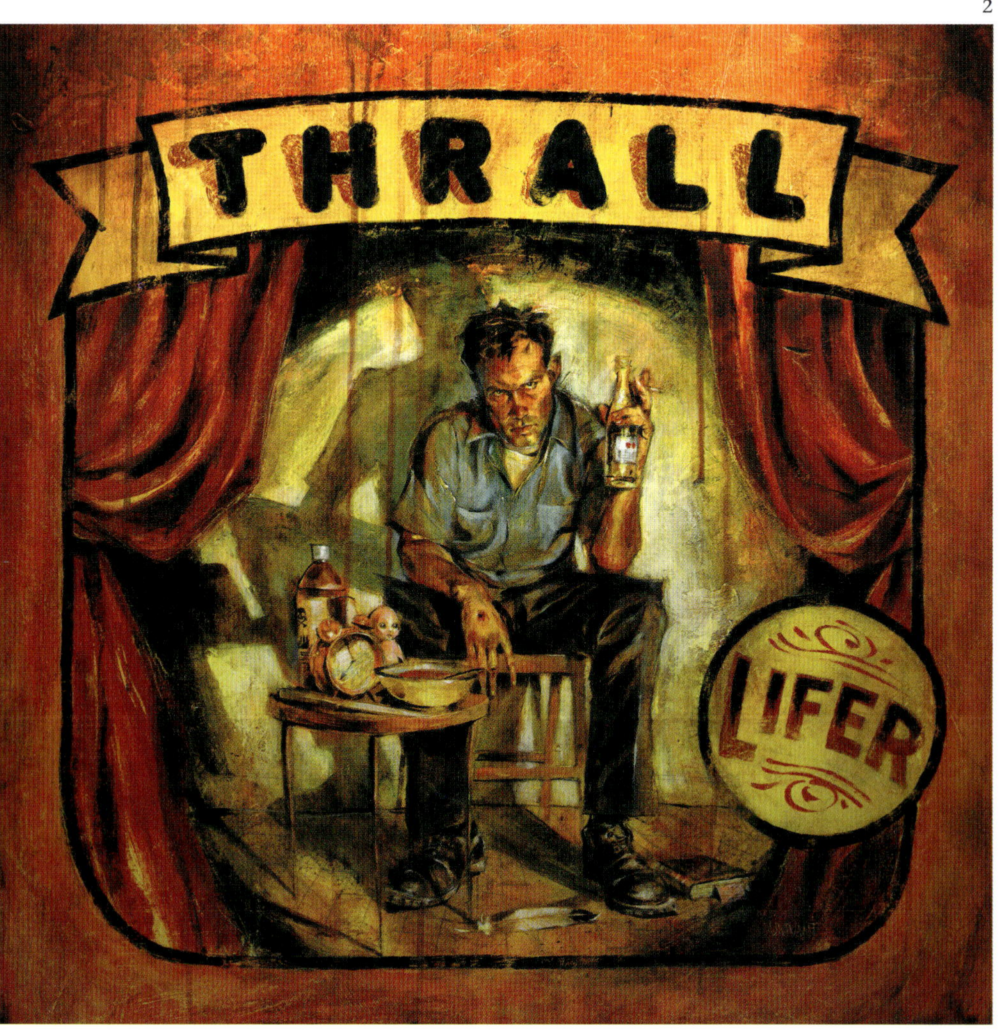

3

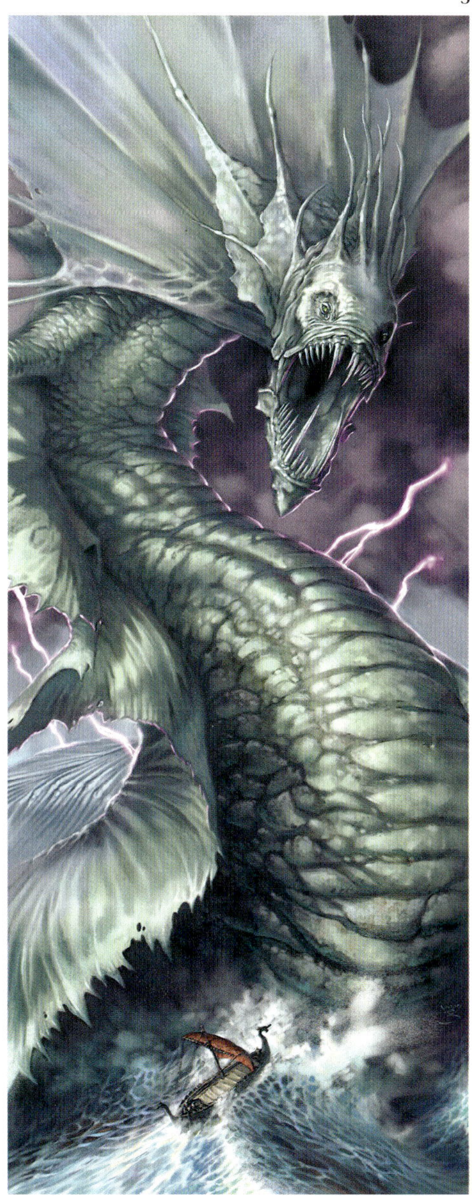

4

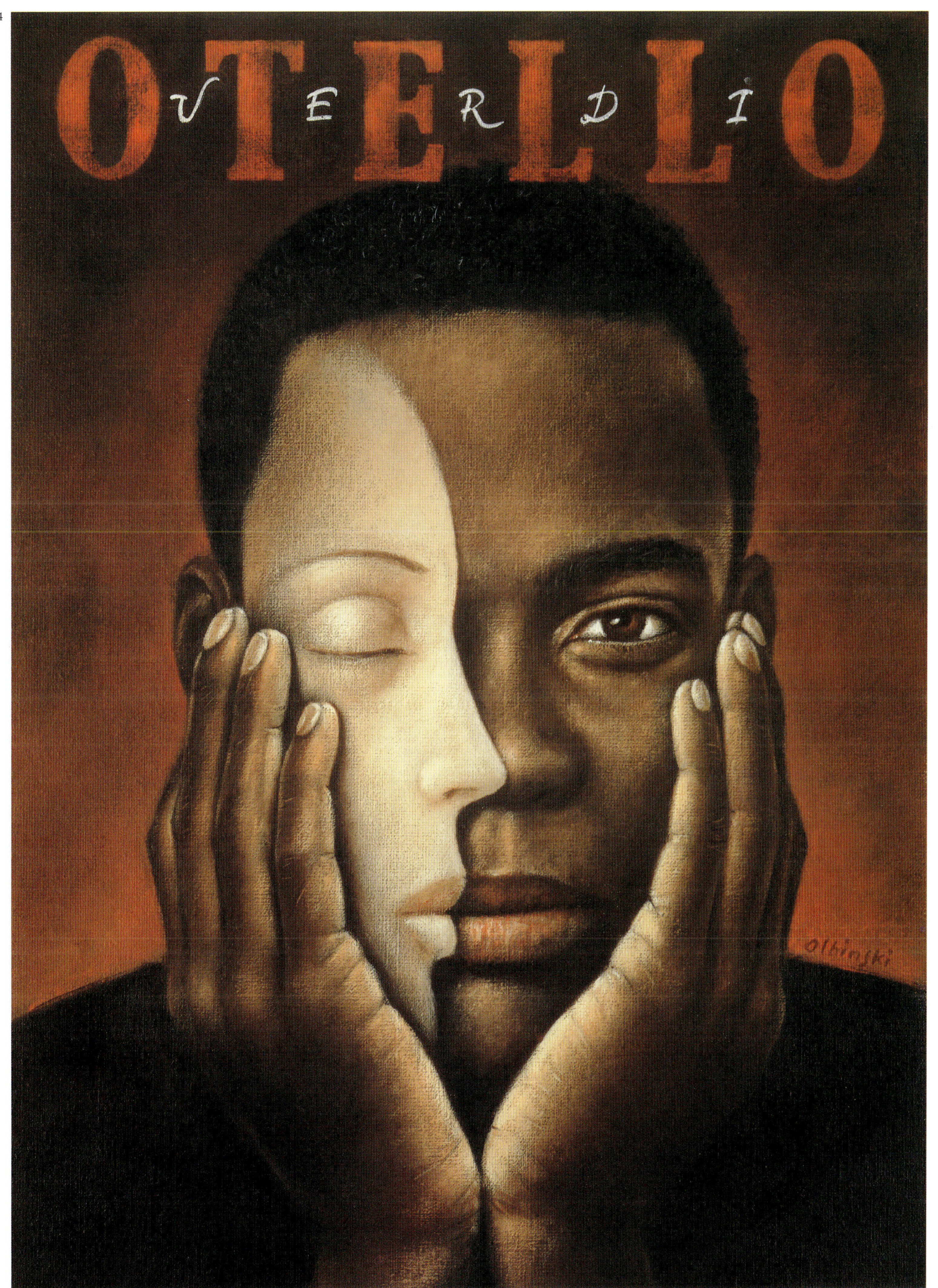

Advertising

1
artist: **Tony DiTerlizzi**
art director: Michelle Montague
designer: Jade Lee
client: Simon & Schuster
title: These Books Are Good!
medium: Gouache *size:* 15″x15″

2
artist: **Rafal Olbinski**
client: Alegro
title: Norma
medium: Acrylic *size:* 20″x30″

3
artist: **Burton**
client: Los Cancioneros
title: 2003-2004 Season
medium: Digital *size:* 8 1/2″x11″

4
artist: **Dave Seeley**
art director: Dave Brzozowski
client: Bluespark Studios–TDK–Disney
title: Pirates of the Caribbean/Gameboy
medium: Digital

5
artist: **Jerry Lofaro**
art director: Kimberly Malleck
client: Celestial Seasonings
title: Marrakesh Express Tea
medium: Digital *size:* 18″x12″

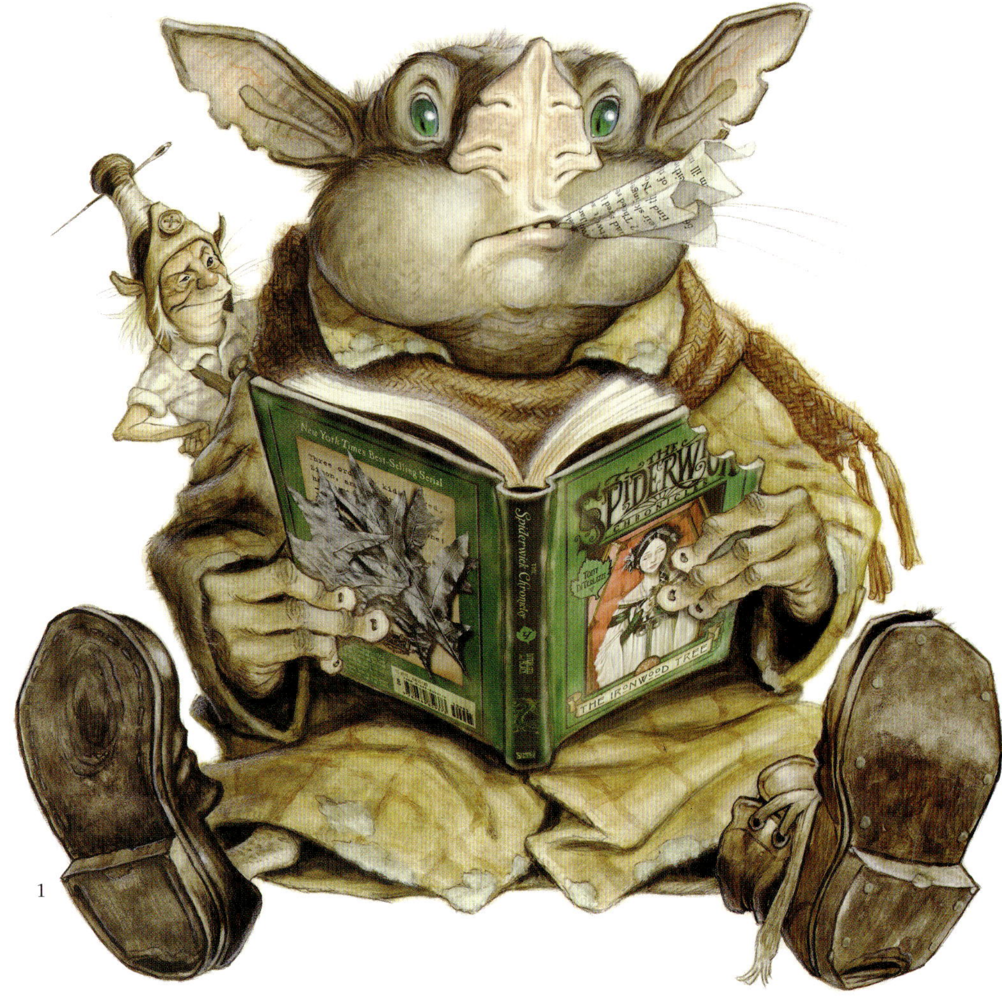

1

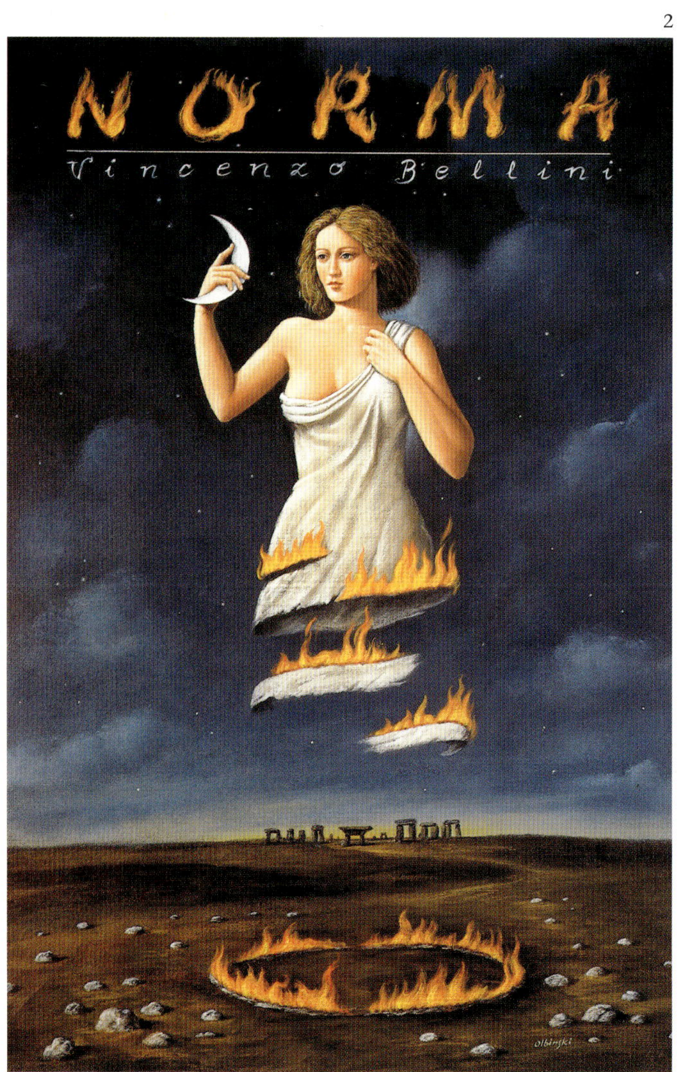

2

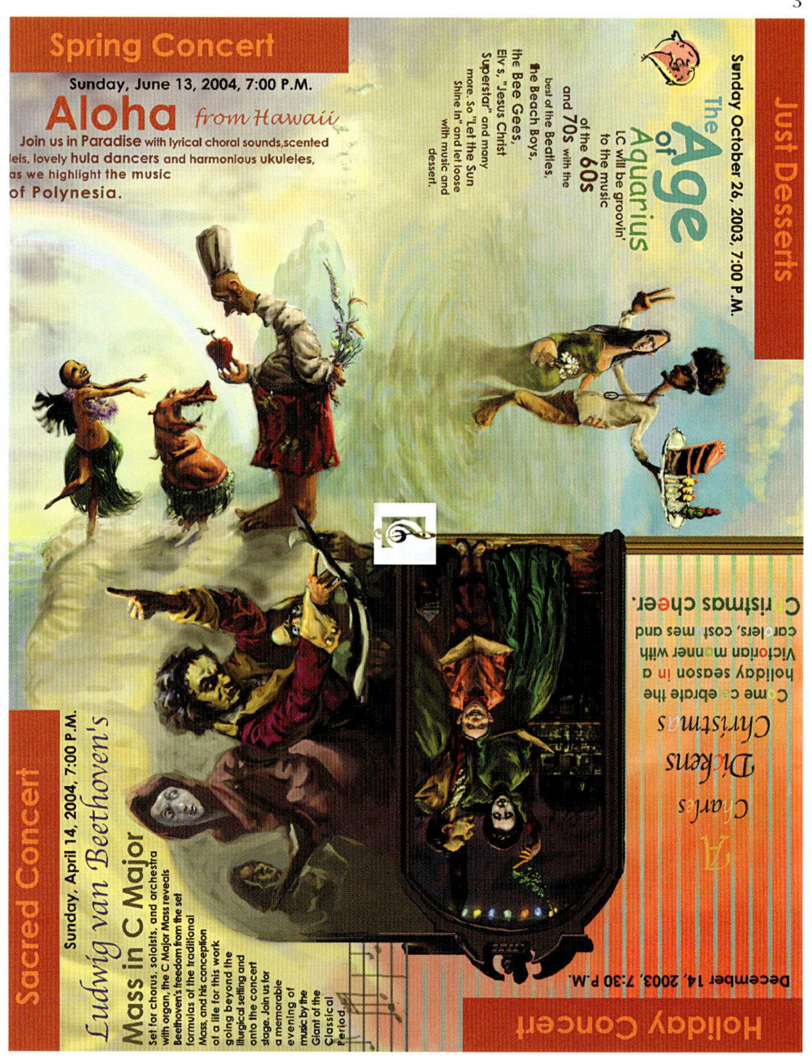

3

4

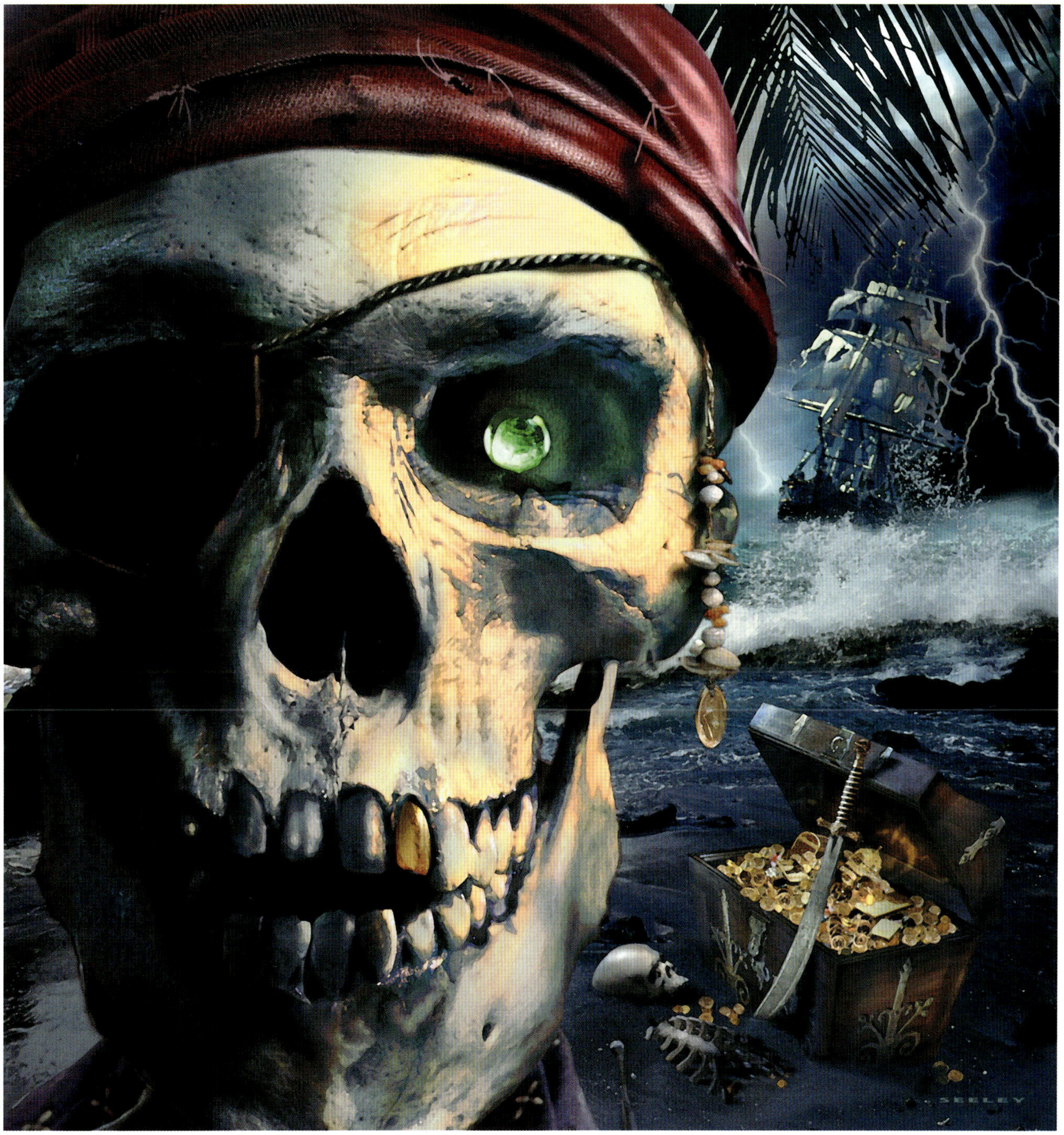

5

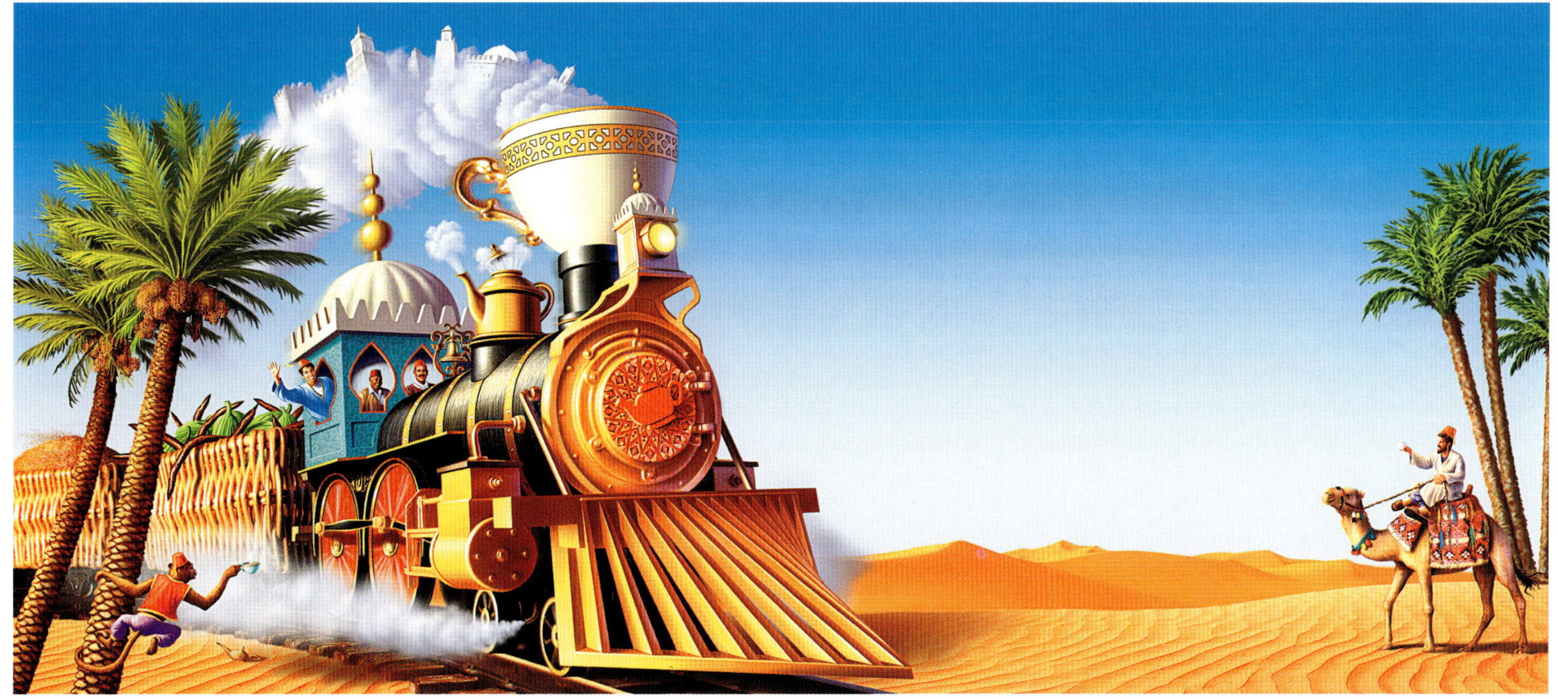

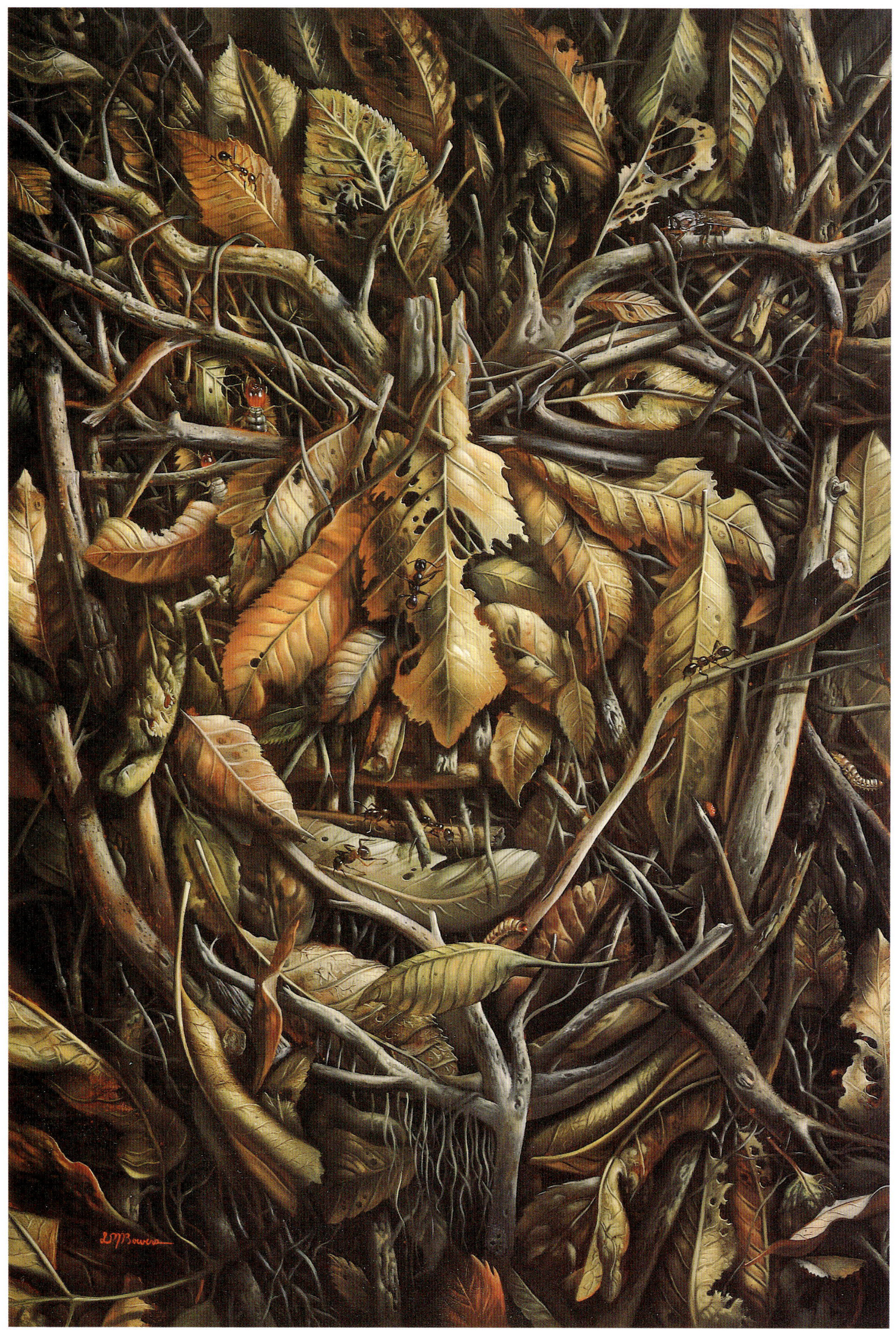

artist: **David Bowers**
art director: Irene Gallo *client:* Tor Books *title:* Twigman *medium:* Oil *size:* 11"x17"

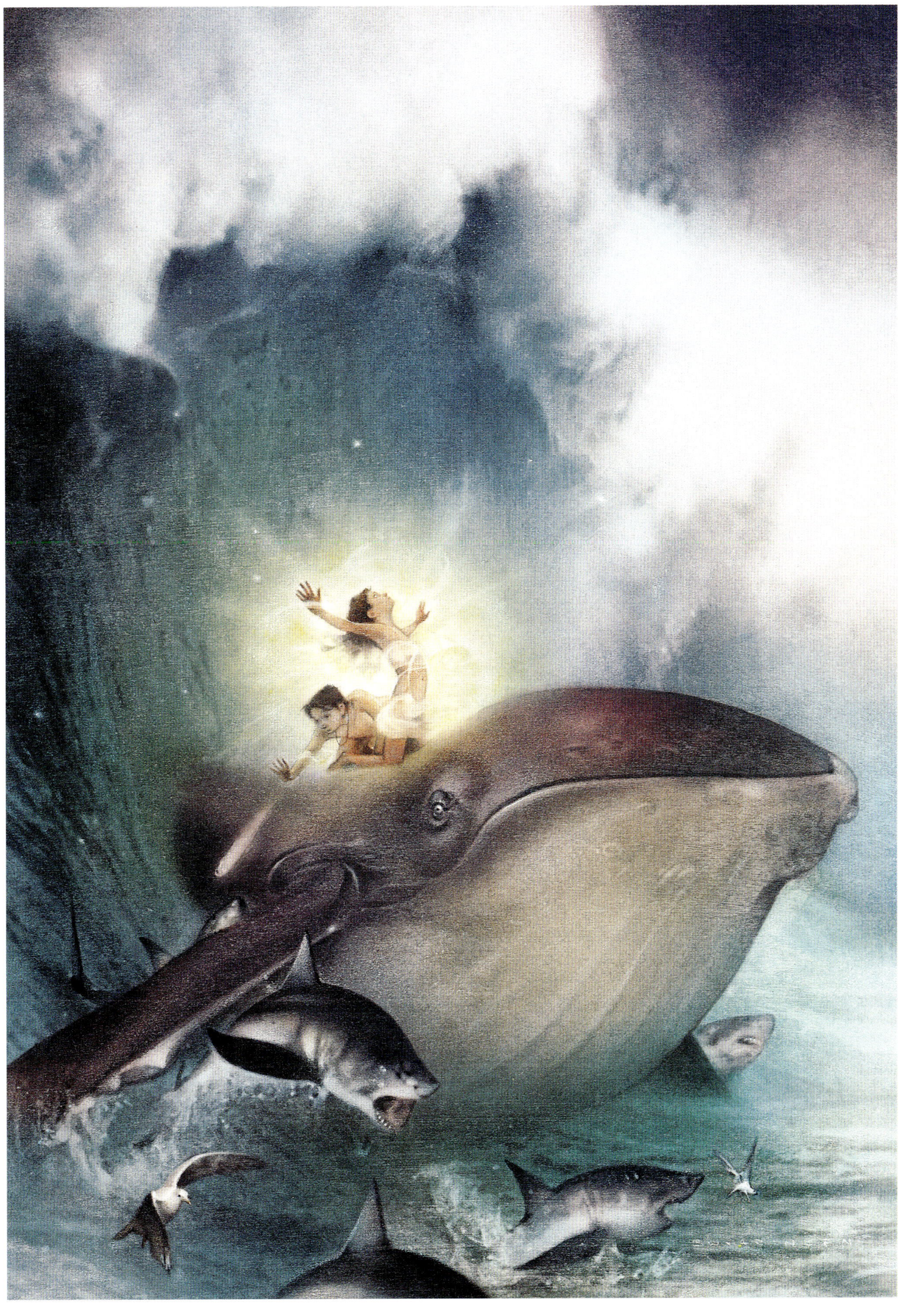

artist: **Greg Swearingen**
art director: Liz Demeter *designer:* Liz Demeter *client:* Harcourt, Inc. *title:* Deep Wizardry
medium: Mixed *size:* 8″x12″

1
artist: **Caniglia**
client: Night Shade Books
title: A Paler Shade of Being
medium: Watercolor
size: 10"x14"

2
artist: **Patrick Arrasmith**
art director: Irene Gallo
client: Orb/Tor Books
title: Agyar
medium: Scratchboard
size: 10$^{1}/_{2}$"x15$^{1}/_{2}$"

3
artist: **Darrel Anderson**
client: Donald M. Grant Publishing, Inc.
title: Birdman
medium: Digital
size: 6"x92"

4
artist: **Michael J. Deas**
art director: Richard Deas
client: Tor Books
title: Hell House
medium: Oil on panel
size: 13"x222"

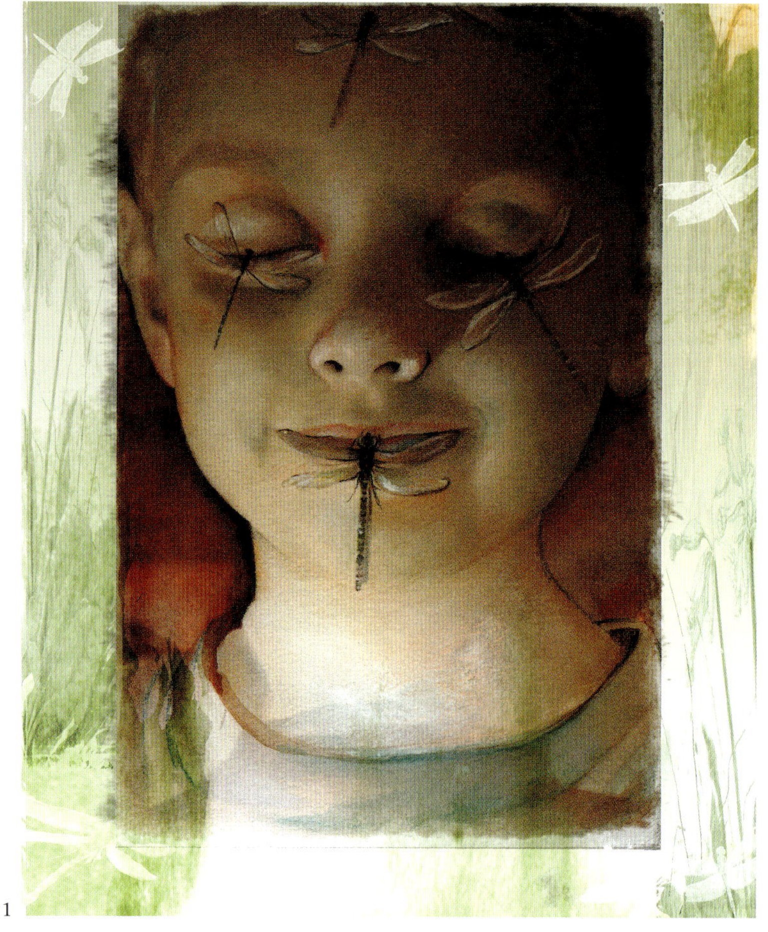
1

2

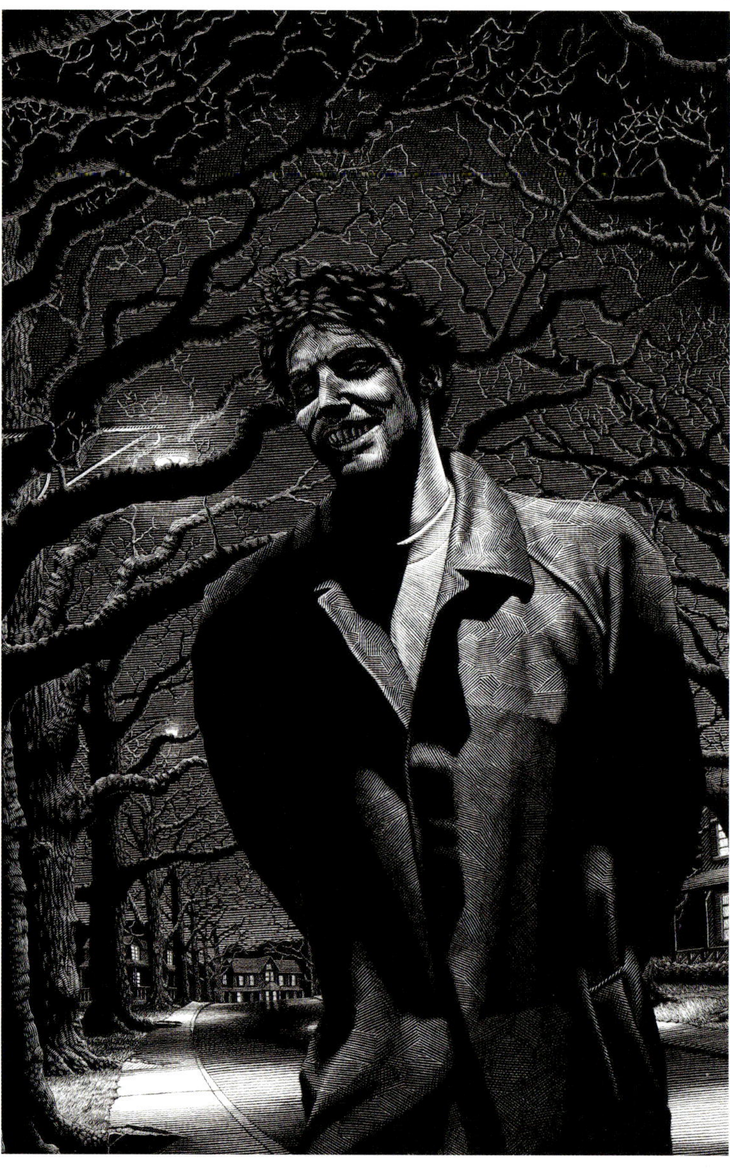

3

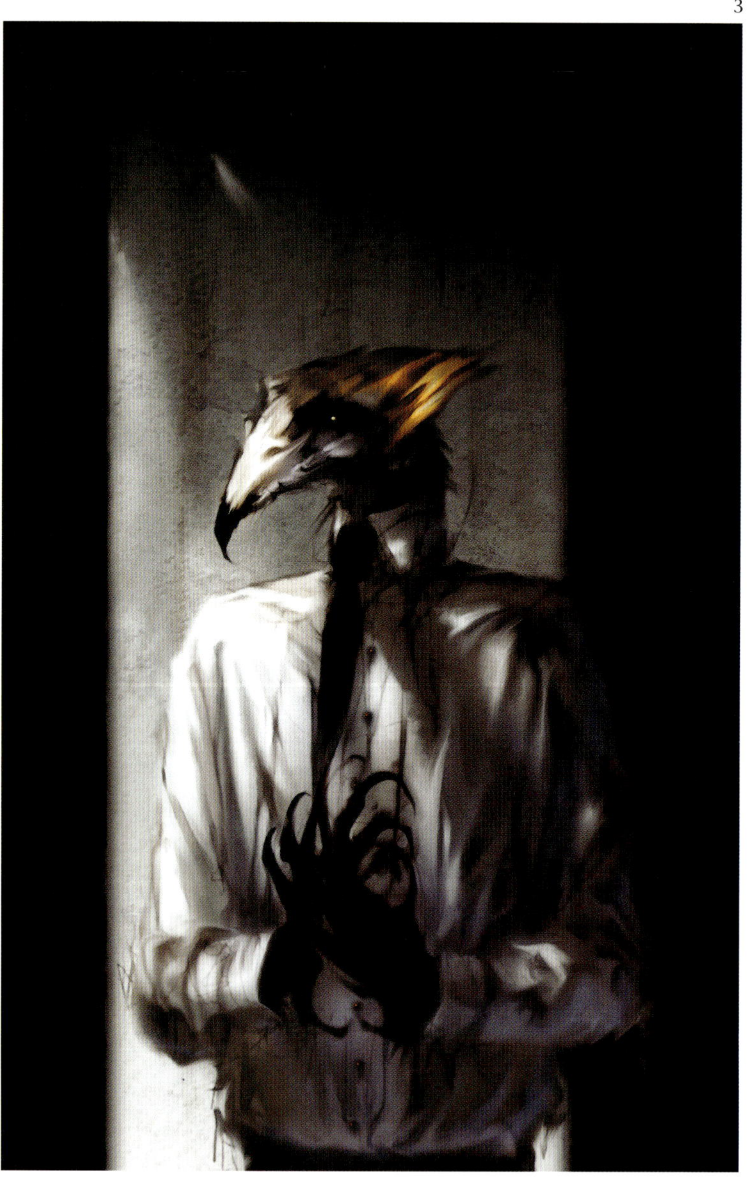

4

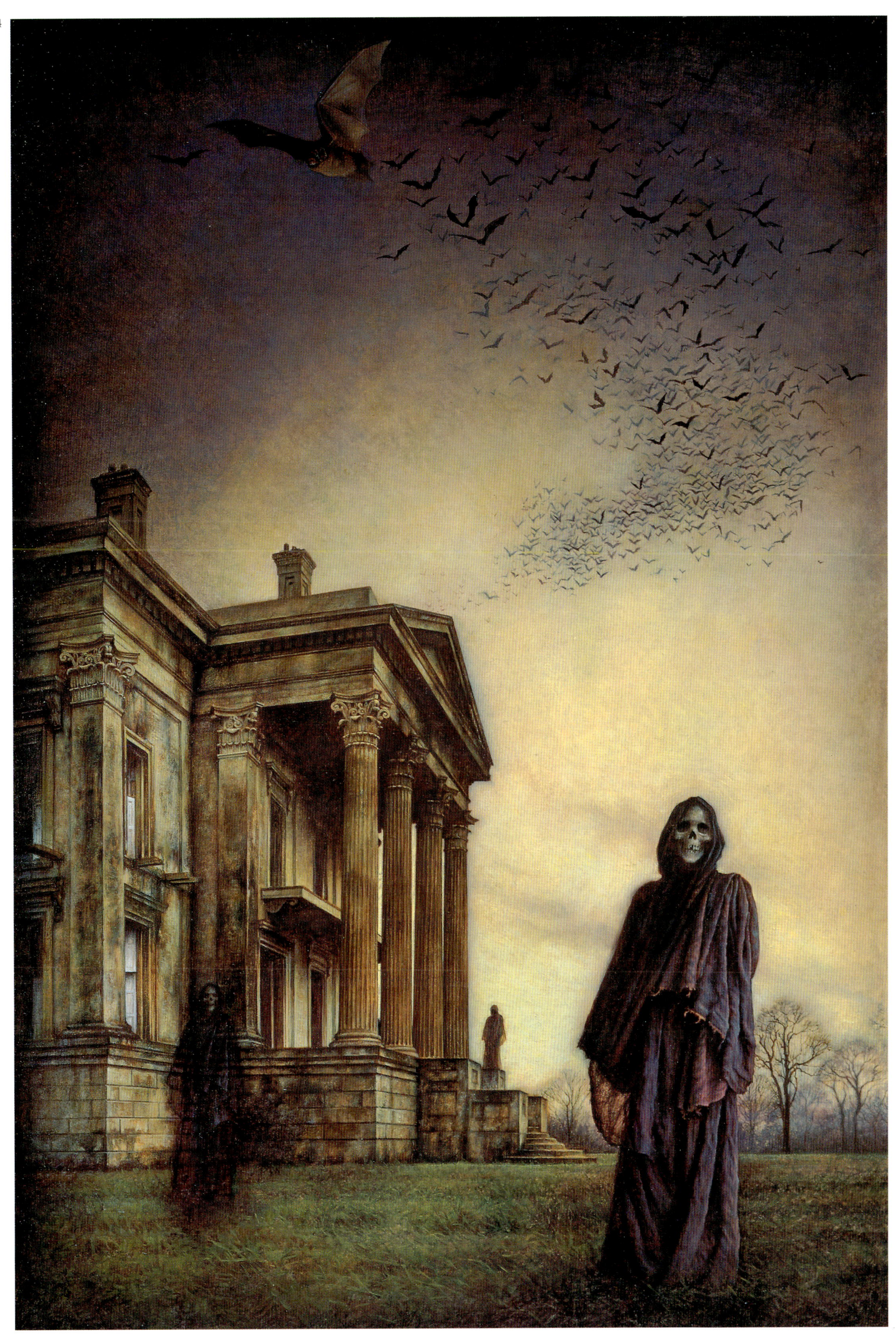

Book

1
artist: **Paul Bonner**
art director: Theodore Bergquist
designer: Paul Bonner
client: Riotminds
title: Drakar Och Demoner
medium: Watercolor
size: 39cmx55cm

2
artist: **Marc A. Fishman**
art director: James Londer
client: Green Knight Publishing
title: Pendragon
medium: Oil on canvas
size: 5′x6′

3
artist: **Todd Lockwood**
client: Paper Tiger
title: Transition
medium: Digital
size: 13″x20″

4
artist: **Paul Bonner**
art director: Theodore Bergquist
designer: Paul Bonner
client: Riotminds
title: Tornödlorna
medium: Watercolor
size: 41cmx56cm

1

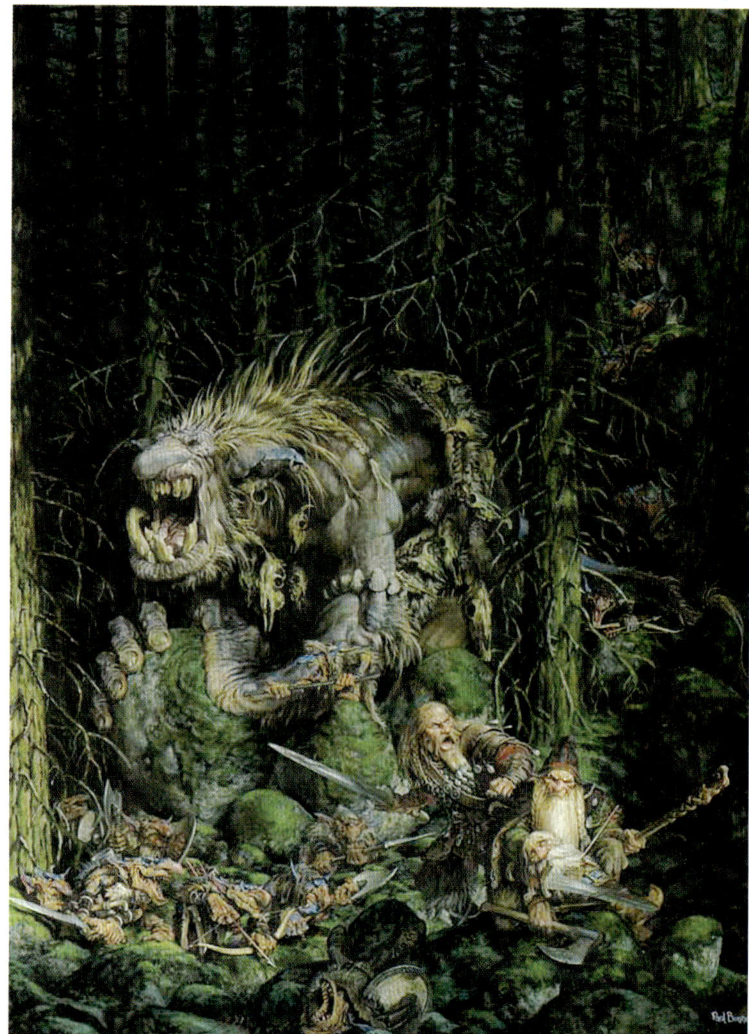

2

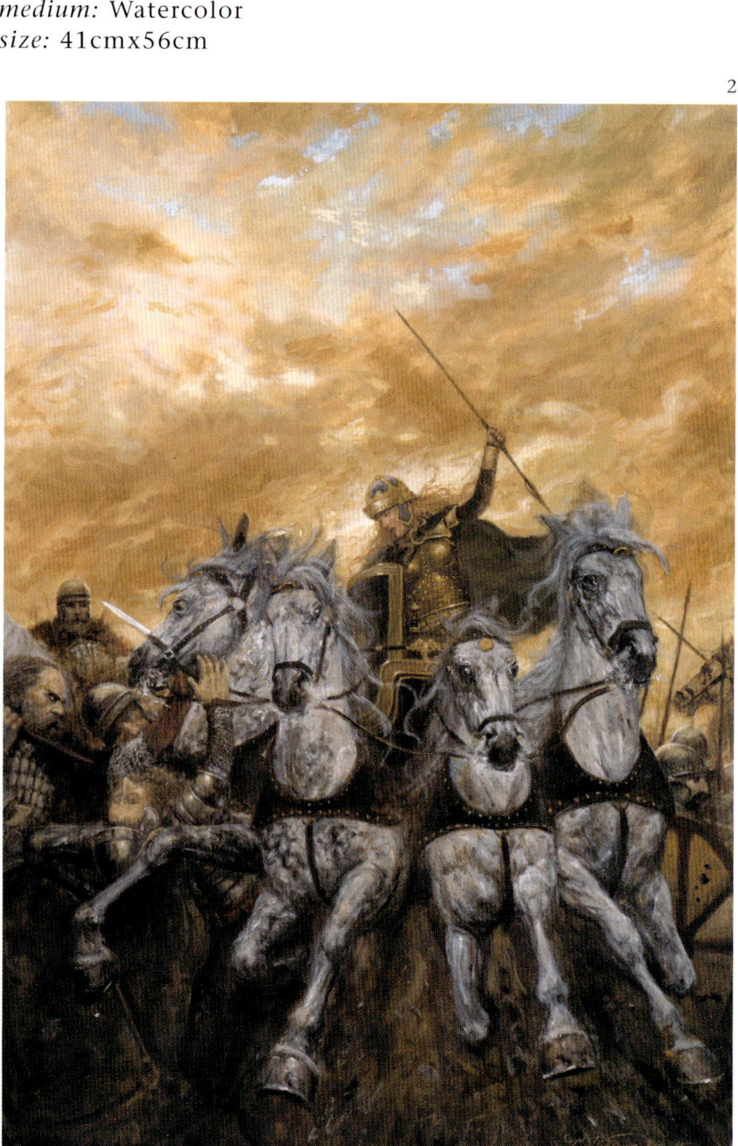

3

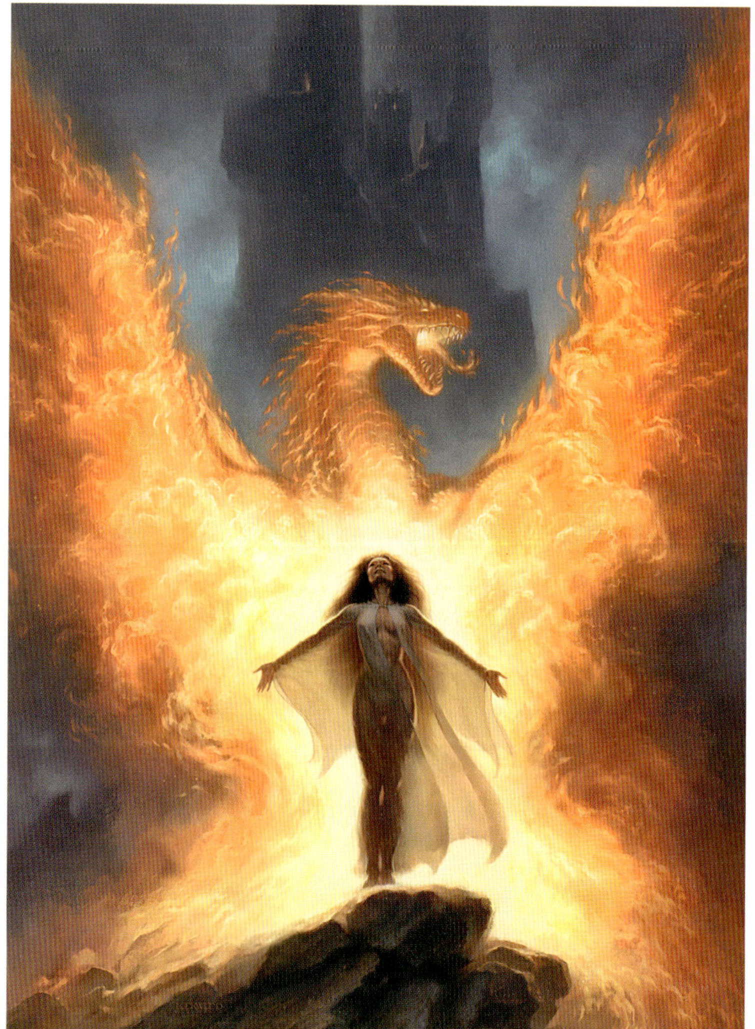

4

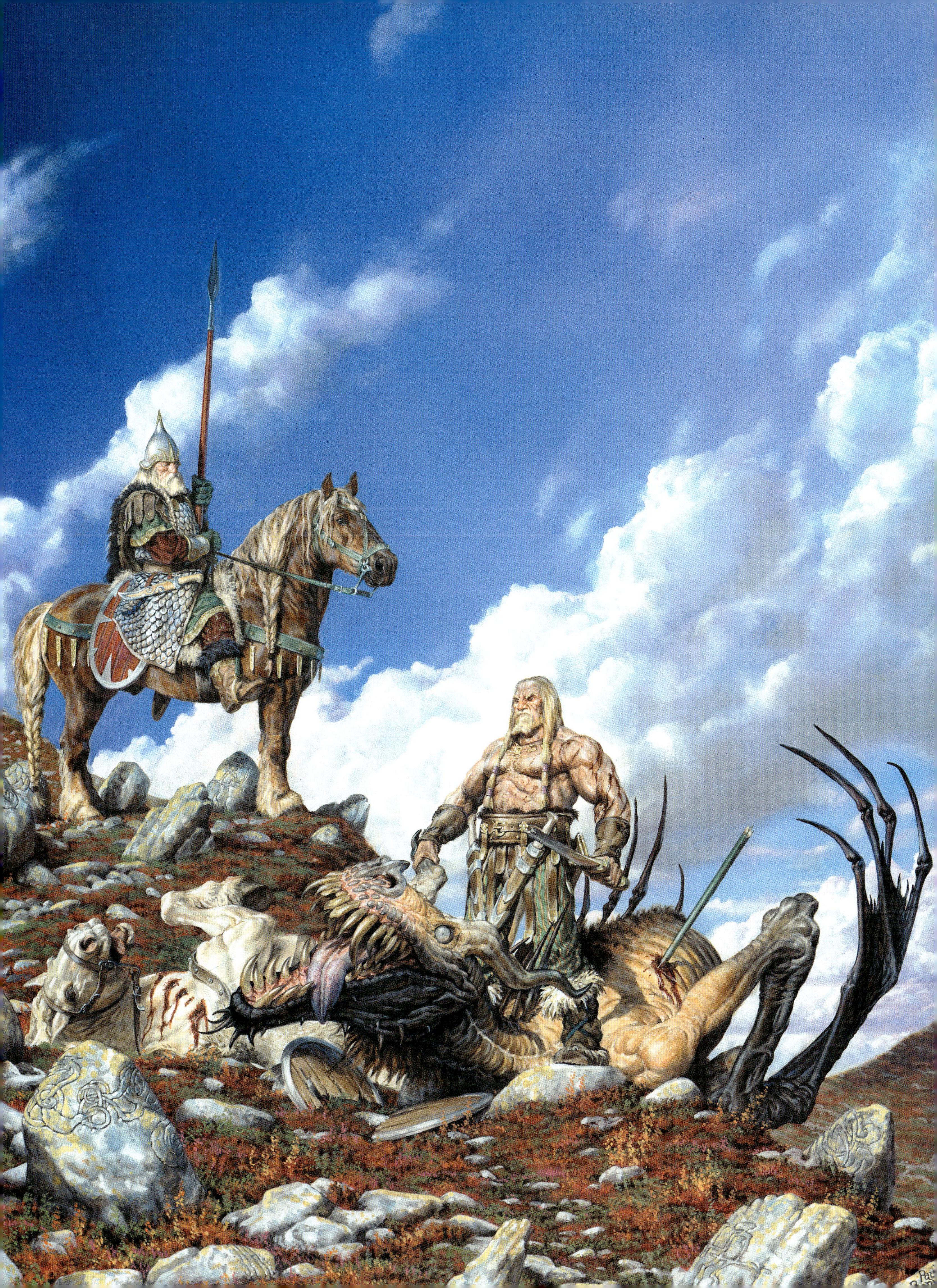

Book

1
artist: **Kurt Miller**
art director: Jim Baen
client: Baen Books
title: The Hero
medium: Digital
size: $6\frac{3}{4}$″x$9\frac{3}{5}$″

2
artist: **Jon Foster**
art director: Dave Dorman
client: Rolling Thunder Press
title: Re-entry
medium: Digital
size: $6\frac{3}{4}$″x$10\frac{1}{4}$″

3
artist: **Scott Grimando**
art director: Judith Murello
client: Ace Books
title: Kris Longknife Mutineer
medium: Mixed
size: 9″x12″

4
artist: **Jon Foster** WITH DAVE DORMAN
art director: Dave Dorman
client: Rolling Thunder Press
title: The Uninvited
medium: Digital
size: $6\frac{3}{4}$″x$10\frac{1}{4}$″

1

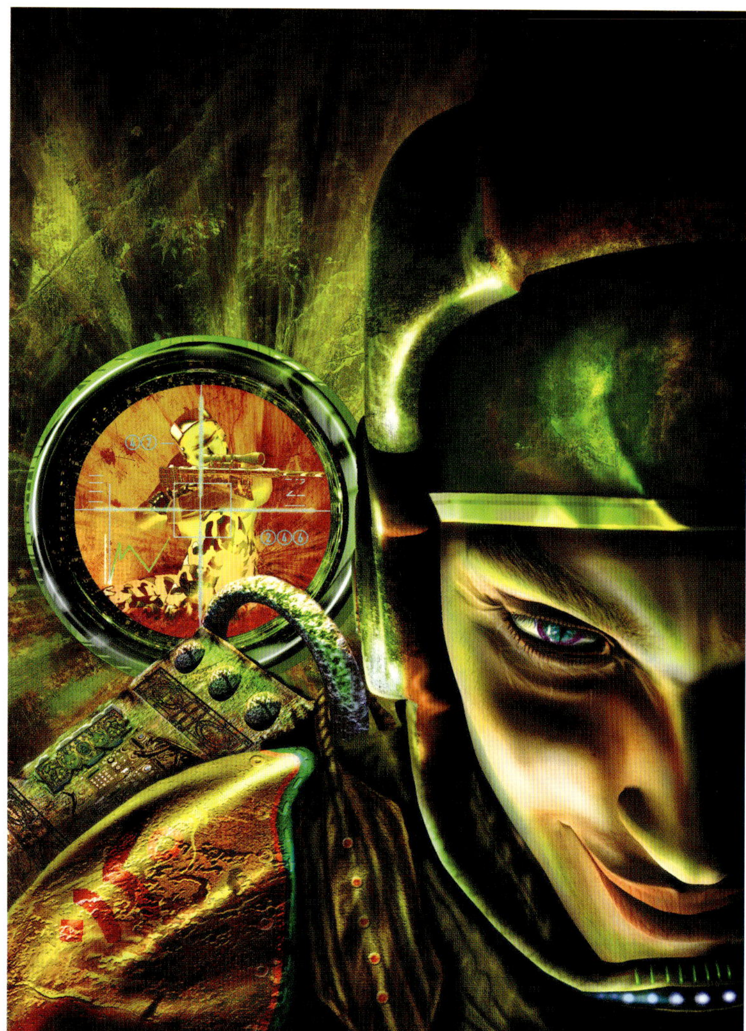

2

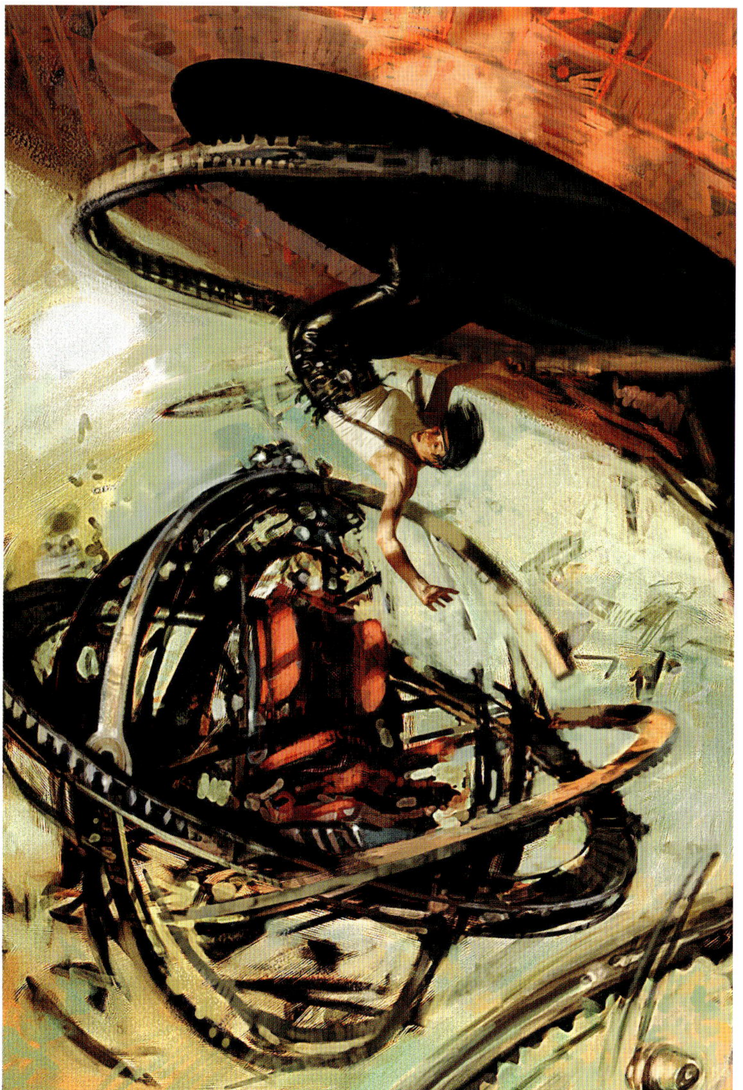

3

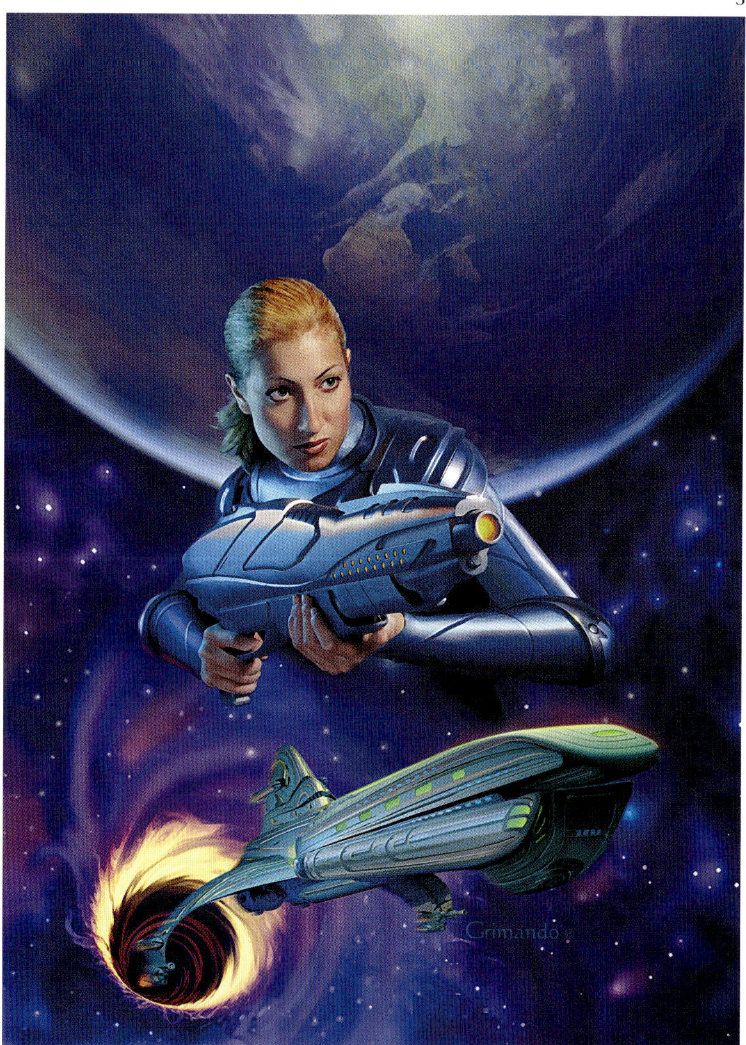

4

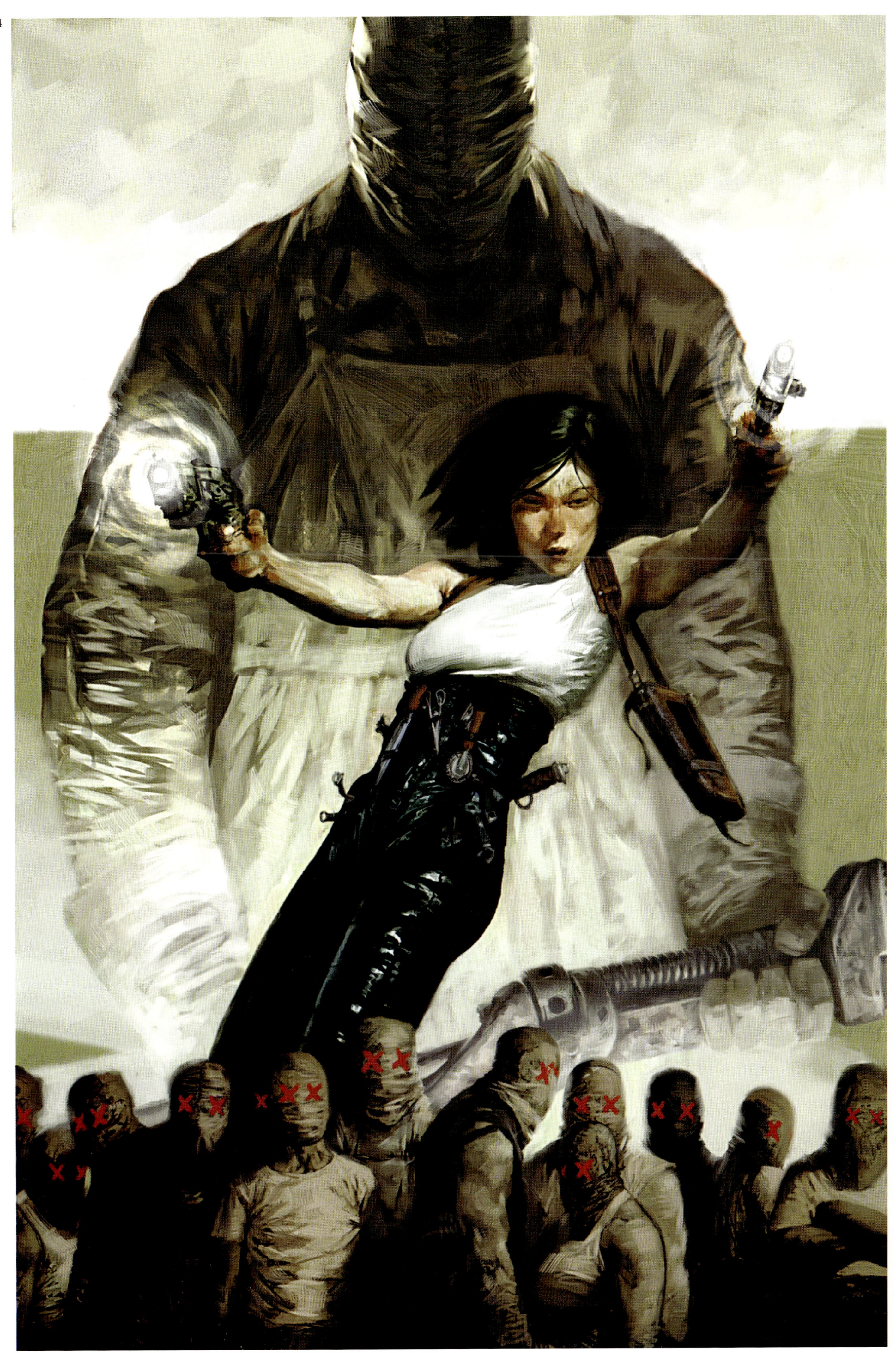

Book

1
artist: **Thomas Thiemeyer**
client: Verlag Nummer 1
title: Sky Needle
medium: Oil on masonite
size: 27"x25"

2
artist: **Stephen Youll**
art director: Don Puckey
designer: Stephen Youll
client: Warner Books
title: Horizon Storms
medium: Digital
size: 9"x8"

3
artist: **J.P. Targete**
art director: Tom Egner
client: Eos Books
title: Contact Imminent
medium: Oils on board
size: 18"x24"

4
artist: **Chris Moore**
art director: Sue Mechniewicz
client: Orion Books
title: The Simulacra
medium: Acrylics
size: 11"x17"

5
artist: **Fred Gambino**
art director: Ray Lundgren
client: Roc Books
title: Fortress of Lies
medium: Digital

6
artist: **David B. Mattingly**
art director: Jim Baen
client: Baen Books
title: The Road to Damascus
medium: Digital

1

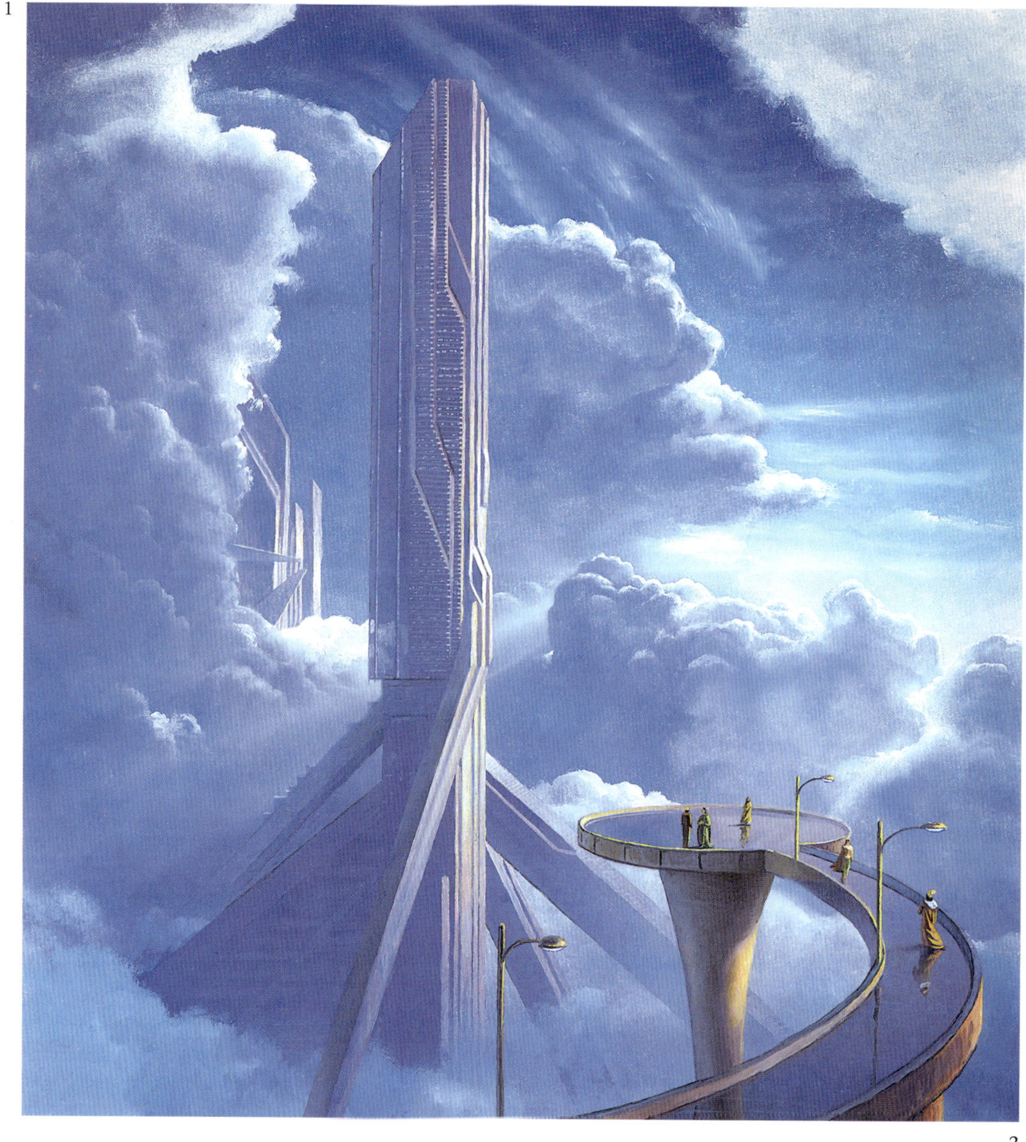

2

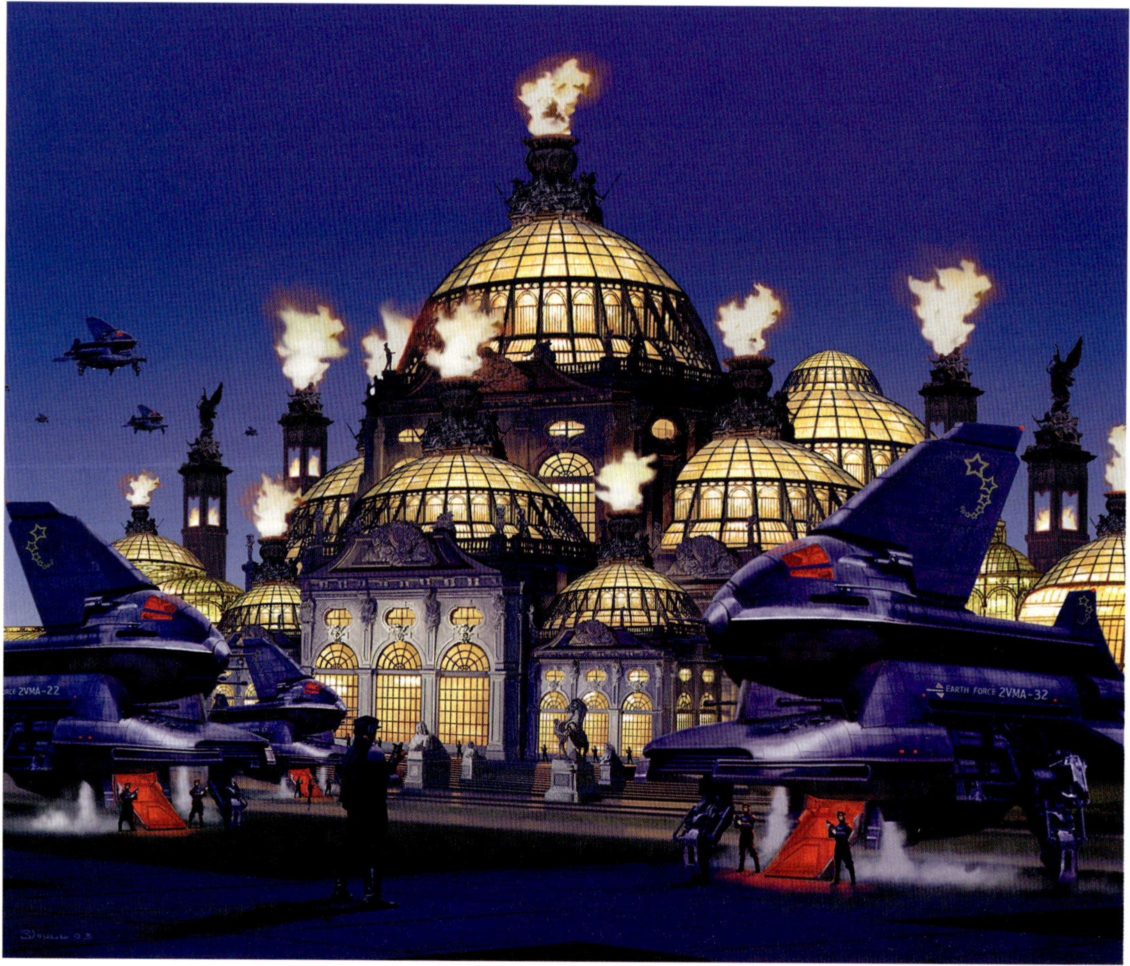

3

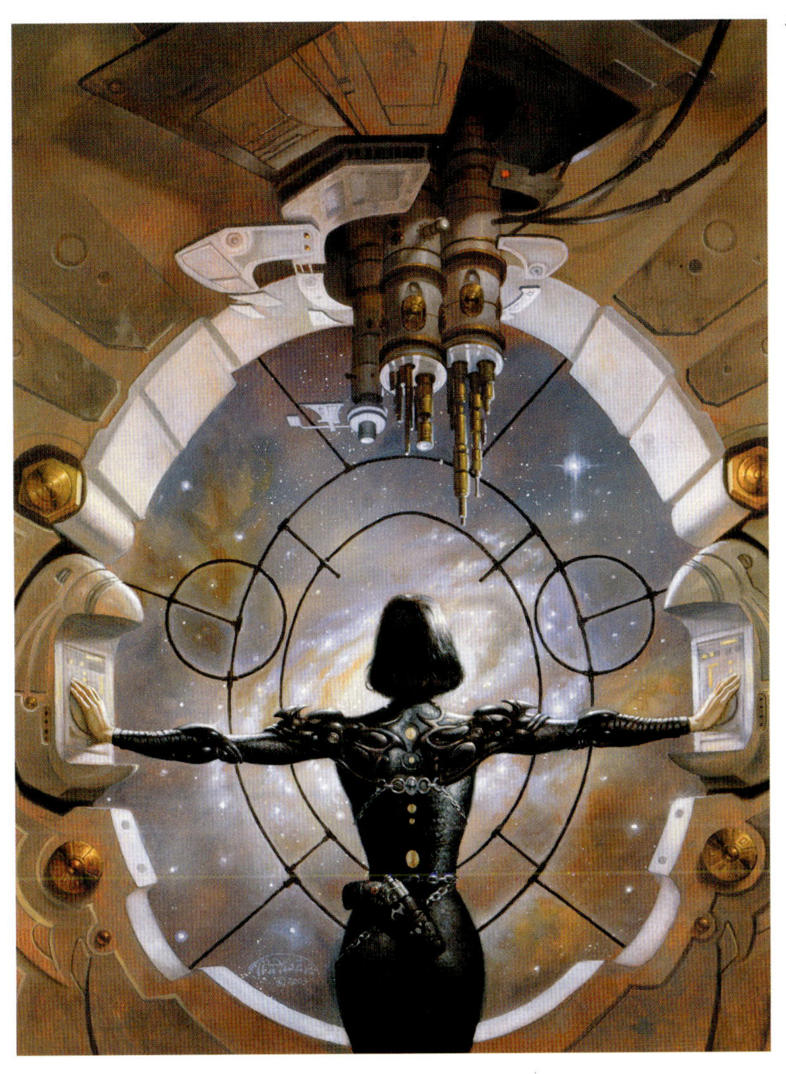

4

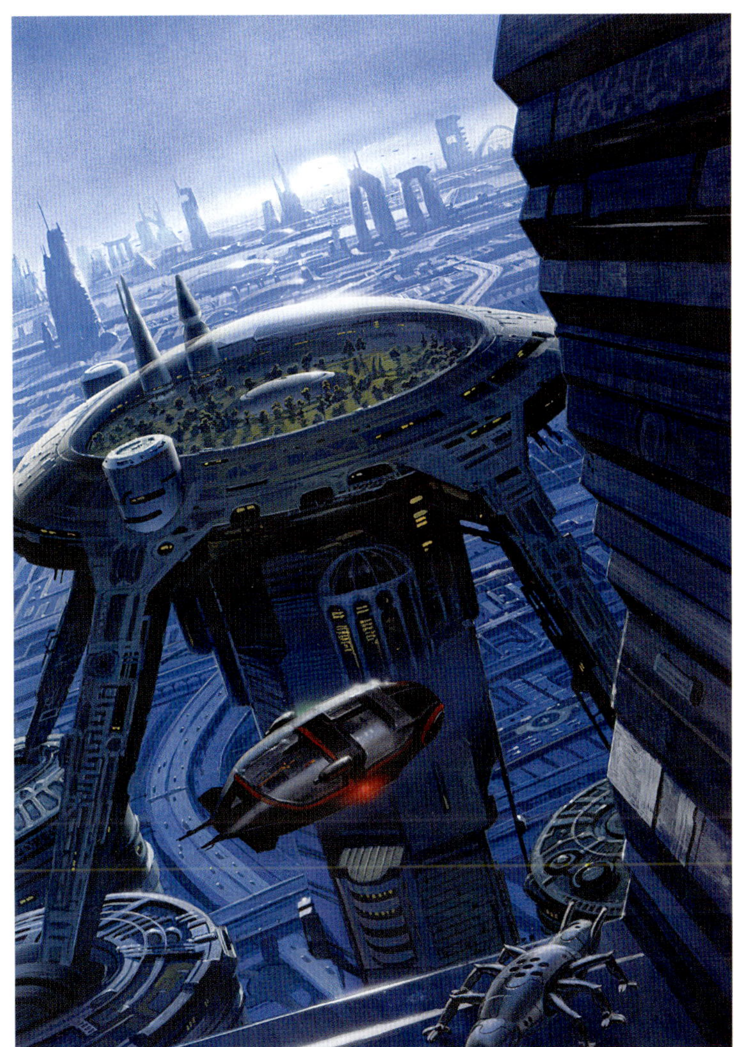

5

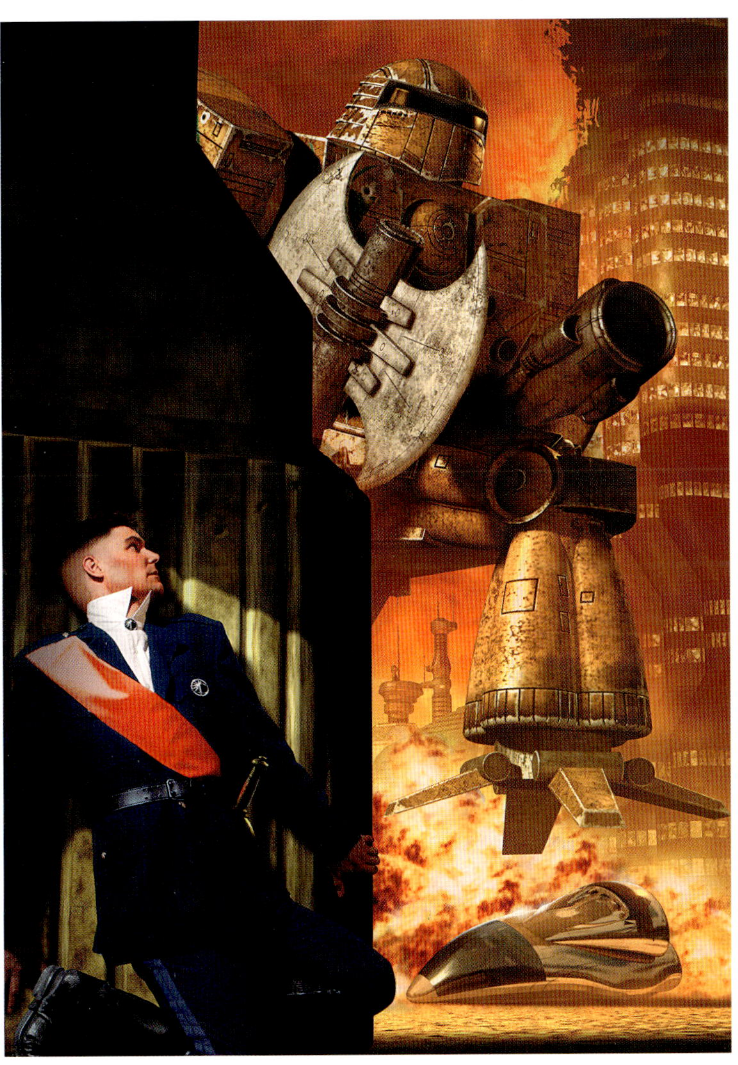

6

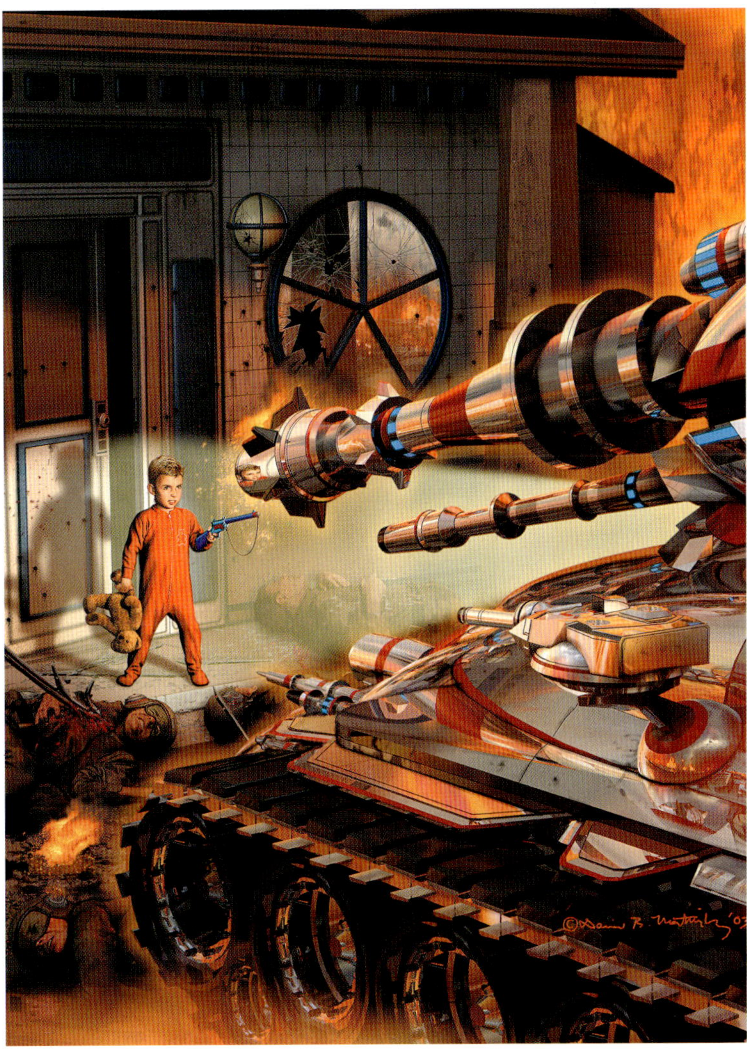

1
artist: **Echo Chernik**
art director: Phil Brucato
client: Smoke, Mirror & Muse
title: Ivy Melavat
medium: Digital
size: 5″x5″

2
artist: **Brom**
client: Wizards of the Coast
title: Avatar
medium: Oil

3
artist: **Chad Michael Ward**
client: NBM
title: The Madness
medium: Digital
size: 9″x12″

4
artist: **Larry Moore**
art director: Irene Gallo
client: Tor Books
title: Inventing Memory
medium: Pastel

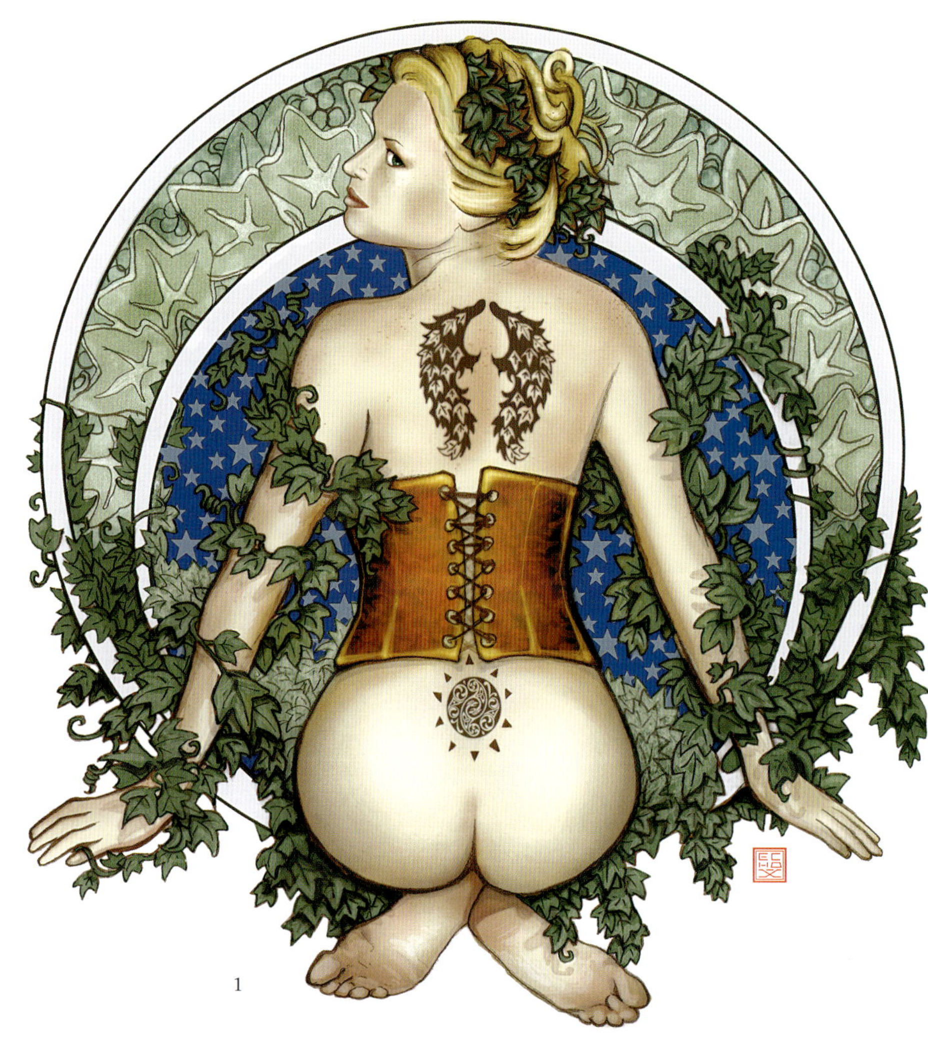

1

2

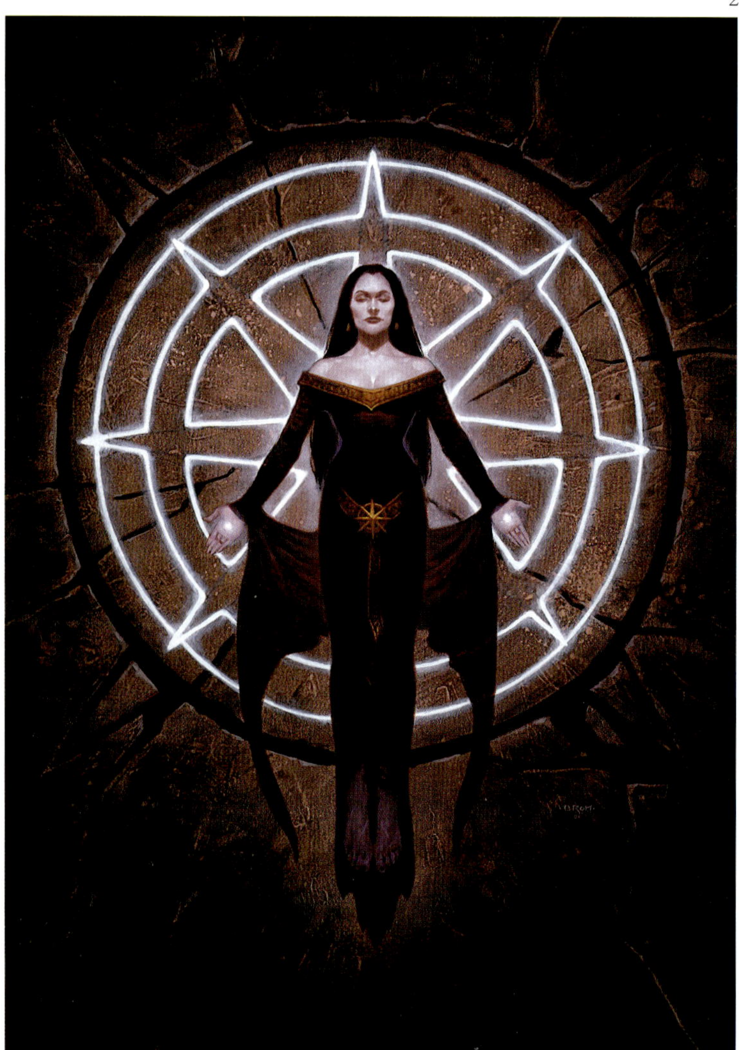

3

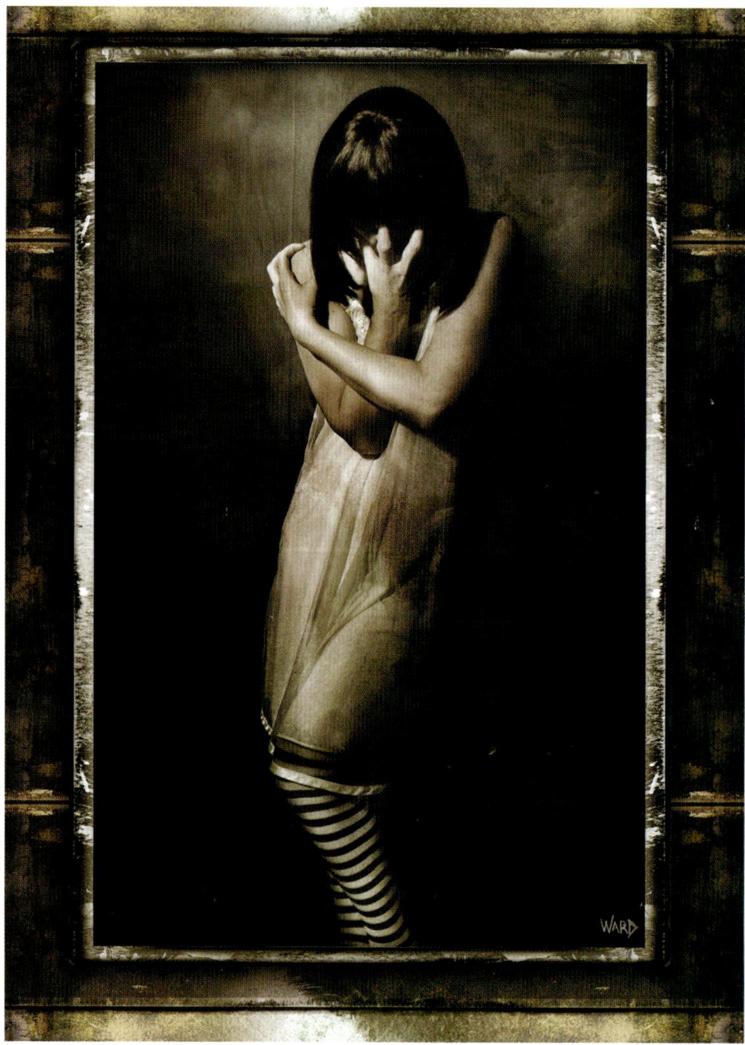

4

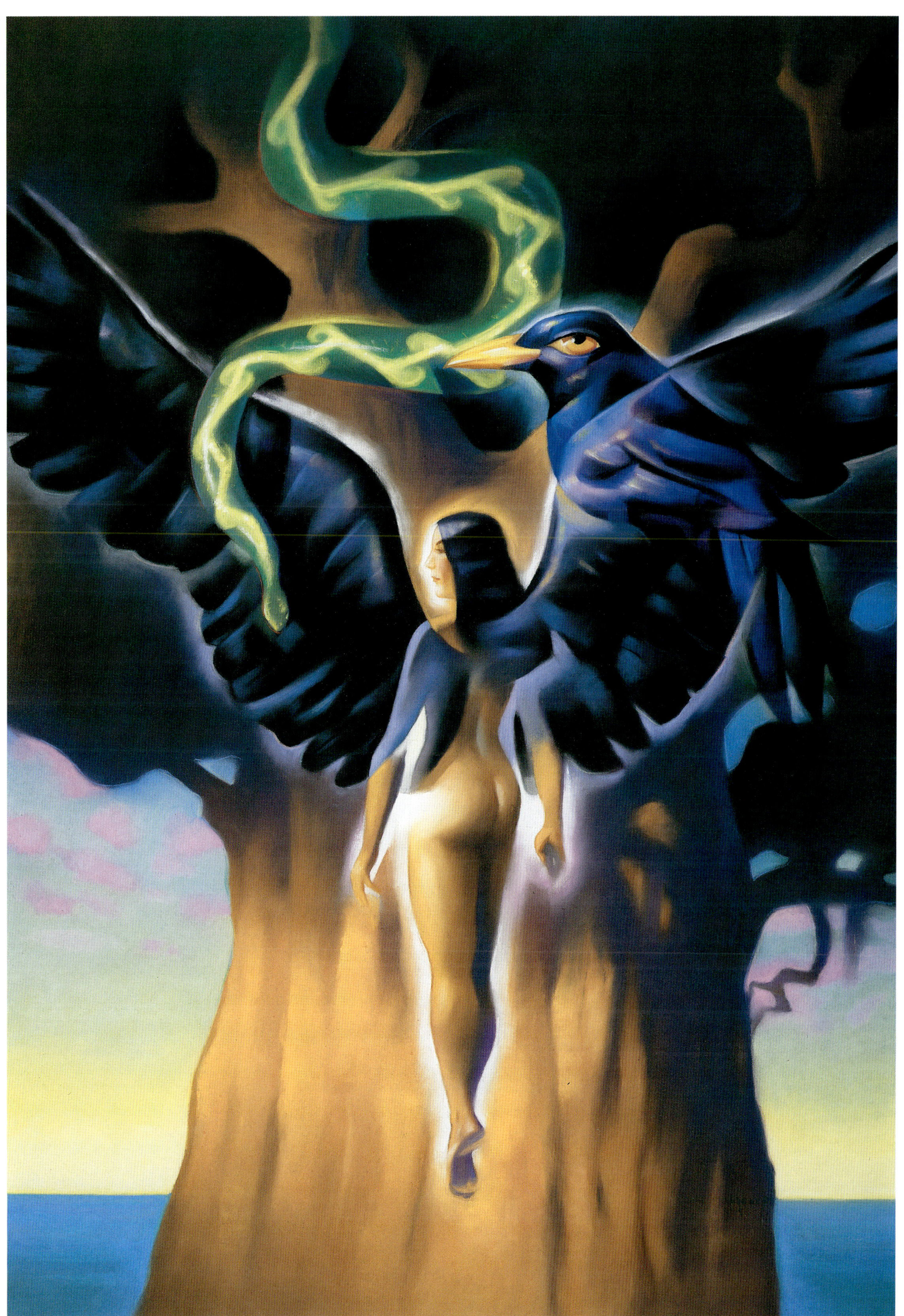

1
artist: **John Rush**
art director: Andrea Spooner
client: Chronicle Books
title: The Last of England
medium: Oil
size: 22″x22″

2
artist: **Yvonne Gilbert**
art director: Yvonne Gilbert
client: iBooks
title: Moonspeaker
medium: Color pencils
size: 8″x12″

3
artist: **David Bowers**
art director: Irene Gallo
client: Tor Books
title: Mother of Poisons
medium: Oil

4
artist: **David Bowers**
art director: Richard Aquan
client: Eos/HarperCollins
title: Paladin of Souls
medium: Oil
size: 14″x19″

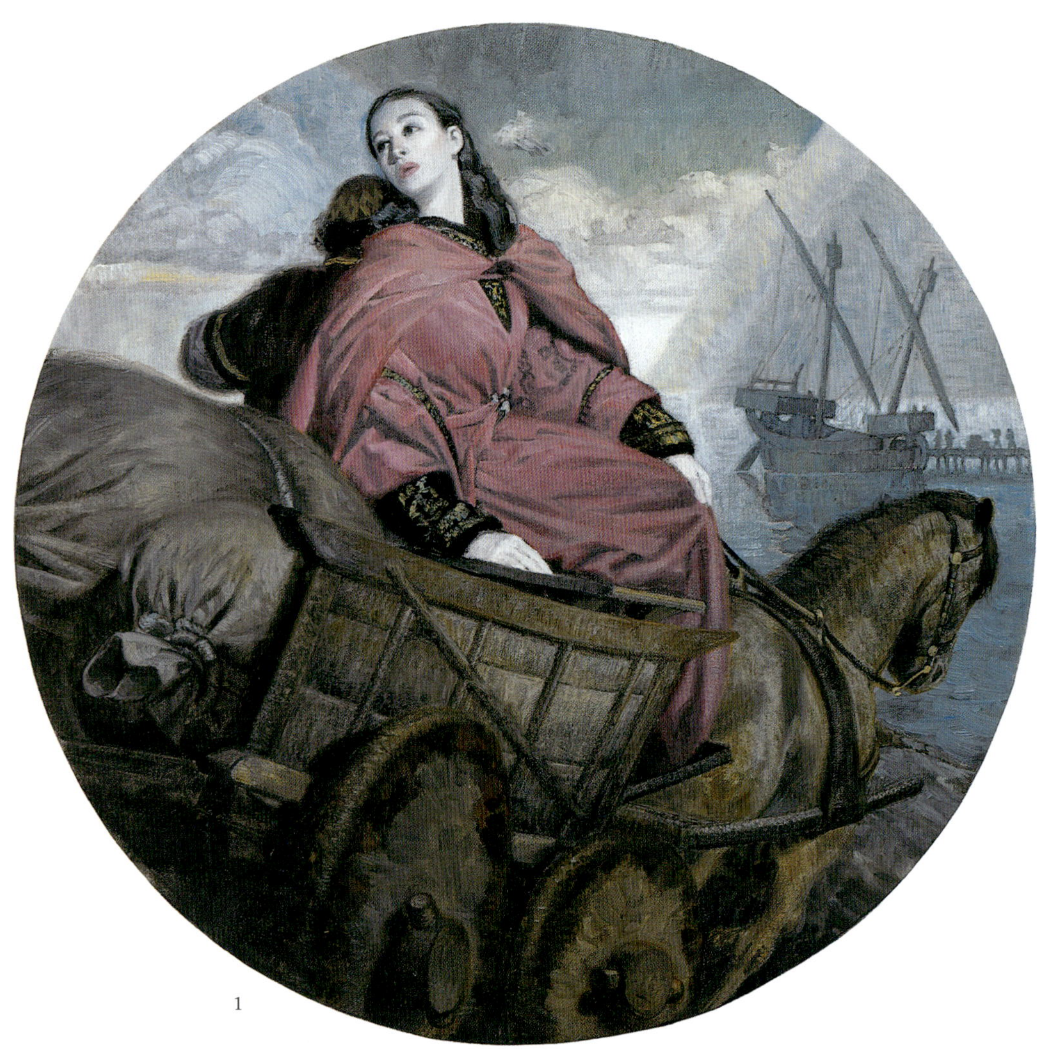

1

2

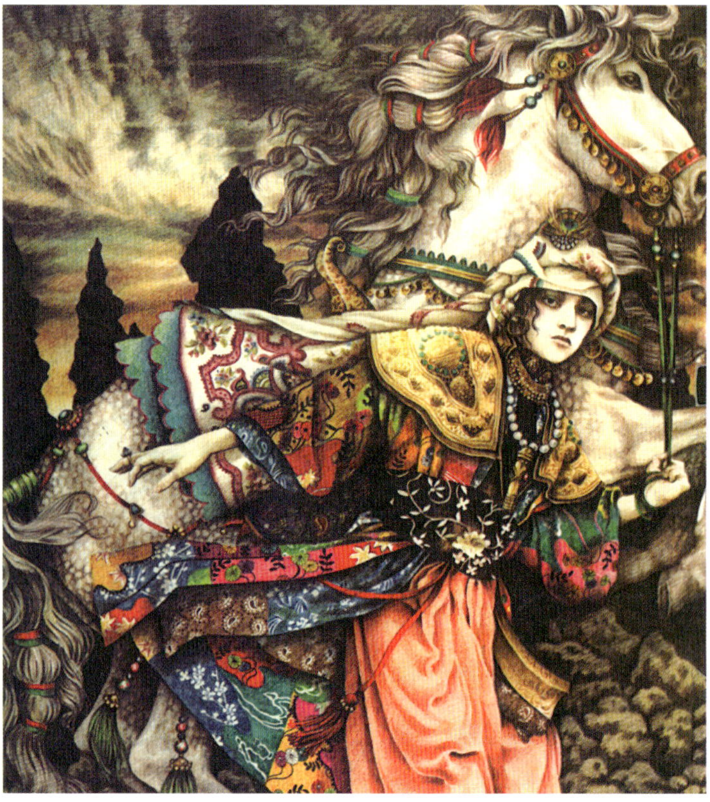

3

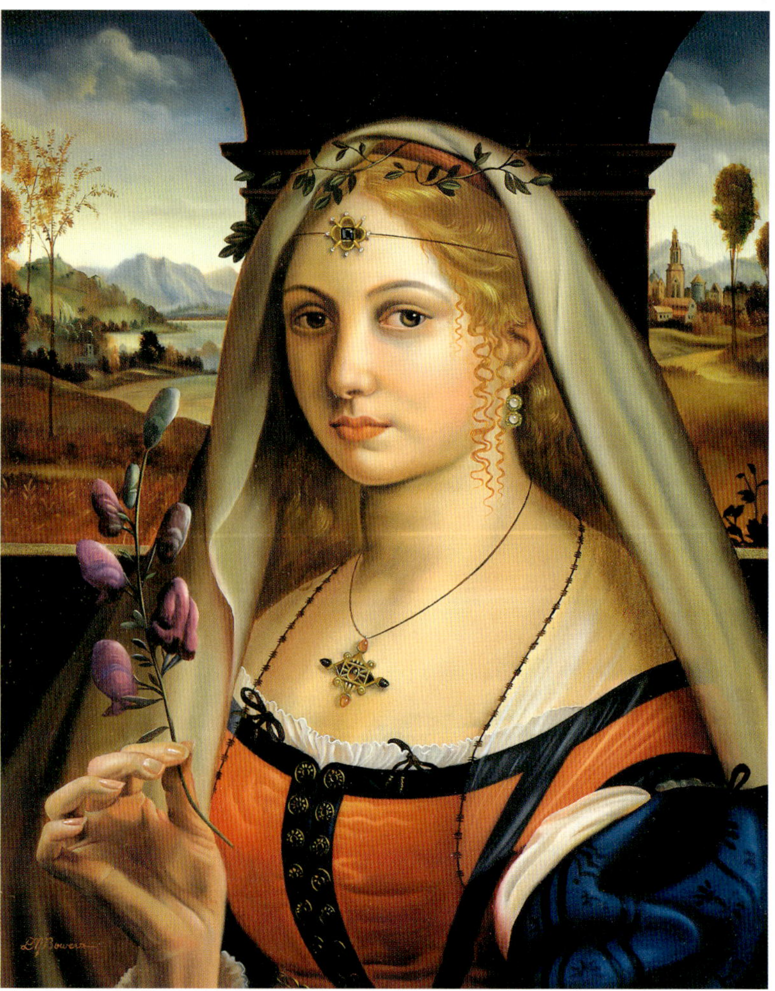

4

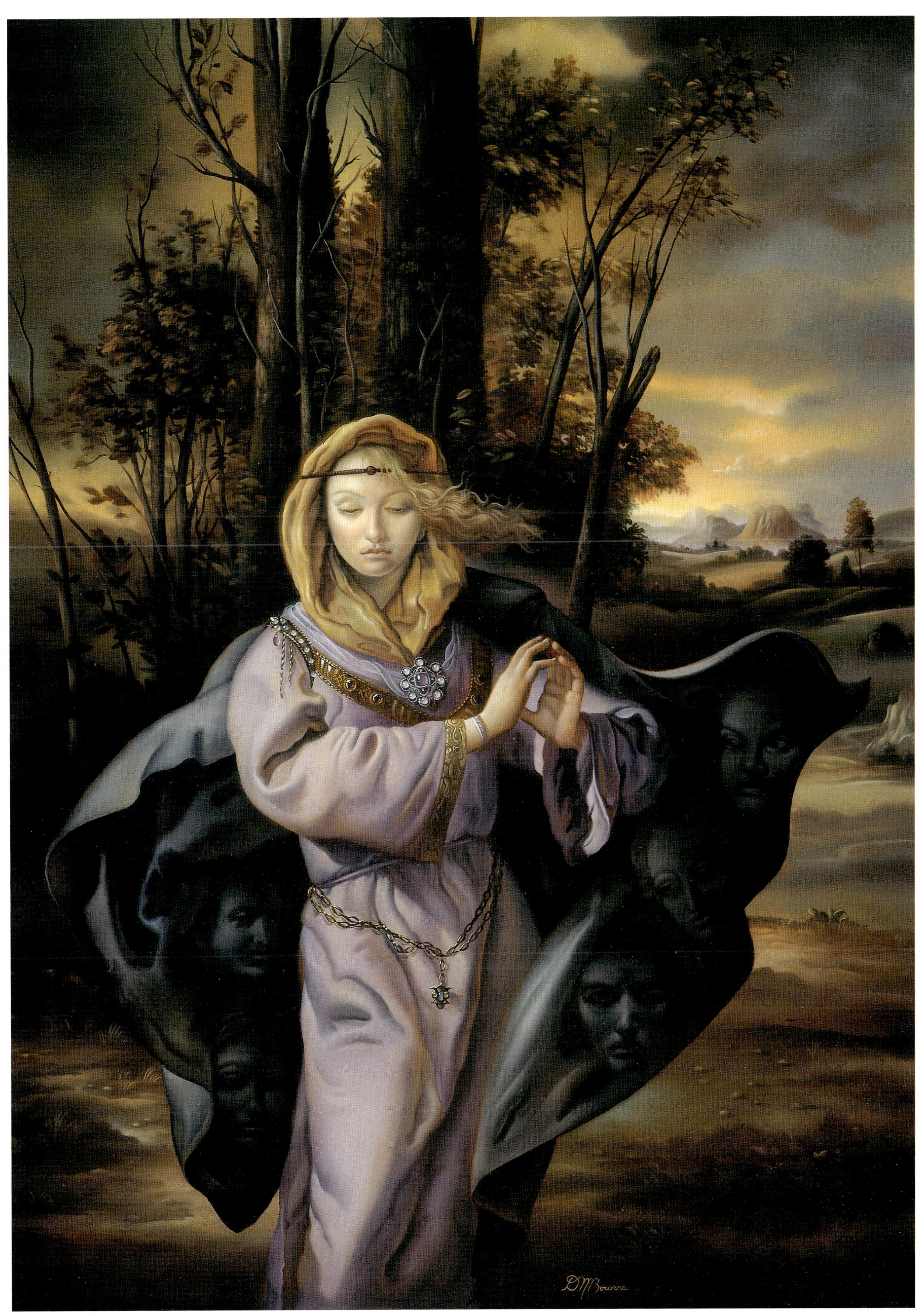

1
artist: **John Jude Palencar**
art director: Isabel Warren-Lynch
client: Alfred A. Knopf
title: Eragon
medium: Acrylic *size:* 14″x16″

2
artist: **Todd Lockwood**
art director: Matt Adelsperger
client: Wizards of the Coast
title: Lone Drow
medium: Digital *size:* 20″x9″

3
artist: **Rebecca Guay**
art director: Alison Keehn
client: Barefoot Books
title: Aphrodite
medium: Acrylic/gouache
size: 10″x17″

4
artist: **J.P. Targete**
art director: Greg Benage
client: Fantasy Flight Games
title: Midnight: Crown of Shadow
medium: Digital *size:* 7″x9″

5
artist: **Daniel Dos Santos**
art director: Irene Gallo
client: Tor Books
title: The Duke's Ballad
medium: Oil
size: 30″x40″

6
artist: **Rick Berry**
art director: Irene Gallo
client: Tor Books
title: Amazon Queen
medium: Mixed

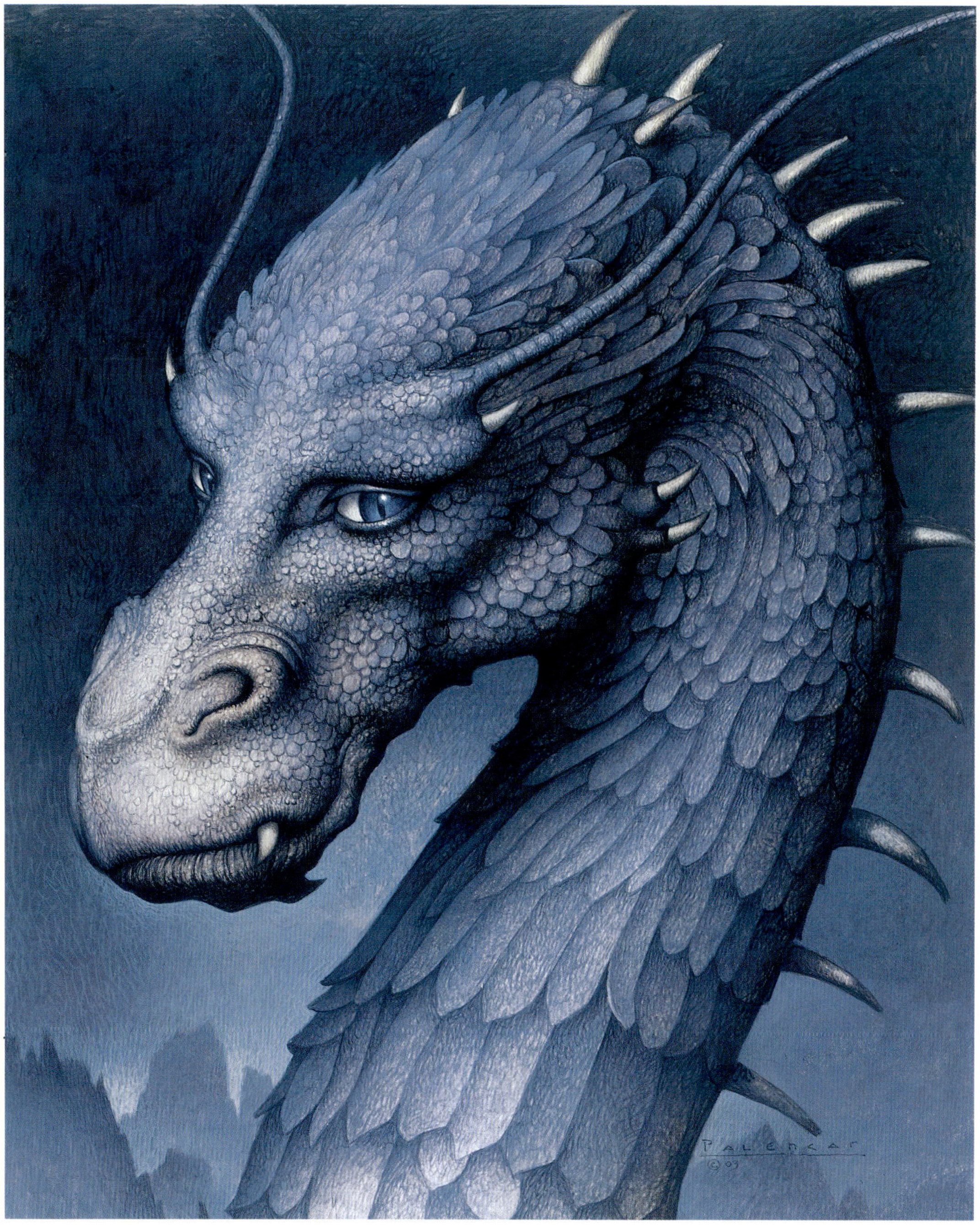

1

2

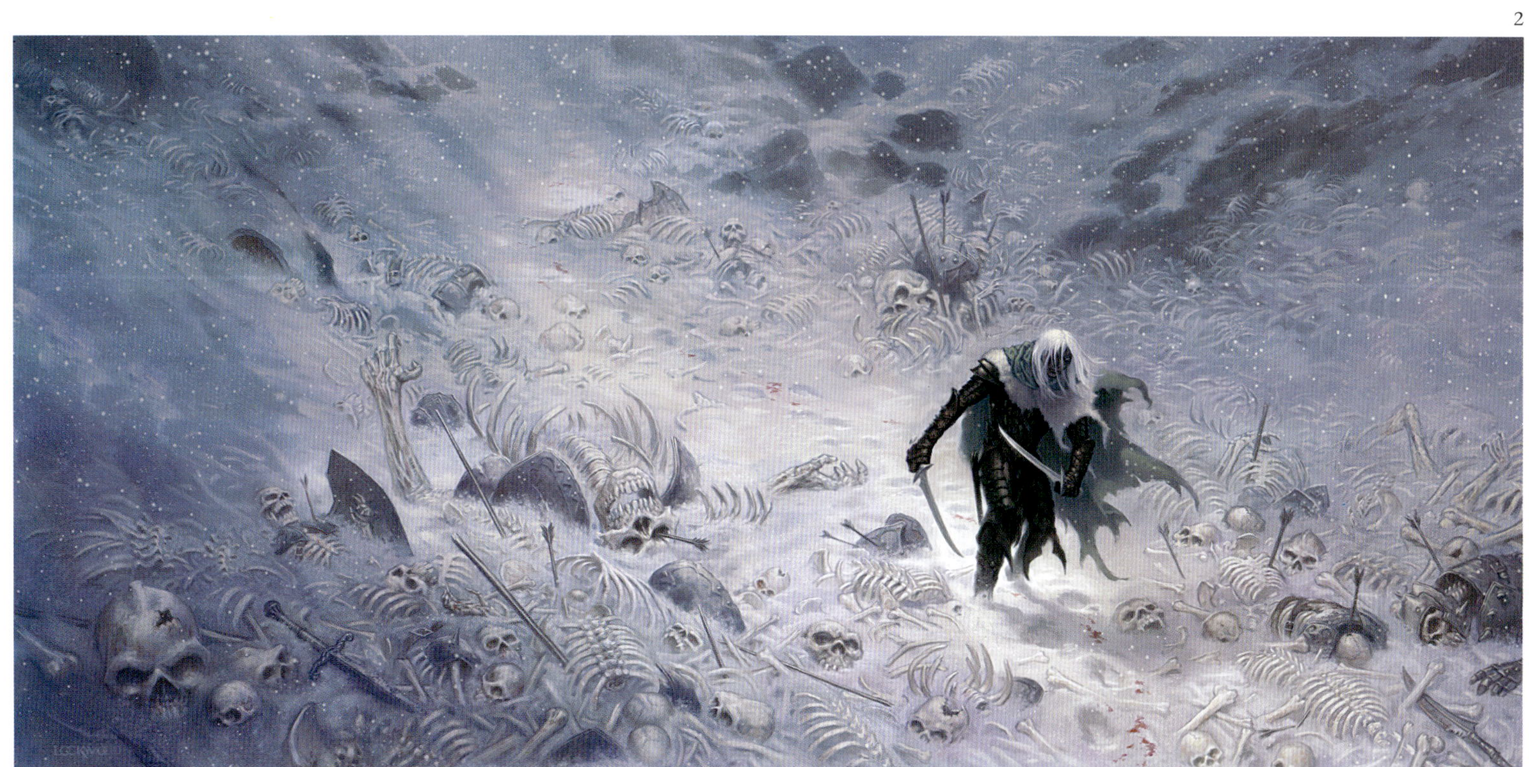

3

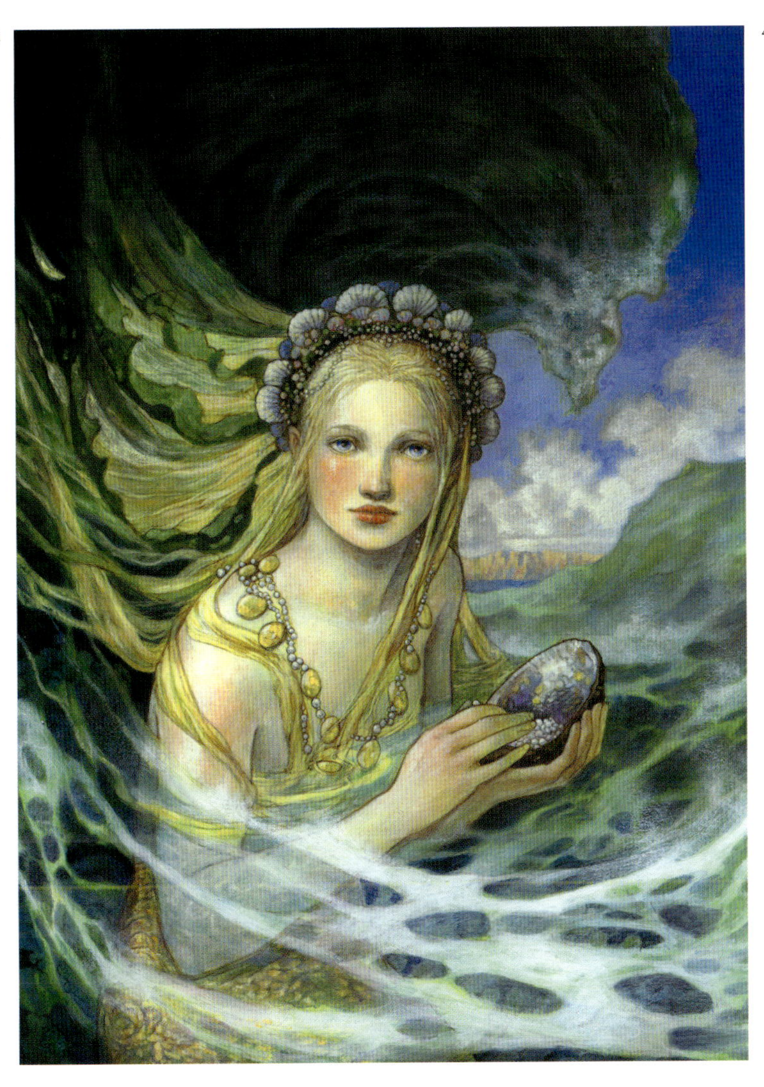

4

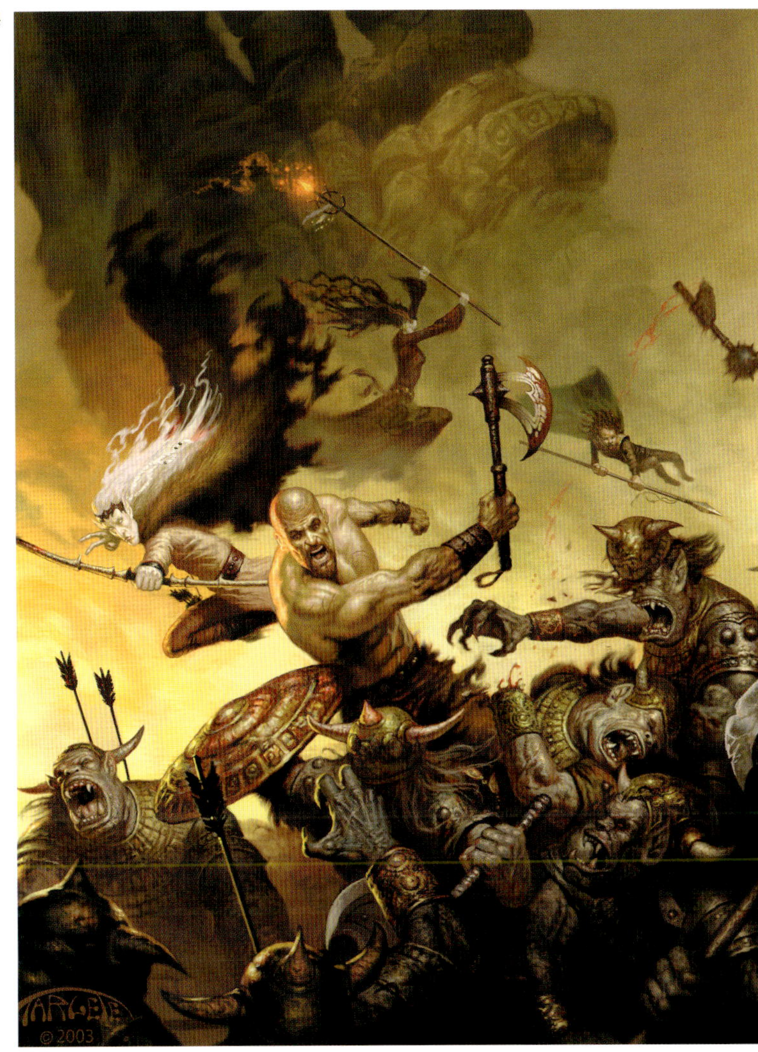

5

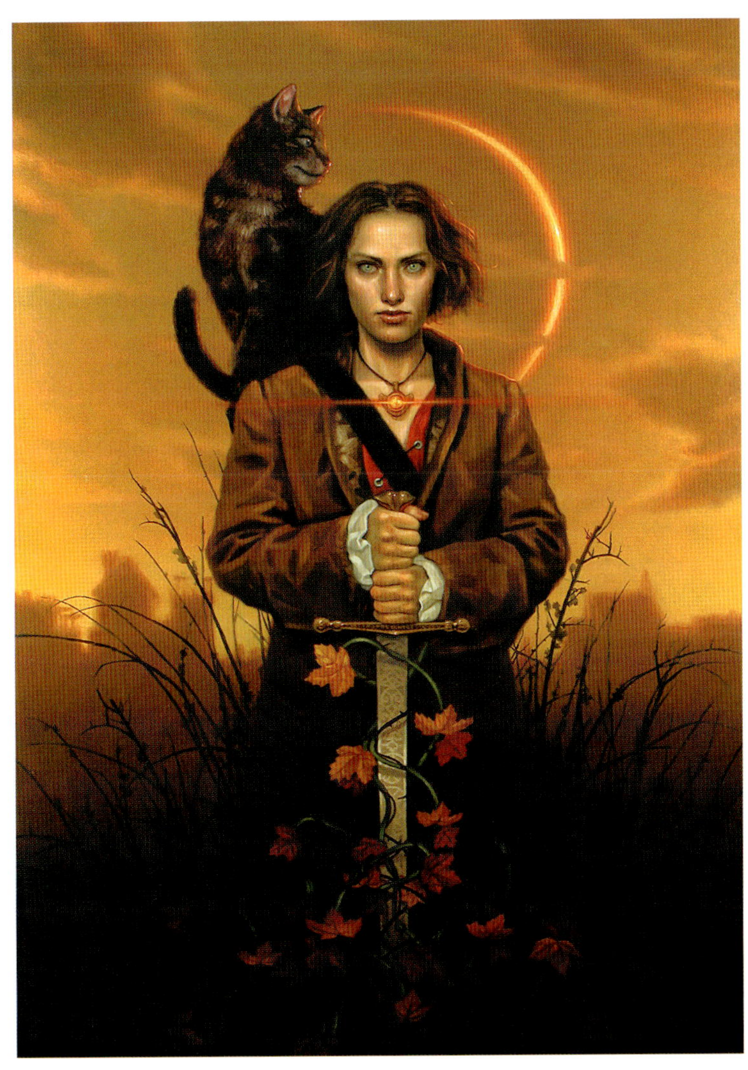

6

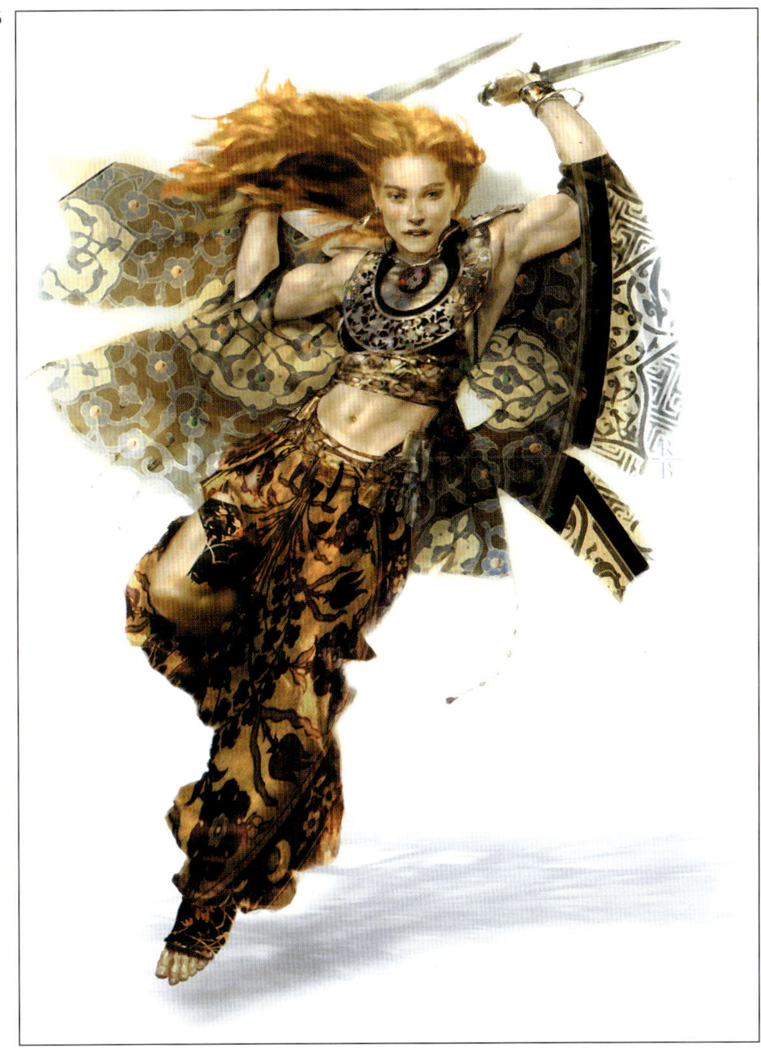

Book

1
artist: **Stephan "Cricket" Martiniere**
art director: Irene Gallo
client: Tor Books
title: Ring World Children
medium: Digital

2
artist: **Jon Foster**
art director: Irene Gallo
client: Tor Books
title: Earthborn
medium: Digital
size: 6 3/4"x10"

3
artist: **Doug Chiang**
client: Robota
title: Kaantur's City
medium: Acrylic
size: 8 1/4"x11 1/2"

4
artist: **Stephan "Cricket" Martiniere**
art director: Irene Gallo
client: Tor Books
title: Hostile Takeover
medium: Digital

1

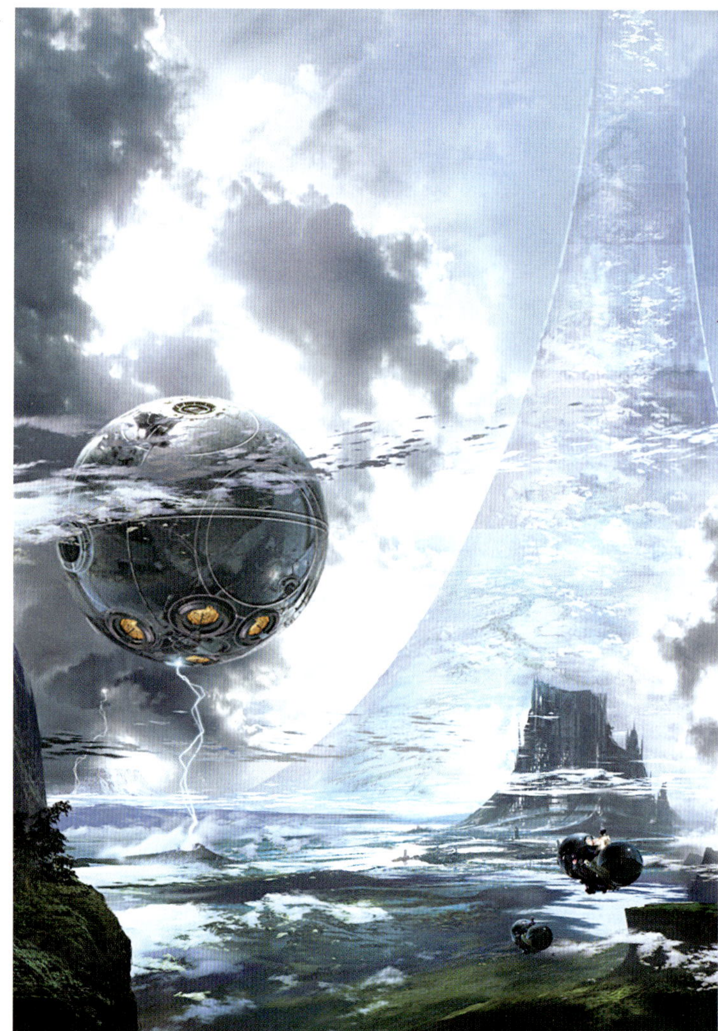

2

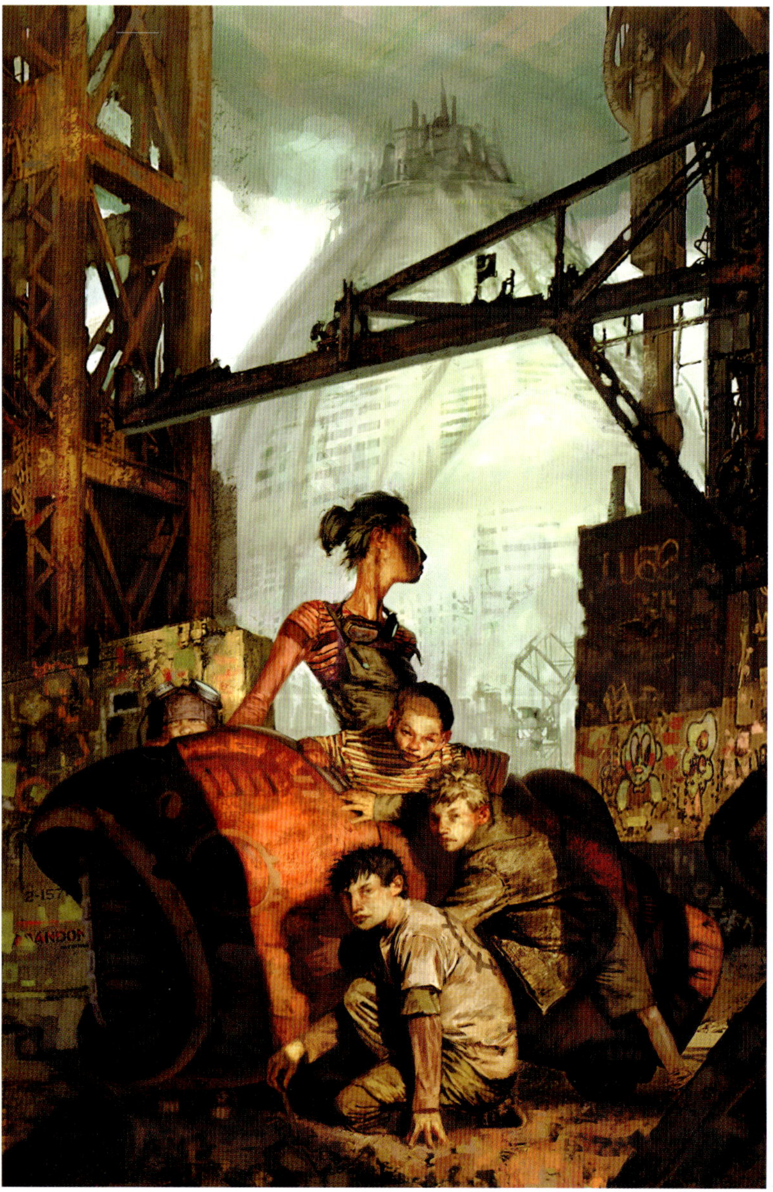

3

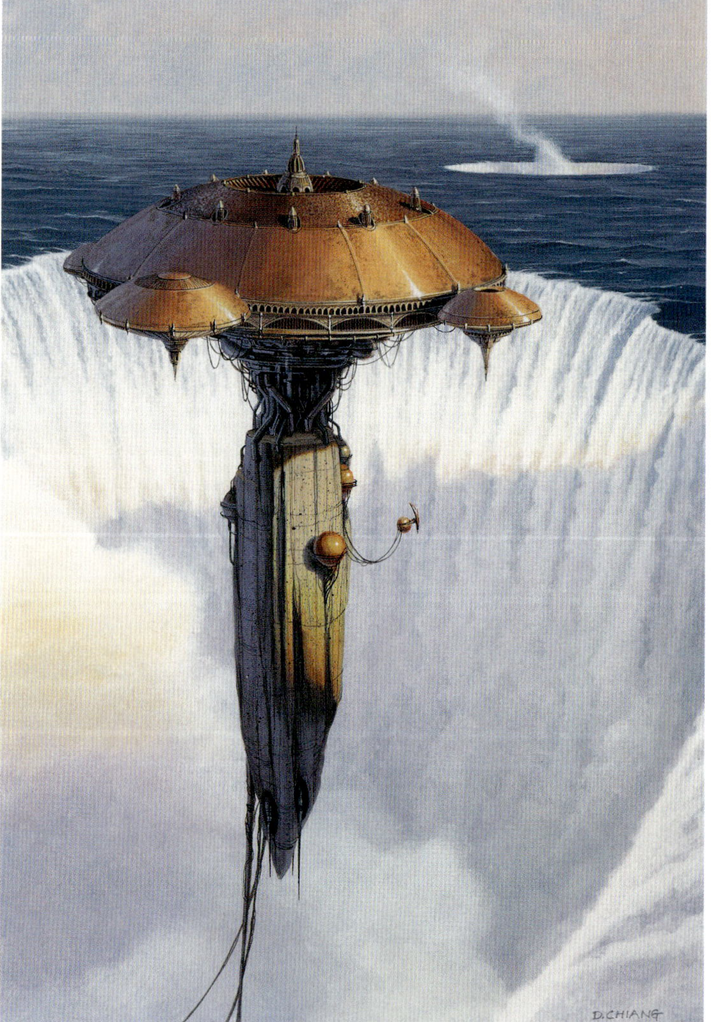

4

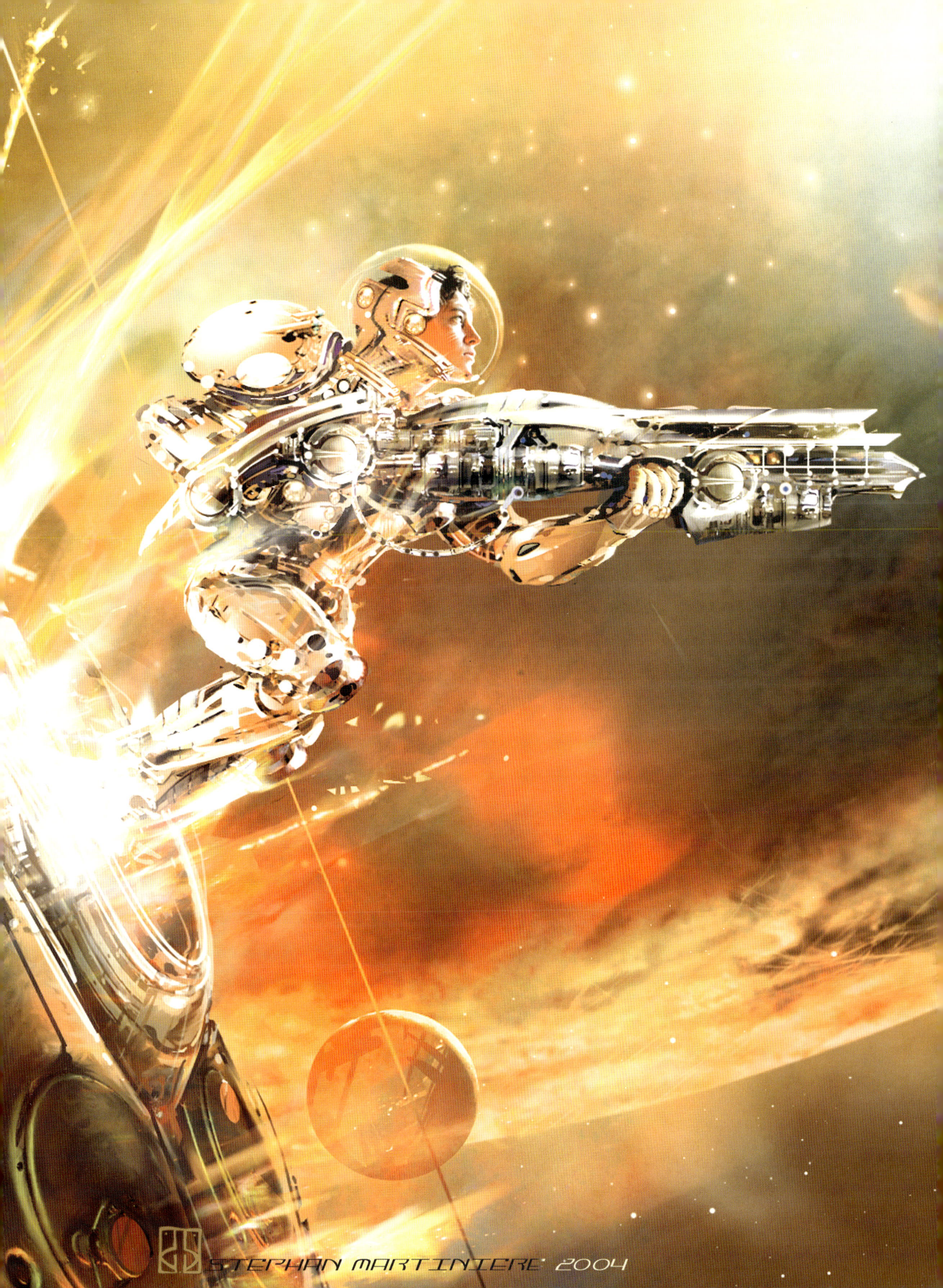
STEPHAN MARTINIERE 2004

Book

1
artist: **Chris McGrath**
art director: Ray Lundgren
client: Roc Books
title: Wyrmhole
medium: Digital
size: 4 1/4"x3 1/4"

2
artist: **Dan Santat**
art director: David Saylor
client: Scholastic Books
title: The Guild of Geniuses
medium: Acrylic & ink
size: 17"x11"

3
artist: **Gnemo**
art director: Tom Kidd/
Betsy Wollheim
client: Spellcaster Press/DAW Books
title: Fitzpatrick's War
medium: Oil

4
artist: **John Harris**
art director: Irene Gallo
client: Tor Books
title: Gateway
medium: Oils on canvas
size: 14"x19"

5
artist: **Terese Nielsen**
art director: David Stevenson
client: Del Rey Books
title: The Final Prophecy
medium: Mixed
size: 9 1/2"x15"

6
artist: **Dan Santat**
art director: David Saylor
client: Scholastic Books
title: The Guild of Geniuses
medium: Acrylic & ink
size: 17"x11"

1

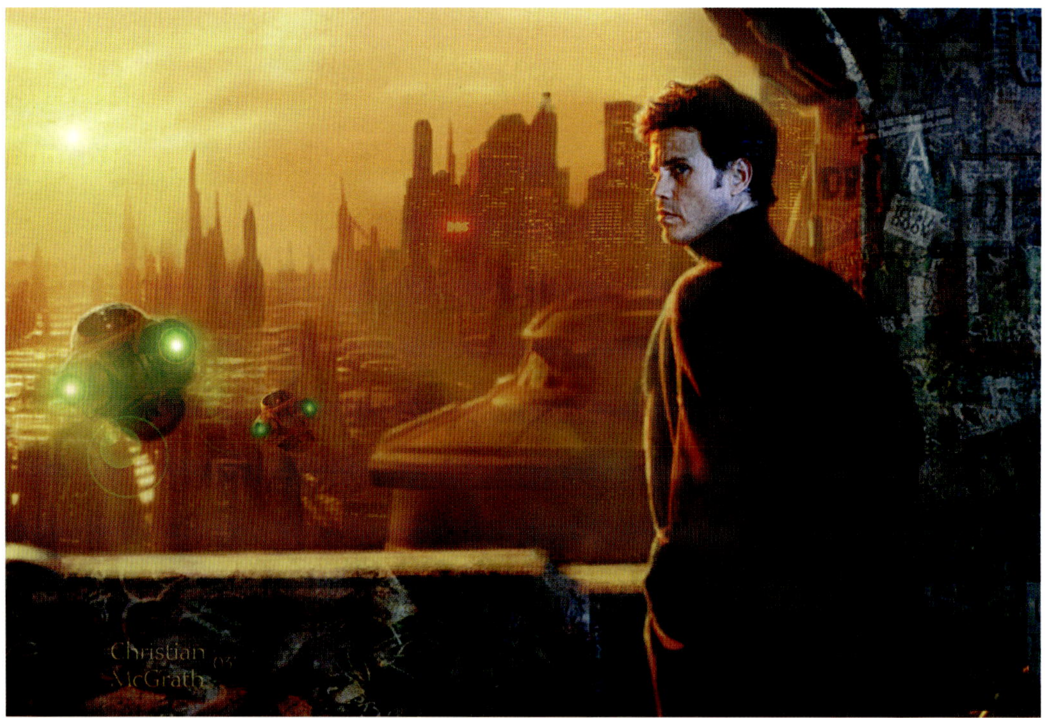

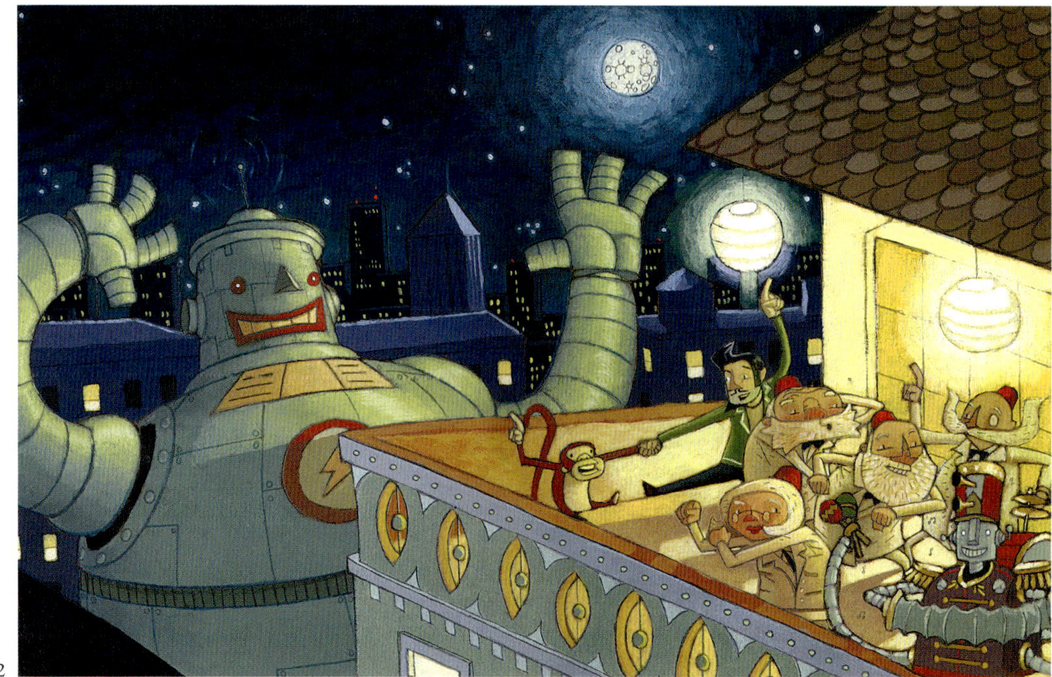

2

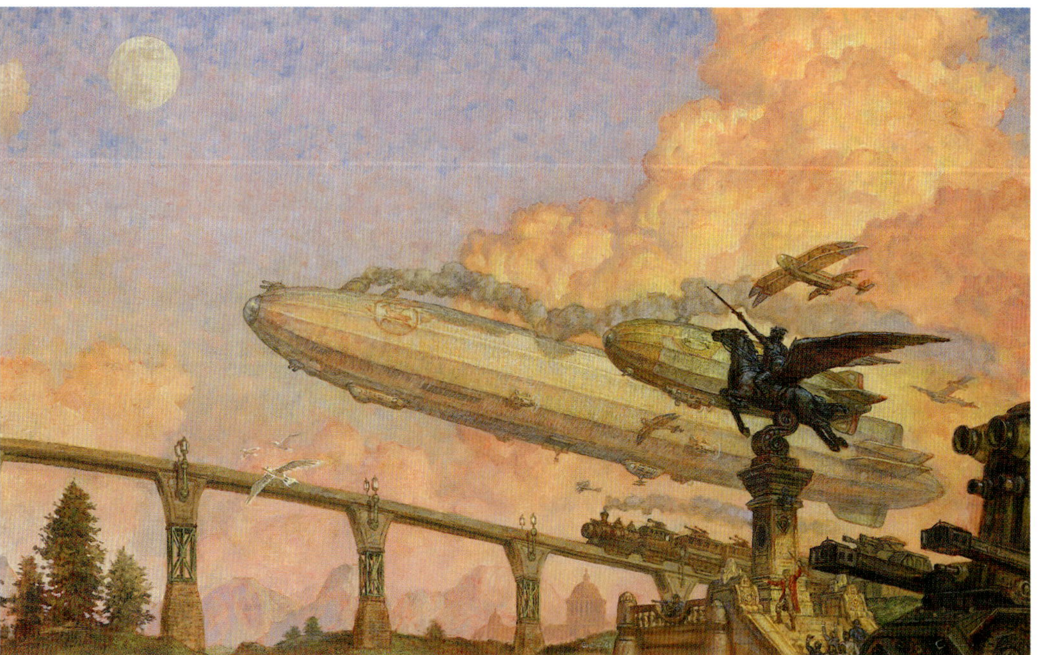

3

4

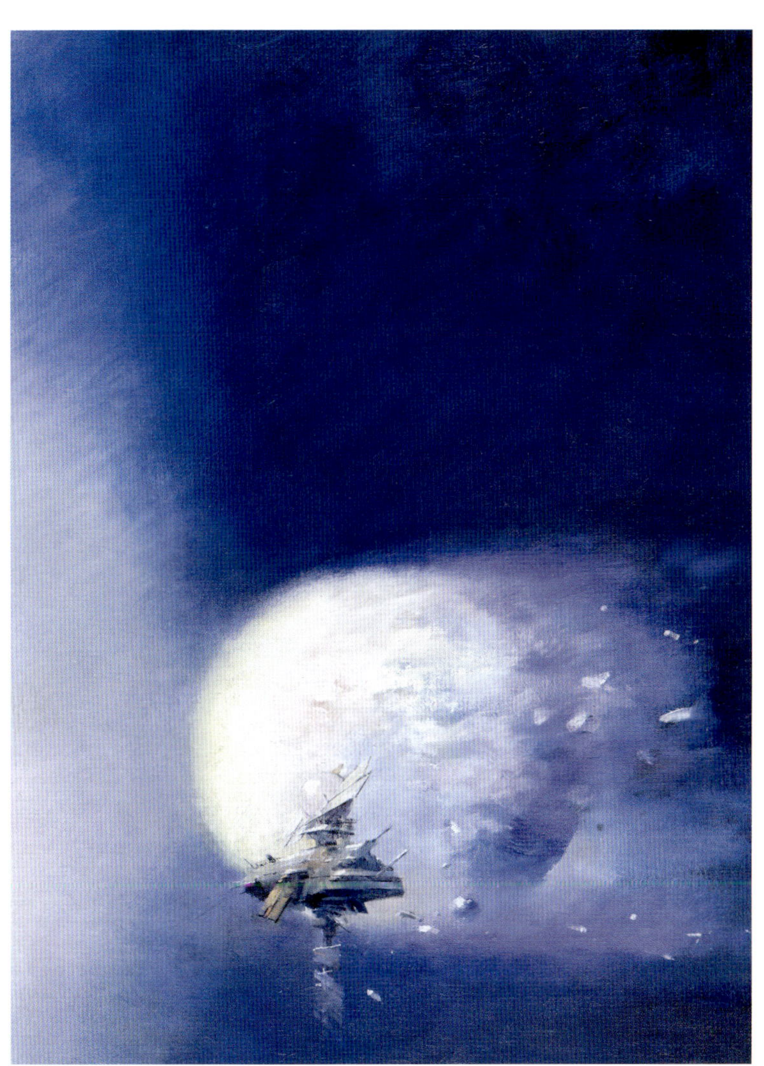

5

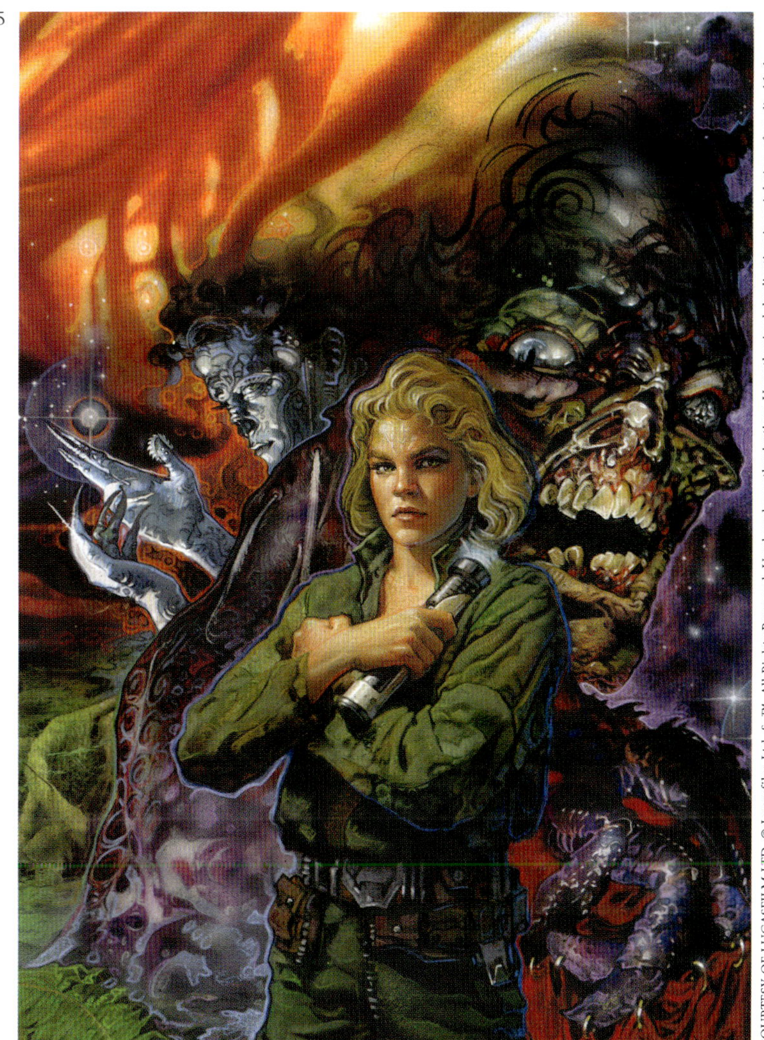

6

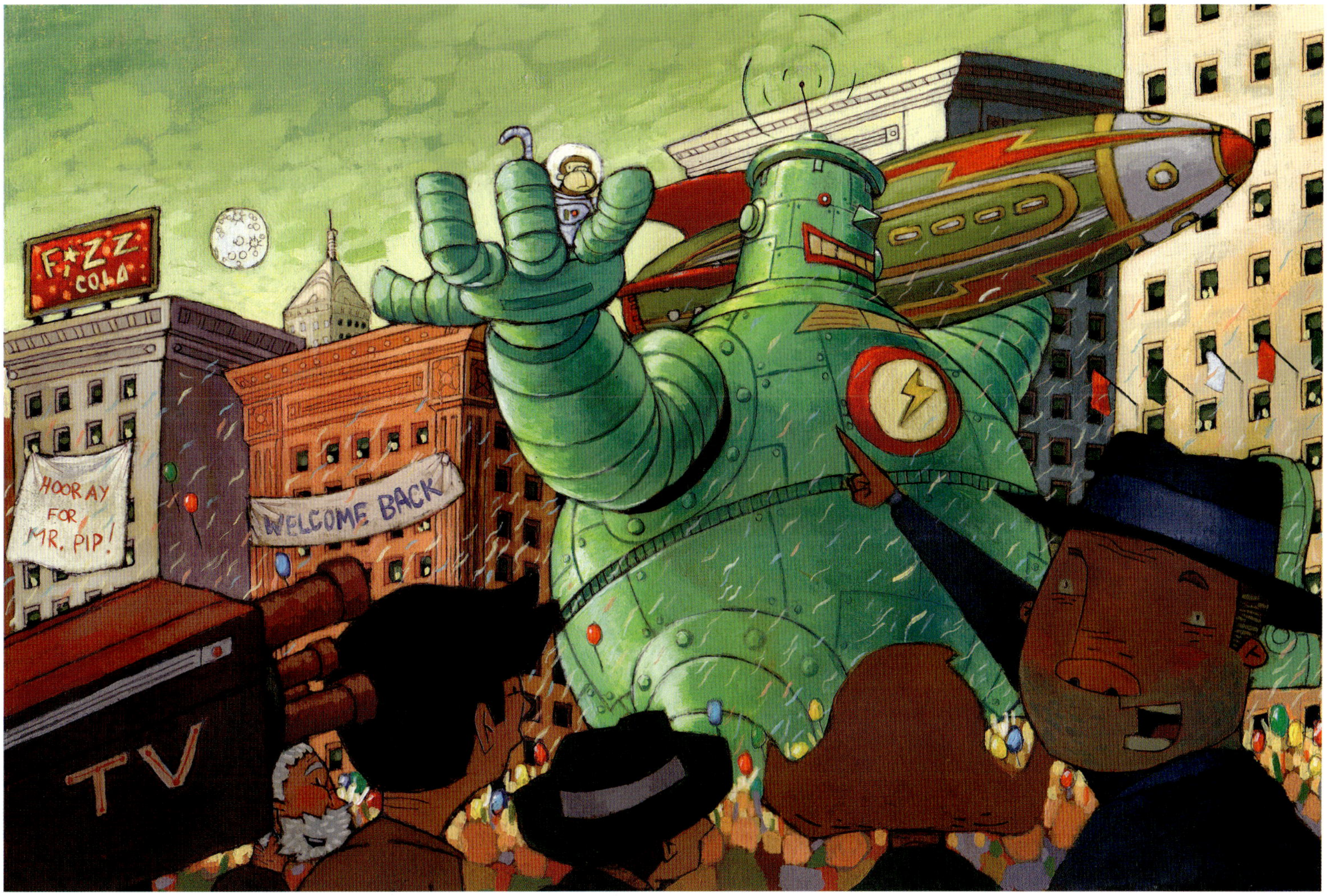

Book

1
artist: **Echo Chernik**
art director: Phil Brucato
client: Smoke, Mirror & Muse
title: Drowned
medium: Digital
size: 5″x7″

2
artist: **Frank Cho**
client: Monkey Boy Press
title: "Hey!"
medium: Ink & wash
size: 11″x17″

3
artist: **Manchu**
client: Mnemos
title: L'ere du Dragon
medium: Acrylic
size: 50cmx65cm

4
artist: **Doug Chiang**
client: Robota
title: Kaantur
medium: Acrylic
size: 8 1/4″x10 1/4″

1

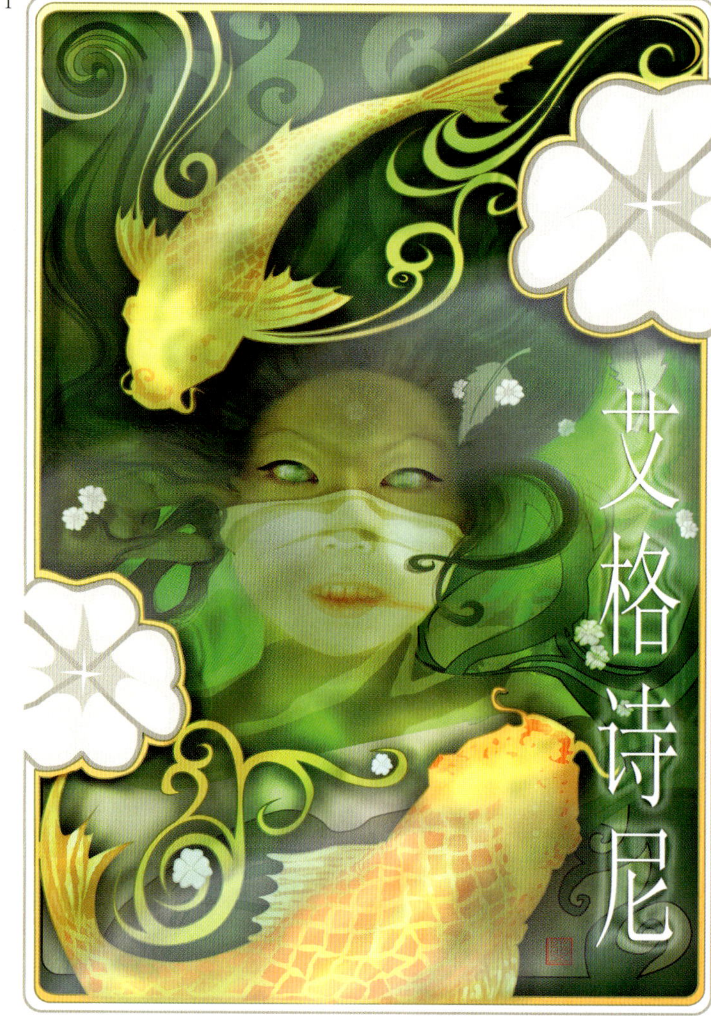

2

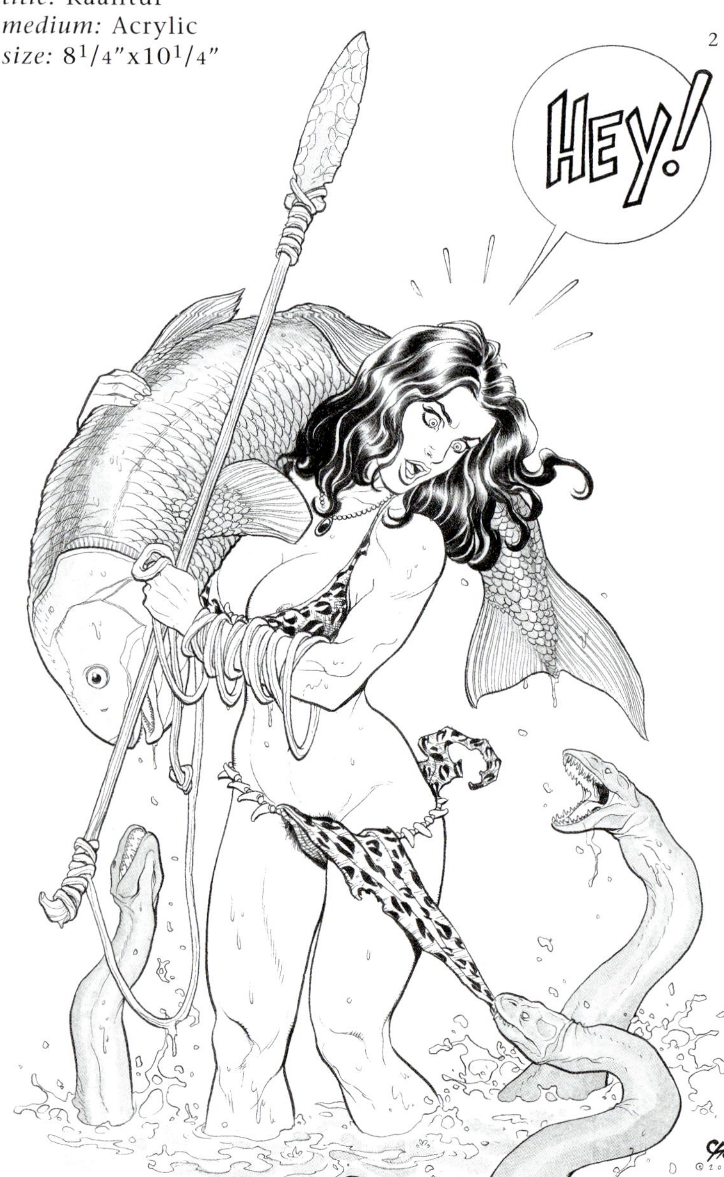

3

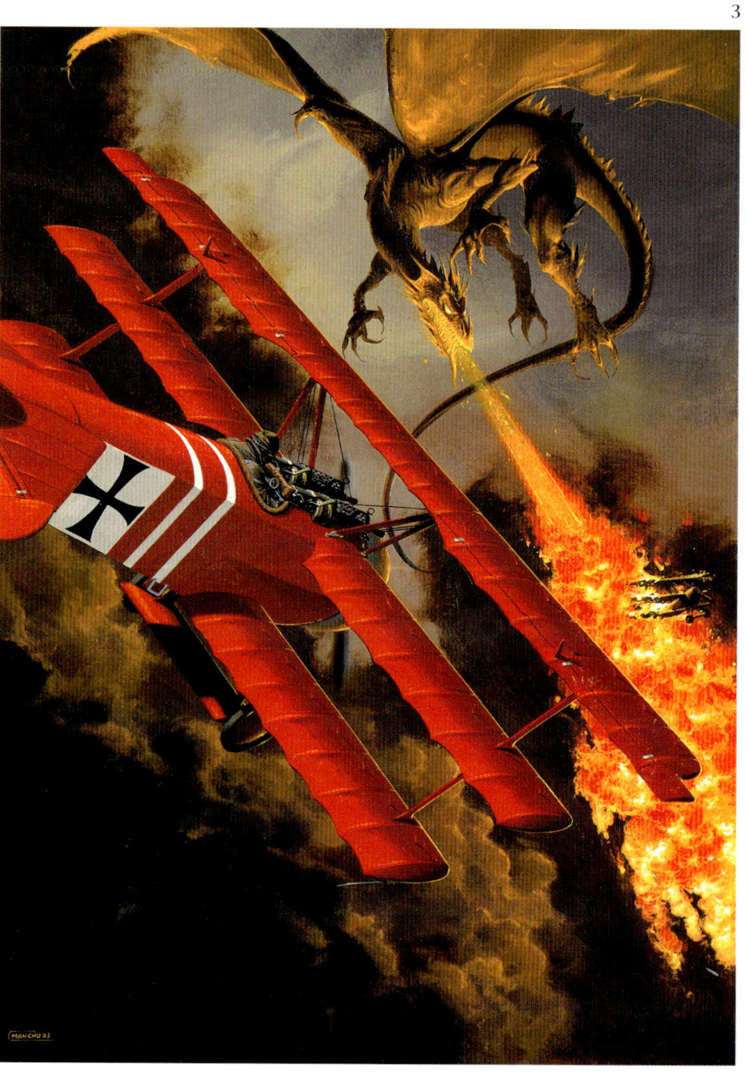

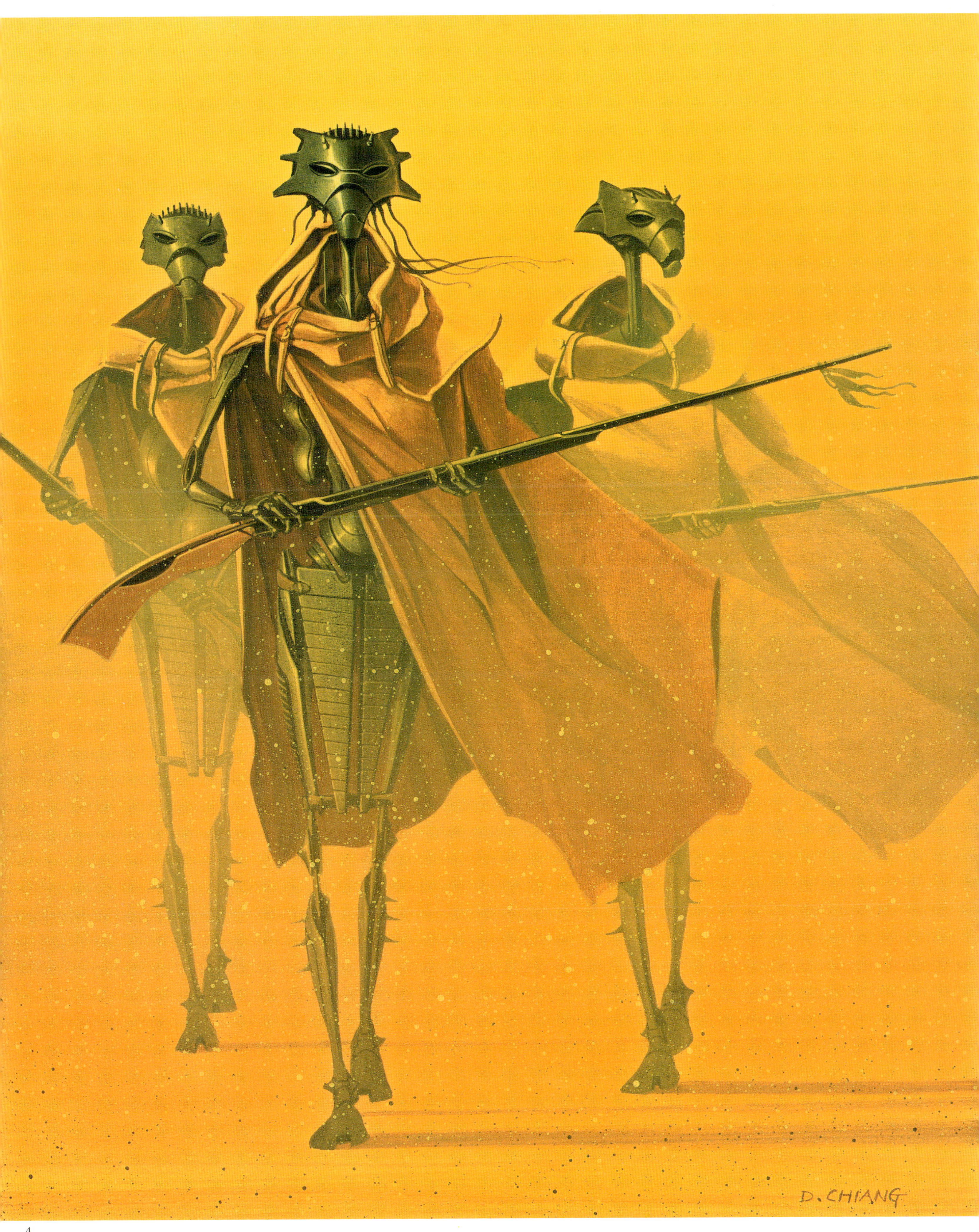

4

Book

1
artist: **Charles Vess**
art director: Nancy Brennan
client: Viking Books
title: The Faery Reel
medium: Colored inks
size: 16″x21″

2
artist: **Todd Lockwood**
art director: Matt Adelsperger
client: Wizards of the Coast
title: The Two Swords
medium: Digital
size: 20″x9″

3
artist: **Charles Vess**
art director: Irene Gallo
client: Starscape Books
title: Peter Pan
medium: Ink on paper

4
artist: **Greg Newbold**
art director: Mark Siegel
client: Simon & Schuster
title: Wheel
medium: Acrylic
size: 9″x13″

5
artist: **Todd Lockwood**
art director: Irene Gallo
client: Tor Books
title: Glass Dragon
medium: Digital
size: 19″x12 1/2″

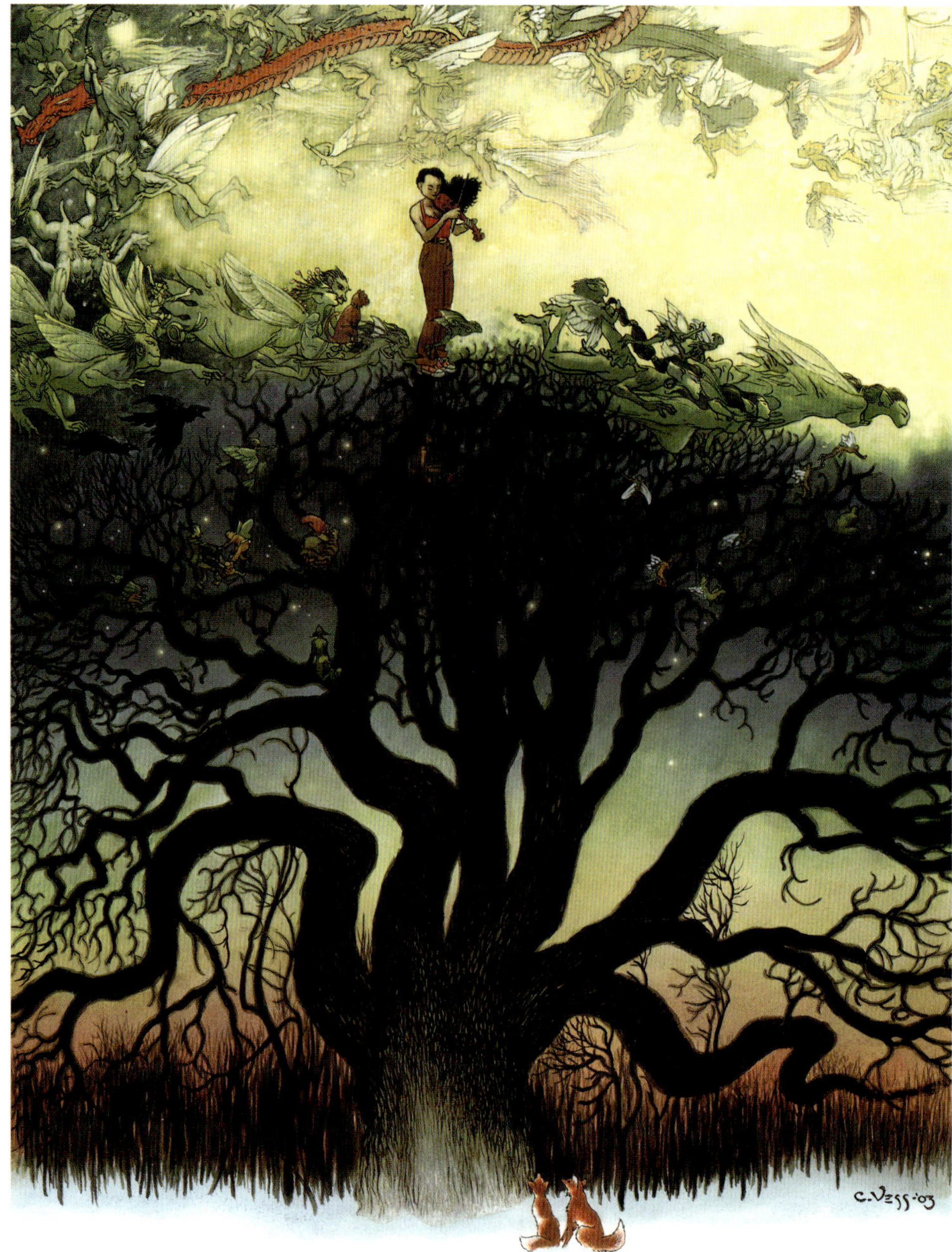

1

2

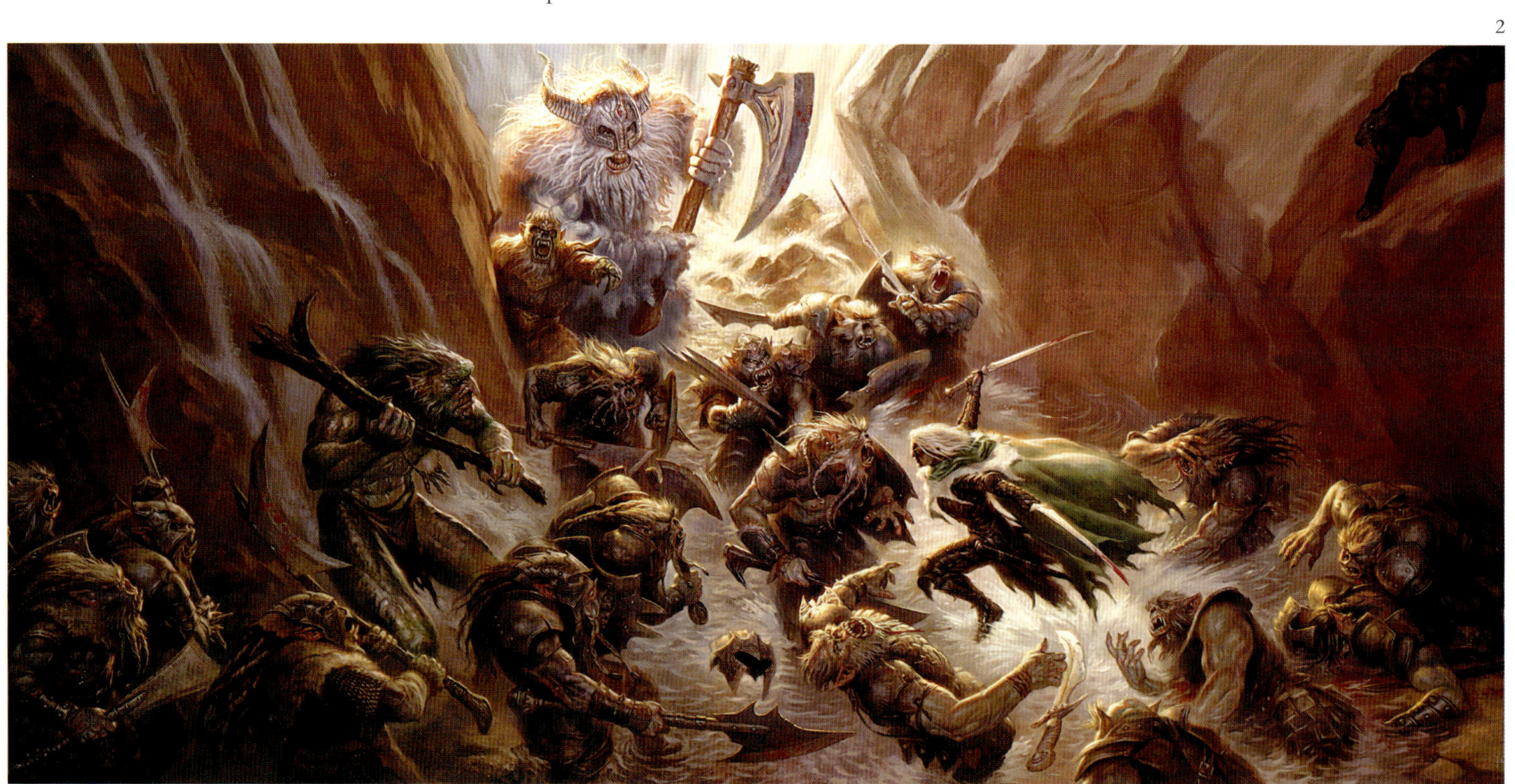

3

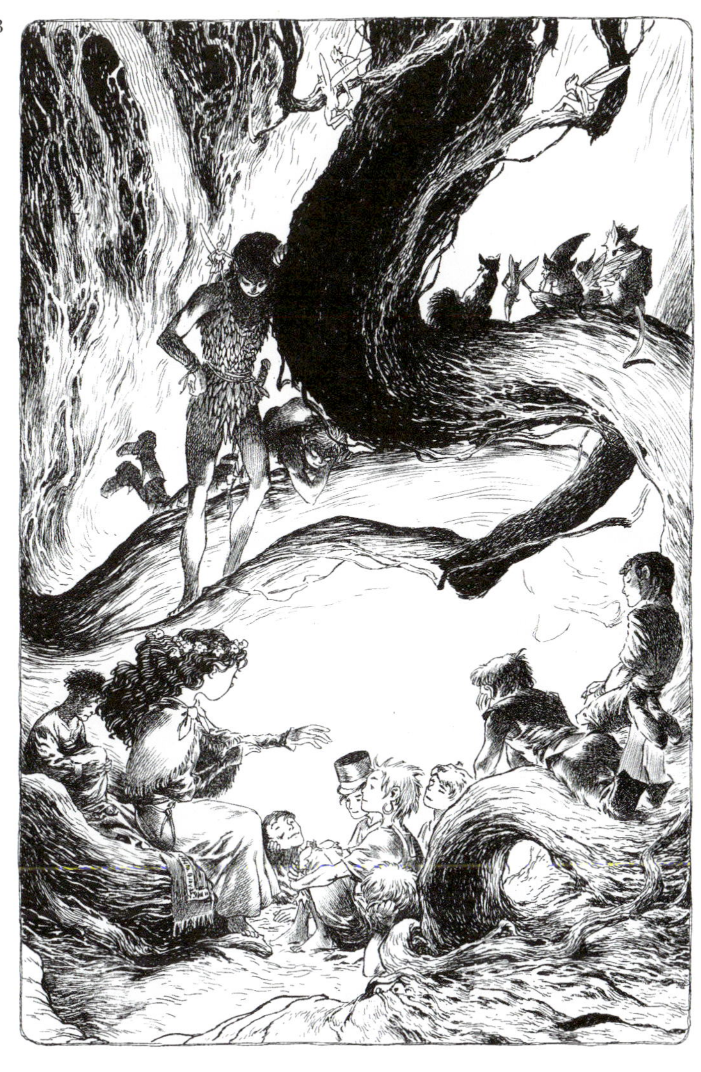

4

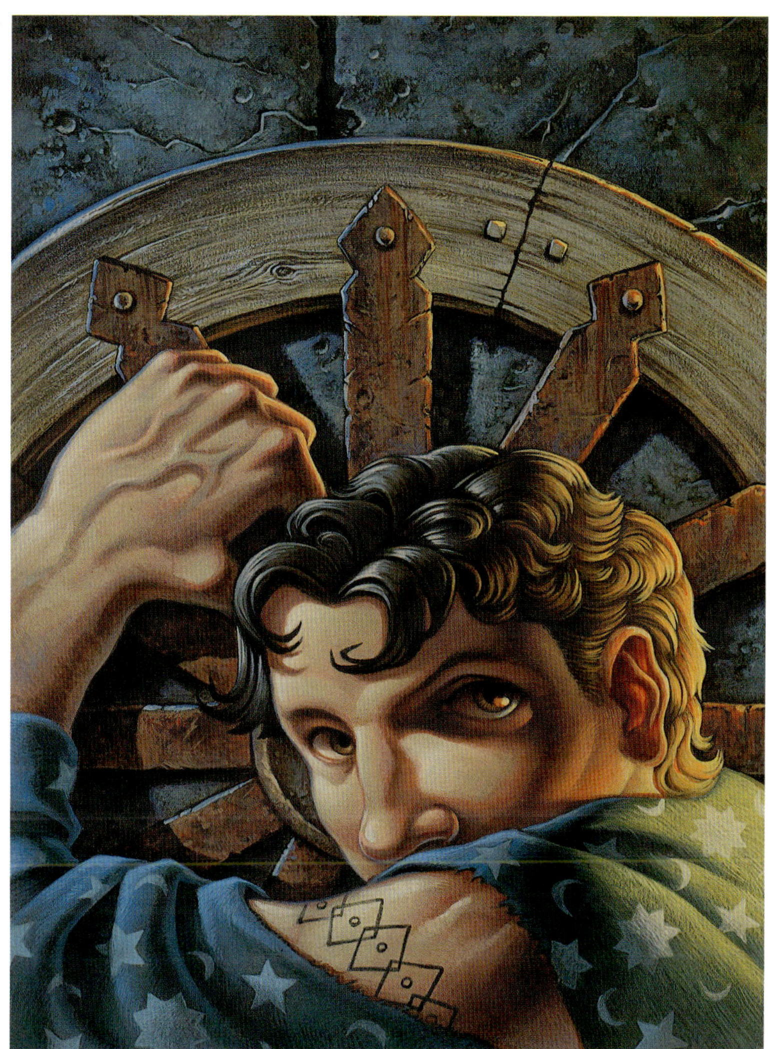

5

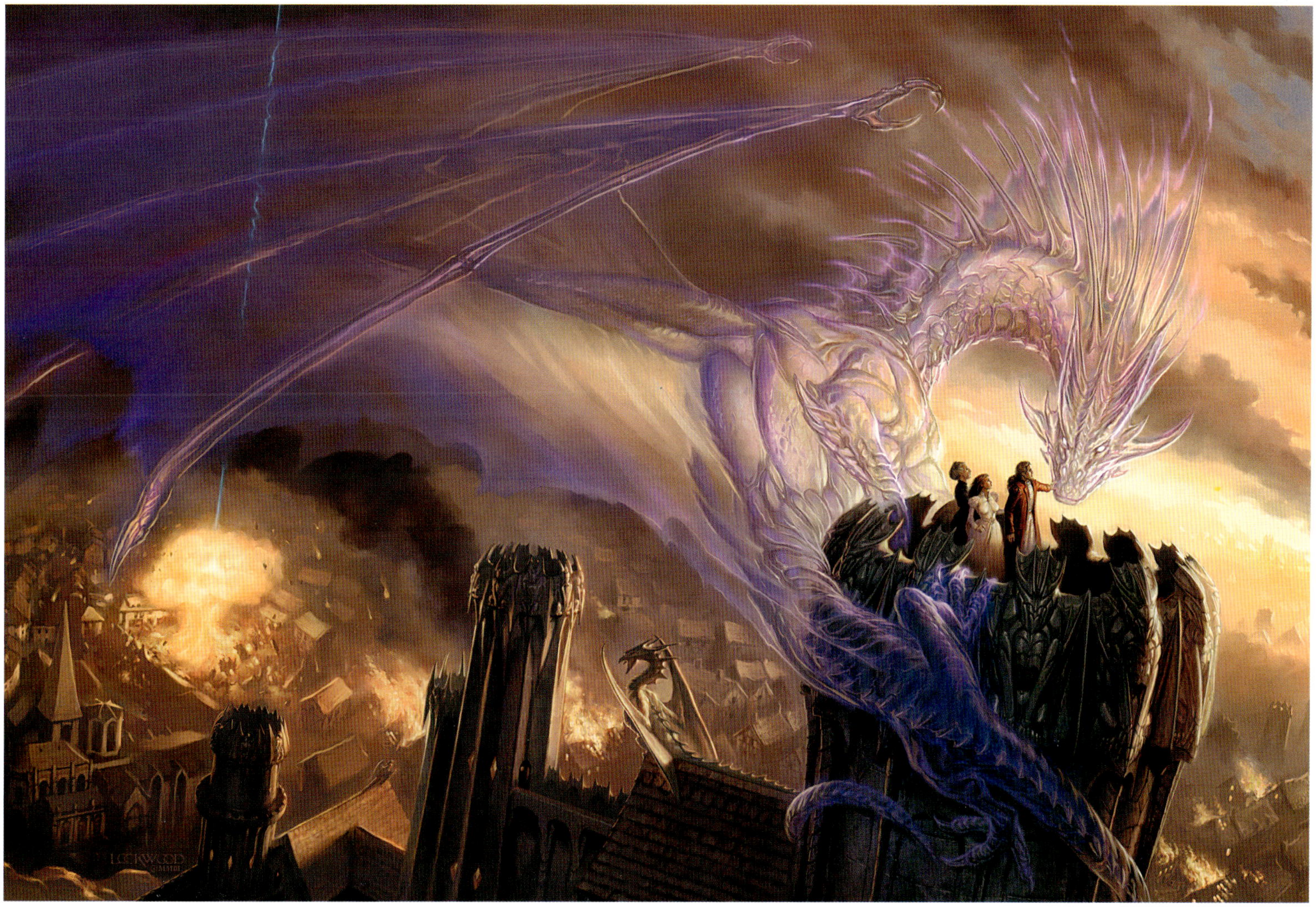

Book

1
artist: **Greg Swearingen**
art director: Liz Demeter
designer: Liz Demeter
client: Harcourt, Inc.
title: So You Want to Be a Wizard
medium: Mixed
size: 8"x12"

2
artist: **Greg Swearingen**
art director: Liz Demeter
designer: Liz Demeter
client: Harcourt, Inc.
title: High Wizardry
medium: Mixed
size: 8"x12"

3
artist: **Bruce Jensen**
art director: Toby Schwartz
client: SF Book Club
title: Other Dimension
medium: Digital

4
artist: **Donato Giancola**
art director: Irene Gallo
client: Tor Books
title: Finger Pointing Solward
medium: Oil on paper
size: 17"x29"

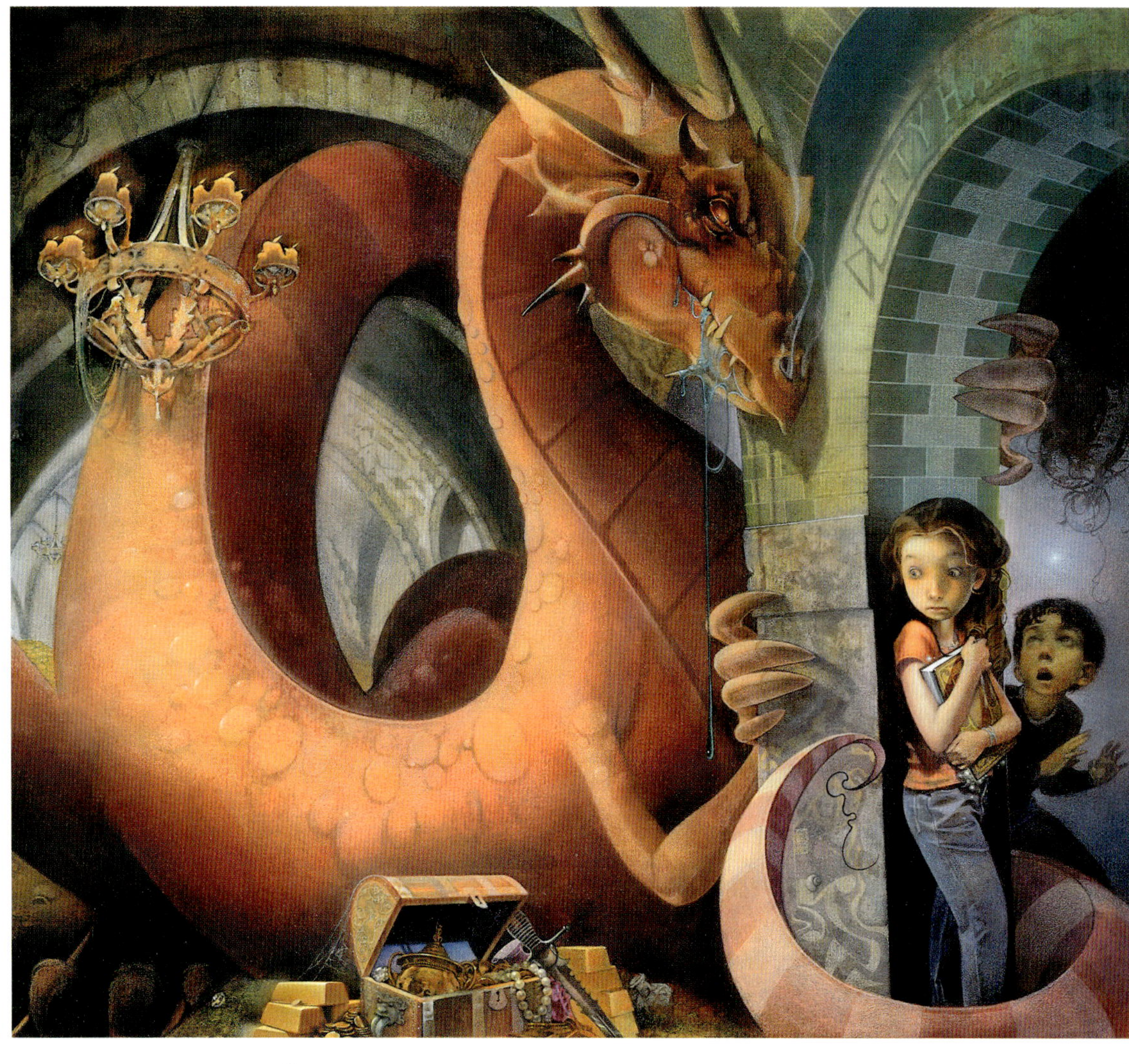

1

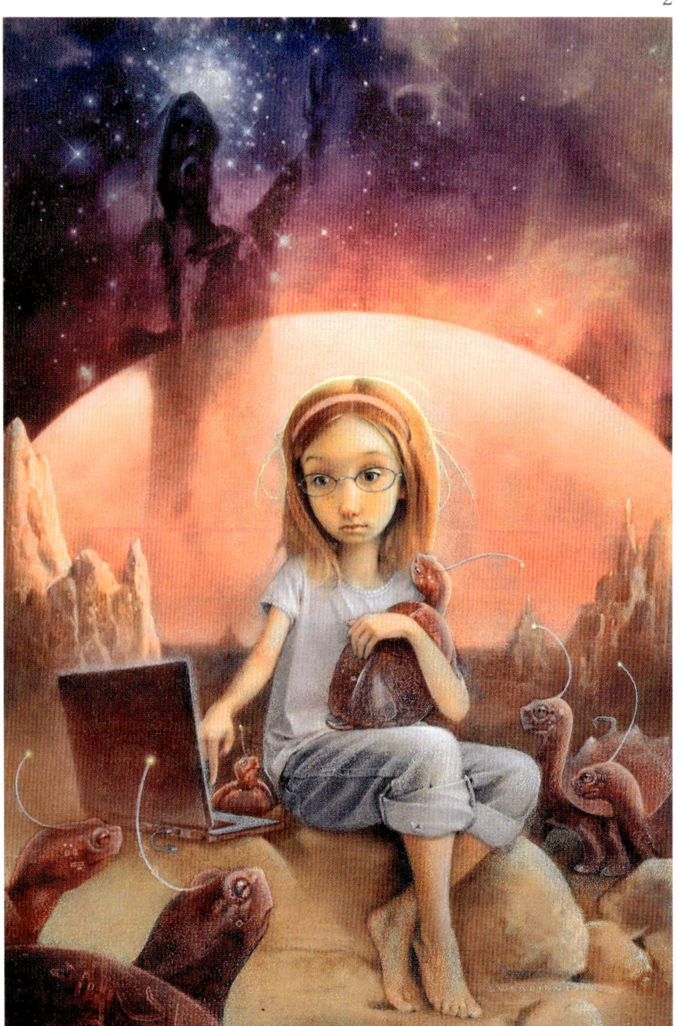

2

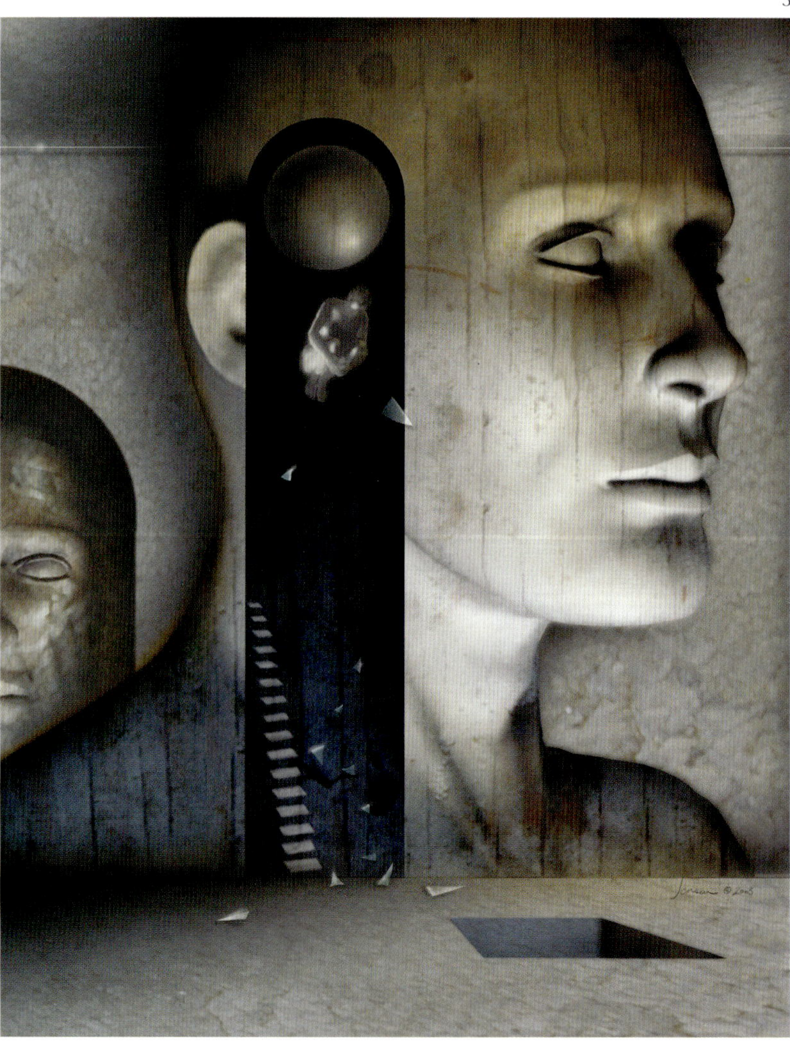

3

4

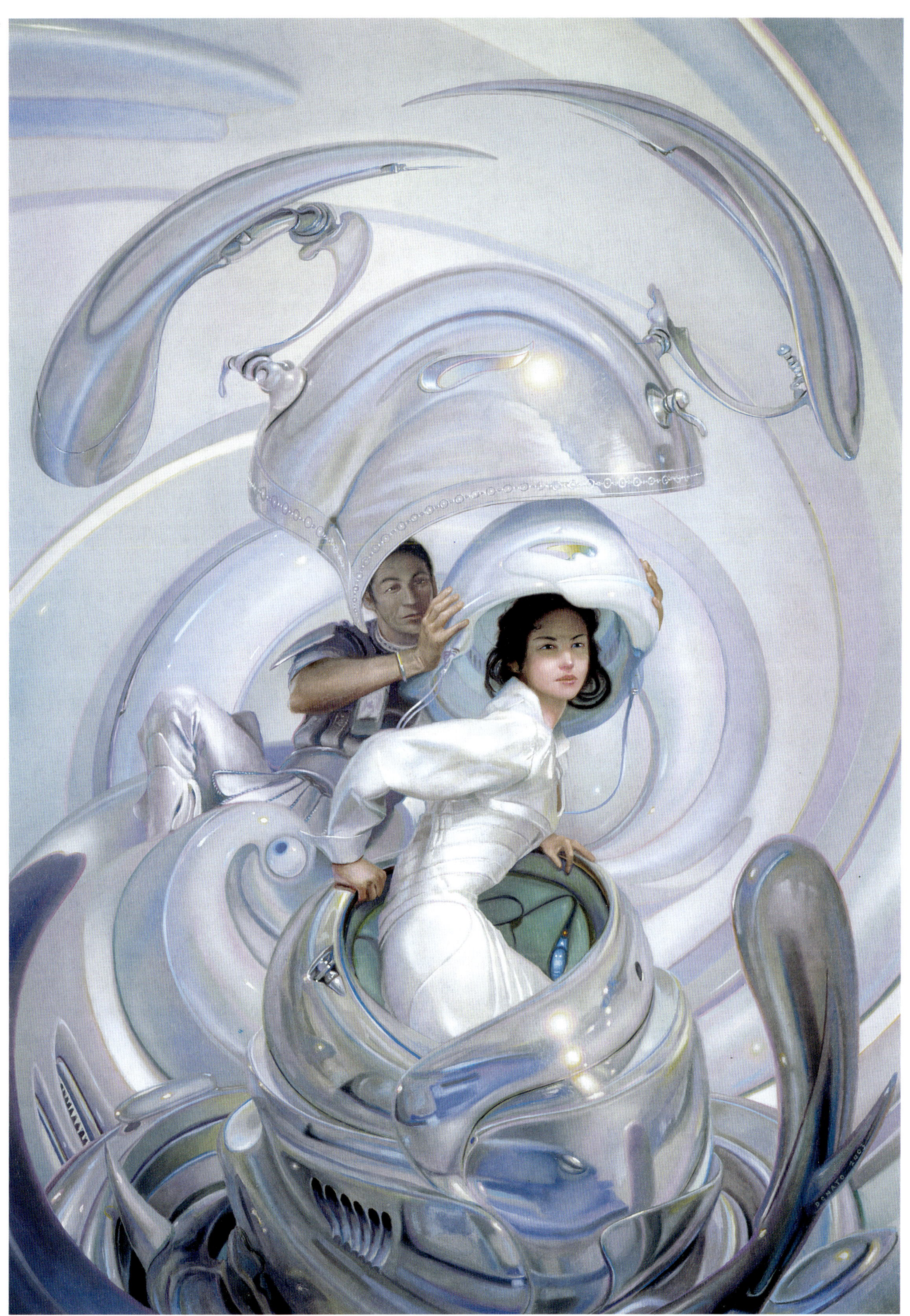

1
artist: **Frank Cho**
client: Monkey Boy Press
title: Babe and Ape
medium: Ink & watercolor
size: 17″x11″

2
artist: **Vince Natale**
art director: Michael Storrings
client: St. Martins Press
title: The Awakening
medium: Oils
size: 19″x8″

3
artist: **Ray-Mel Cornelius**
art director: Allyson Bradley
client: Half-Price Books Pub.
title: Jonathan Swift and the Martians
medium: Acrylic

4
artist: **John Steven Gurney**
art director: Joyce White
client: Scholastic
title: Snow Monster Mystery
medium: Oils
size: 19″x27″

5
artist: **Brad Weinman**
art director: Patrick Carman
designer: Liz Demeter
client: Patrick Carman
title: The Dark Hills Divide
medium: Oil on paper
size: 11″x14″

6
artist: **John Picacio**
client: Monkeybrain Books
title: Heroes & Monsters
medium: Oil/digital
size: 25″x18½″

1

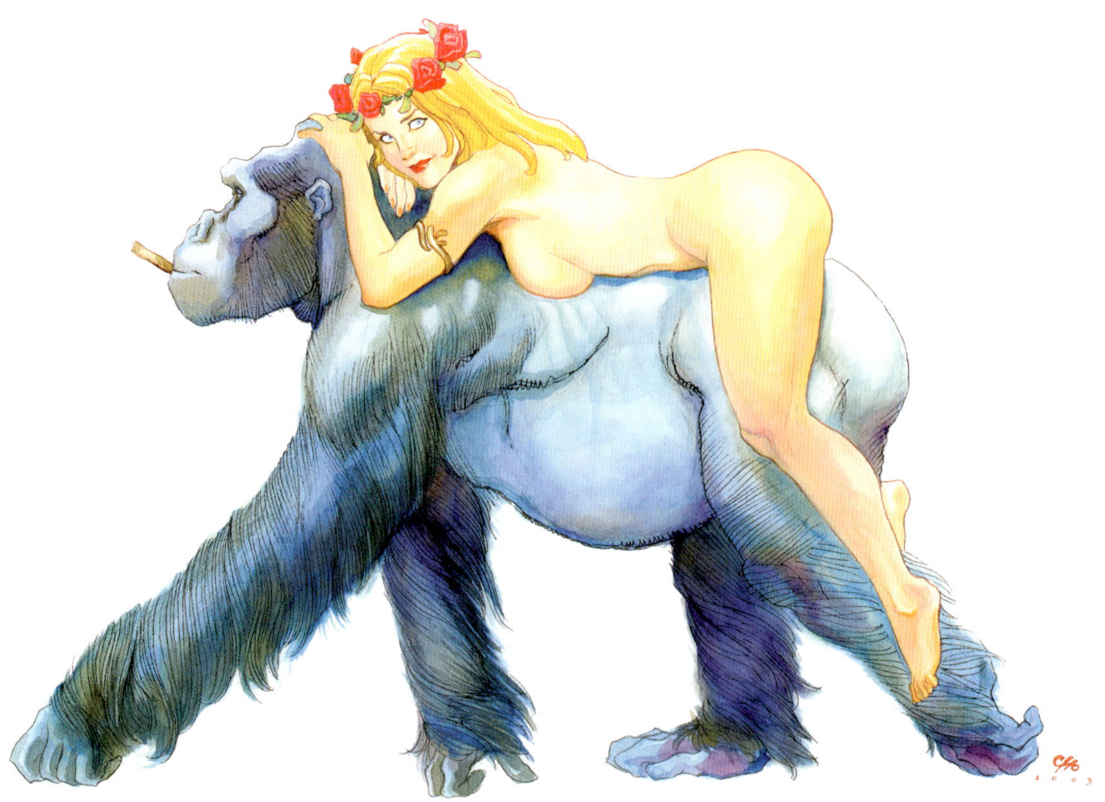

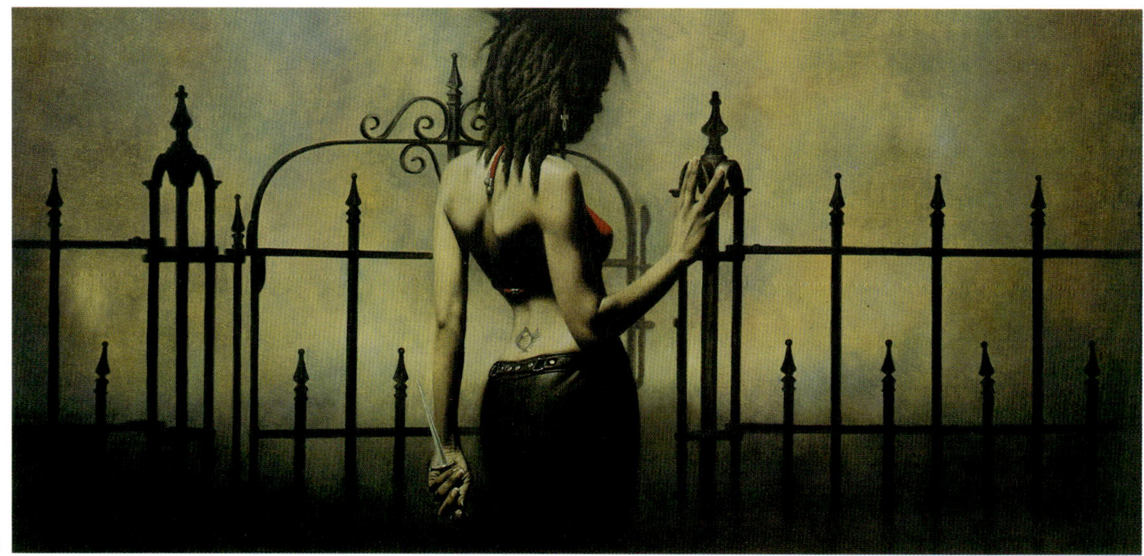

2

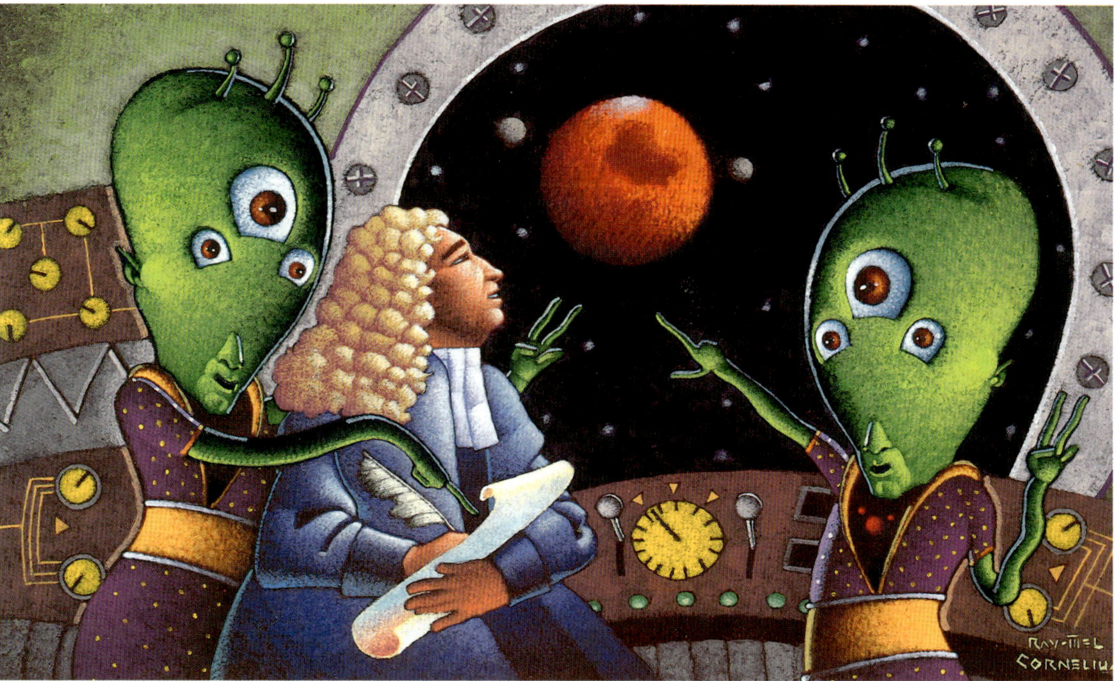

3

4

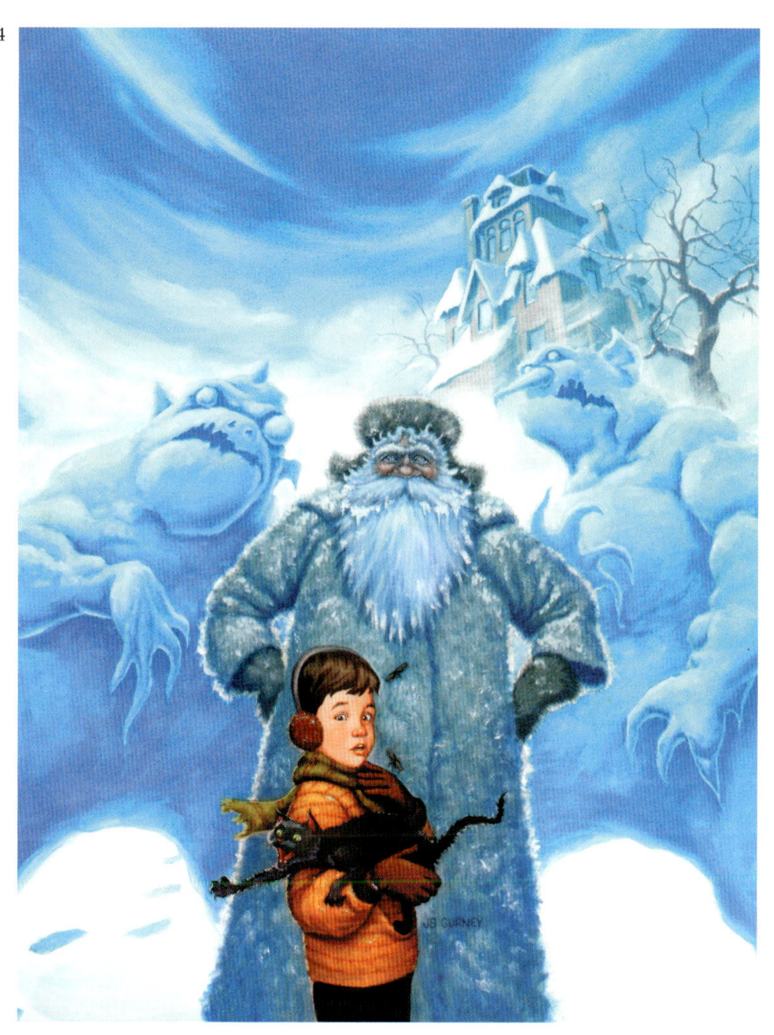

5

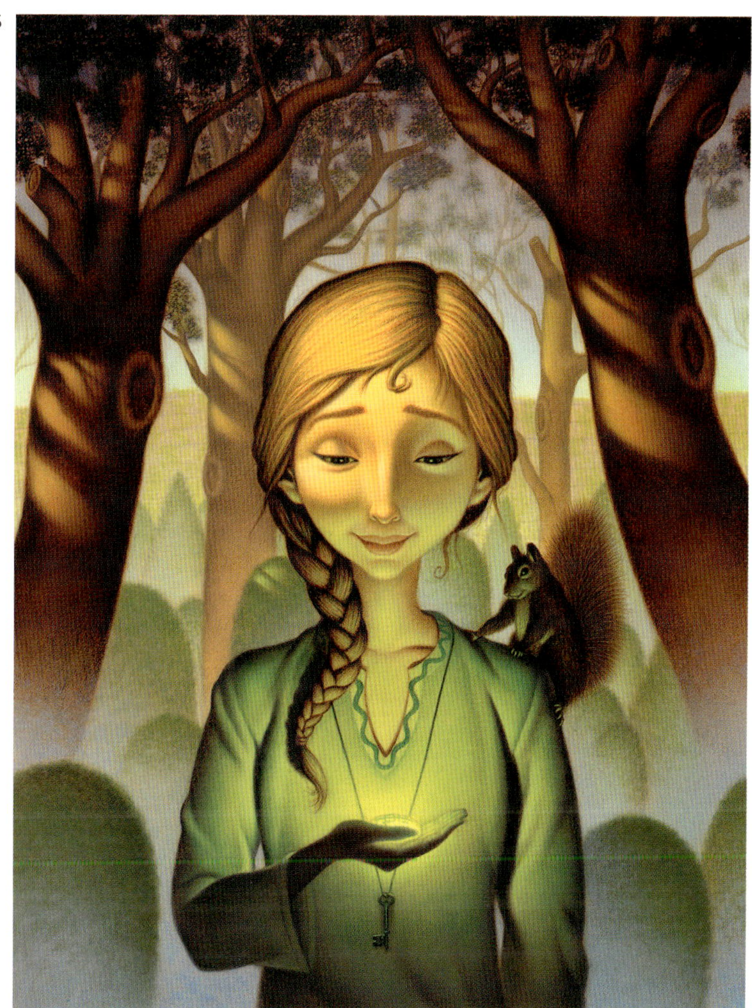

6

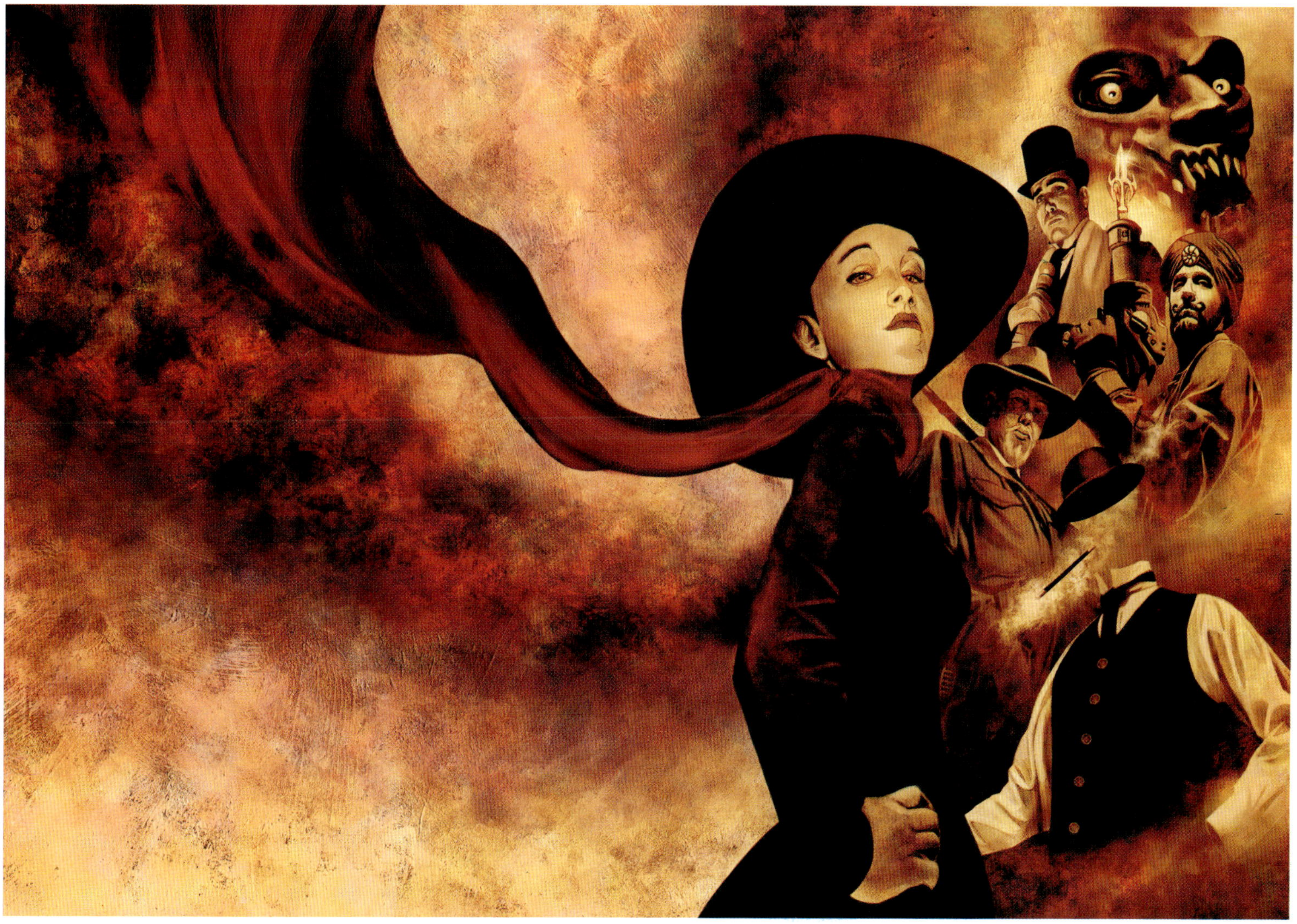

Book

1
artist: **Scott Gustafson**
art director: Wendy Wentworth
designer: Scott Gustafson
client: The Greenwich Workshop
title: The Step Sisters
medium: Oils
size: 22″x16″

2
artist: **Scott Gustafson**
art director: Wendy Wentworth
designer: Scott Gustafson
client: The Greenwich Workshop
title: Gretel and the Witch
medium: Oils
size: 22″x16″

3
artist: **John Jude Palencar**
art director: Sheila Gilbert
client: DAW Books
title: Smoke & Shadows
medium: Acrylic
size: 19″x27″

4
artist: **Duane O. Myers**
art director: Matt Adelsperger
client: Wizards of the Coast
title: Weasel's Luck
medium: Digital

5
artist: **Hala Wittwer**
art director: Irene Gallo
designer: Irene Gallo
client: Starscape Books
title: Squaring the Circle
medium: Acrylics & oils
size: 10 1/4″x15″

6
artist: **Peter de Sève**
art director: Peter de Sève/ Lori Barra
designer: Lori Barra
client: Editions Paquet
title: An Idle Mind
medium: Watercolor & ink

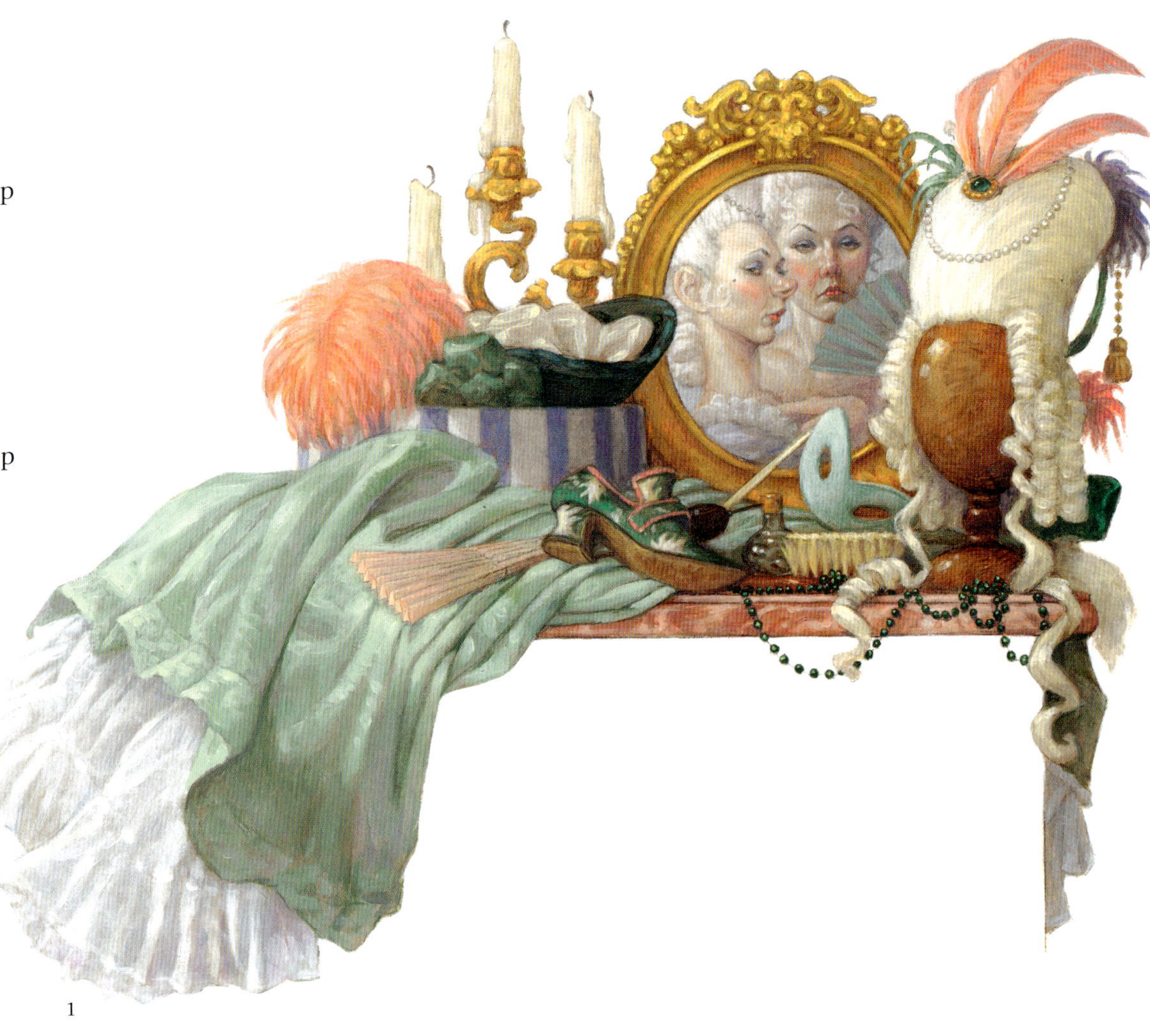

1

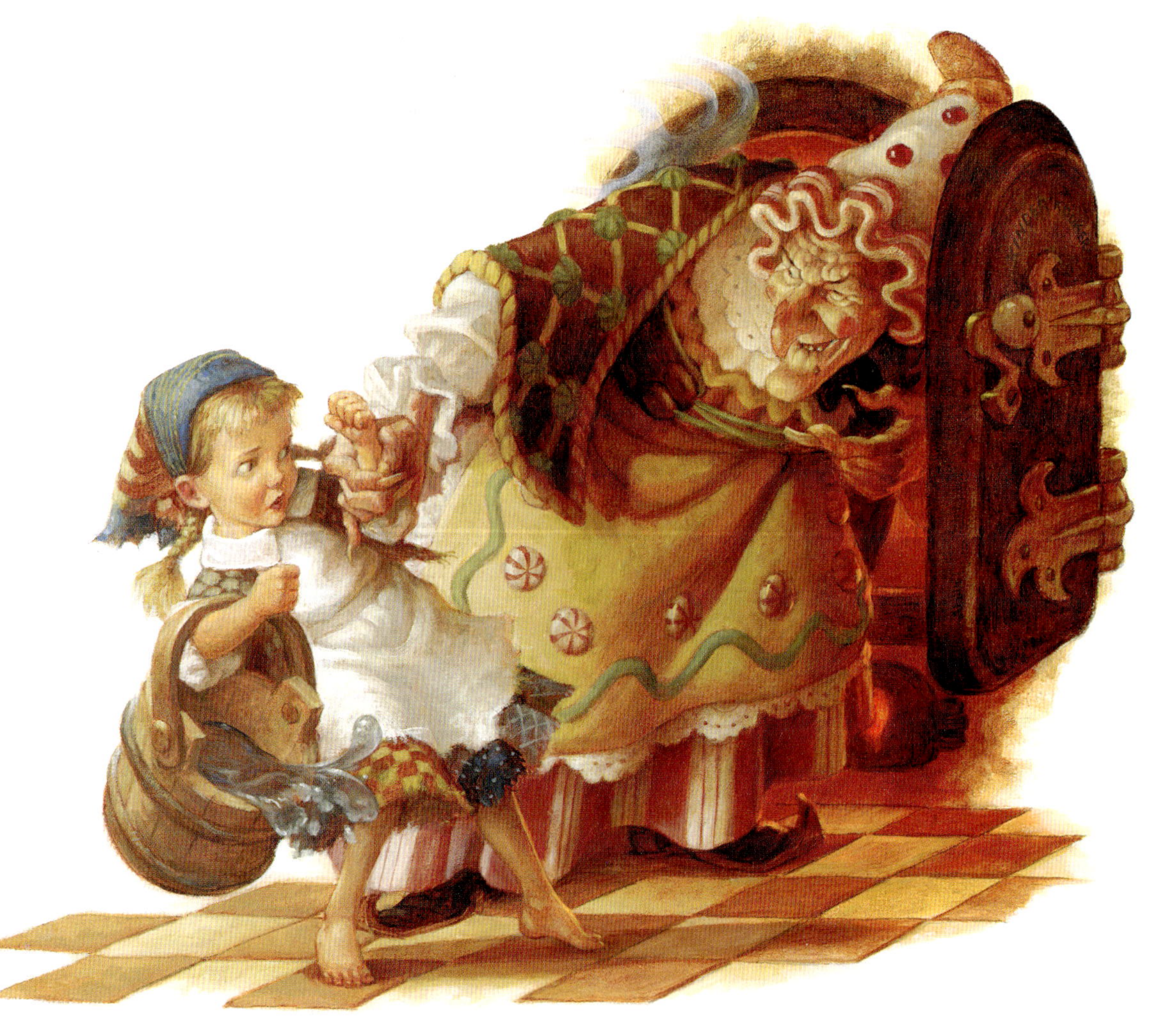

2

3

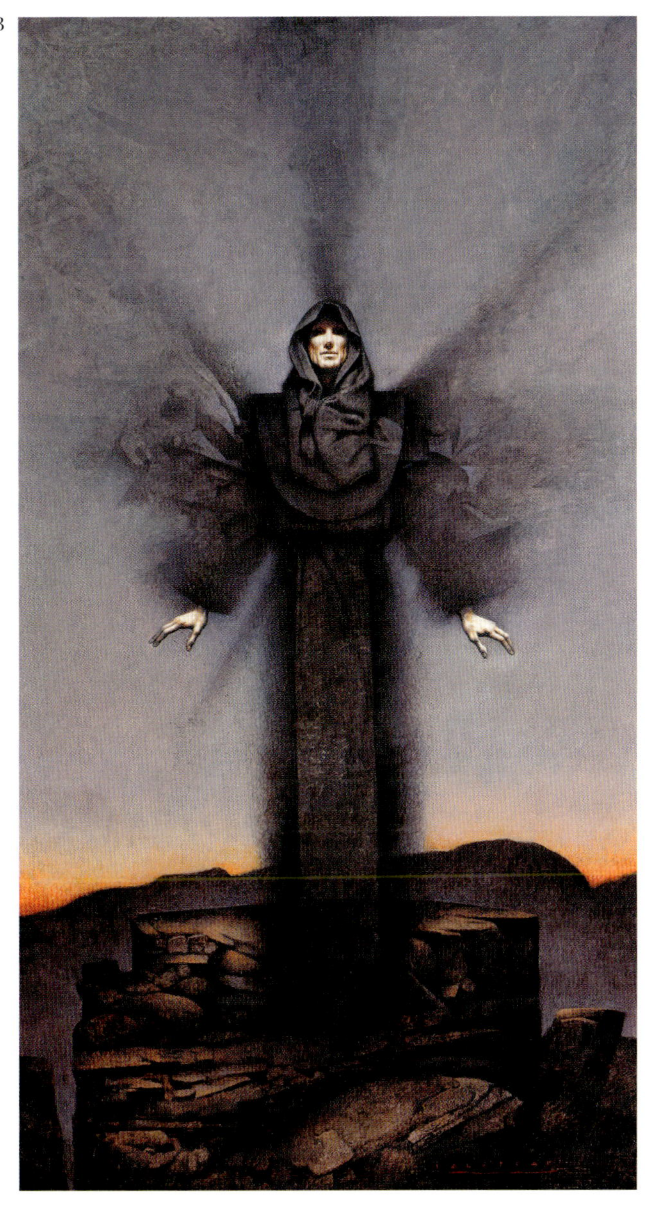

4

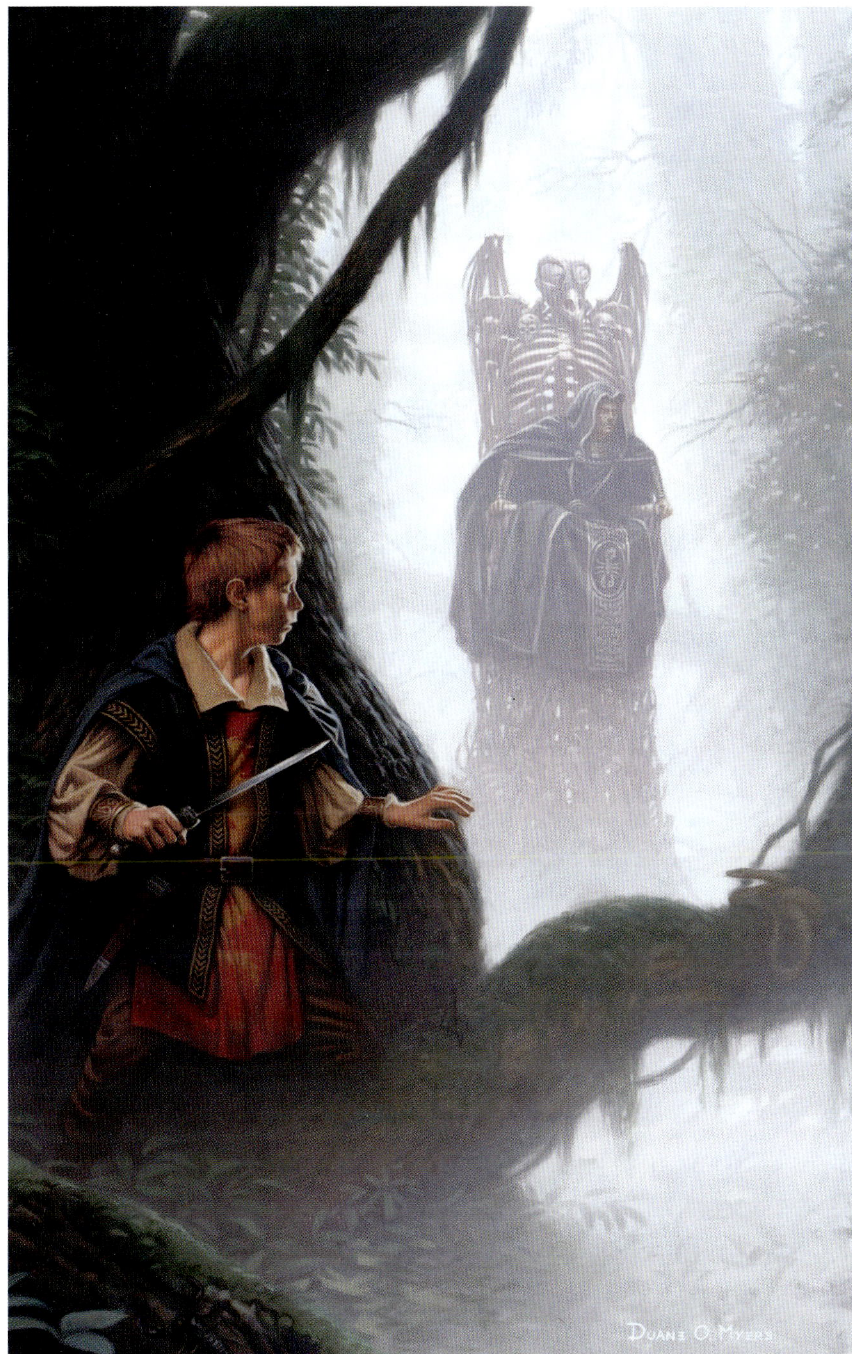

5

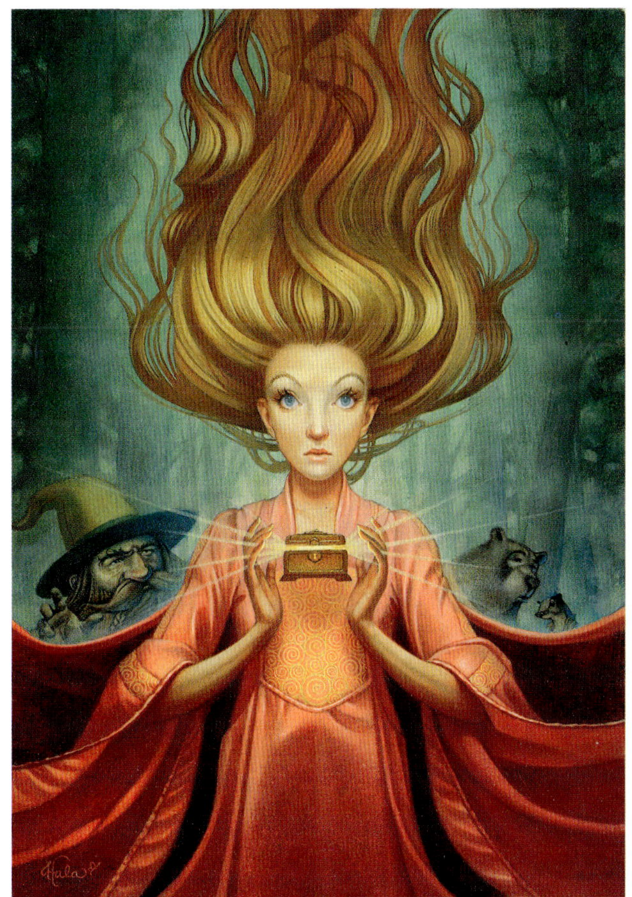

6

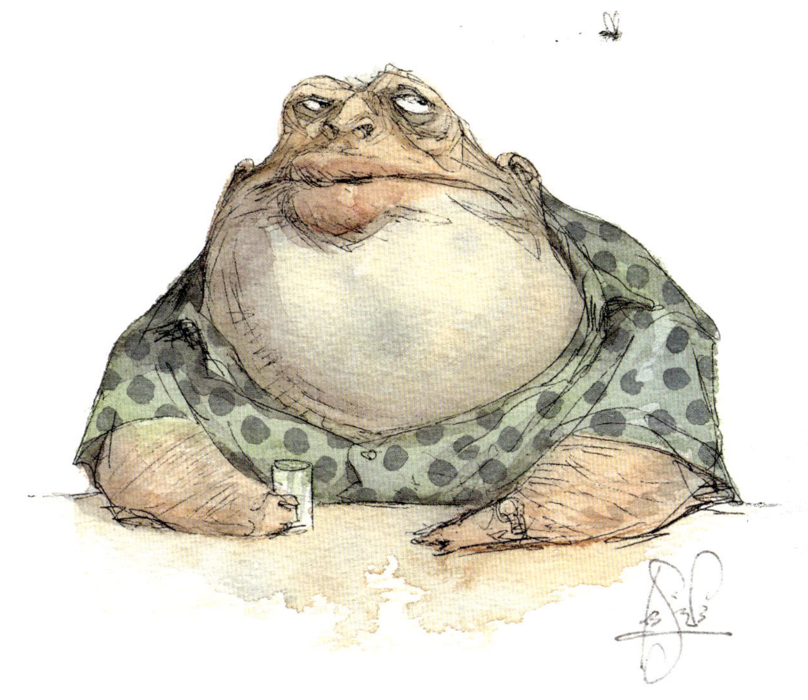

Book

1
artist: **Jon Foster**
art director: Dave Dorman
client: Rolling Thunder Press
title: Lady of Northside
medium: Digital
size: 6 3/4"x10 1/4"

2
artist: **Matt Wilson**
client: Privateer Press
title: Walk Softly...
medium: Oil on board
size: 44"x24"

3
artist: **Michael Deas**
art director: Daniel Rembert
client: Villard Books
title: David Blaine: Mysterious Stranger
medium: Oil on panel
size: 18"x22"

4
artist: **Donato Giancola**
art director: Irene Gallo
client: Tor Books
title: The Nameless Day
medium: Oil on paper
size: 36"x48"

5
artist: **Kinuko Y. Craft**
art director: Judith Murello
client: Berkley/Penguin/Putnam
title: The Alphabet of Thorn
medium: Oil over watercolor
size: 24"x18"

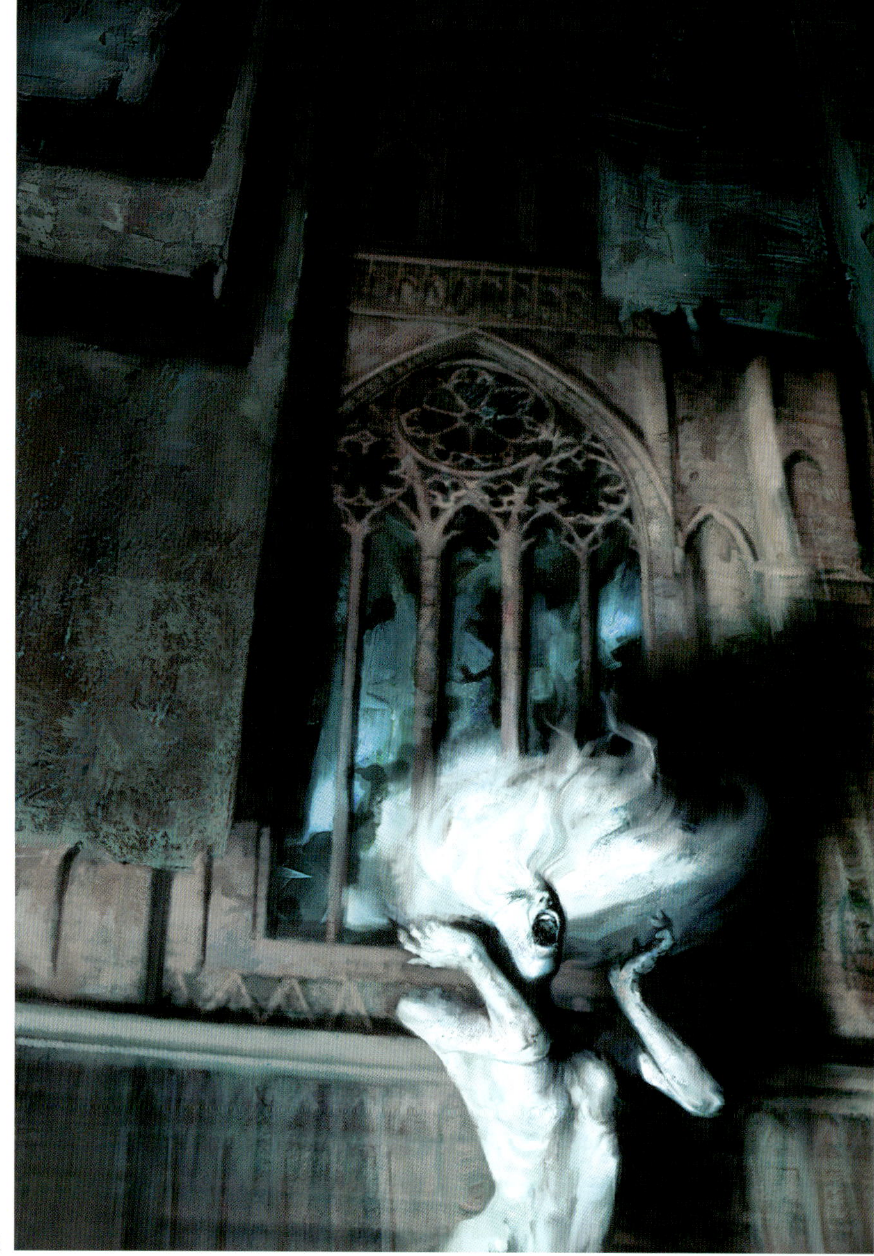

1

2

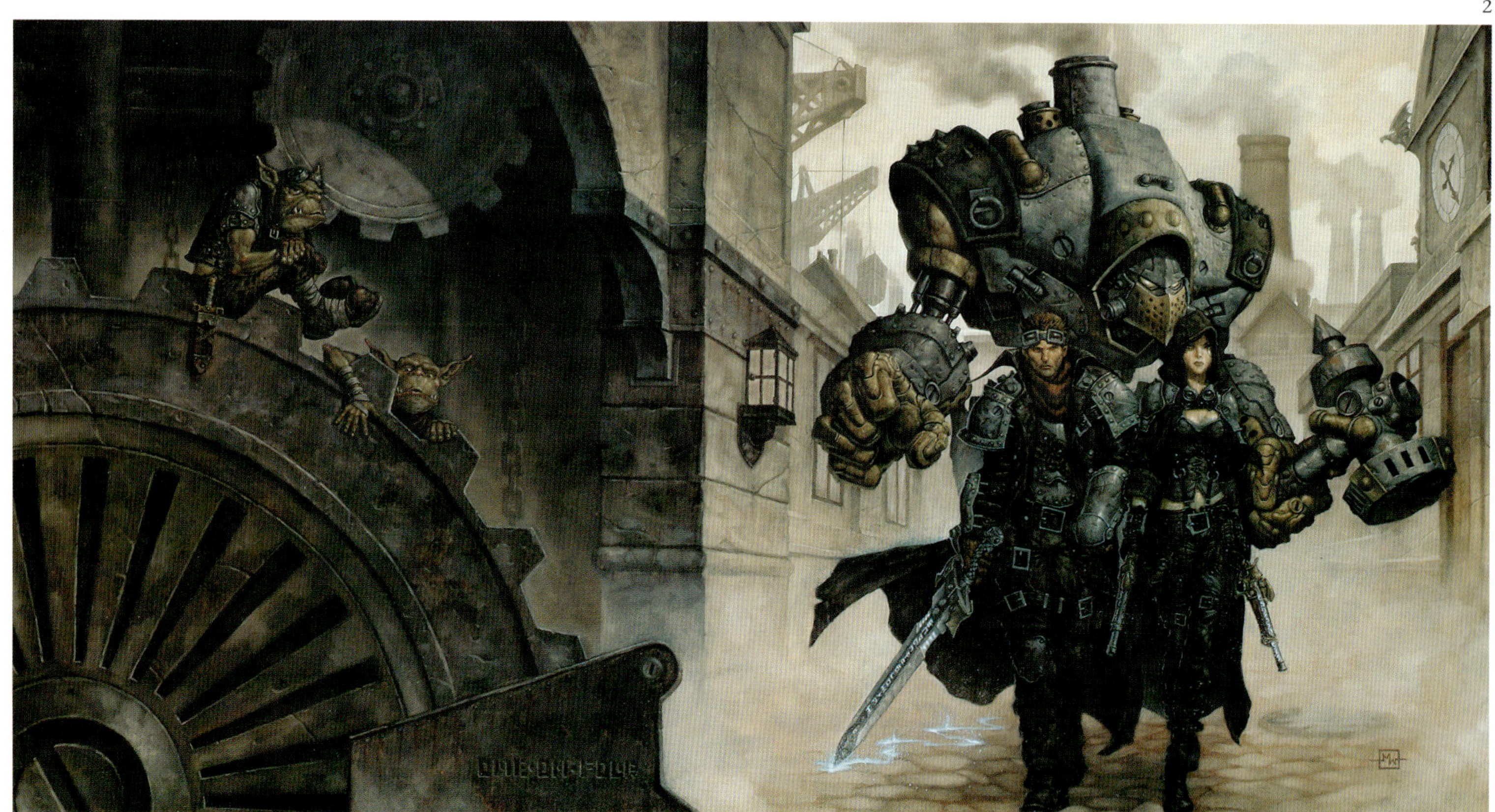

3

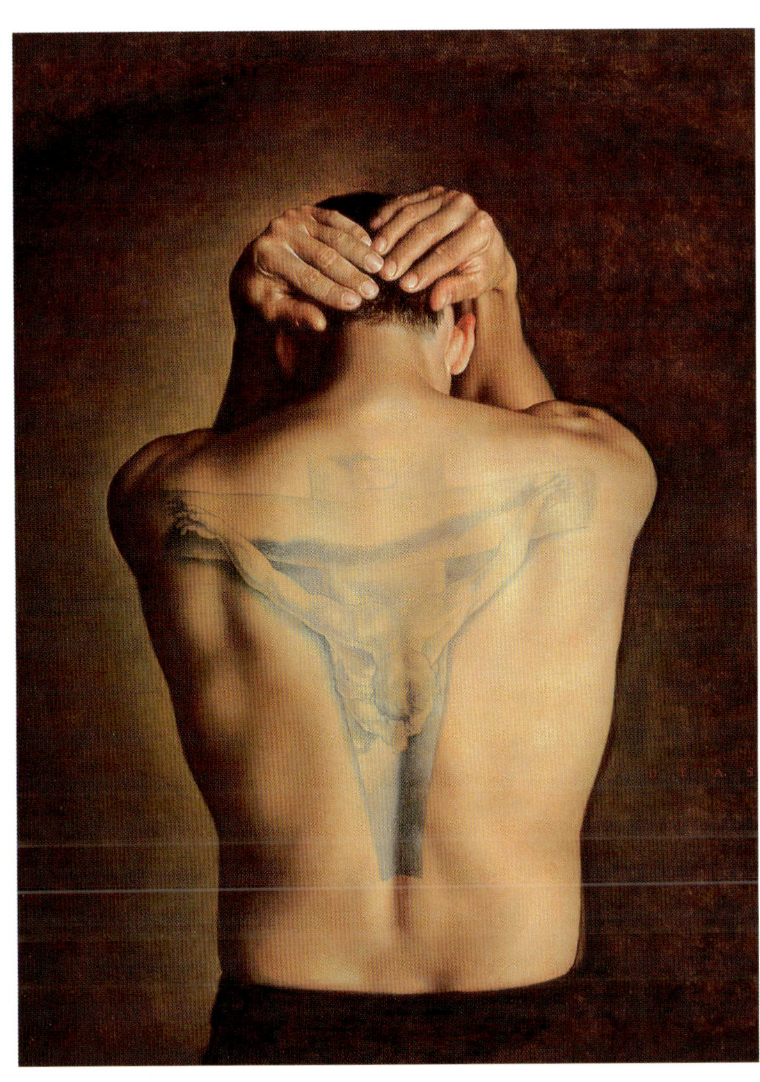

4

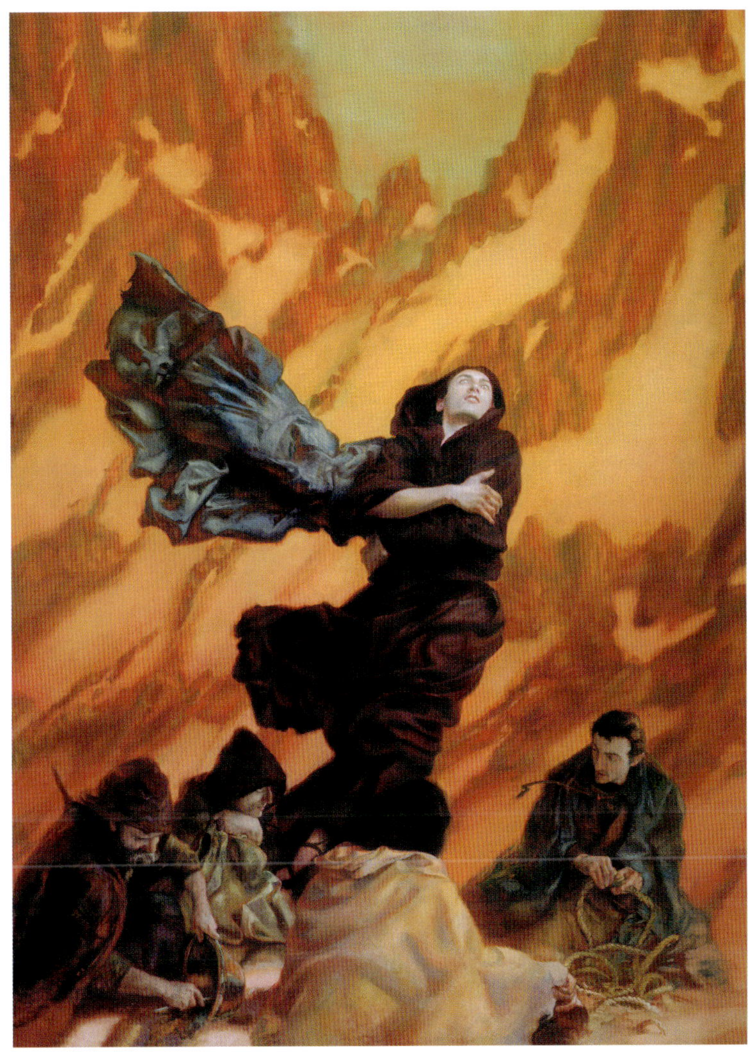

5

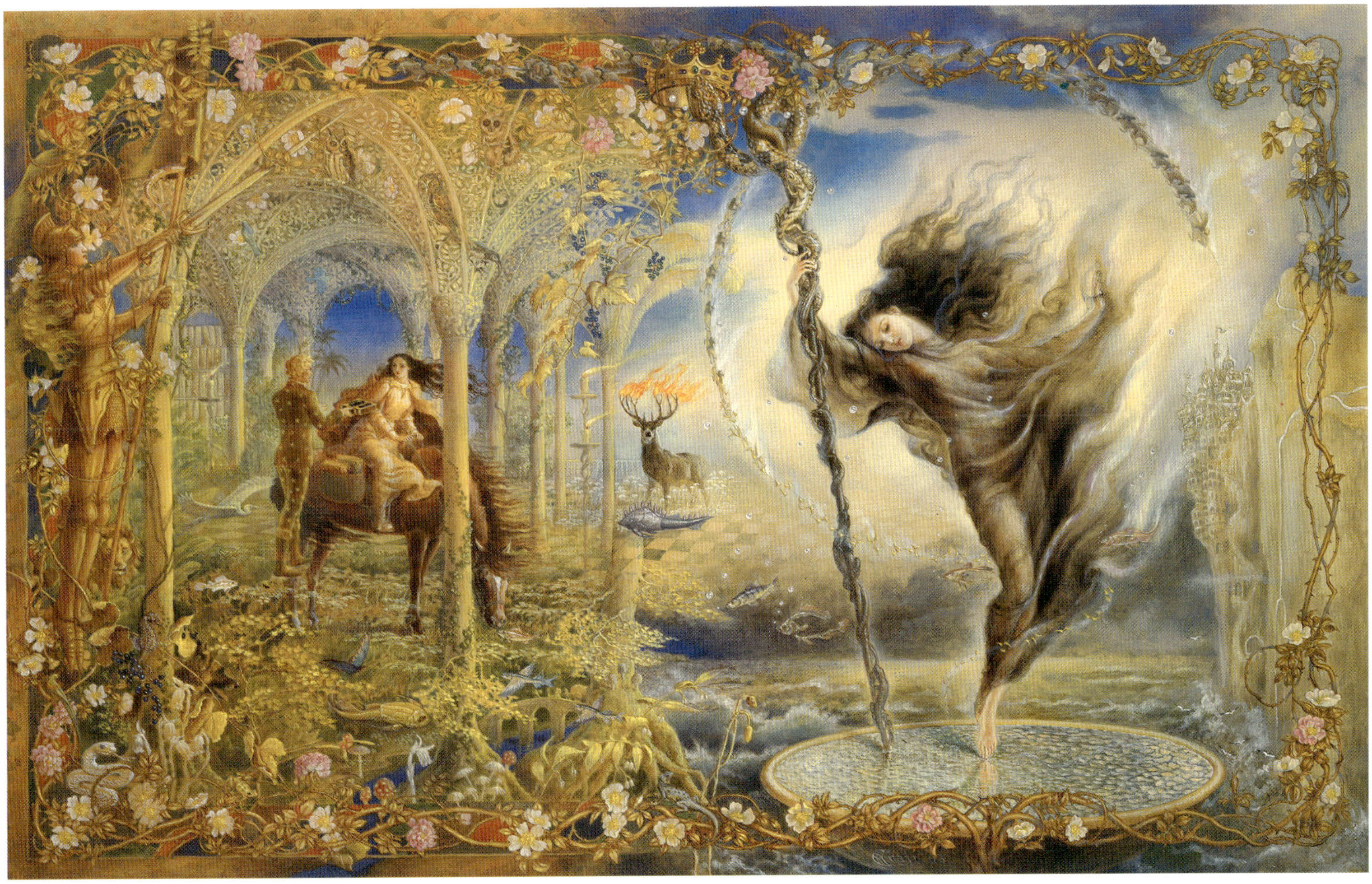

1
artist: **Gnemo**
art director: Tom Kidd/Irene Gallo
client: Spellcaster Press
title: Black Brillion
medium: Oils

2
artist: **Greg Spalenka**
art director: Elizabeth Parissi
client: Scholastic Books
title: Daughter of the Wind
medium: Mixed *size:* 8 1/2"x11"

3
artist: **Jon Sullivan**
client: Millennium Fantasy
title: Blue Moon Rising
medium: Oil *size:* 12"x20"

4
artist: **Kinuko Y. Craft**
art director: Irene Gallo
client: Tor Books
title: Fox Mask
medium: Oils *size:* 16 1/8"x23 1/2"

1

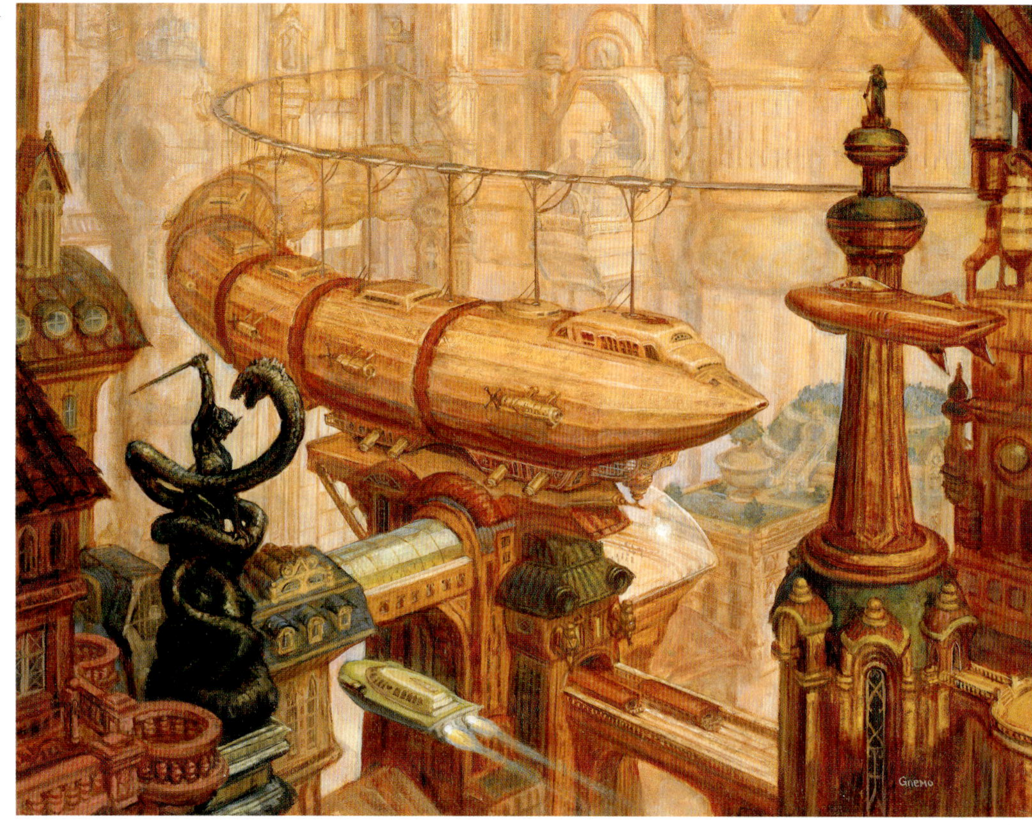

2

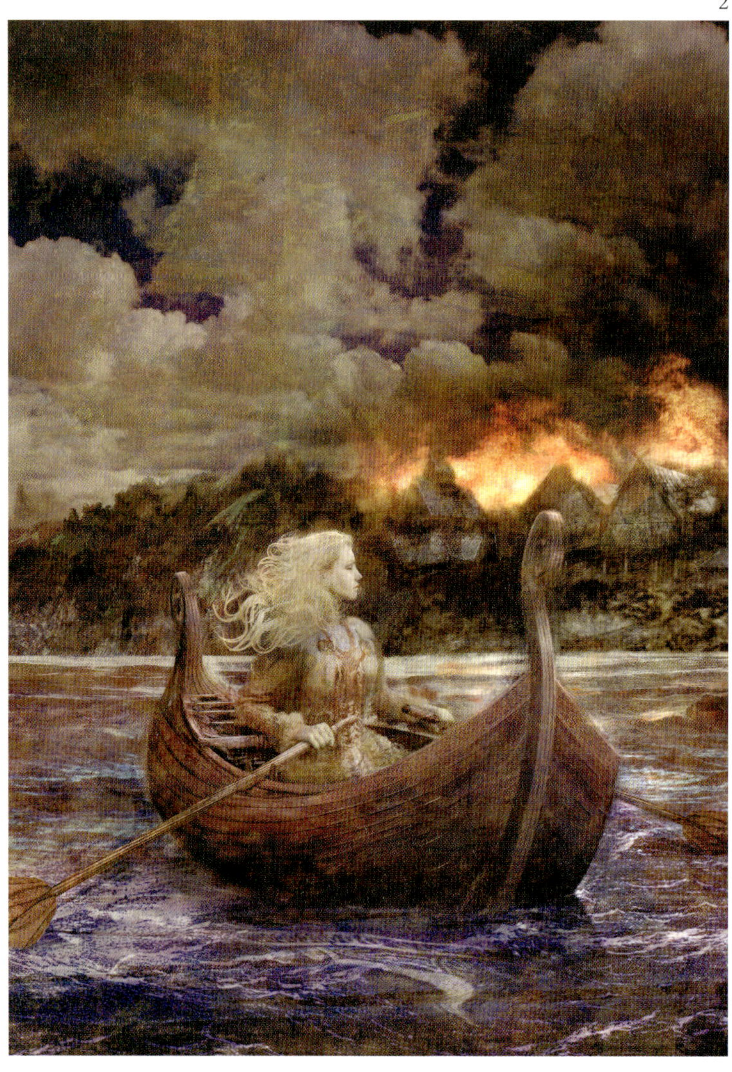

3

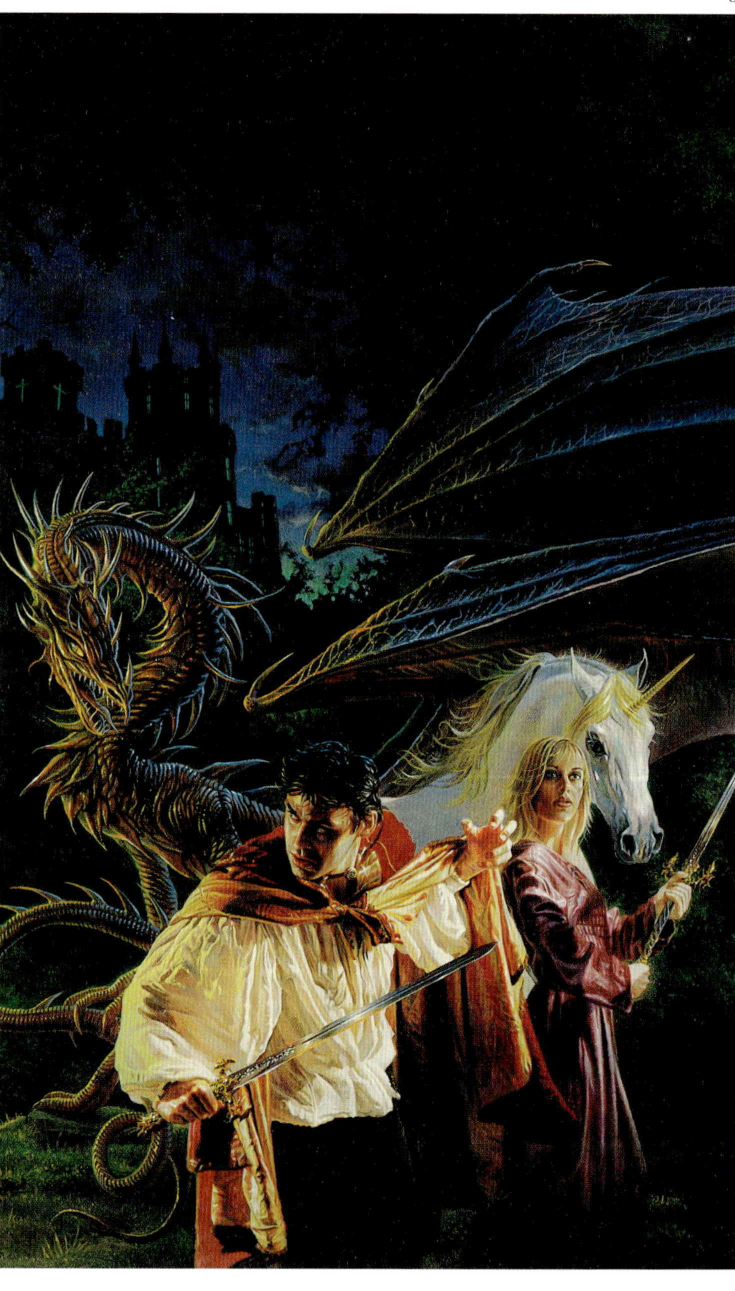

4

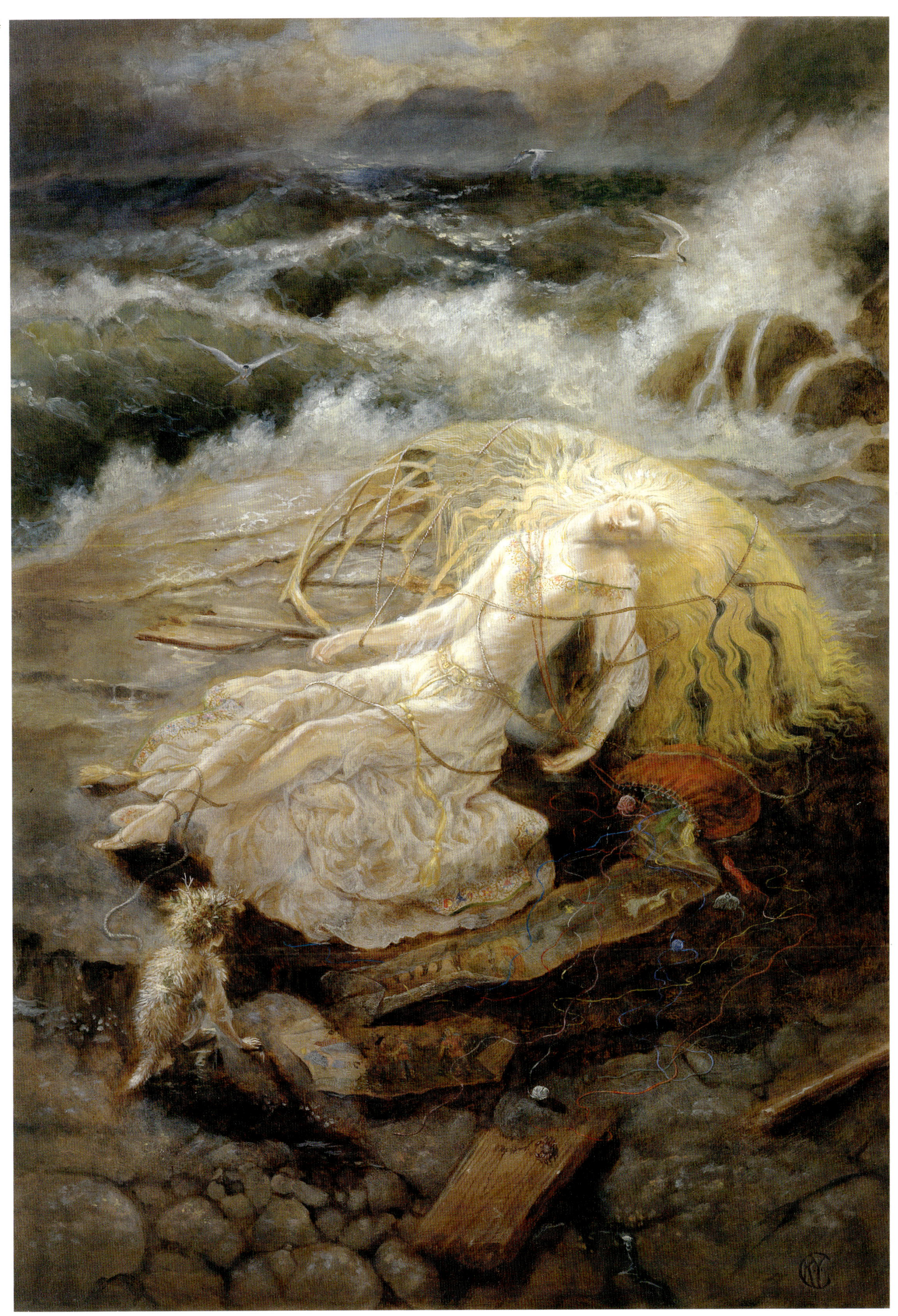

1
artist: **Roxana Villa**
art director: Susan Oyama
designer: Corinda Cook
client: Running Press
title: Spring
medium: Acrylics on board
size: 12"x18"

2
artist: **Rick Berry**
client: Donald M. Grant Books
title: Bad Attitude
medium: Oils/mixed

3
artist: **Brad Weinman**
art director: Kathleen Flanigan
designer: Kathleen Flanigan
client: HarperCollins
title: Stink Files 001
medium: Oils on paper
size: 11"x14"

4
artist: **Julie Bell**
art director: Irene Gallo
client: Tor Books
title: Earth Logic
medium: Oils

1

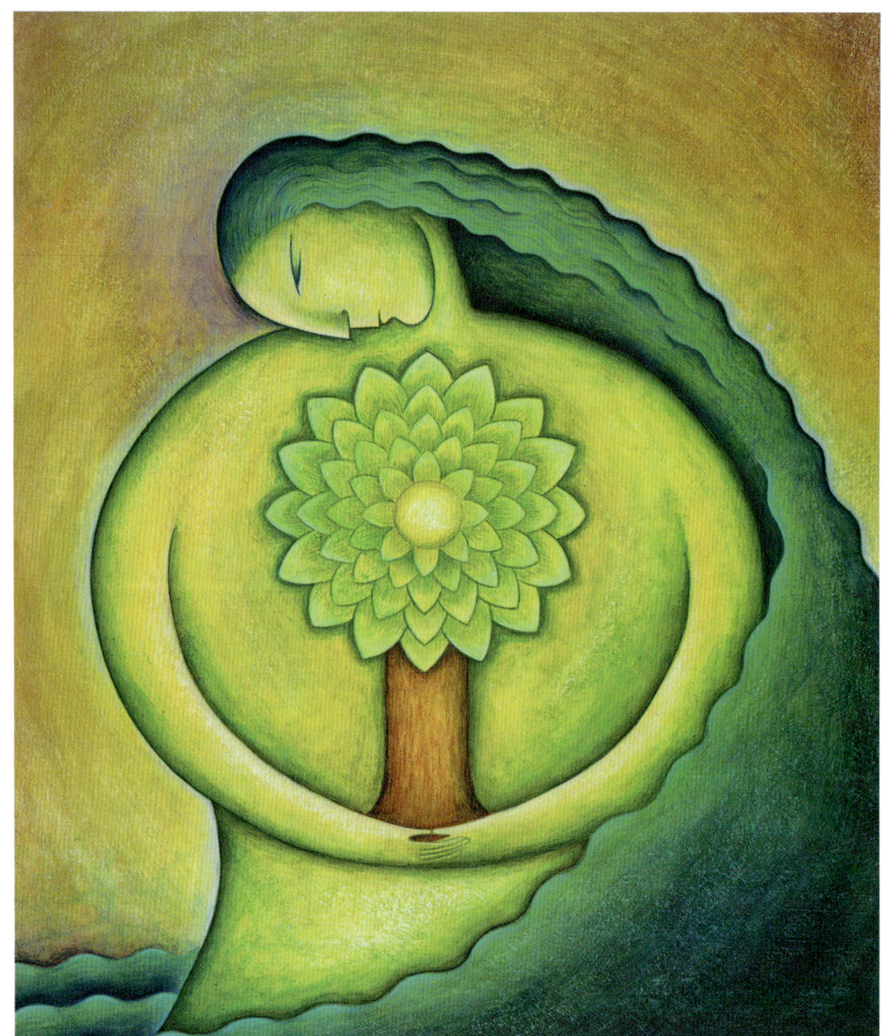

2

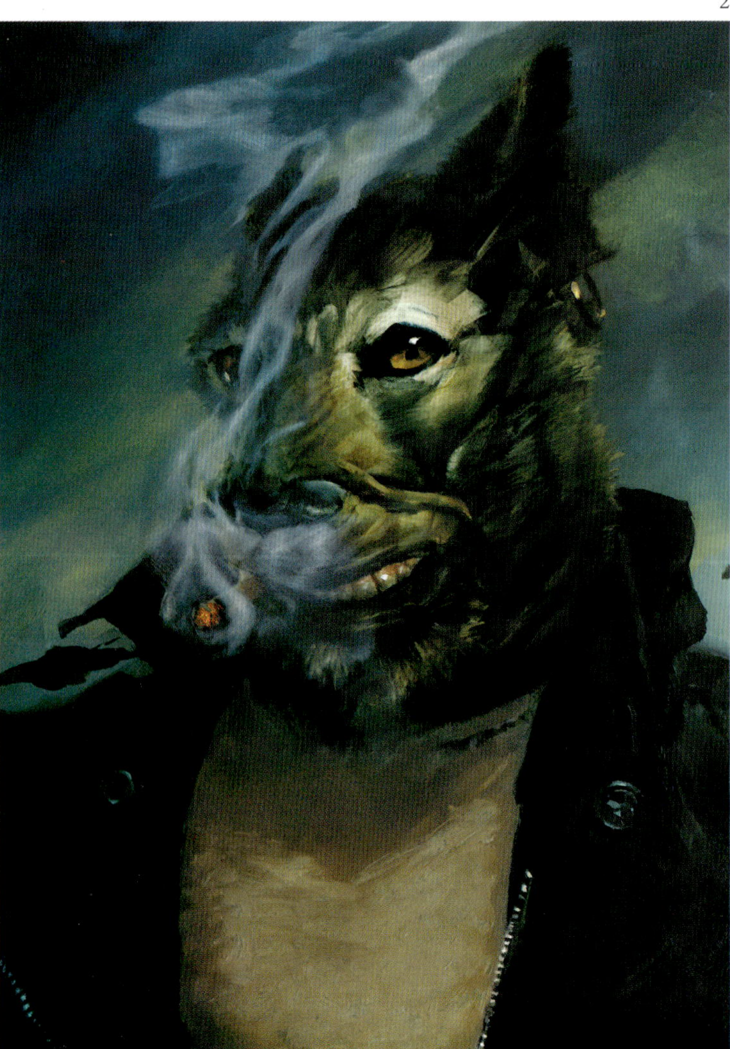

3

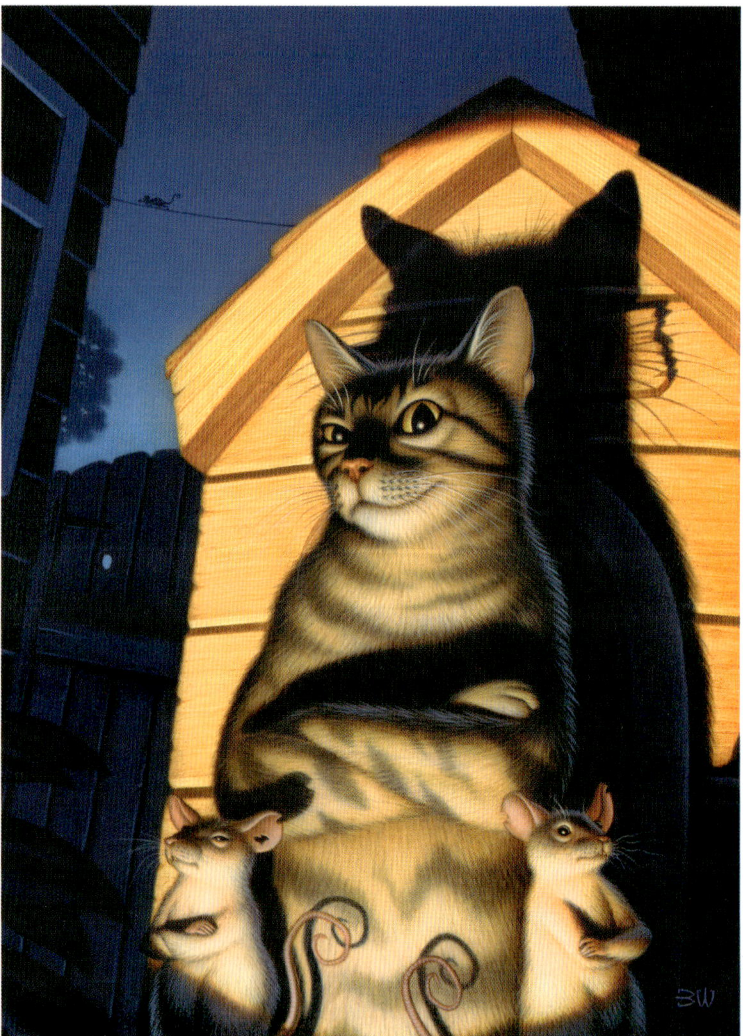

4

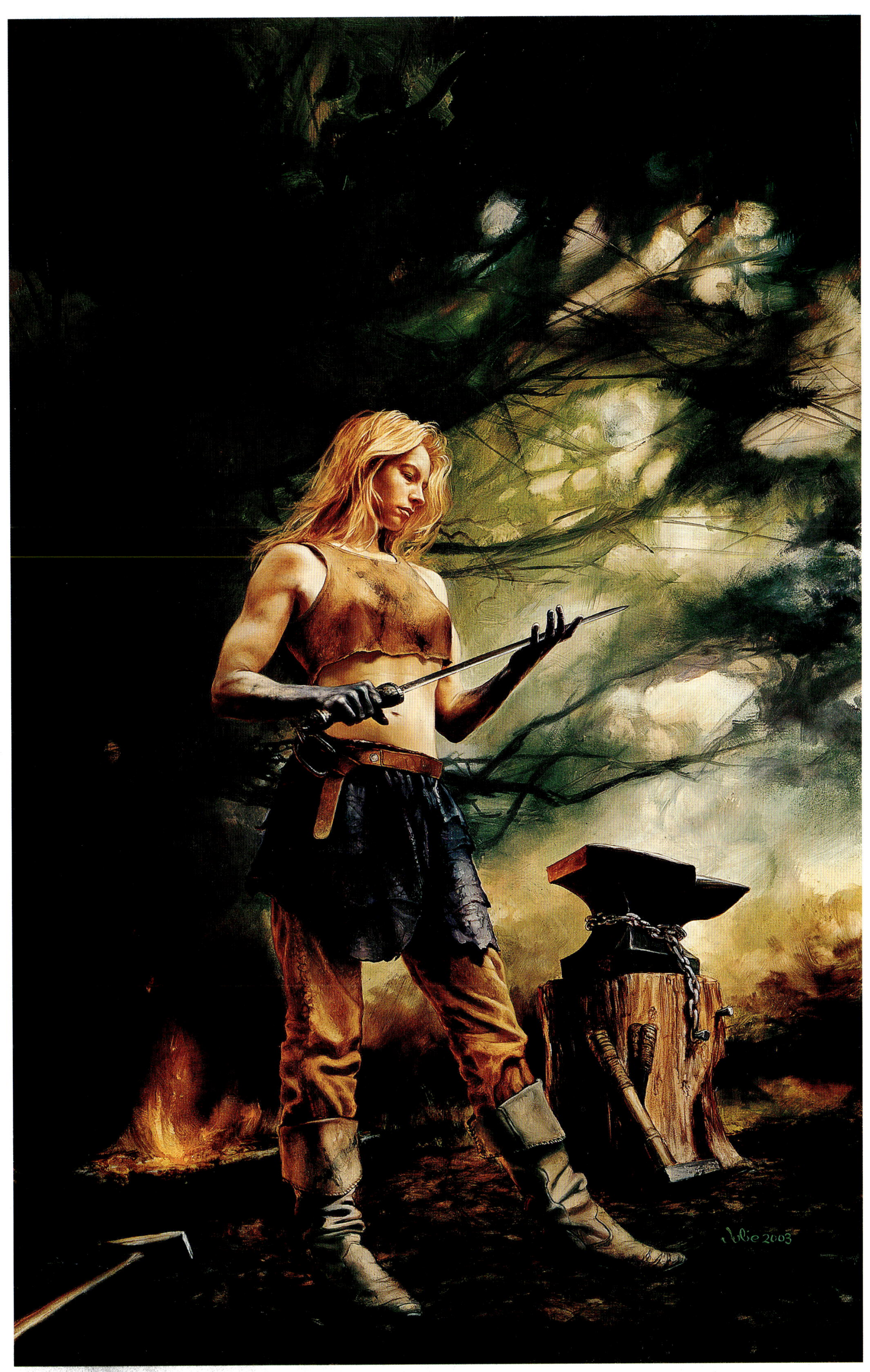

Book

1
artist: **Eric Bowman**
art director: Irene Gallo
client: Tor Books
title: The Buried Pyramid
medium: Oil

2
artist: **Edward Miller**
art director: Paul Miller
client: Earthling Publications
title: Exorcising Angels
medium: Acrylics
size: 28"x20"

3
artist: **William O'Connor**
art director: Justin Drolsbaugh
client: MBI/Easton Press
title: Empire from the Ashes
medium: Oil
size: 15"x23"

4
artist: **Daniel Dos Santos**
art director: Irene Gallo
client: Starscape Books
title: The Red Unicorn
medium: Oil

5
artist: **Bob Eggleton**
art director: Irene Gallo
client: Tor Books
title: Jaws of Darkness
medium: Acrylics
size: 24"x18"

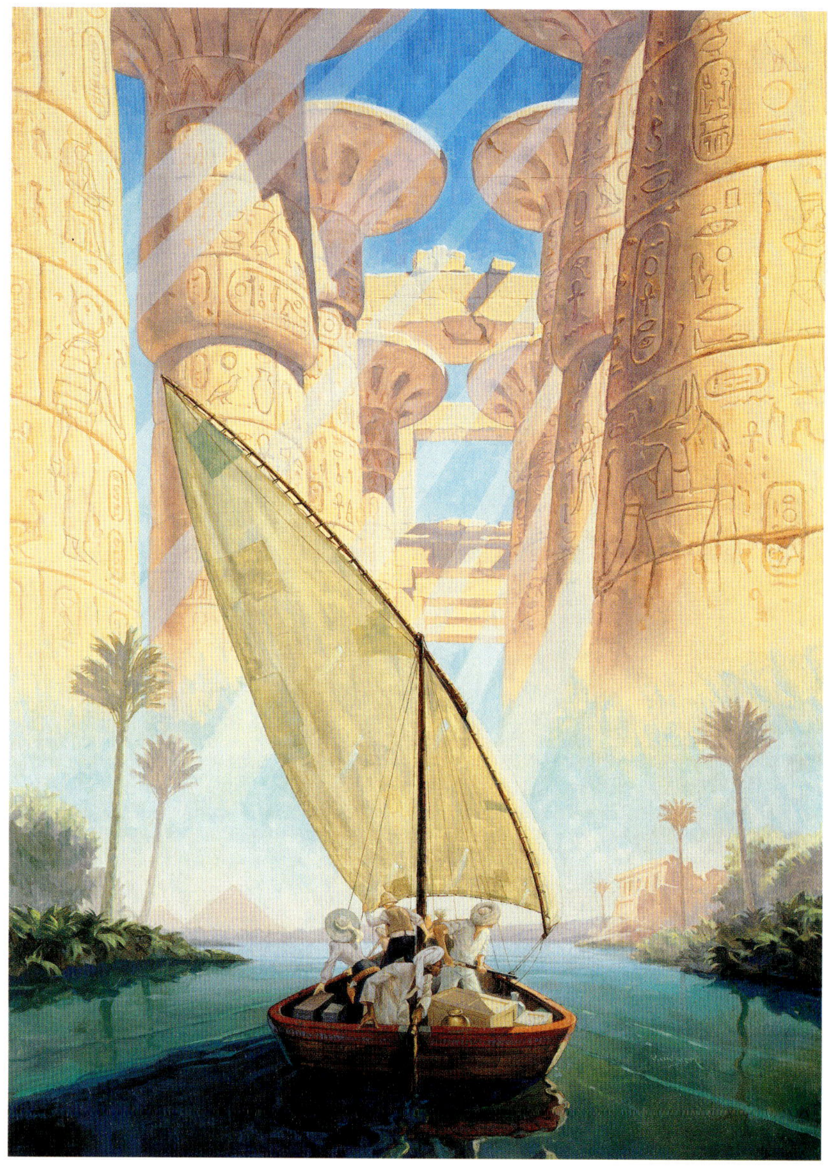

1

2

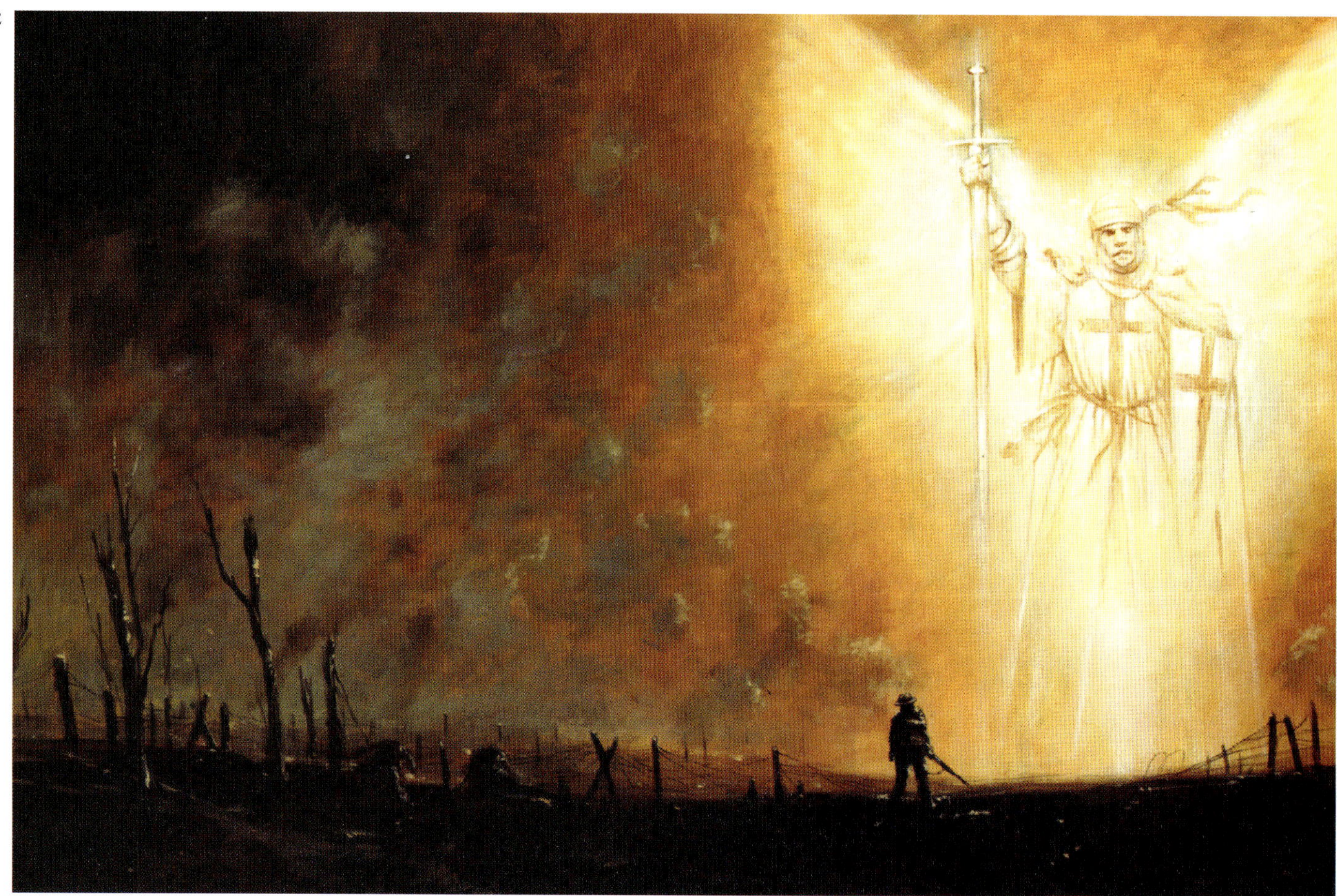

3

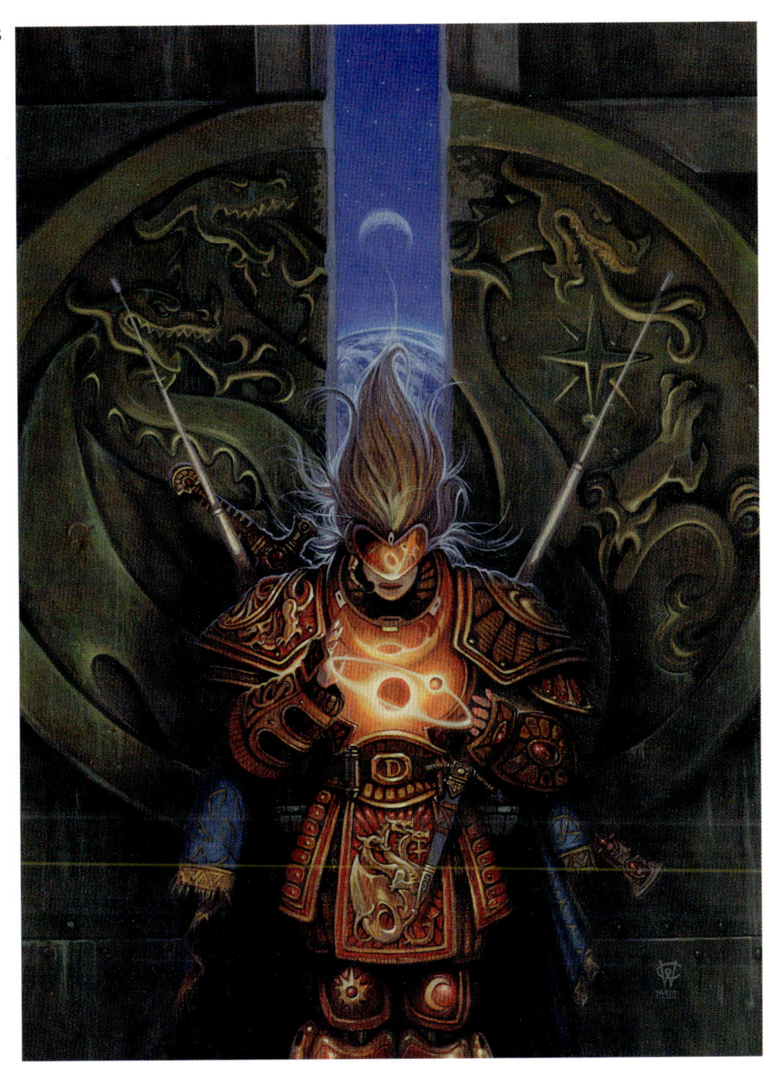

4

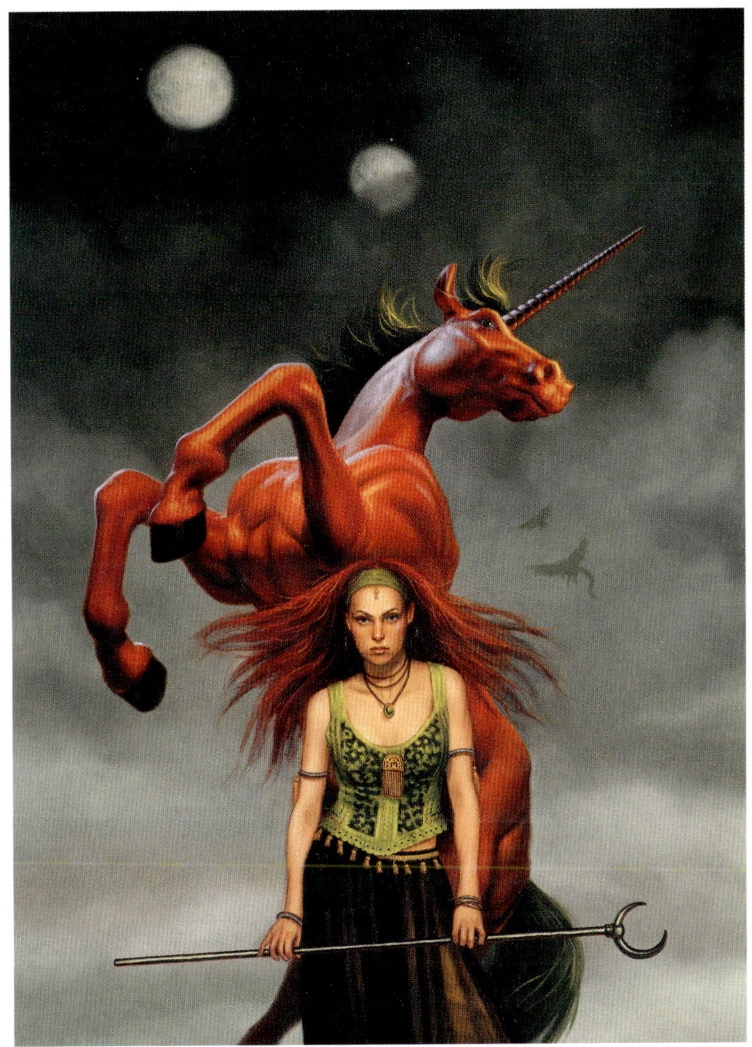

5

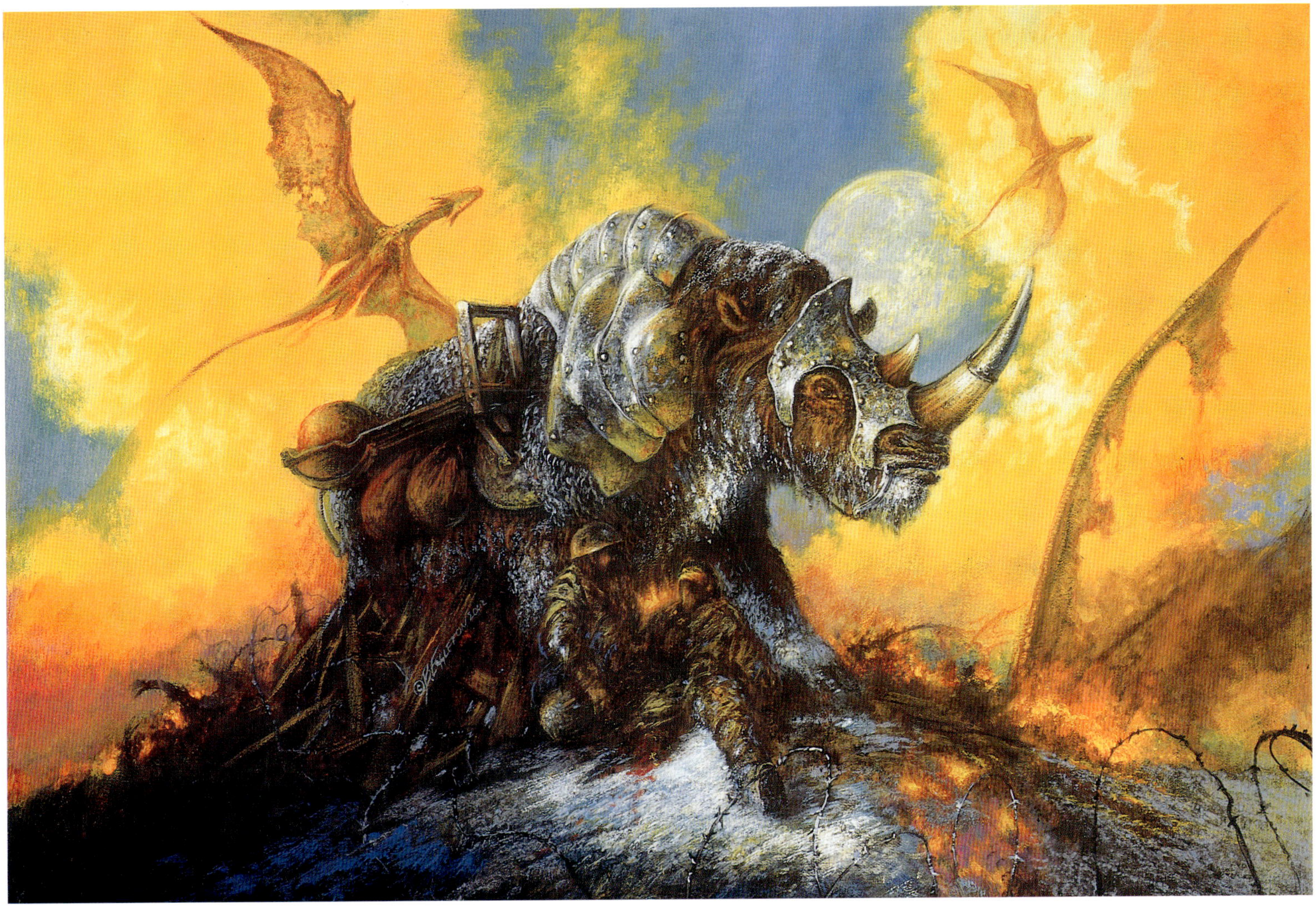

Book

1
artist: **Tristan Elwell**
art director: Irene Gallo
client: Tor Books (Starscape)
title: Obernewtyn
medium: Oils on canvas
size: 12″x16″

2
artist: **Matt Stawicki**
art director: Matt Adelsperger
client: Wizards of the Coast
title: Amber and Ashes
medium: Digital

3
artist: **J.P. Targete**
art director: Greg Benage
client: Fantasy Flight Games
title: Midnight: Minions of the Shadows
medium: Digital
size: 7″x9″

4
artist: **John Rush**
art director: Andrea Spooner
client: Chronicle Books
title: Attack on the Castle
medium: Oils
size: 20″x28″

5
artist: **John Jude Palencar**
art director: David Stevenson
client: Del Rey Books
title: The New Lovecraft Circle
medium: Acrylics
size: 29″x19″

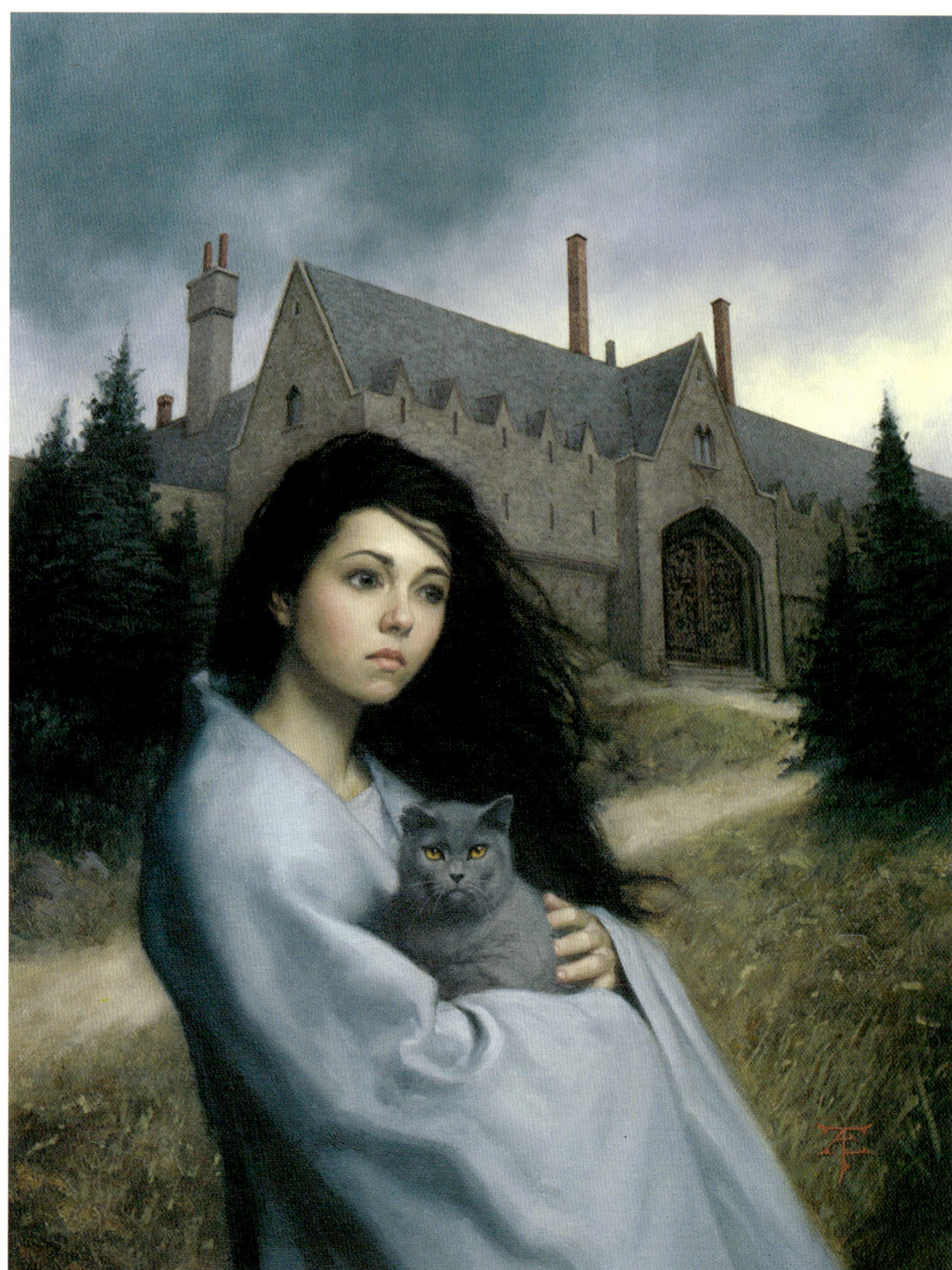
1

2
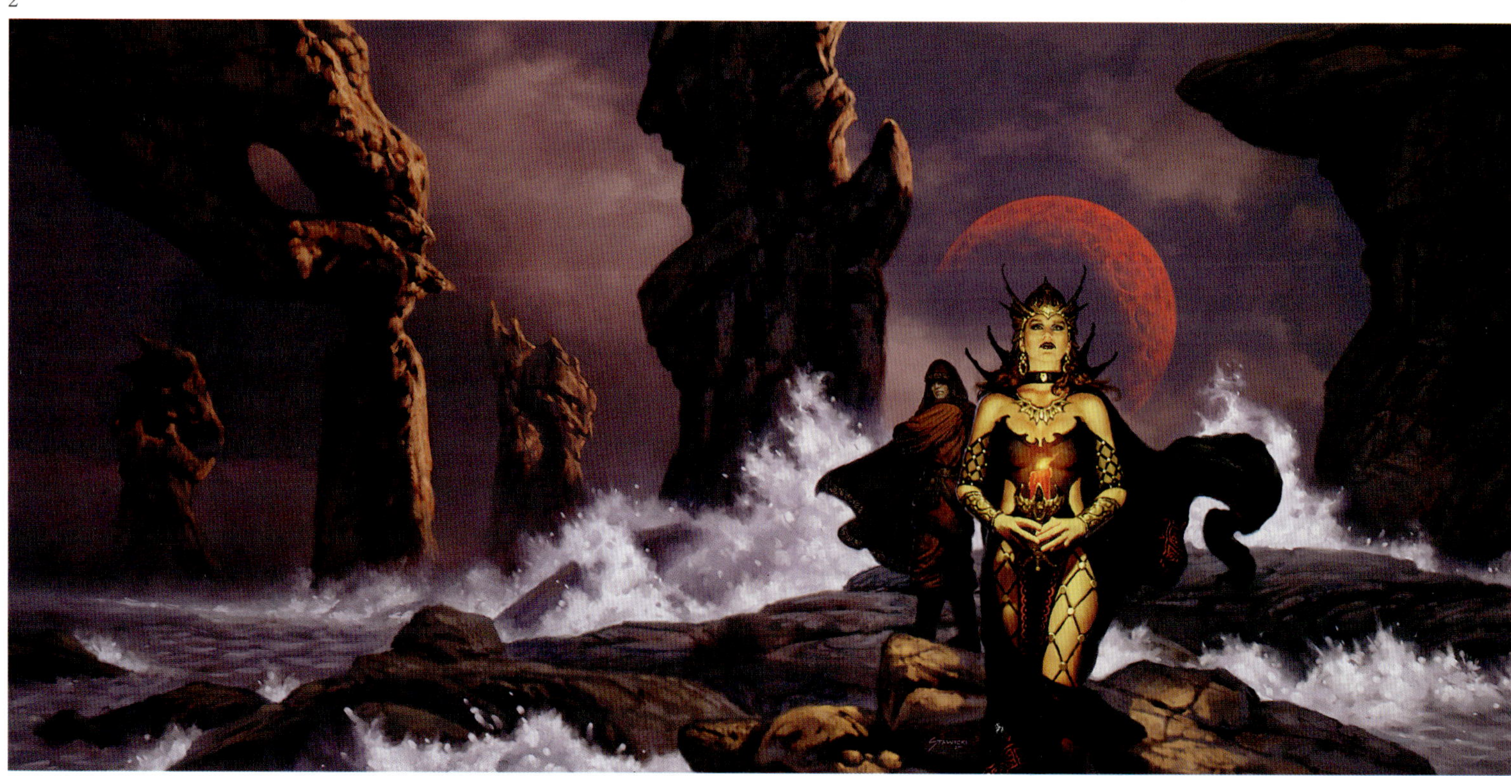

3

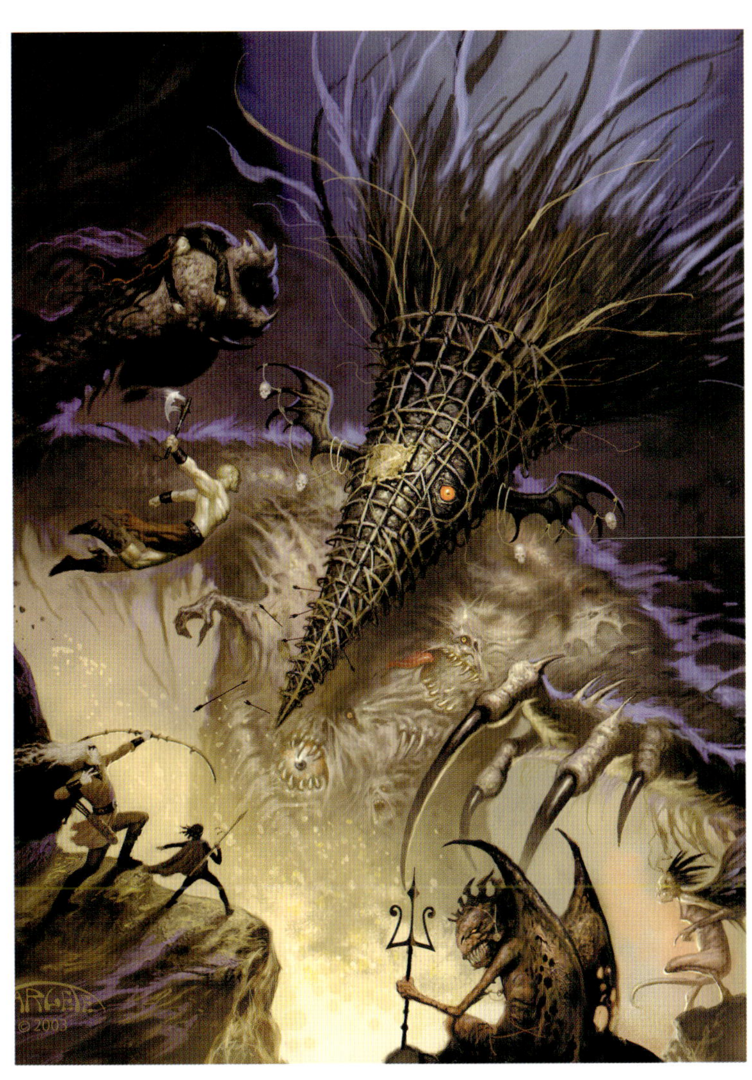

4

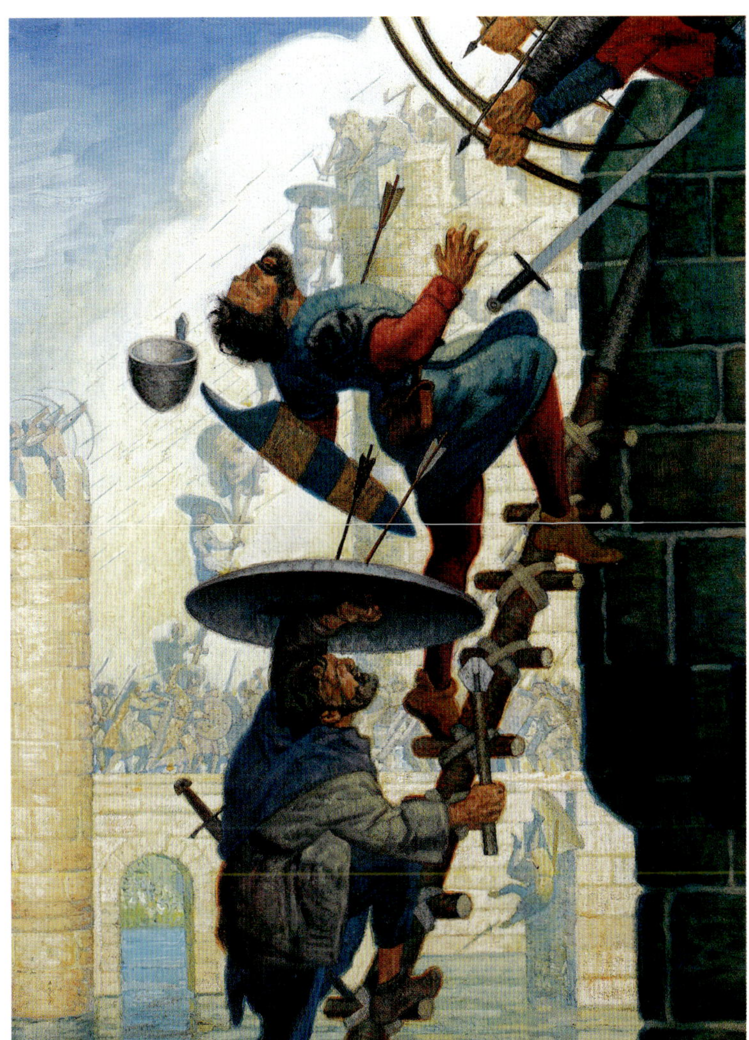

5

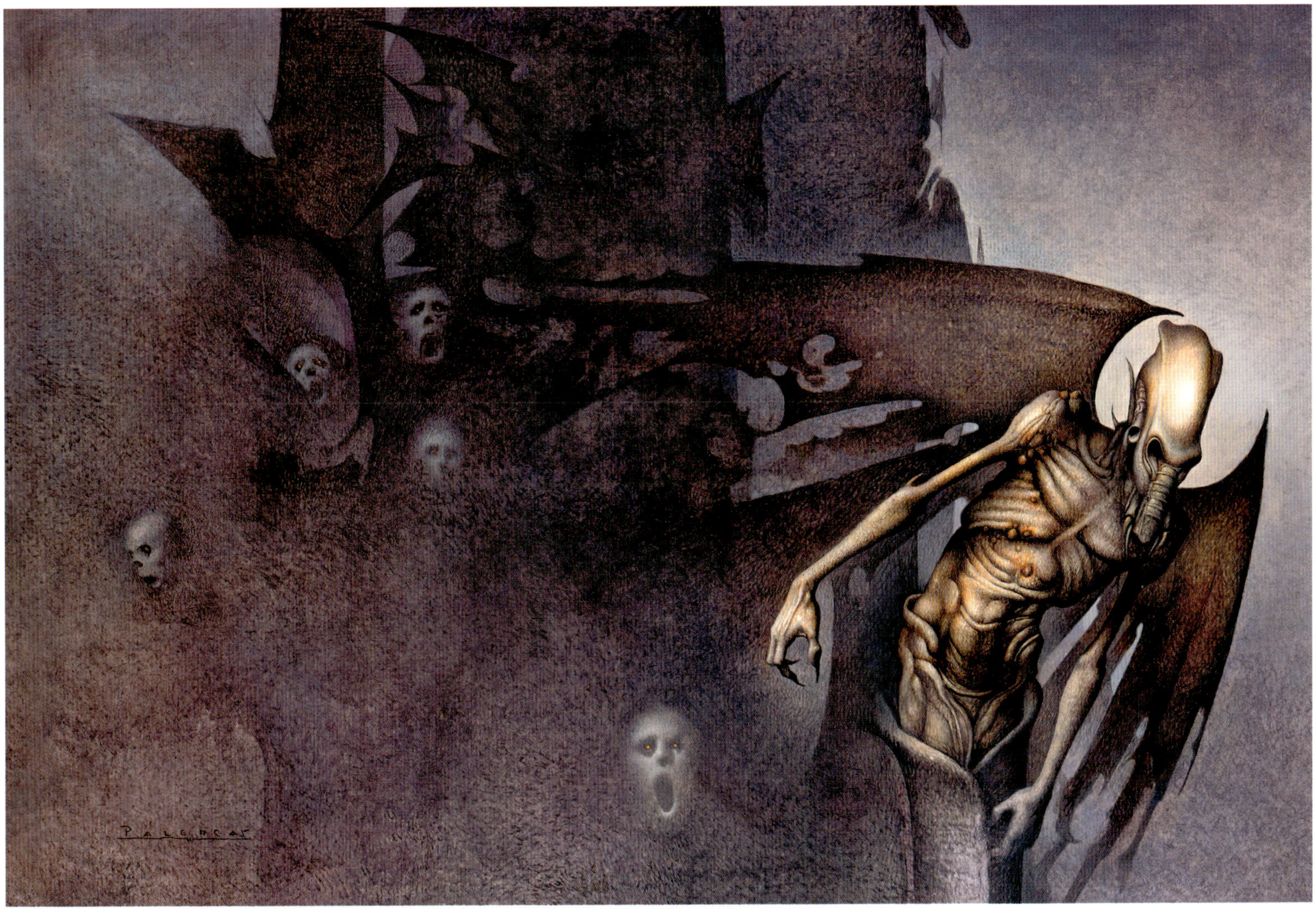

Book

1-2 & 4-5
artist: **Greg Couch**
art director: Marc Cheshire
designer: Cheshire Studio
client: North-South Books
title: Halloween
medium: Colored pencils & acrylic wash
size: 17"x14"

3
artist: **Ezra Tucker**
client: Walker & Co.
title: Big Friends #5
medium: Acrylics
size: 17"x11"

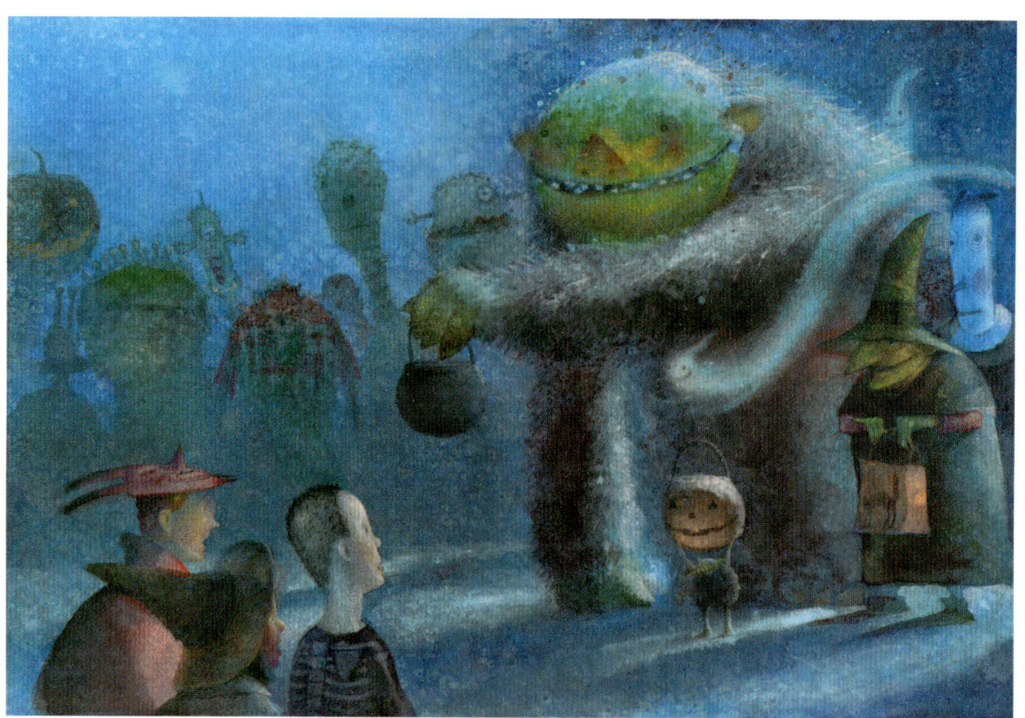

1

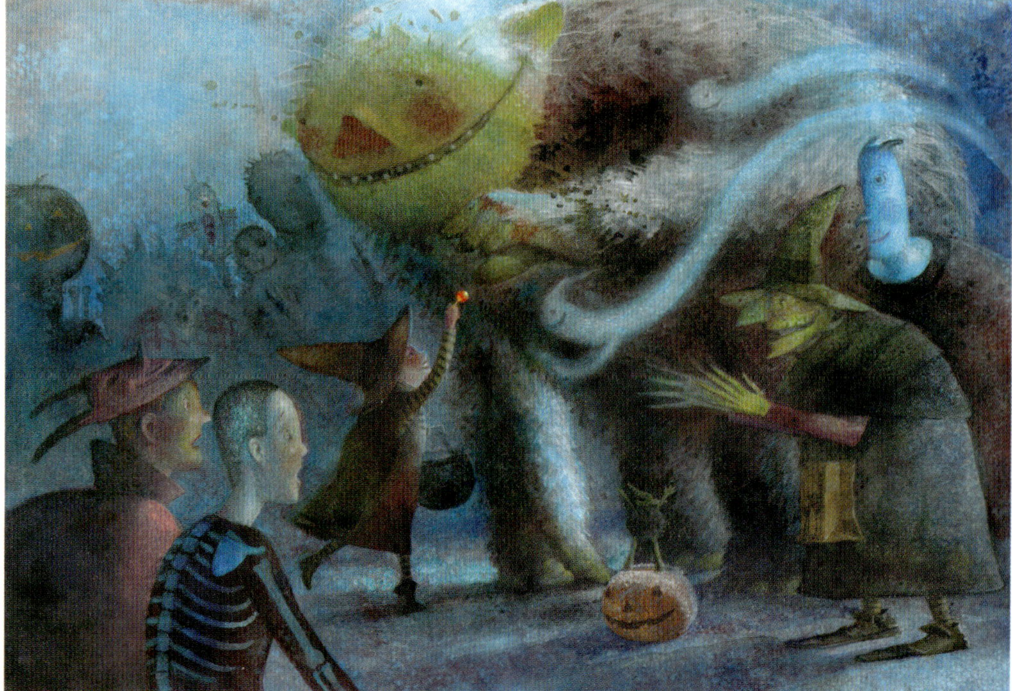

2

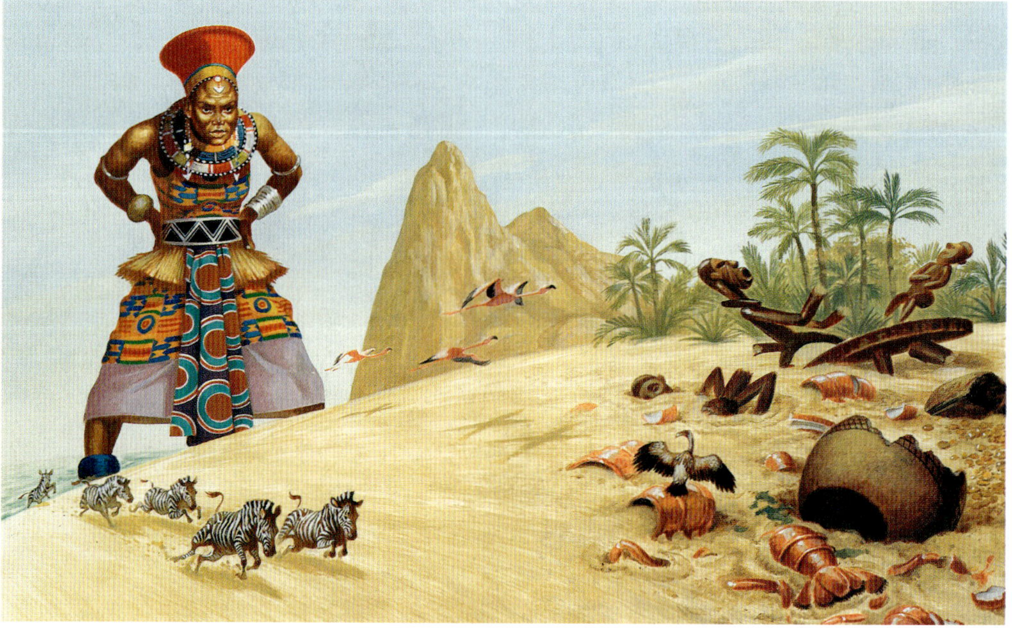

3

4

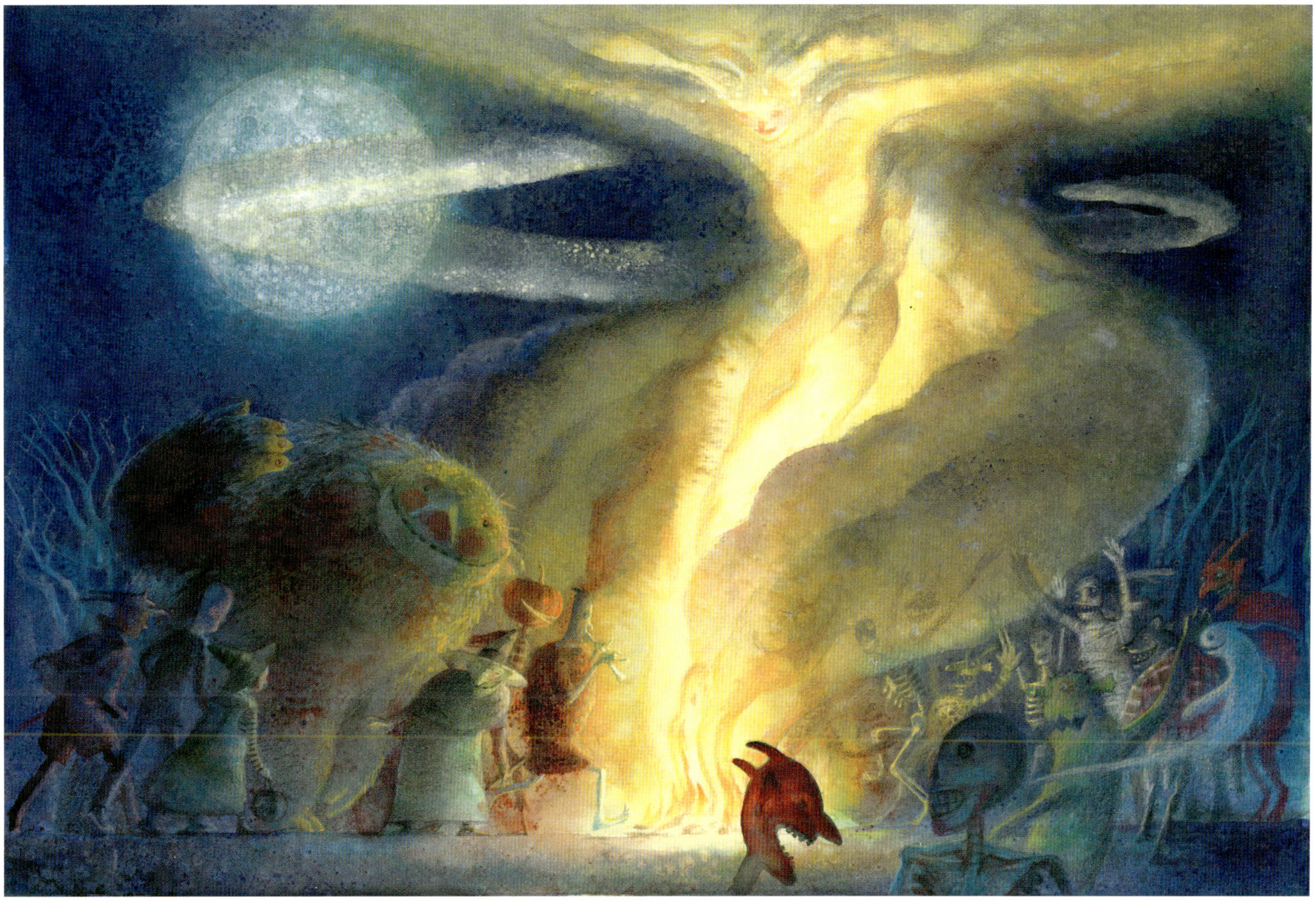

5

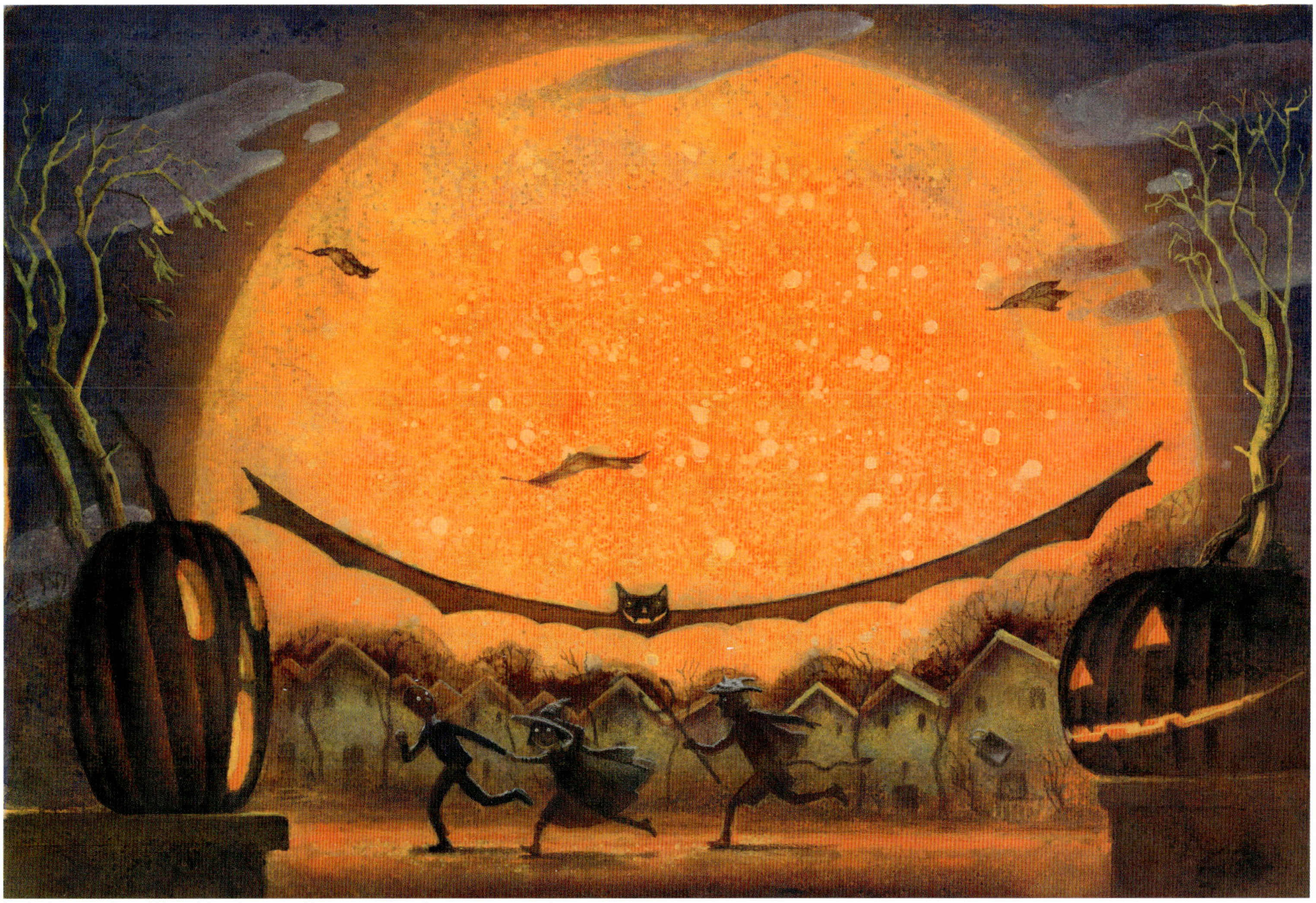

Book

1
artist: **Fiedler**
art director: Mark Murphy
designer: Mark Murphy
client: Murphy Design, Inc.
title: Heaven
medium: Mixed
size: 4"x4"

2
artist: **Robin Muller**
art director: Helen Mah
designer: Helen Mah
client: Moonstar Pub.
title: The Night Wood
medium: Ink & pencil crayon
size: 9 1/2"x13"

3
artist: **Gregory Manchess**
art director: Irene Gallo
client: Tor Books
title: Grania
medium: Oil on linen
size: 20"x24"

4
artist: **Gregory Manchess**
art director: Irene Gallo
client: Tor Books
title: The Knight
medium: Oil on linen

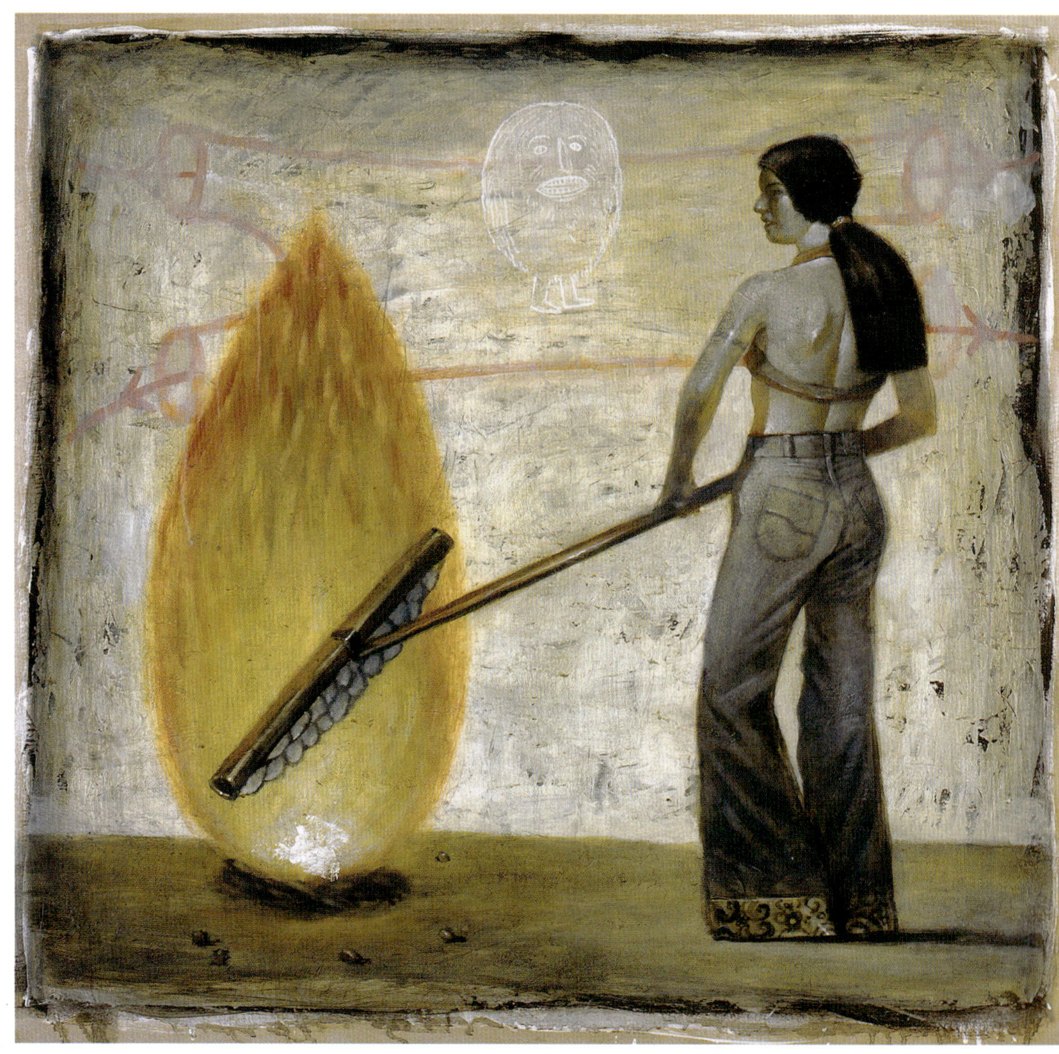

1

2

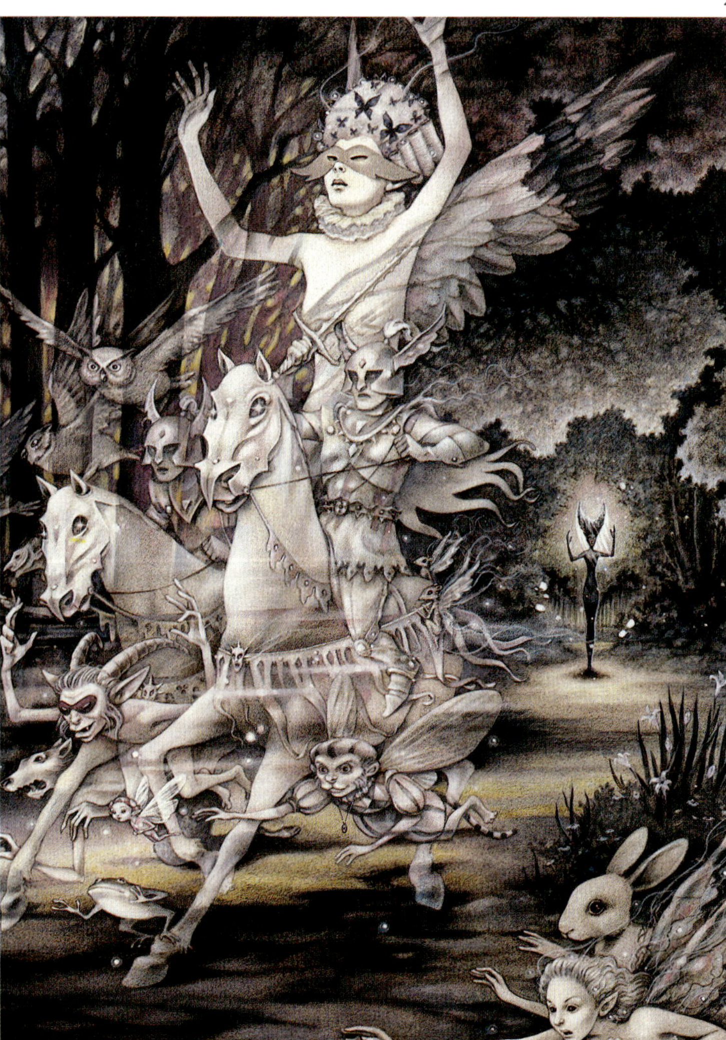

3

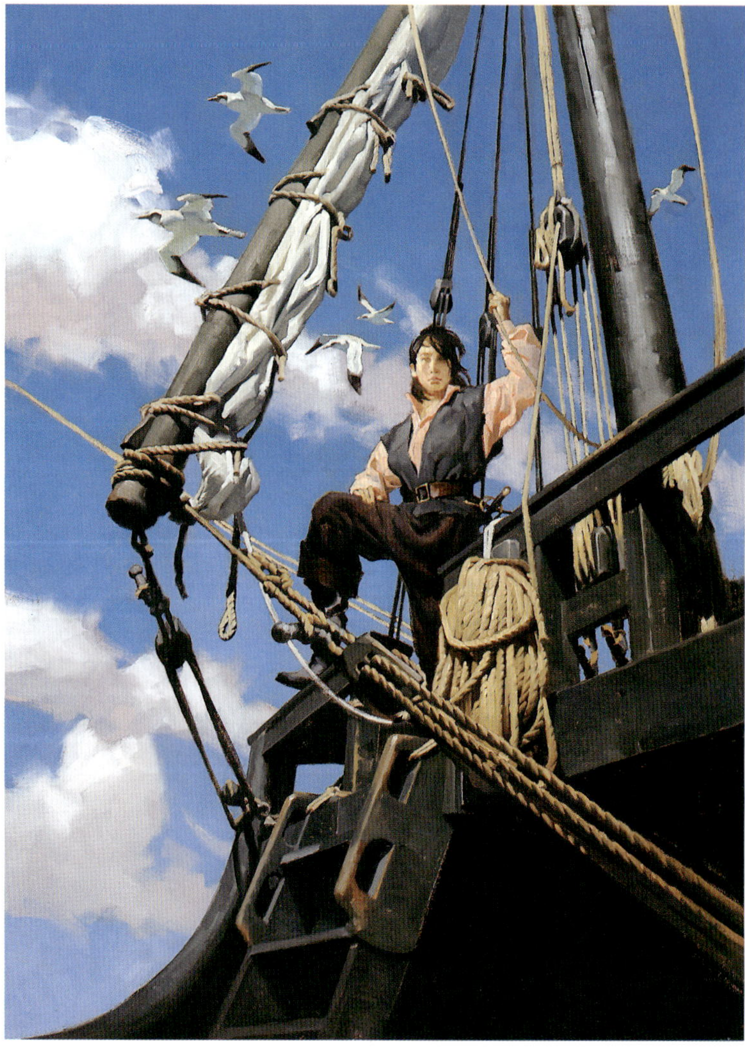

4

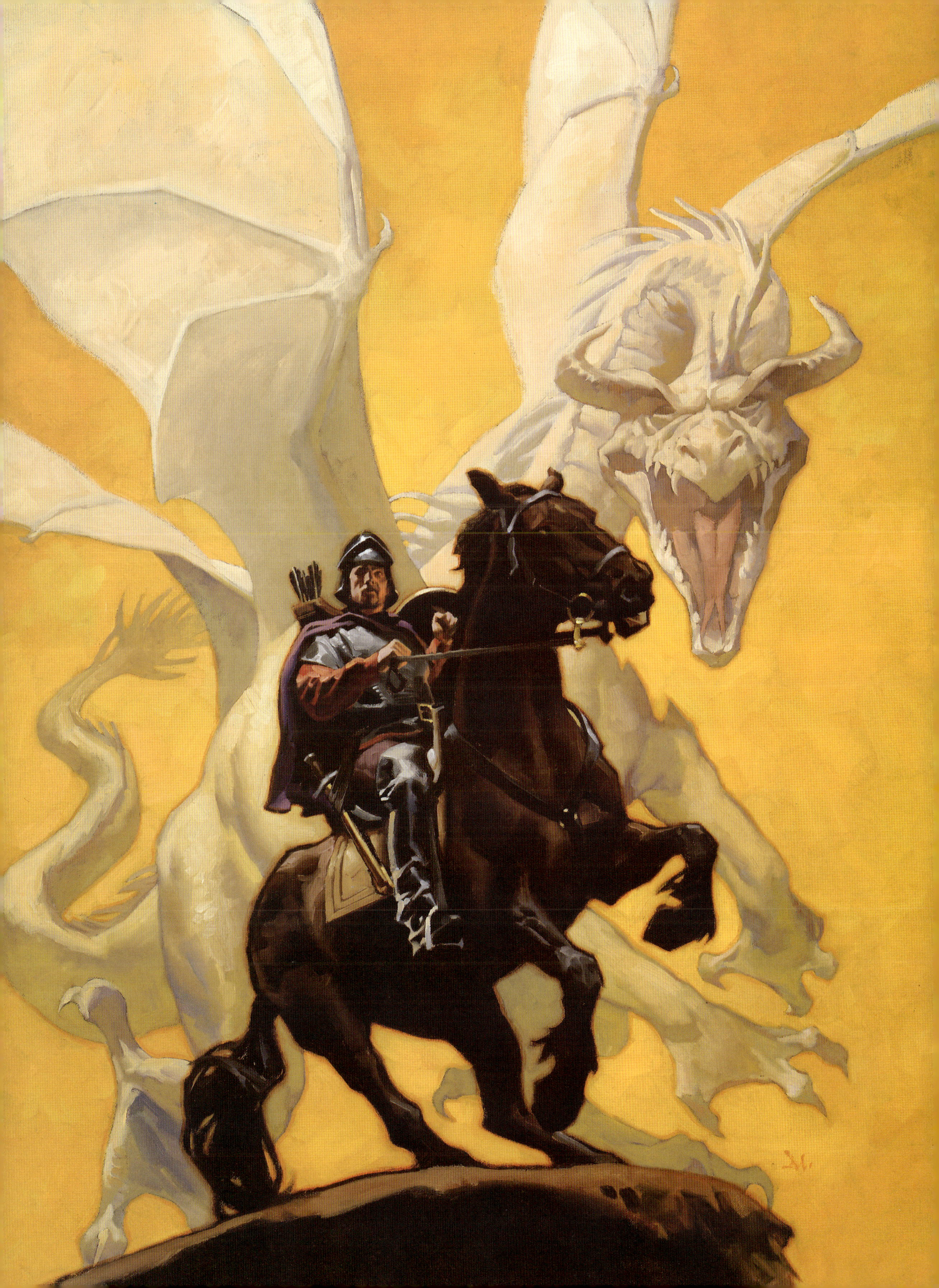

Book

1
artist: **Wayne Reynolds**
art director: Dawn Murin
client: Wizards of the Coast
title: Fensirs and Rakka
medium: Acrylics
size: 6¾"x5"

2
artist: **Adam Rex**
art director: Robert Raper
client: Wizards of the Coast
title: Winter Storm
medium: Oils
size: 37"x12"

3
artist: **Mark Zug**
art director: Matt Adelsperger
client: Wizards of the Coast
title: The Alabaster Staff
medium: Oils
size: 14"x18"

4
artist: **Stephen Youll**
art director: Irene Gallo
designer: Stephen Youll
client: Tor Books
title: The Dragon's Son
medium: Mixed
size: 16"x22"

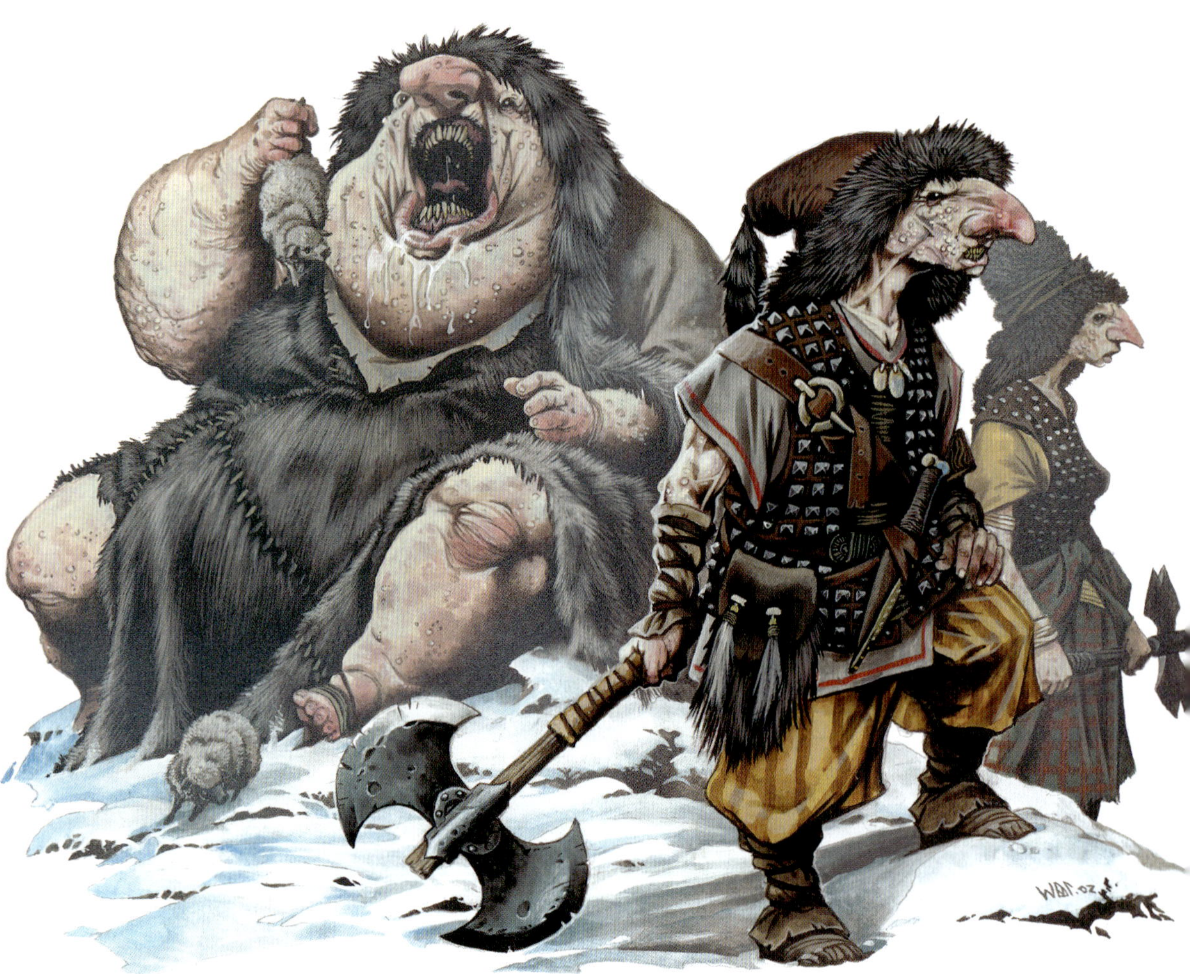

1

2

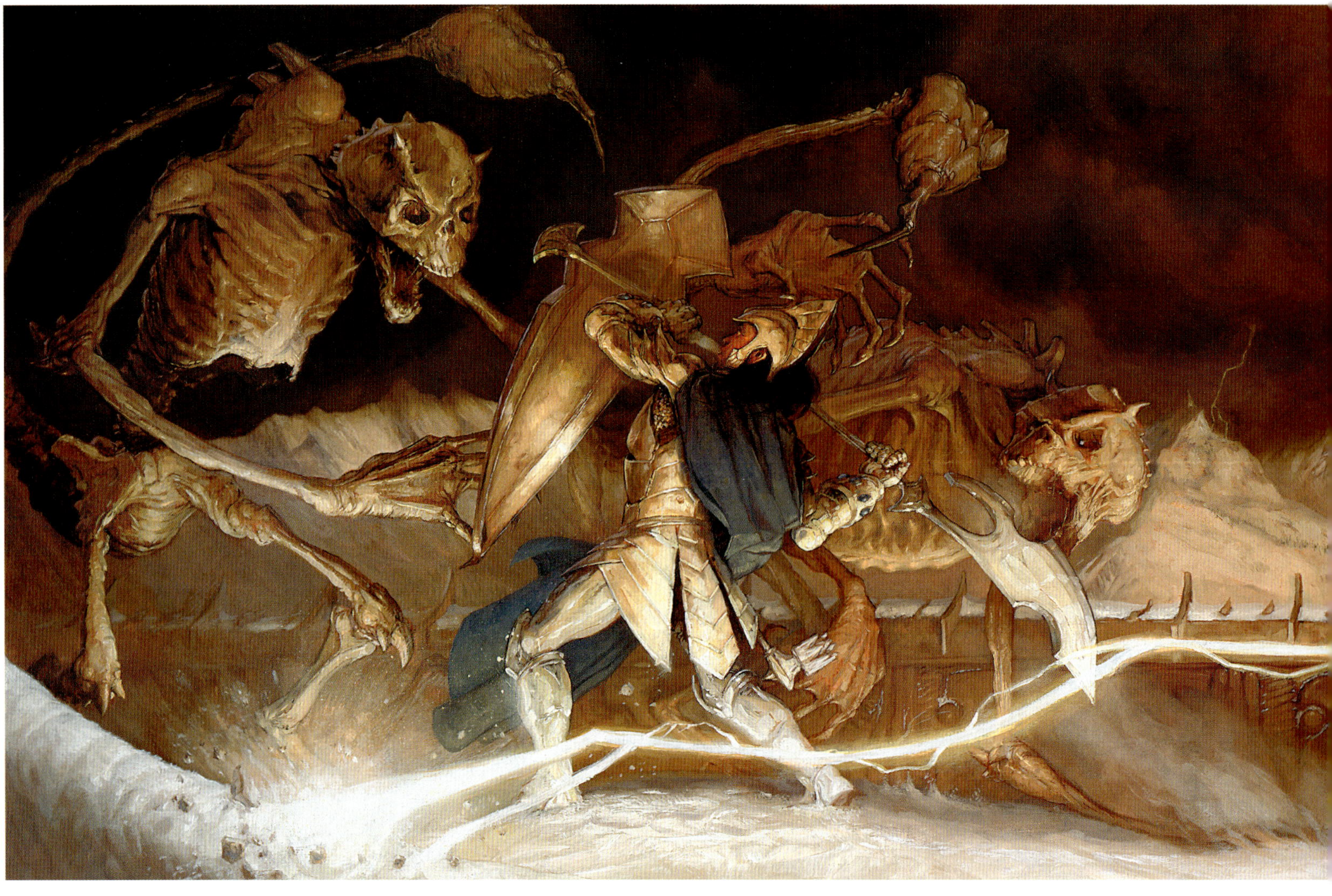

3

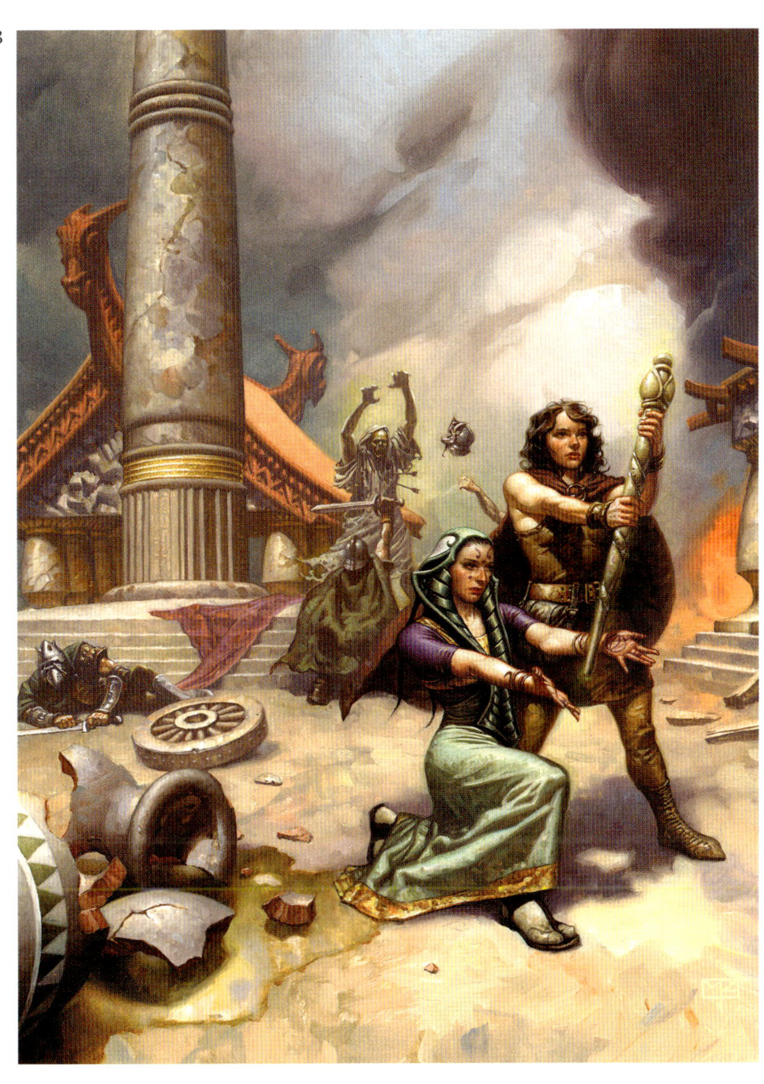

4

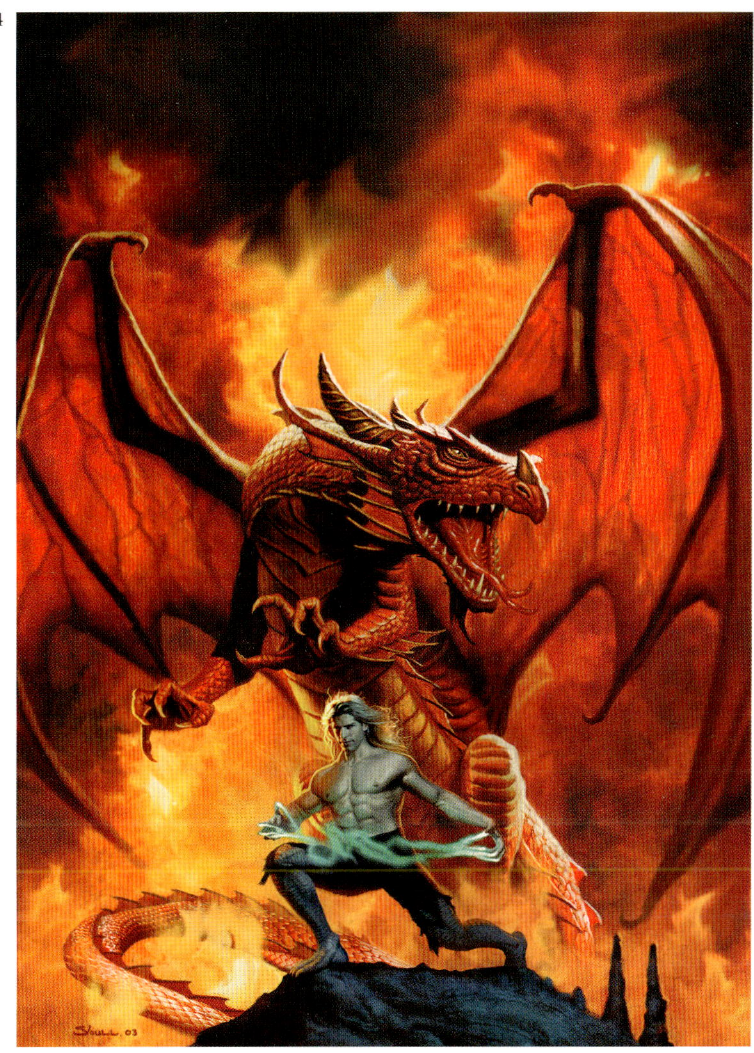

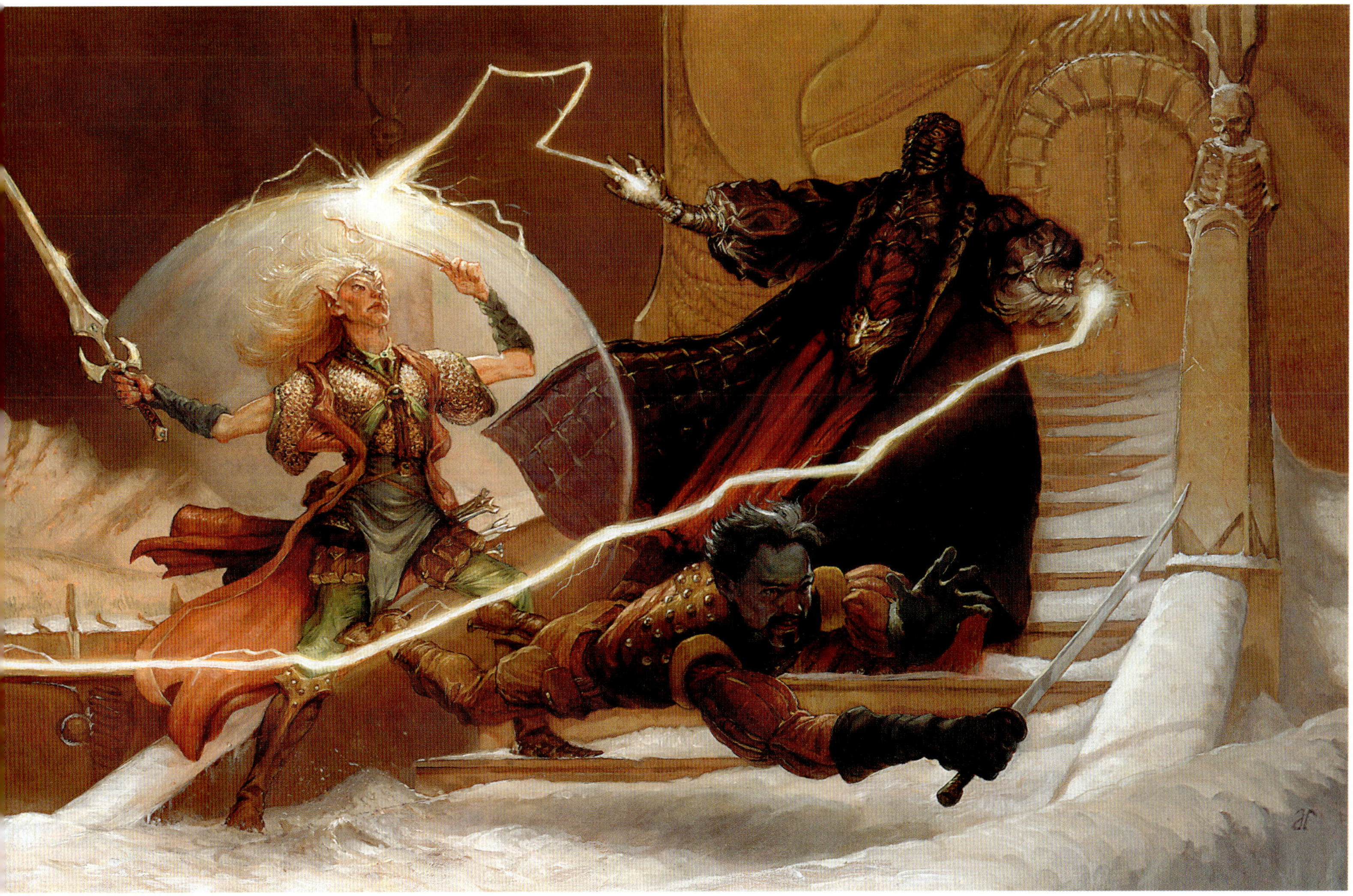

1
artist: **Gris Grimly**
client: Baby Tattoo Books
title: Wicked Nursery Rhymes
medium: Ink and watercolor
size: 7 1/2"x7 1/2"

2
artist: **Cos Koniotis**
client: Fantasy Flight Games
title: Dawnforce: Path of Legend
medium: Digital

3
artist: **Justin Sweet**
art director: Irene Gallo
client: Tor Books
title: The Last Guardian of Everness
medium: Oil/digital
size: 30"x42"

4
artist: **Ruth Sanderson**
art director: Tracy Shaw
client: Little, Brown & Co.
title: The Snow Princess
medium: Oils
size: 16"x20"

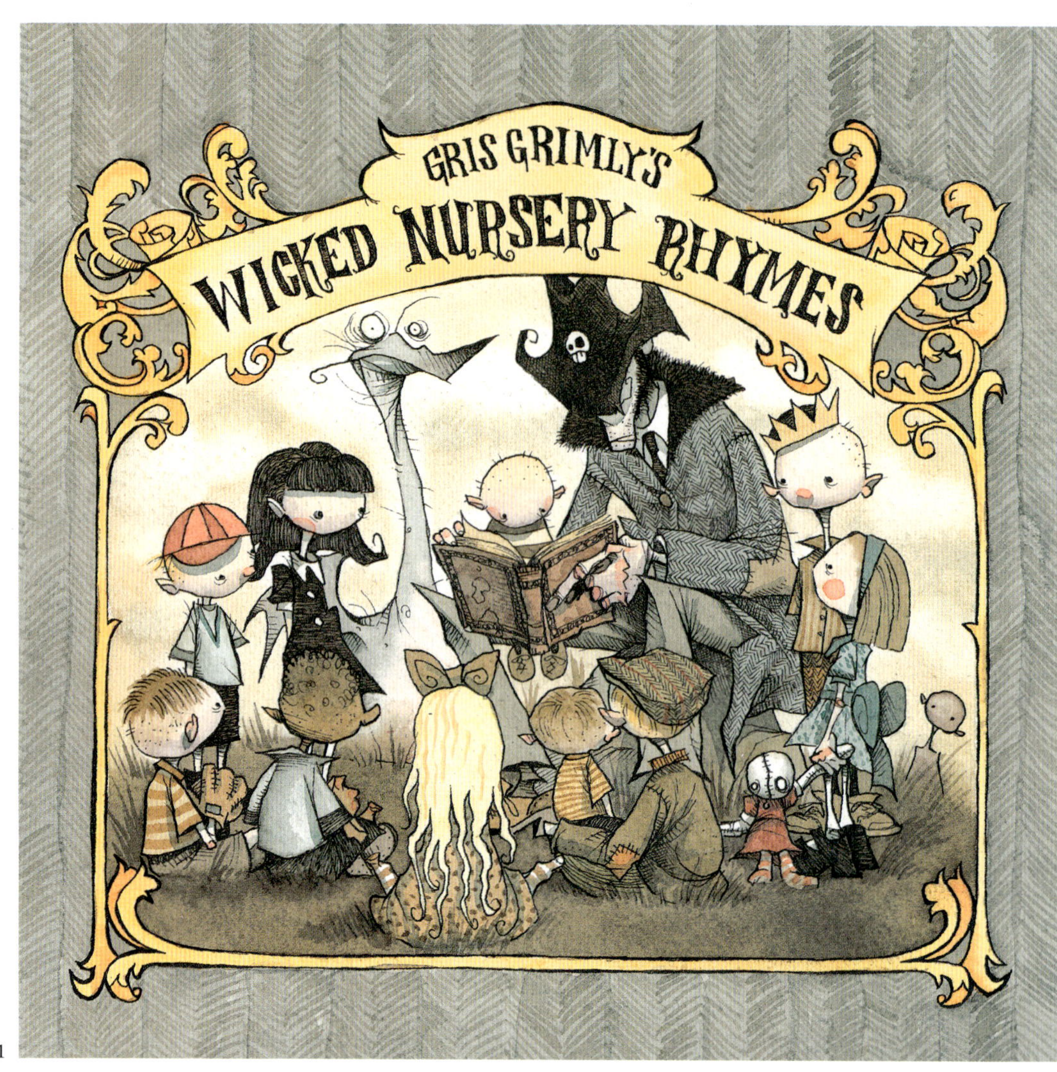

1

2
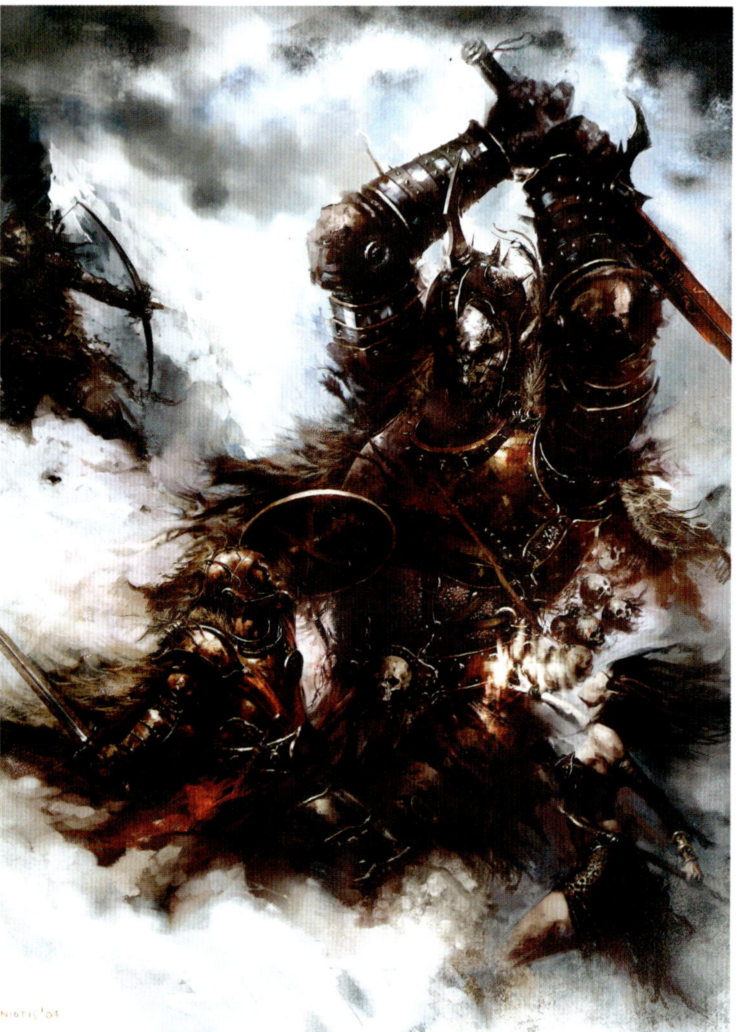

3
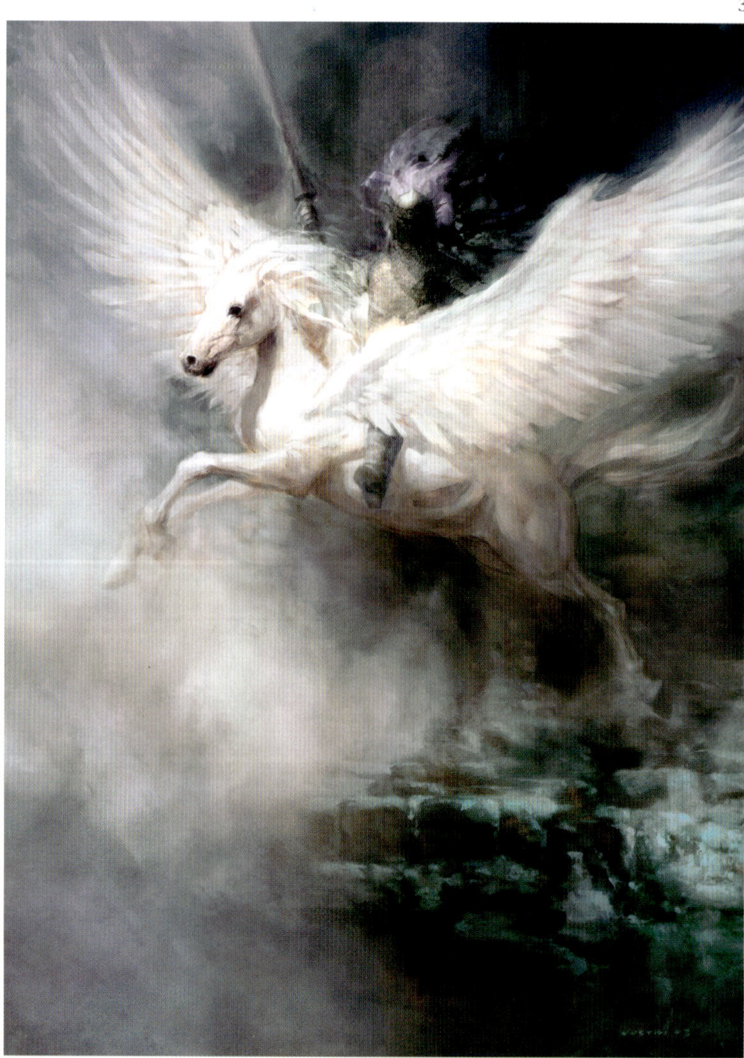

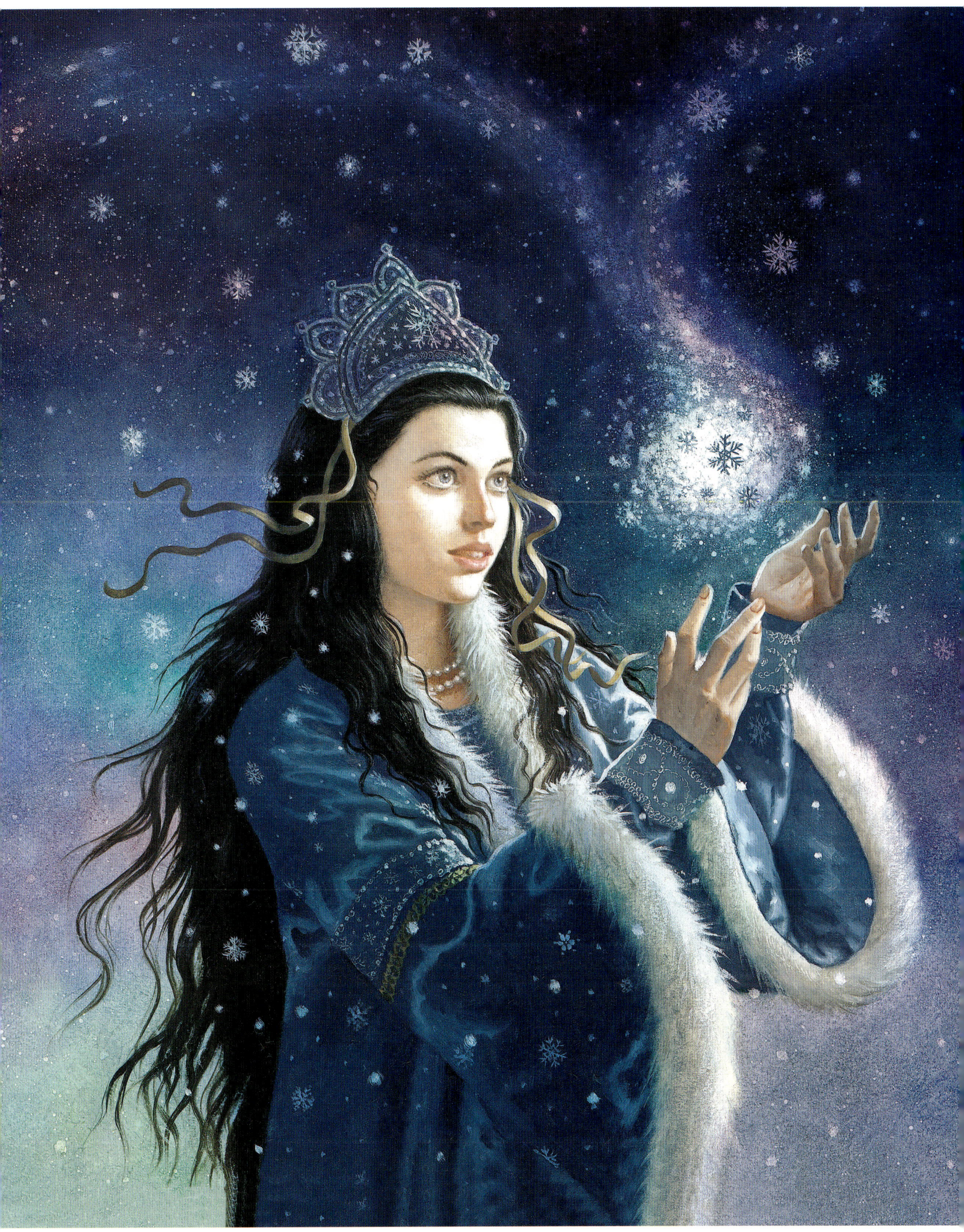

4

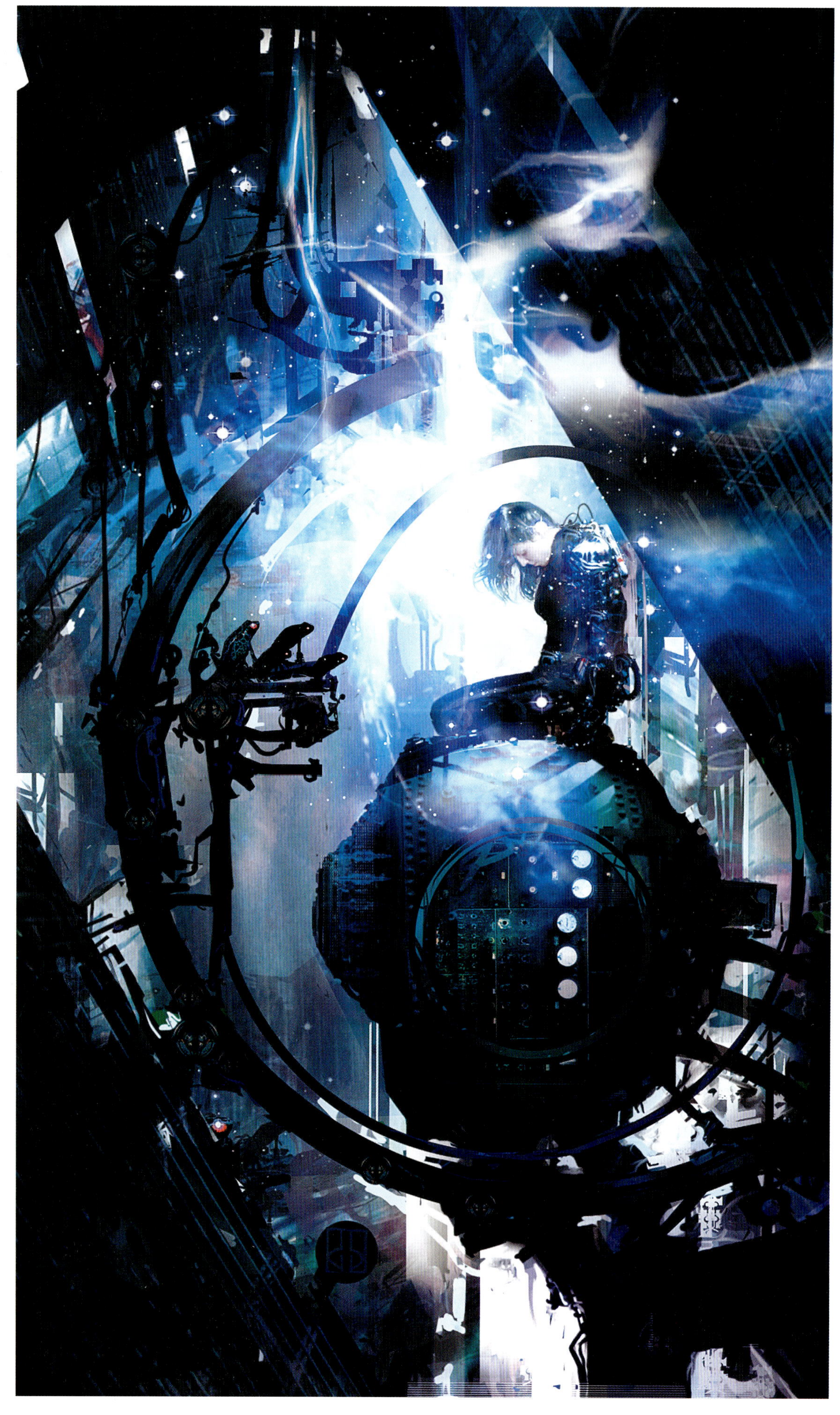

artist: **Stephan "Cricket" Martiniere**
art director: Teal Chimblo *client:* Penny-Farthing Press *title:* Para 2 *medium:* Digital/mixed *size:* 11"x17"

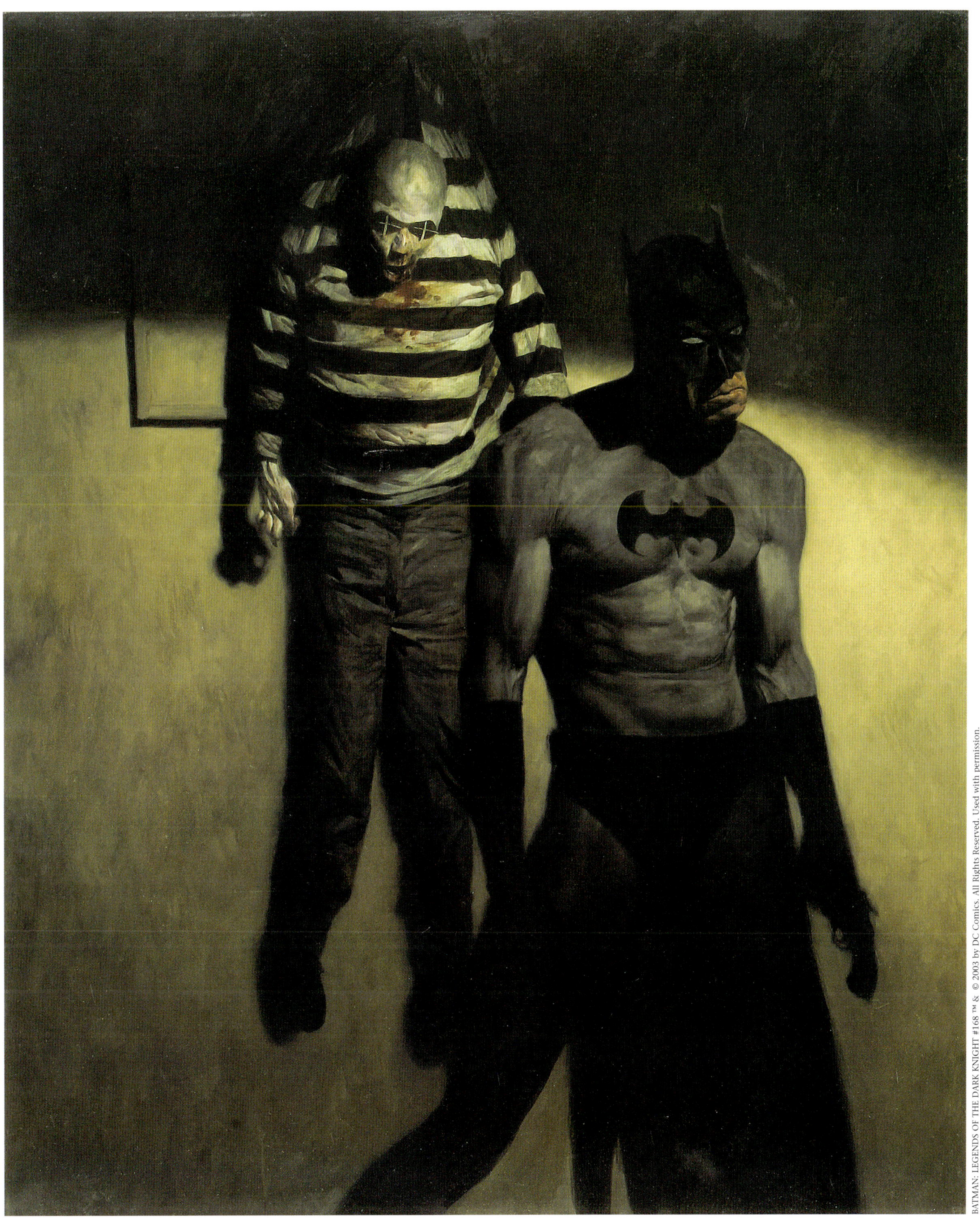

artist: **Phil Hale**
art director: Mark Chiarello *client:* DC Comics *title:* Batman: Urban Legend
medium: Oil on canvas *size:* 36″x48″

1
artist: **Frazer Irving**
art director: Alan Barnes
client: Rebellion
title: Ssmile...
medium: Ink/digital
size: 210mmx276mm

2
artist: **Brian Horton**
art director: Scott Allie
client: Dark Horse Comics
title: Buffy #61: A Stake to the Heart
medium: Digital
size: 6"x9"

3
artist: **Mark Wheatley**
client: Image Comics/Insight Studios
title: Frankenstein Mobster #0
medium: Mixed/digital
size: 12"x18"

4
artist: **William Stout**
art director: Scott Allie
designer: William Stout
client: Dark Horse Comics
title: Hellboy At the Mountains of Madness
medium: Mixed
size: 10"x15 1/2"

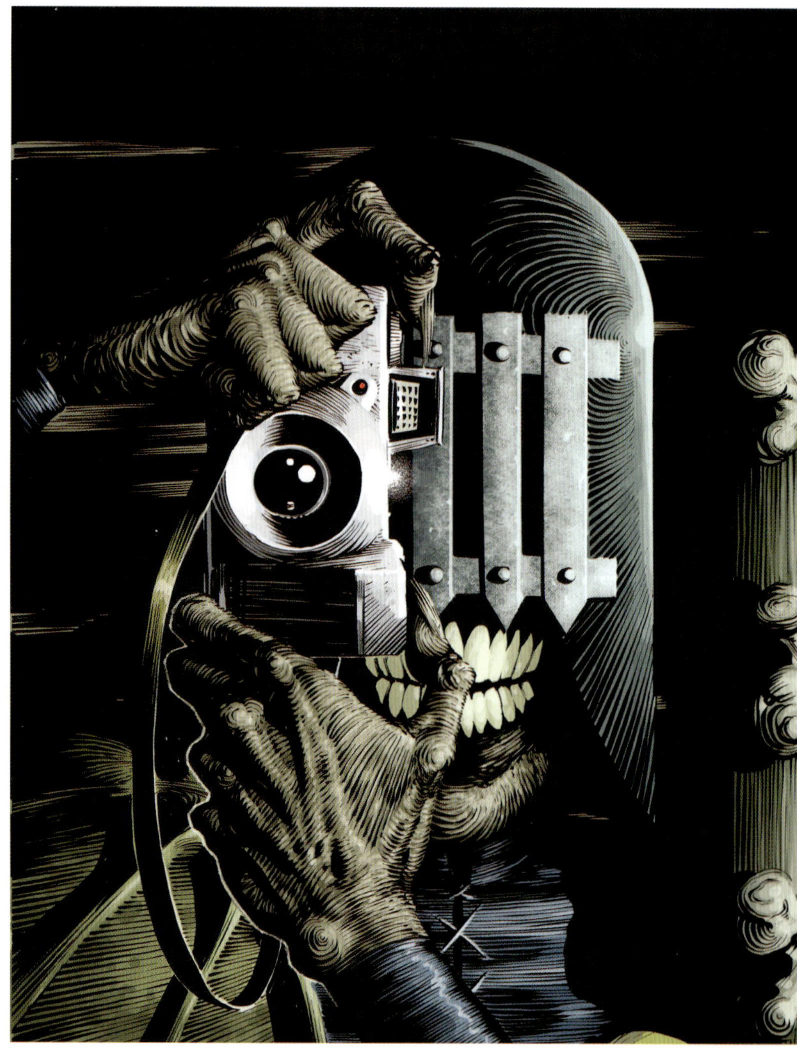

1

2

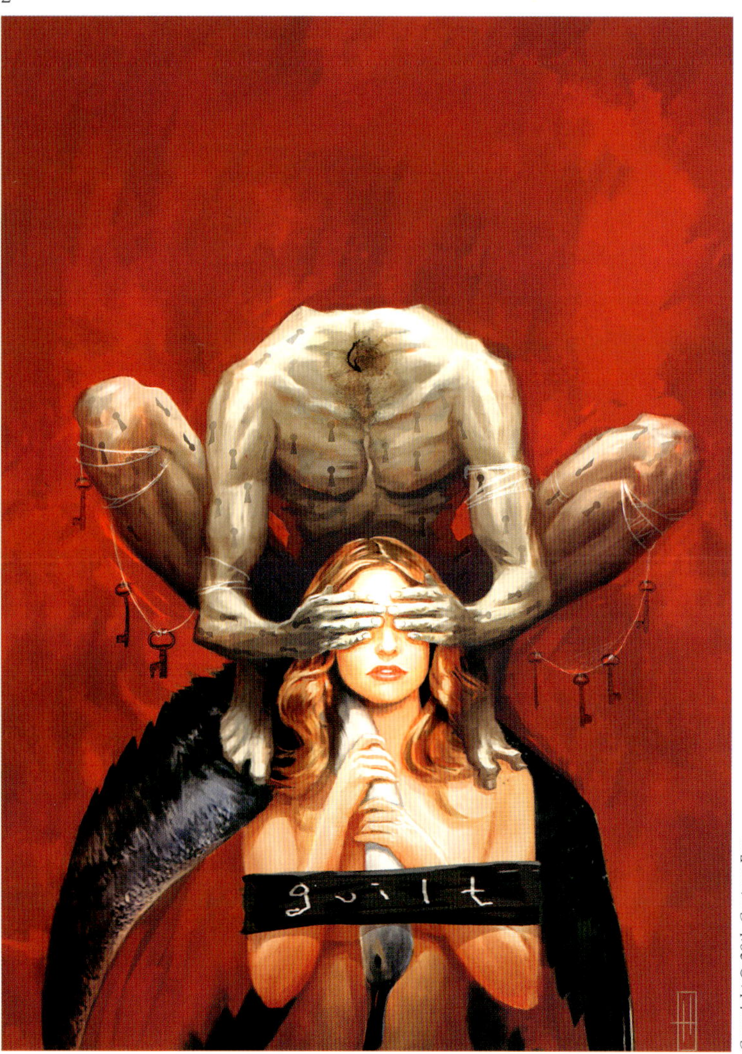

3

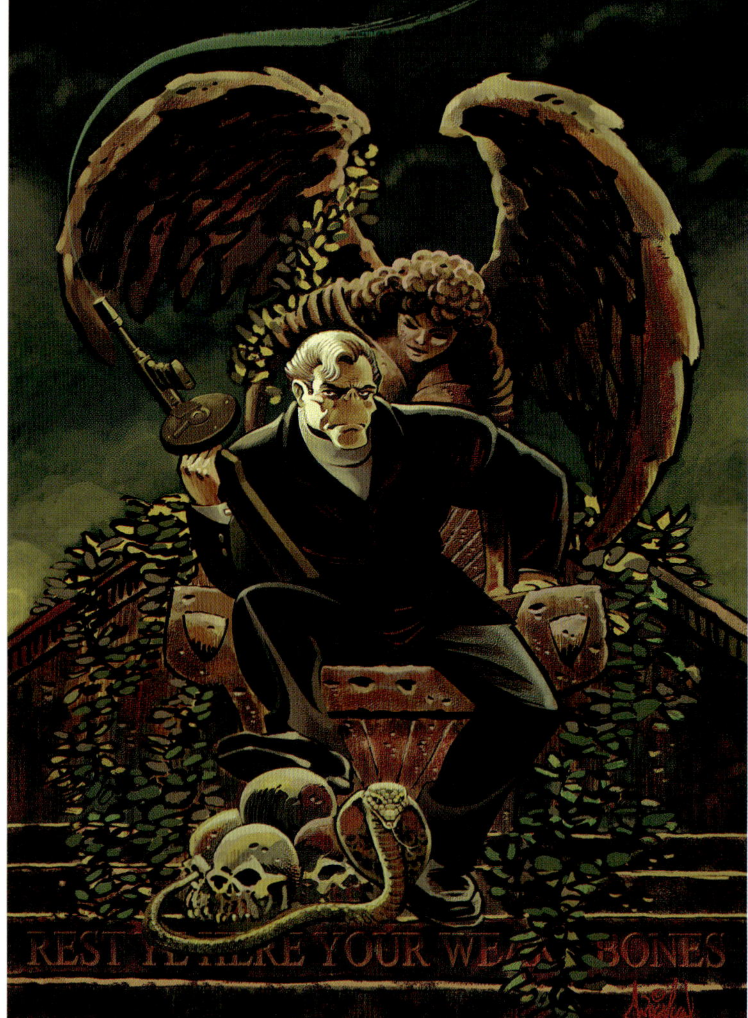

4

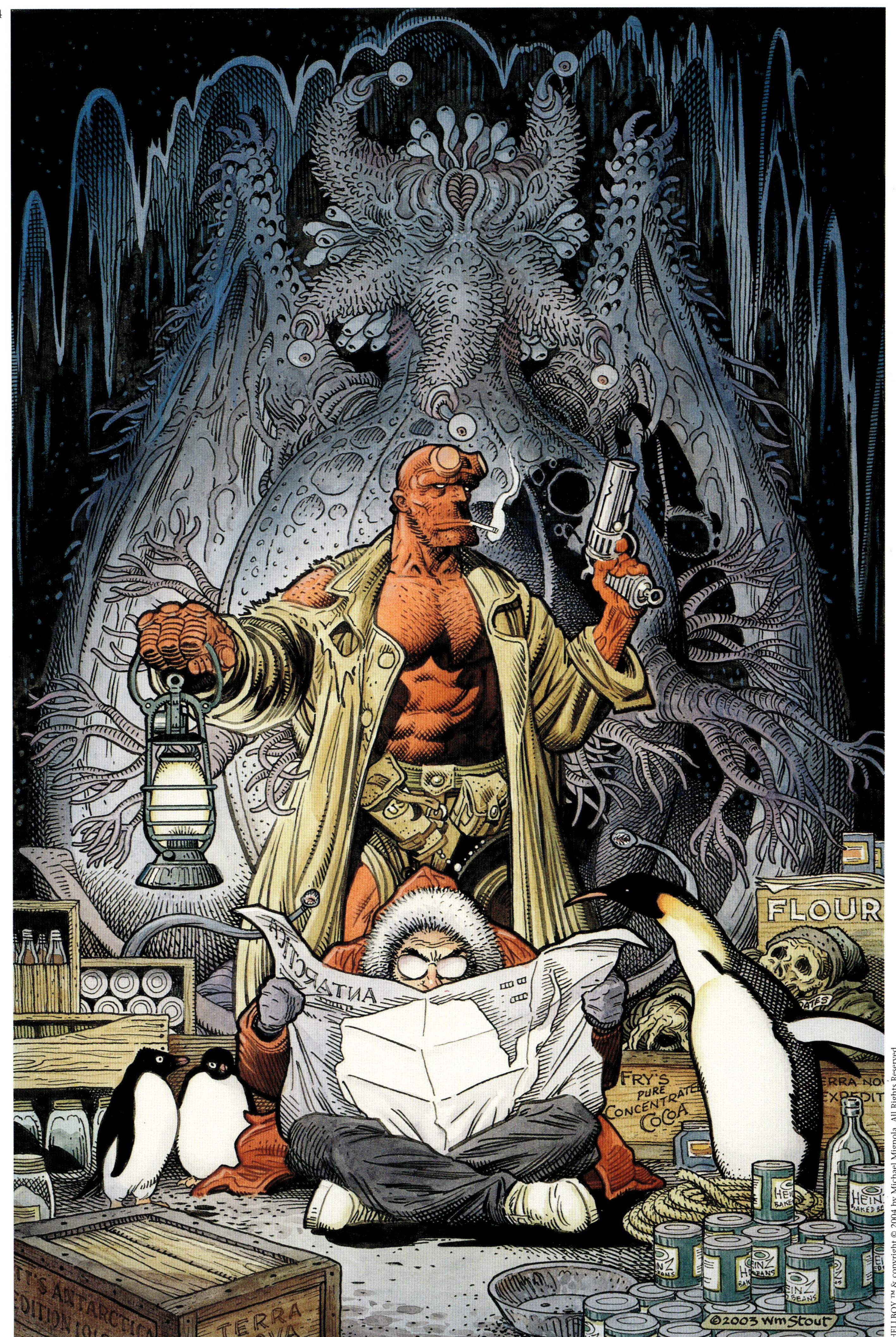

Comics

1
artist: **Frank Cho**
art director: Brett Evans
designer: Frank Cho
colorist: Brett Evans
client: Image Comics
title: Jen's Revenge
medium: Pen & ink/digital color
size: 11"x17"

2
artist: **Mark Texeira**
client: Harris Comics
title: Vampirella

3
artist: **John Van Fleet**
art director: Peter Tomasi
designer: John J. Hill
client: DC Comics
title: H-E-R-O #8
medium: Mixed
size: 8"x10"

4
artist: **Francis Tsai**
art director: Dave Wilkins
client: Dave Wilkins
title: El Zombo
medium: Digital
size: 11"x17"

5
artist: **Glen Orbik**
art director: Shelly Bond
client: DC Comics
title: American Century #26
medium: Oil
size: 13"x16"

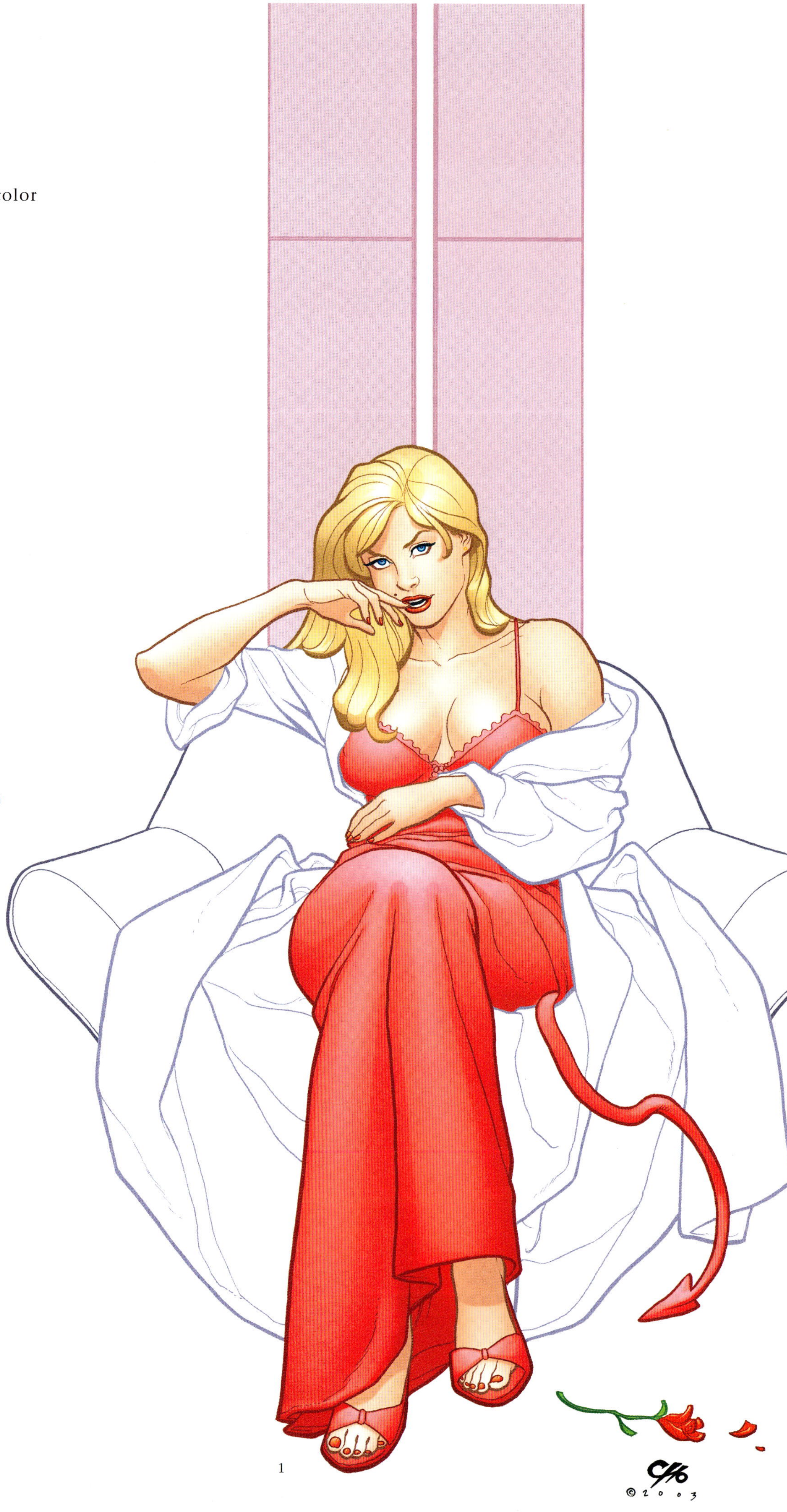

1

2

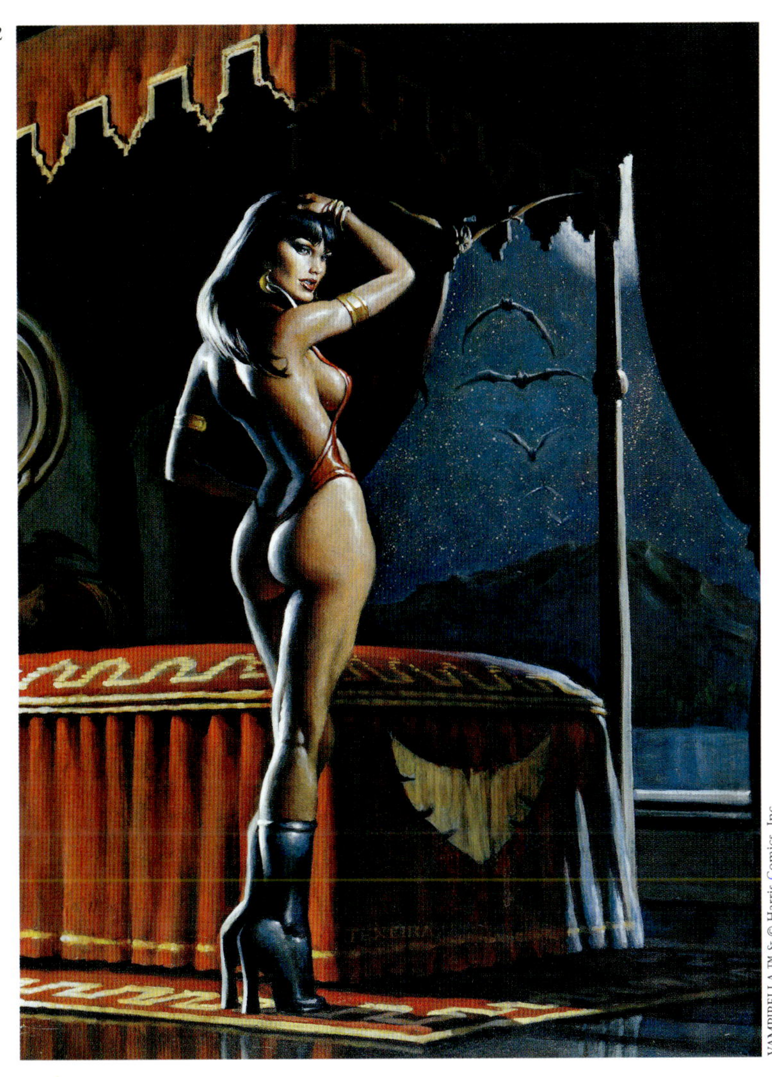

VAMPIRELLA ™ & © Harris Comics, Inc.

3

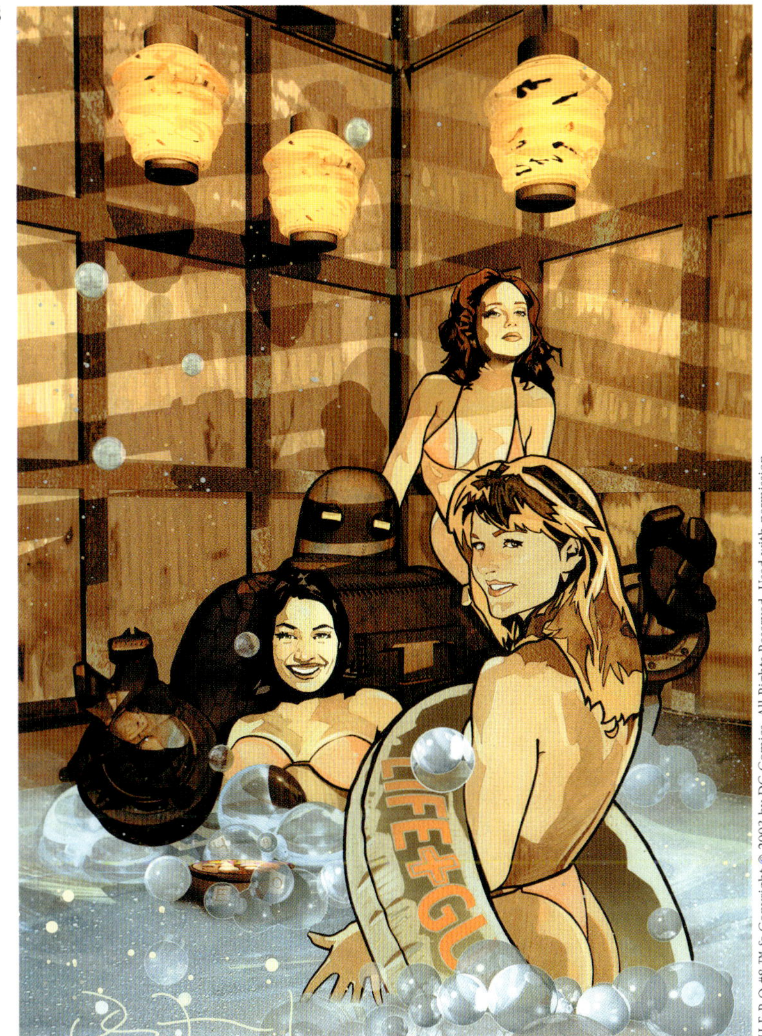

H-E-R-O #8 ™ & Copyright © 2003 by DC Comics. All Rights Reserved. Used with permission.

4

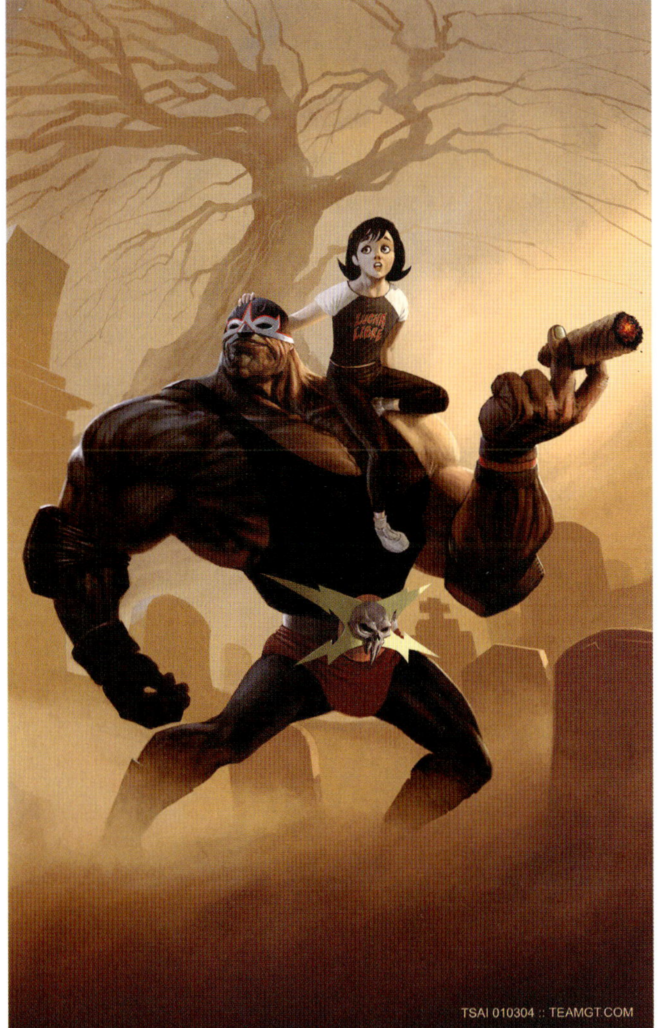

5

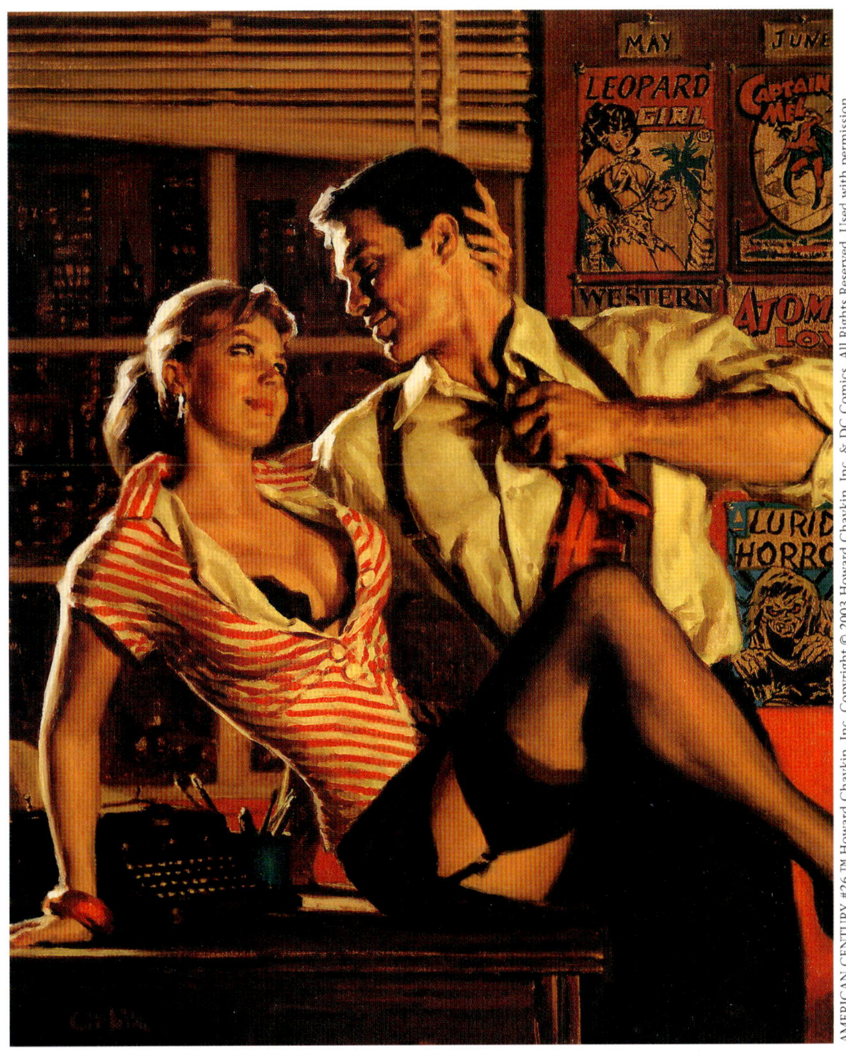

AMERICAN CENTURY #26 ™ Howard Chaykin, Inc. Copyright © 2003 Howard Chaykin, Inc. & DC Comics. All Rights Reserved. Used with permission.

Comics

1
artist: **A. Davison**
client: A. Davison
title: Spiral Dreams 3
medium: Ink/digital
size: 8 1/2"x11"

2
artist: **Cathy Wilkins**
art director: Pauline Benny
client: White Wolf Publishing
title: Saved
medium: Digital

3
artist: **Christopher Moeller**
art director: Shelly Bond
client: DC Comics
title: Lucifer #43
medium: Acrylics
size: 20"x30"

4
artist: **E.M. Gist**
client: Dark Horse Comics
title: Grave Danger
medium: Oils
size: 20"x30"

5
artist: **Alex "Horley" Orlandelli**
art director: Dan Didio
client: DC Comics
title: Lobo Unbound #1
medium: Acrylics/oils
size: 11"x17"

6
artist: **Greg Ruth**
client: Dark Horse Comics
title: Freaks of the Heartland #1
medium: Mixed
size: 8 1/2"x11"

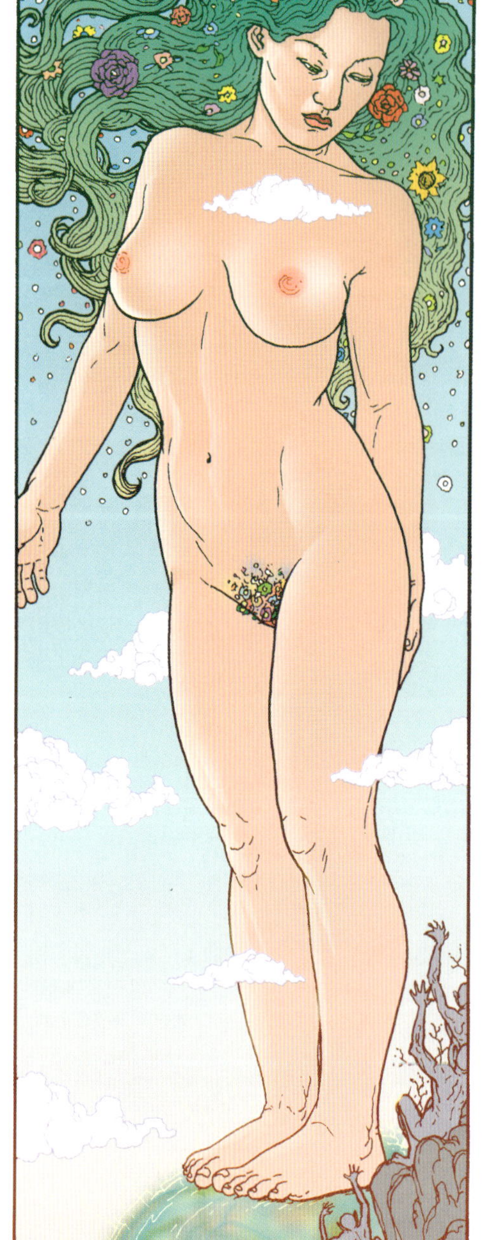
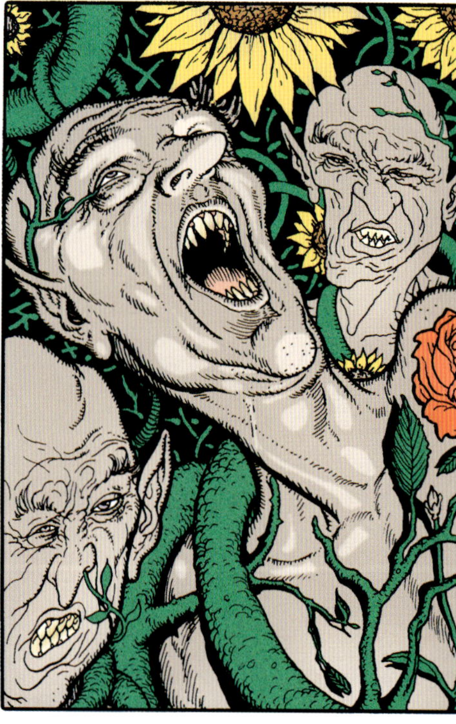
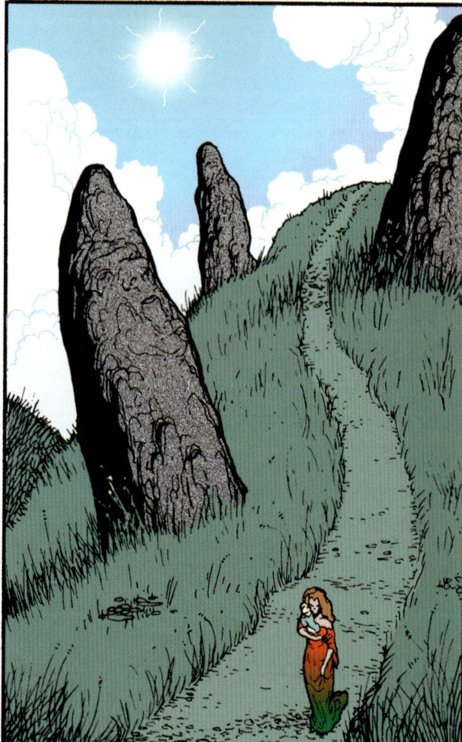

1

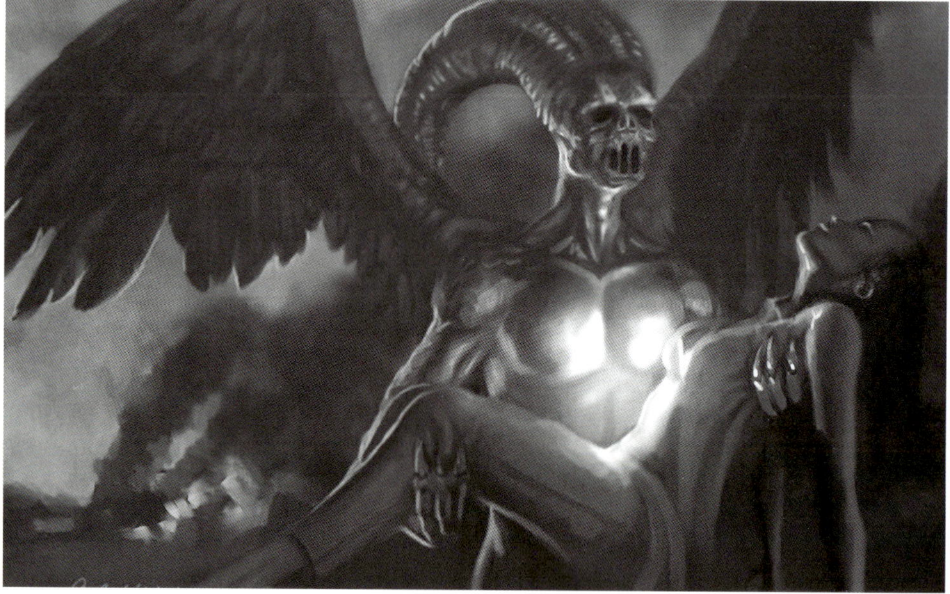

2

3

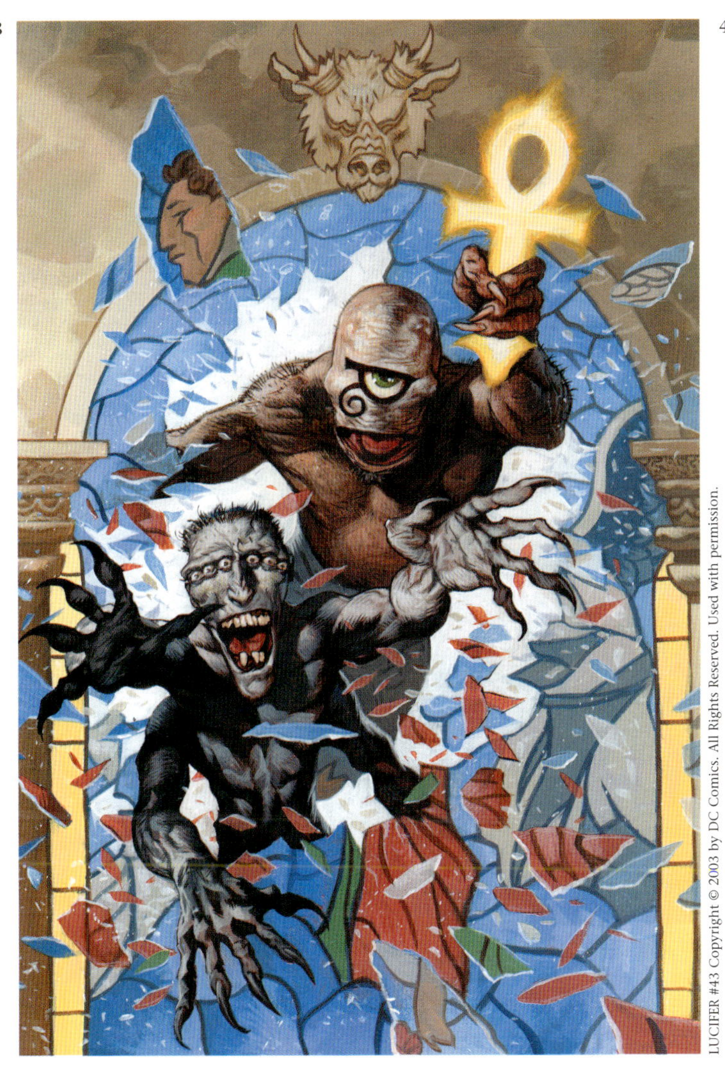

LUCIFER #43 Copyright © 2003 by DC Comics. All Rights Reserved. Used with permission.

4

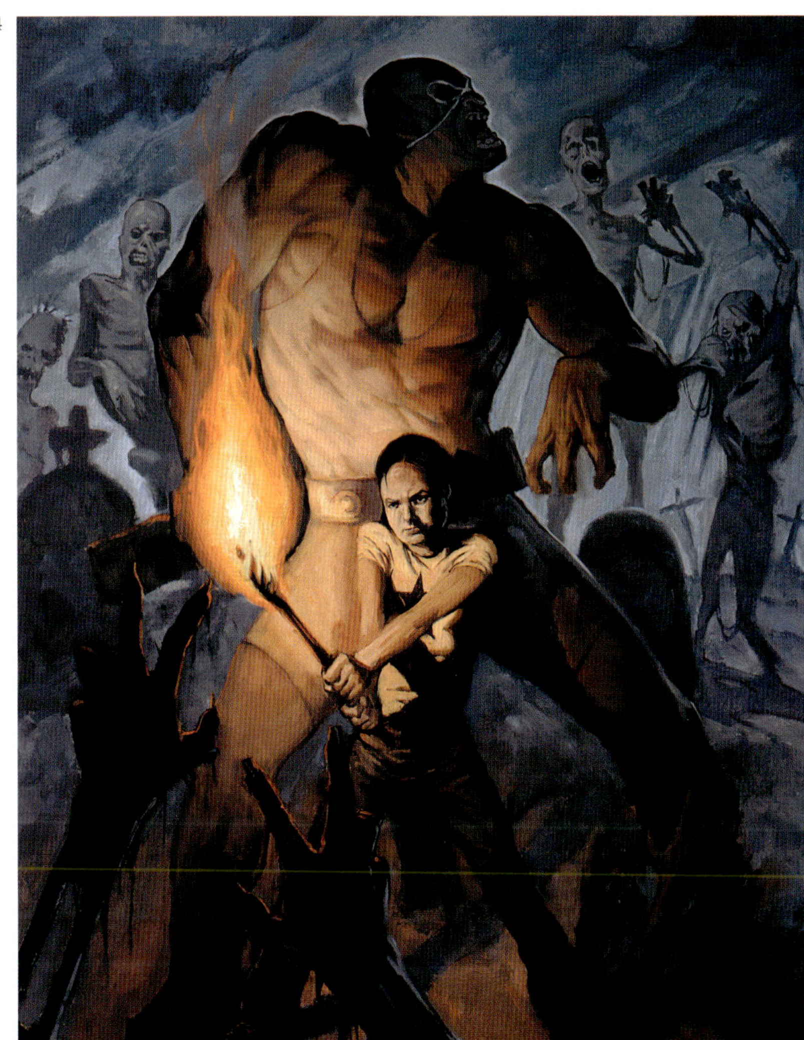

5

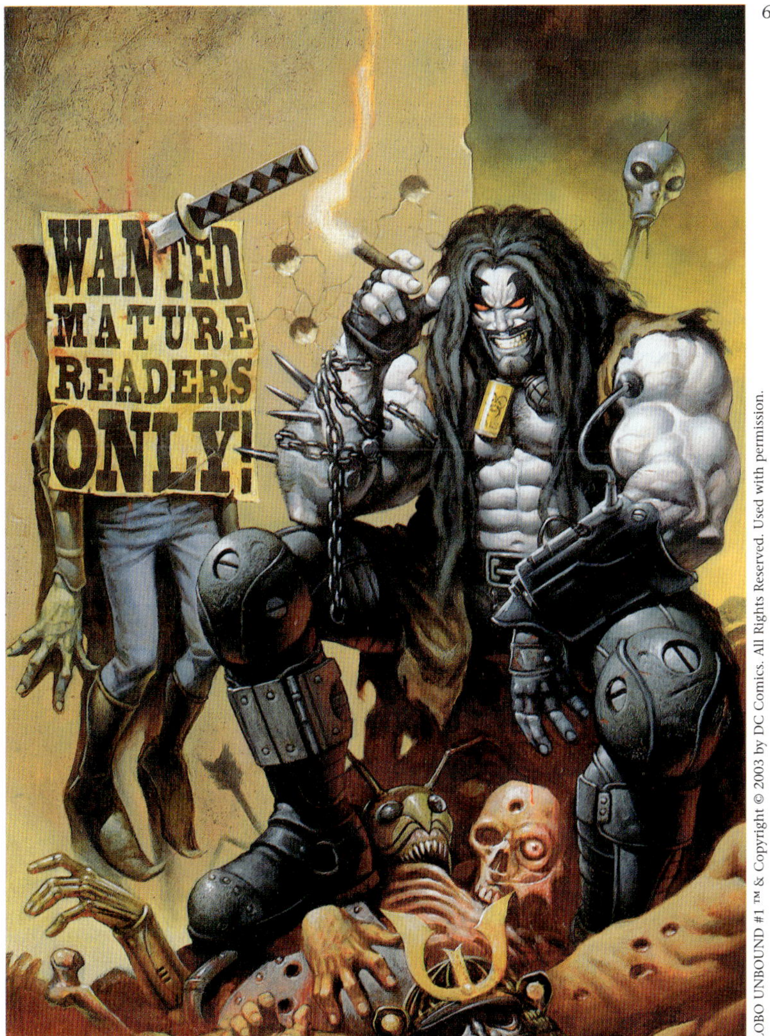

LOBO UNBOUND #1 ™ & Copyright © 2003 by DC Comics. All Rights Reserved. Used with permission.

6

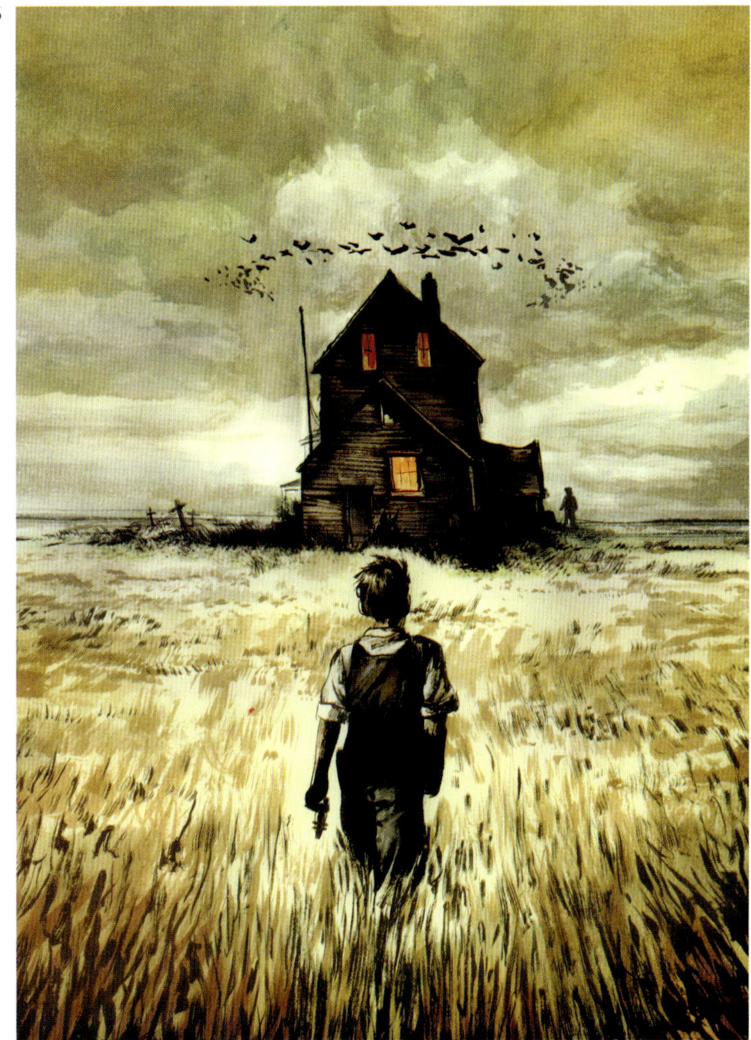

Comics

1
artist: **Colleen Doran**
art director: Amie Brockway Meltcalf
client: DC Comics
title: Orbiter
medium: Watercolor
size: 12"x18"

2
artist: **Erik Siador**
client: culpritresearchproject.com
title: Monkey Trouble
medium: Pen & ink/digital
size: 15"x16"

3
artist: **Raymond Swanland**
art director: Matt Alford
client: TokyoPop
title: The Wanderer
medium: Digital

4
artist: **Michael Kaluta**
art director: Teal Chimblo
client: Penny-Farthing Press
title: Self-Estrangement
medium: Mixed
size: 15"x20"

5
artist: **David Rankin**
art director: Terry Nantier
client: NBM Publishing
title: The Fallen Vol. 2
medium: Oils/mixed
size: 15"x20"

6
artist: **Raymond Swanland**
art director: Matt Alford
client: TokyoPop
title: Sacrifice
medium: Digital

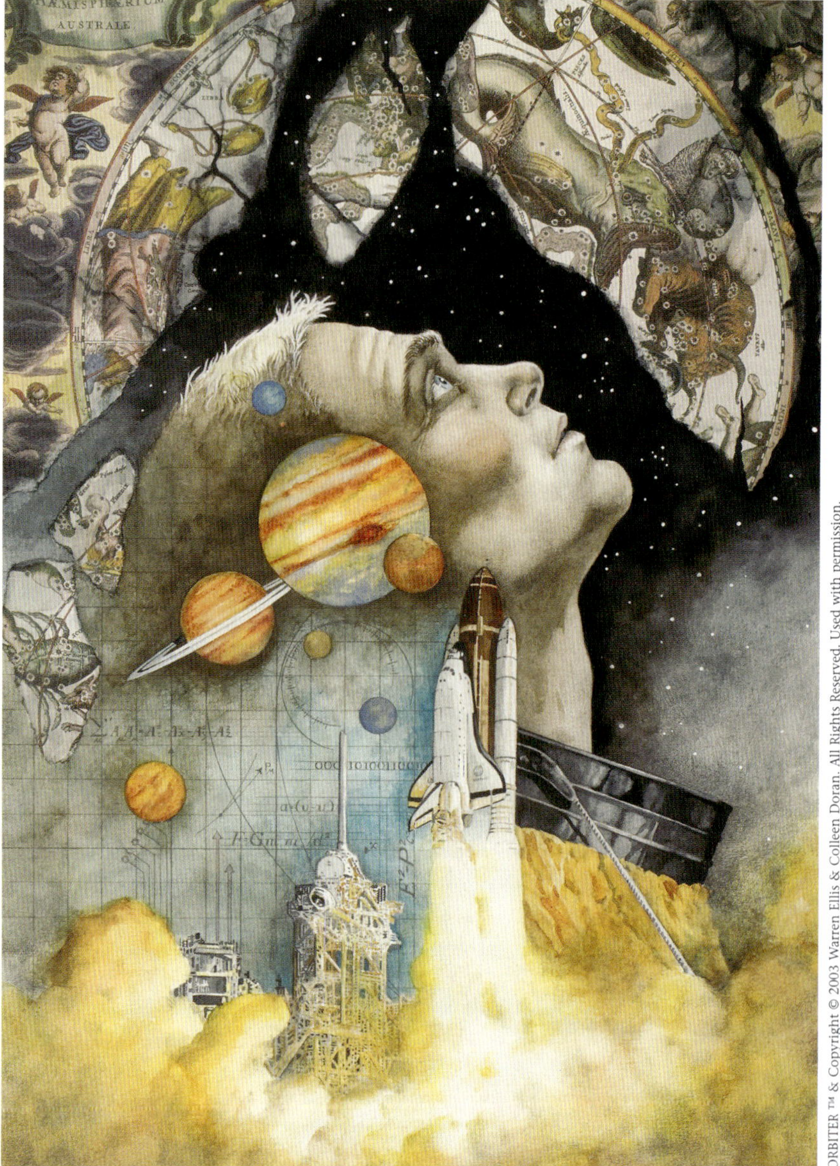

1

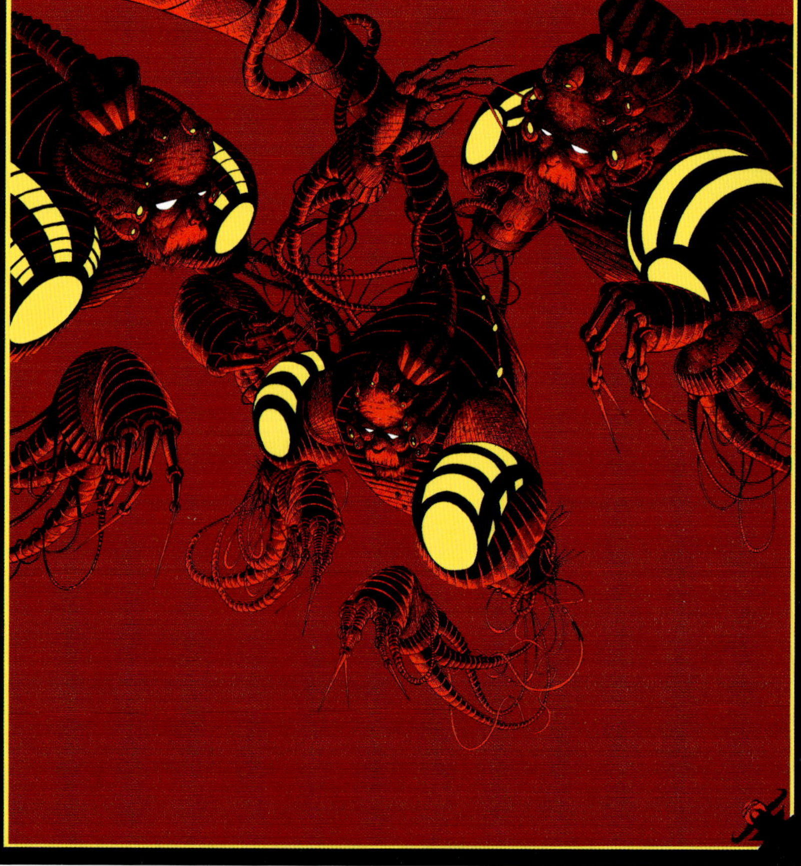

2

3

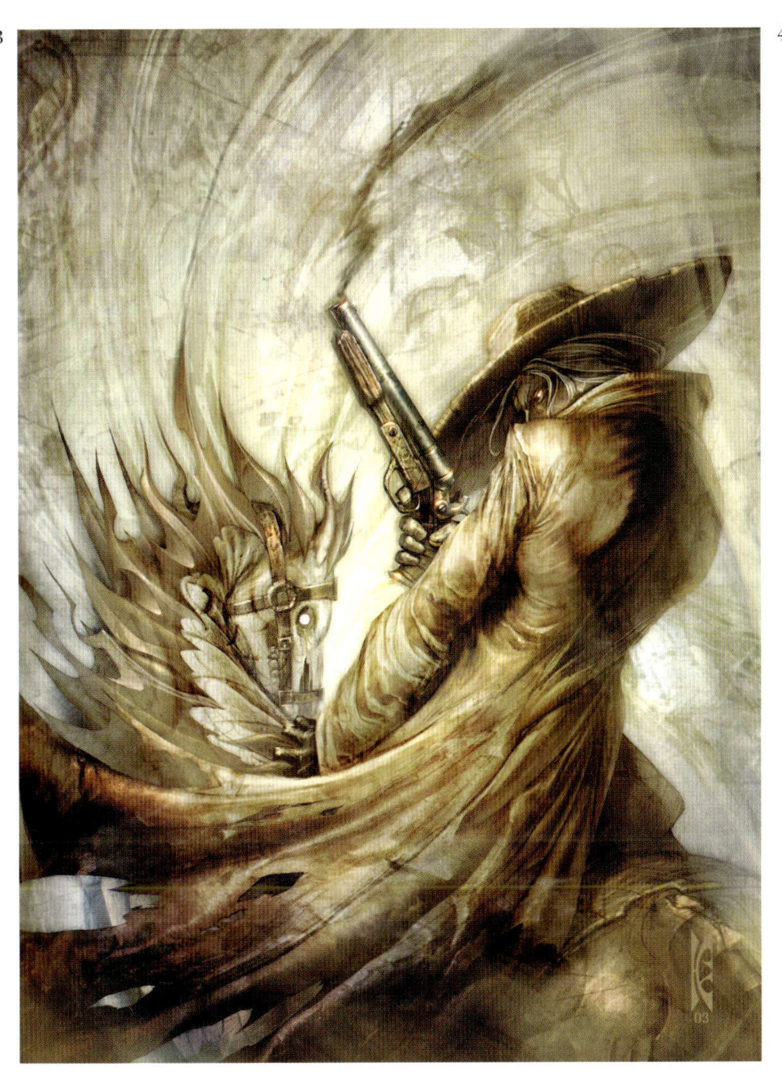

4

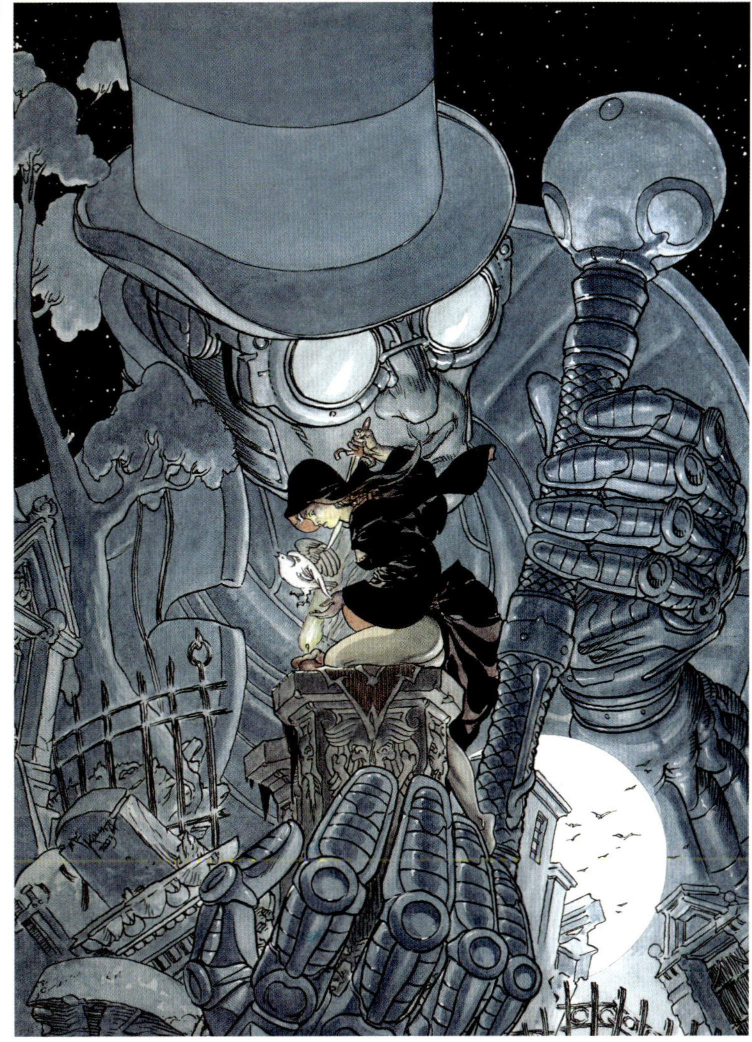

5

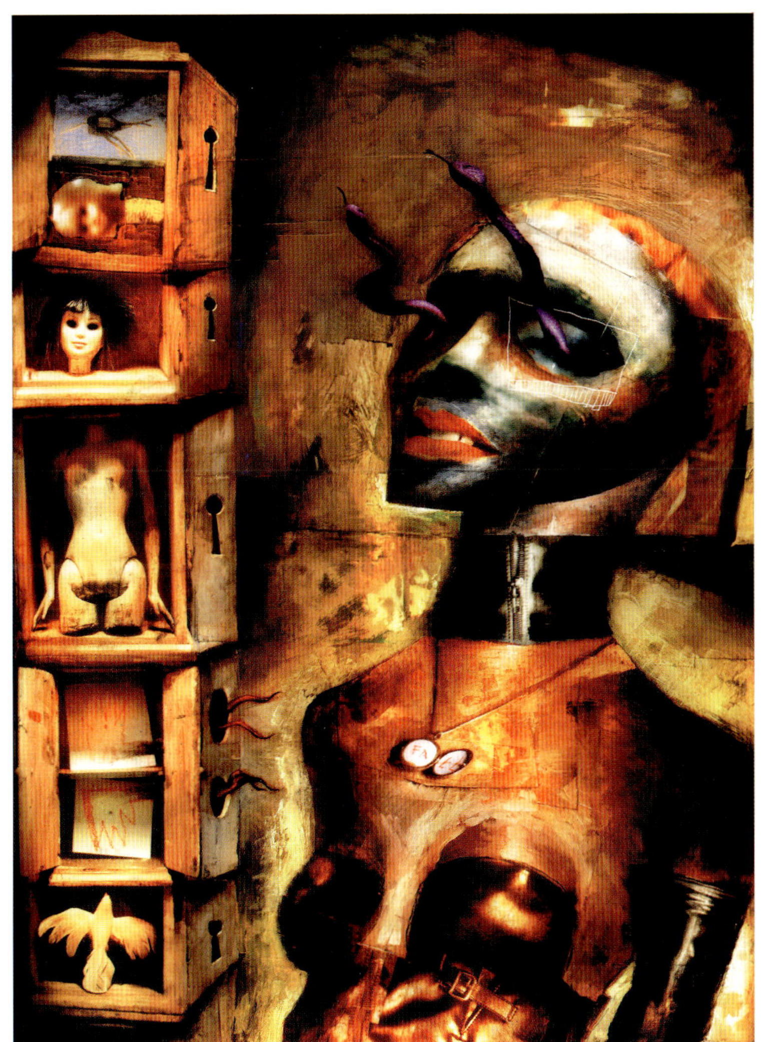

6

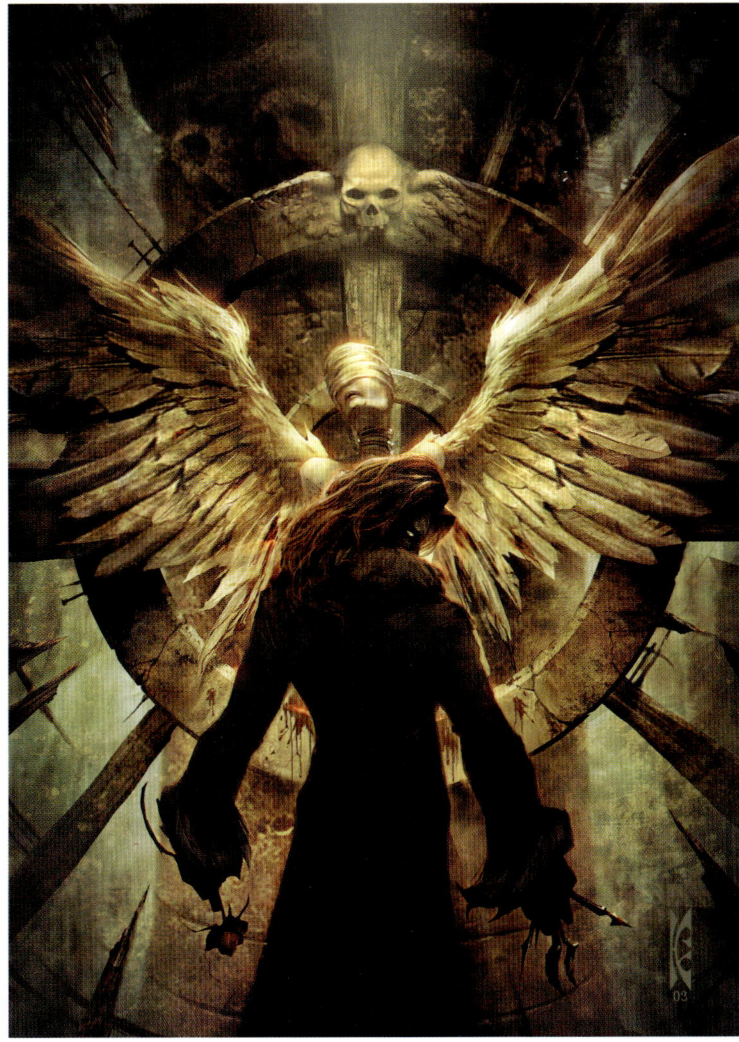

1
artist: **Brian Horton**
art director: Scott Allie
client: Dark Horse Comics
title: Buffy #60: A Stake to the Heart
medium: Digital
size: 6″x9″

2
artist: **Arthur Adams**
client: More Fund Comics/Skydog Press
title: Monkey Man and O'Brien Go Diving
medium: Pen & ink
size: 22″x17″

3
artist: **John Van Fleet**
art director: Joey Cavalieri
designer: John J. Hill
client: DC Comics
title: Poison Ivy: Cast Shadows
medium: Acrylics
size: 10″x16½″

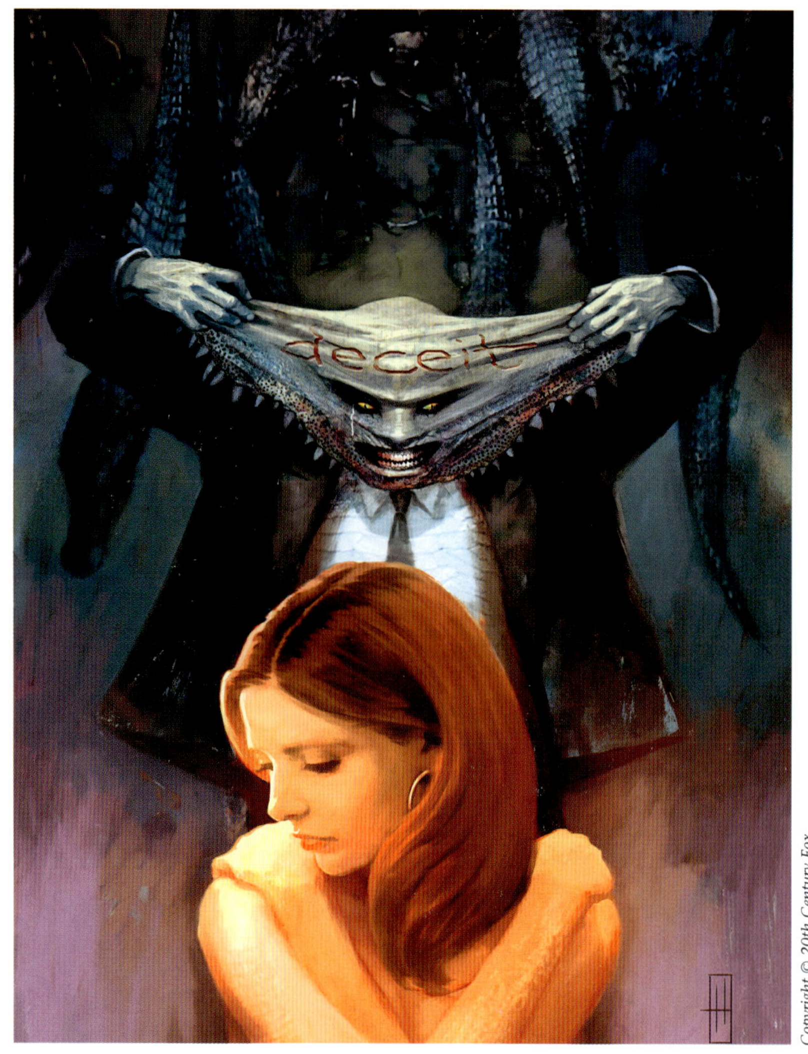

1

2

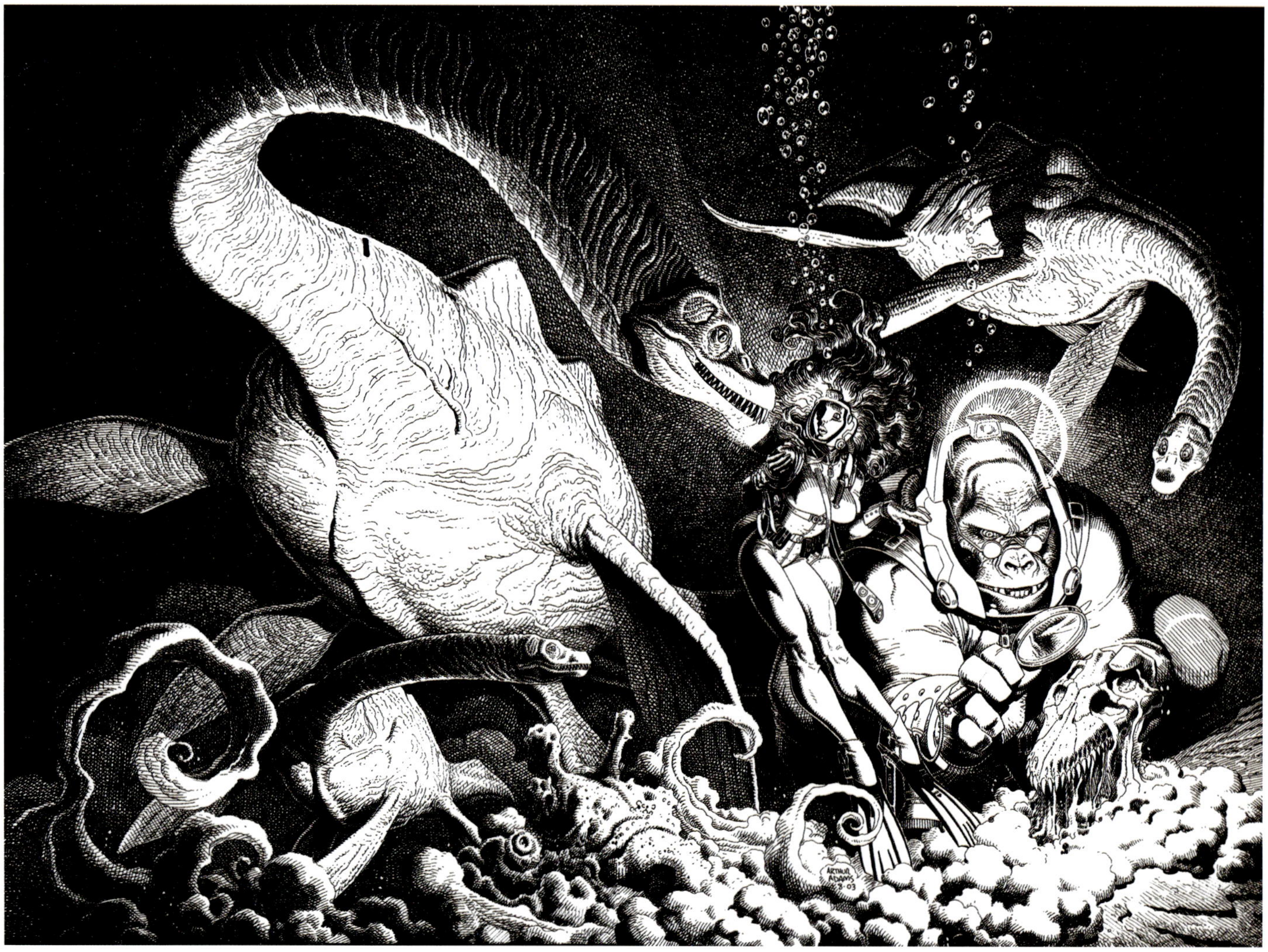

3

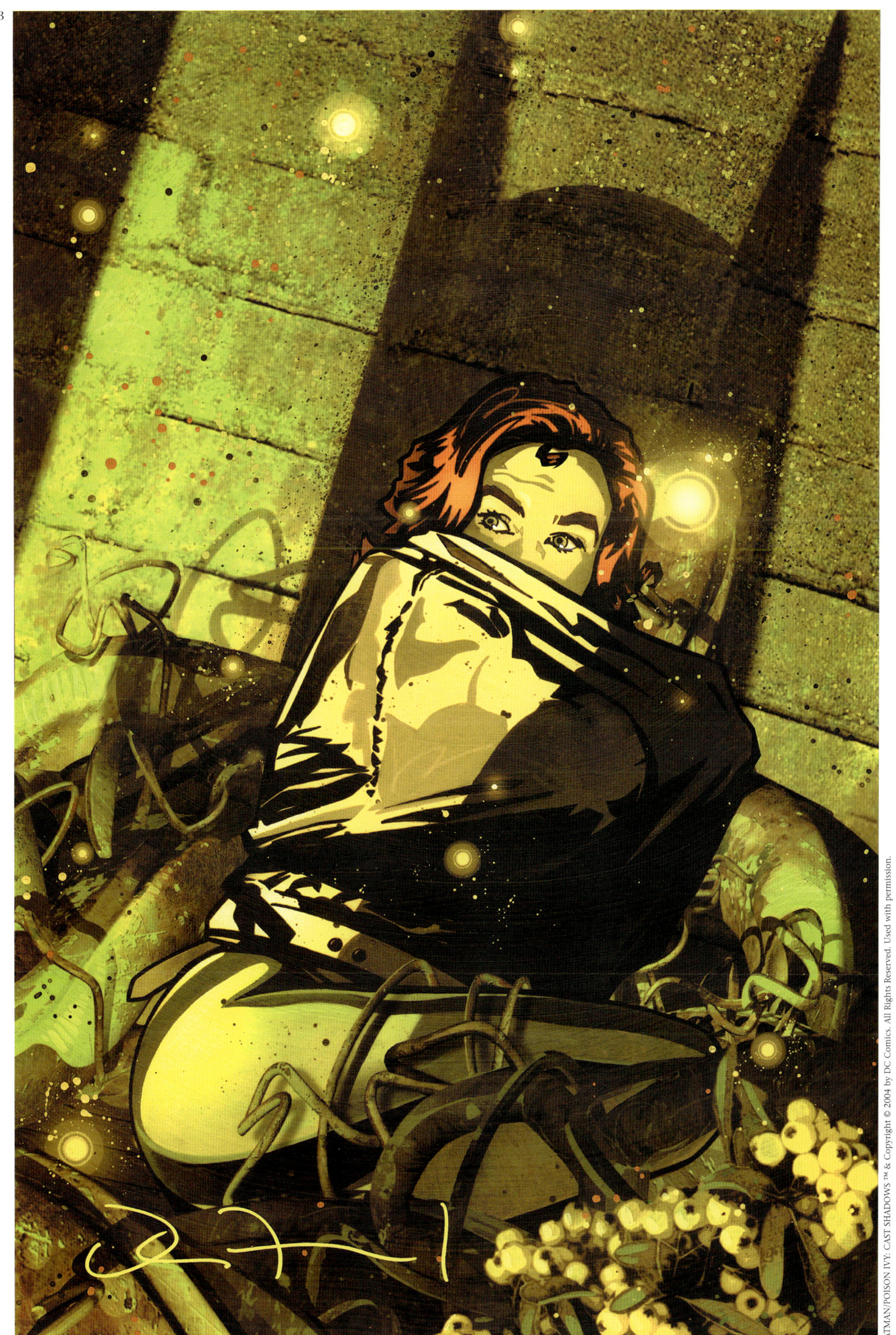

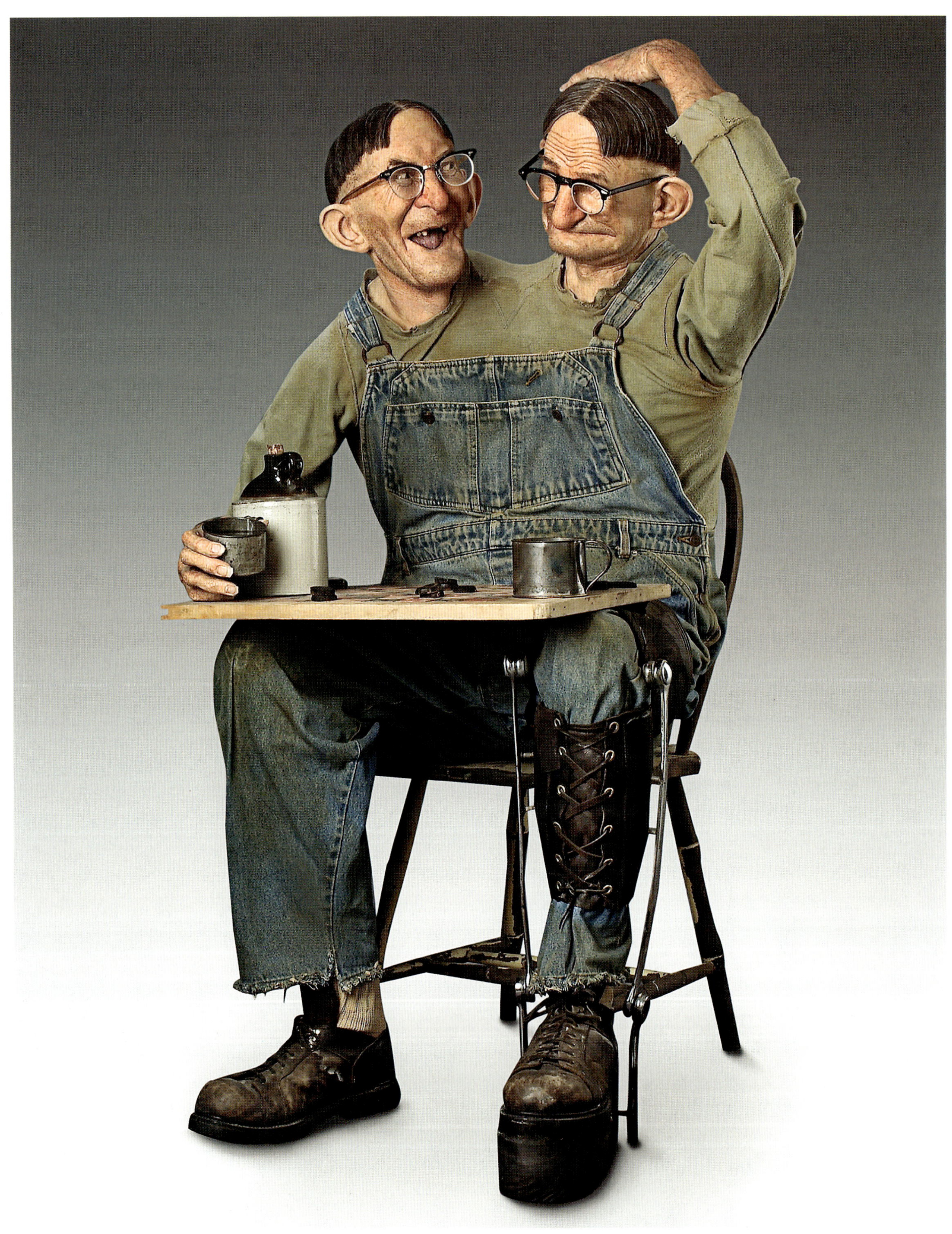

artist: **Thomas S. Kuebler**
title: Cletus and Shorty Play Checkers *medium:* Silicone/mixed *size:* Life-size

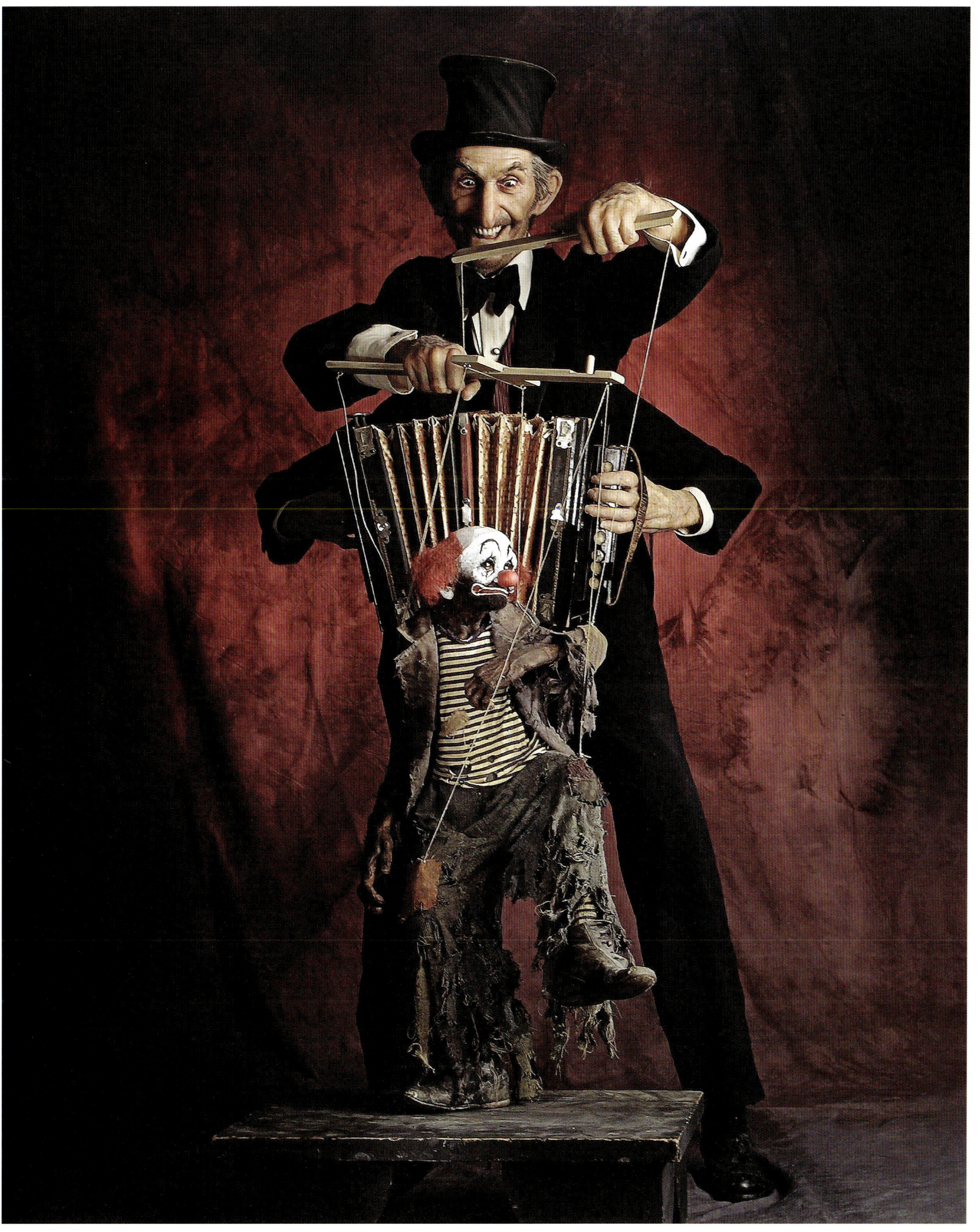

artist: **Thomas S. Kuebler**
title: The Puppeteer *medium:* Silicone/mixed *size:* Life-size

1
artist: **Tim Holter Bruckner**
art director: Georg Brewer
designer: Alex Ross
client: DC Direct
title: Shazam/Kingdom Come
medium: Painted resin
size: 6 7/8" tall

2
artist: **Jonathan Matthews**
art director: Ed Bolkus
designer: Jill Thompson
colorist: Plan B Toys
client: DC Direct
title: Manga Death Maquette
medium: Cold-cast porcelain
size: 8"tall

3
artist: **Tim Holter Bruckner**
art director: Georg Brewer
designer: Jim Lee
client: DC Direct
title: Batman/Hush
medium: Painted resin
size: 6 3/4" tall

4
artist: **Tim Holter Bruckner**
art director: Georg Brewer
designer: Adam Hughes
client: DC Direct
title: Wonder Woman
medium: Painted resin
size: 11 3/4" tall

1

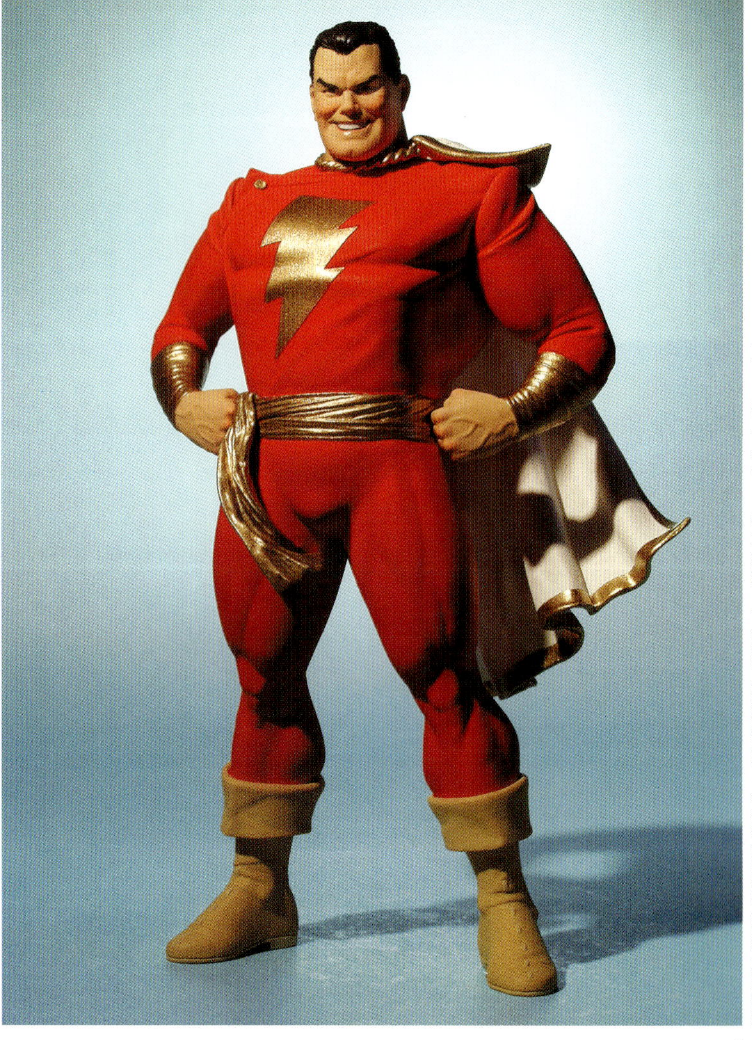

2

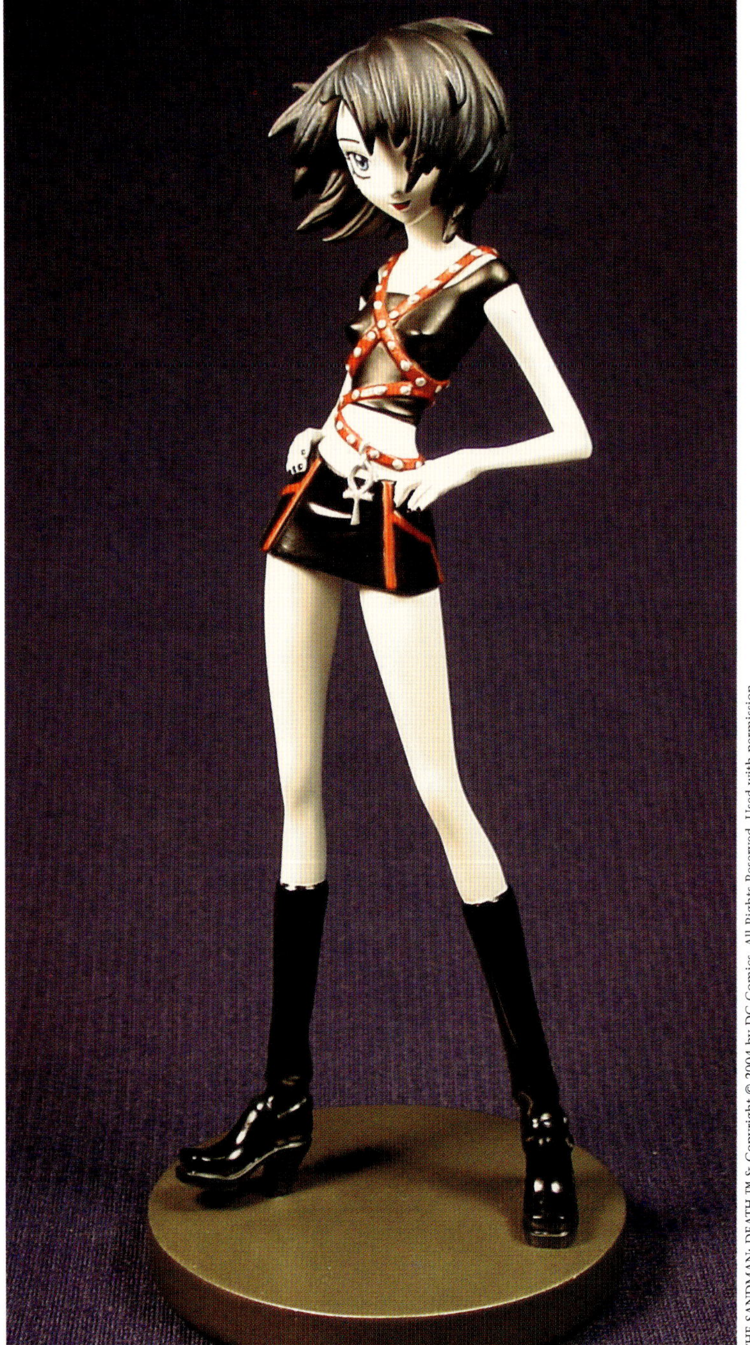

3

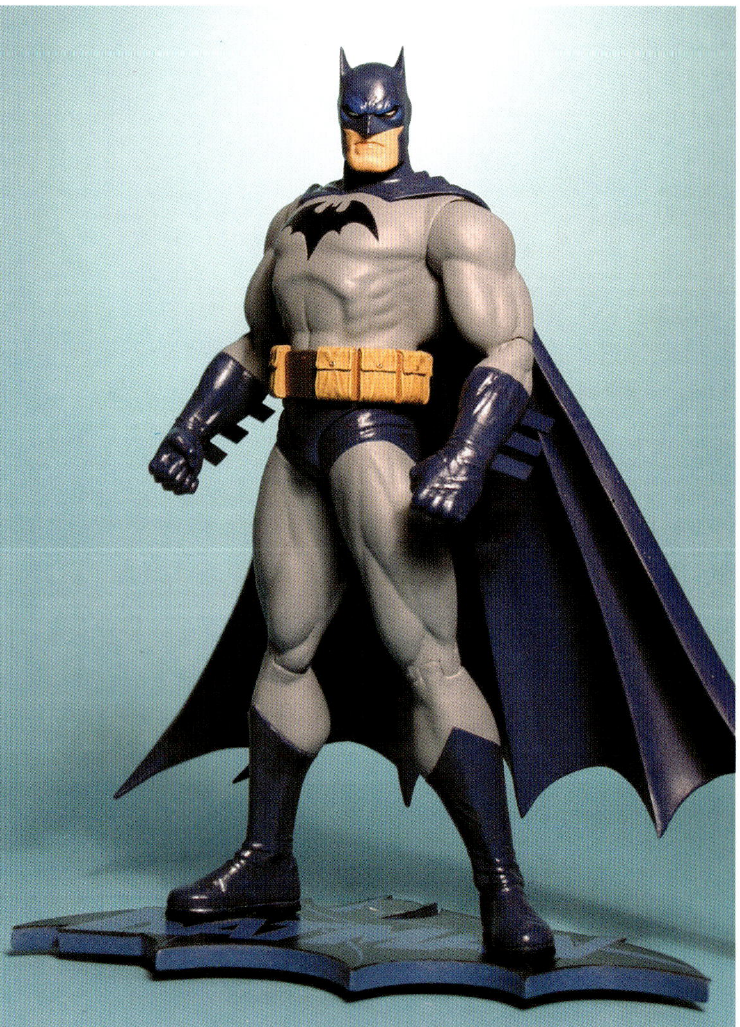

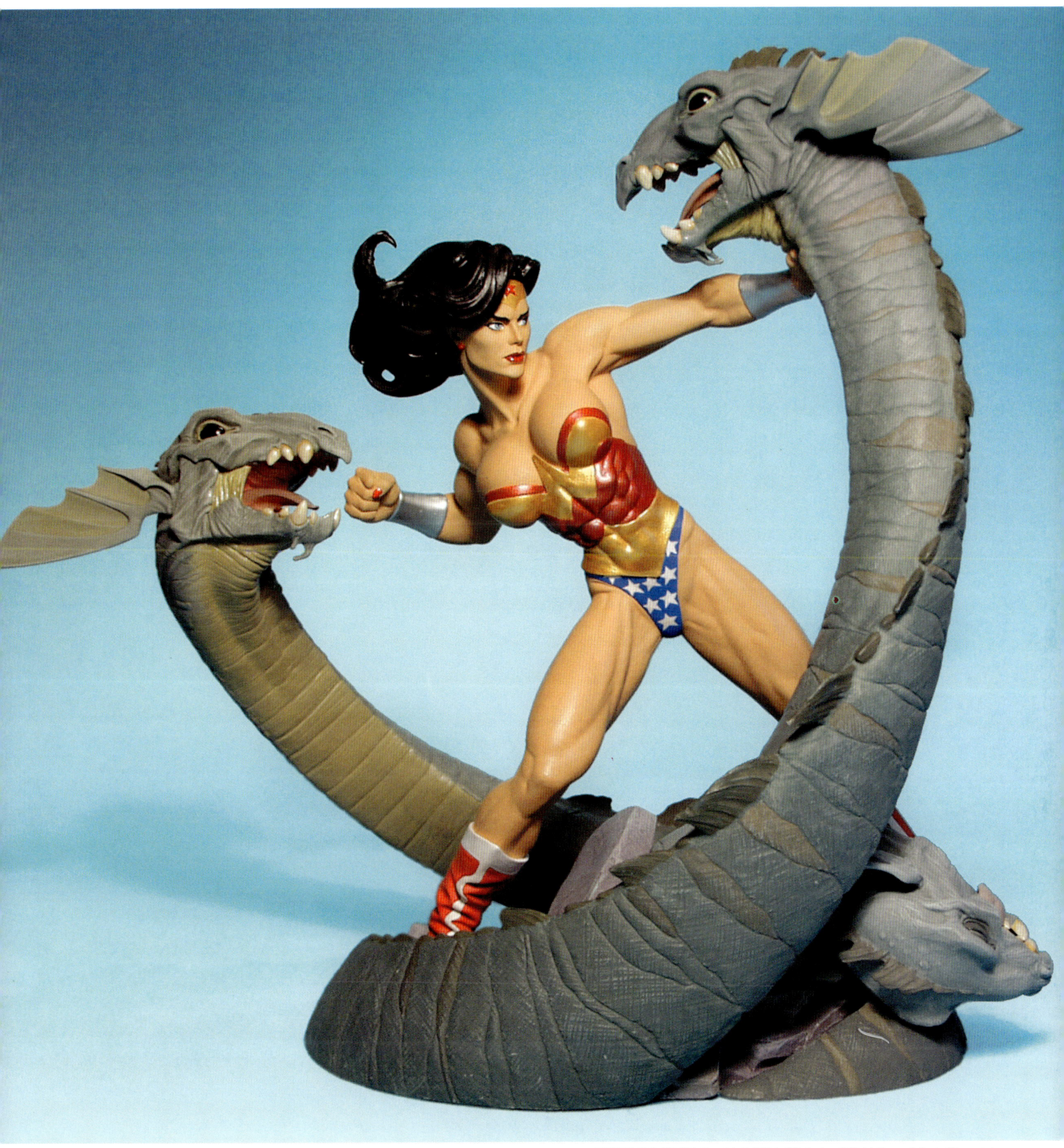

4

1
artist: **James Hakola**
client: MrDandy.com
title: Sikk at the Circus™: The Ringmeister & "Meester"
medium: Sculpey, wax
size: 3 1/2"tall

2
artist: **Kevin Slice**
art director: Kyle Cross
designer: Tom Keever
title: Muruz Lizard
medium: Sculpey
size: 35"long x 10"tall

3
artist: **Alejandra Jorquera**
art director: Gonzalo Vecino
photographer: Martin Sigal
client: BBDO Argentina/NIKE
title: David 1—Goliath 0
medium: Epoxy clay, sculpey
size: 14"long x 8"tall x 12"wide

4
artist: **Angela Giovanna Loroux**
title: Eden
medium: Polymer clay
size: 11"tall x 15"long x 12"wide

5
artist: **Alejandra Jorquera**
art director: Gustavo Chiocconi
photographer: Martin Sigal
client: BBDO Argentina
title: Speed to Everyone
medium: Epoxy clay, sculpey
size: 14"long x 10"tall x 12"wide

6
artist: **Eric Nocella**
art director: Lesean Thomas
photographer: Sym 7
client: Whet Paper Bag
title: Philly the Kid
medium: Wax
size: 8" tall

7
artist: **Sean Olmos**
client: Opifex
title: F'n Guy
medium: Sculpey, wax
size: 13" tall

1

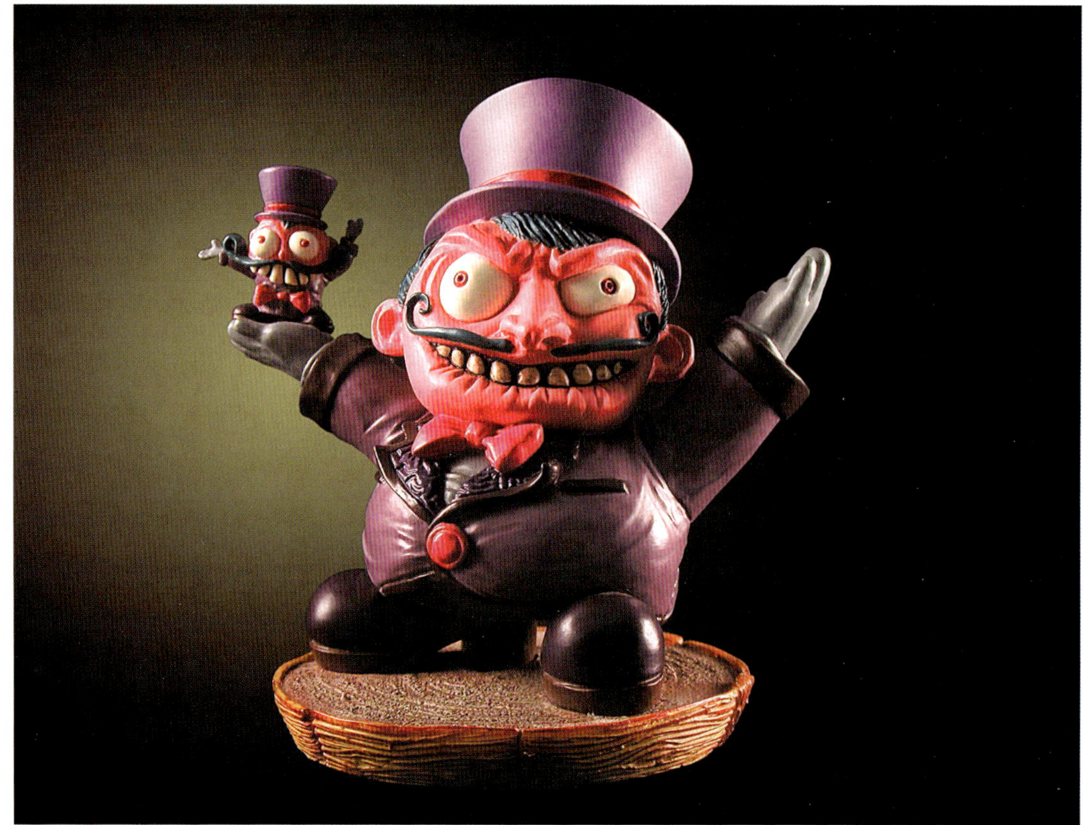

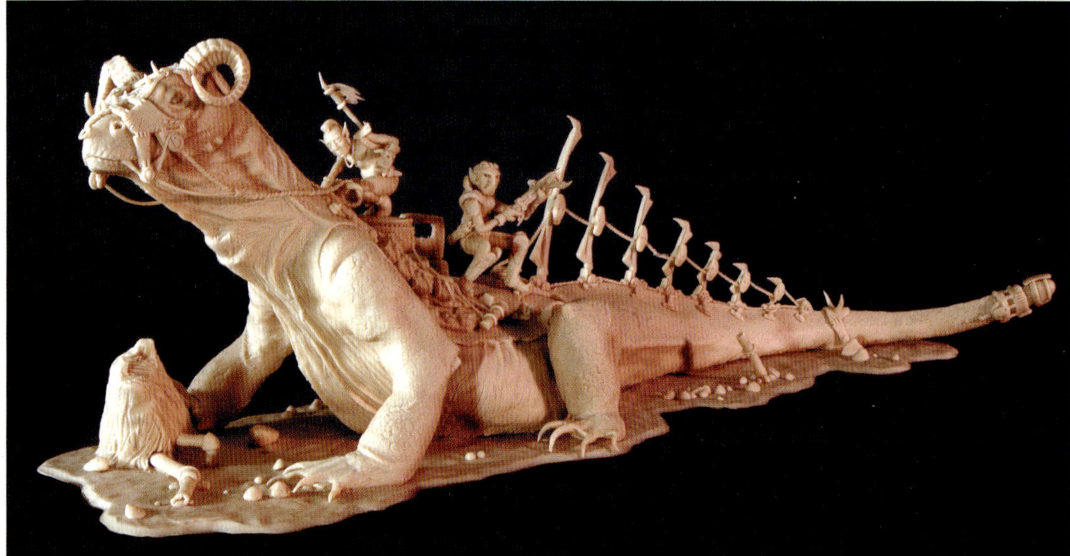

2

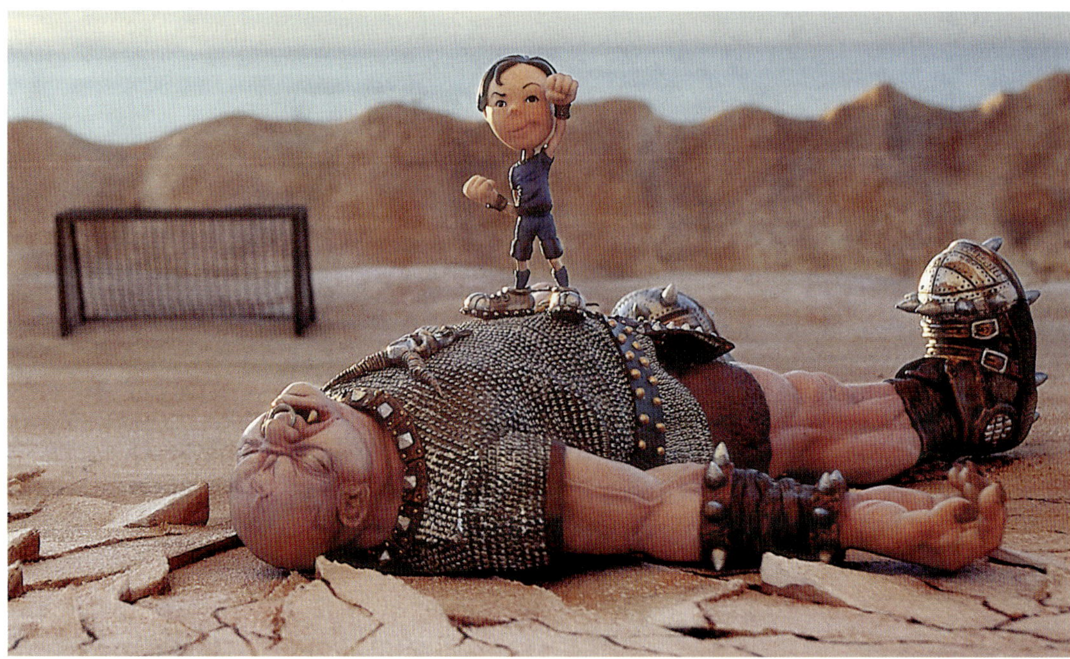

3

4

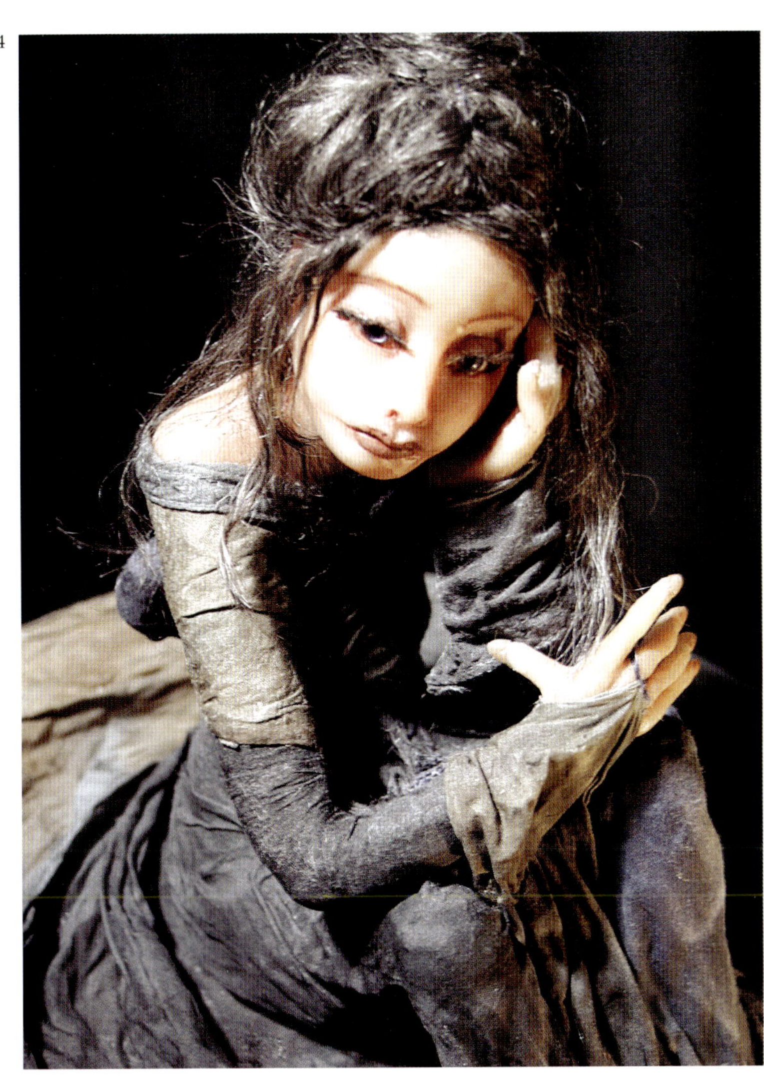

5

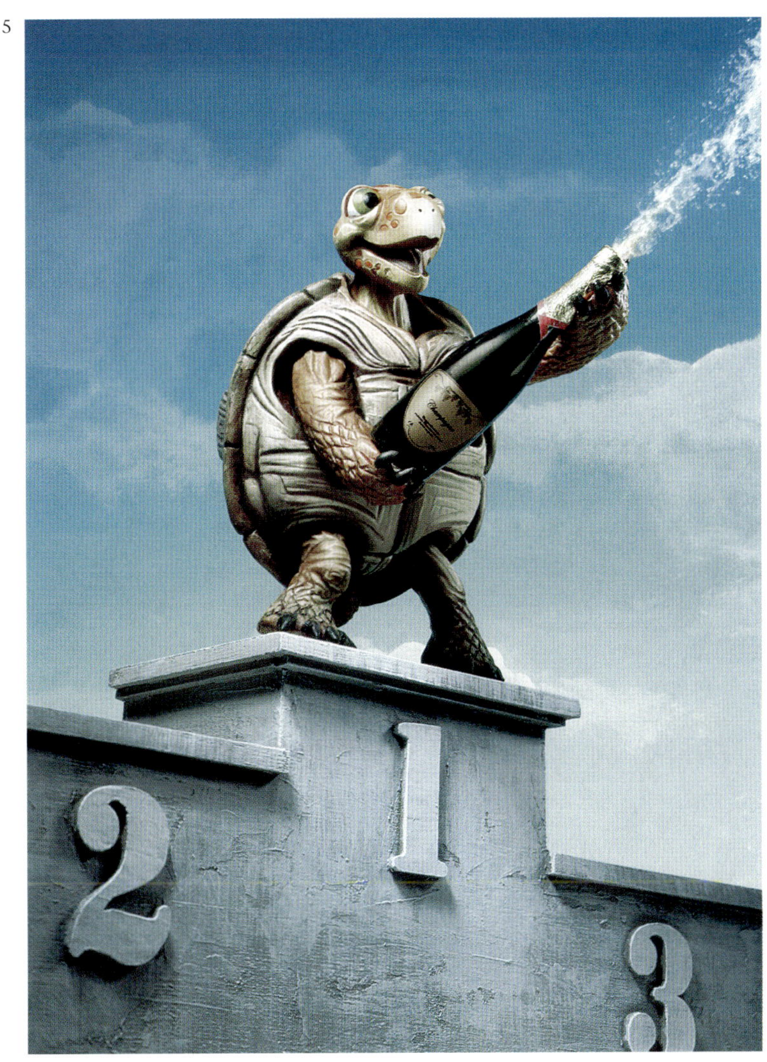

6

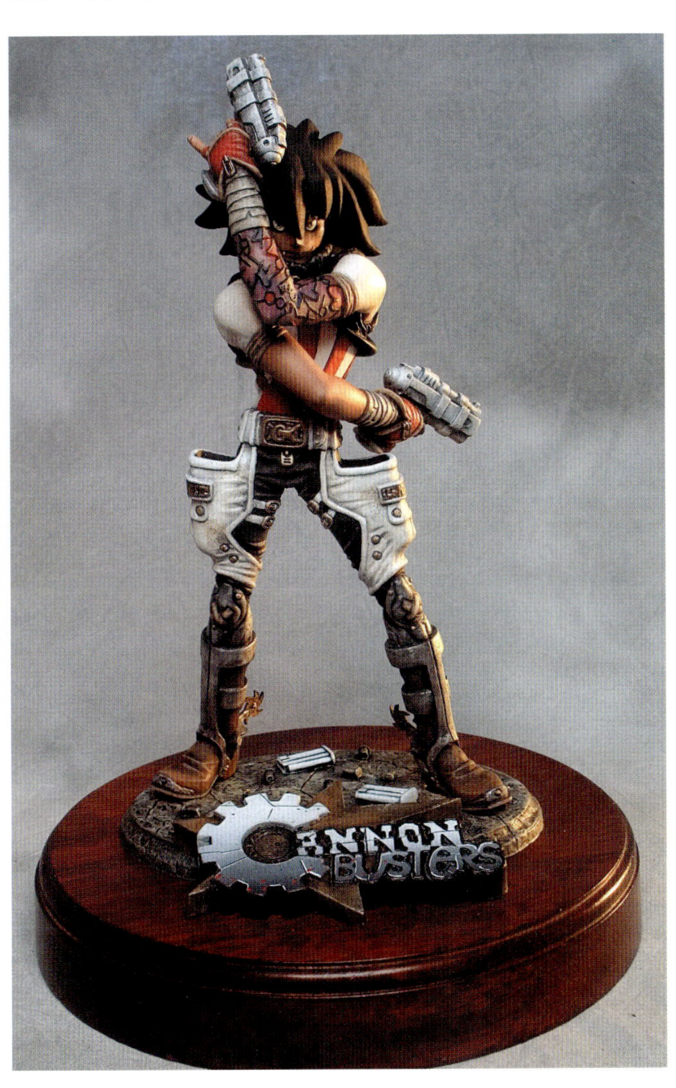

7

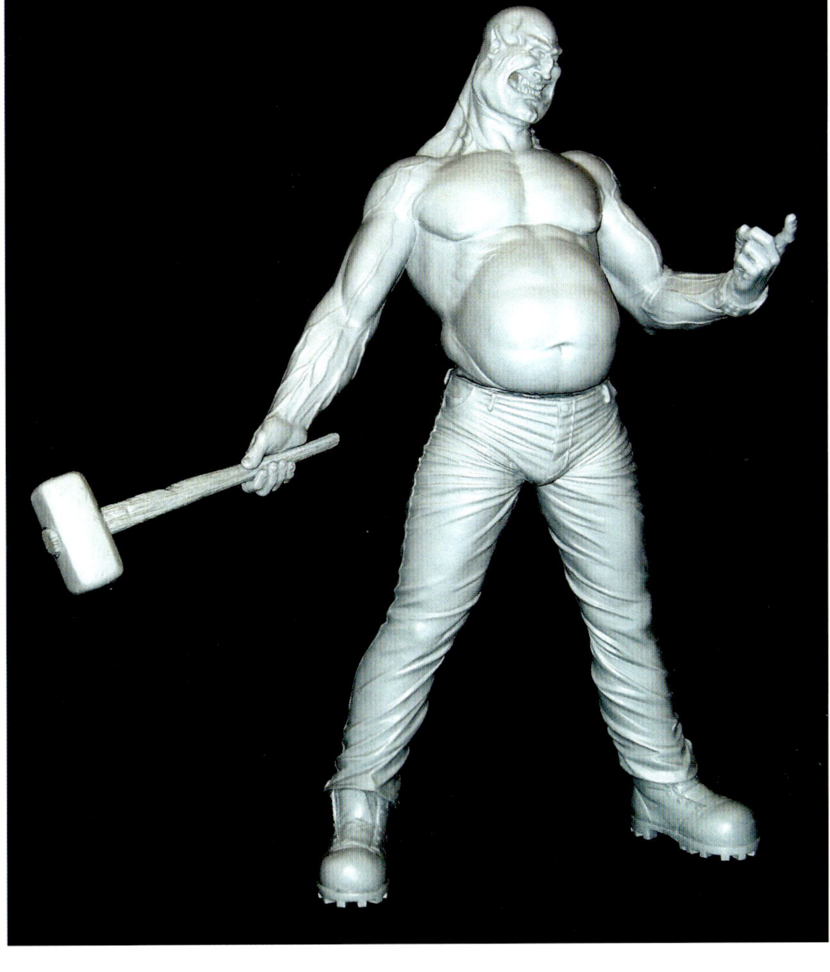

1
artist: **Kenneth M. Faraoni**
title: Fairy: The Other White Meat
medium: Bronze with patina
size: $7^{1}/_{2}$″tall x$4^{5}/_{8}$″wide

2
artist: **Tim Baker**
title: Instruments of Secrets Vol. One
medium: Mixed
size: 11″ tall

3
artist: **Fernando Favila**
client: Edge FX
title: Hyde–LXG
medium: Bronze
size: 12″long x 8″tall

4
artist: **David Cheng Lu**
art director: Monte Moore
designer: Monte Moore
client: Tradex-Germany
title: Guardians
medium: Resin
size: 11″ tall

5
artist: **Pablo Viggiano**
art director: Gore Group
designer: Pablo Viggiano/Juan Bobillo
colorist: Alejandra Jorquera
client: Dynamic Forces
title: Hulk
medium: Resin
size: 7″ tall

6
artist: **Alterton**
photographer: Martin Canale
title: "Next time, Reed...Next time..."
medium: Epoxy putty

7
artist: **David Cheng Lu**
art director: Monte Moore
designer: Monte Moore
client: Tradex-Germany
title: Draconis
medium: Resin
size: 24″ tall

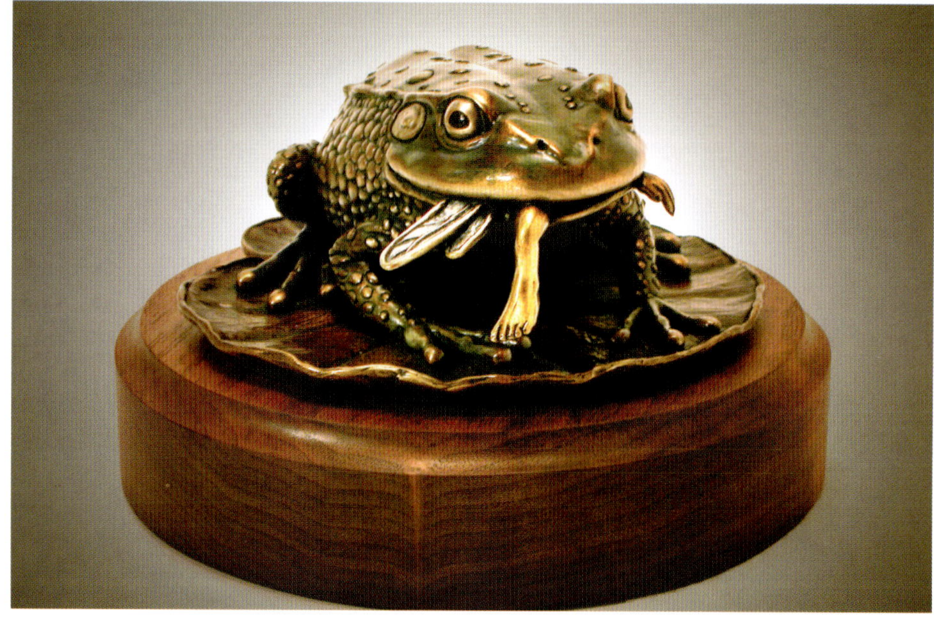
1

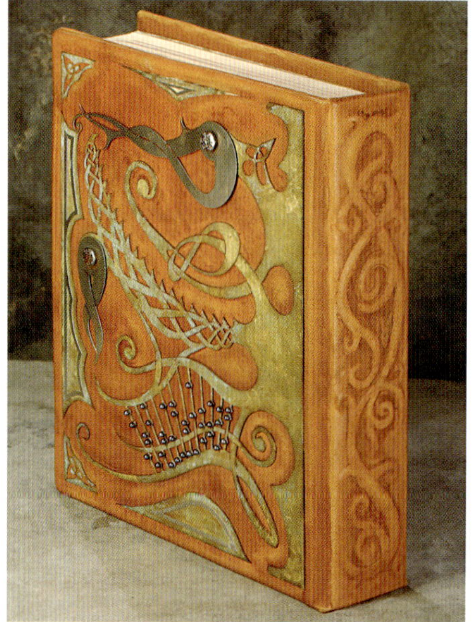
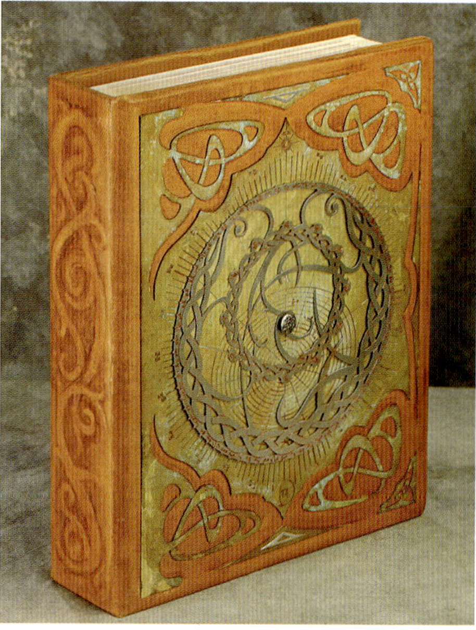
2

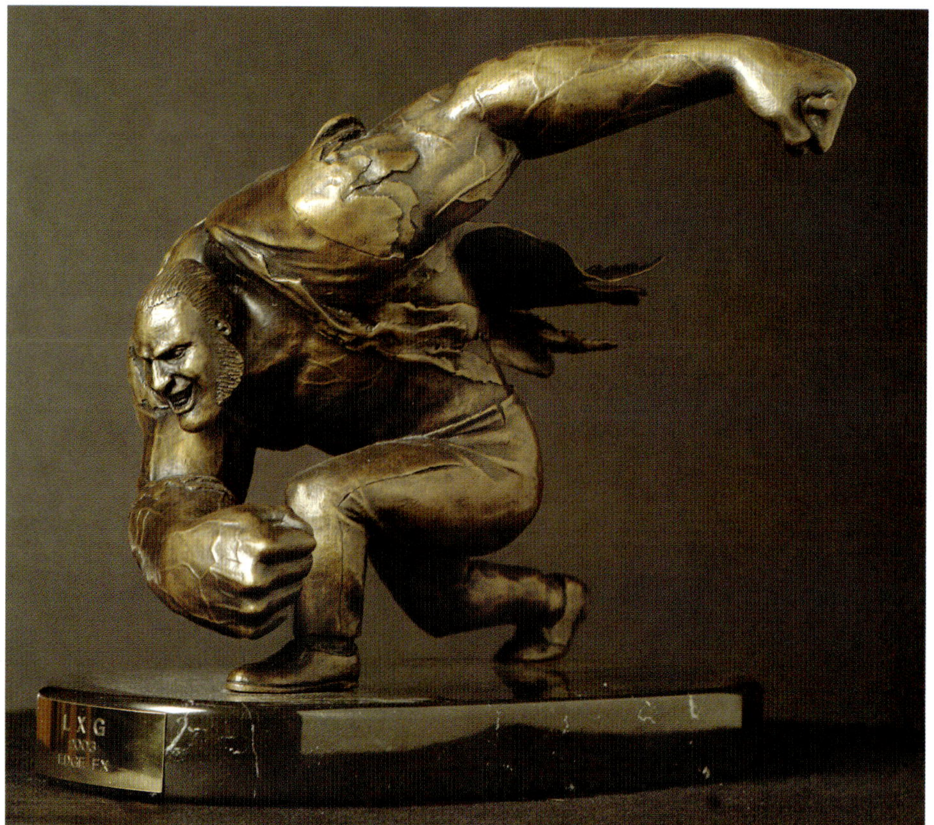

3

4

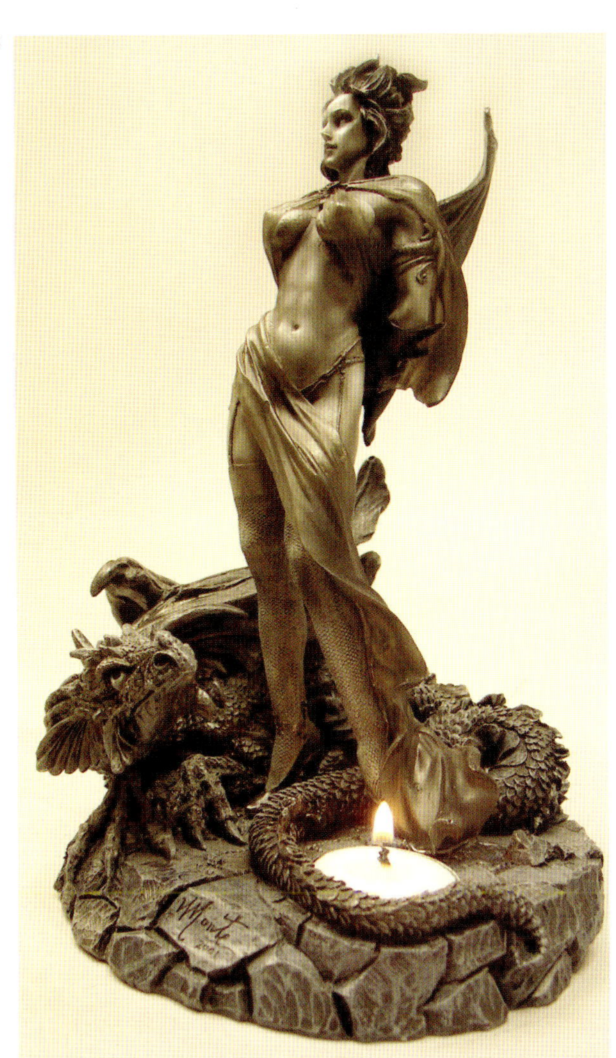

5

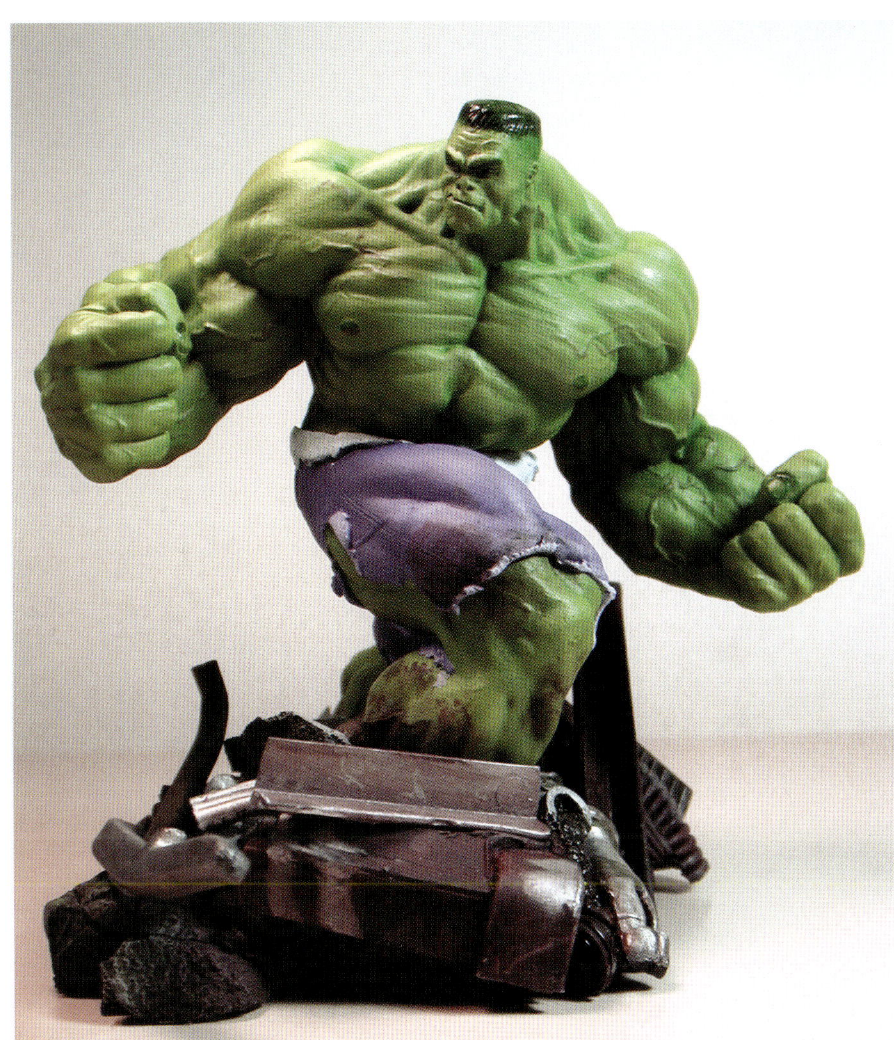

6

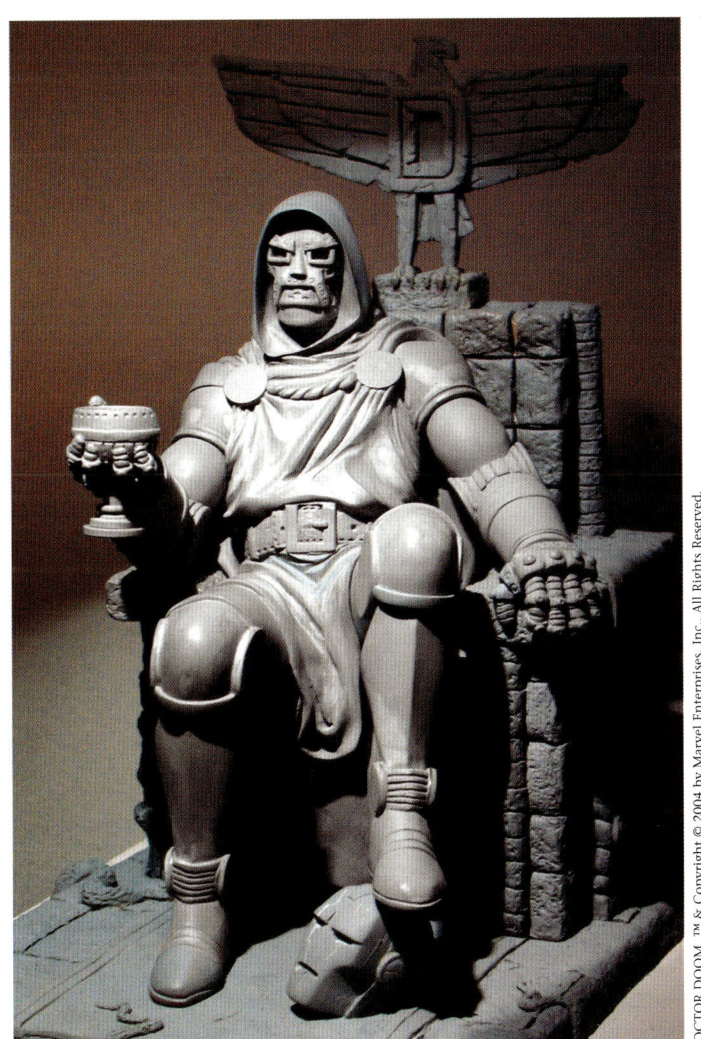

7

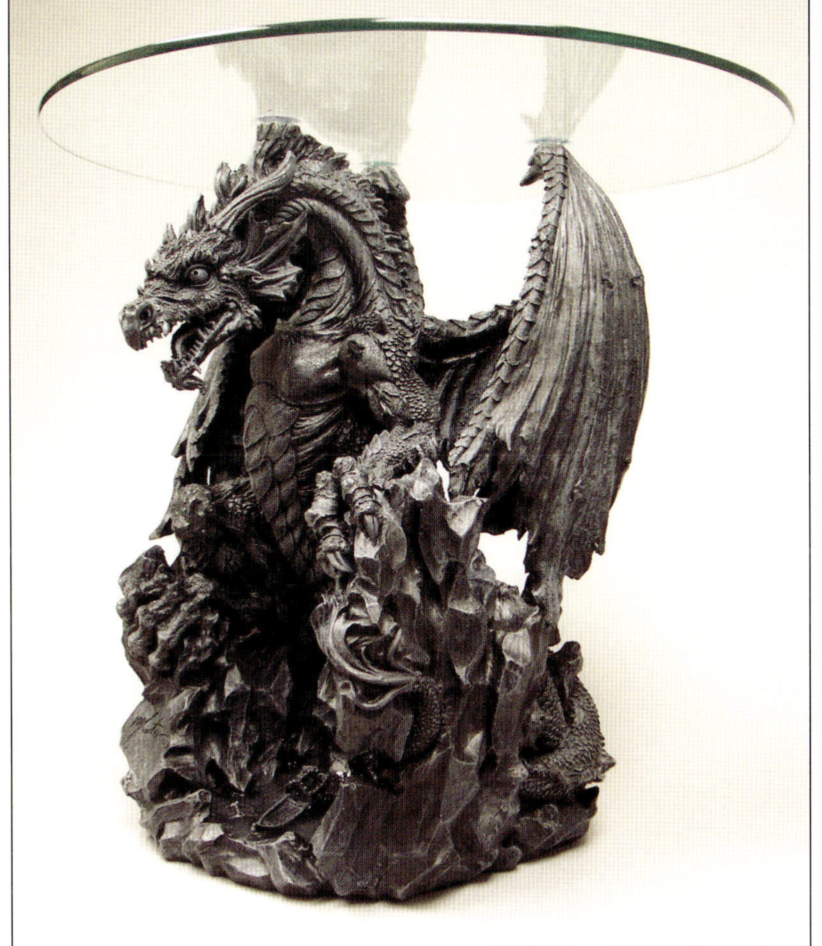

1
artist: **Thomas S. Kuebler**
title: Guru
medium: Silicone/mixed
size: 23"x23"

2
artist: **William Basso**
photographer: Paul Mejias
client: Eldritch Design, Inc.
title: The Ambassador
medium: Painted resin
size: 8 1/4" tall

3
artist: **A. Brent Armstrong**
photographer: Spatola Designer Images
title: The Mummy
medium: Fiberglass & acrylics
size: Life-size

4
artist: **Miles Teves**
art director: Innumerable
client: Universal Studios
title: Overlord—concept
medium: Resin
size: 14"tall x 11"wide

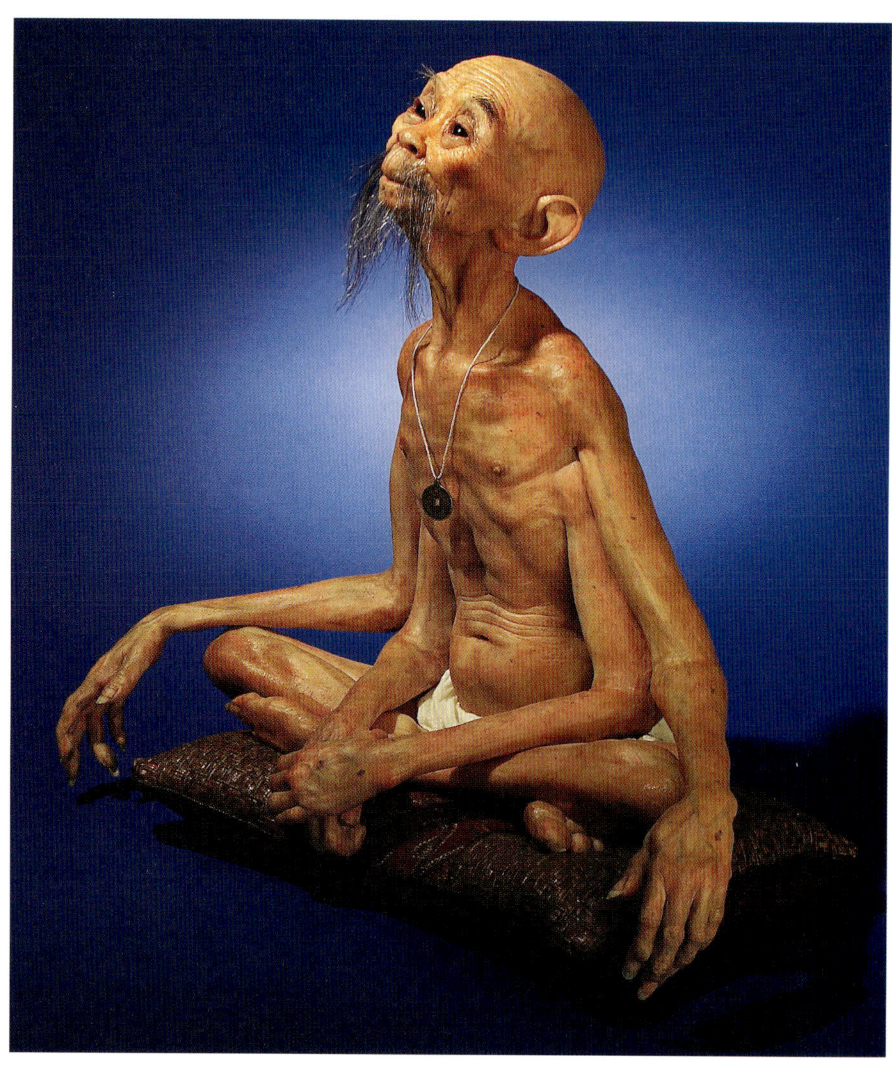

1

2

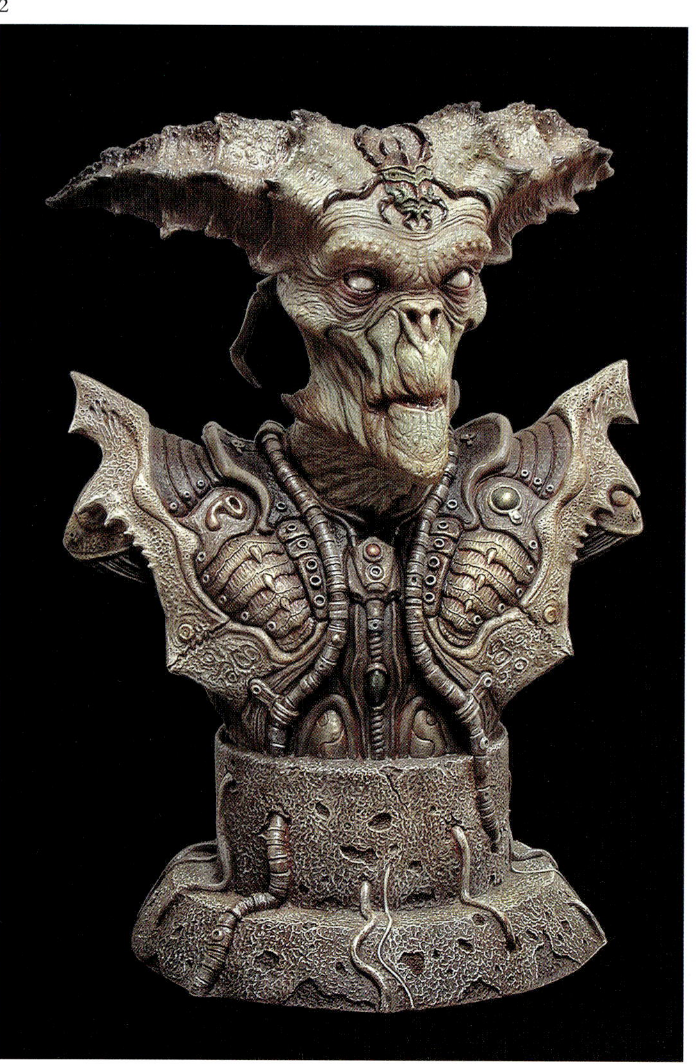

3

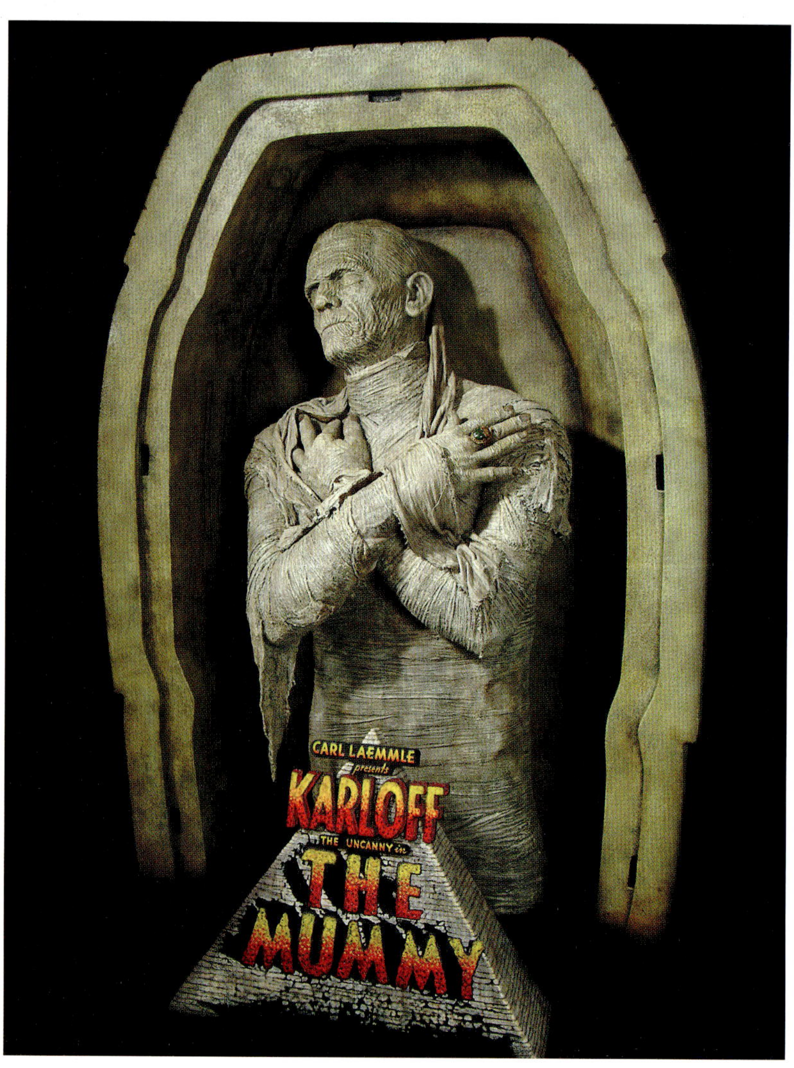

4

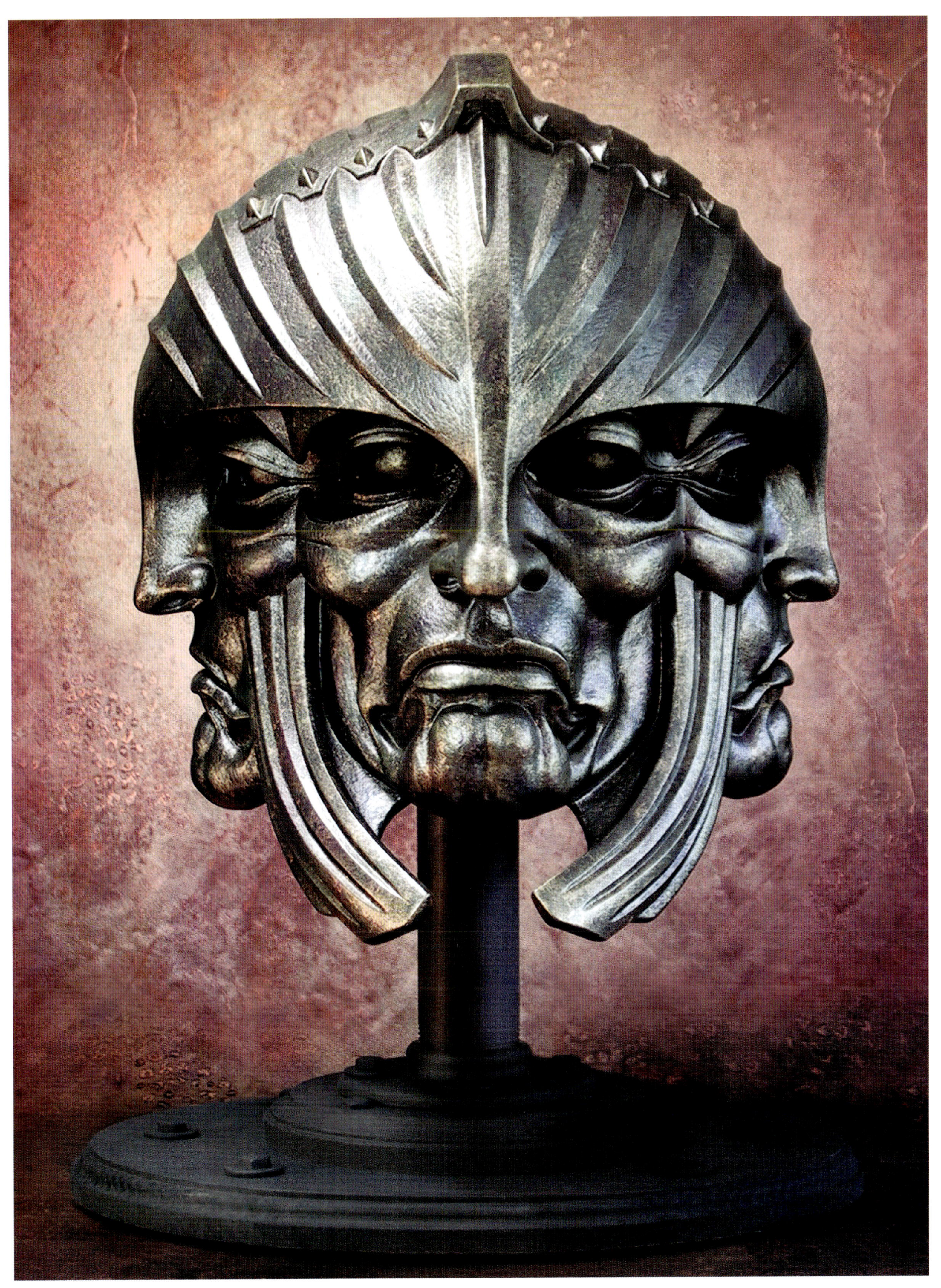

1
artist: **Jean-Marc Laroche**
client: Private collection
title: Coffre à Secrets
medium: Resin/Mixed
size: 18"x14"x9"

2
artist: **Greg Polutanovich**
client: Kirk Dilbeck
title: Thunder God
medium: Roma clay
size: 21"x17"x16"

3
artist: **Gary A Lippincott**
art director: R.J. Vansickle
client: Distinctive Collections
title: Jack
medium: Lost-wax bronze
size: 7" tall

4
artist: **Shaun Gentry**
client: Bandersnatch Prod.
title: Ignatius the Ancient
medium: Super sculpey
size: 17" tall

5
artist: **Jonathan Matthews**
art director: Ed Bolkus
designer: Jill Thompson
client: DC Direct
title: Manga Sandman
medium: Wax
size: 9" tall

6
artist: **Jay Stuckwisch**
art director: Art Vogt
title: Leonequs
medium: Super Sculpey
size: 11"tall x 8 1/2" wide

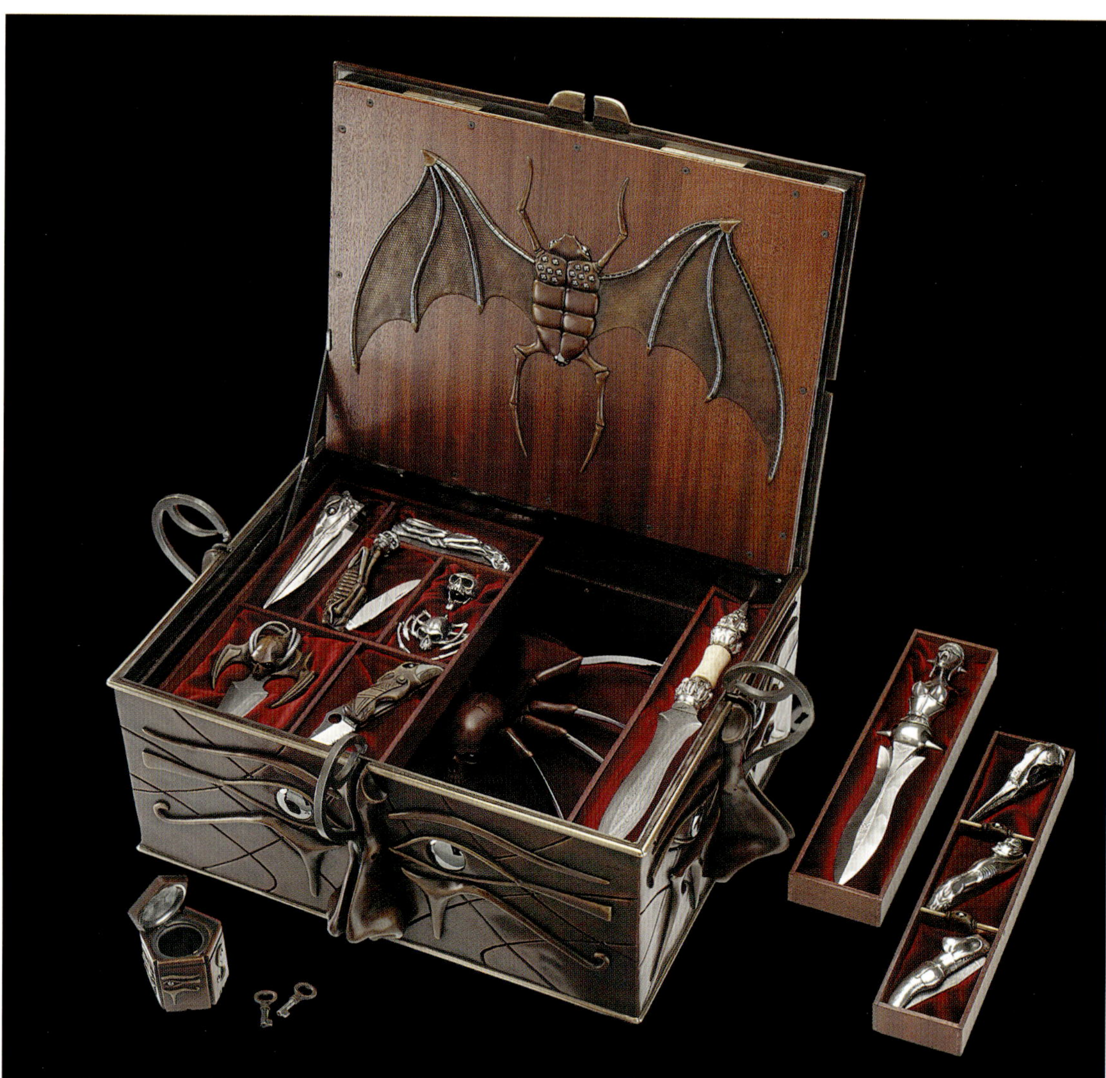

1

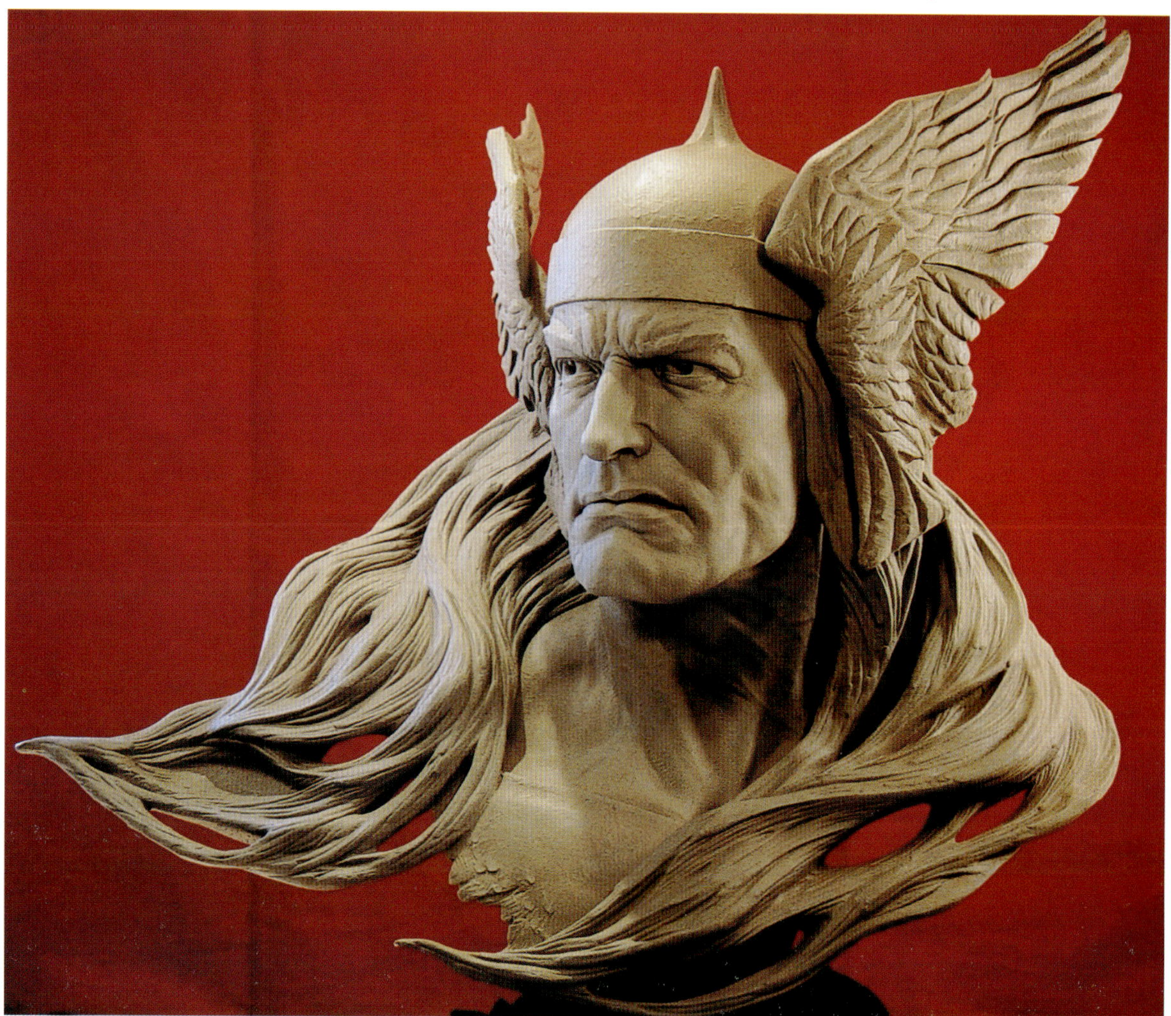

2

3

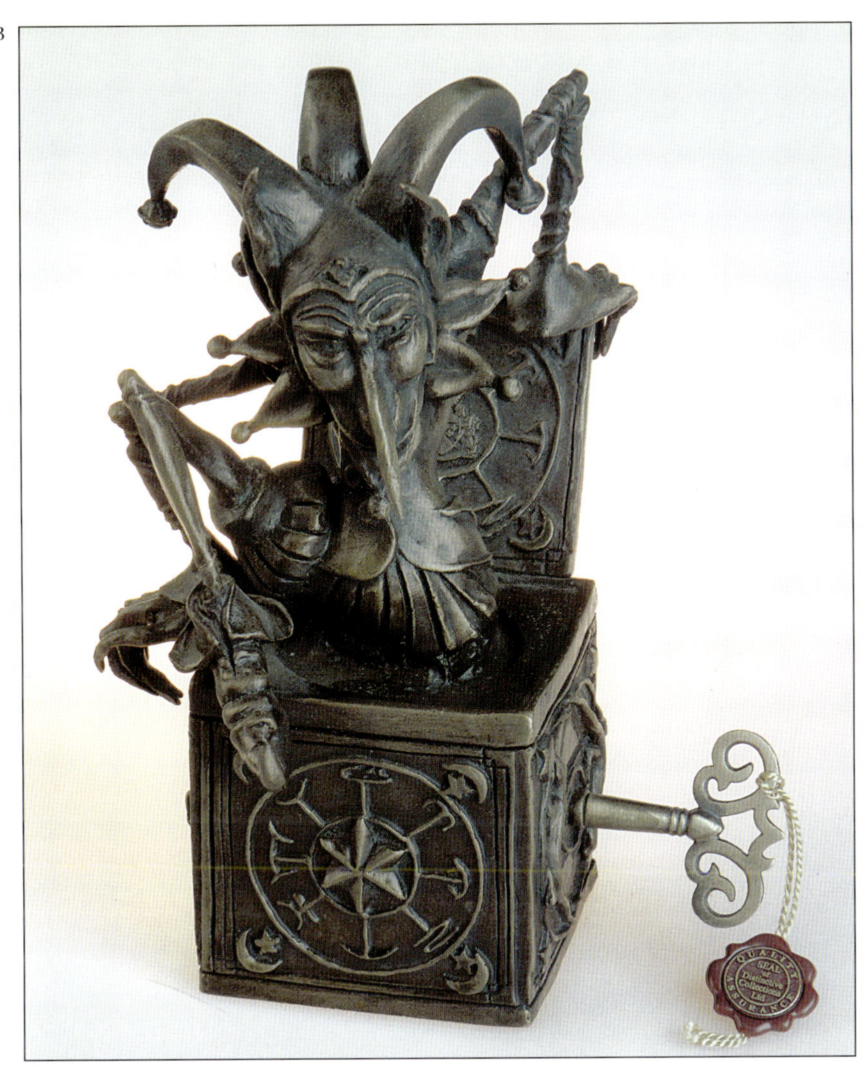

4

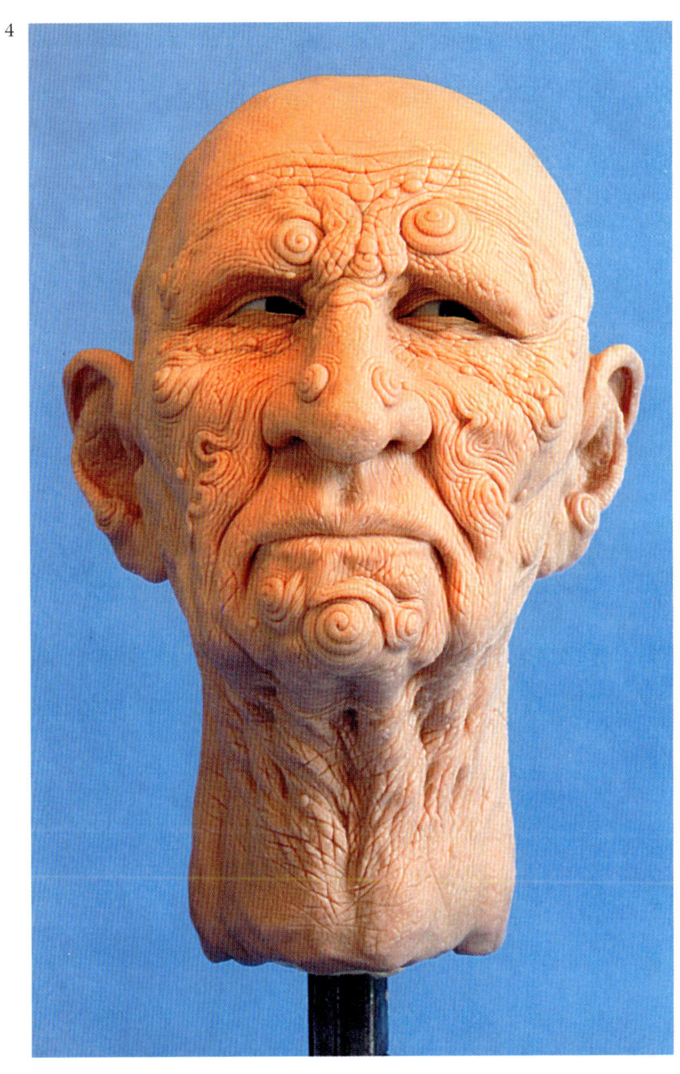

5

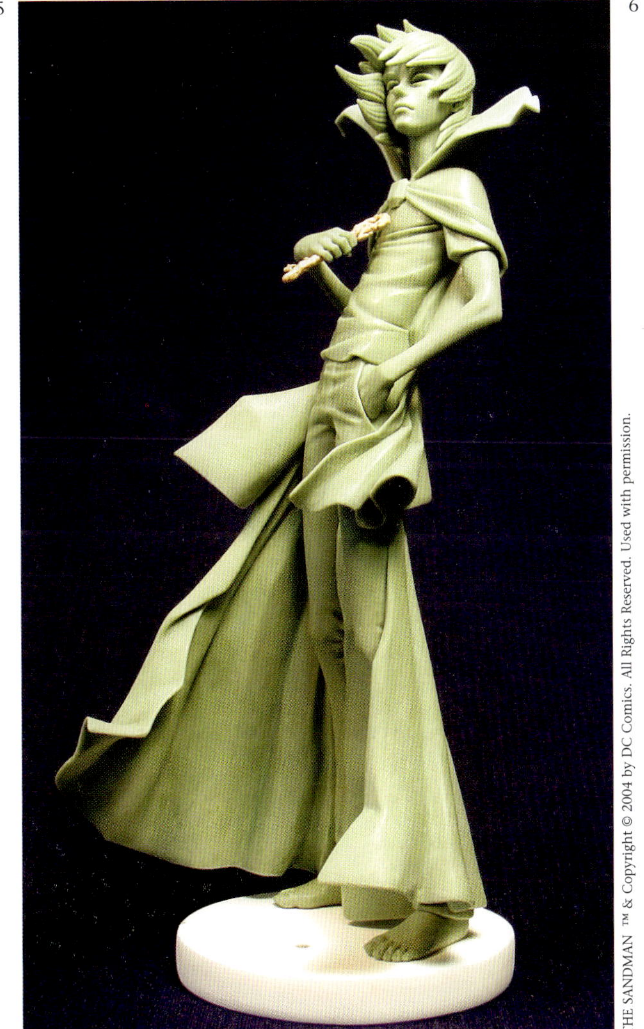

6

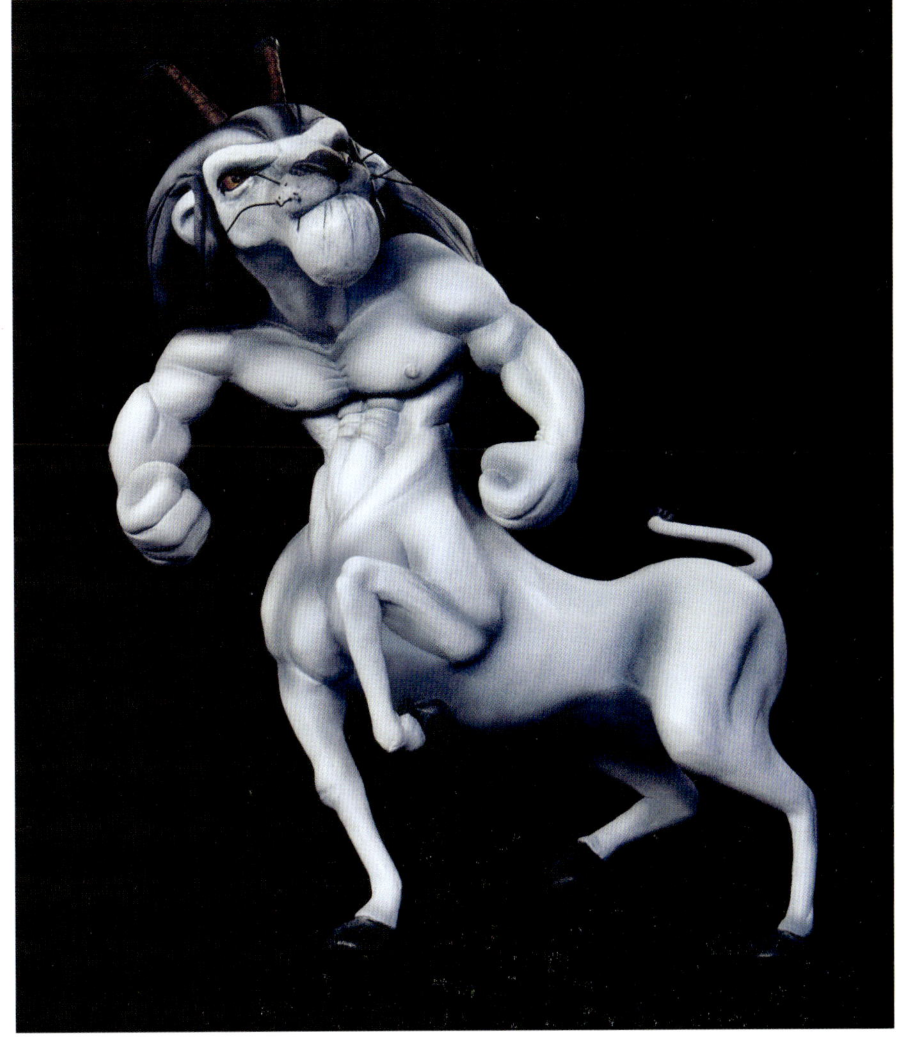

1
artist: **Lawrence Northey**
client: Albert Folsom
title: AF-Z4 The Duke an' Blinky
medium: Metal and glass
size: 27" tall

2
artist: **Lawrence Northey**
client: www.robotart.net
title: Teen Tokyo Koneko-chan (Little Kitty)
medium: Metal and resin
size: 27" tall

3
artist: **Martin Canale**
art director: Gore Group
designer: Martin Canale
client: Pegaso Models
title: Full Moon Breed
medium: Resin
size: 9" tall

4
artist: **Martin Canale**
art director: Gore Group
designer: Martin Canale
client: Pegaso Models
title: Demon Lord
medium: Resin
size: 9" tall

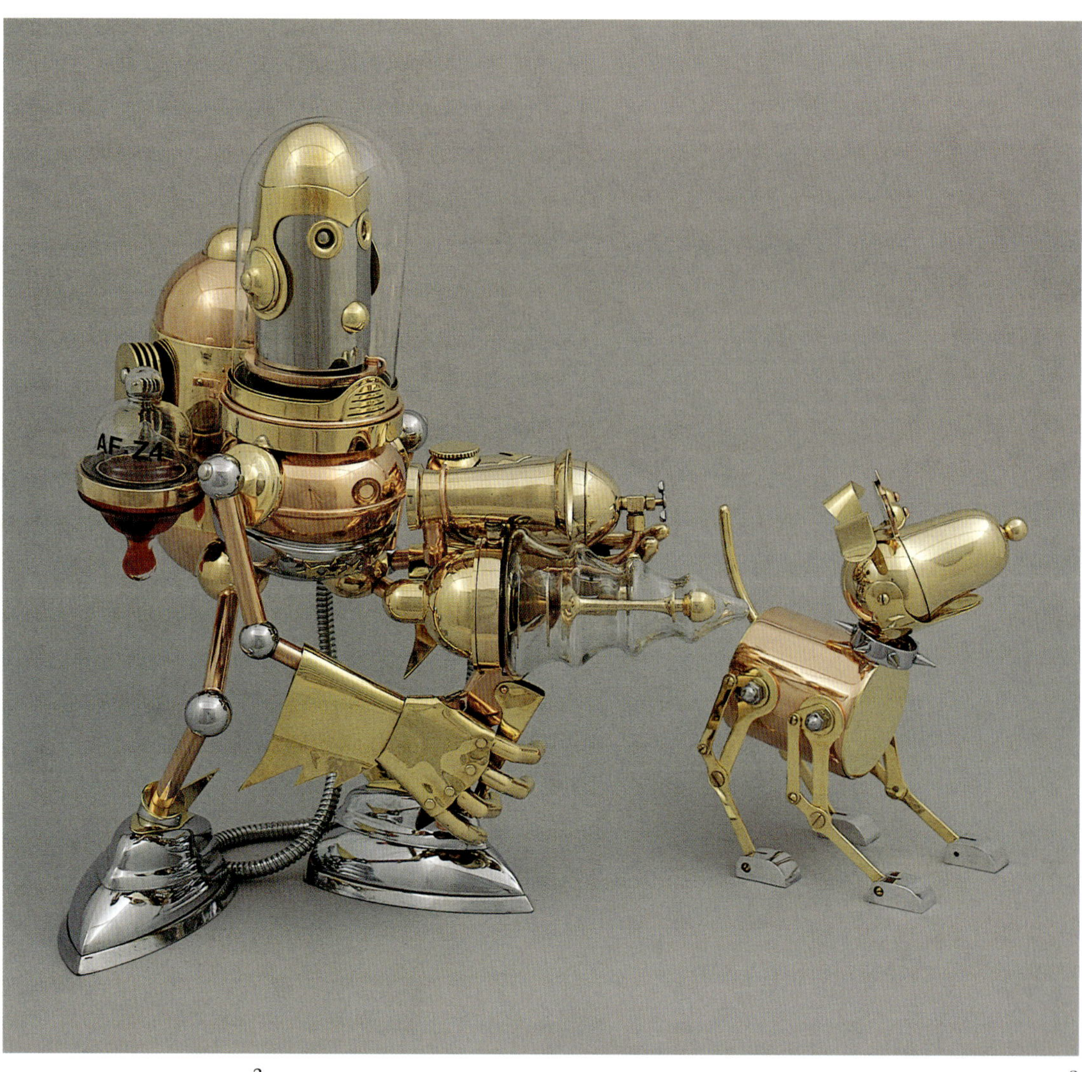

1

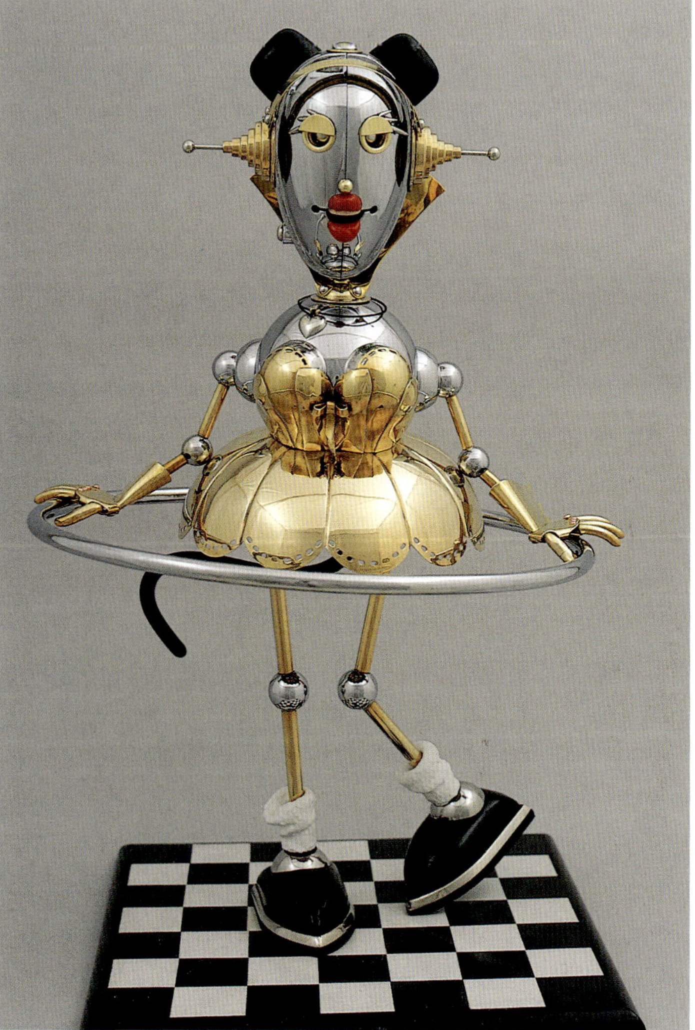
2

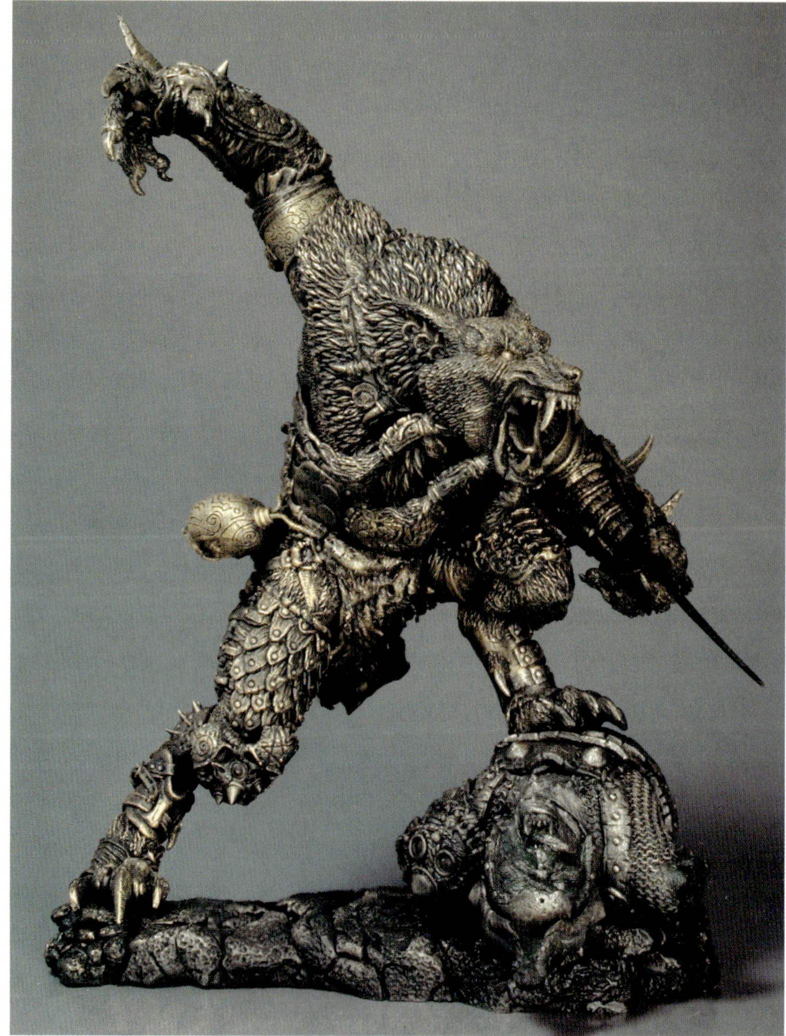
3

4

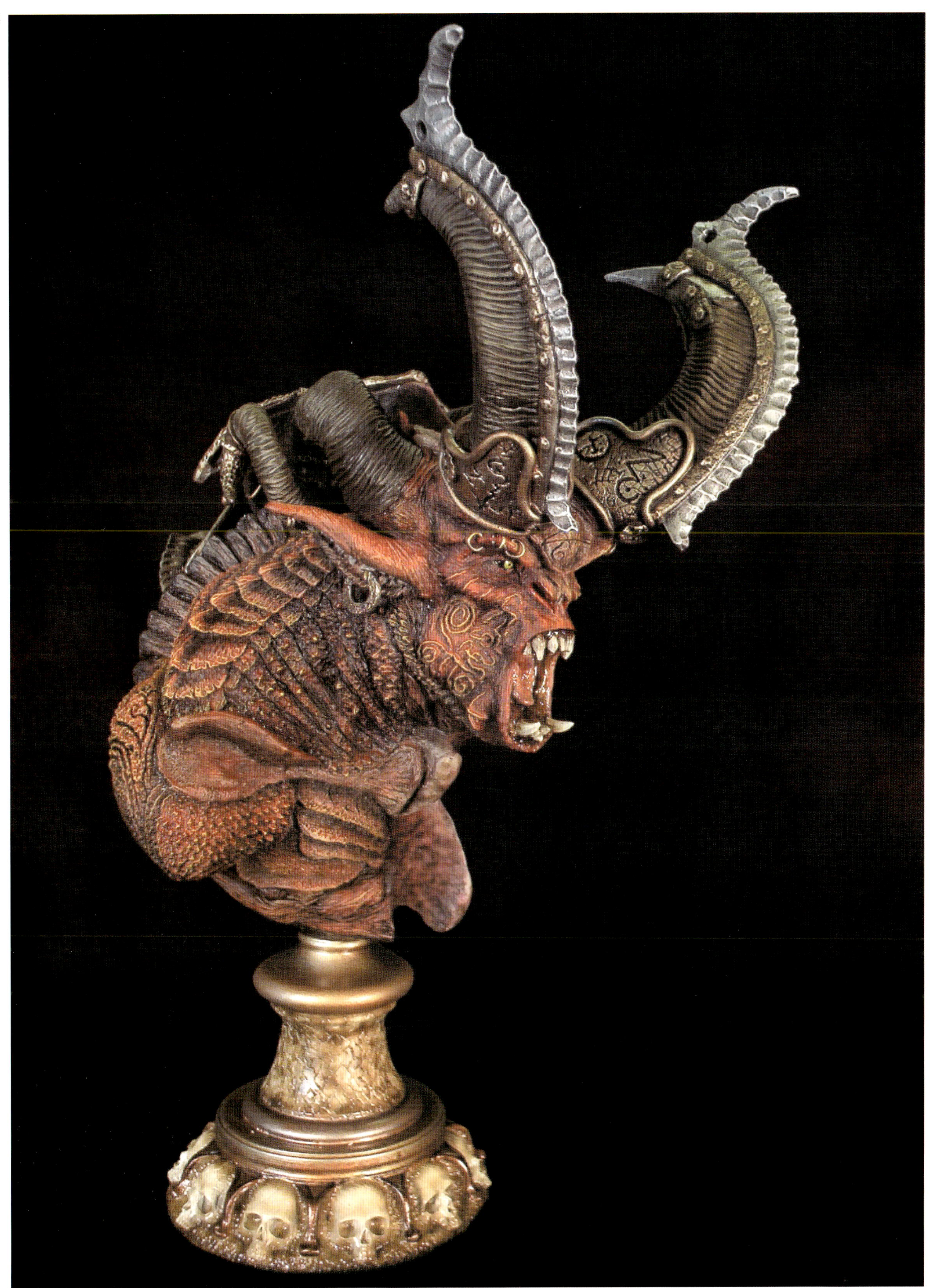

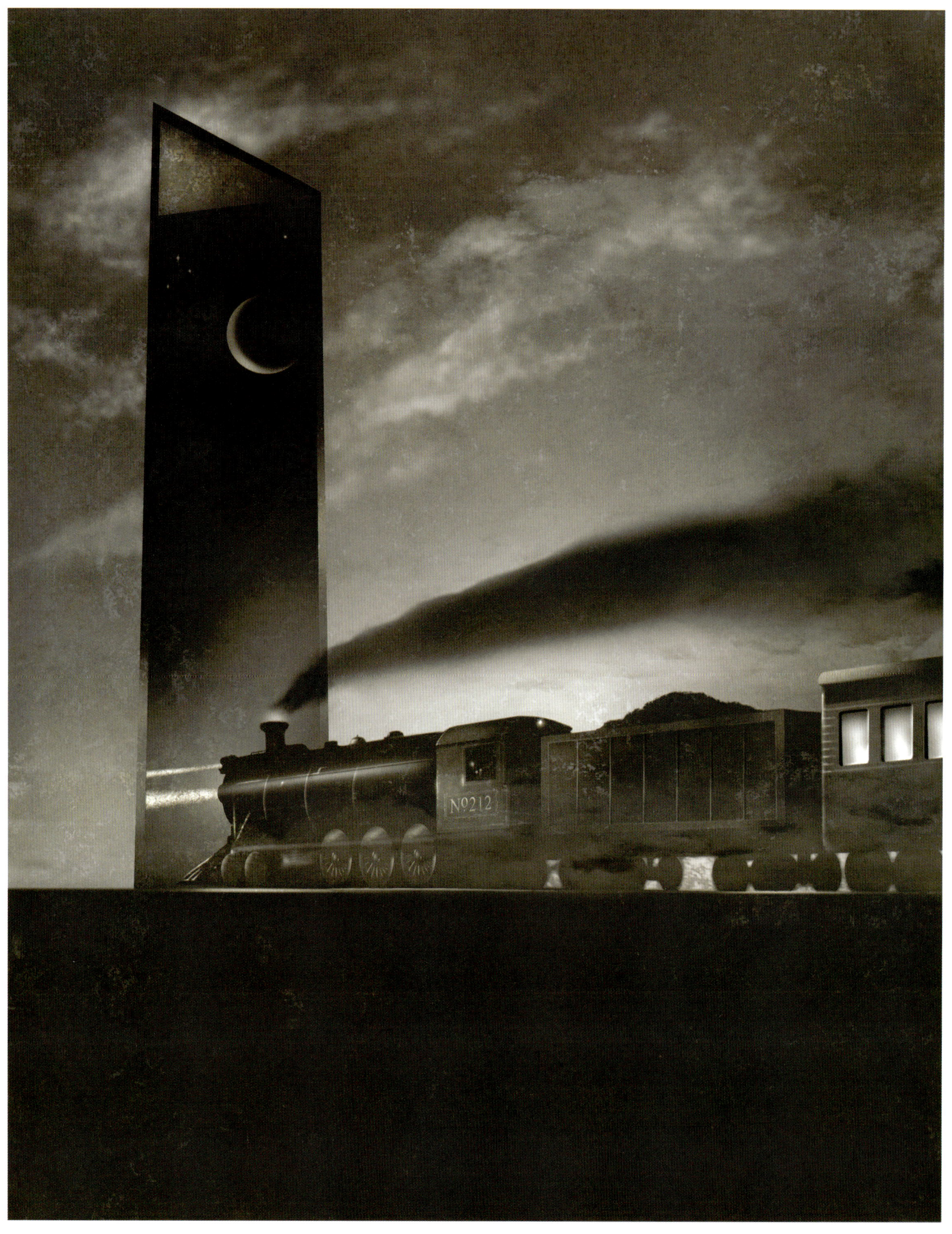

artist: **Michael Gibbs**

art director: Carl Gnam/Laura Cleveland *client:* Realms of Fantasy *title:* Blink *medium:* Digital *size:* 8 1/2"x11"

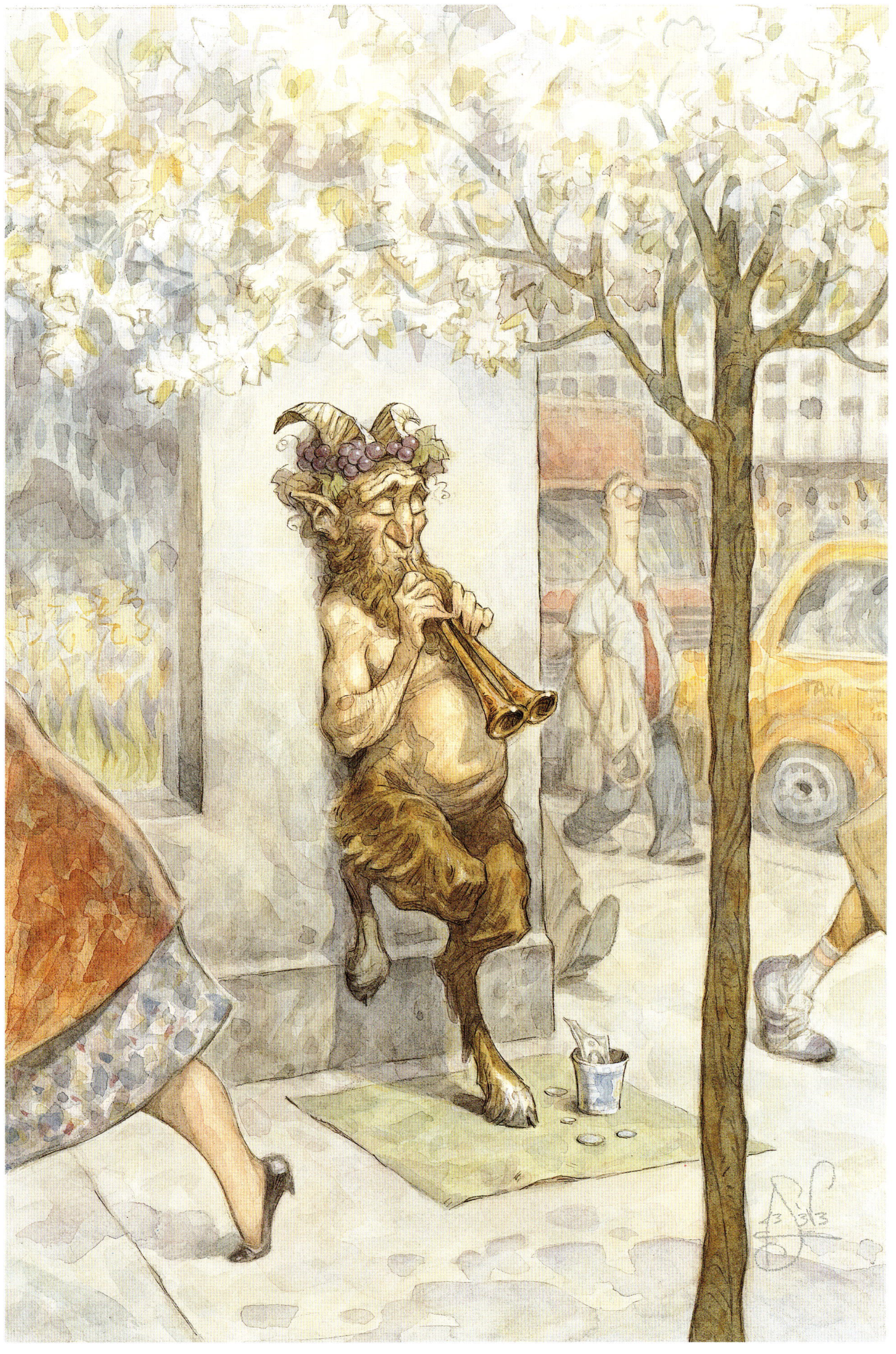

artist: **Peter de Sève**
art director: François Mouly *client:* The New Yorker *title:* Pan *medium:* Watercolor and ink

1
artist: **Todd Lockwood**
art director: Laura Cleveland
client: Realms of Fantasy
title: Not So Byzantine (Crossing Into the Empire)
medium: Digital
size: 15″x15″

2
artist: **Stephen Johnson**
art director: Laura Cleveland
client: Realms of Fantasy
title: A Hunter's Ode to His Bait
medium: Pastel
size: 24″x30″

3
artist: **Douglas Klauba**
art director: Tom Hook
client: Breakaway Magazine
title: Ghost Pirates
medium: Acrylics
size: 15″x20″

4
artist: **Marc Gabbana**
title: Spica–The Divine Draconic Spark
medium: Digital

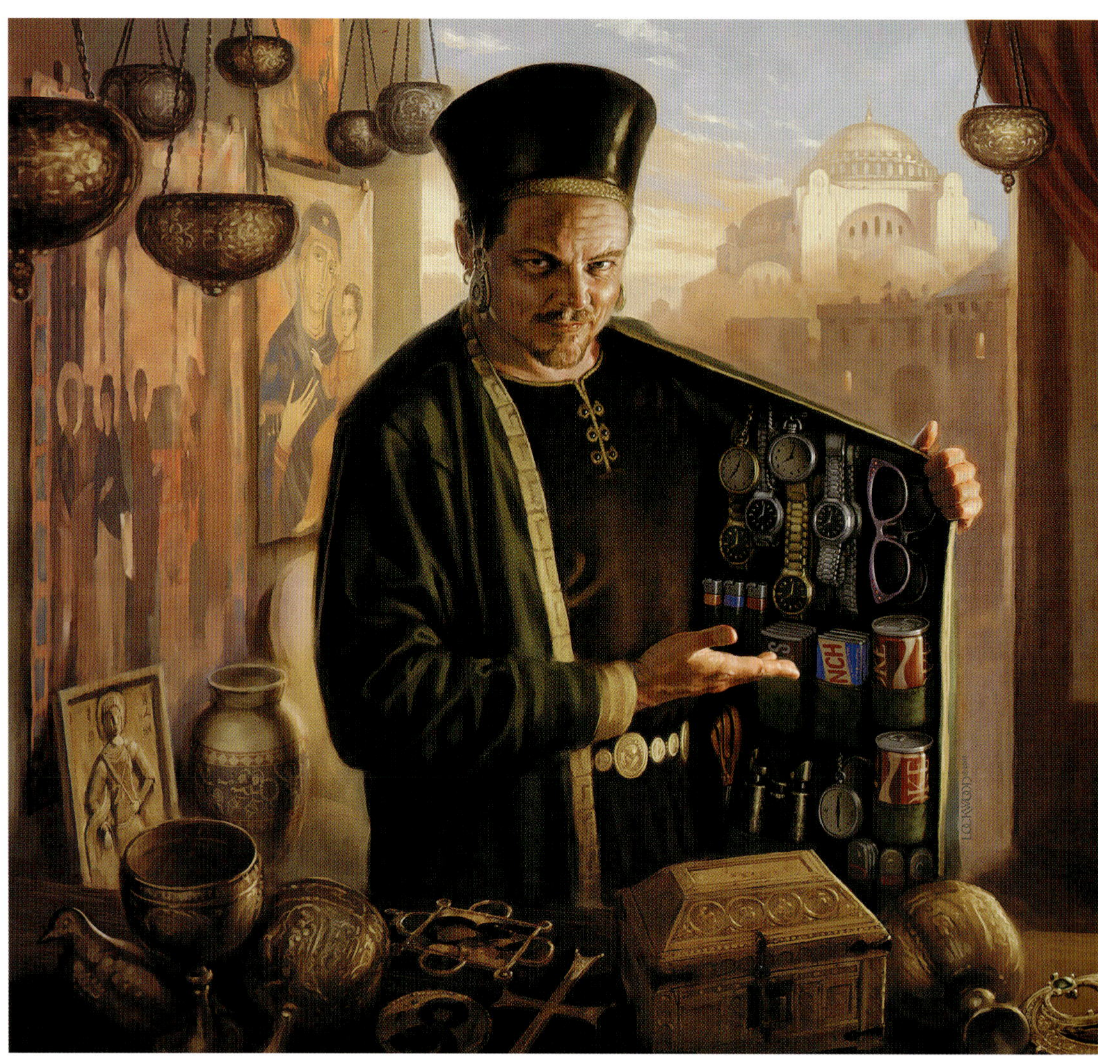

1

2

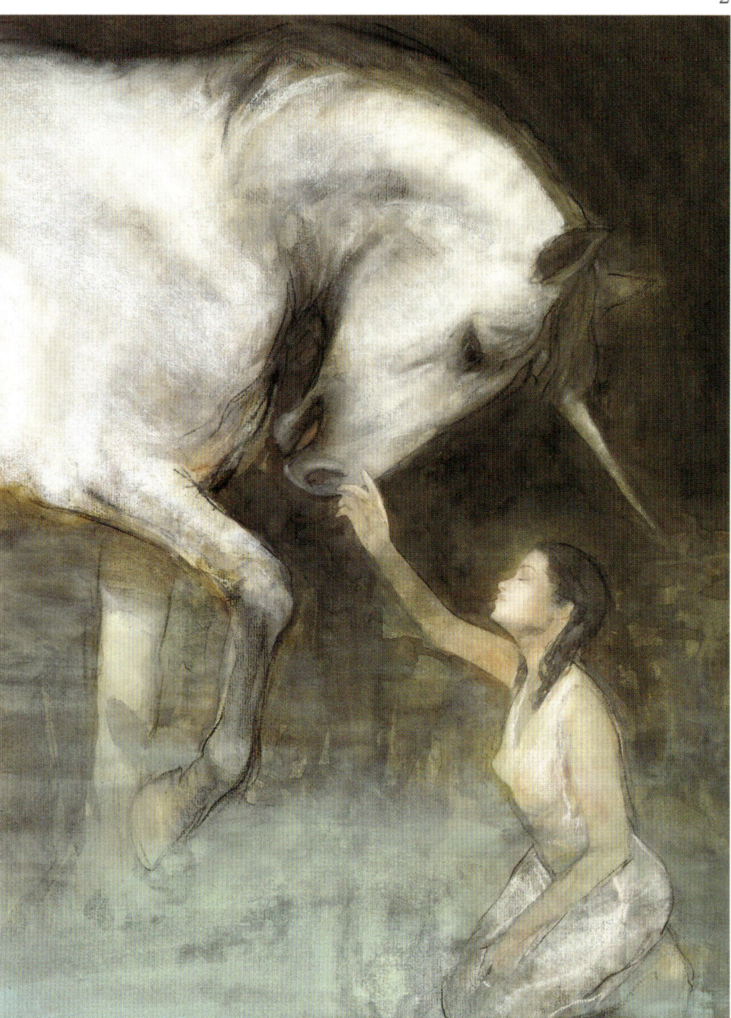

3

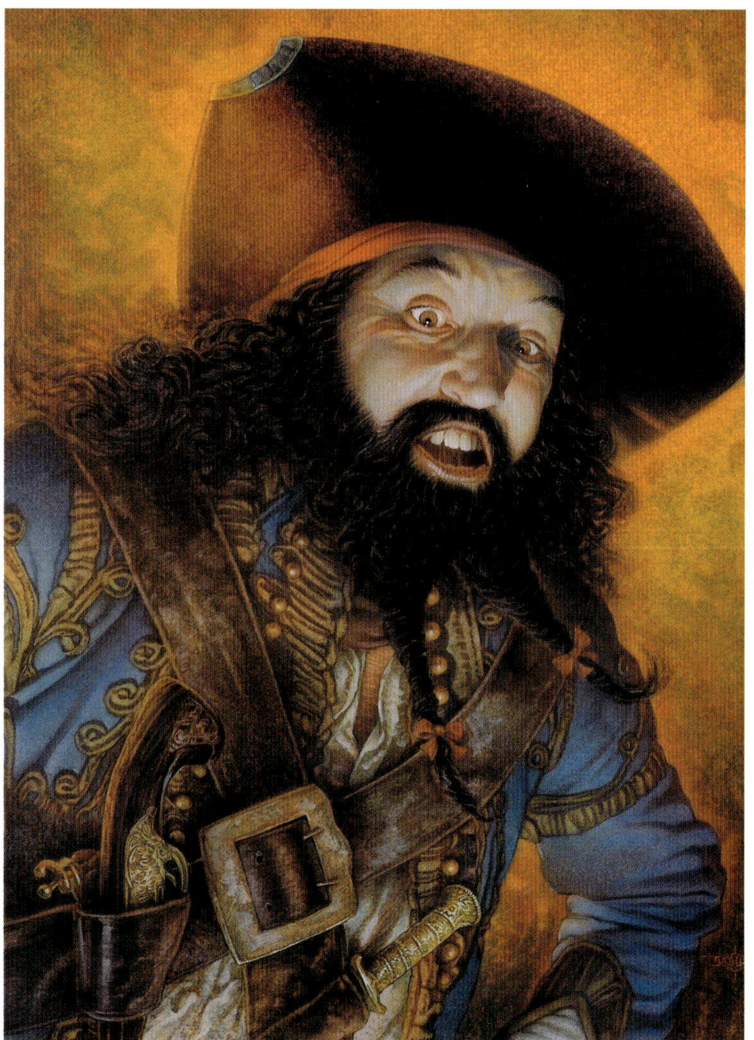

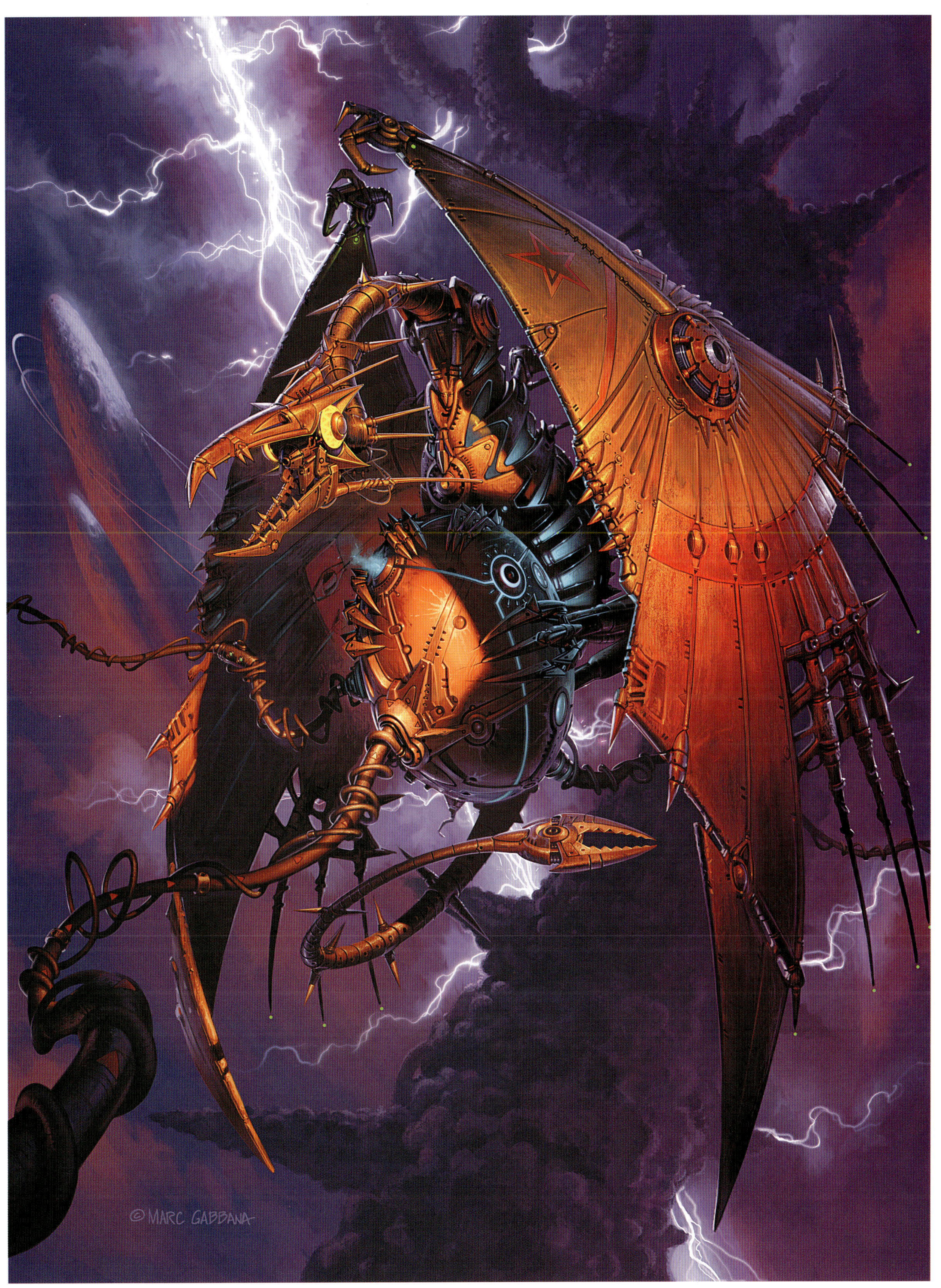
©MARC GABBANA

Editorial

1
artist: **Katherine Jones**
client: Harlequin
title: Harlequin
medium: Oils
size: $8^{1}/_{2}$″x12″

2
artist: **Howard Lyon**
art director: Lisa Chido
client: Paizo Publishing
title: Brotherhood of the Burning Heart
medium: Digital

3
artist: **Sandrine Gestin**
client: Faiseurs Editions
title: Galadriel
medium: Oils on canvas
size: $23^{1}/_{2}$″x32″

4
artist: **Jim Burns**
art director: Howard Jurofsky
designer: Jim Burns
client: Heavy Metal
title: Threlxepia's Little Sister
medium: Acrylics
size: 24″x36″

1

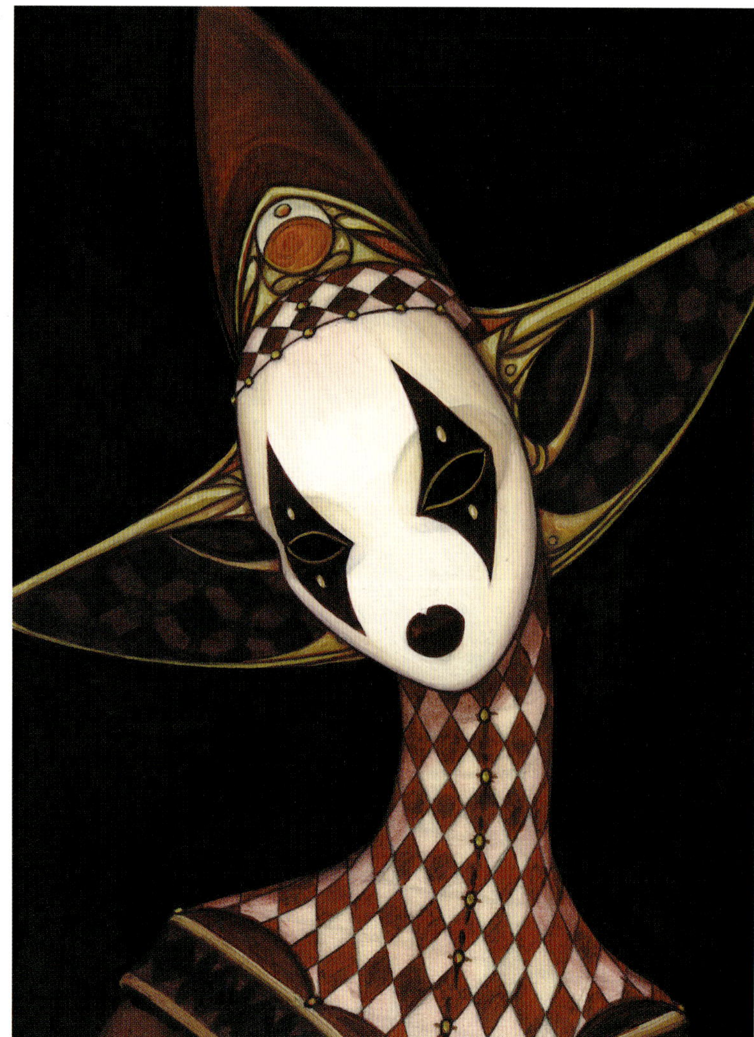

2

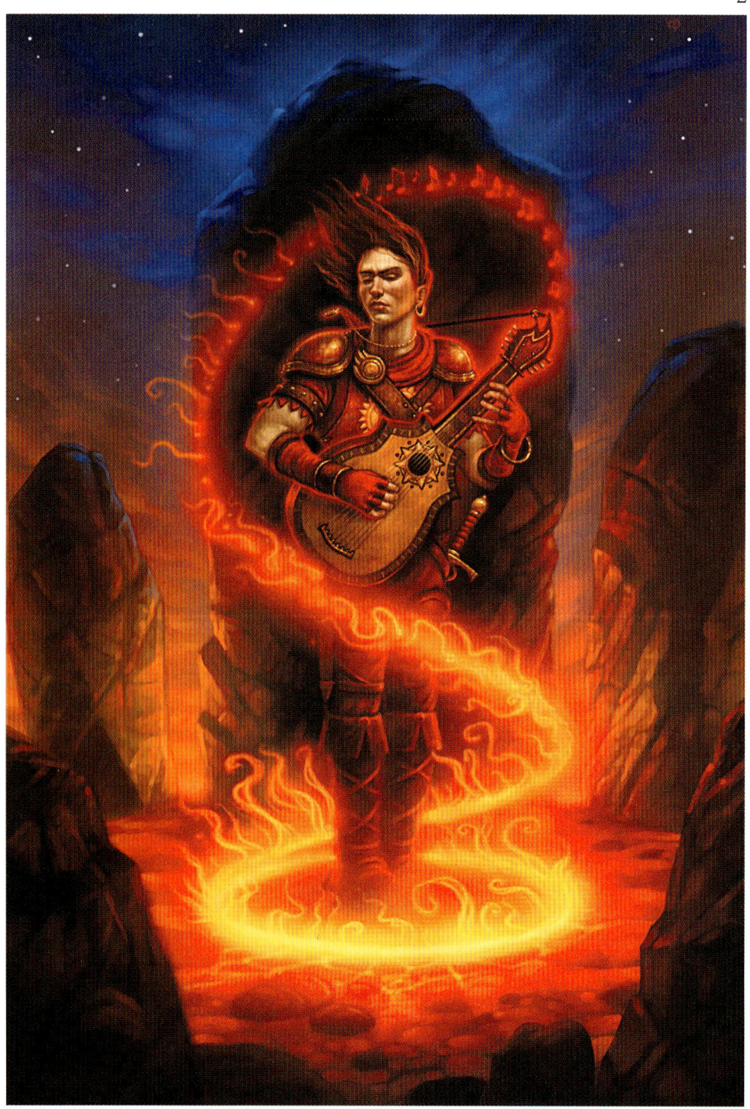

3

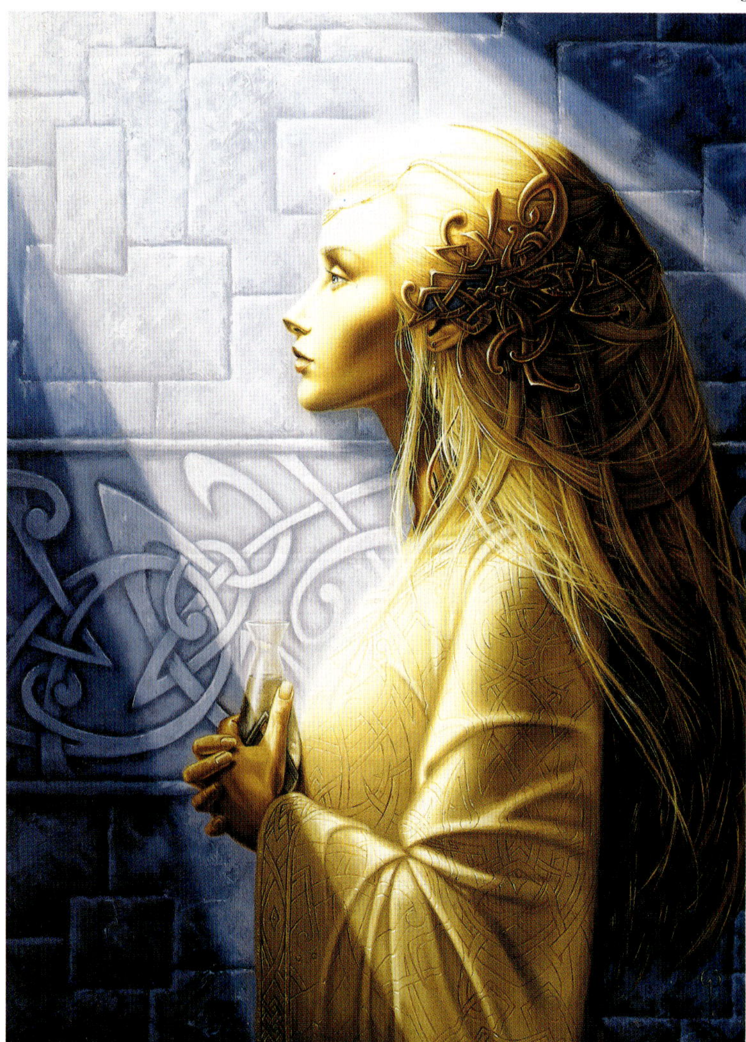

4

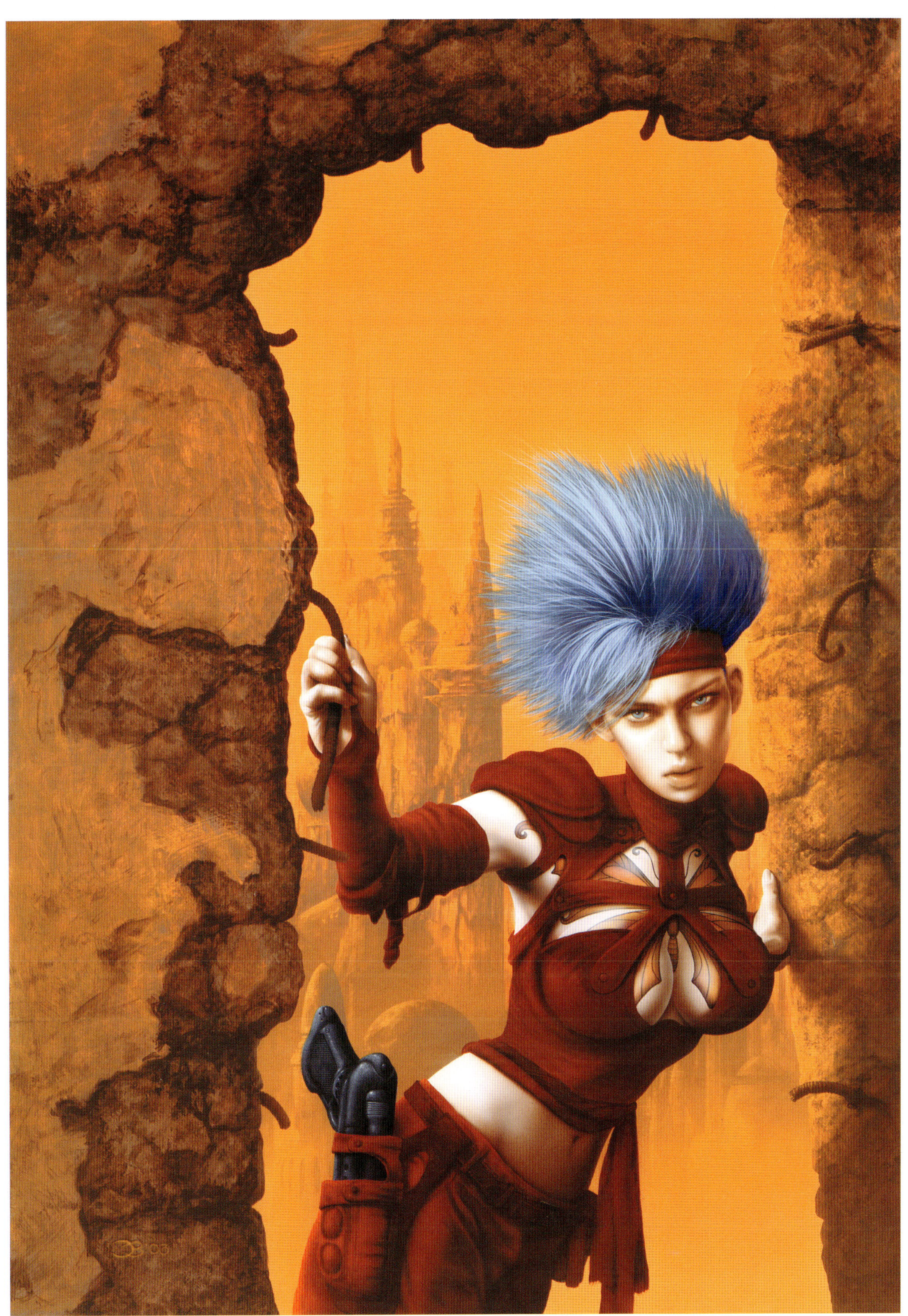

Editorial

1
artist: **Lori Koefoed**
art director: Laura Cleveland
client: Realms of Fantasy
title: The Seamstress
medium: Acrylics/digital
size: 8″x11″

2
artist: **Stephan "Cricket" Martiniere**
client: Phobos
title: Hitting the Skids in Pixeltown
medium: Mixed/digital

3
artist: **Larry Price**
art director: Arnie Fenner
client: Locus
title: Spring
medium: Digital
size: 7 1/2″x9″

4
artist: **Maurizo Manzieri**
art director: Gordon Van Gelder
client: The Magazine of Fantasy & Science Fiction
title: Pictures From an Expedition
medium: Digital

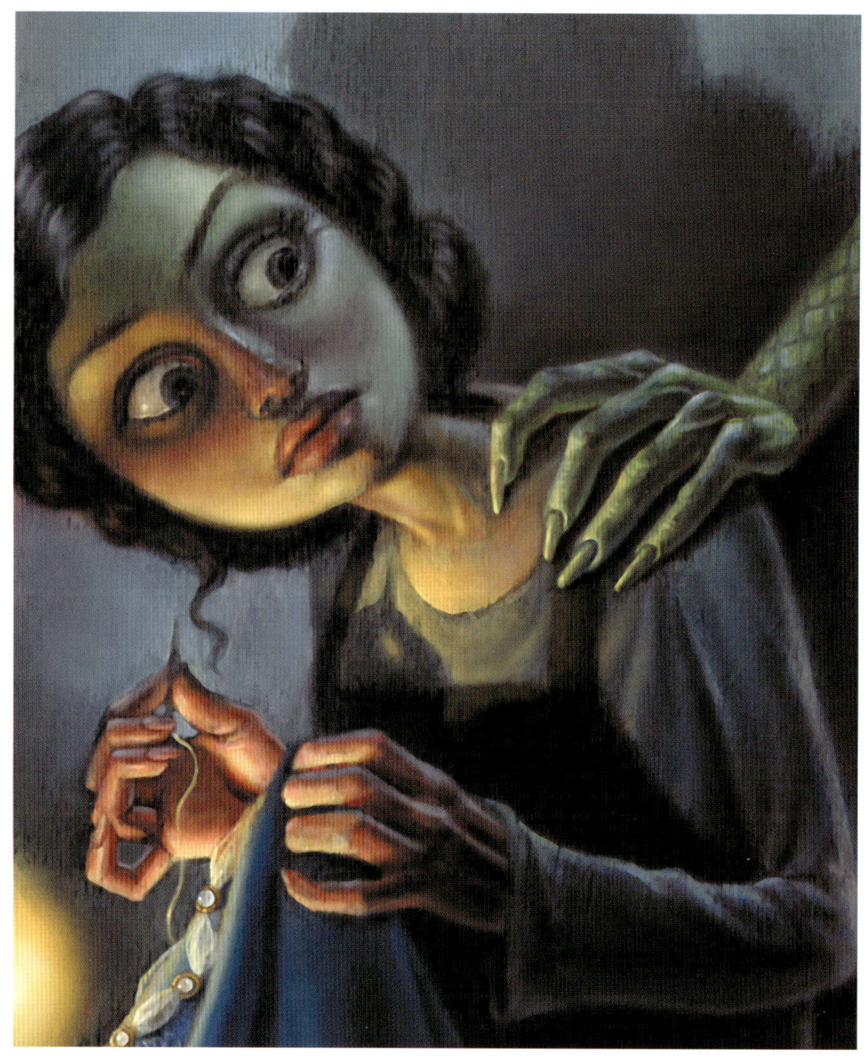

1

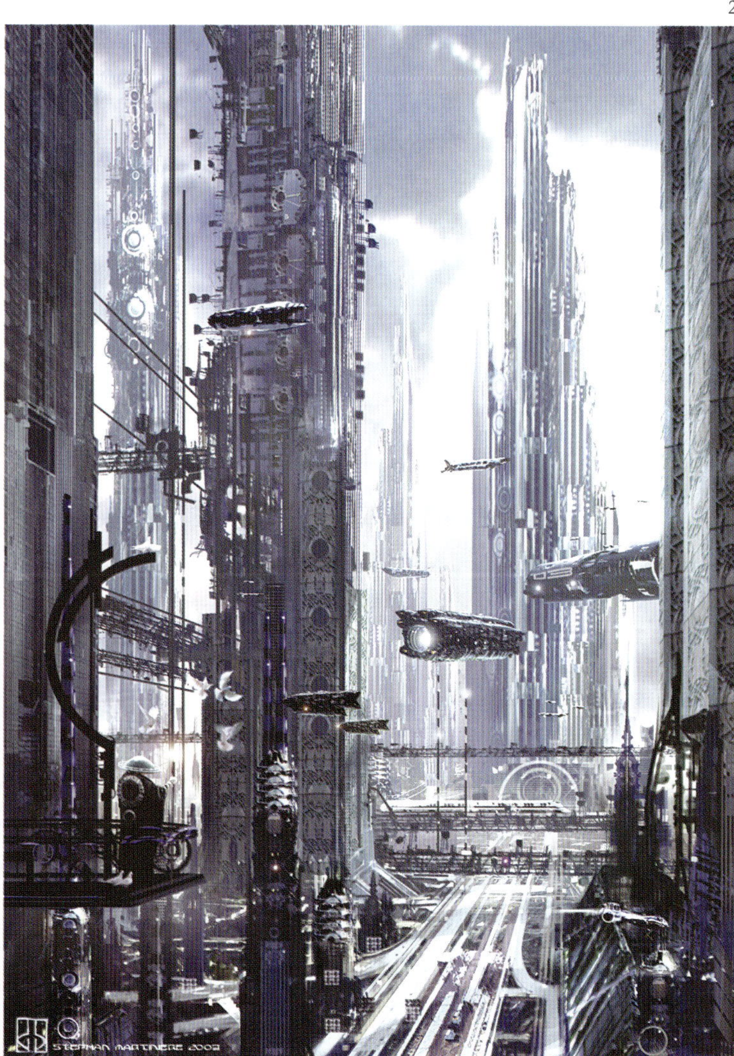

2

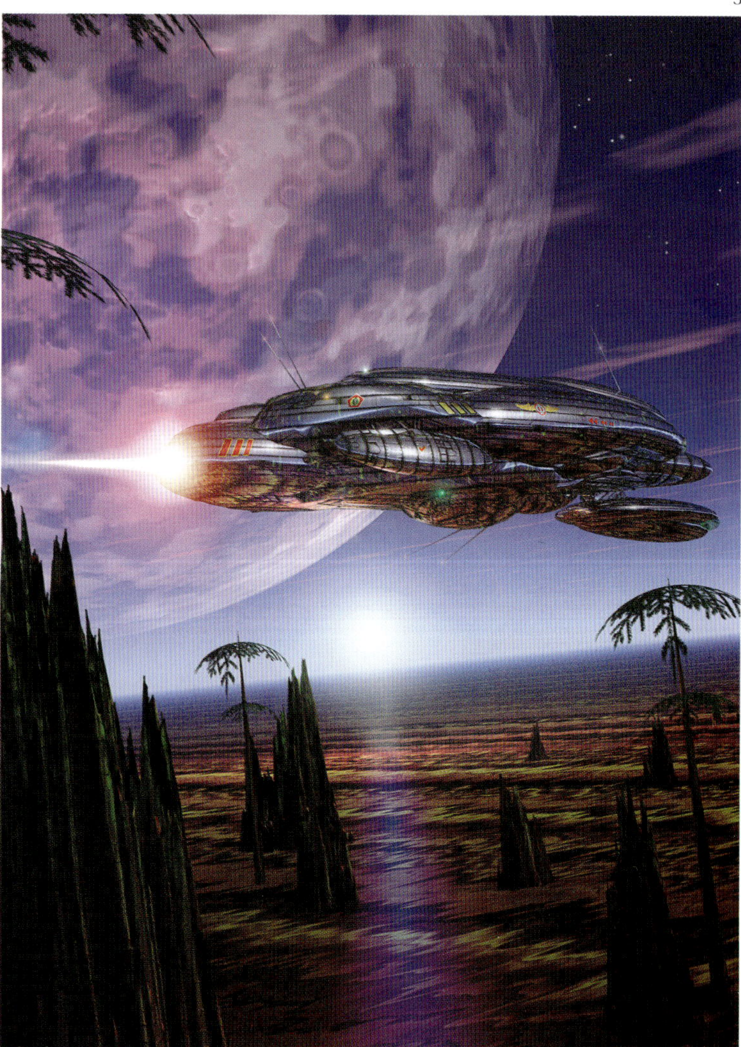

3

4

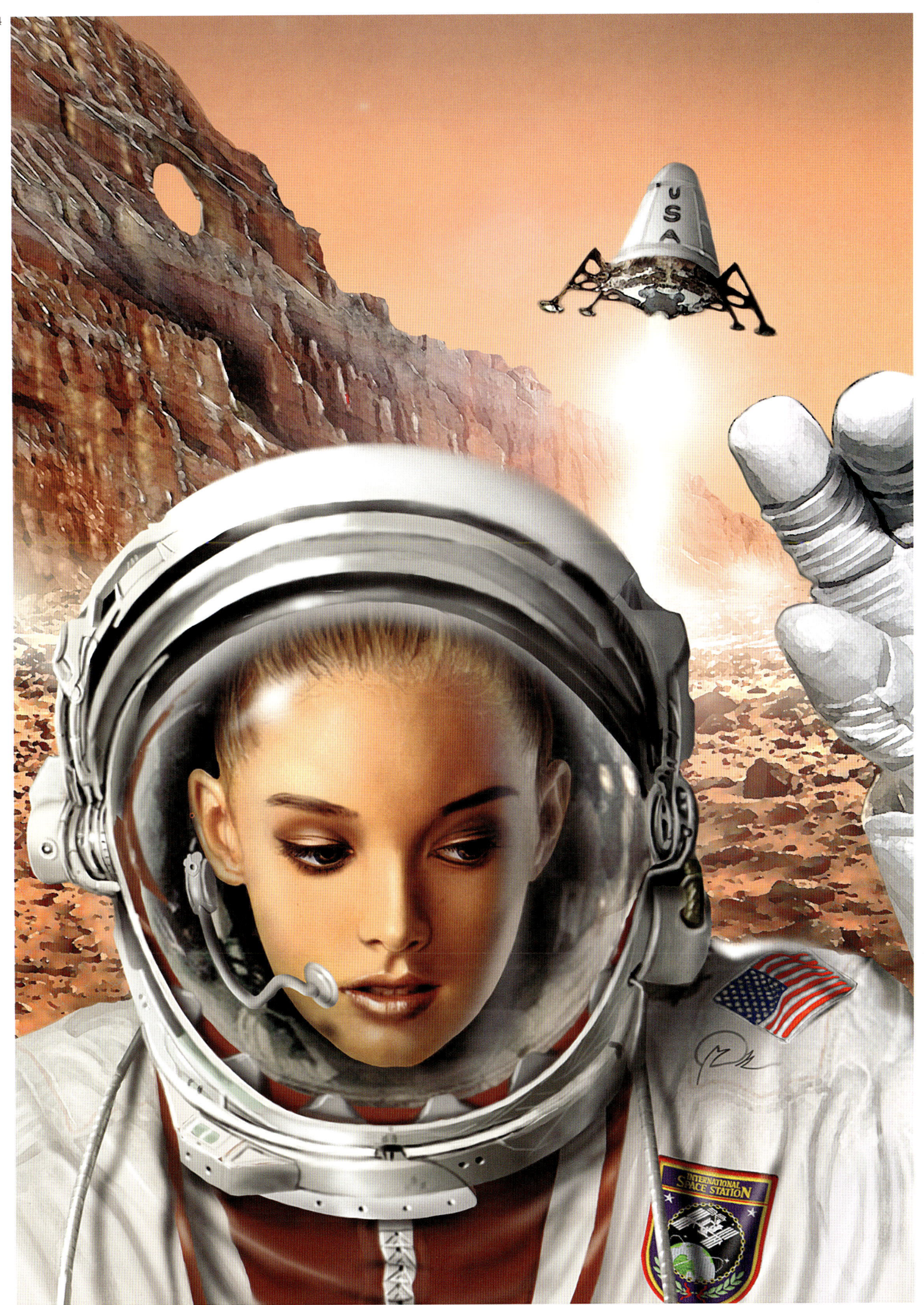

1
artist: **Yoshihito Tomobe**
client: Vibes Magazine
title: Black & White
medium: Acrylics
size: 9″x12″

2
artist: **Greg Horn**
client: Wizard
title: Super Hero Movie Opener
medium: Digital

3
artist: **Brian Horton**
art director: Laura Cleveland
client: Realms of Fantasy
title: Still Man
medium: Digital
size: 11″x10″

4
artist: **William Stout**
art director: Ron McCutchan
client: Cricket Magazine
title: Love's Labors Lost
medium: Mixed
size: 32″x20″

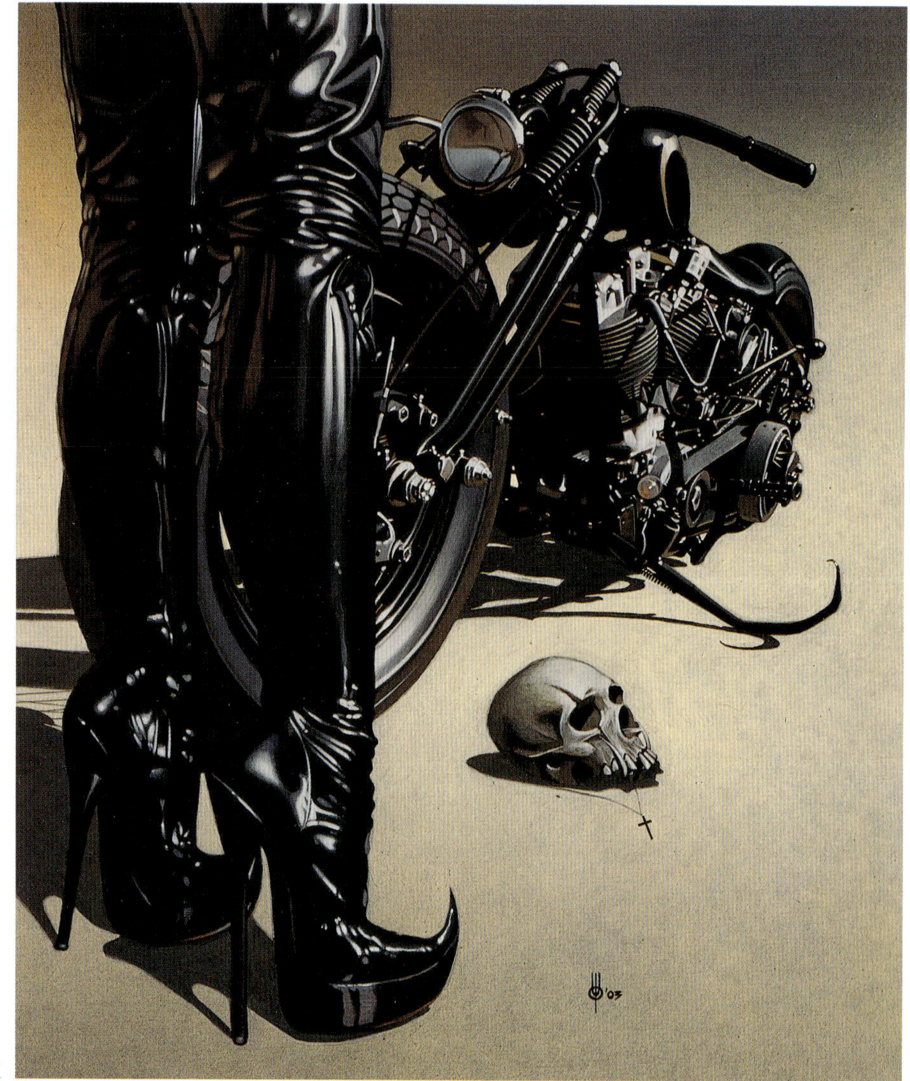
1

2
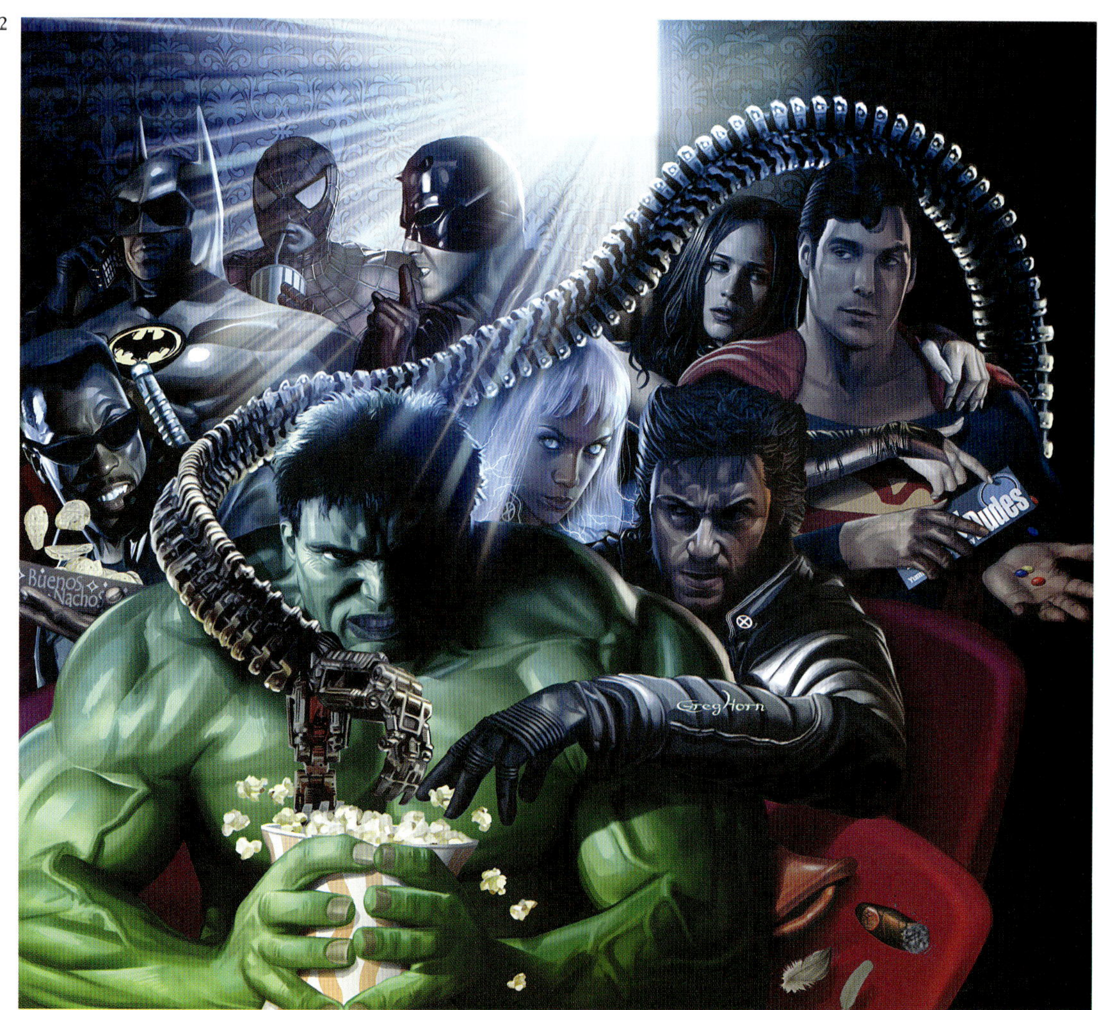

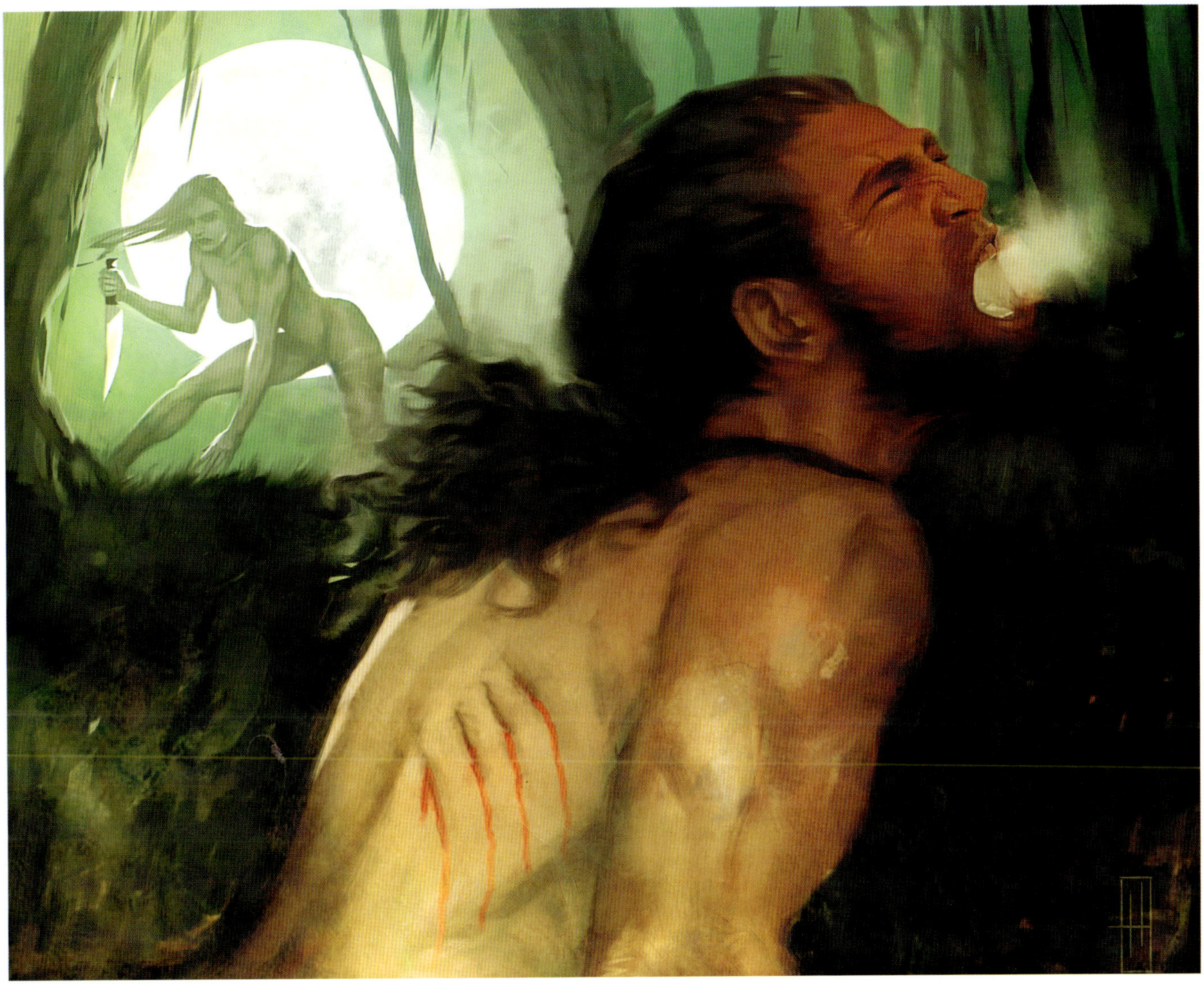

3

4

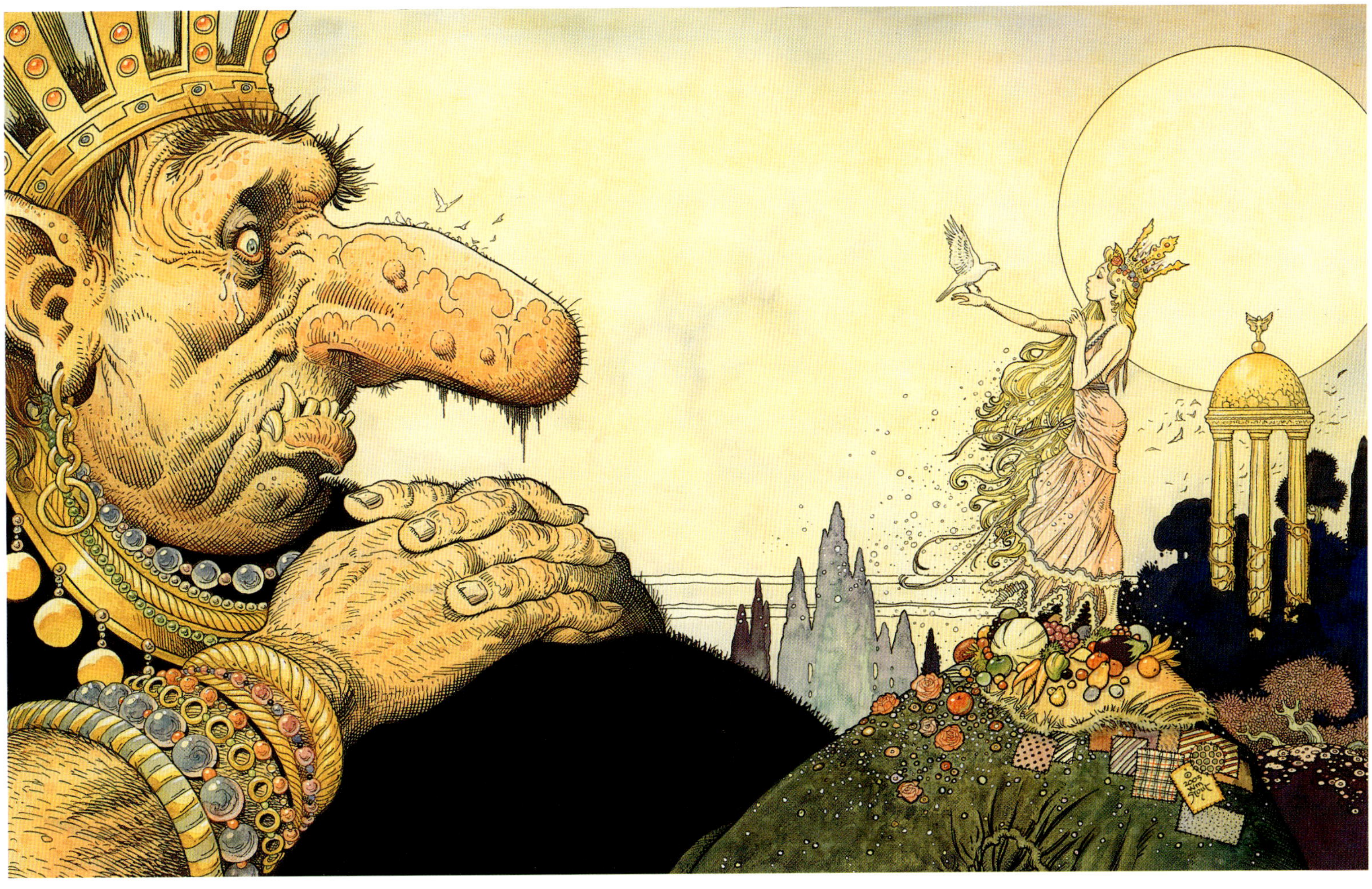

1
artist: **James Gurney**
art director: Michael Mrak
client: Discover
title: Dinosaur Family Values
medium: Oils
size: 12″x14″

2
artist: **Eric Fortune**
art director: Laura Cleveland
client: Realms of Fantasy
title: Divided by Time
medium: Acrylics
size: 12″x16″

3
artist: **Bryn Barnard**
art director: Tony Jacobson
client: Spider Magazine
title: Ozymandius
medium: Oils on board
size: 18″x24″

4
artist: **Richard Bernal**
art director: Tony Jacobson
client: Spider Magazine
title: Joy To The World
medium: Oils
size: 12″x15″

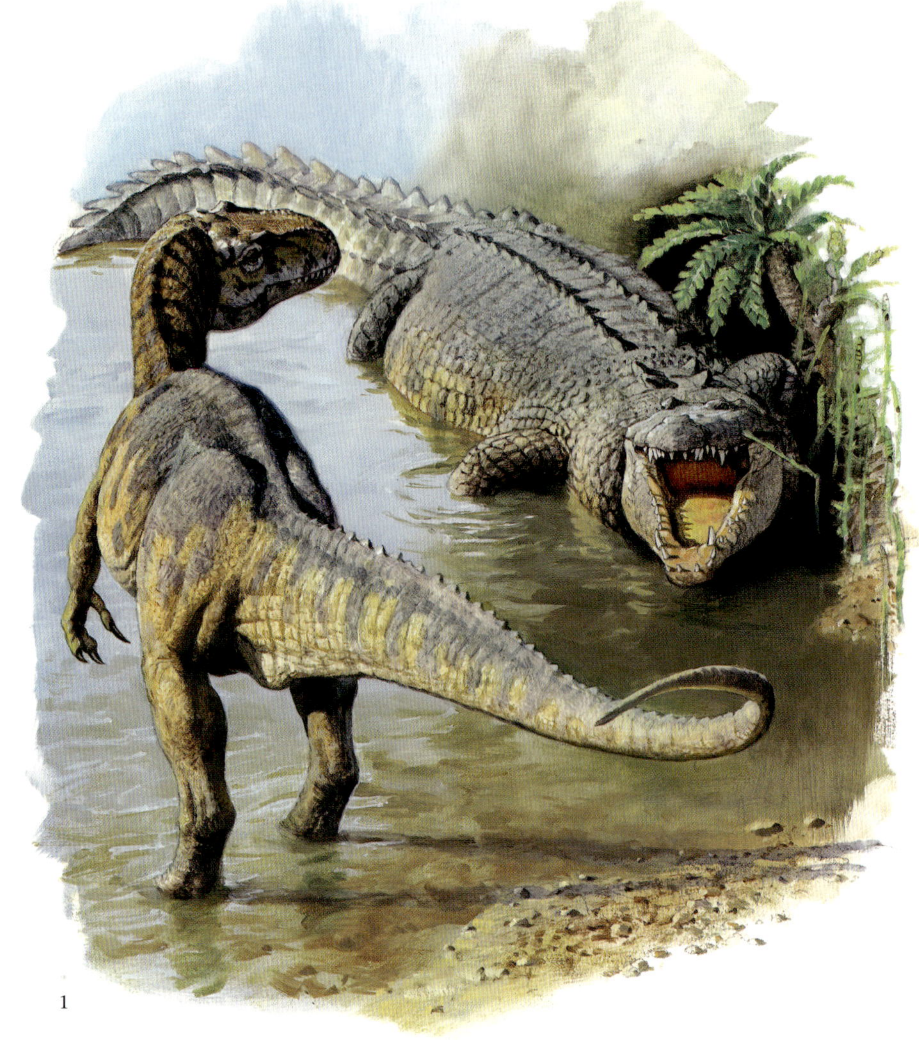

1

2

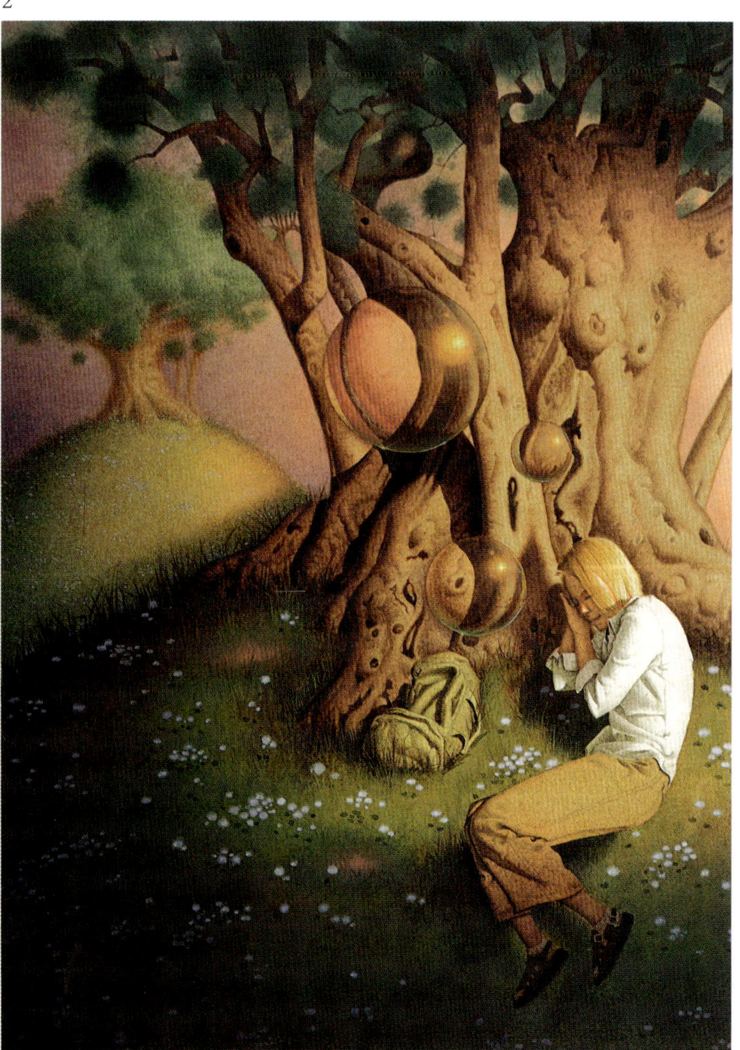

3

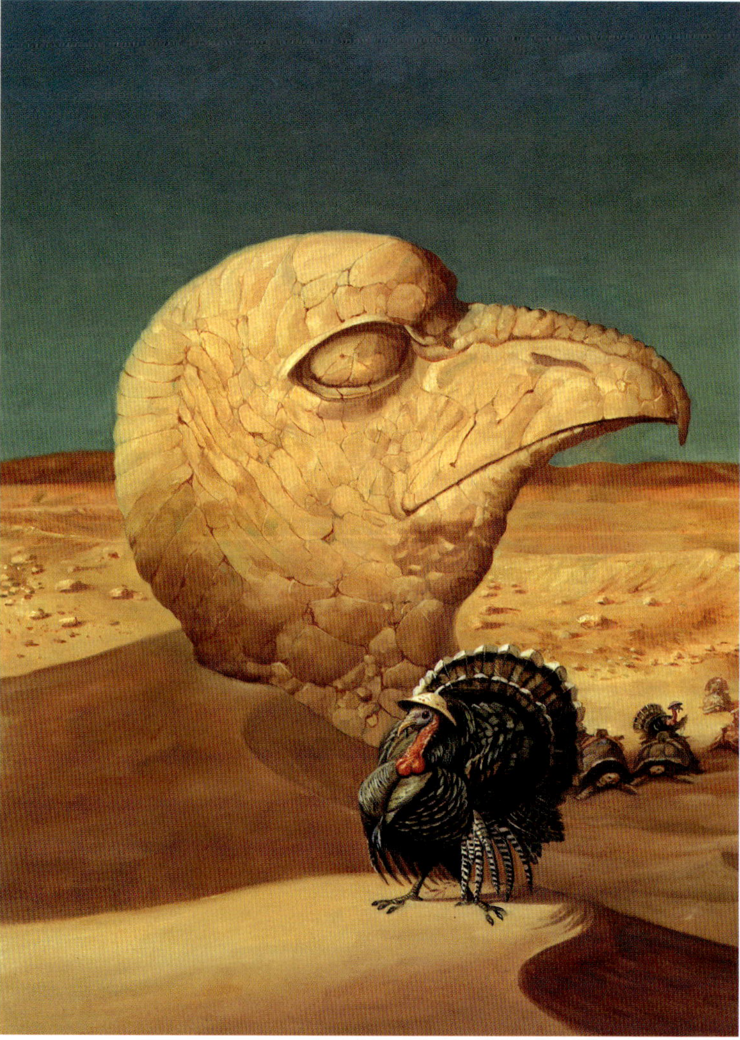

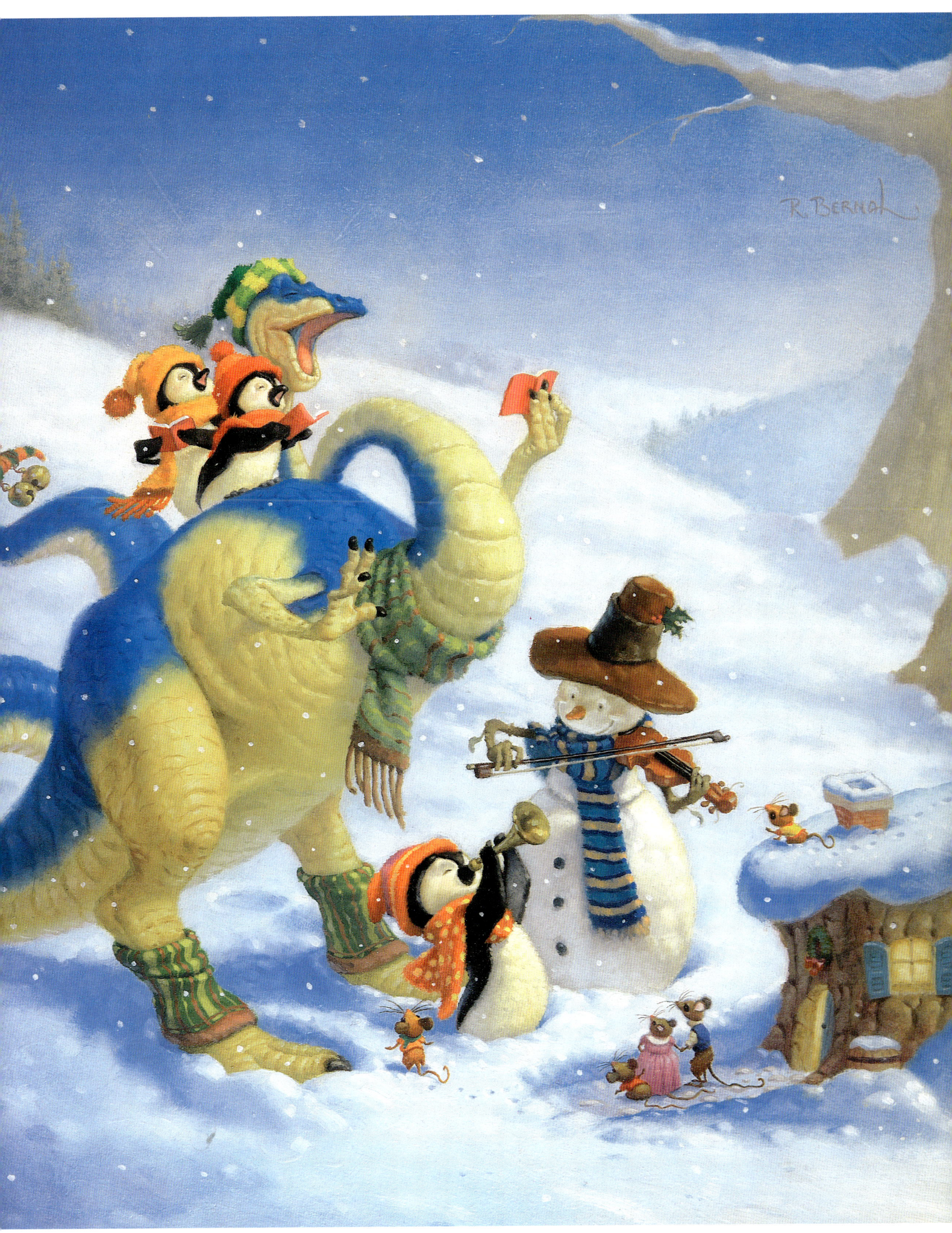

4

1
artist: **William Stout**
art director: Darrie Whitney
designer: William Stout
client: Fantagraphics Books
title: William Stout: A Visual History
medium: Mixed
size: 18″x18″

2
artist: **Kent Williams**
art director: Tom Staebler
client: Playboy
title: Tuba City
medium: Mixed
size: 24″x18″

3
artist: **David Ho**
client: Ezonils
title: Letting Go
medium: Digital
size: 8 1/2″x11″

4
artist: **Michael Gibbs**
art director: Laura Cleveland
client: Realms of Fantasy
title: The Man Who Did Nothing
medium: Digital
size: 8 1/2″x11″

5
artist: **Kent Williams**
art director: Tom Staebler
client: Playboy
title: Assignment in Havana
medium: Mixed
size: 24″x18″

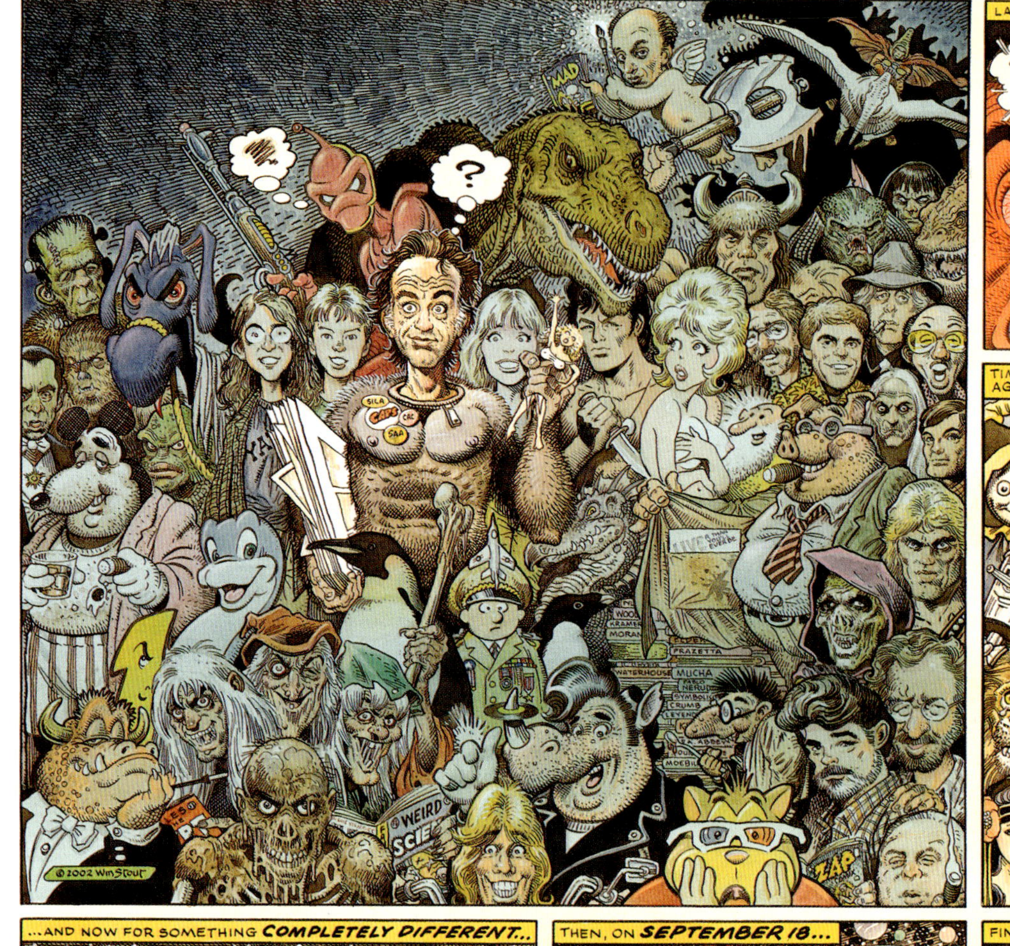

1

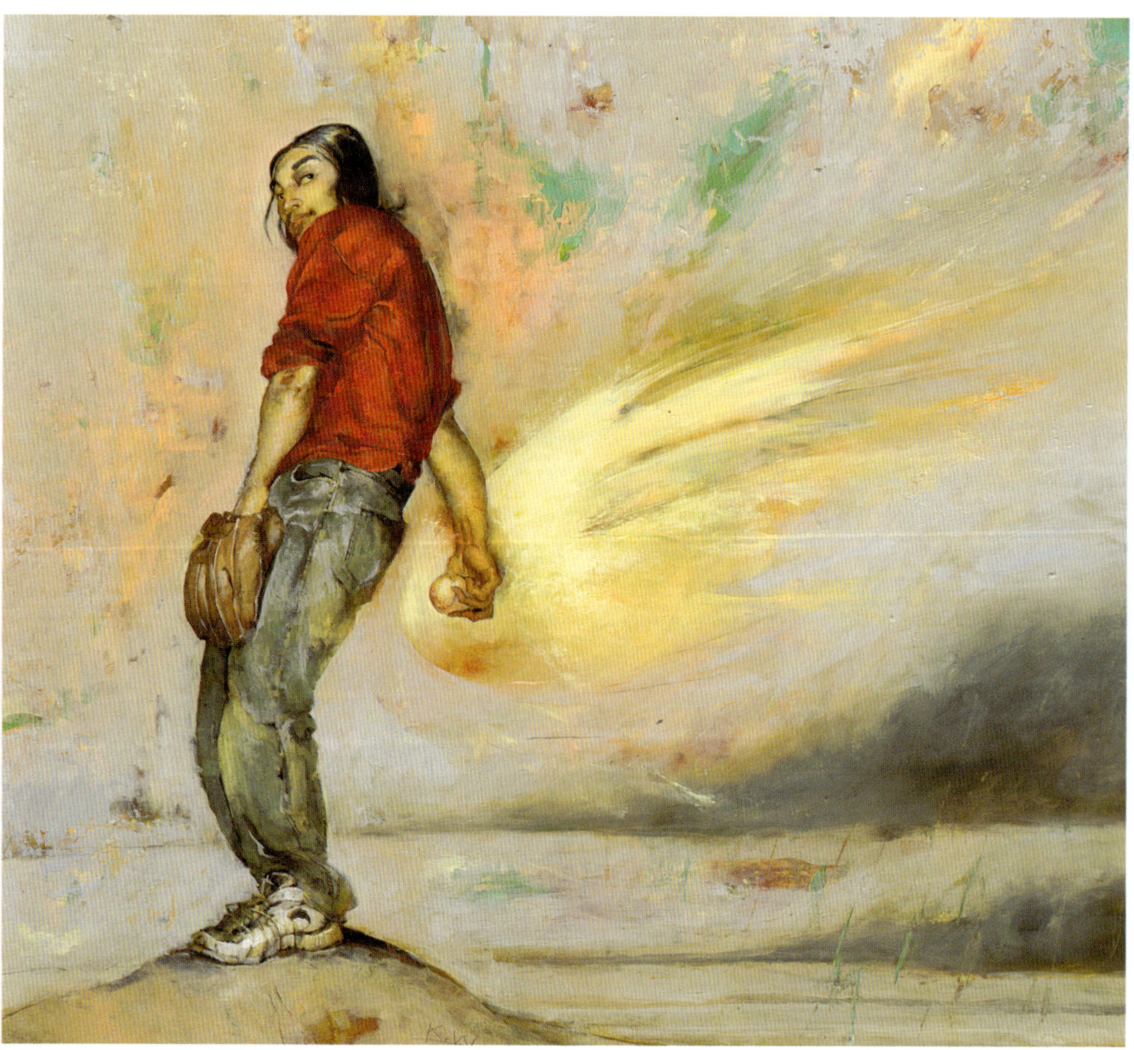

2

3

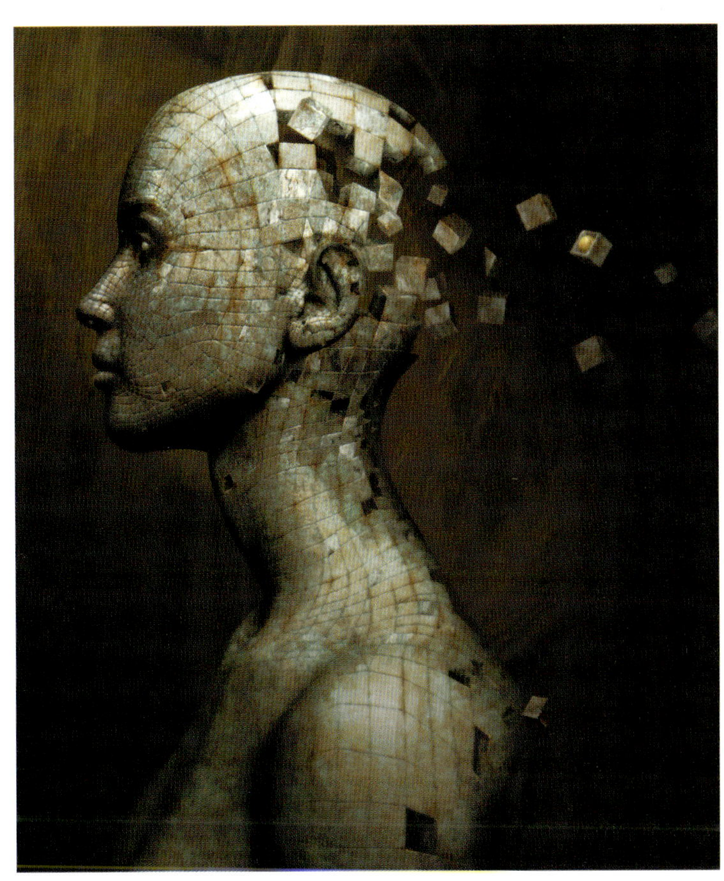

4

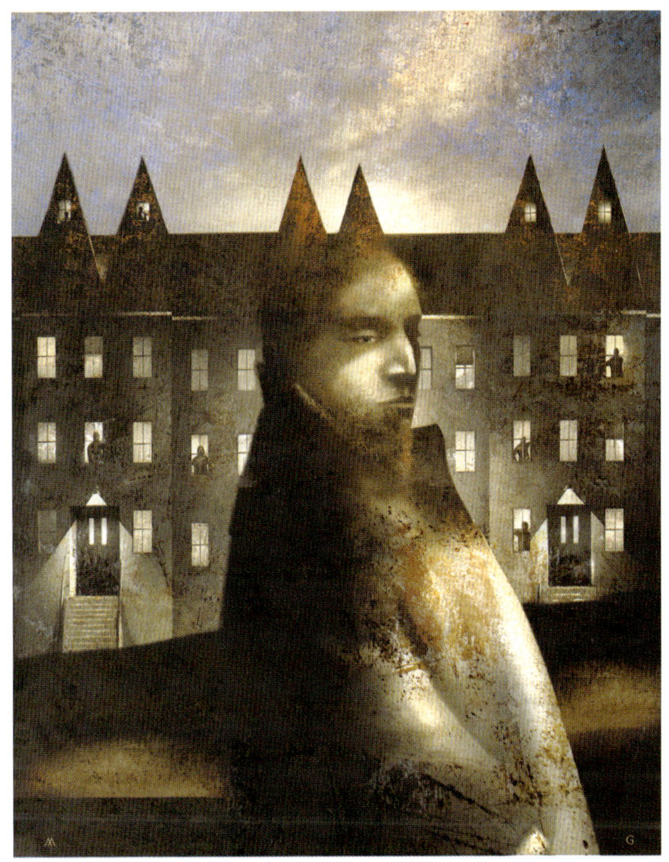

5

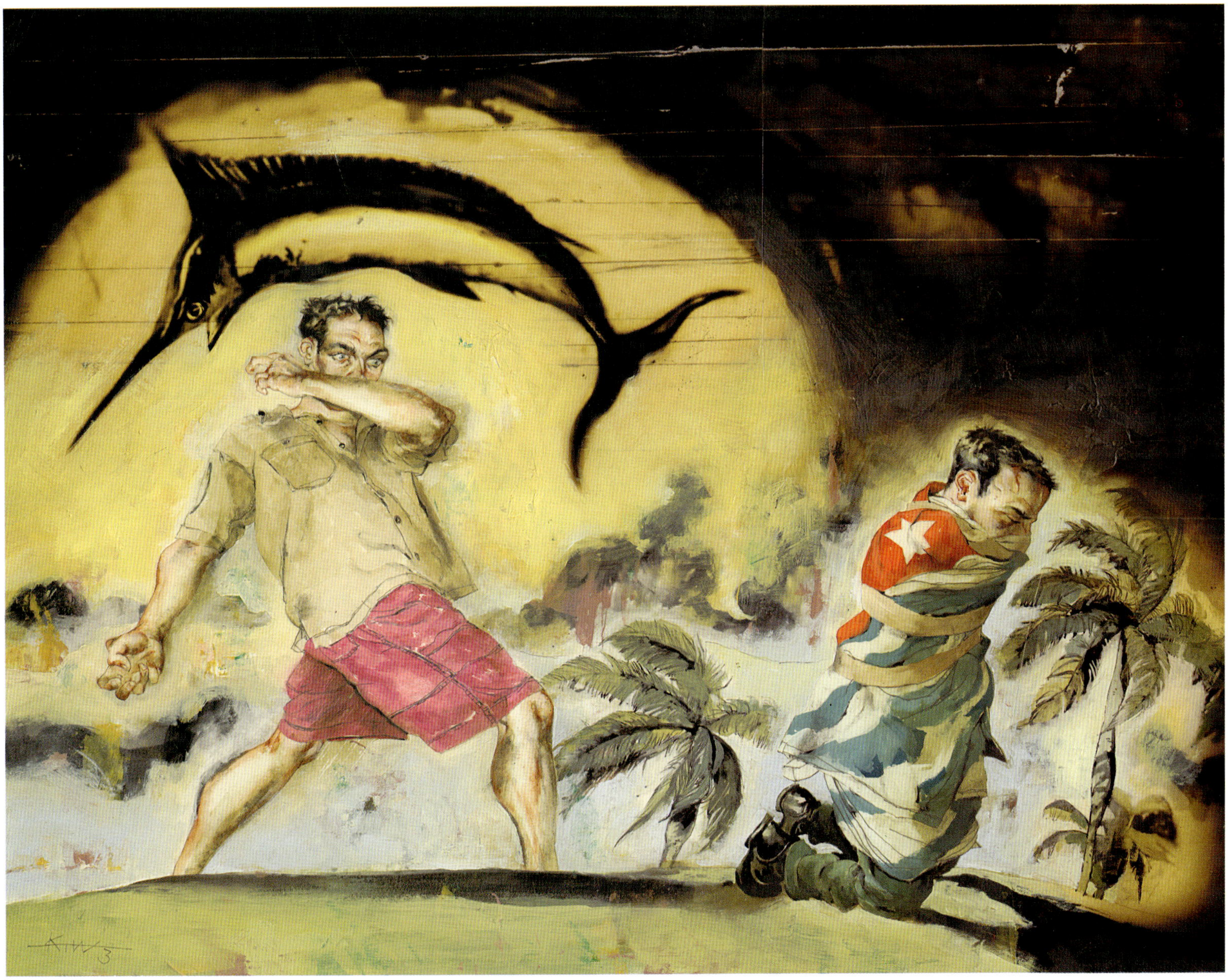

1
artist: **Griesbach/Martucci**
art director: Minh Unong
designer: Ted Keller
client: The Village Voice
title: Father of the Year
medium: Pils on board
size: 11″x14″

2
artist: **John Picacio**
art director: Mark Mahorsky
client: Texas Parks & Wildlife
title: A Texas Childhood
medium: Mixed/digital
size: 16 3/4″x10 7/8″

3
artist: **Patrick Arrasmith**
art director: Laura Cleveland
client: Realms of Fantasy
title: Runesmith
medium: Scratchboard/digital
size: 8″x11″

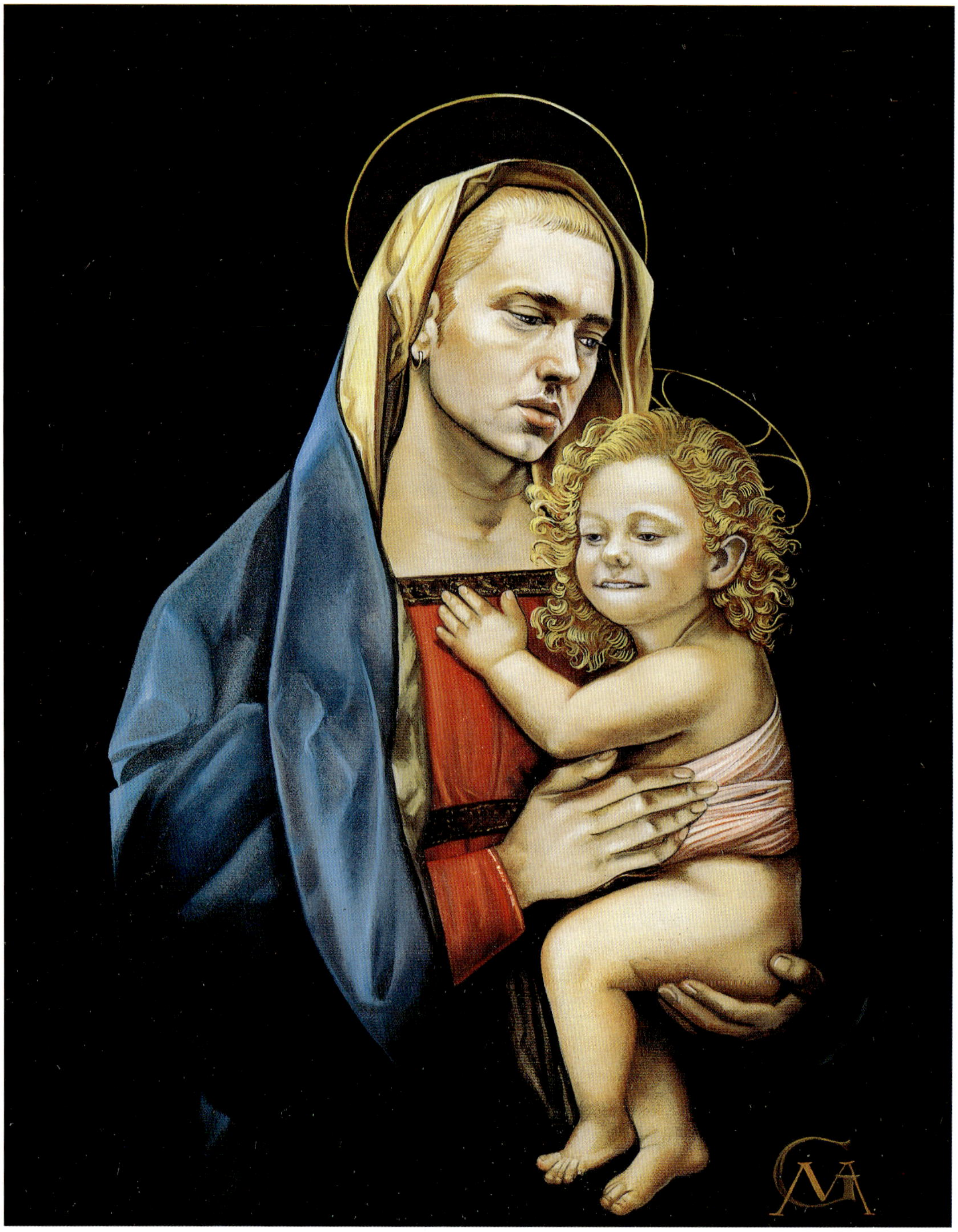

1

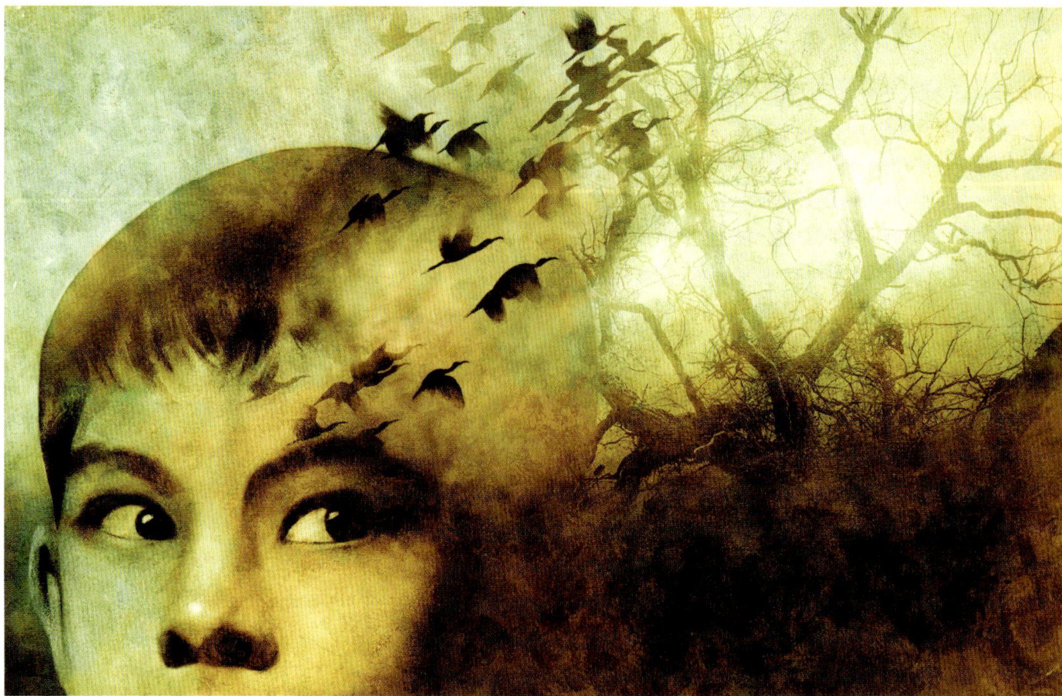

2

3

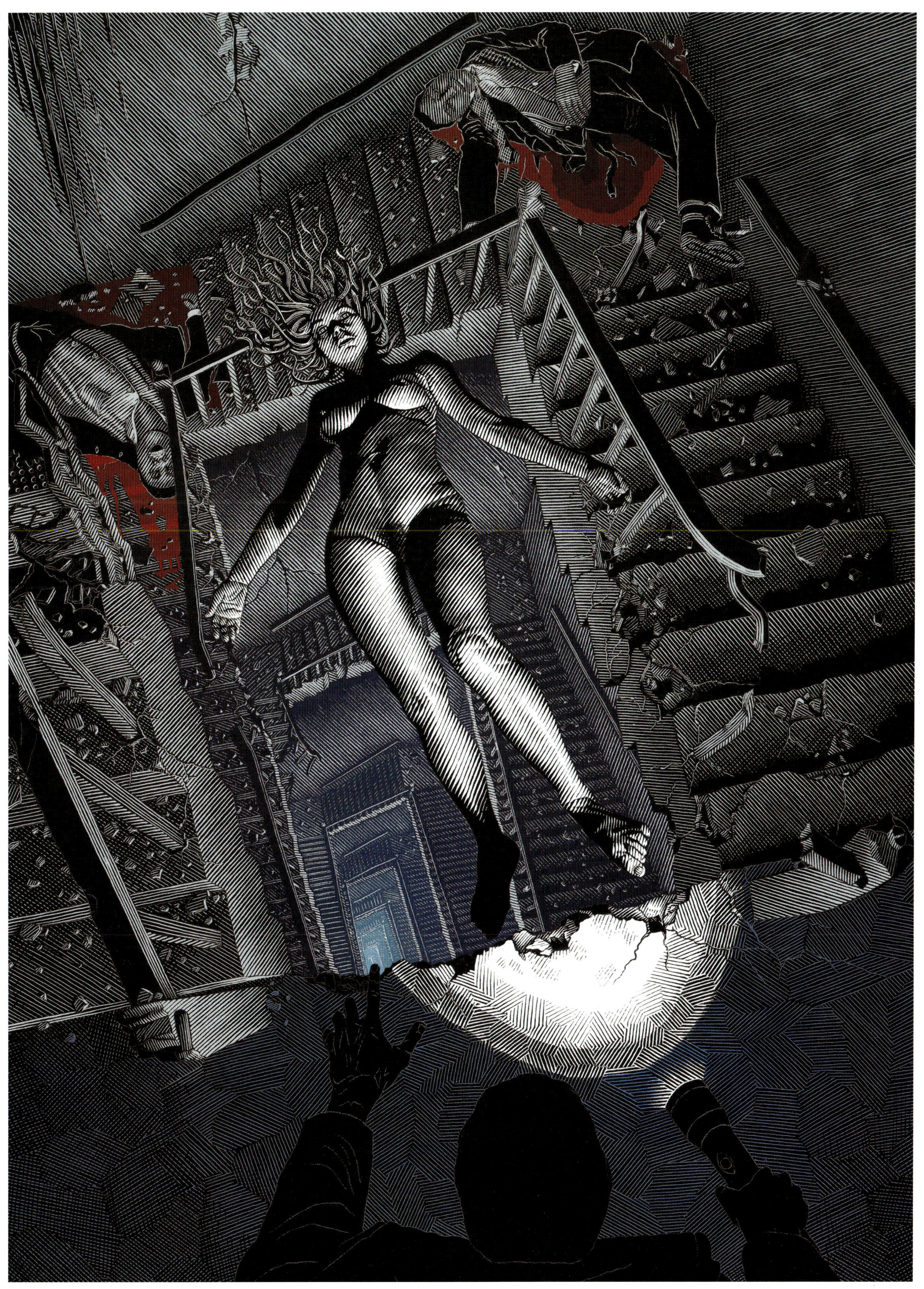

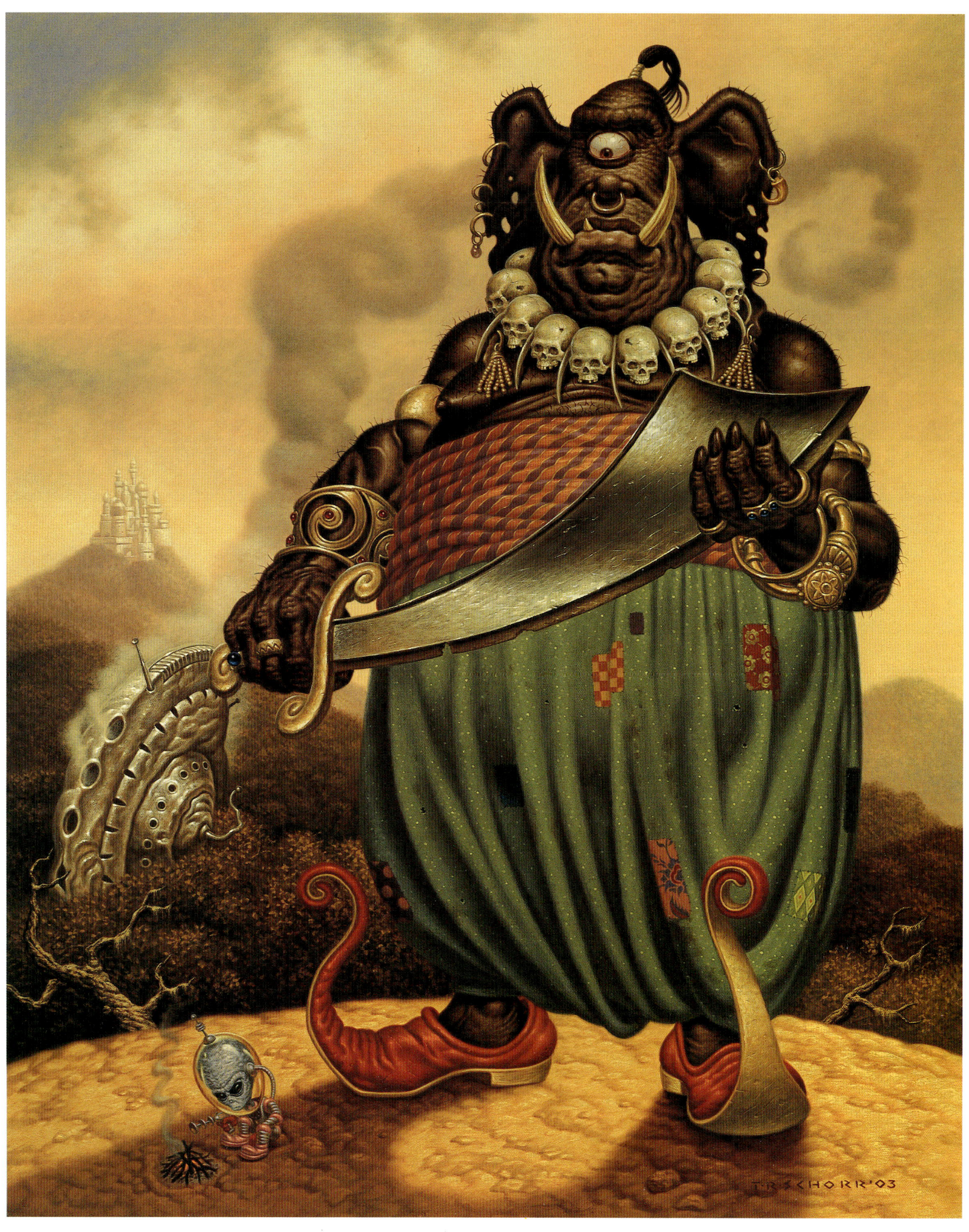

artist: **Todd Schorr**
client: Merry Karnowsky Gallery *title:* An Alien in the Land of Make-Believe
medium: Acrylics on canvas *size:* 24"x30"

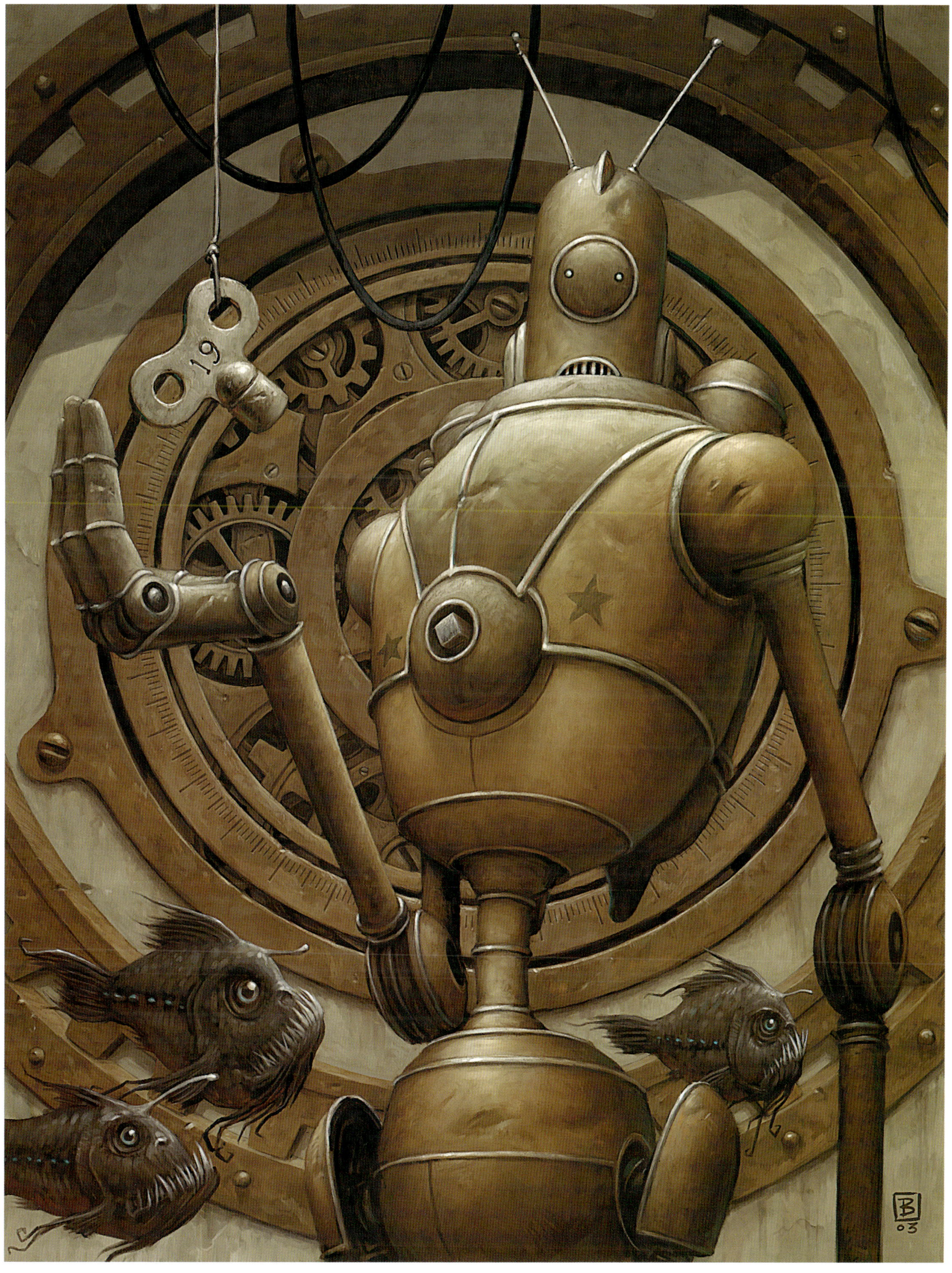

artist: **Brian Despain**
title: Pisces Ex Machina *medium:* Digital *size:* 6"x8"

1
artist: **Andrew Bawidamann**
art director: Steve Kessler
client: Fantasy World Studios
title: Dino Girl
medium: Digital
size: 12″x12″

2
artist: **Chris Spollen**
client: Moonlightpress Studio
title: Little Devil
medium: Mixed/digital
size: 16″x20″

3
artist: **Andrew Bawidamann**
client: Echo Gallery
title: Bad Habit
medium: Enamel on gessoed masonite
size: 36″x48″

4
artist: **Andrew Bawidamann**
art director: Steve Kessler
client: Fantasy World Studios
title: Robot Girl
medium: Digital
size: 8 1/2″x11″

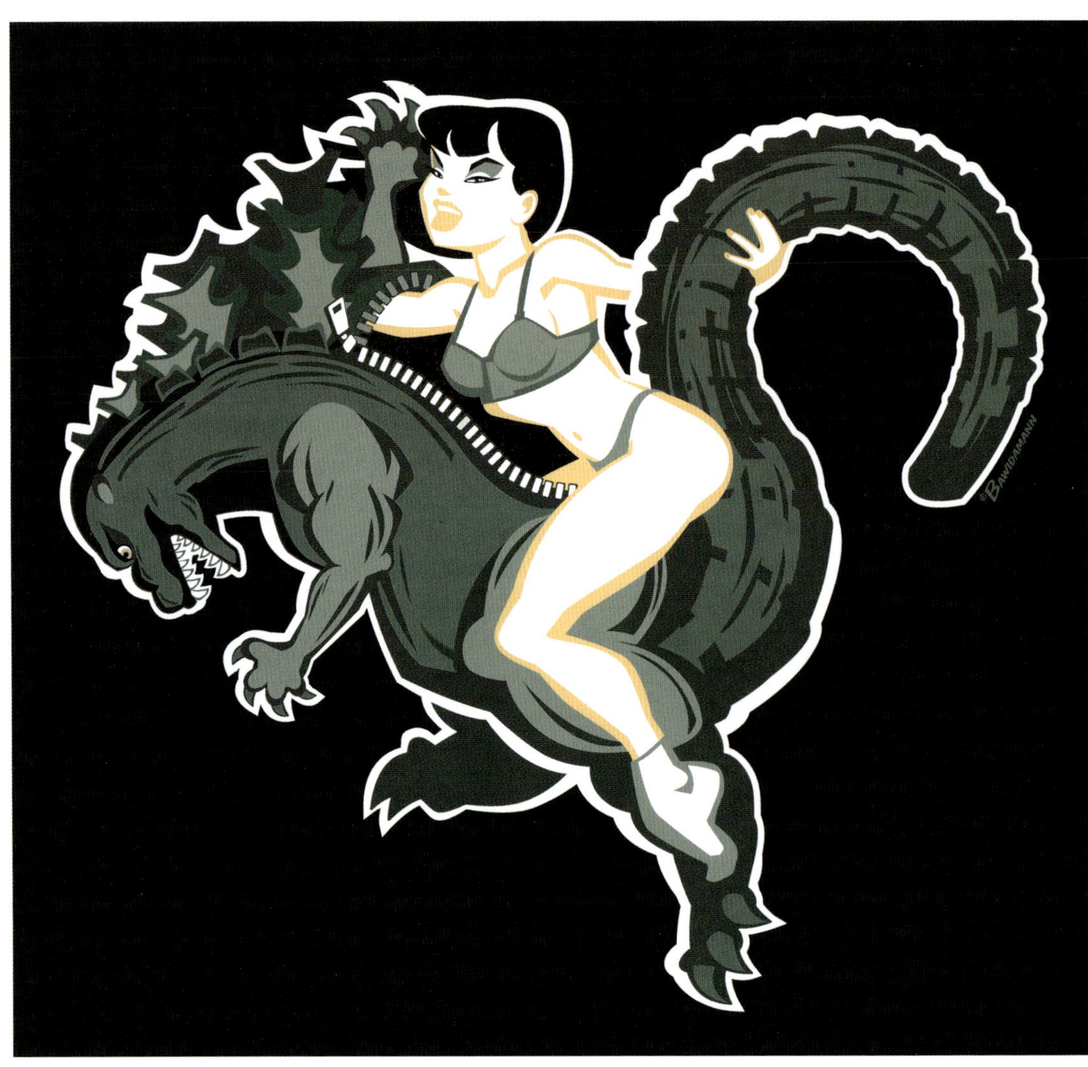

1

2

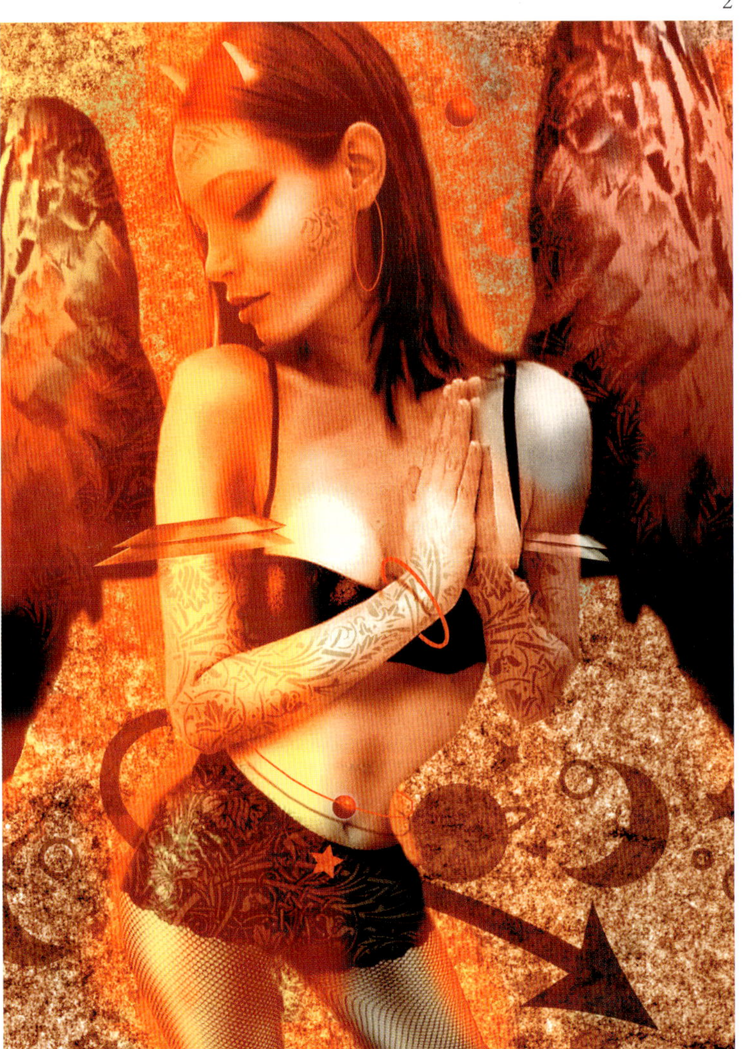

3

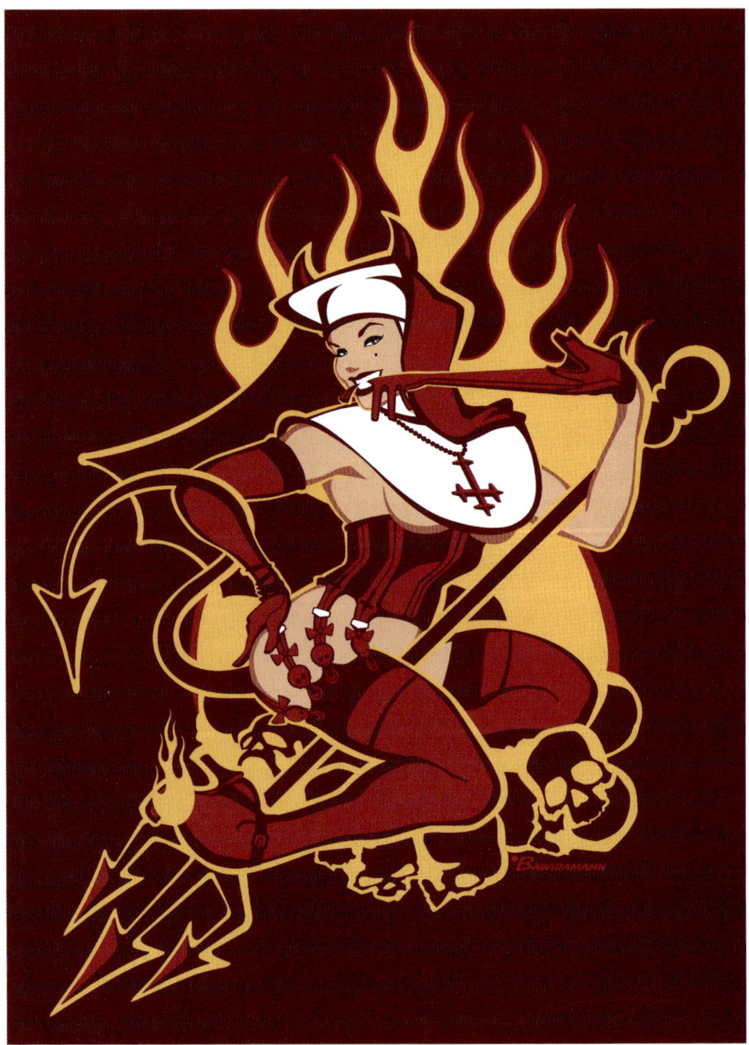

4

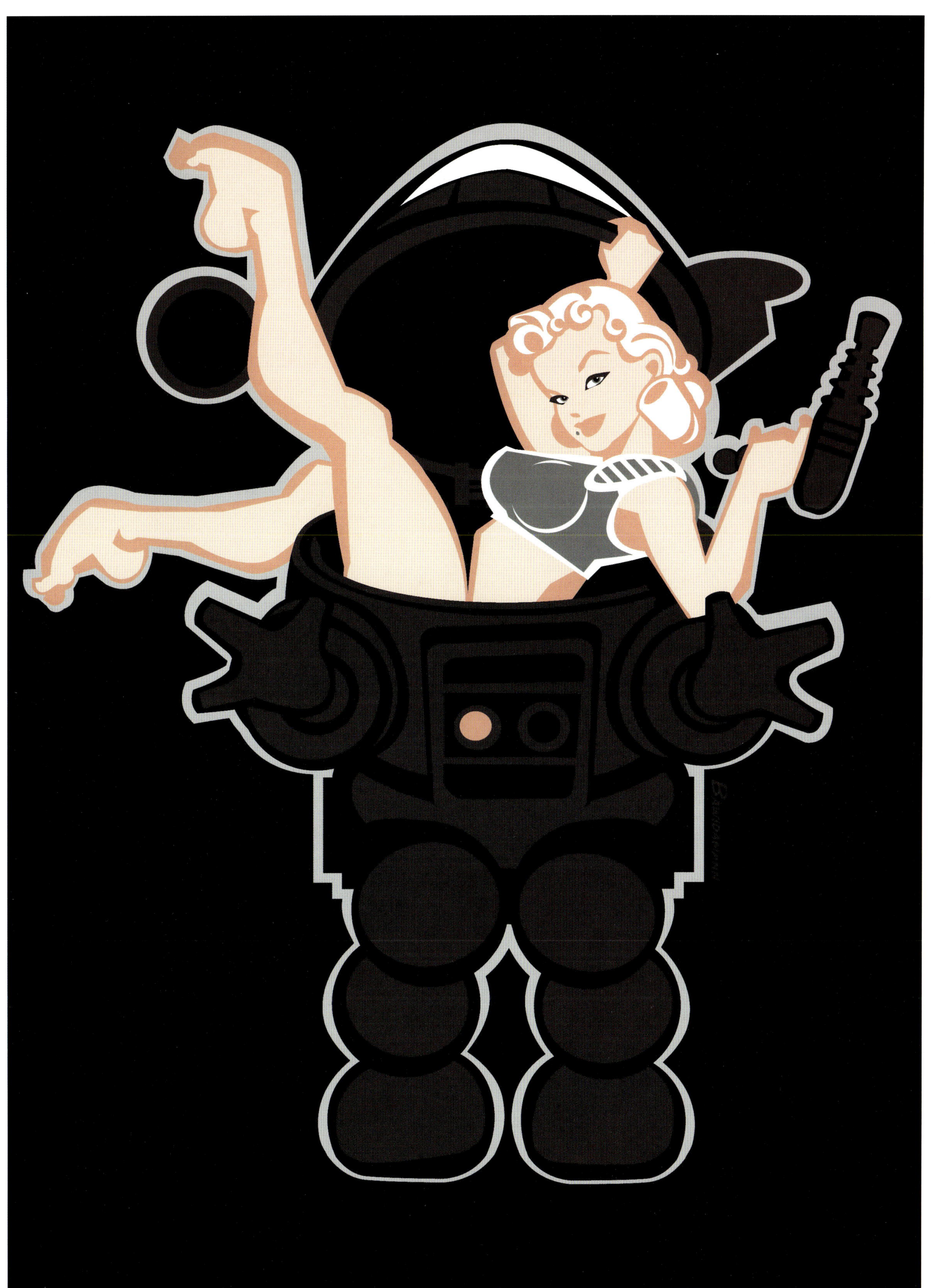

Institutional

1
artist: **Carl Critchlow**
art director: Jeremy Cranford
client: Wizards of the Coast
title: Darksteel Colossus
medium: Acrylics
size: 16"x12"

2
artist: **Jonathan Wayshak**
title: Iron Stigmata
medium: Digital

3
artist: **Rick Berry, Brom, Phil Hale**
art director: Cosimo Panlini
client: Lucca Hospital Charity Memorial Calendar
title: Paint Performance #1
medium: Oils
size: 20"x30"

4
artist: **Brian Despain**
title: The Icarus Fish
medium: Digital
size: 6"x8"

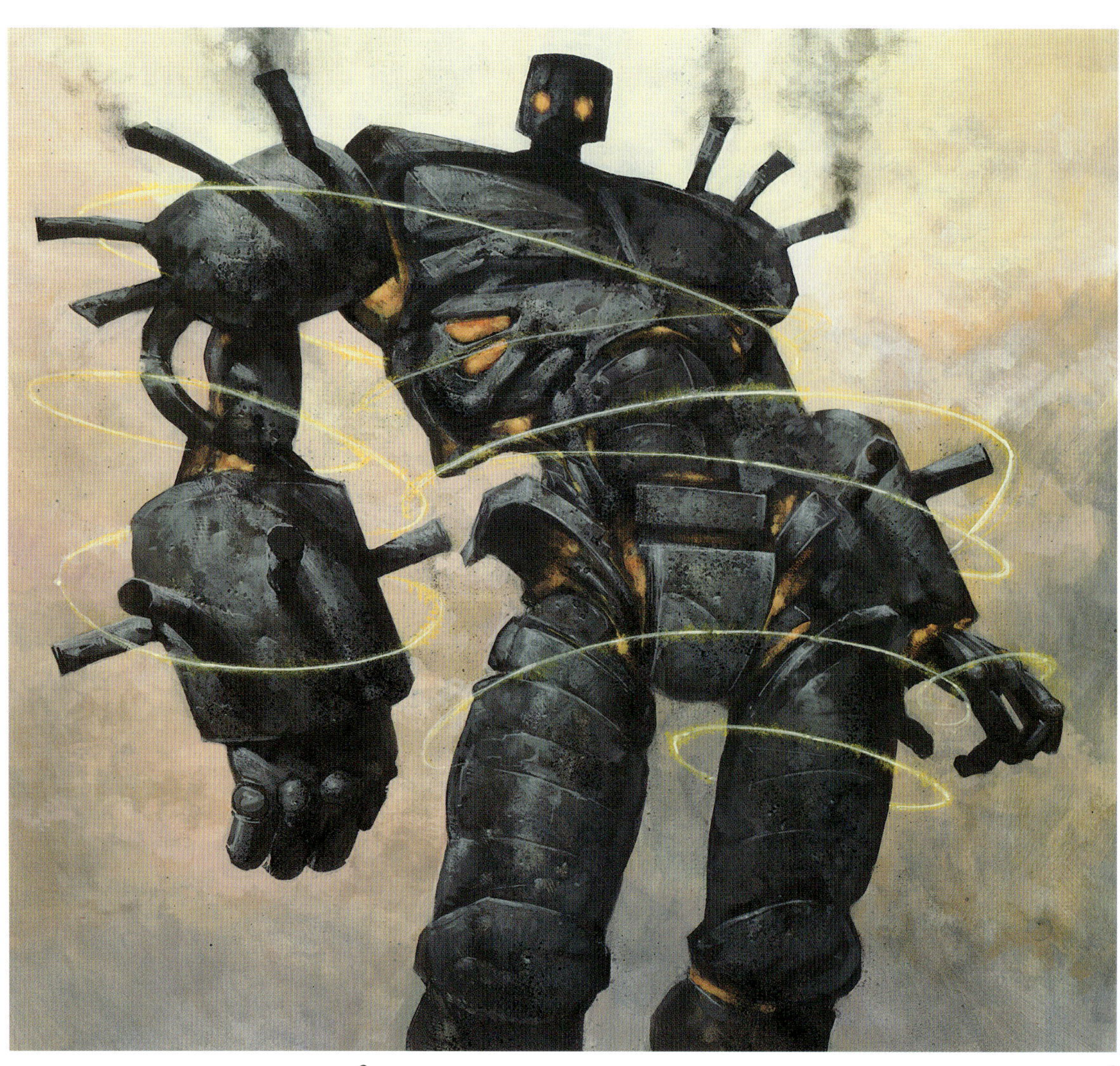

1

2

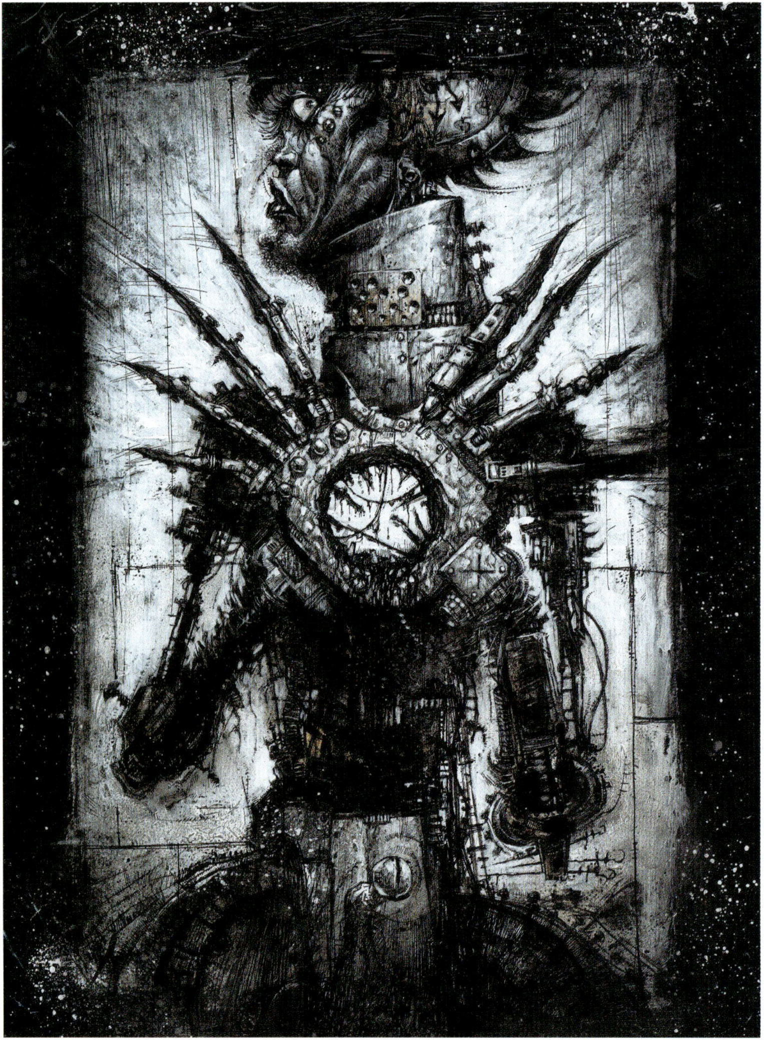

3

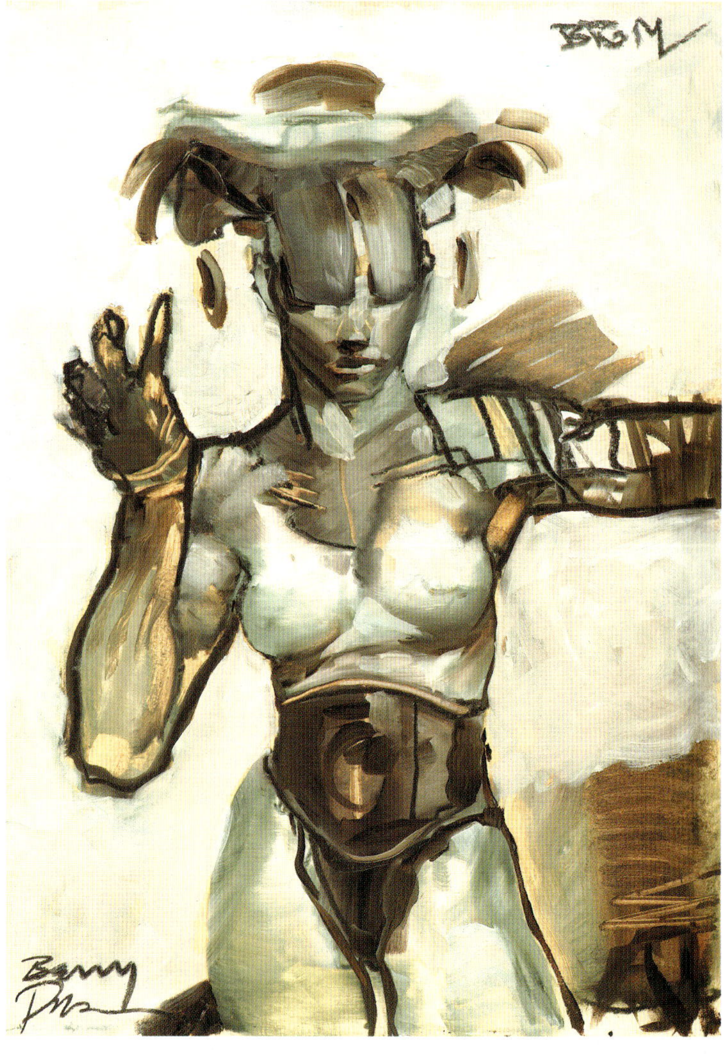

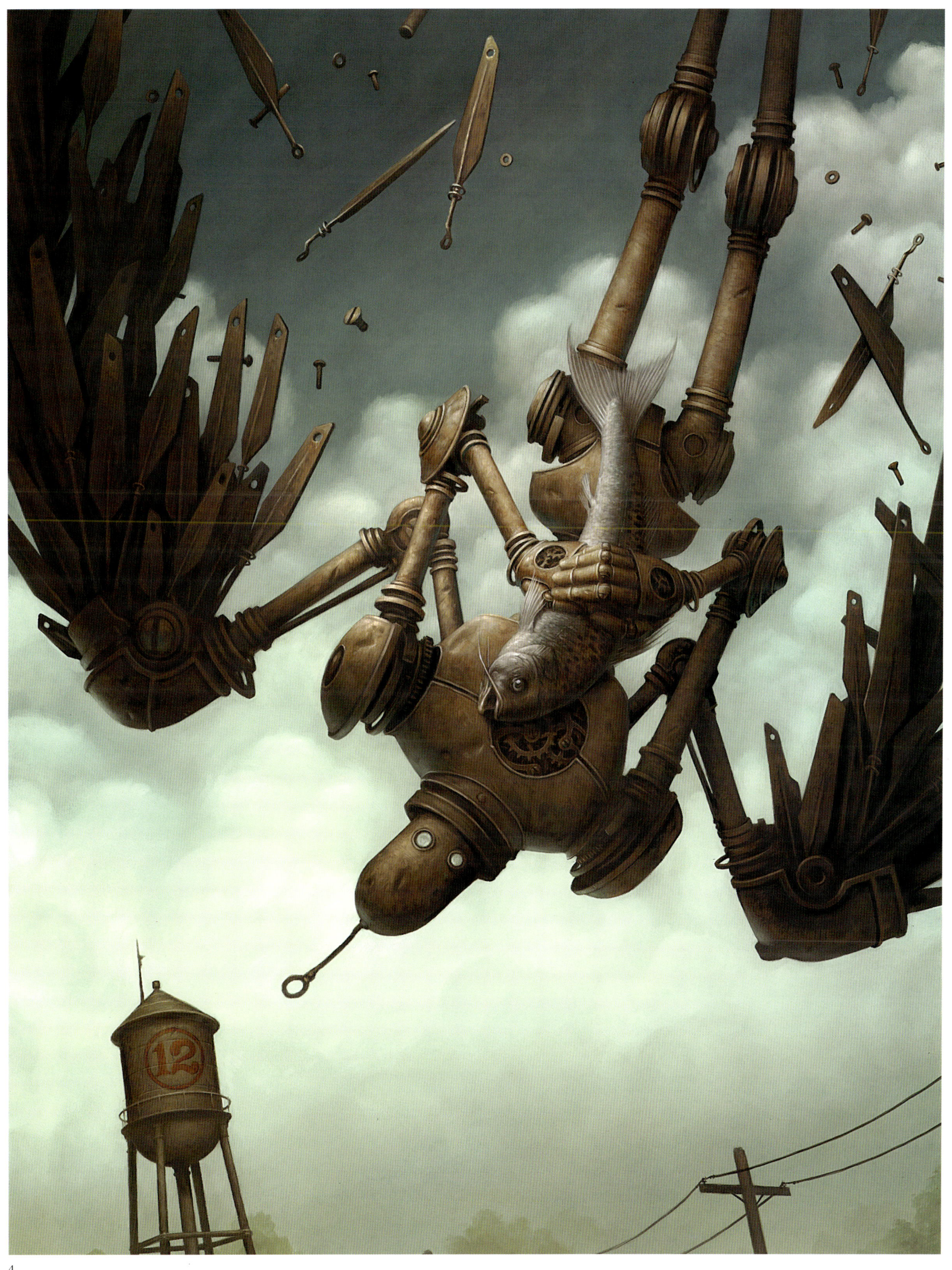

4

Institutional

1
artist: **Jeremy Jarvis**
art director: Jeremy Cranford
client: Wizards of the Coast
title: Loxodon Warhammer
medium: Watercolor
size: 8″x5 7/8″

2
artist: **Philip Straub**
title: Crossroads
medium: Digital
size: 13″x7″

3
artist: **Lars Grant-West**
art director: Jeremy Cranford
client: Wizards of the Coast
title: Trash for Treasure
medium: Digital
size: 2″x1 1/2″

4
artist: **Mike Sass**
client: Atari Interactive
title: Balorfight
medium: Digital
size: 8 3/4″x11 1/4″

5
artist: **Michael Phillippi**
art director: Franz Vohwinkel
client: Kosmos Games
title: Lonus Mightius
medium: Digital
size: 5 3/4″x10″

6
artist: **Franz Vohwinkel**
art director: Imelda Vohwinkel
client: Kosmos Verlag
title: Demegodas the Odd
medium: Digital
size: 6″x10″

7
artist: **Impact/Nick Greenwood**
art director: Nick Greenwood
client: The Games Machine
title: Spirits
medium: Digital
size: 48″x72″

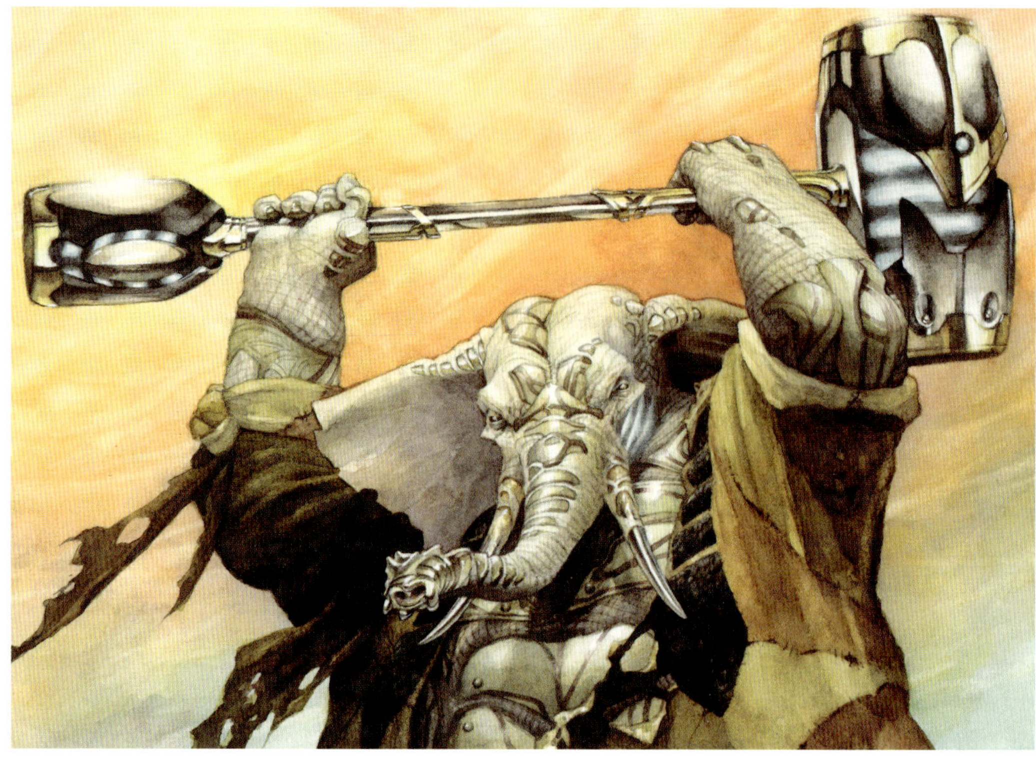
1

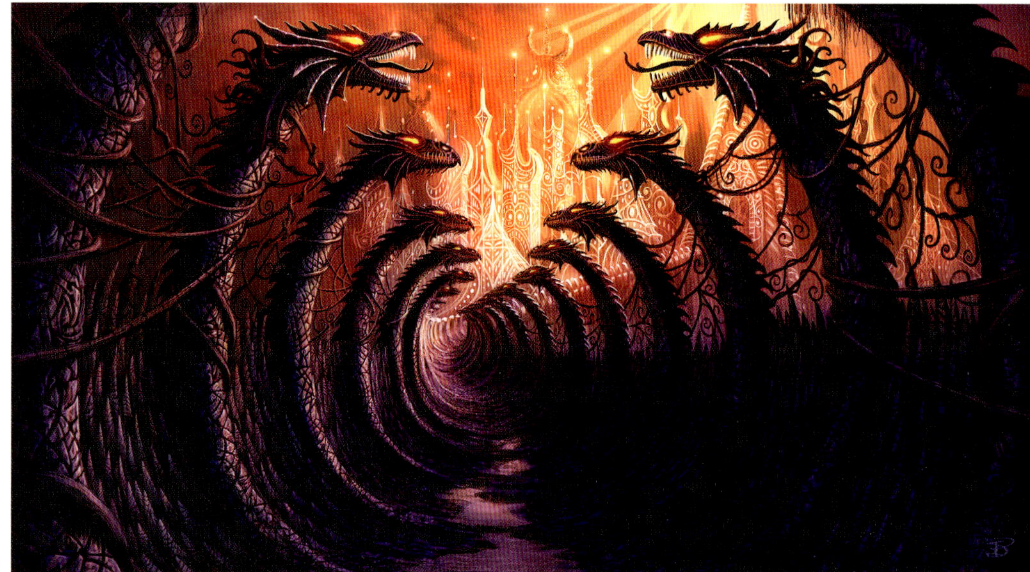
2

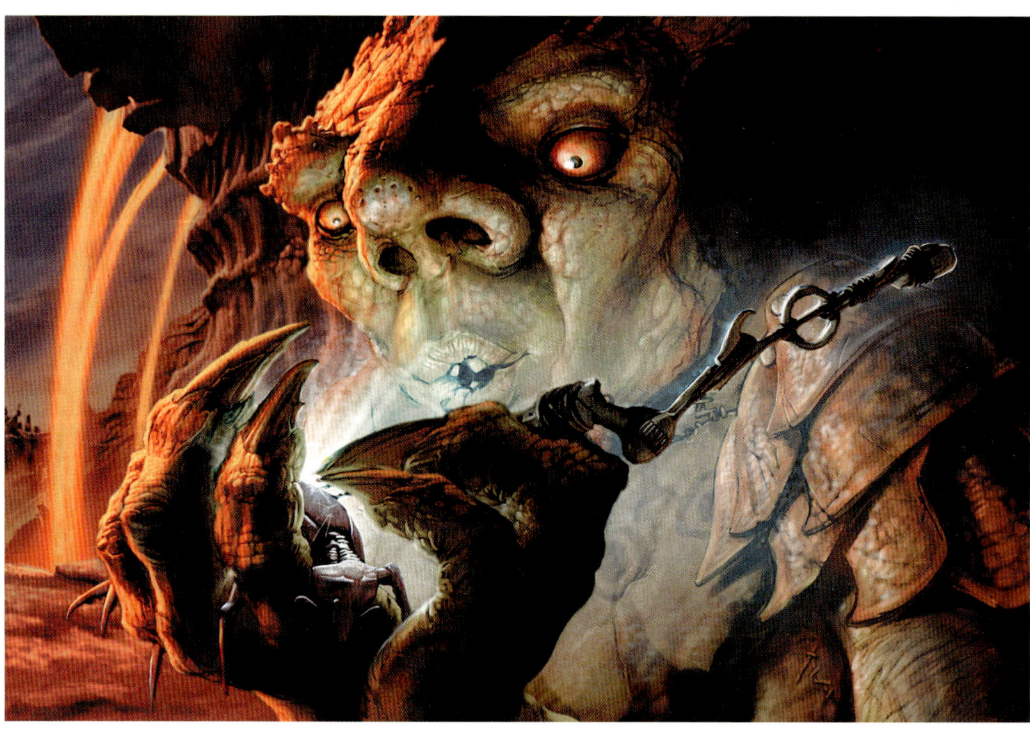
3

4

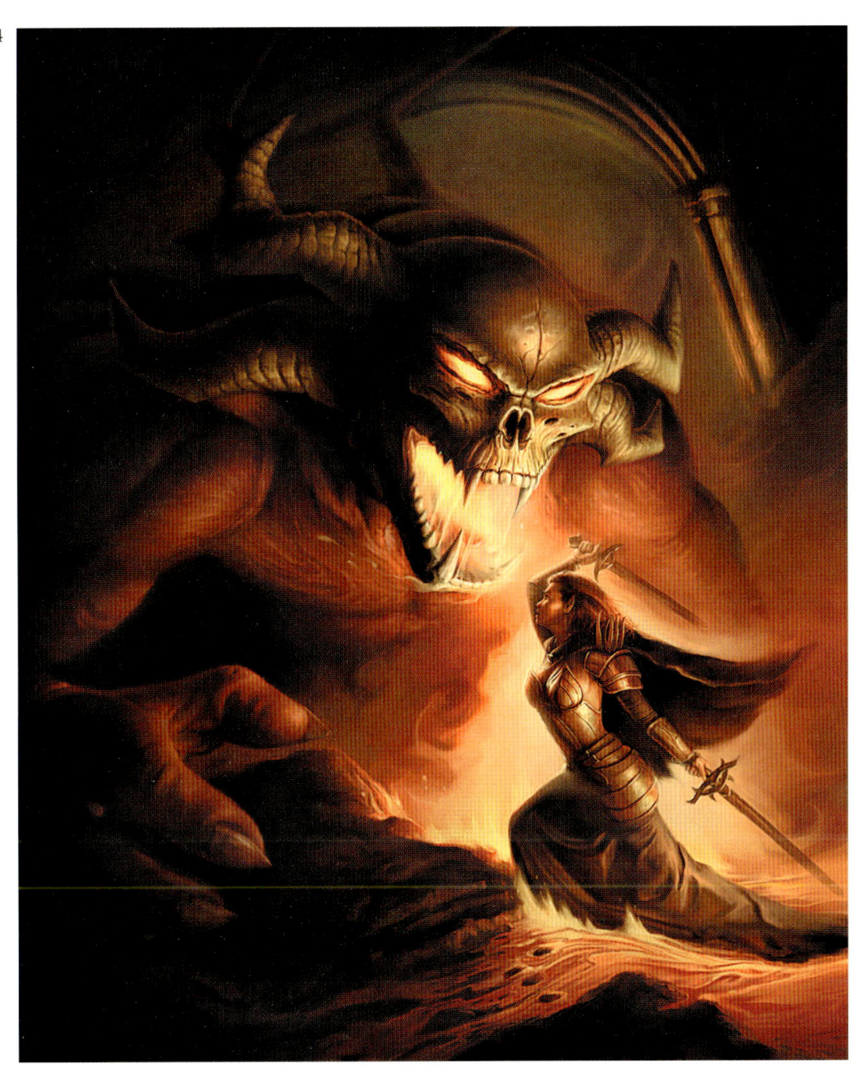

5

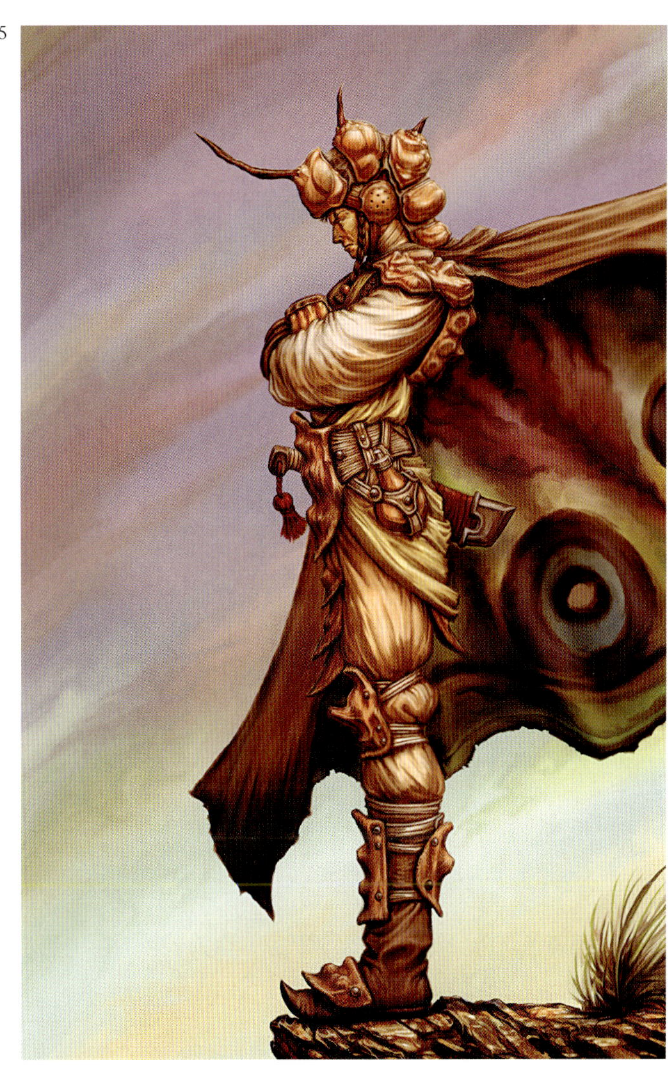

6

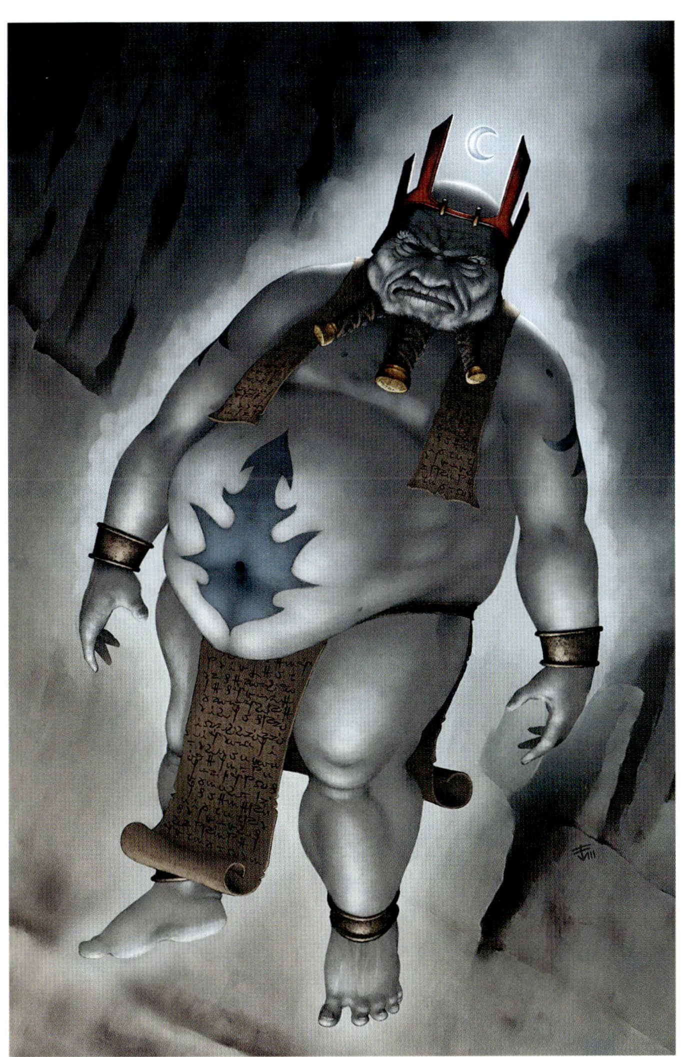

7

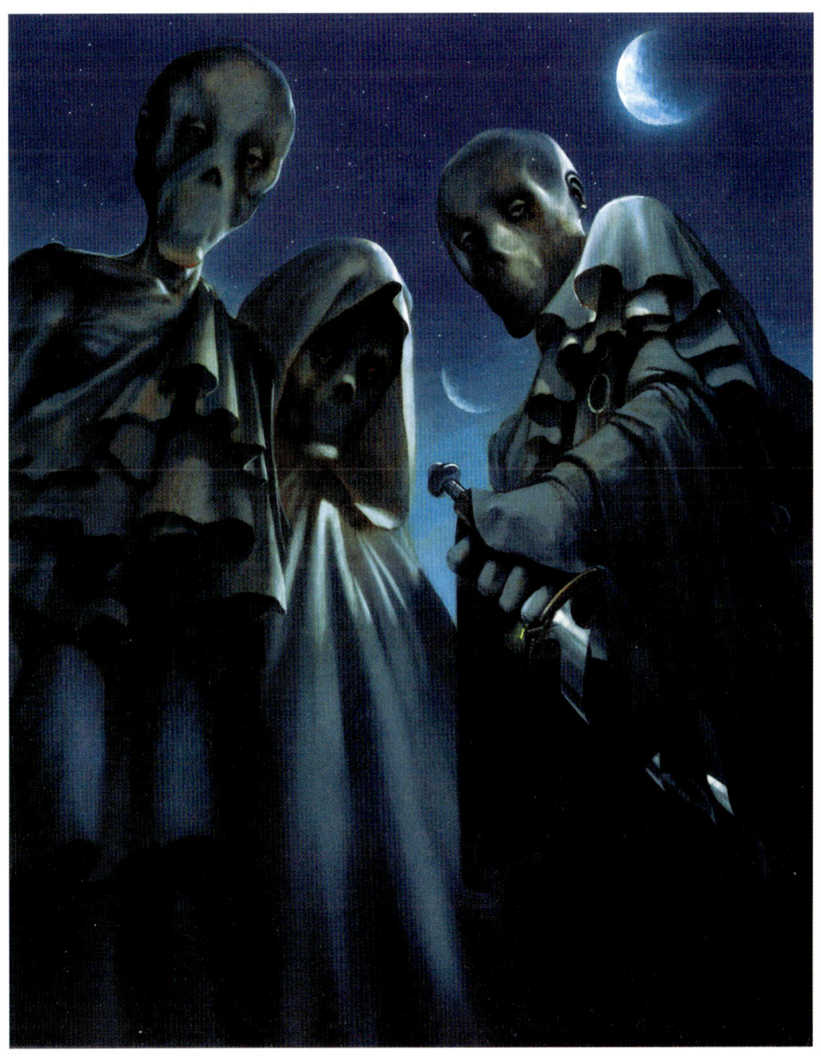

Institutional

1
artist: **Dave Stevens**
title: La of Opar Head Study
medium: Graphite

2
artist: **Scott M. Fischer**
art director: Teresa Green
client: Green Fisch Studios
title: Dobro
medium: Mixed

3
artist: **Scott M. Fischer**
art director: Teresa Green
client: Green Fisch Studios
title: Touched
medium: Mixed

4
artist: **Scott M. Fischer**
art director: Teresa Green
client: Green Fisch Studios
title: Java
medium: Mixed

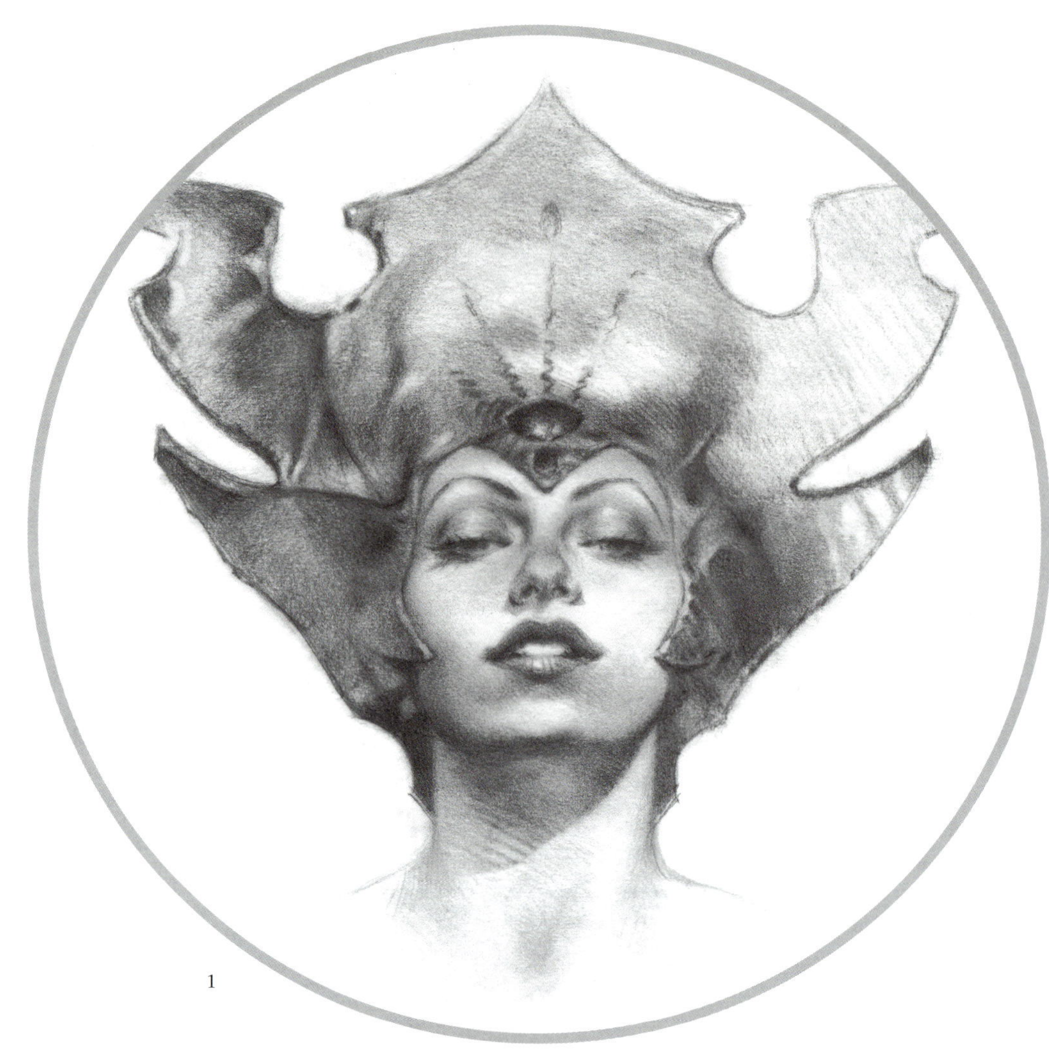

1

2

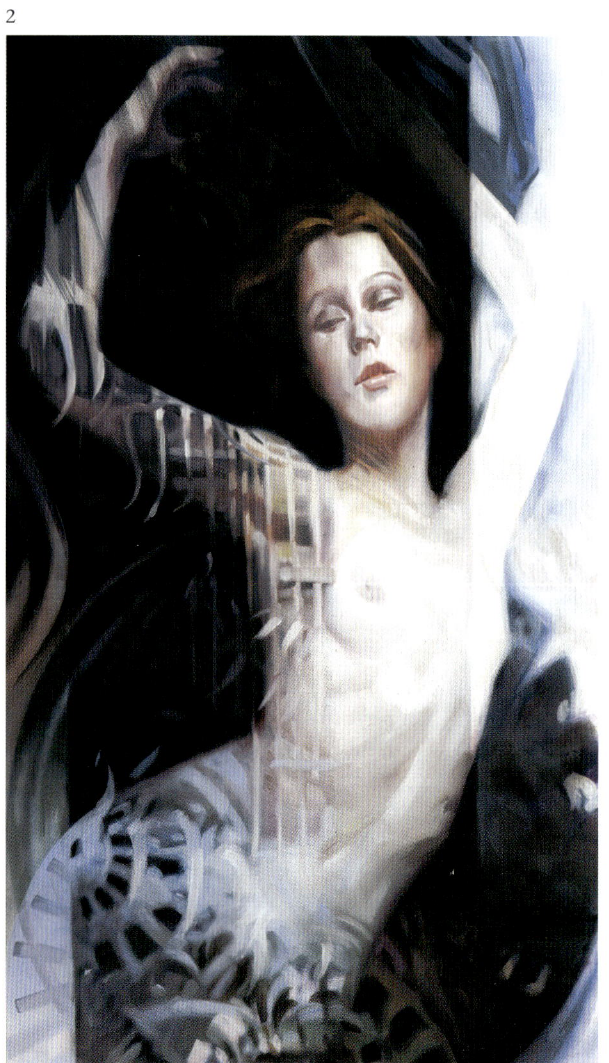

3

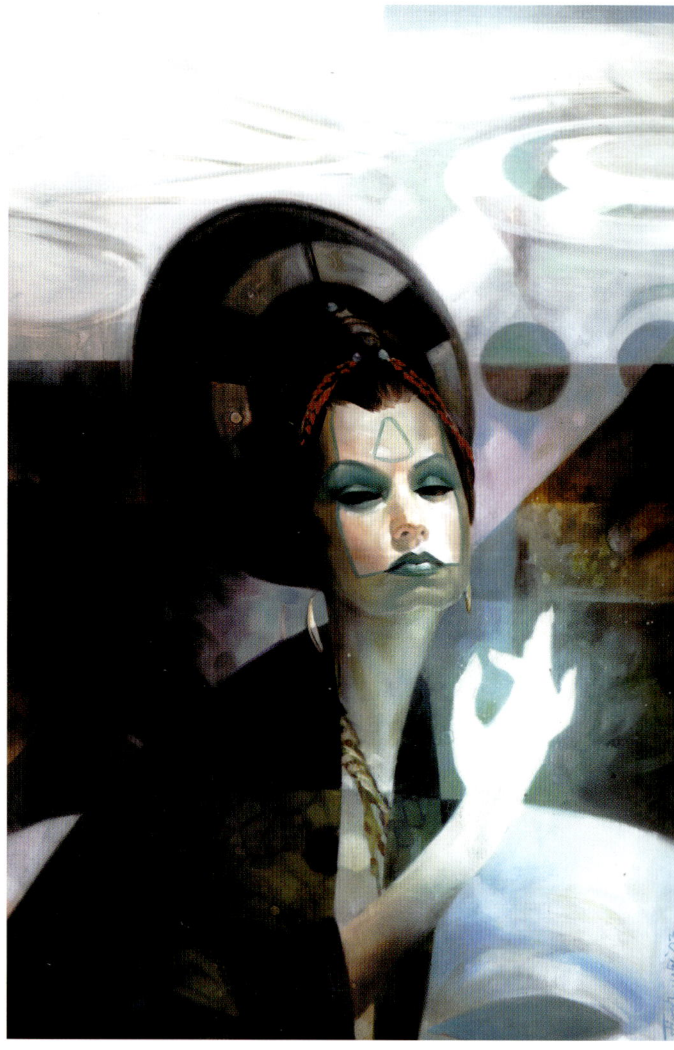

4

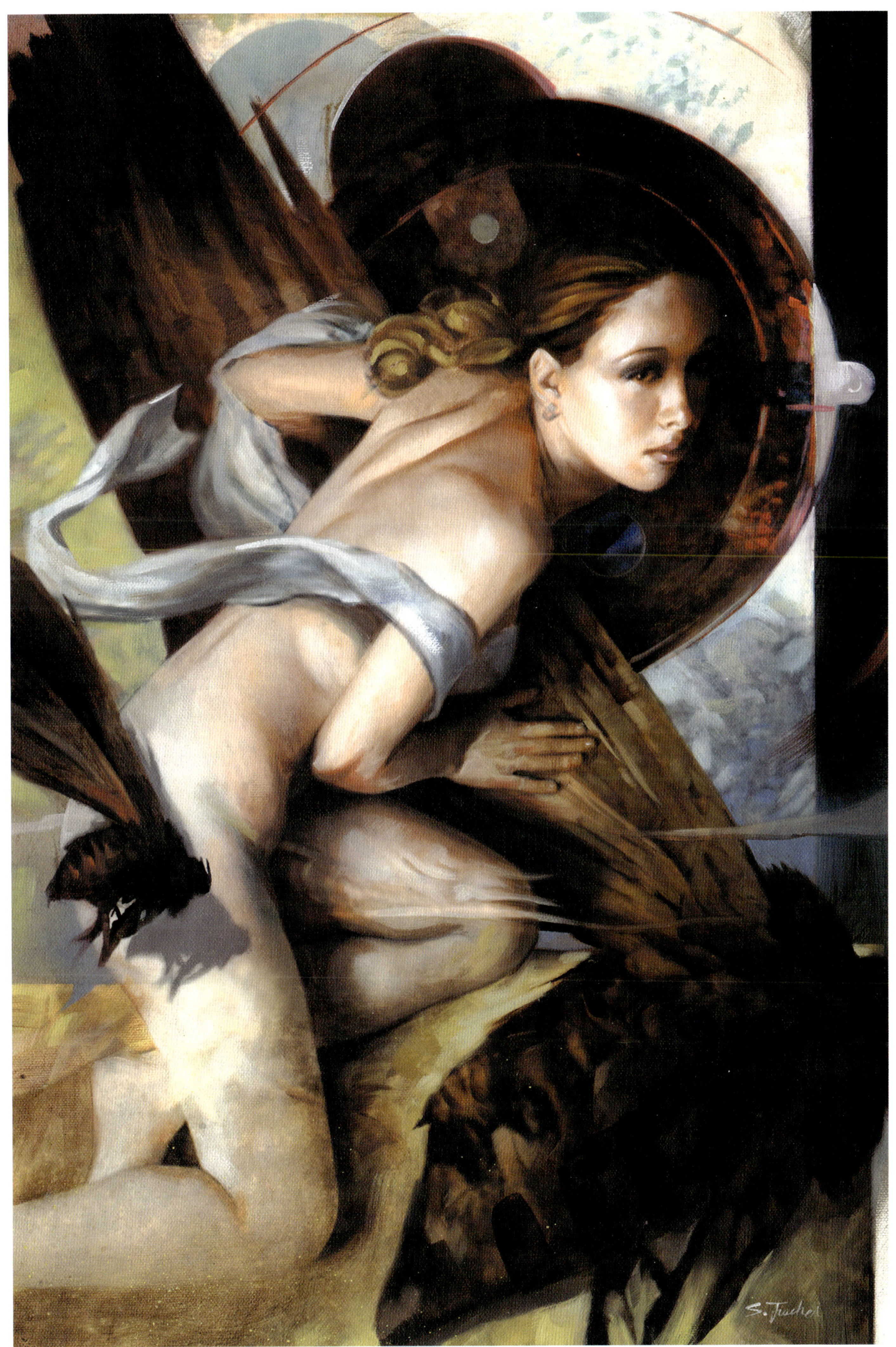

1
artist: **Chet Phillips**
title: Infinity's Back Yard
medium: Digital
size: 8 3/4"x11 3/4"

2
artist: **Tony DiTerlizzi**
designer: Ken Meyer, Jr.
client: RAINN
title: Black Swan
medium: Color pencil & watercolor
size: 14"x17"

3
artist: **Roxana Villa**
designer: Andy Bernstein
client: The Work of Byron Katie Journal
title: Lotus
medium: Acrylics on board
size: 19"x21"

4
artist: **Jos. A. Smith**
designer: Tom Burke
client: MCS Gallery
title: The Tree
medium: India ink on Arches watercolor paper
size: 24"x18"

5
artist: **Rogério Viela**
client: Fábrica de Quandrinhos
title: Passage
medium: Acrylics on canvas
size: 51"x35"

1

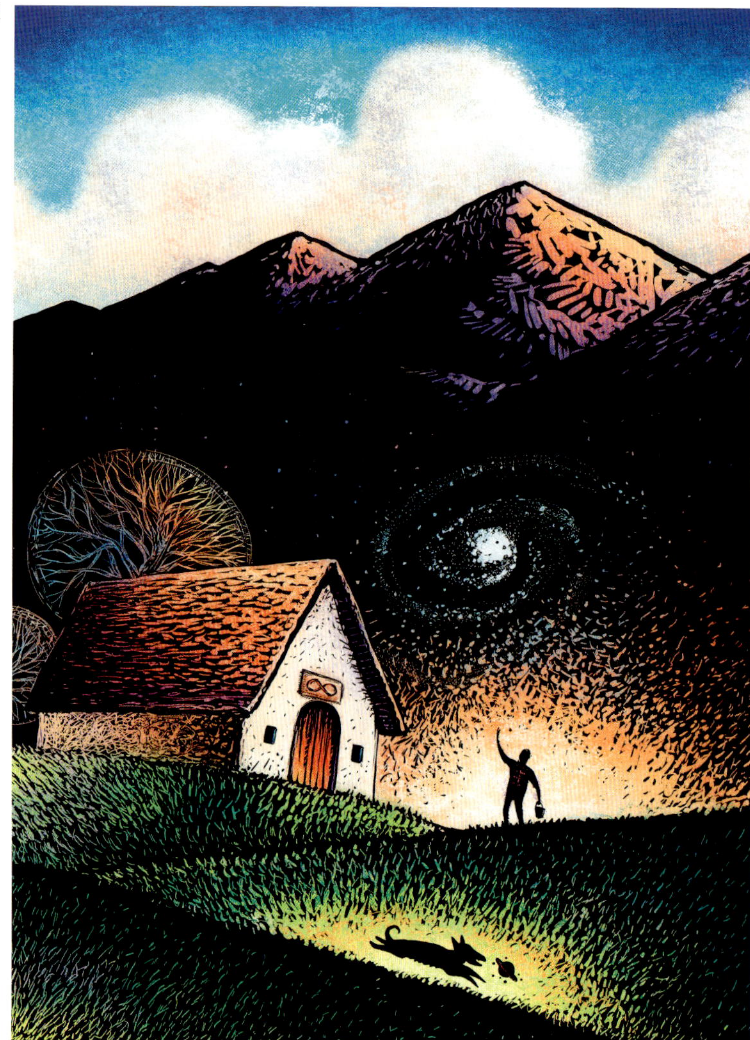

2

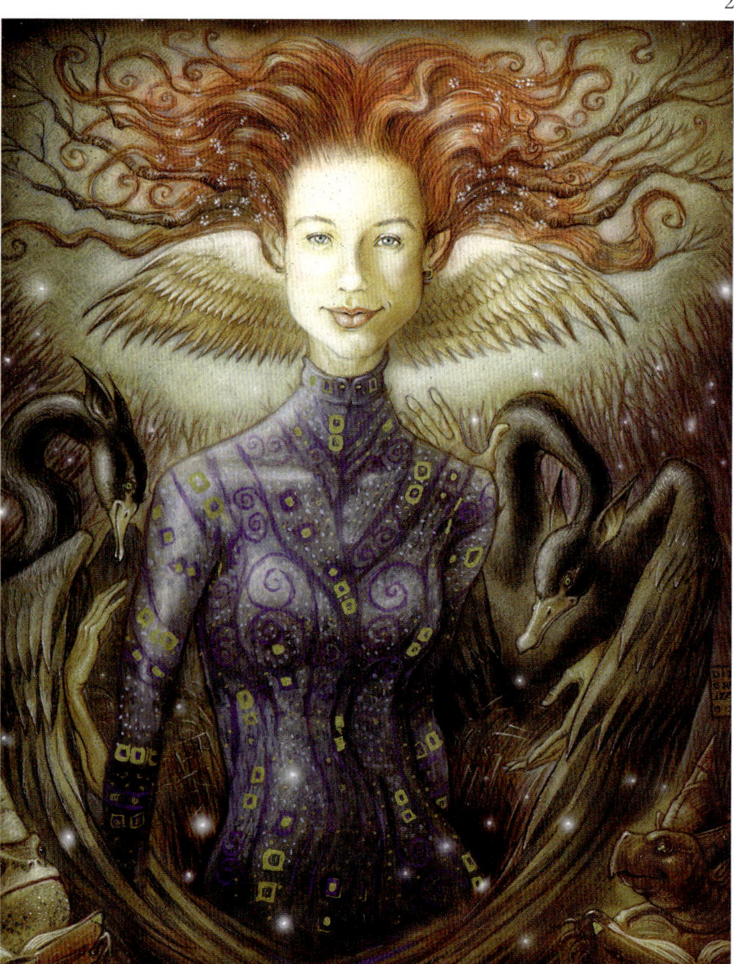

3

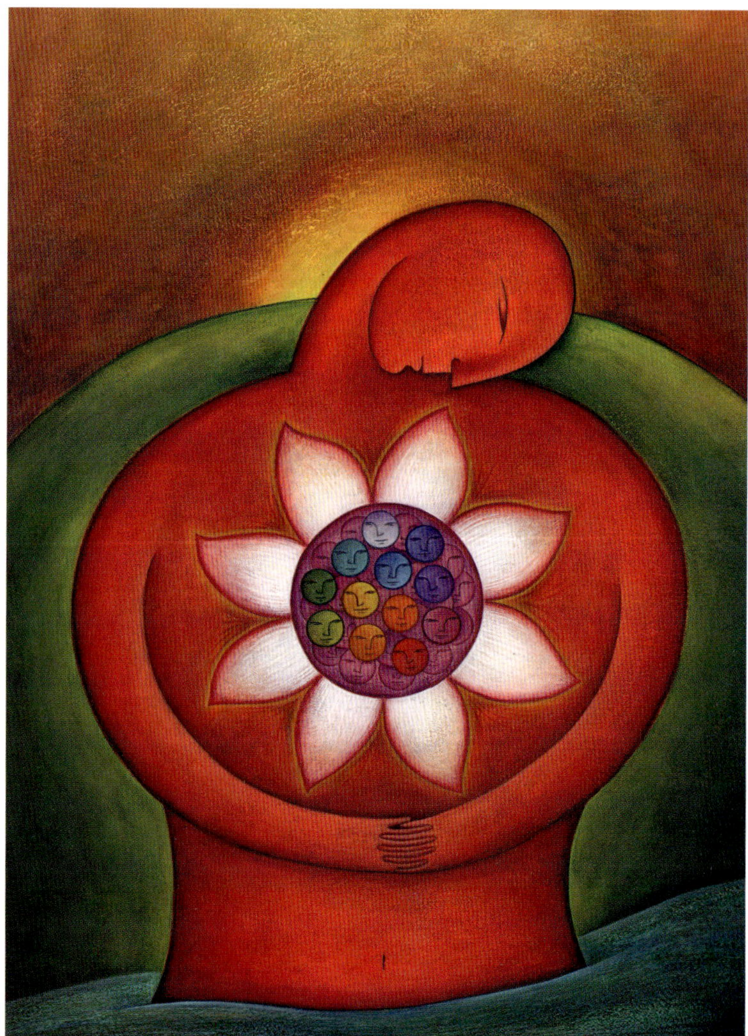

4

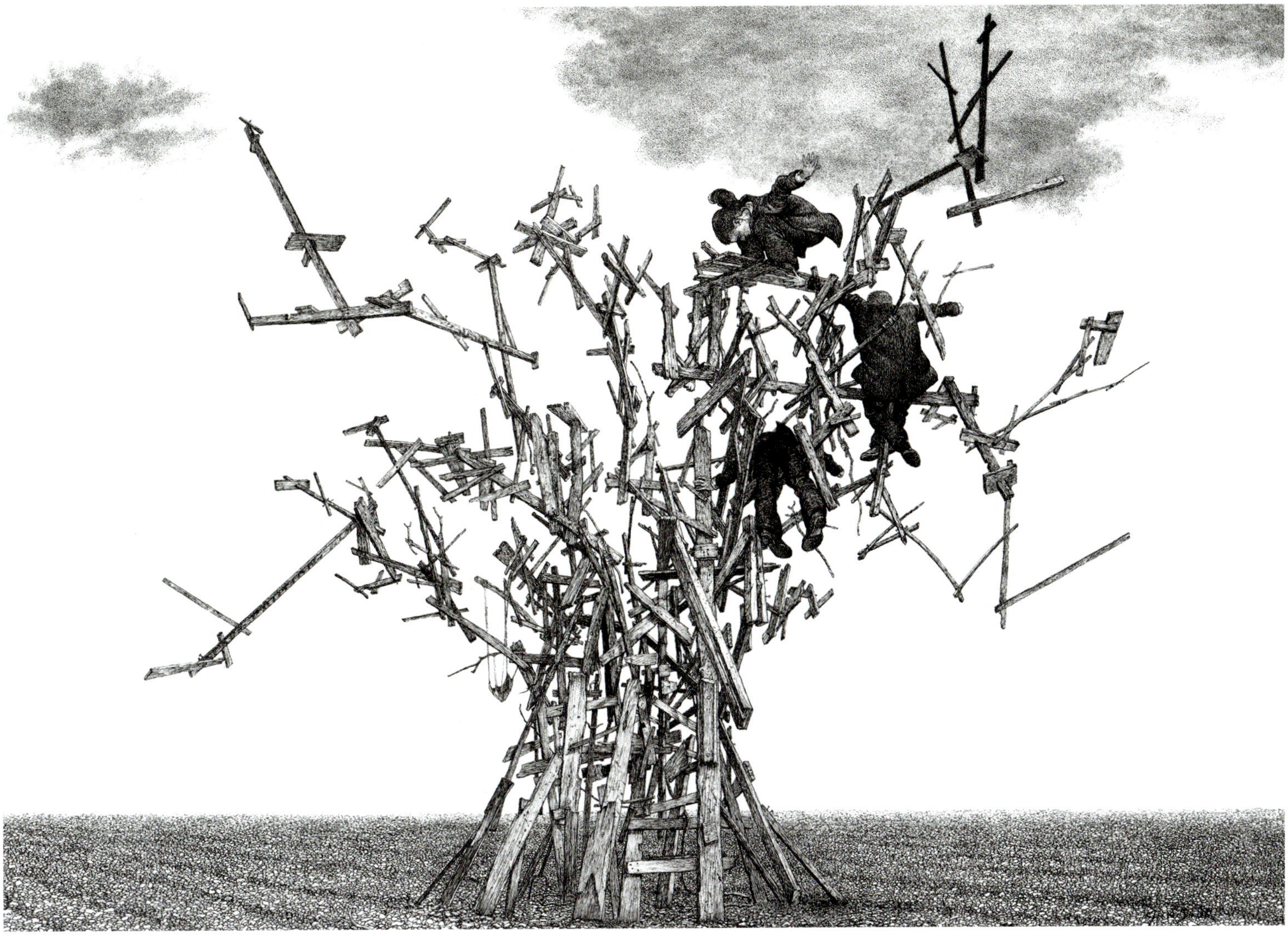

5

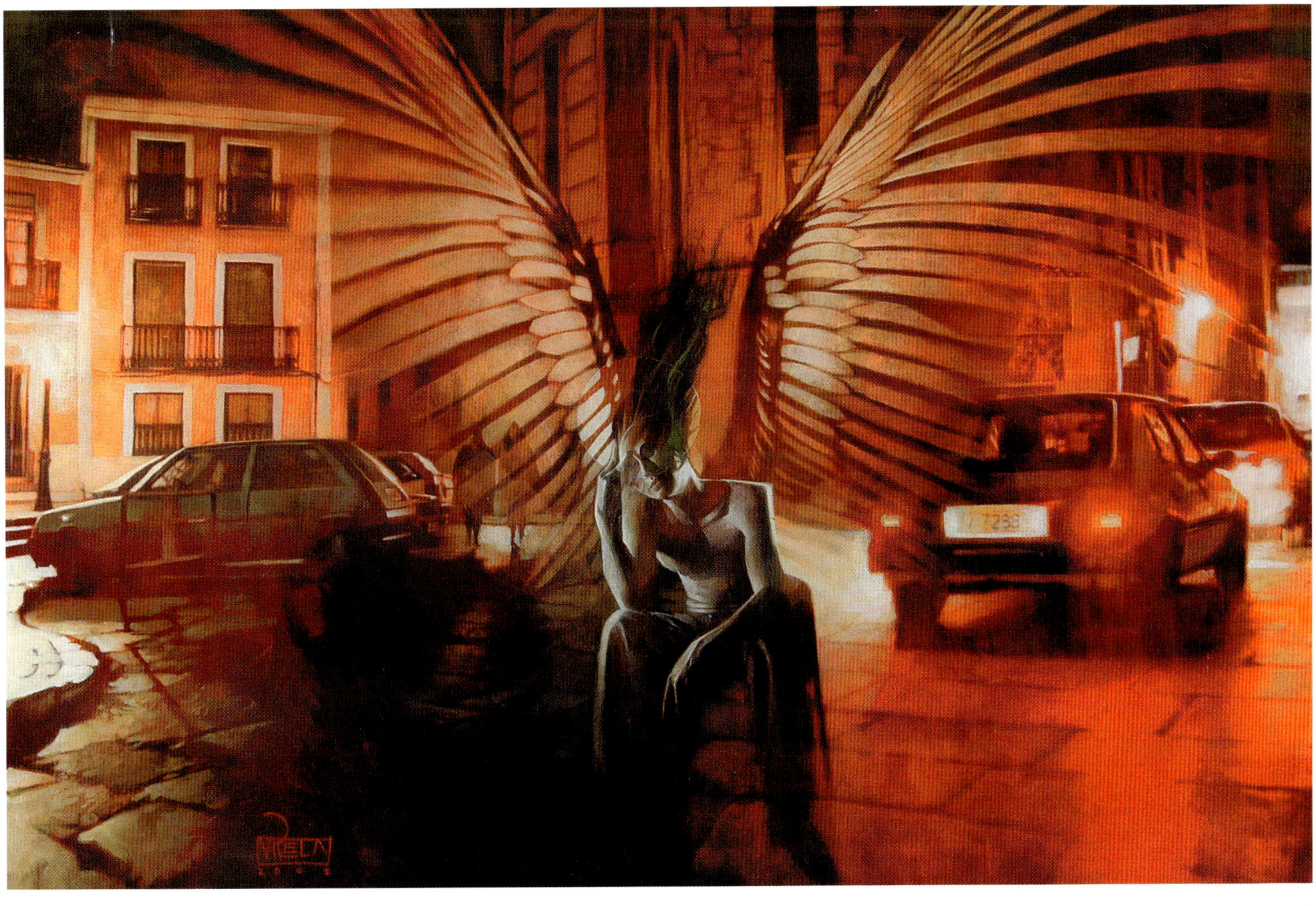

Institutional

1
artist: **Silvio Aebischer/Oddworld CG Dept**
art director: Lorne Lanning
designer: Silvio Aebischer
client: Oddworld Inhabitants
title: The Outlaws
medium: Digital
size: 8″x10″

2
artist: **Owen Richardson**
art director: Kellan Hatch
client: Sony Computer Entertainment America, Inc.
title: War of the Monsters–Goliath Concept
medium: Digital

3
artist: **Oddworld Production Design & CG Departments**
art director: Raymond Swanland/ Lorne Lanning
designer: Raymond Swanland
client: Oddworld Inhabitants
title: Stranger Intro Movie
medium: Digital
size: 8″x6″

4
artist: **Owen Richardson**
art director: Kellan Hatch
client: Sony Computer Entertainment America, Inc.
title: War of the Monsters Poster #3
medium: Digital

1

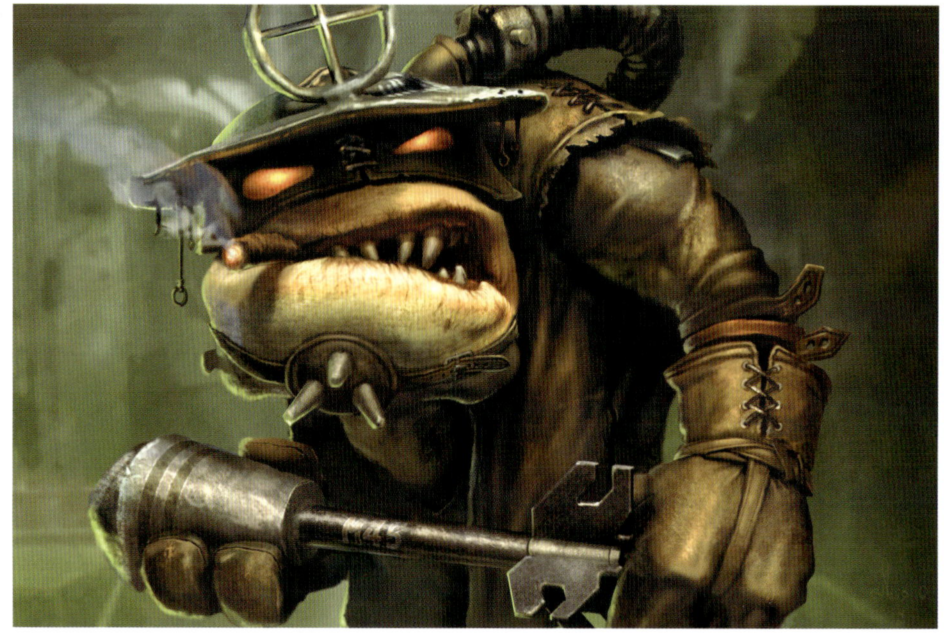

2

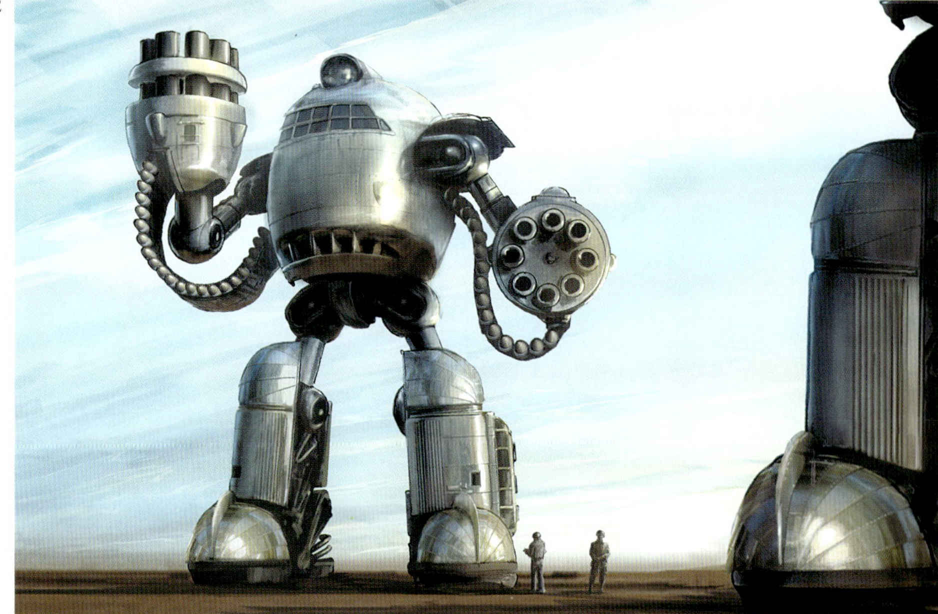

3

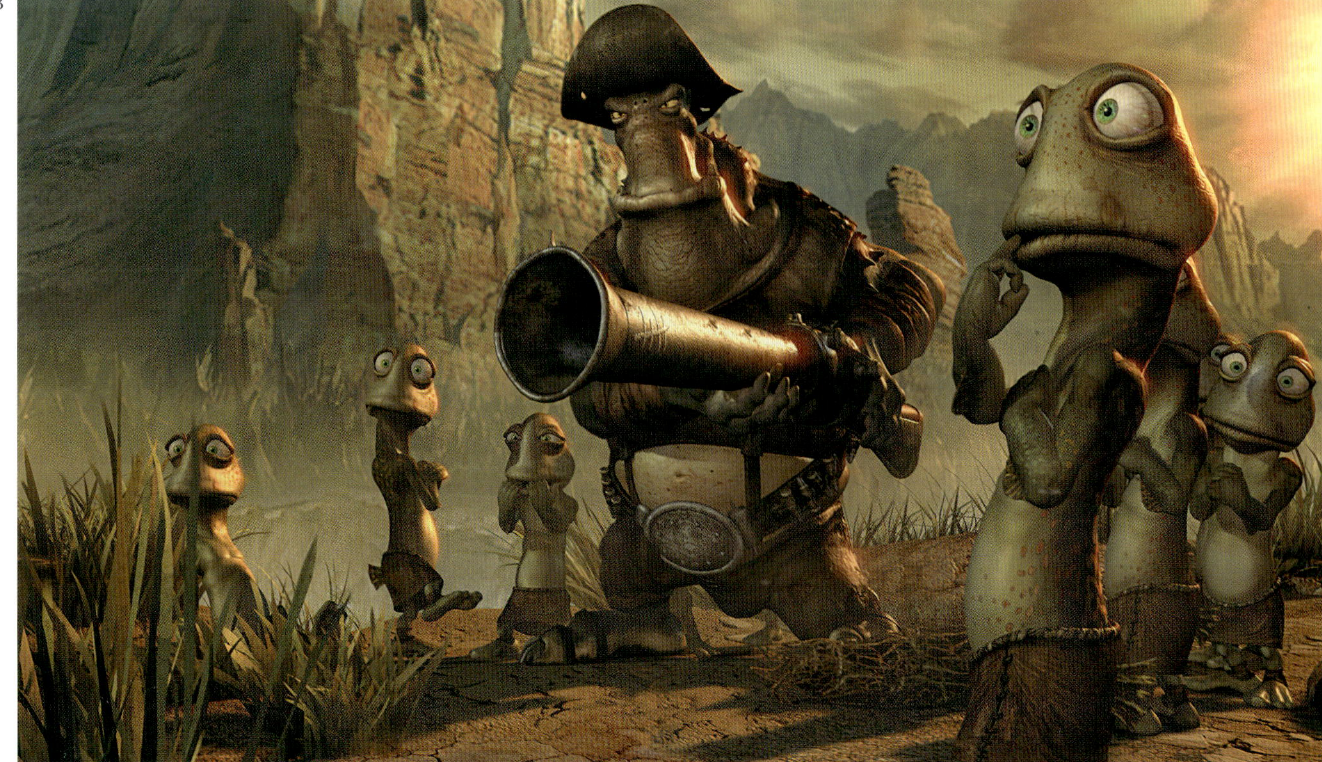

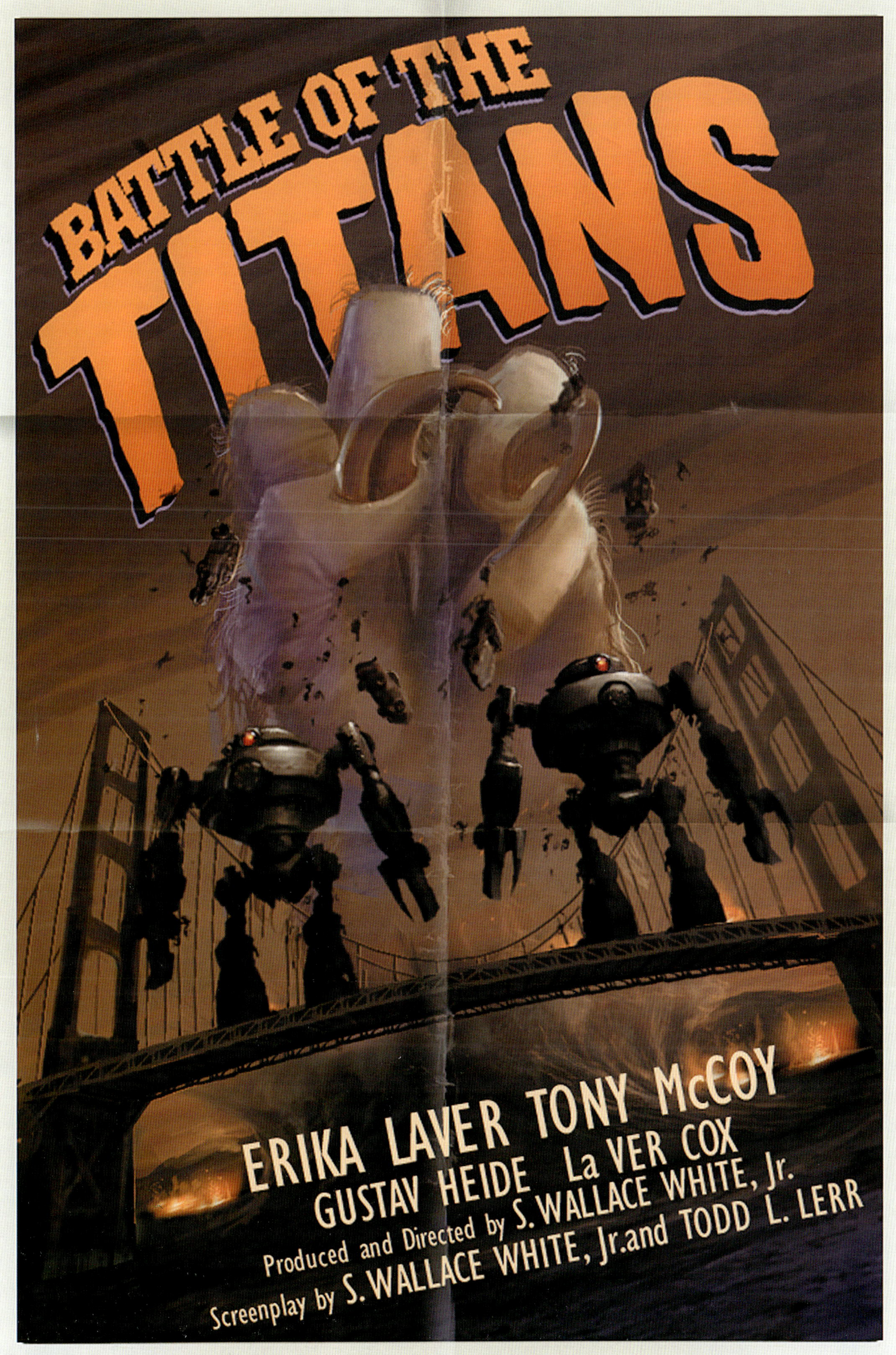
BATTLE OF THE
TITANS
ERIKA LAVER TONY McCOY
GUSTAV HEIDE La VER COX
Produced and Directed by S. WALLACE WHITE, Jr.
Screenplay by S. WALLACE WHITE, Jr.and TODD L. LERR

1
artist: **Edward Binkley**
client: Stark-Raving Studios
title: Exhumer
medium: Digital
size: 14"x11"

2
artist: **Edward Binkley**
client: Stark-Raving Studios
title: Argus
medium: Digital
size: 14 1/2"x11"

3
artist: **Edward Binkley**
client: Stark-Raving Studios
title: Flamen
medium: Digital
size: 9 1/2"x16"

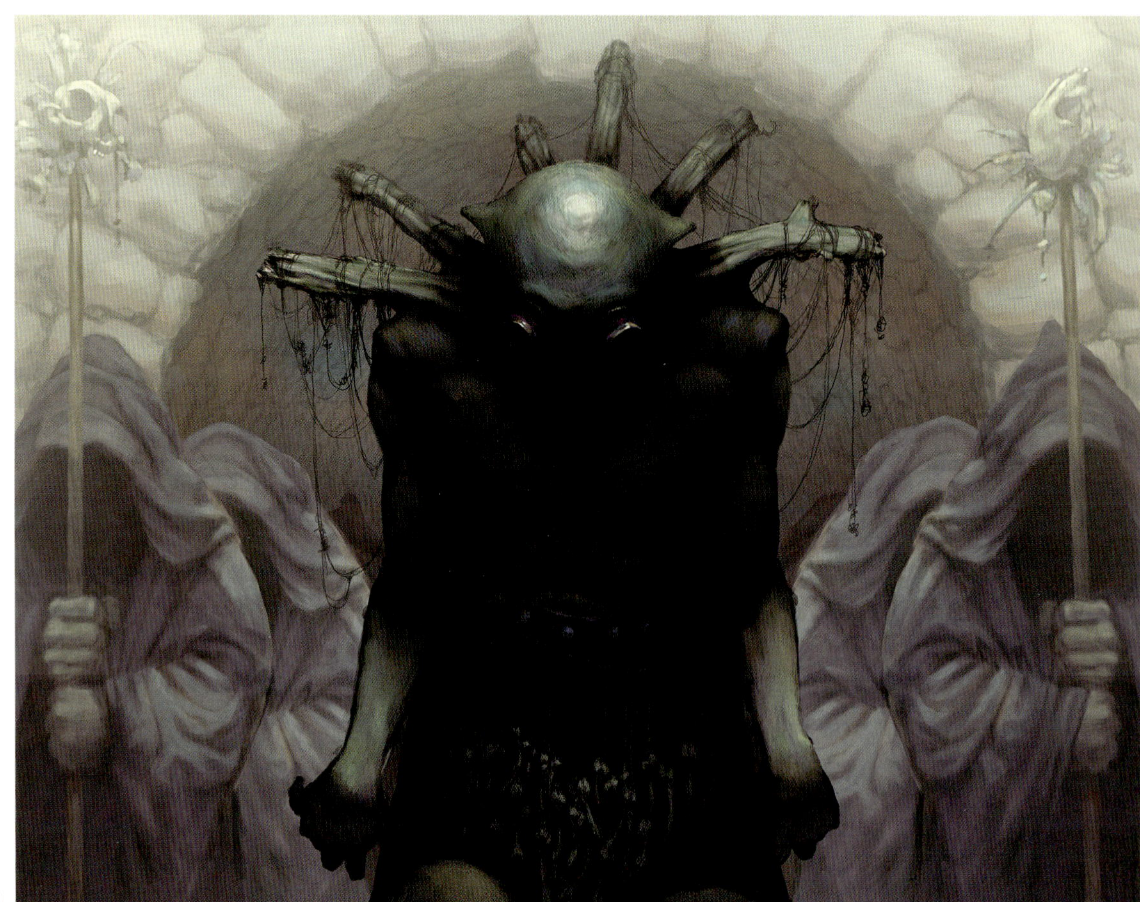

1

2

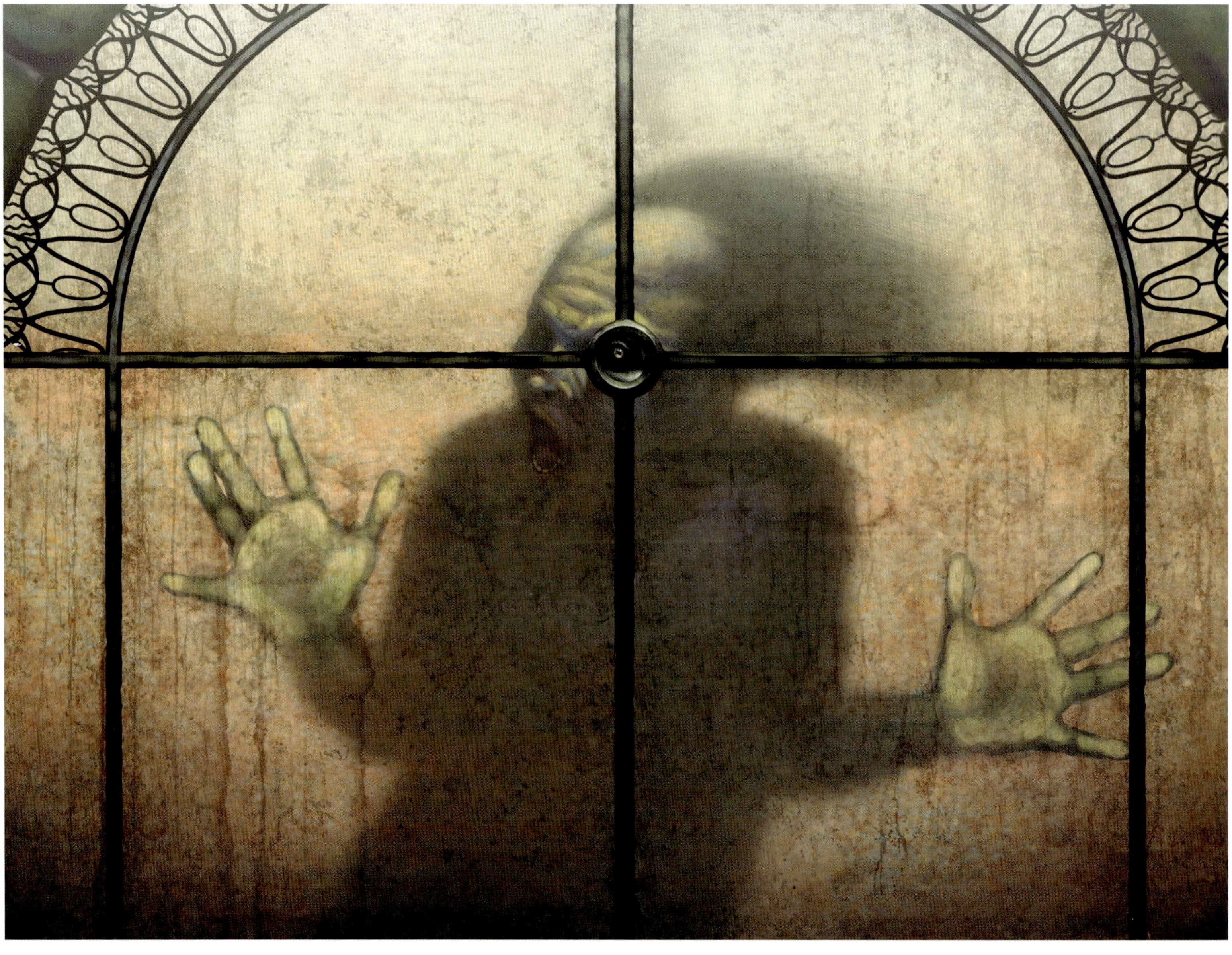

3

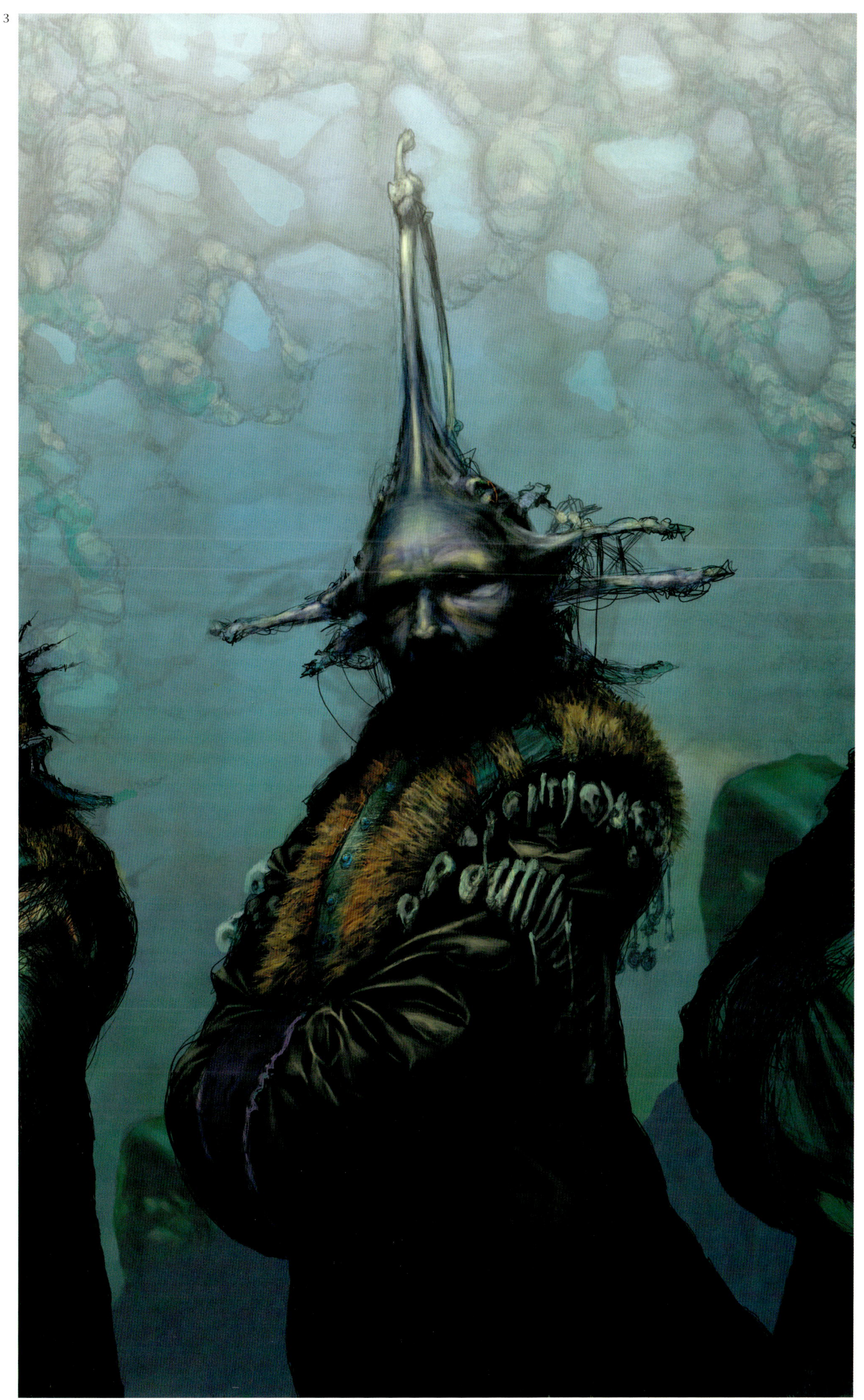

1
artist: **Eric Joyner**
client: ericjoyner.com
title: Robokong
medium: Oils on canvas
size: 24″x48″

2
artist: **Owen Richardson**
art director: Kellan Hatch
client: Sony Computer Entertainment America, Inc.
title: War of the Monsters–Agalmo Attacks
medium: Digital

3
artist: **Silvio Aebischer**
art director: Lorne Lanning
designer: Silvio Aebischer
client: Oddworld Inhabitants
title: Corporate Blimp
medium: Digital
size: 5″x7″

4
artist: **Eric Joyner**
client: thesneeze.com
title: The Final Blow
medium: Oils on panel
size: 32″x26″

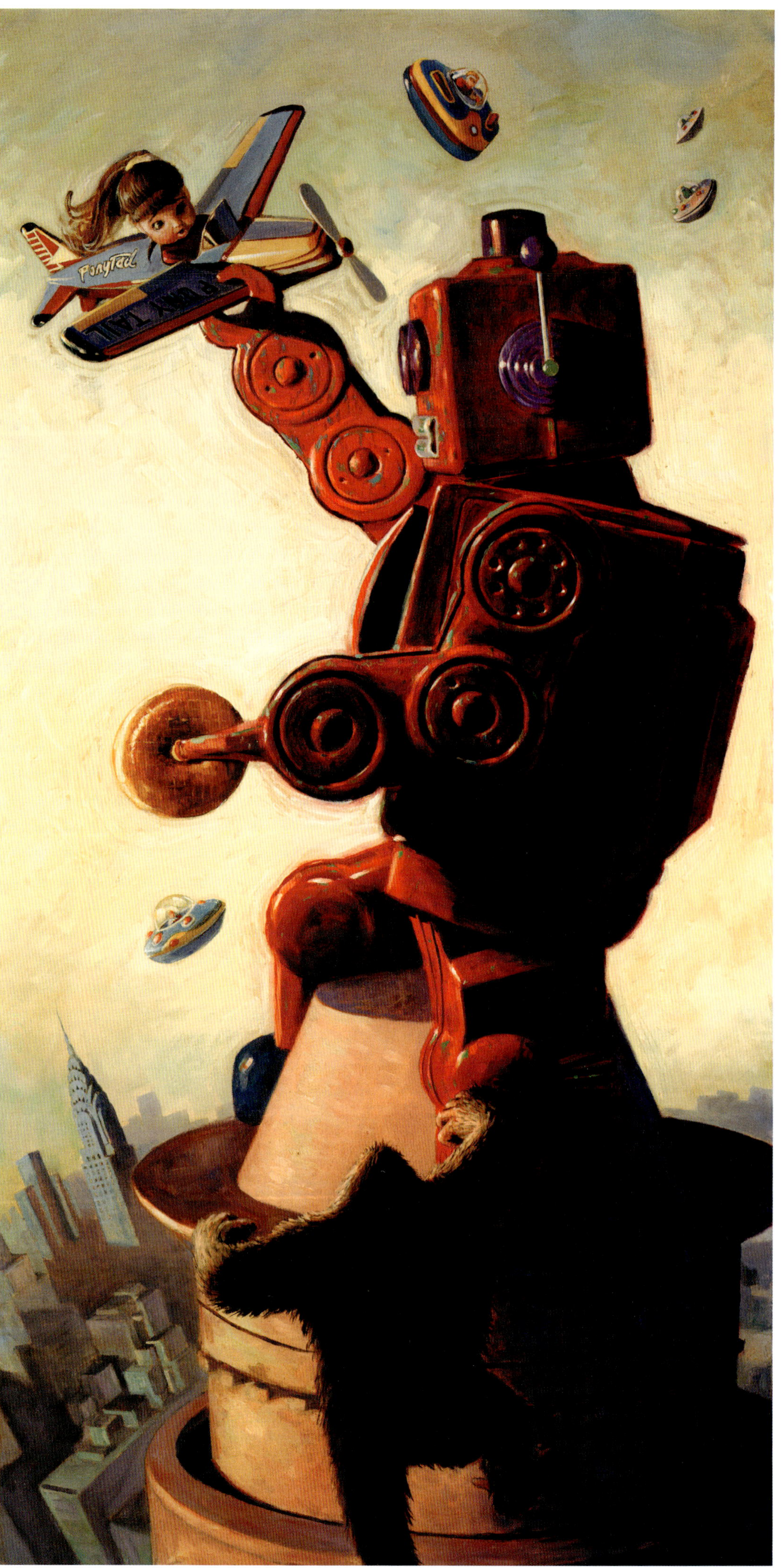

1

2

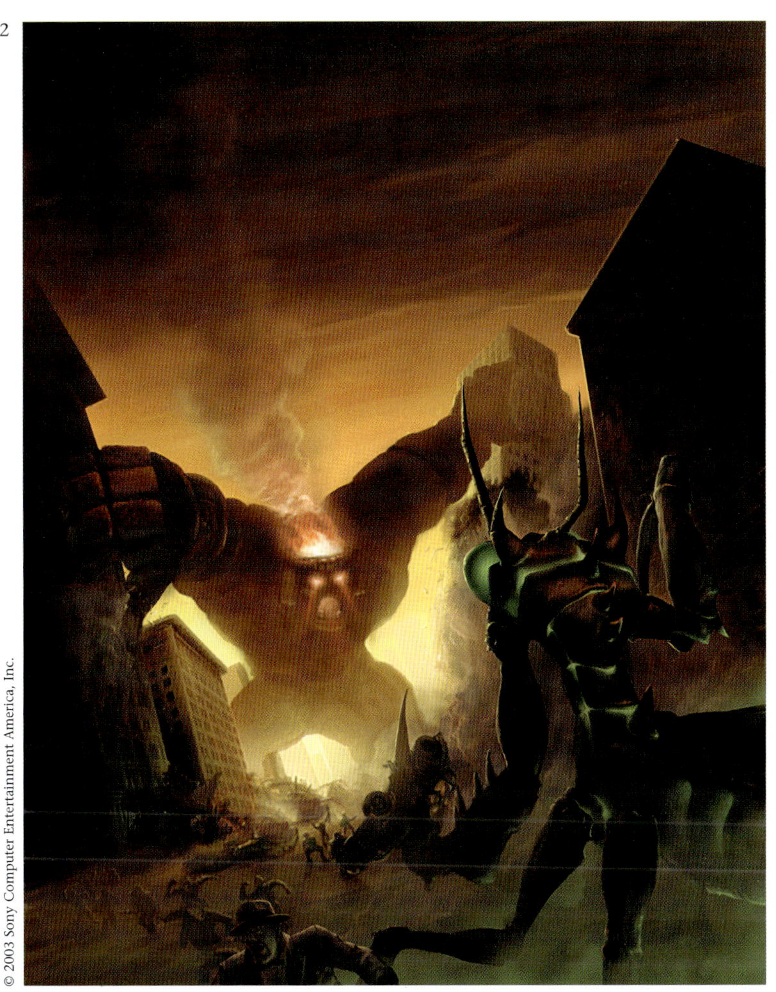

3

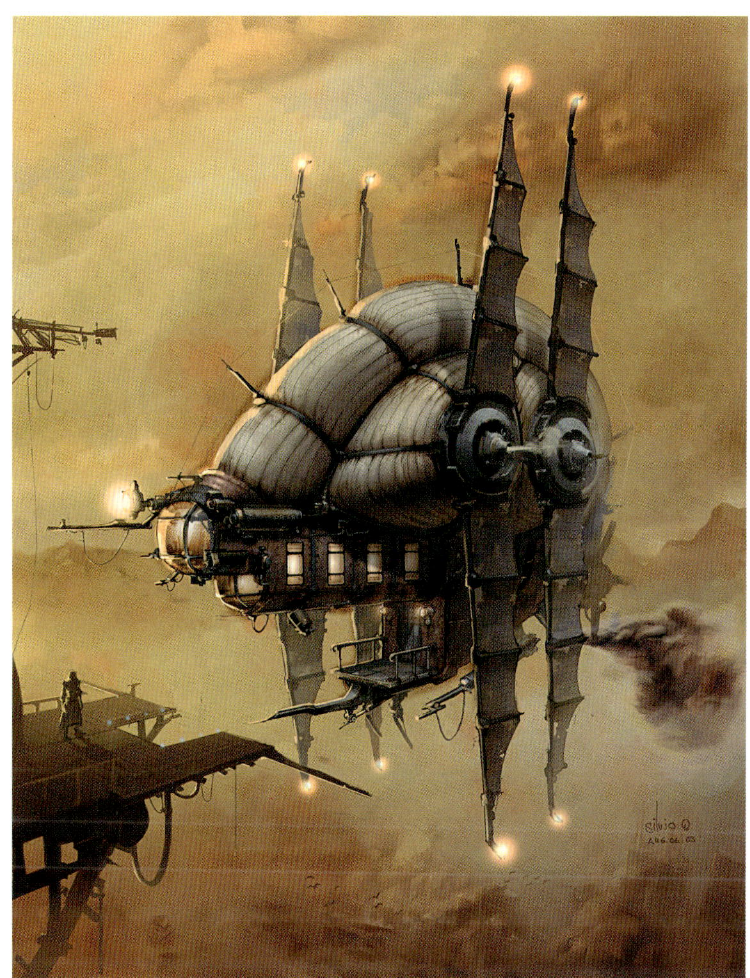

4

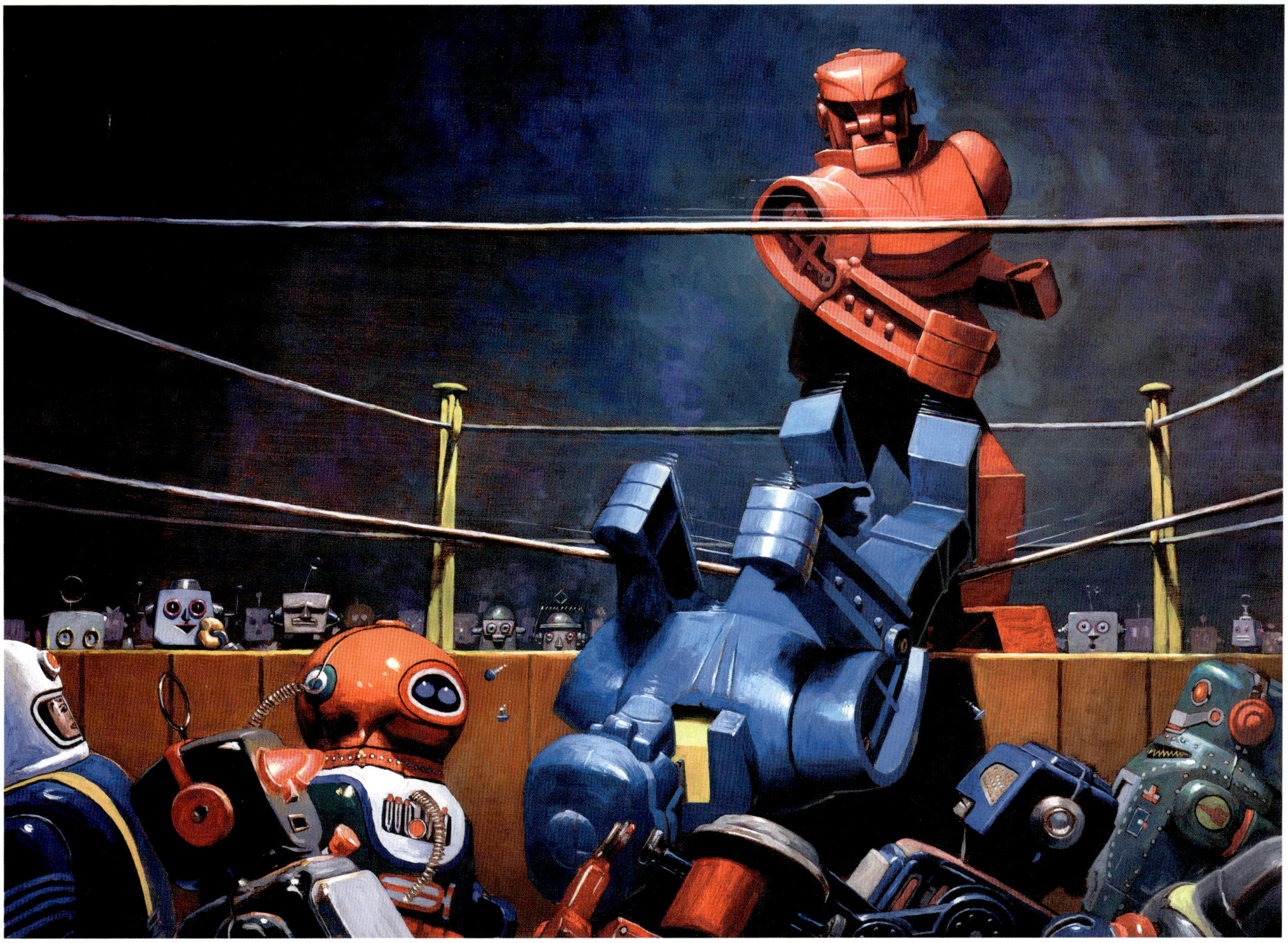

1
artist: **Farzad Varahramyan**
client: Sammy Studios
title: Nightmare
medium: Digital
size: 11″x17″

2
artist: **Matt Wilson**
art director: Jeremy Cranford
client: Wizards of the Coast
title: Fallen Angel
medium: Oils on board
size: 27″x36″

3
artist: **Chad Michael Ward**
art director: Brian Glass
designer: Chad Michael Ward
client: White Wolf
title: Petra
medium: Digital
size: 8″x10″

4
artist: **Cam de Leon**
client: Happy Pencil
title: Ghost .01
medium: Digital

1

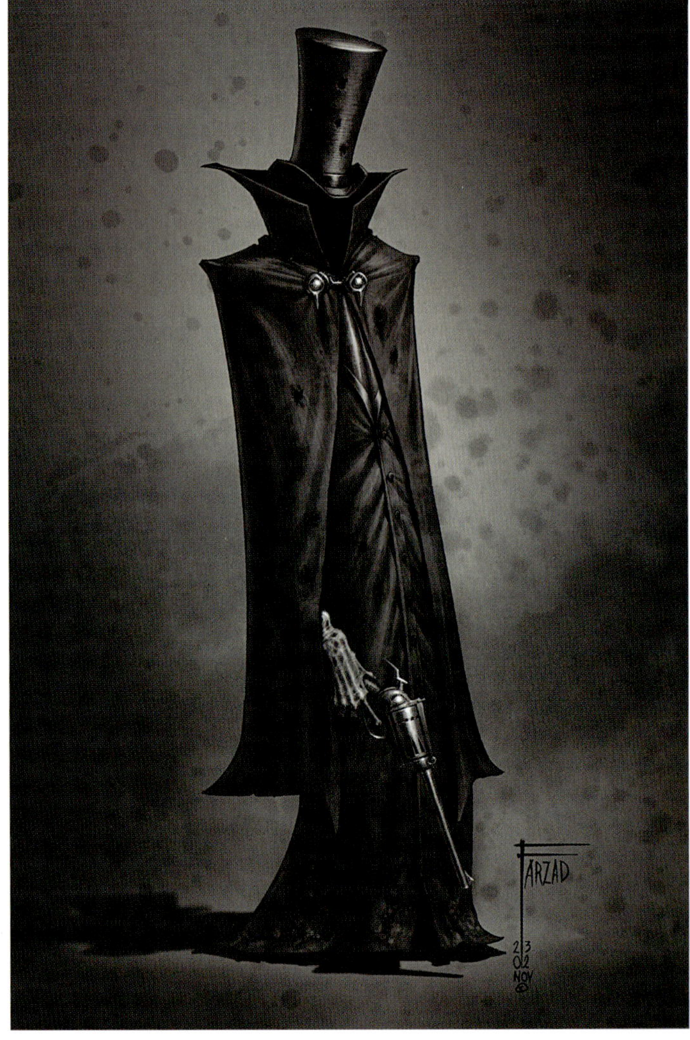

2

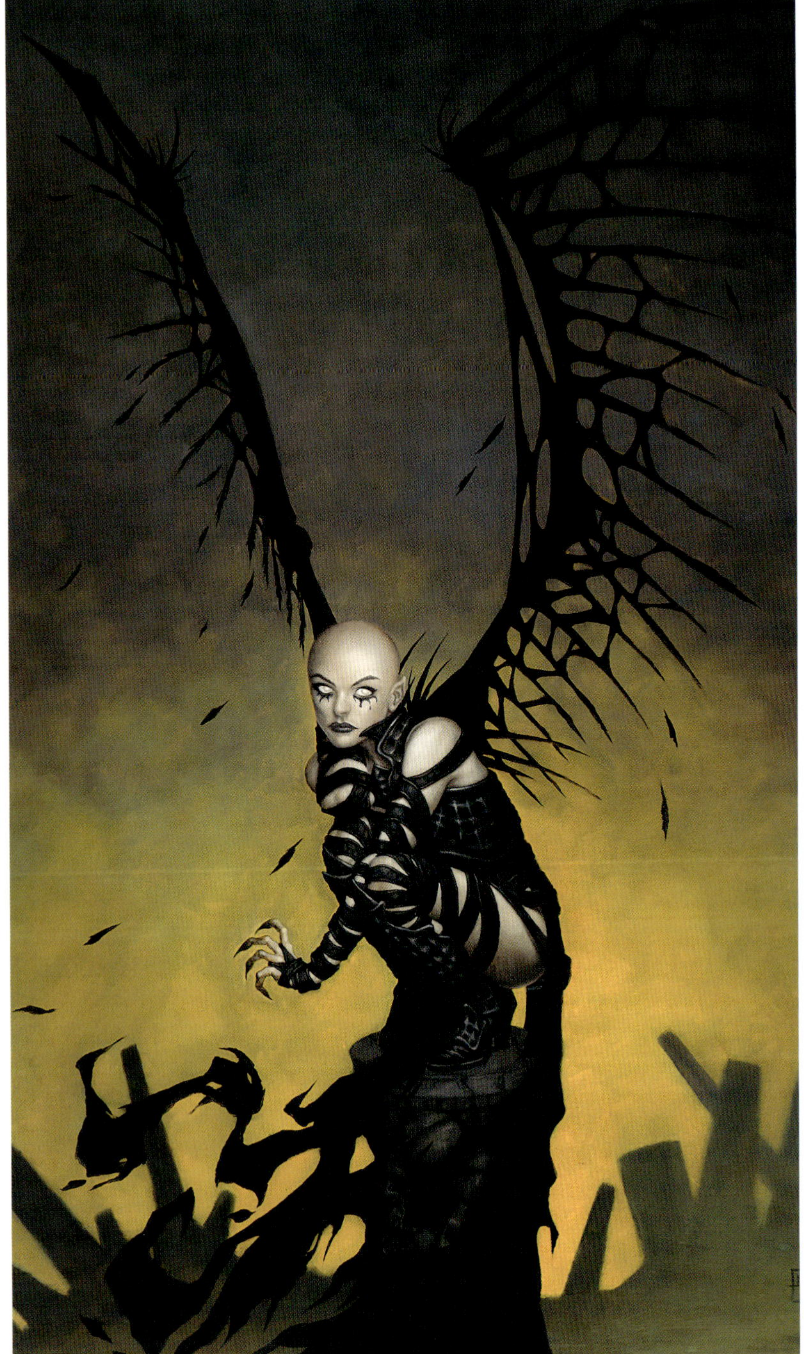

3

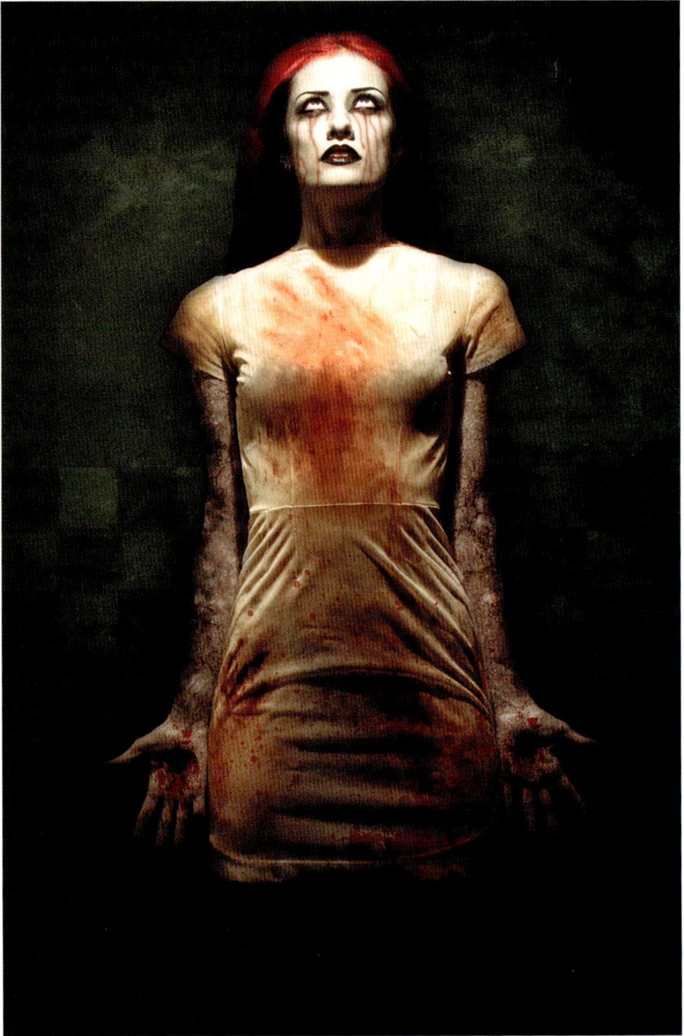

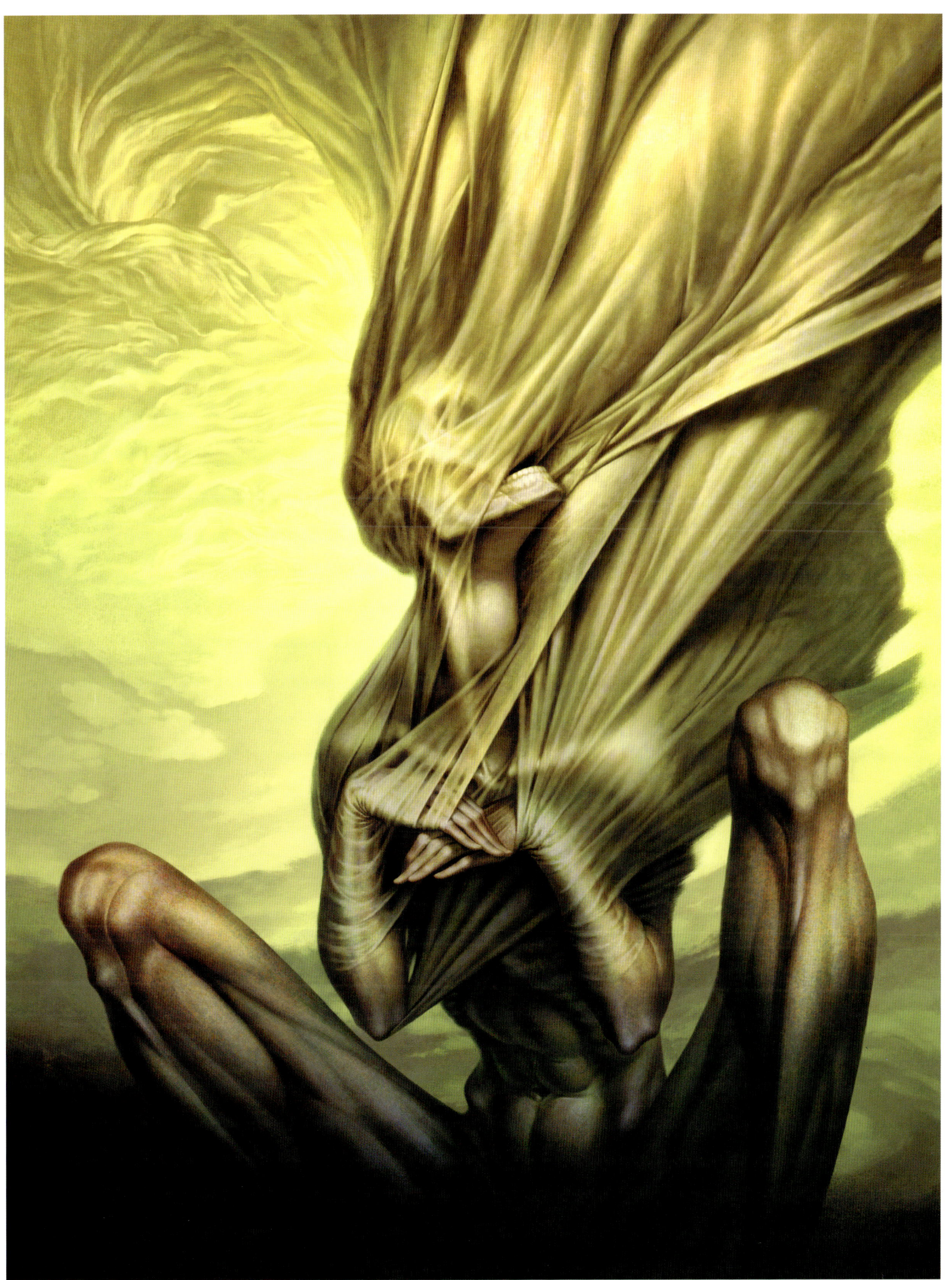

Institutional

1
artist: **Matthew S. Armstrong**
art director: Jim Pinto
client: AEG
title: Ravin Moon
medium: Digital
size: 11 1/4"x9 1/4"

2
artist: **Joe Chiodo**
art director: Dan Herman
designer: Joe Chiodo
client: Hermes Press
title: Pleasure and Pain
medium: Mixed
size: 30"x17"

3
artist: **Rob Alexander**
art director: Jeremy Cranford
client: Wizards of the Coast
title: The Great Razor Plains
medium: Watercolor
size: 20"x8"

4
artist: **Andrew Bawidamann**
art director: Doug Griffith
client: Macsking
title: Byte in Space
medium: Digital
size: 11 1/4"x9"

5
artist: **Ken Wong**
art director: American McGee
client: Waxploitation
title: Alice vs the Matrix
medium: Digital

6
artist: **Chris Hopkins**
art director: Chris Hopkins/ Phil Howe
client: Illustrated Images
title: Hervor
medium: Oils on canvas
size: 22"x34"

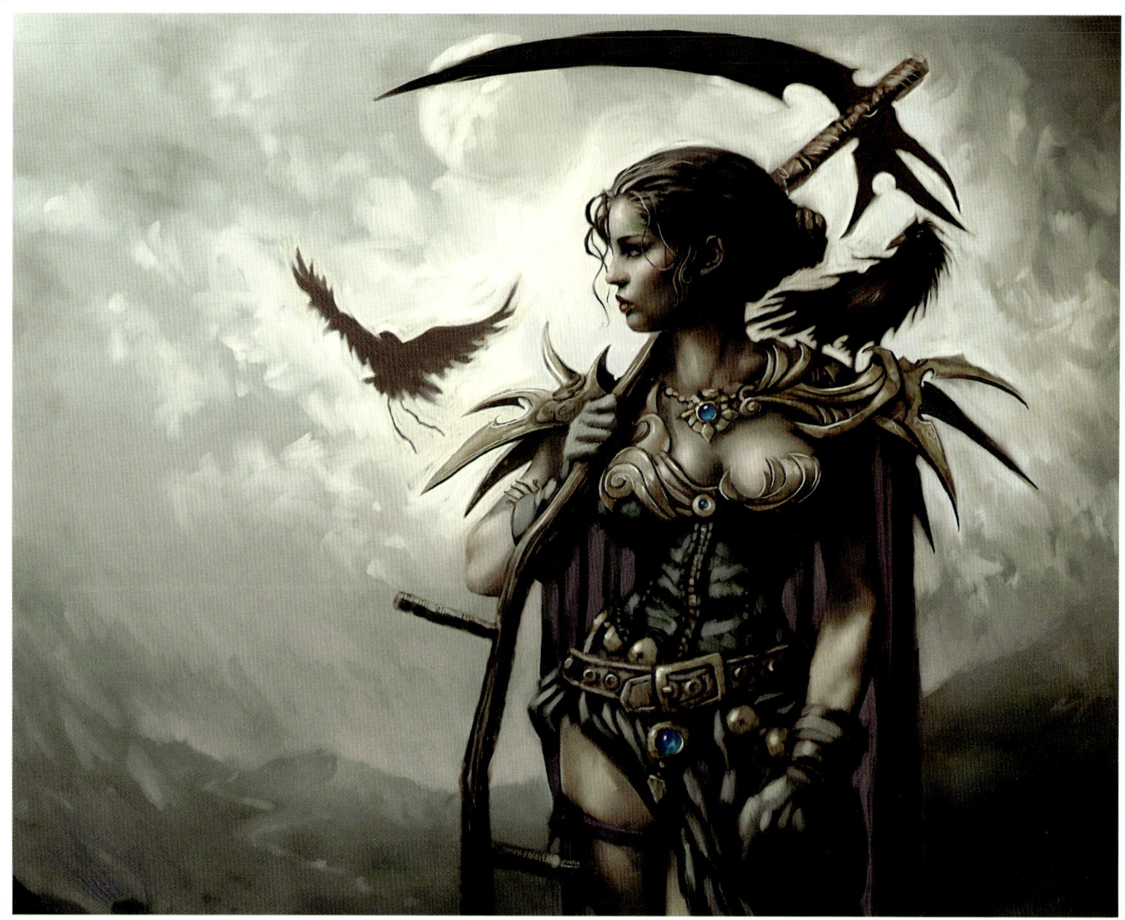
1

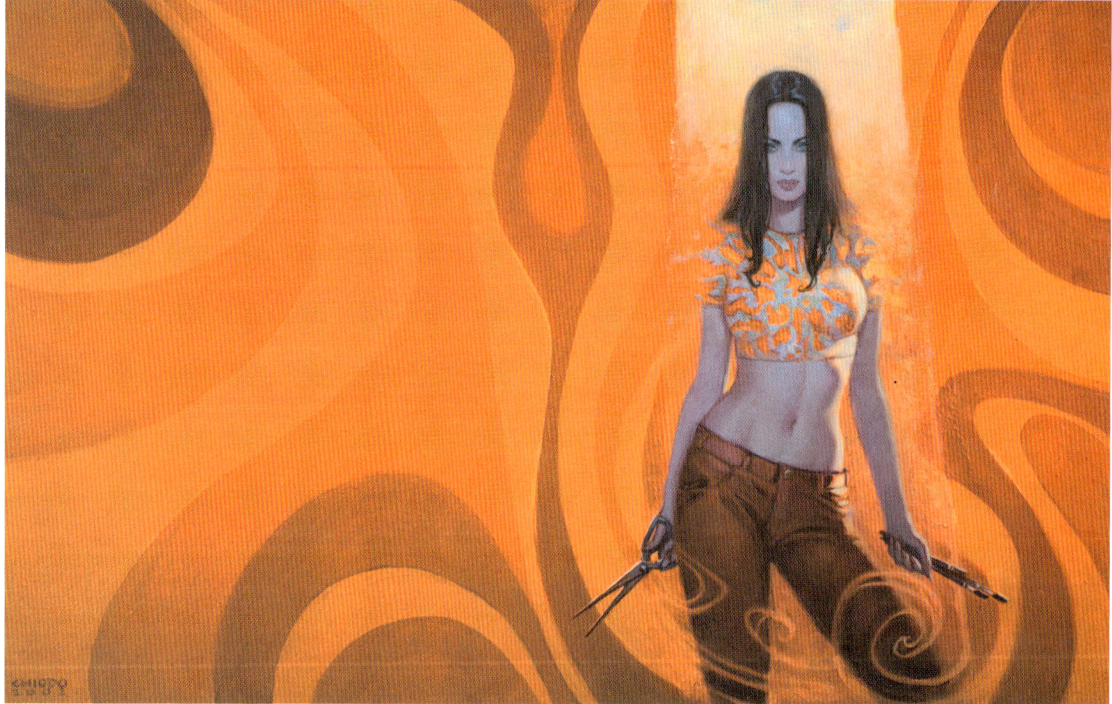
2

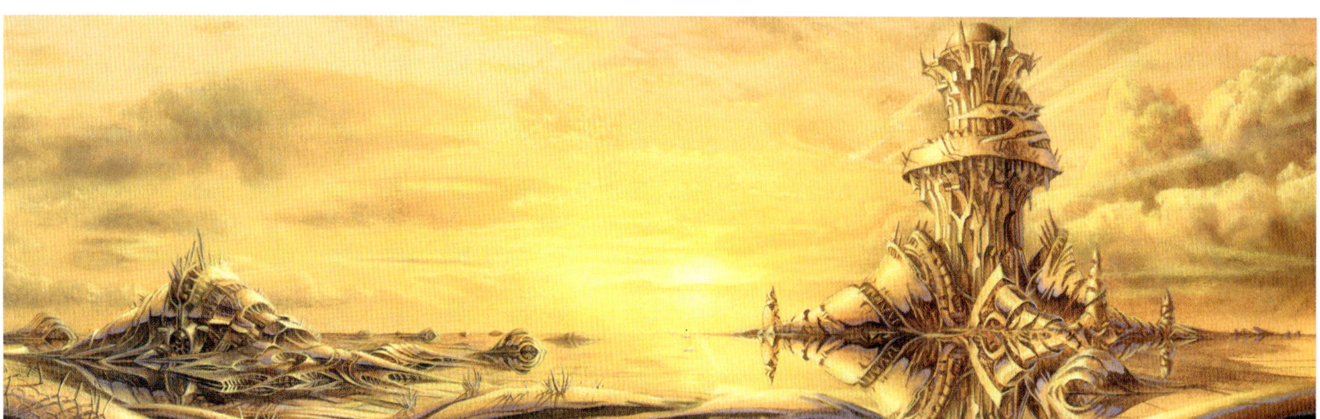
3

4

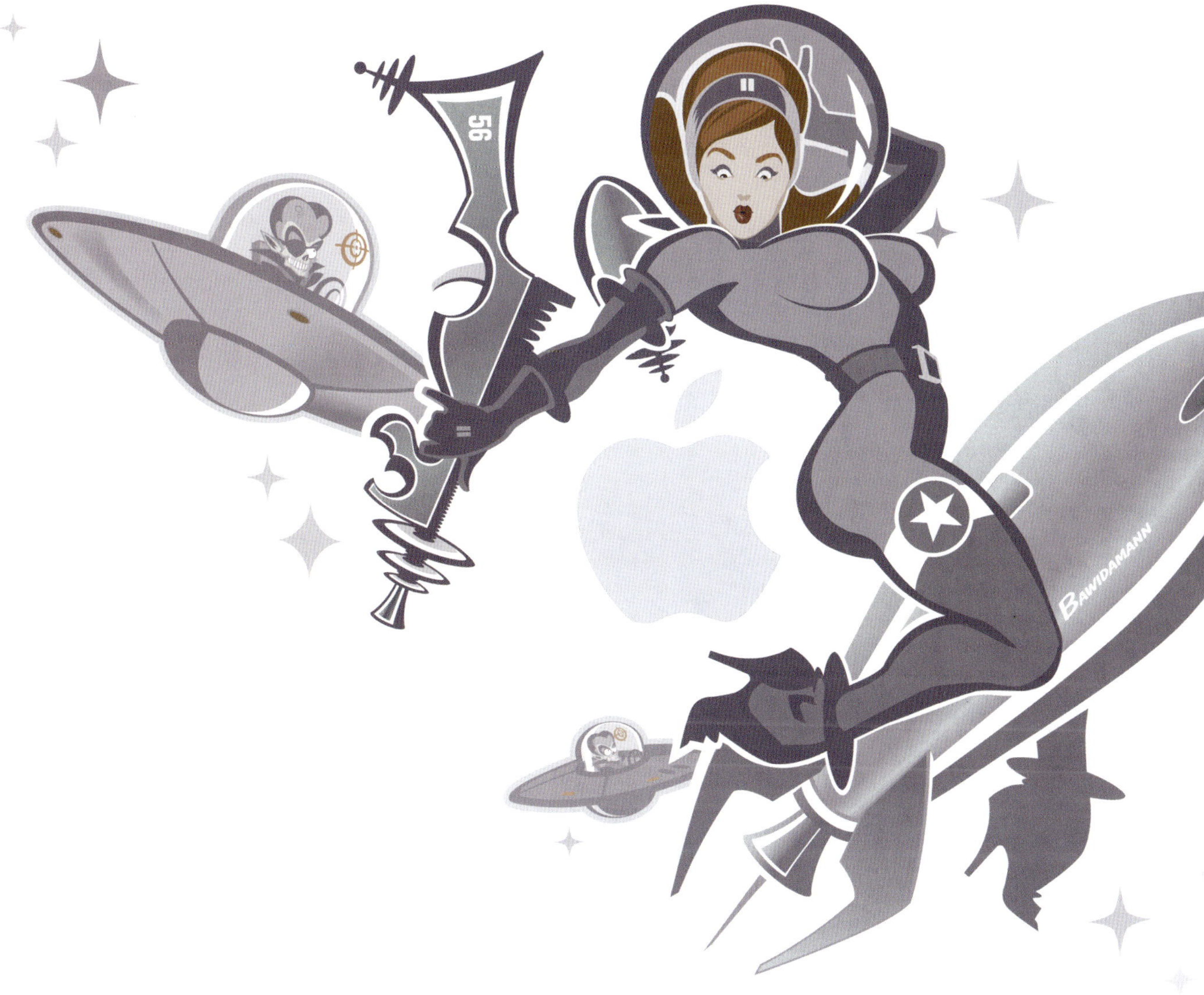

5

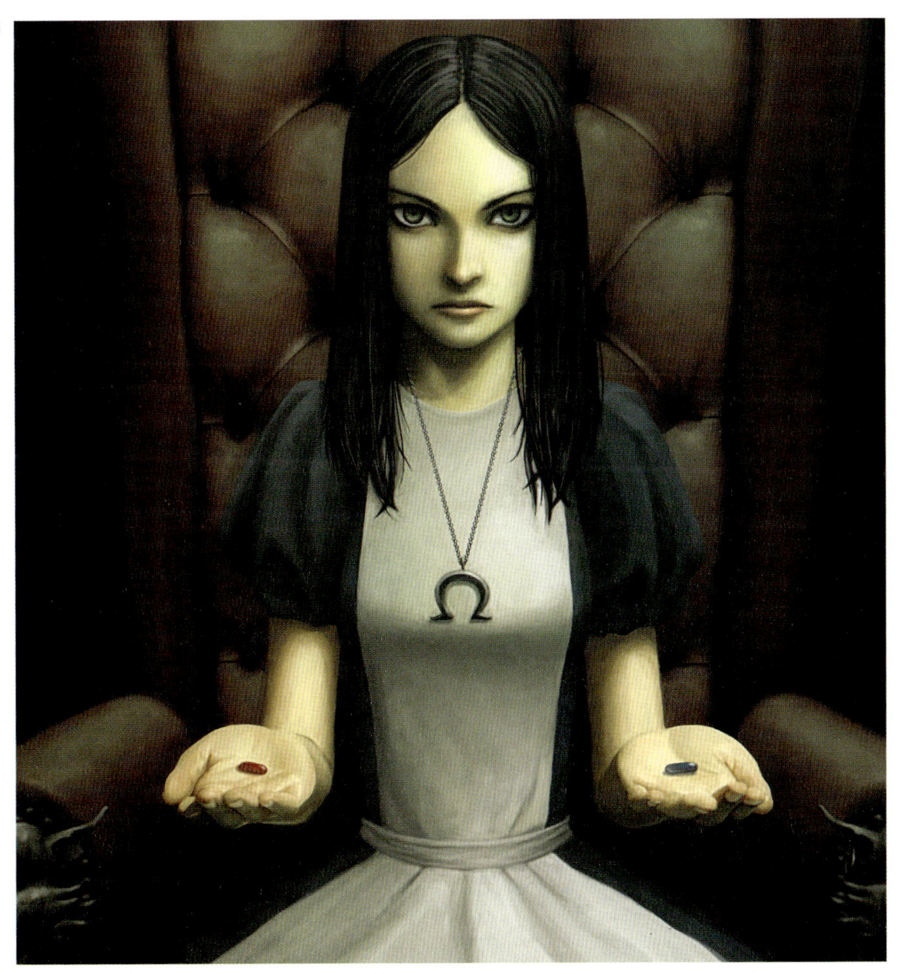

6

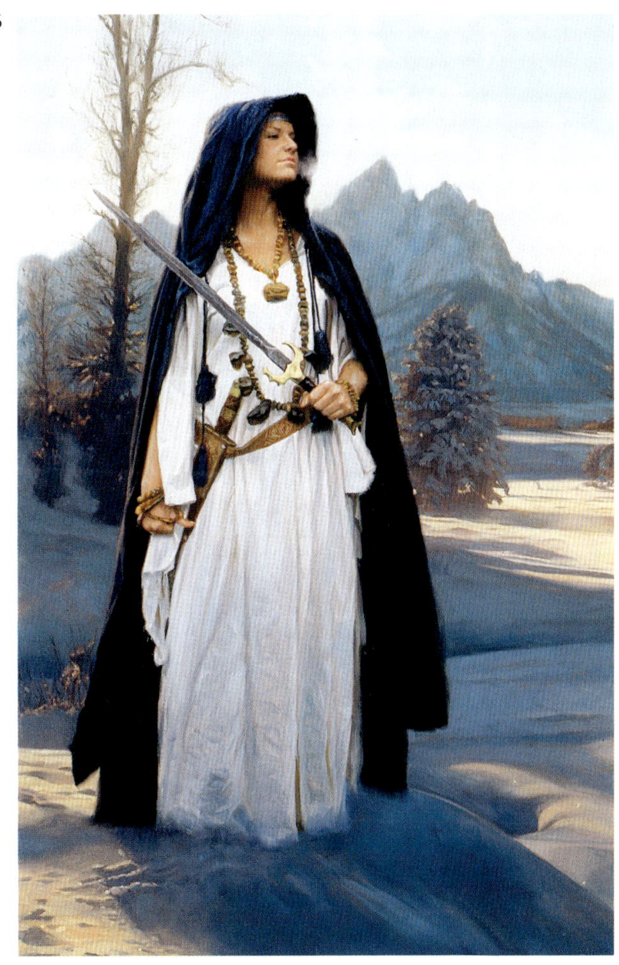

Institutional

1
artist: **Kirk Reinert**
art director: Lilli Farrell/
Kirk Reinert
client: Harmony Art USA
title: Pisces
medium: Acrylics
size: 40″x30″

2
artist: **R.K. Post**
client: White Wolf
title: Lucita
medium: Digital
size: $8\frac{1}{2}$″x11″

3
artist: **Scott Fischer**
art director: Jeremy Cranford
client: Wizards of the Coast
title: Pristine Angel
medium: Mixed
size: $13\frac{1}{2}$″x20″

4
artist: **Luis Royo**
client: Heavy Metal
title: Alia and the Valley
of Doom
medium: Acrylics
size: 10″x16″

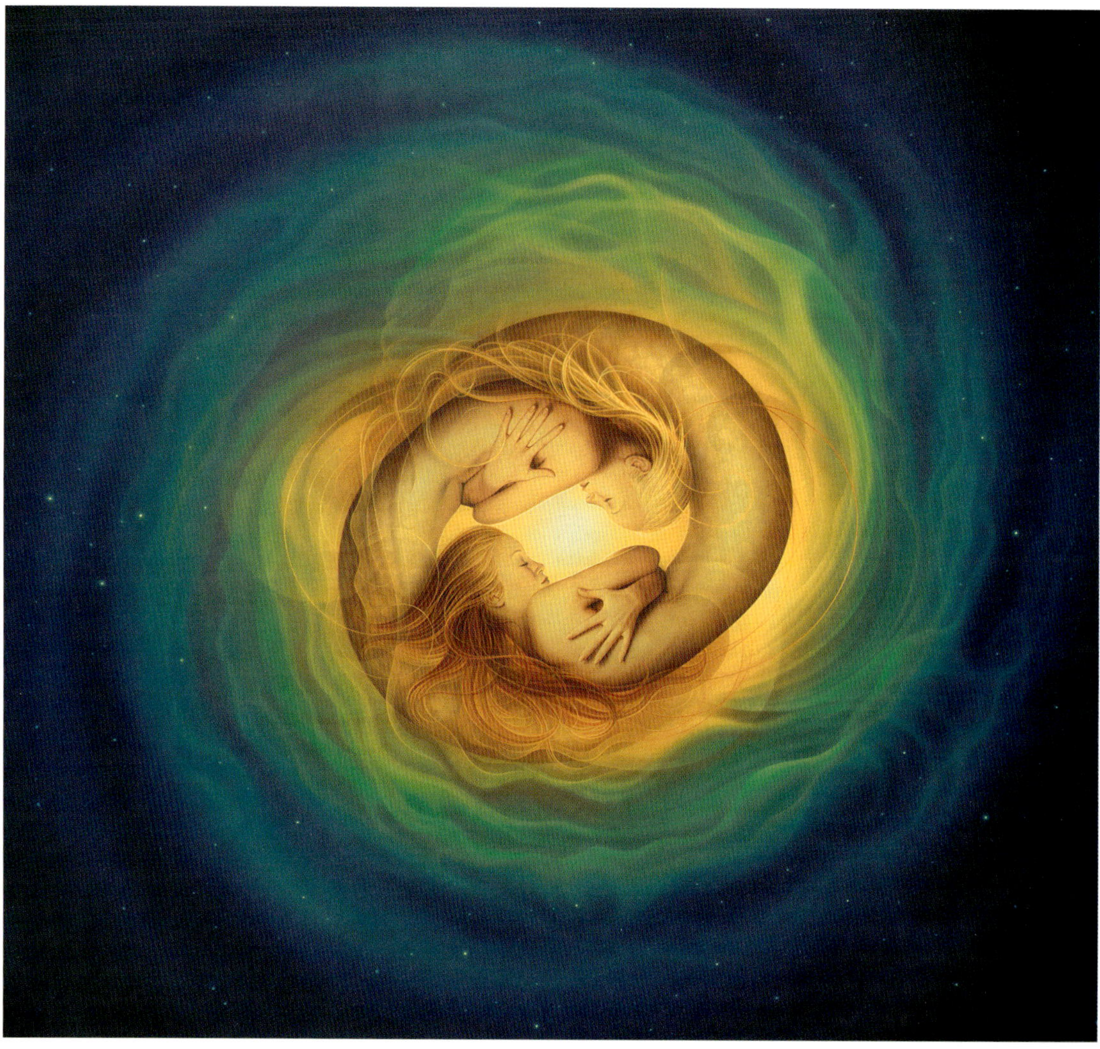

1

2

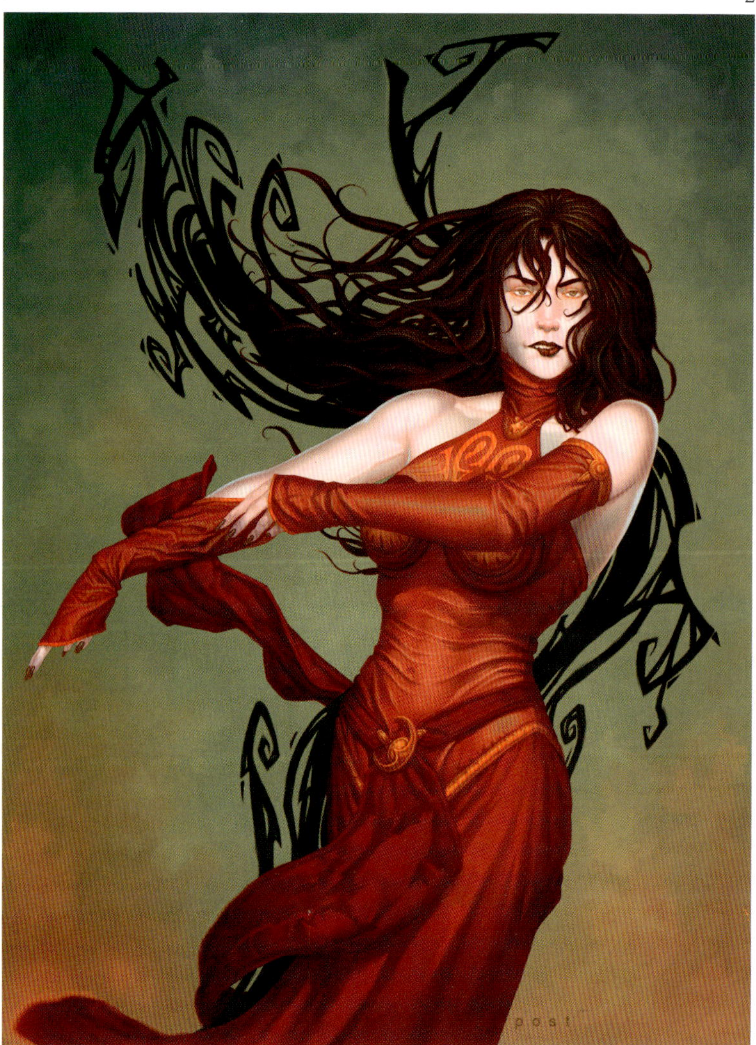

3

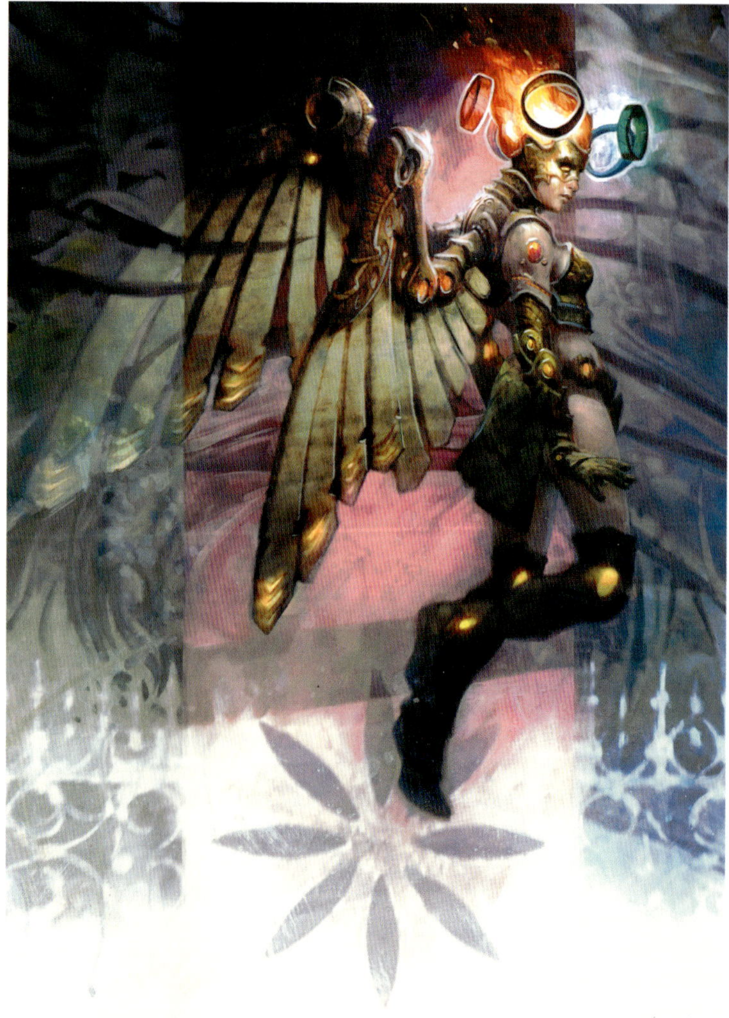

4

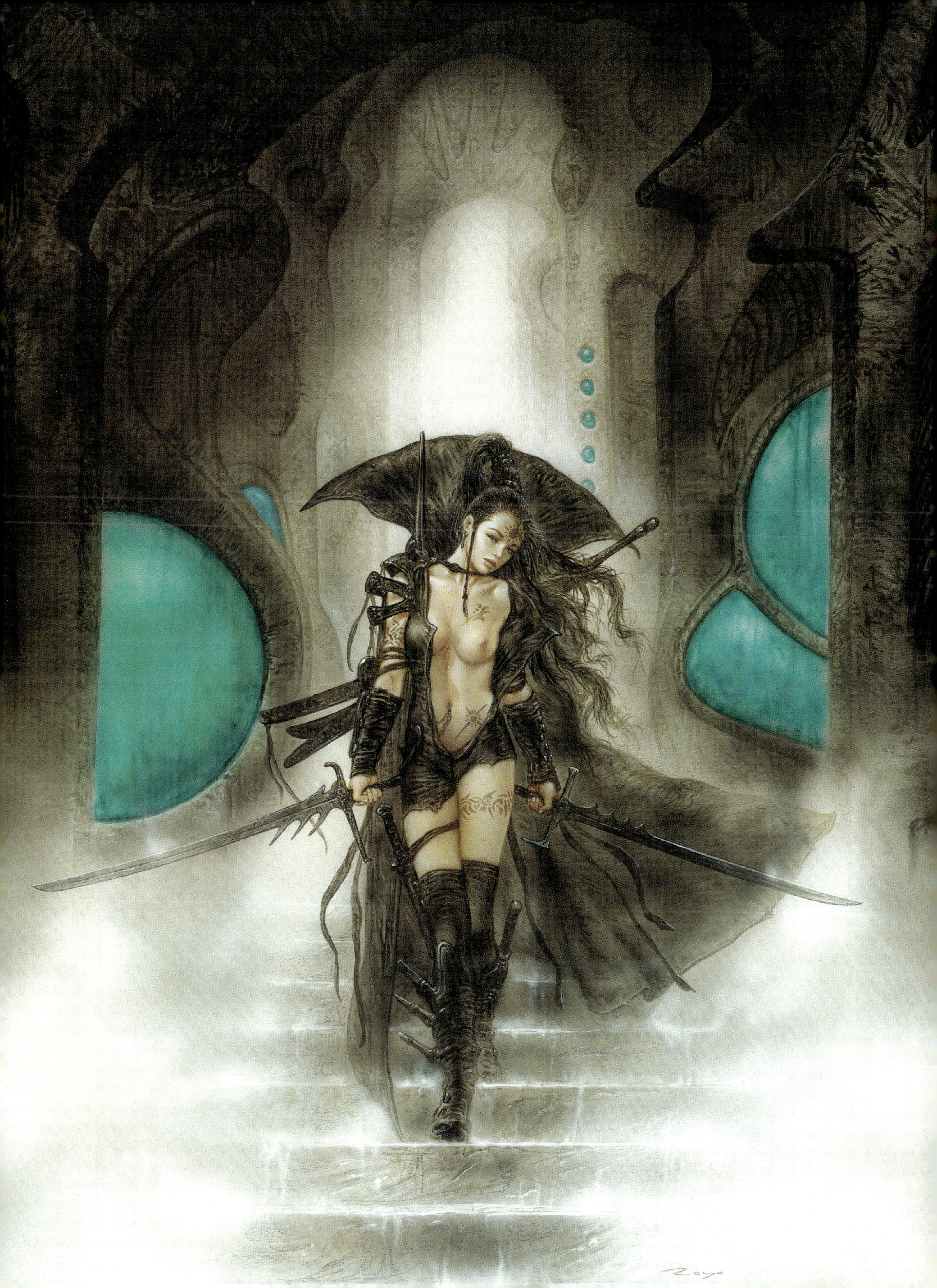
Royo

Institutional

1
artist: **Richard Laurent**
client: Laurent Design
title: Evolution
medium: Oils
size: 16″x20″

2
artist: **William Stout**
art director: Eric Poesch
client: Uncle Milton Industries, Inc.
title: Jurassic & Cretaceous Dinosaurs
medium: Oils on canvas
size: 45″x14″

3
artist: **Jerry Lofaro**
art director: Duy Nguyen
client: Hallmark Entertainment
title: Chasmosaur Senate (Dinotopia Style Guide)
medium: Digital
size: 9″x12″

4
artist: **Shaun Ye Zhonqyi**
title: Blood Wolf
medium: Digital
size: 19″x32″

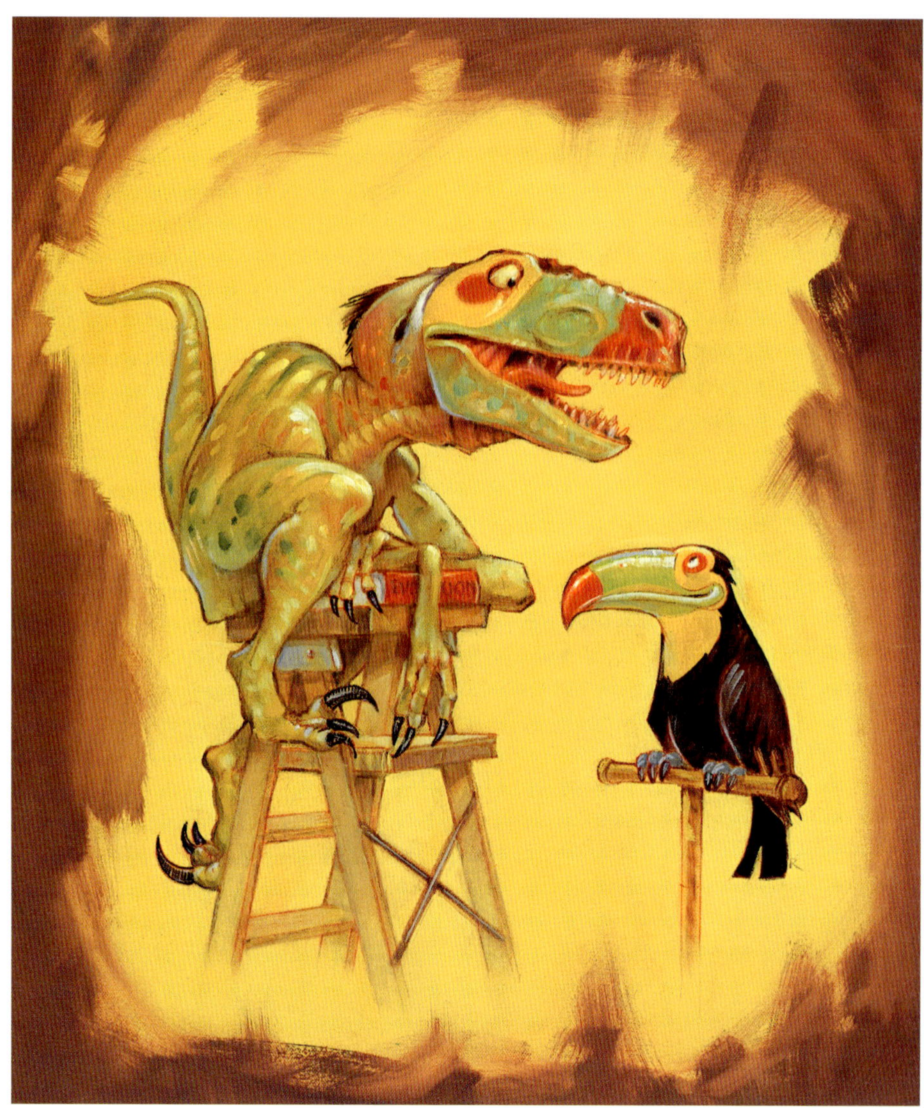

1

2

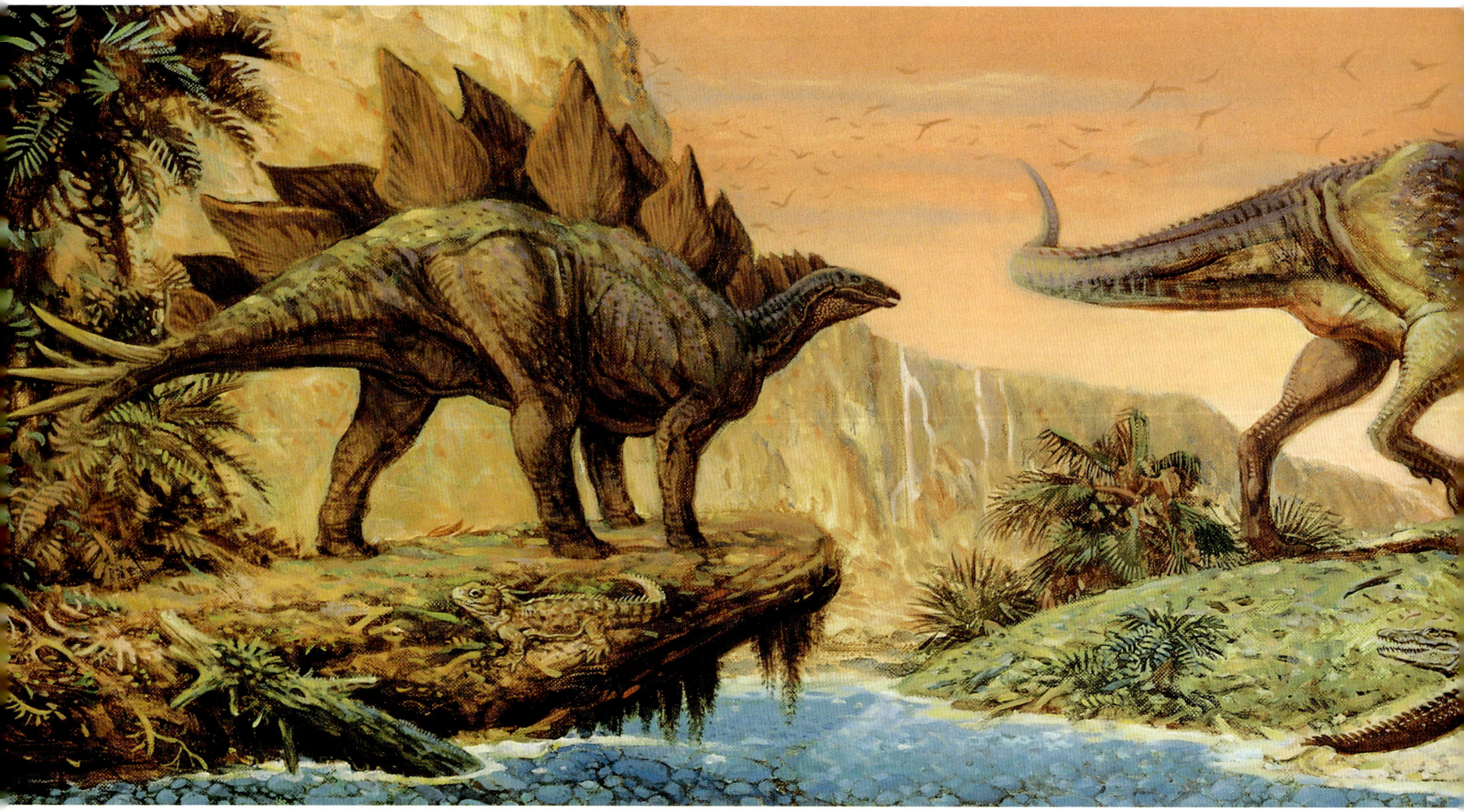

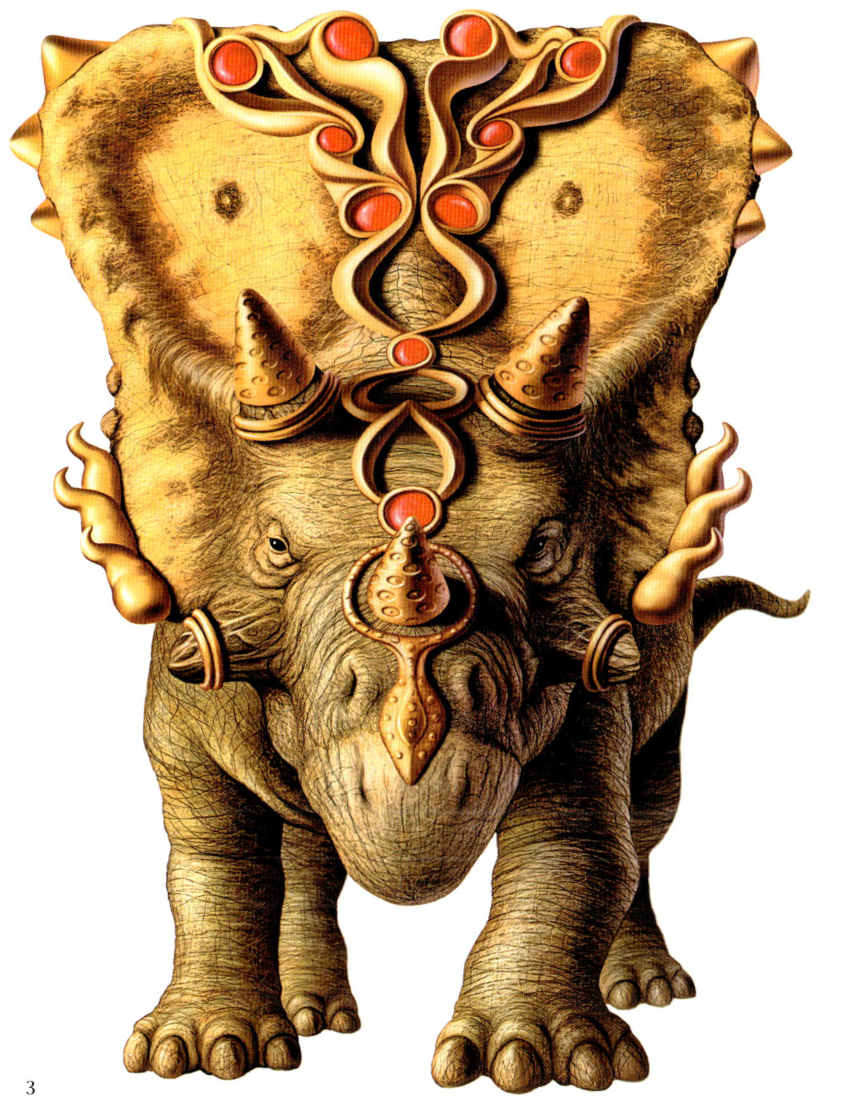

3

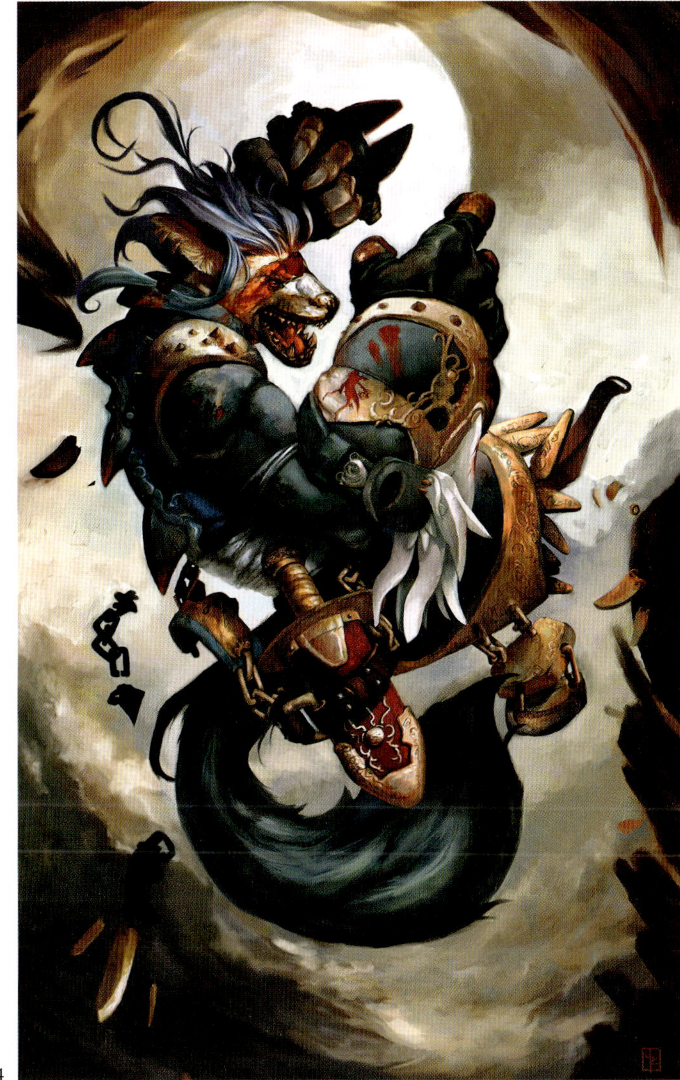

4

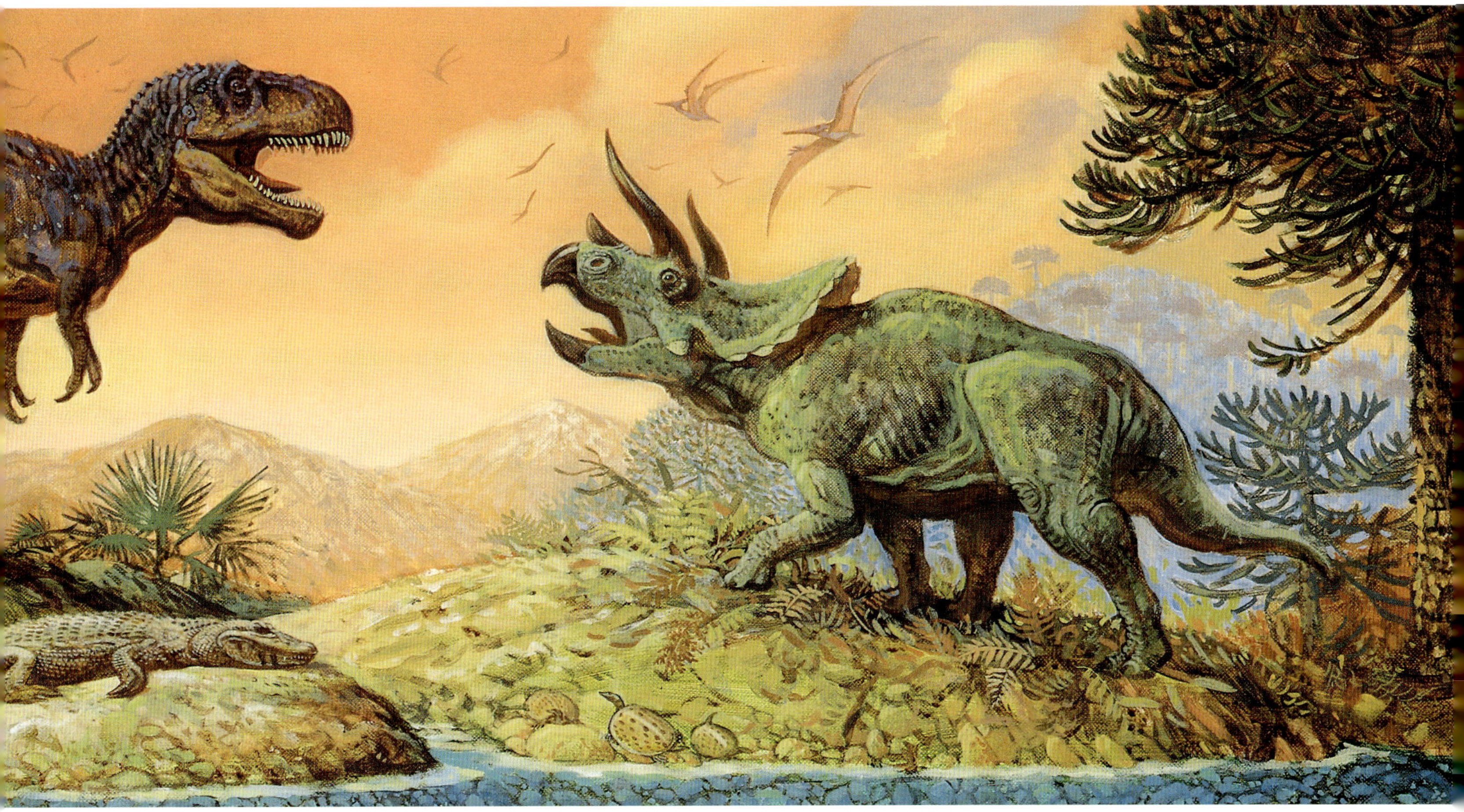

Institutional

1
artist: **Peter de Sève**
art director: Ralph Eggelston
client: Pixar
title: Little Nemo Character Design
medium: Pencil

2
artist: **Peter de Sève**
art director: Ralph Eggelston
client: Pixar
title: Little Nemo Character Design
medium: Pencil

3
artist: **Tony DiTerlizzi**
designer: Francine Kass
client: Simon & Schuster
title: Let Loose This Holiday Season
medium: Pen & ink, watercolor
size: 14"x17"

4
artist: **Peter de Sève**
art director: Peter de Sève/ Lori Barra
designer: Lori Barra
client: Tremaine Gallery
title: An Idle Mind
medium: Ink & watercolor

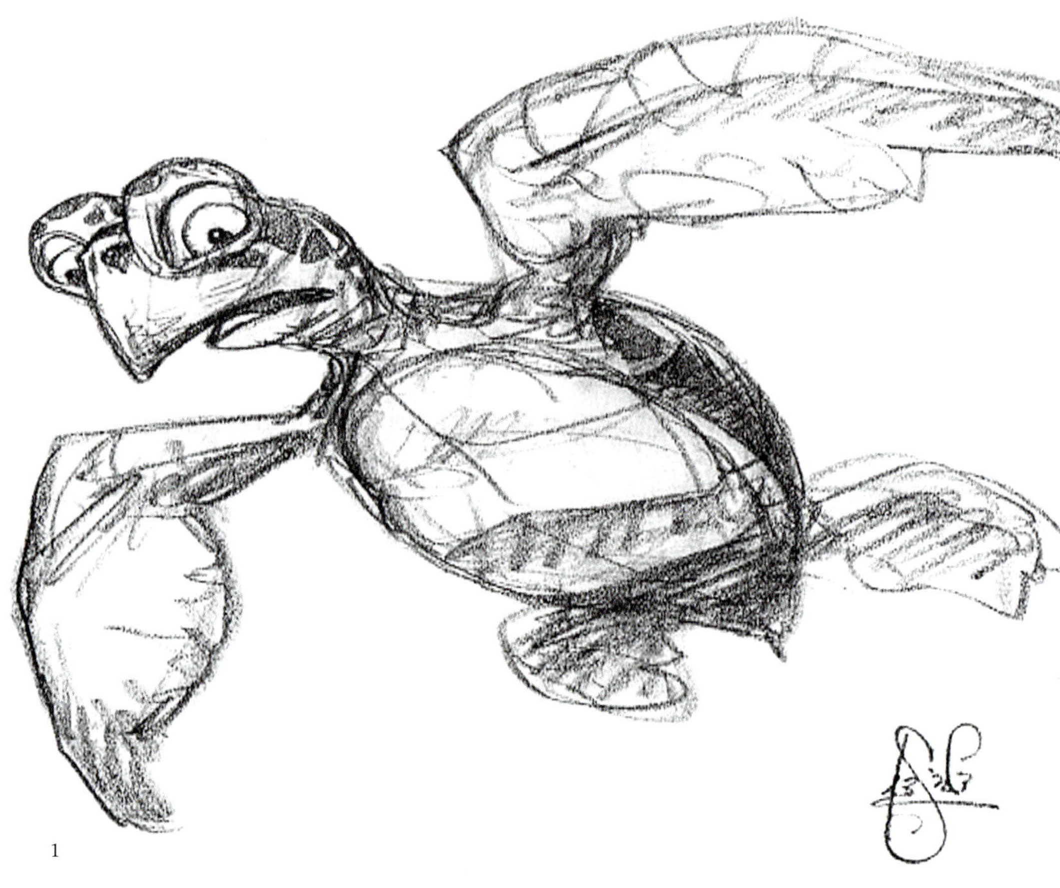

1

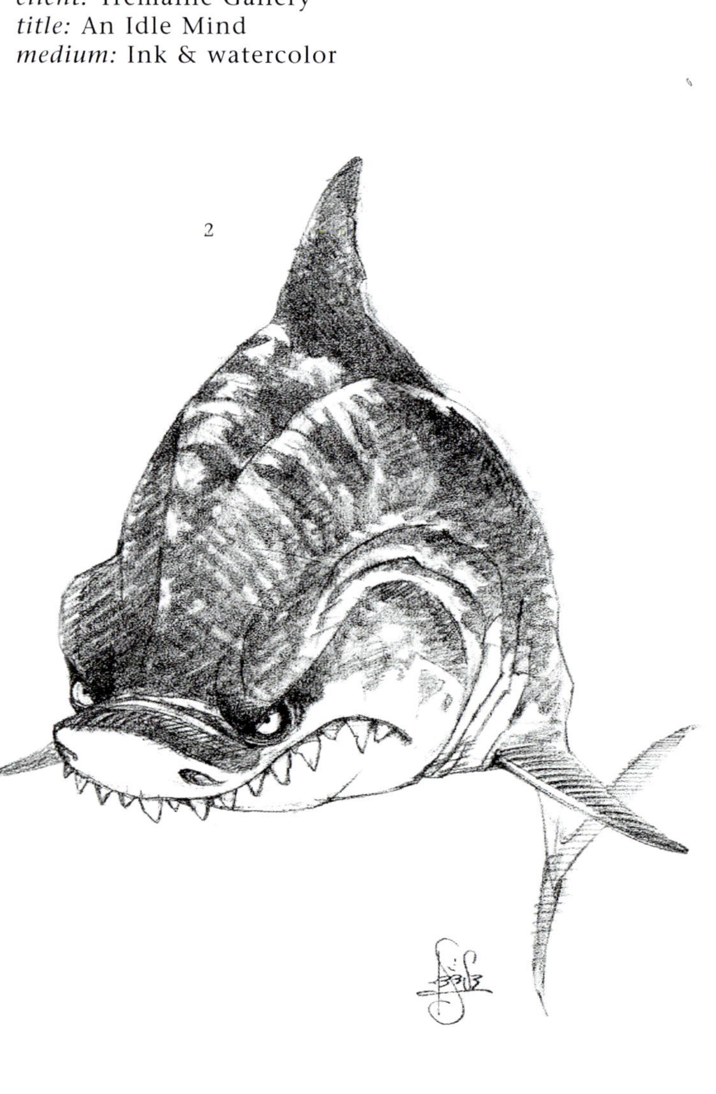

2

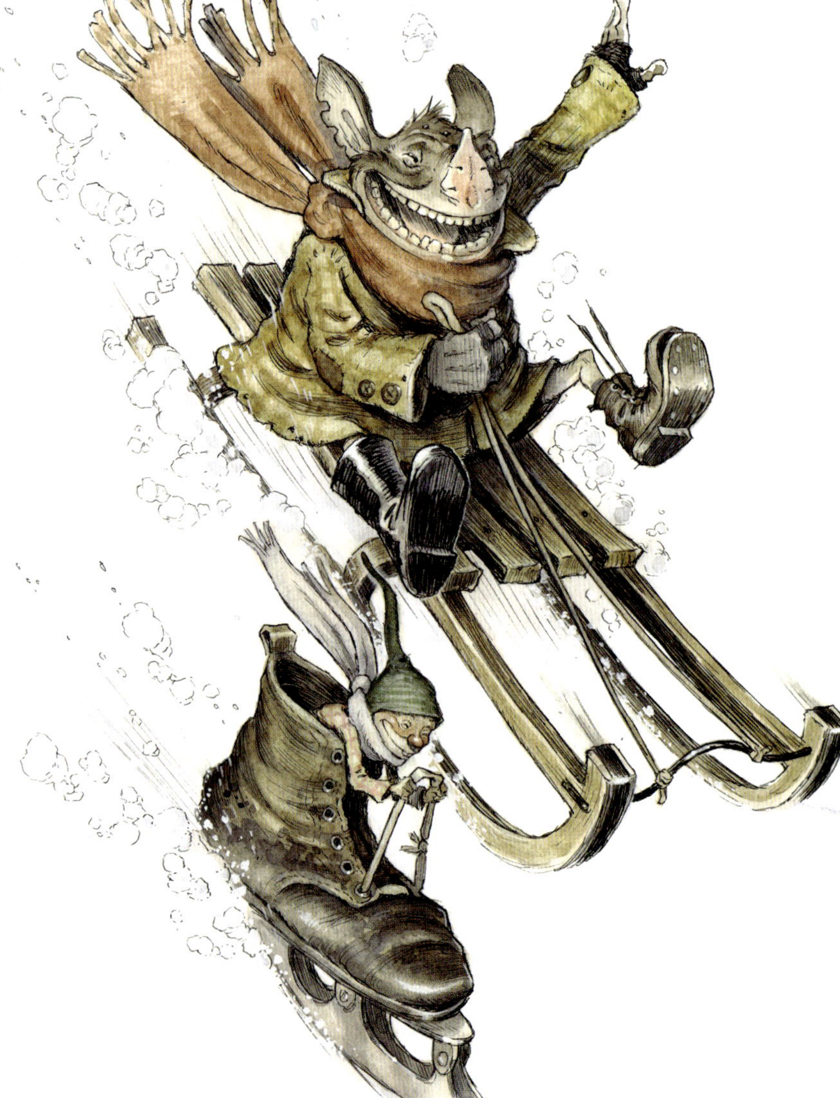

3

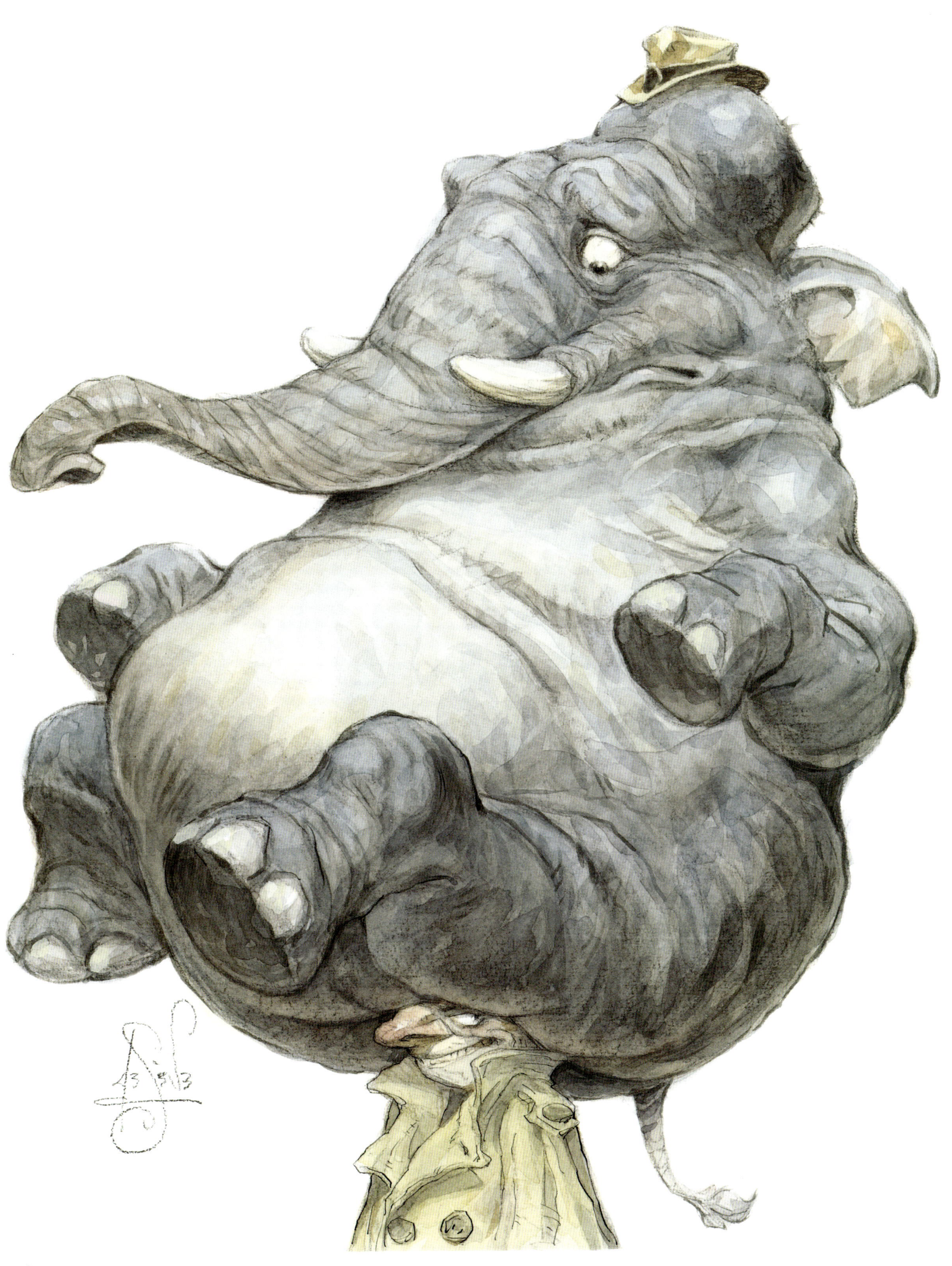

4

Institutional

1
artist: **Anthony S. Waters**
art director: Dana Knutson
client: Wizards of the Coast
title: Cinder Wall
medium: Digital
size: 12″x9″

2
artist: **Mark Covell**
title: The Way
medium: Oils/digital
size: 20″x16″

3
artist: **Brainzoo Studios**
art director: Farzad Varahramyan
client: Sammy Studios
title: High Moon Town
medium: Mixed/digital
size: 11″x8 1/2″

4
artist: **Vincent Di Fate**
title: 50th Anniversary of The Creature
medium: Acrylics
size: 13″x17″

5
artist: **Miles Teves**
art director: Keith Vanderlaan
client: Captive Audience
title: Man-Made Monster Concept
medium: Pencil
size: 11″x17″

6
artist: **Francis Tsai**
art director: Chris Ulm
client: Sammy Studios
title: High Moon
medium: Digital
size: 17″x11″

1

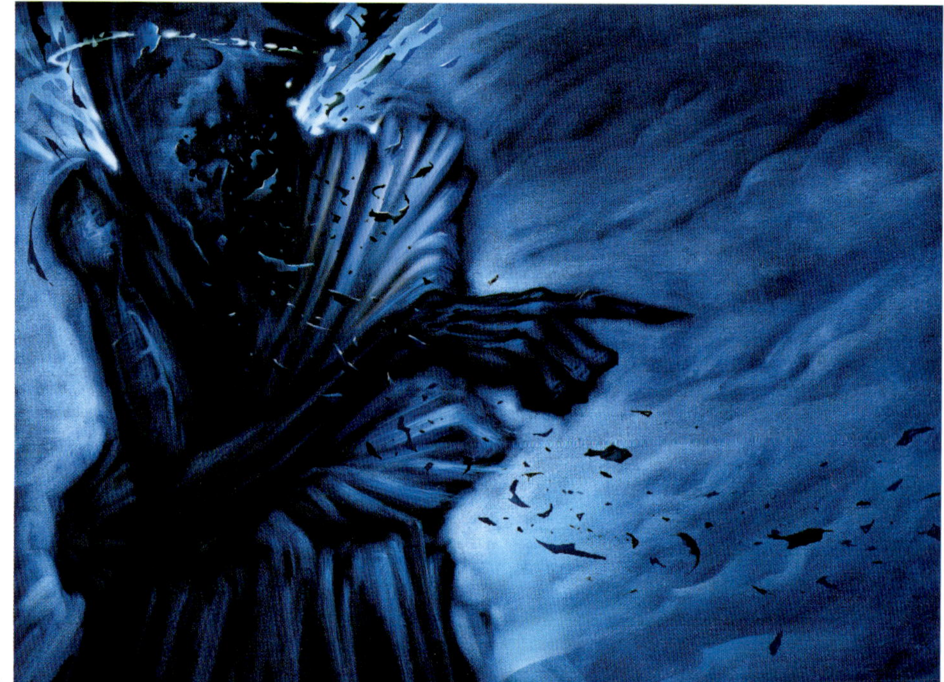

2

3

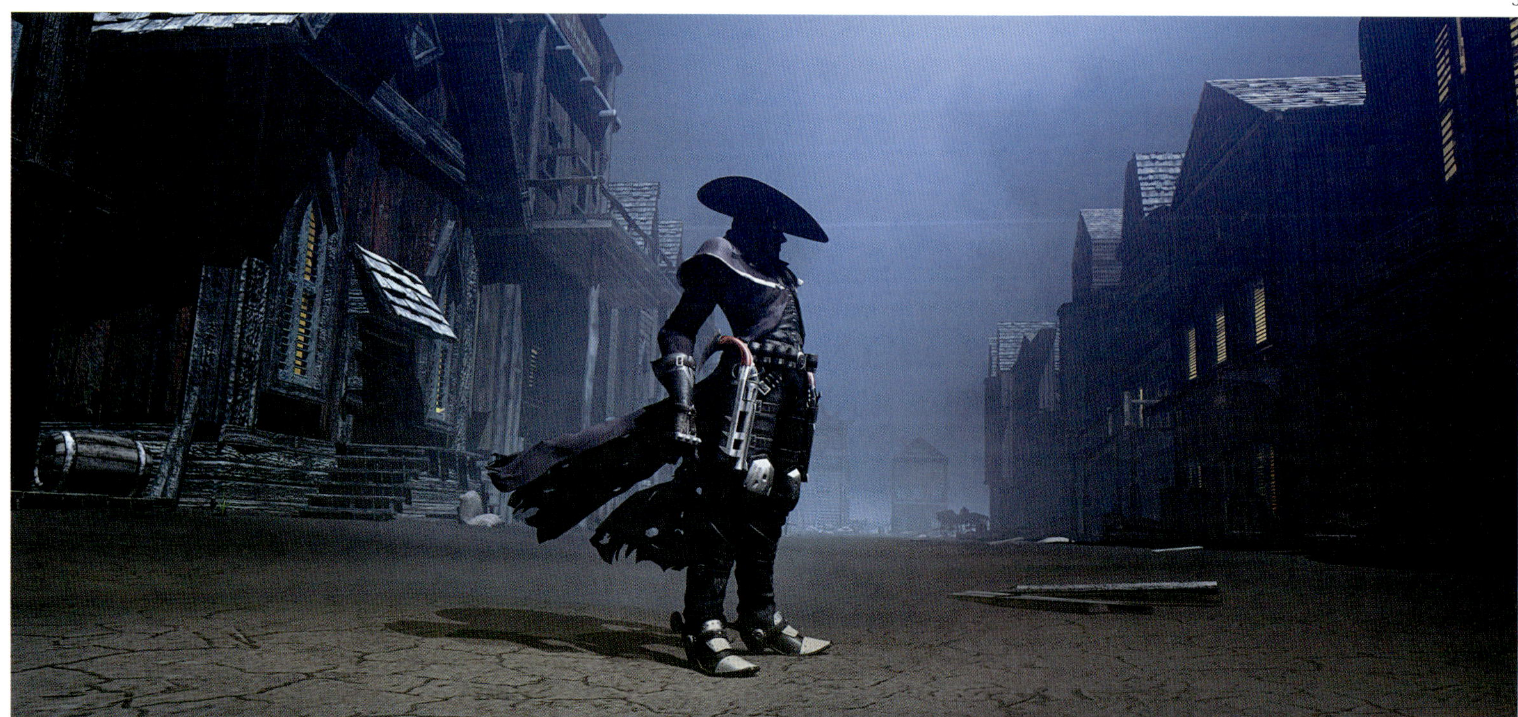

4

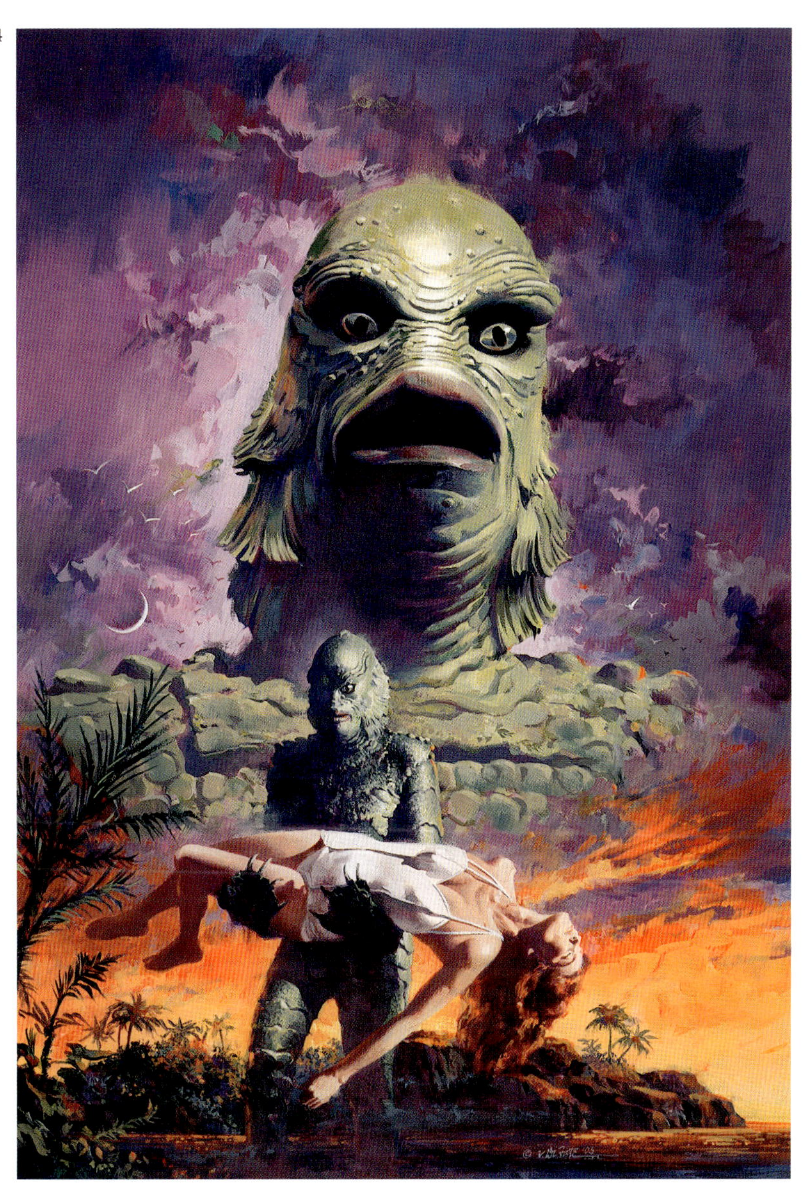

5

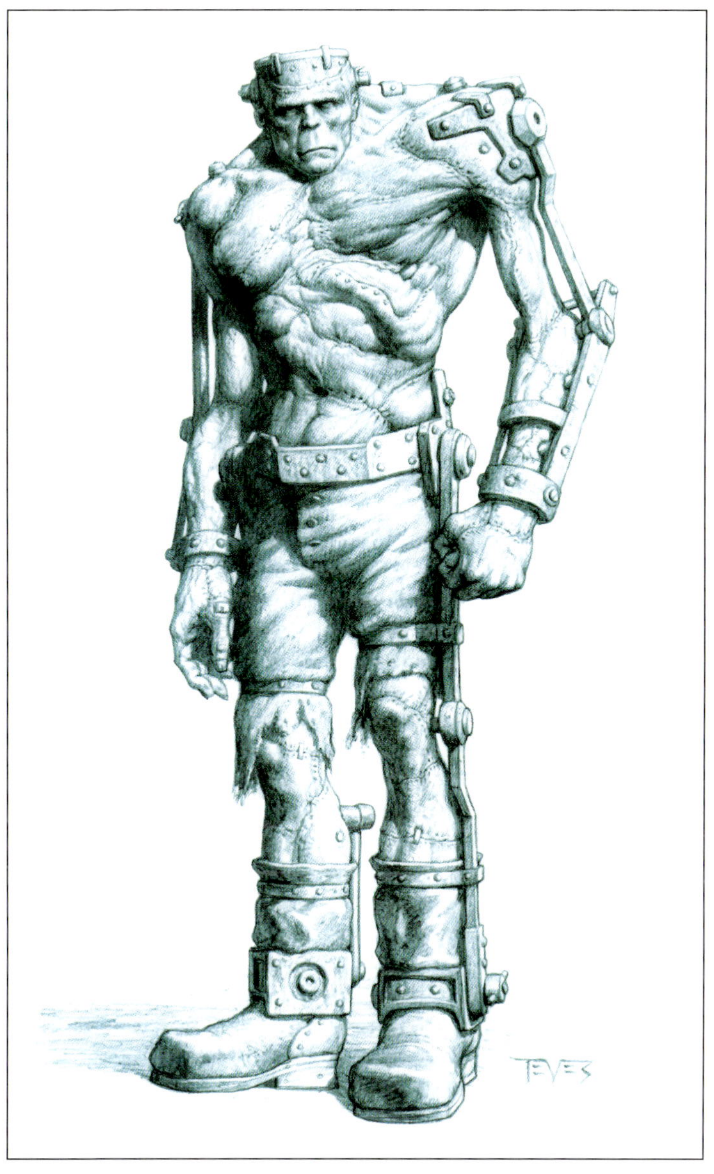

6

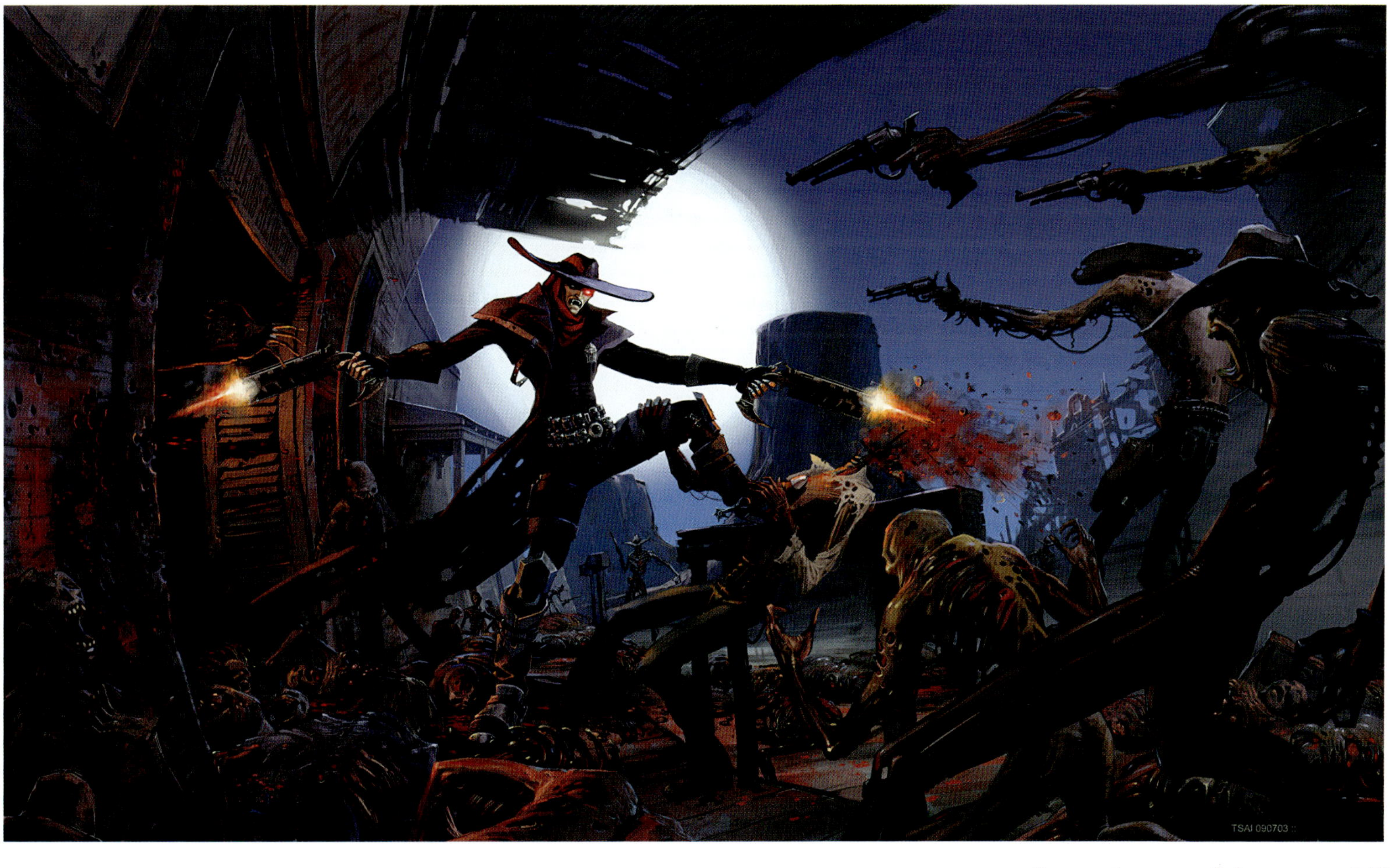

Institutional

1
artist: **David Hudnut**
art director: Daniel Kaufman
client: Sabretooth Games
title: Heavy Support Squad
medium: Digital
size: 10″x8″

2
artist: **Christopher Moeller**
art director: Jeremy Cranford
client: Wizards of the Coast
title: Bloodstoke Howler
medium: Acrylics
size: 12″x9″

3
artist: **Raymond Swanland**
art director: Lorne Lanning
designer: Raymond Swanland
client: Oddworld Inhabitants
title: Steef
medium: Digital
size: 10 1/2″x8″

4
artist: **Paul Bonner**
art director: Jean Bey
designer: Paul Bonner
client: Rackham
title: Bran-ô-kor Orcs
medium: Watercolor
size: 57cmx41cm

5
artist: **Ciruelo**
client: Dac Editions
title: Hobsyllwin
medium: Oils on canvas
size: 28″x20″

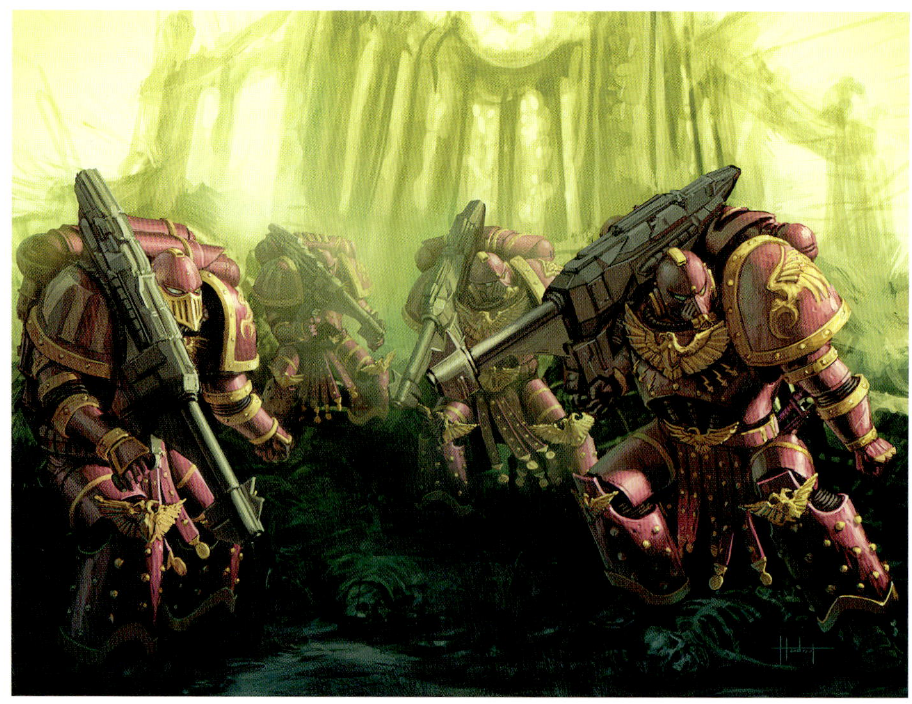

1

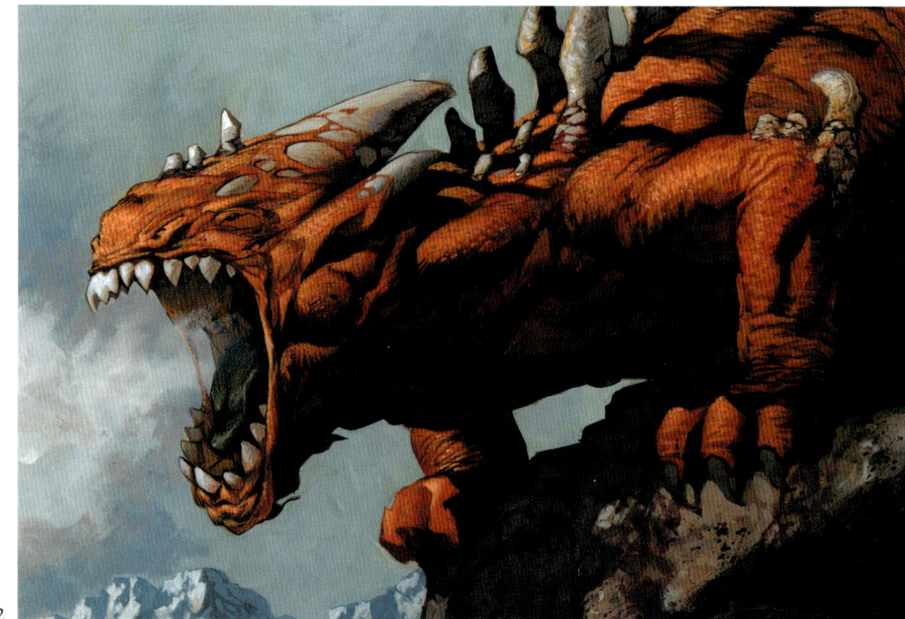

2

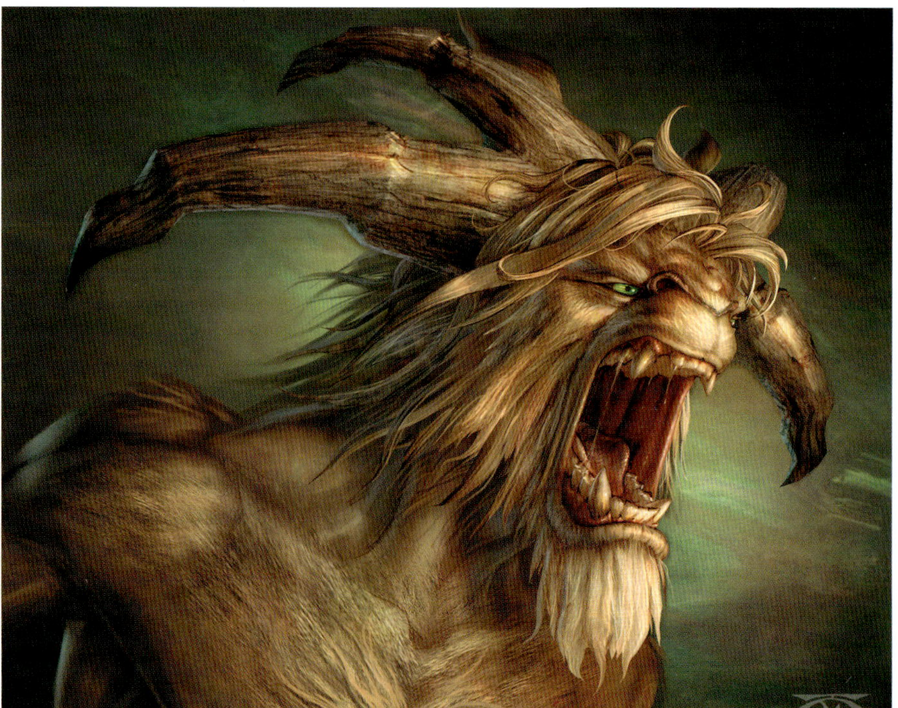

3

4

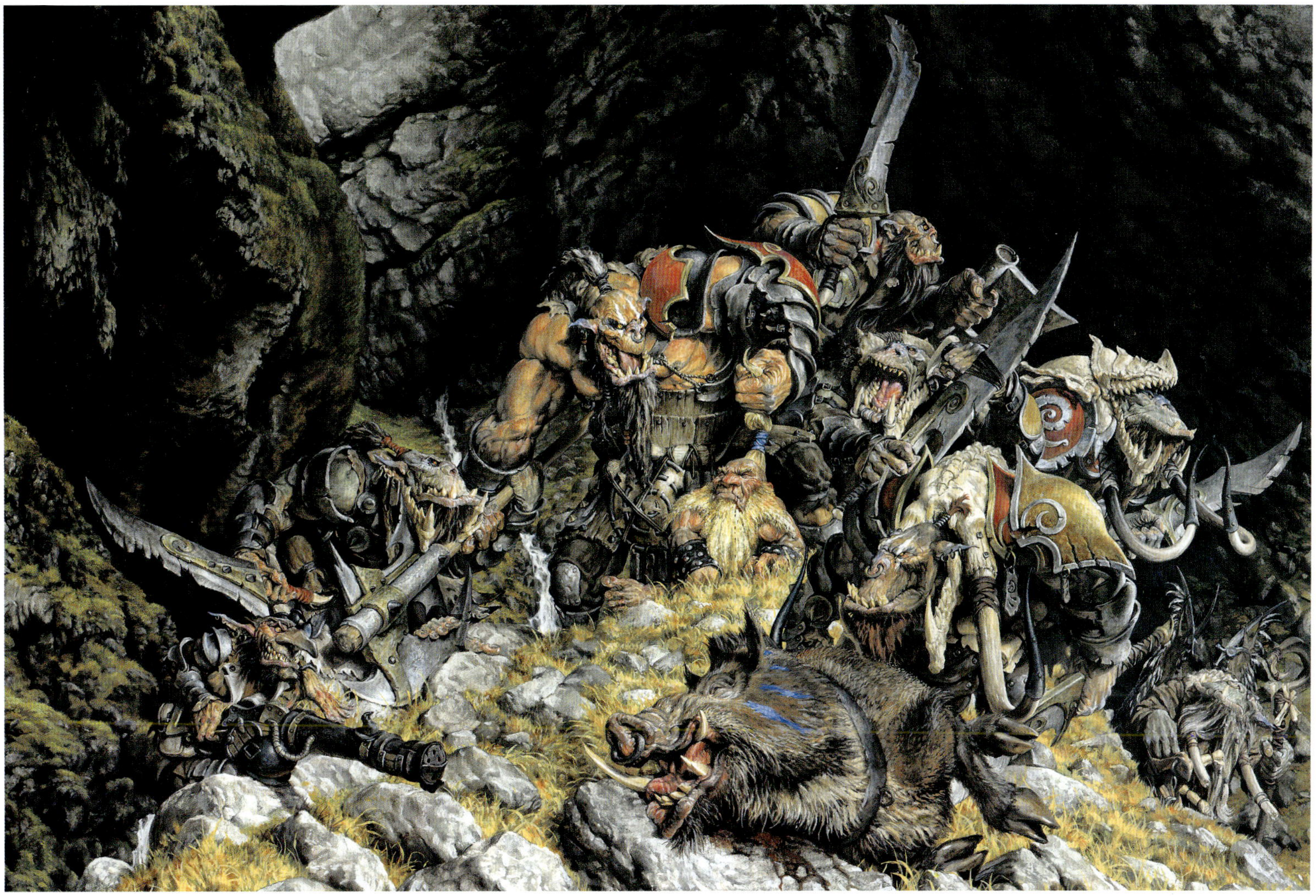

5

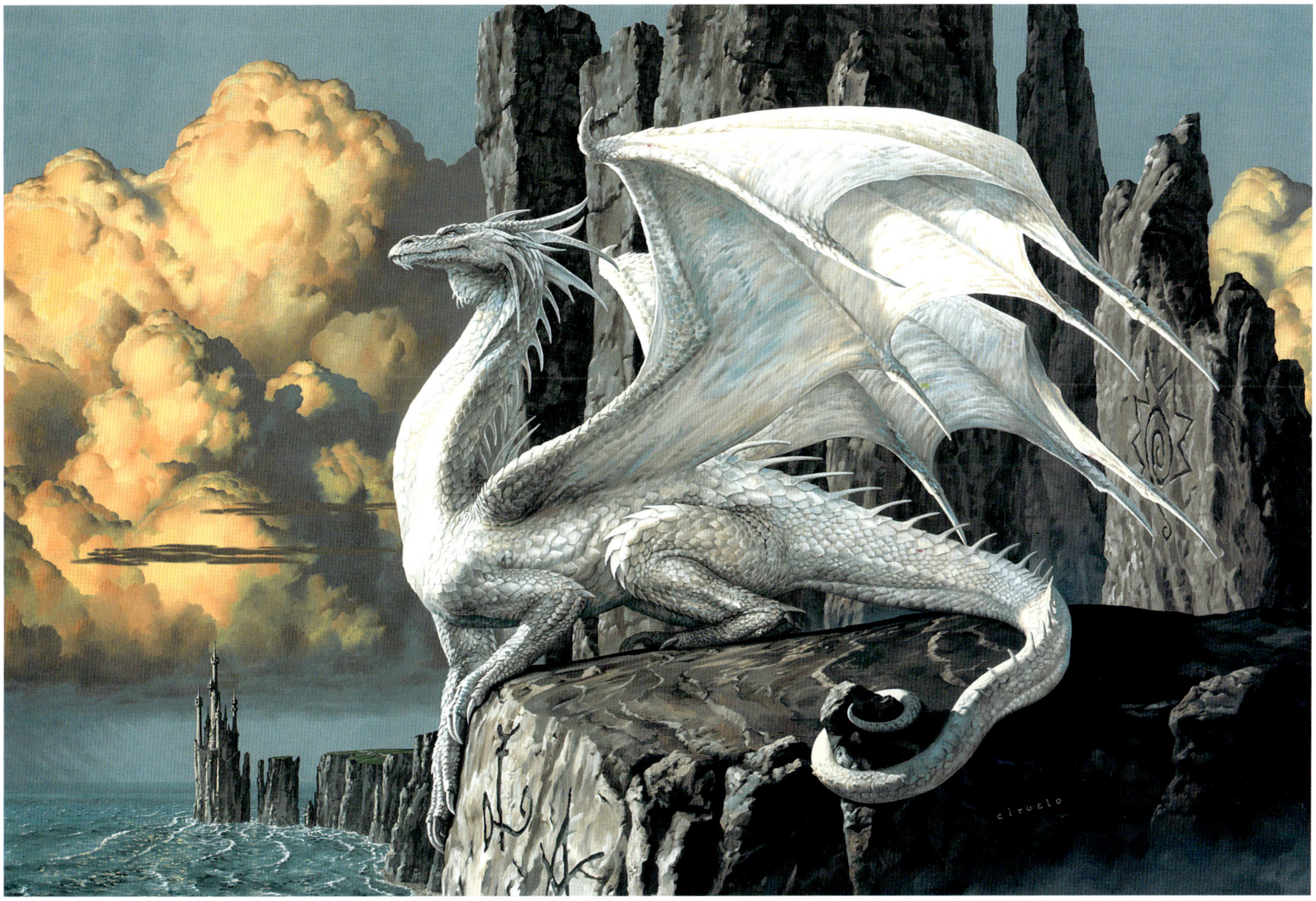

Institutional

1

artist: **John Zeleznik**
client: Palladium Books
title: Bhlaze
medium: Acrylics
size: 12″x18″

2
artist: **Michael Phillippi**
client: Sloth Productions LLC
title: Rorschack
medium: Mixed
size: 19″x15″

3
artist: **Joe Chiodo**
art director: Dan Herman
client: Hermes Press
title: Gun Patrol
medium: Mixed
size: 11″x15″

4
artist: **Terese Nielsen**
client: Rook Steel Storage
title: Archangel Michael
medium: Mixed
size: 6 1/2″x17″

5
artist: **Randy Gallegos**
art director: Jeremy Cranford
client: Wizards of the Coast
title: Tsuki-bito
medium: Oils
size: 11″x17″

6
artist: **Matt Wilson**
art director: Jeremy Cranford
client: Wizards of the Coast
title: Soul Collector
medium: Oils on board
size: 27″x36″

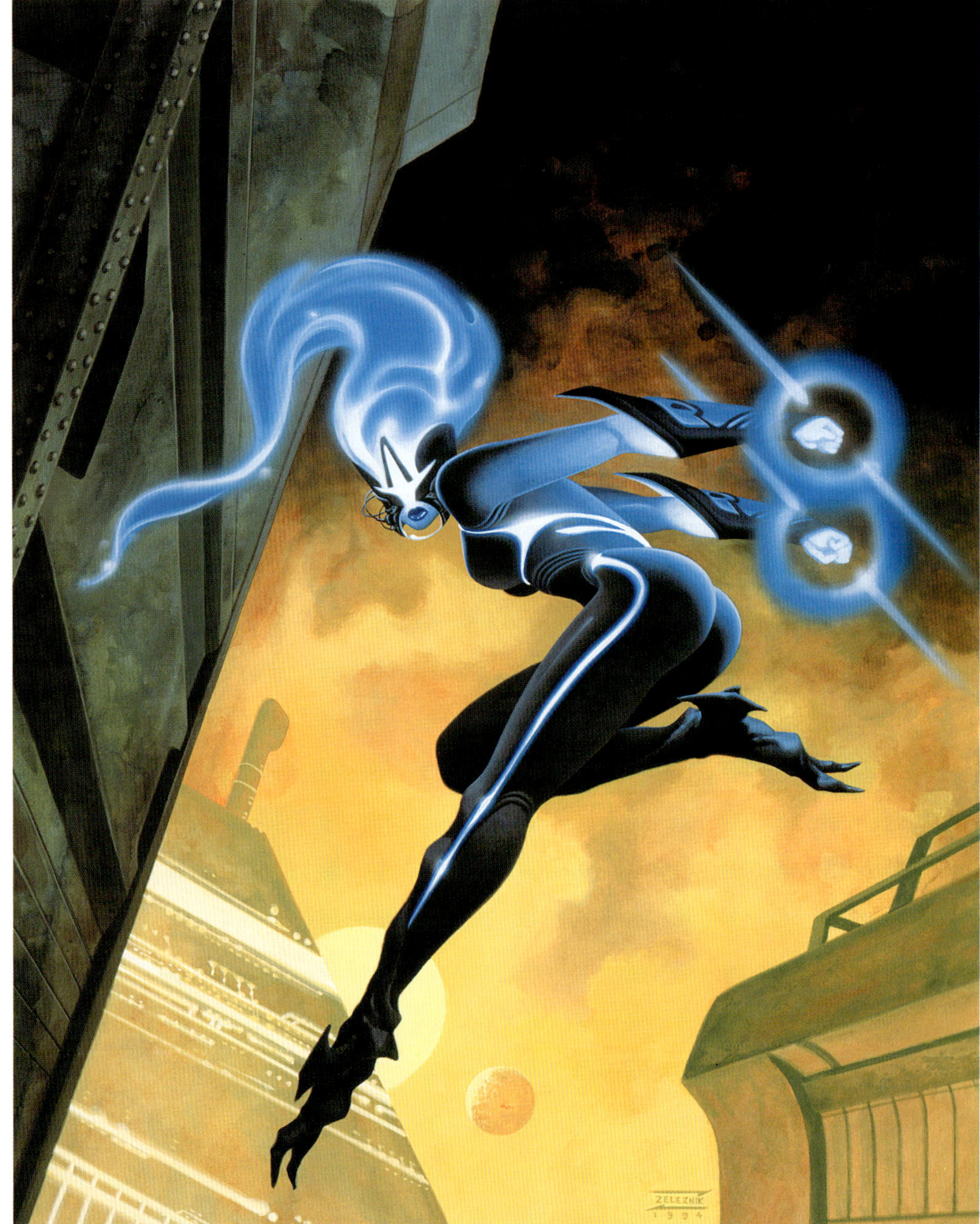

1

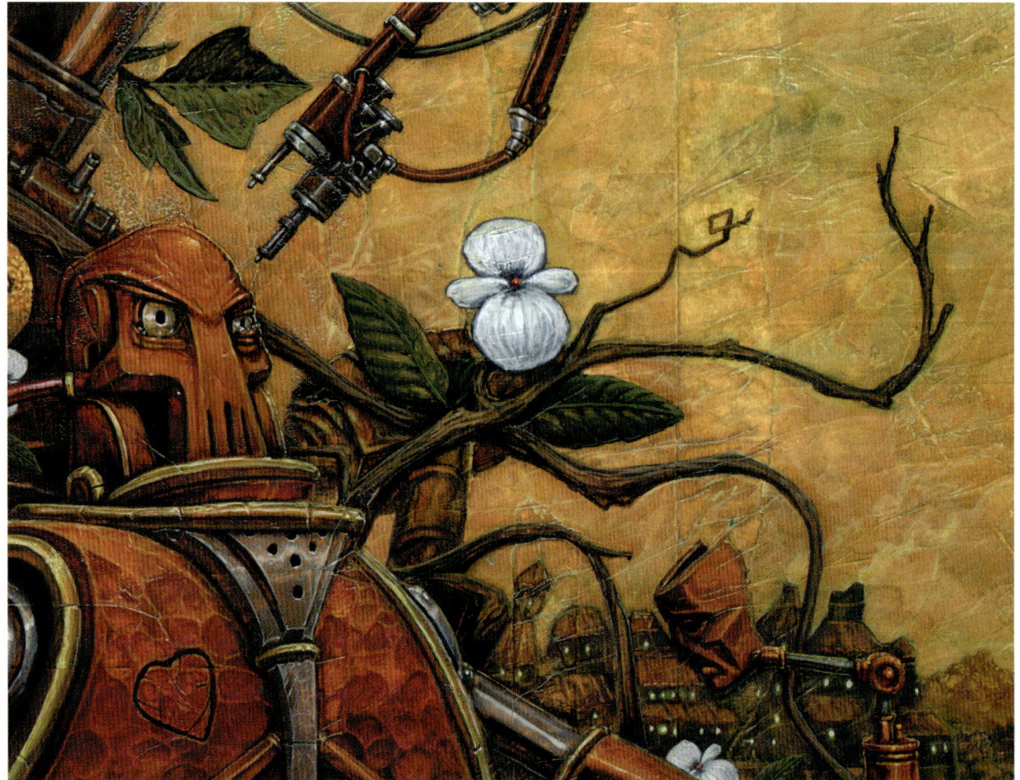

2

3

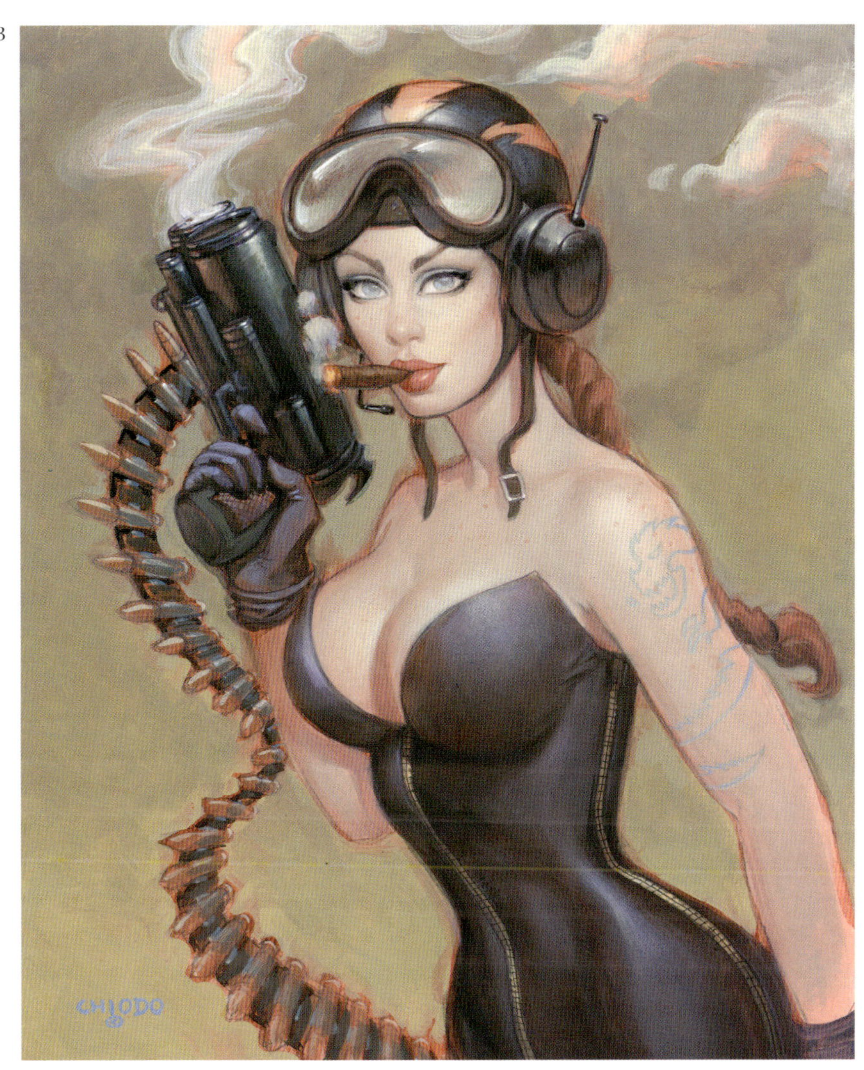

4

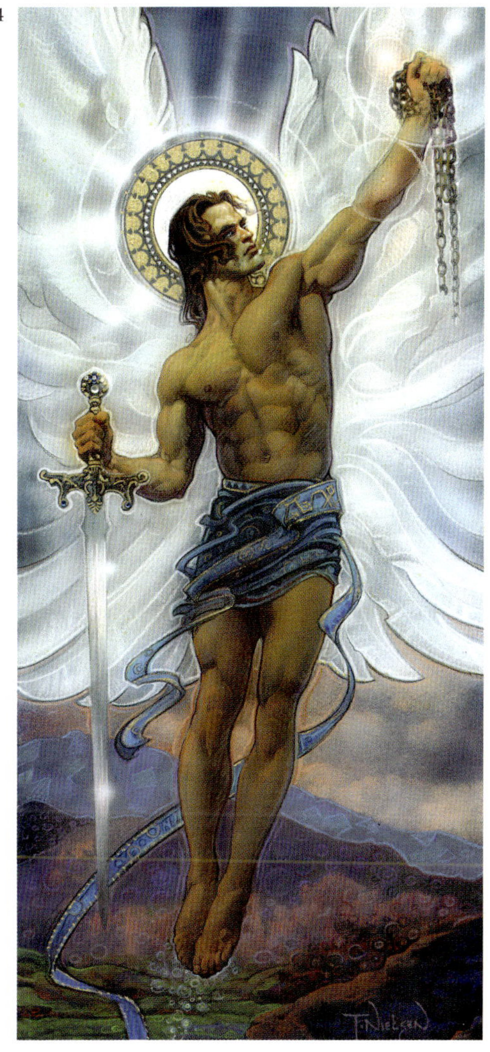

5

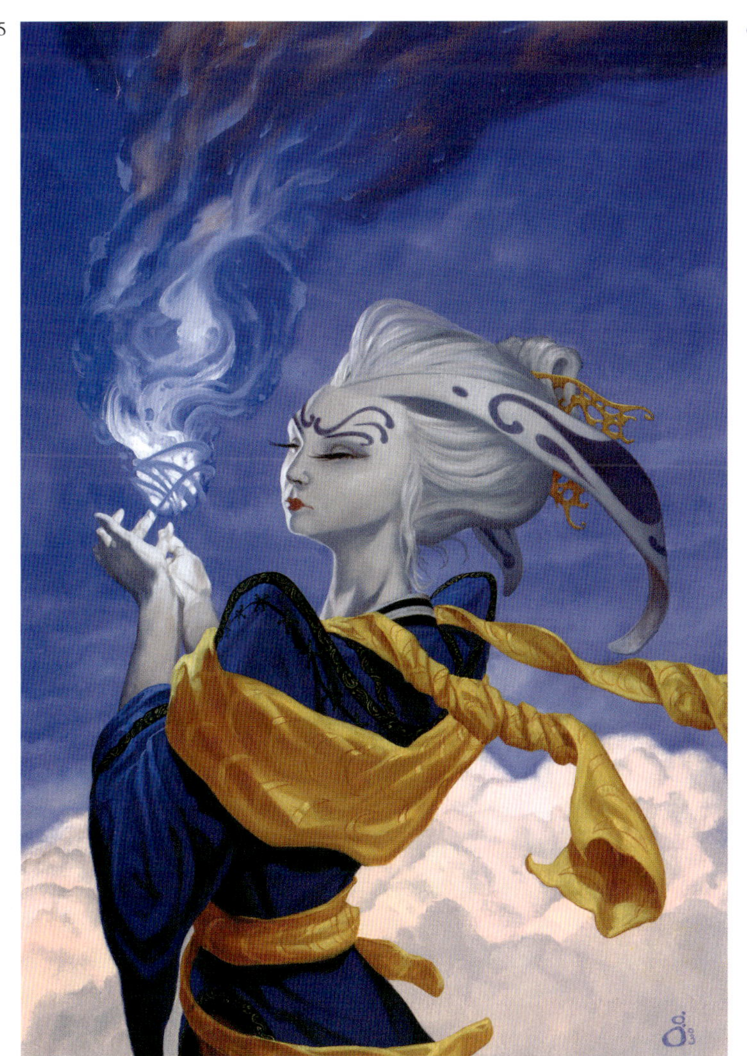

6

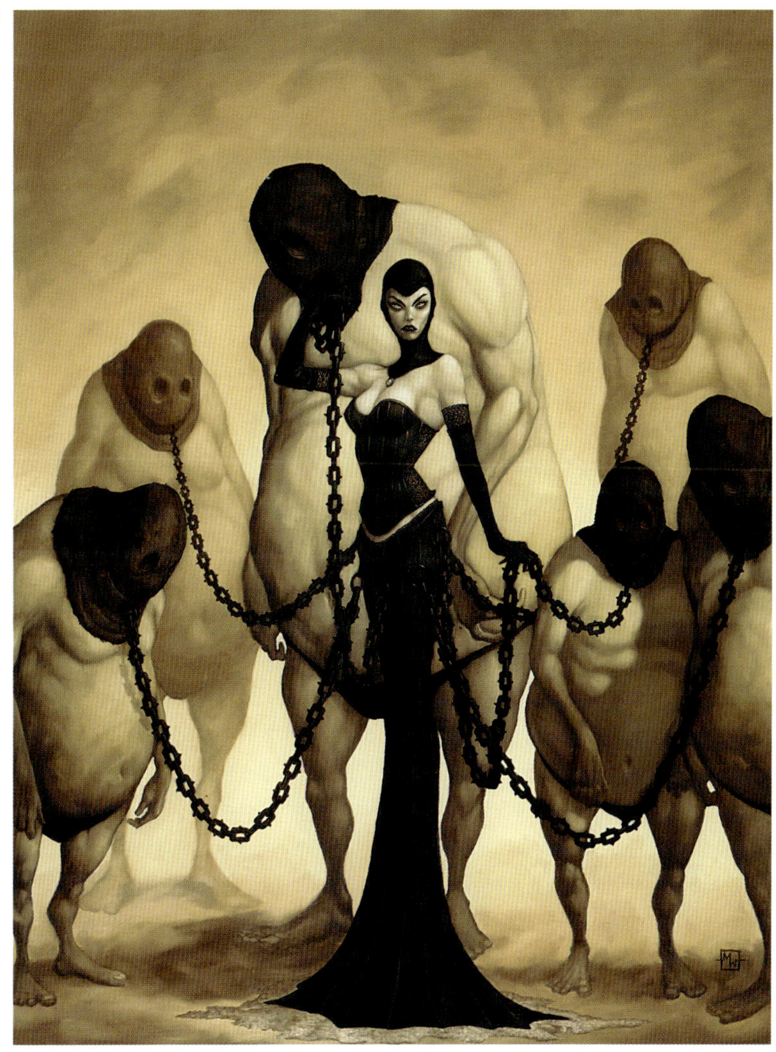

Institutional

1
artist: **Will Bulas**
art director: Elizabeth Johnson
client: Oberthur Gaming Technologies
title: Bearing Gifts...
medium: Watercolor
size: 14"x10"

2
artist: **René Milot**
art director: Bill Urseth/René Milot
client: Norshield Financial Group
title: "...we take nothing at face value..."
medium: Oils on canvas
size: 29"x23"

3
artist: **Patricia Lewis**
client: Underhill Studio
title: Instinct
medium: Pencil/digital

4
artist: **Leah Palmer Preiss**
client: Directory of Illustration
title: Fruit
medium: Acrylics & oils
size: 8"x8"

5
artist: **Jeff Faerber**
art director: Bill Hanjorgiris
designer: Jeff Faerber
client: Bill Hanjorgiris
medium: Acrylics
size: 14"x18"

6
artist: **Victor Powell**
client: victorpowell.com
title: Salad Bar
medium: Oils
size: 48"x48"

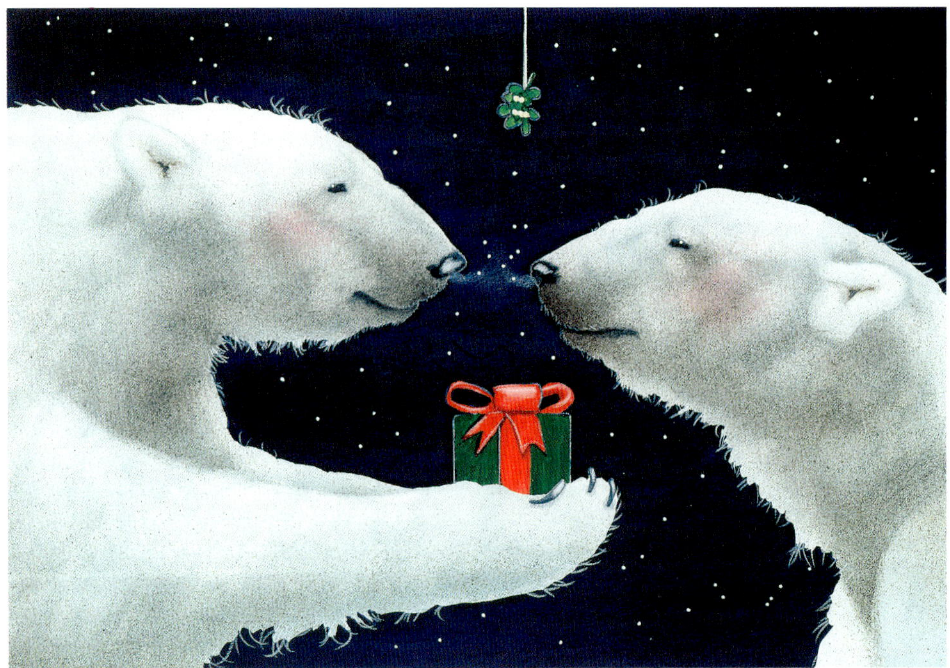
1

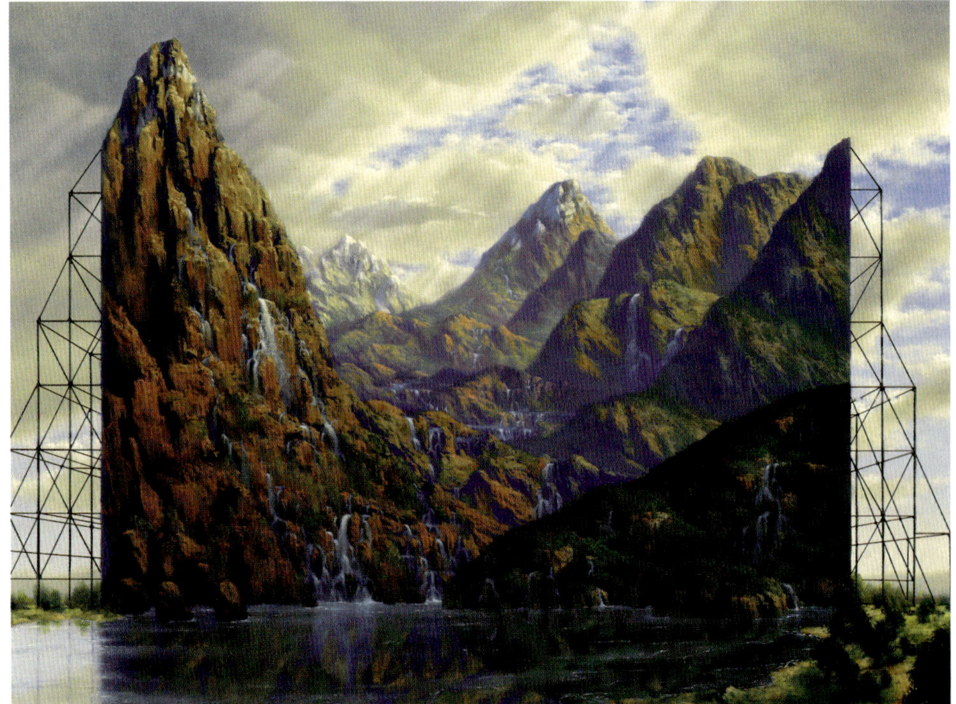
2

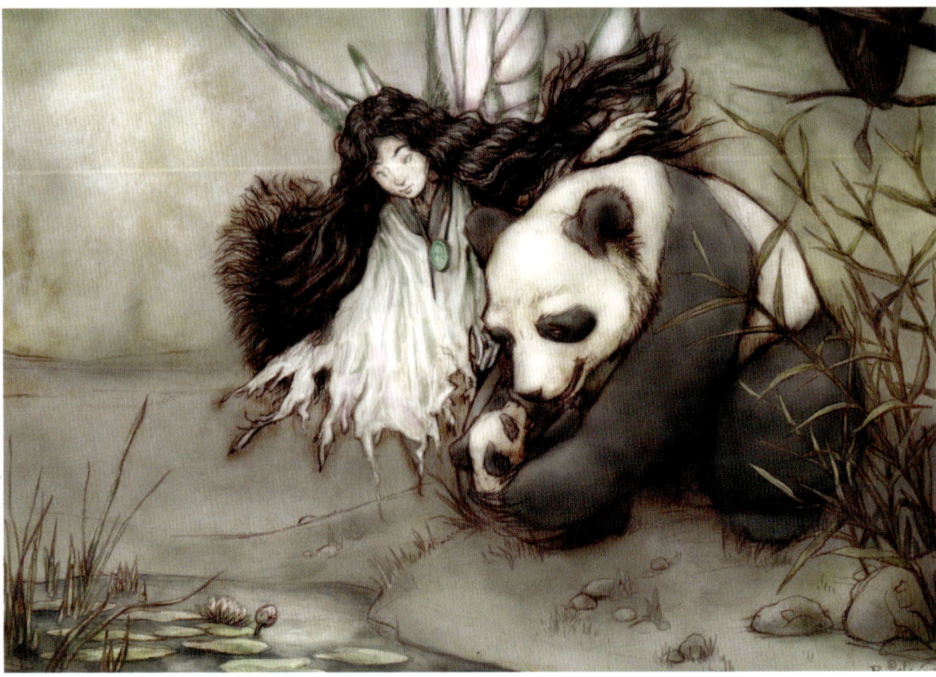
3

4

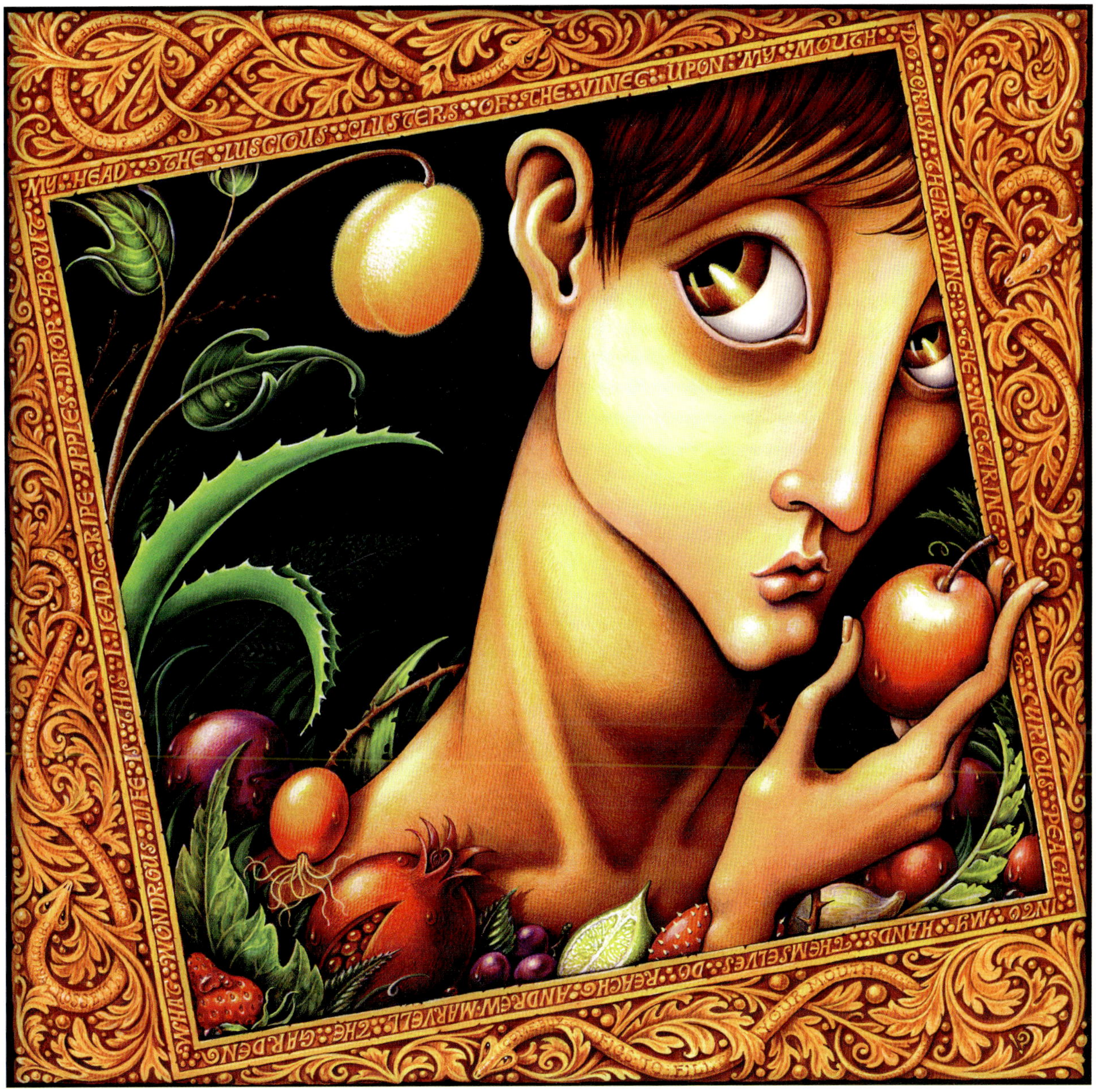

MY HEAD ~ THE LUSCIOUS CLUSTERS OF THE VINE UPON MY MOUTH DO CRUSH THEIR WINE; THE NECTARINE & CURIOUS PEACH INTO MY HANDS THEMSELVES DO REACH ~ ANDREW MARVELL ~ THE GARDEN ~ WHAT WONDROUS LIFE IS THIS I LEAD! RIPE APPLES DROP ABOUT

5

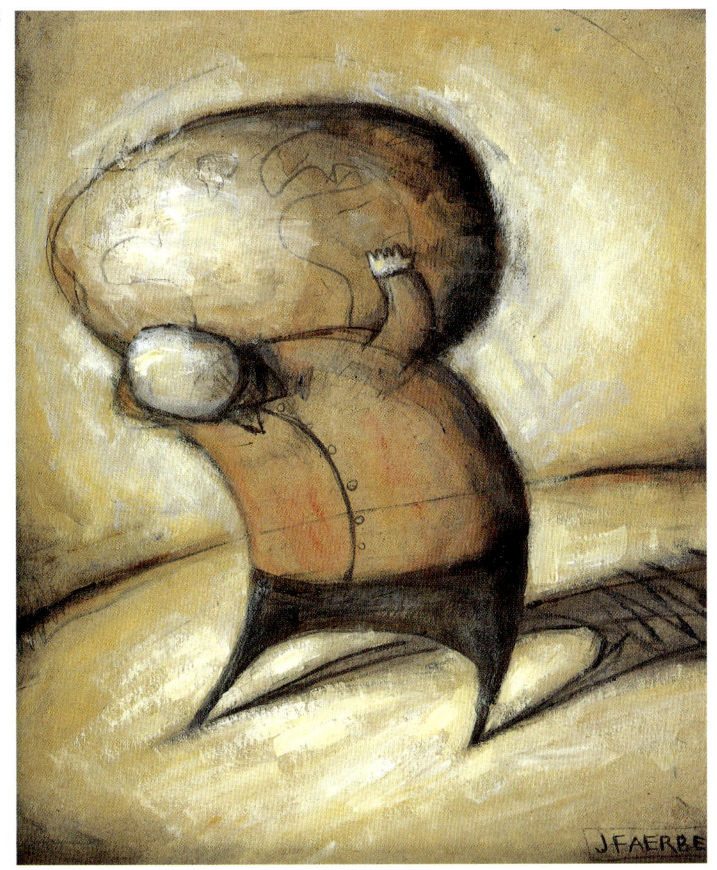
J FAERBE

6

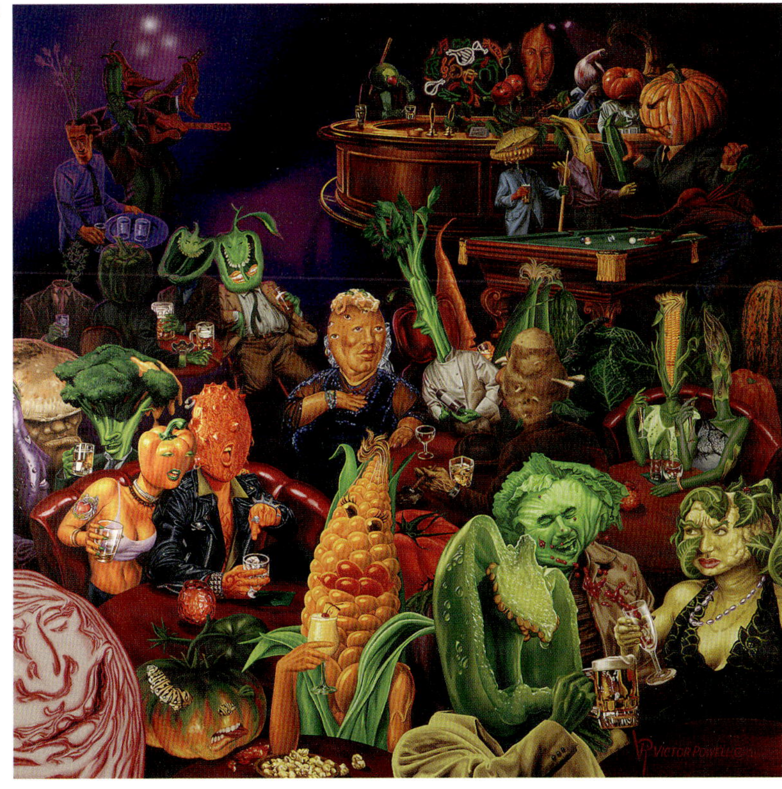

1
artist: **Mark Zug**
art director: Dana Knutson
client: Wizards of the Coast
title: Avatar of Hope
medium: Oils
size: 15″x13½″

2
artist: **Scott Gustafson**
art director: Jim Keegan
designer: Scott Gustafson
client: Wandering Star Press
title: Breckinridge Elkins
medium: Oils
size: 22½″x30″

3
artist: **Paul Bonner**
art director: Jean Bey
designer: Paul Bonner
client: Rackham
title: Ragnorak
medium: Watercolor
size: 90cmx41cm

4
artist: **Justin Sweet**
art director: Jeremy Cranford
client: Wizards of the Coast
title: Green Kami
medium: Digital

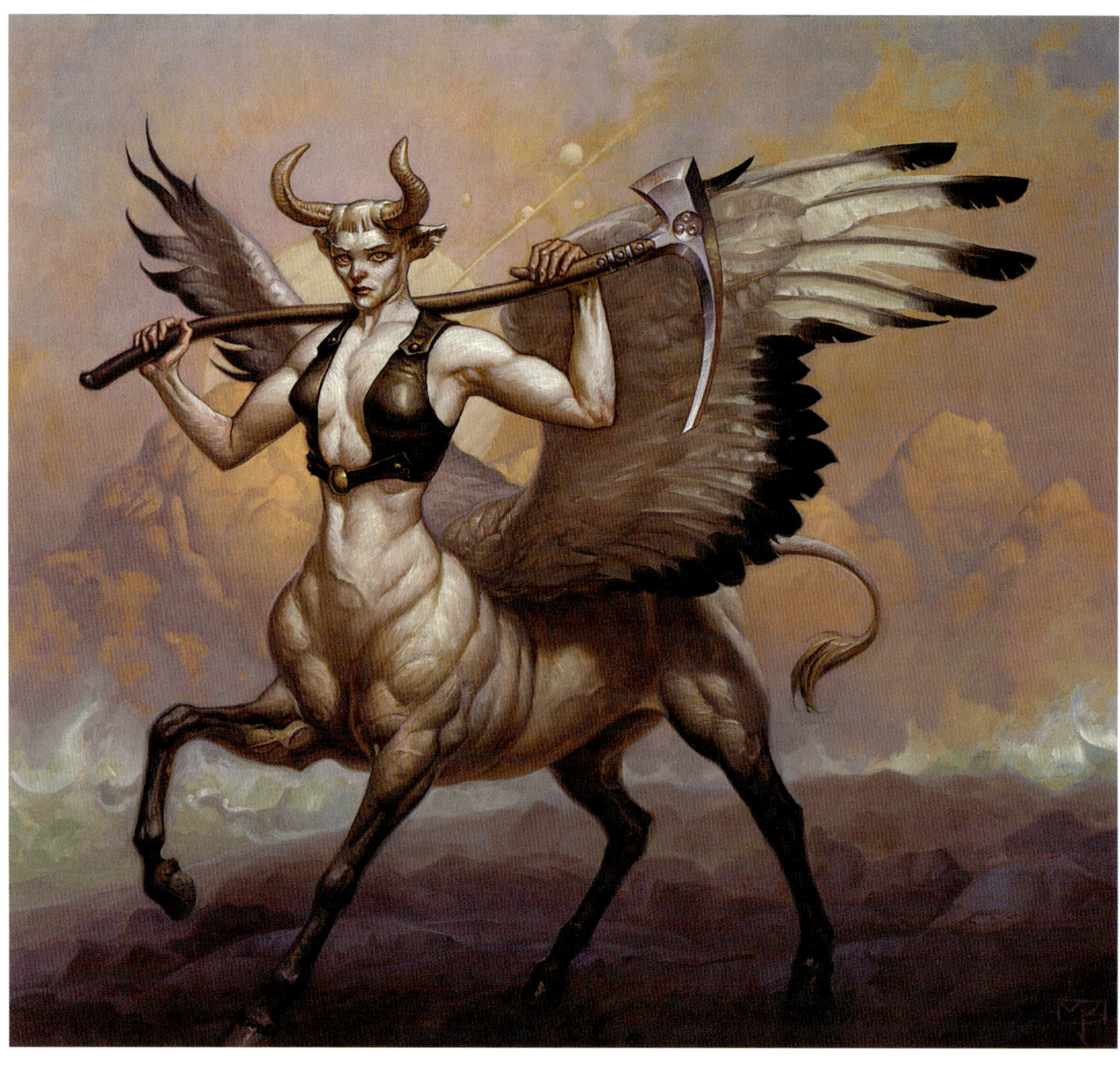
1

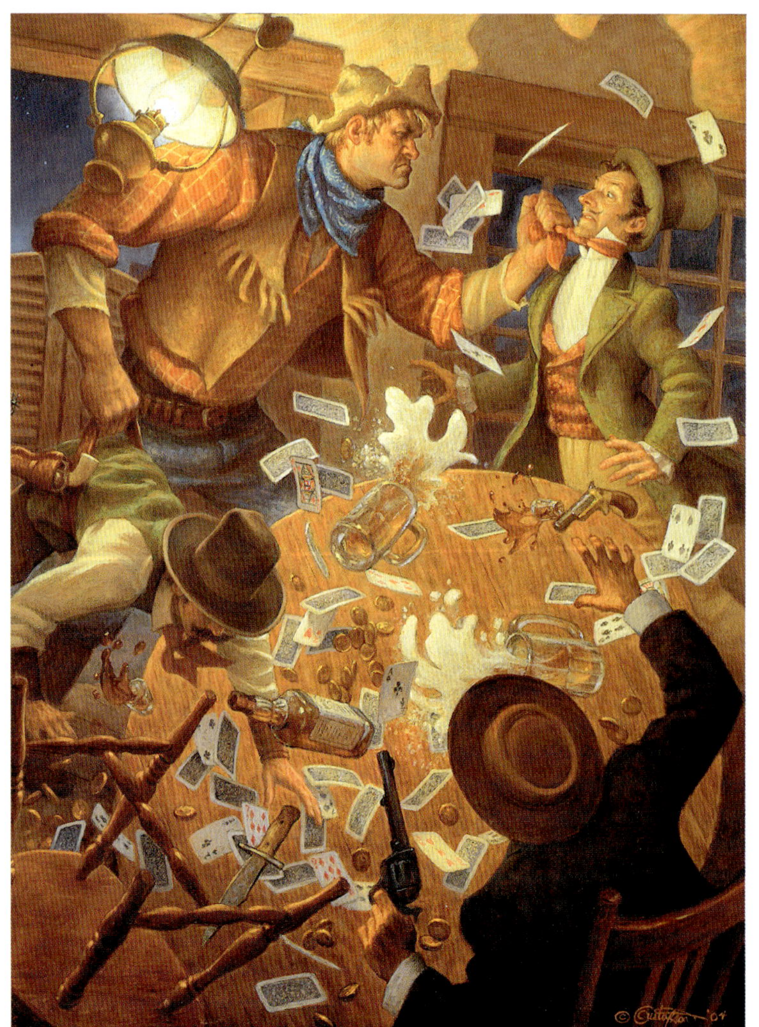
2

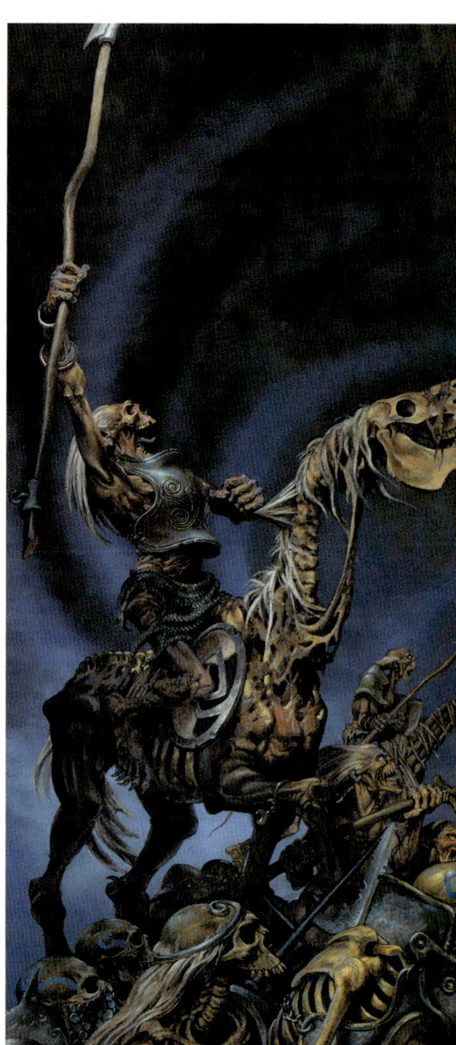
3

4

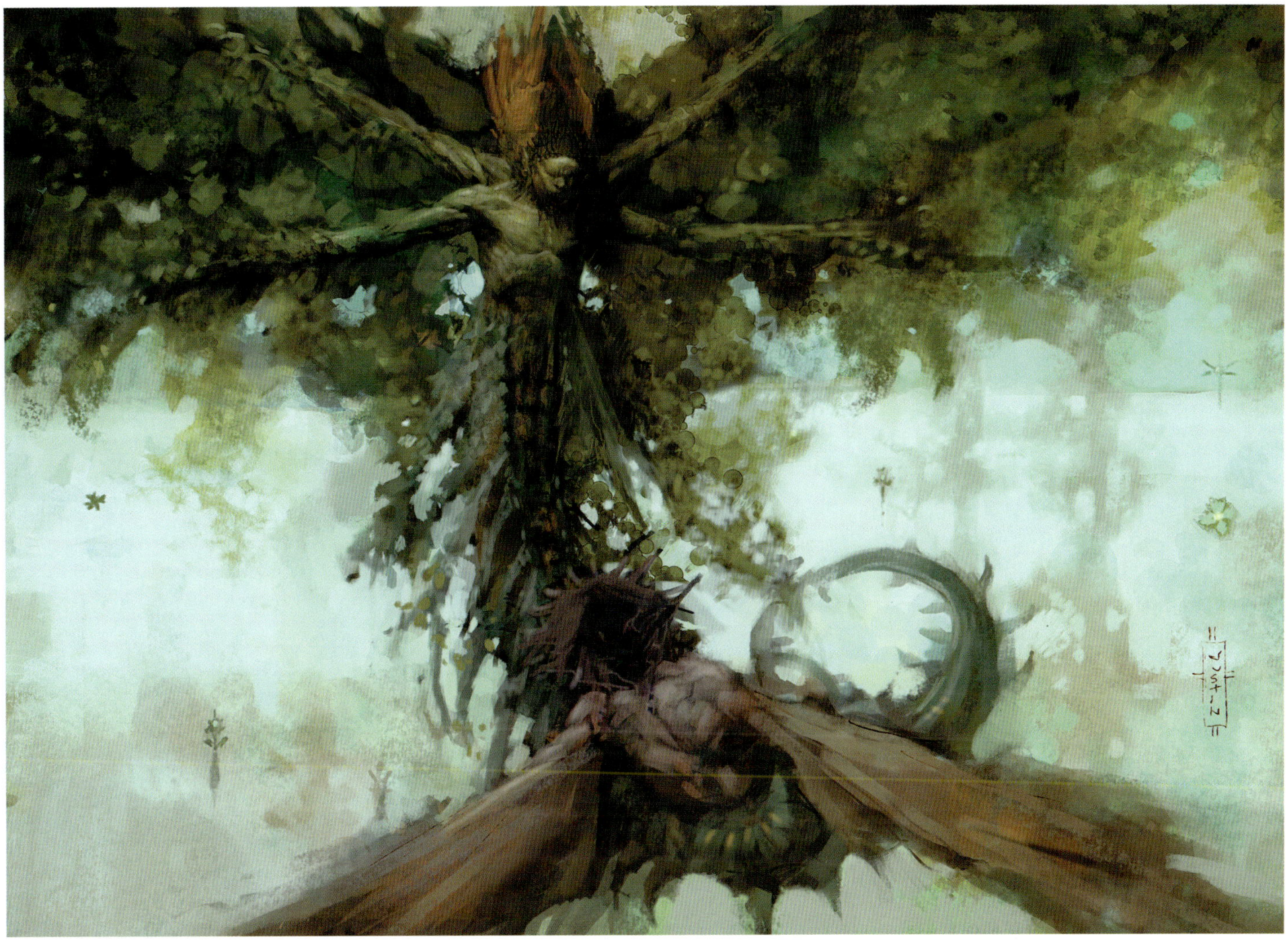

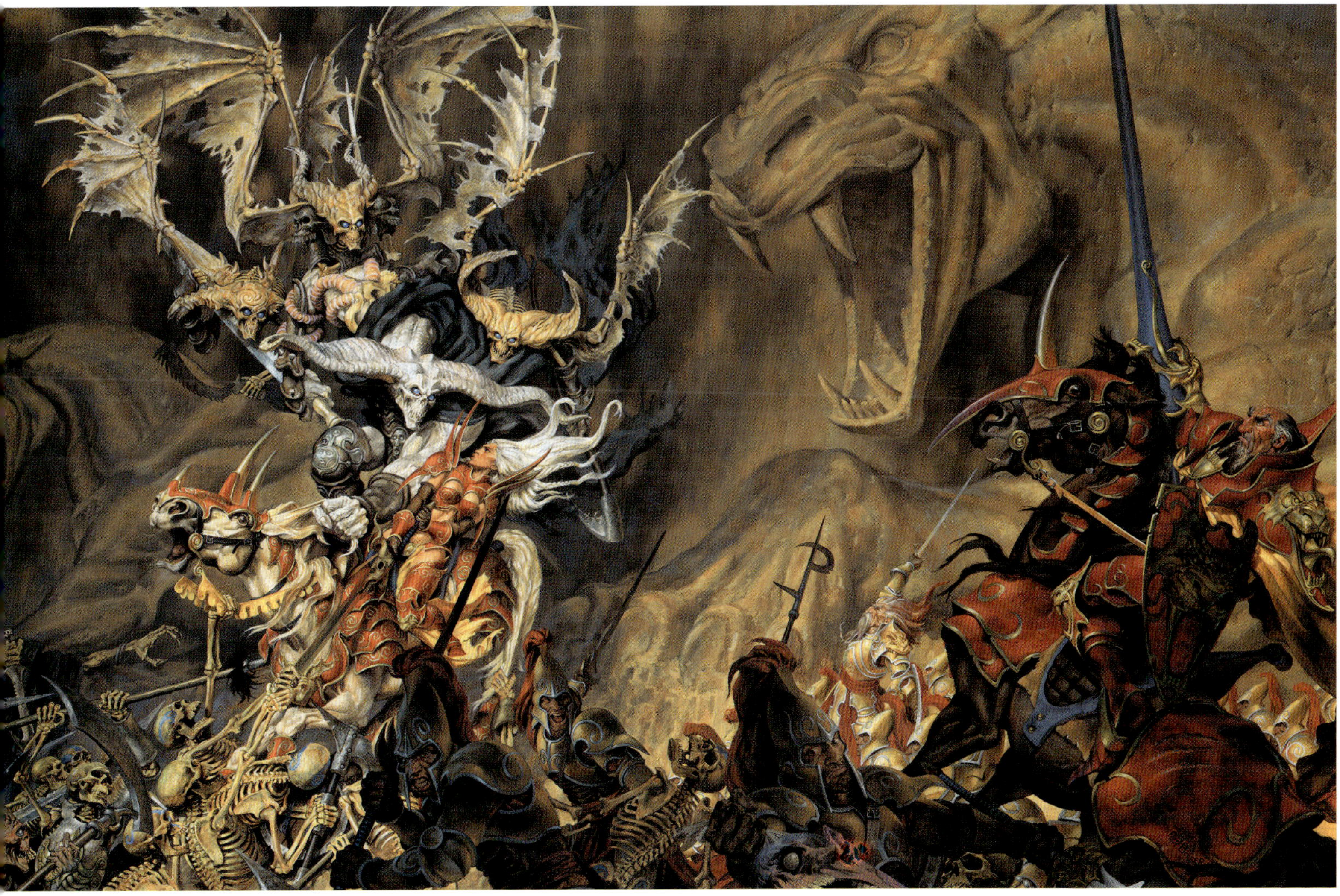

Institutional

1
artist: **Rafal Olbinski**
designer: S. Zaremba
client: Datinae, Inc.
title: Olbinski Calendar
medium: Acrylics
size: 28"x22"

2
artist: **Raoul Vitale**
client: Taharaa Fine Art
title: Lost Horizon
medium: Oils
size: 28"x19"

3
artist: **Greg Spalenka**
art director: Anthony Padilla
designer: Jon Coy
client: Laguna College of Art & Design
title: Lotus Faeries
medium: Mixed/digital
size: 18"x12"

4
artist: **Greg Spalenka**
art director: Anthony Padilla
designer: Jeff Burne
client: Laguna College of Art & Design
title: Emerge
medium: Mixed/digital
size: 24"x36"

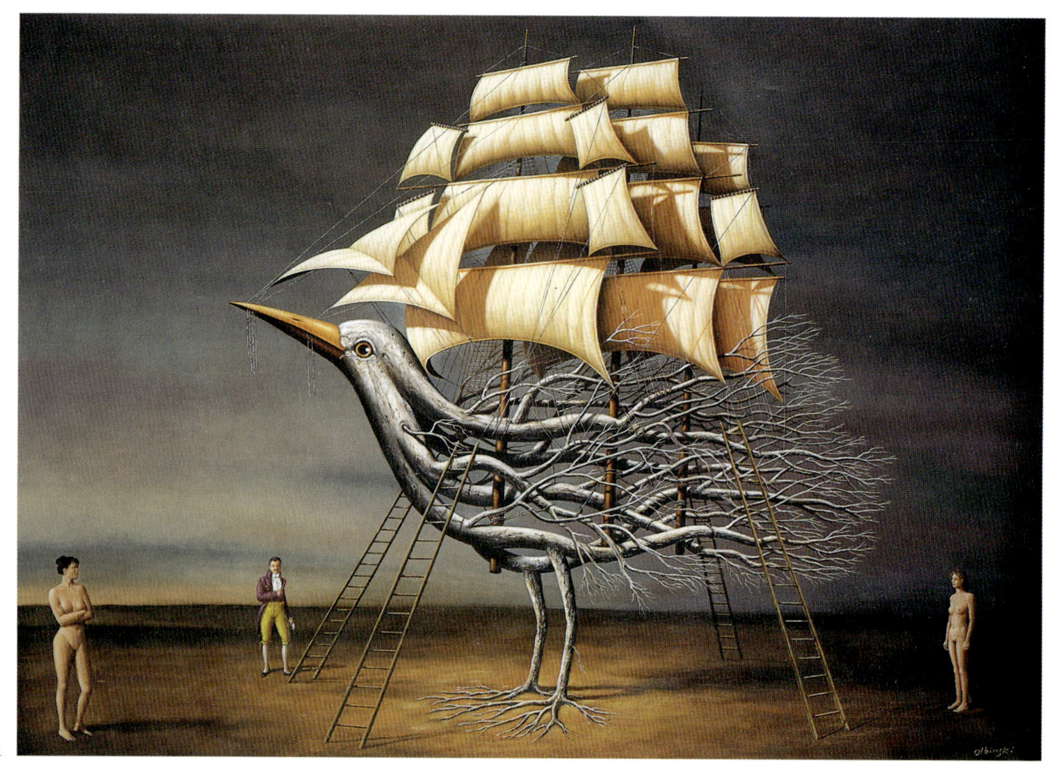
1

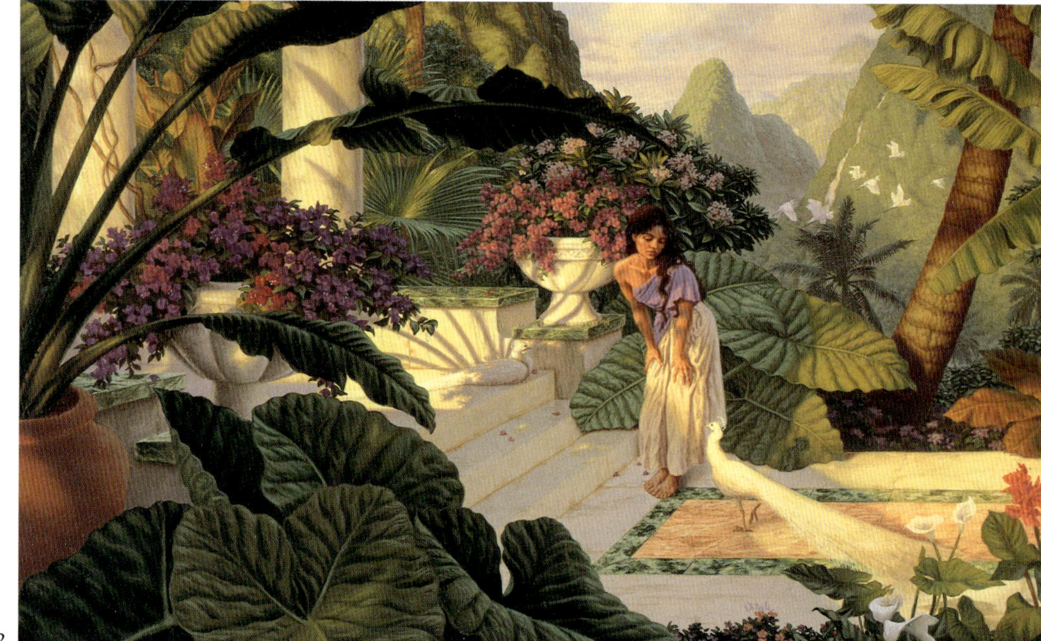
2

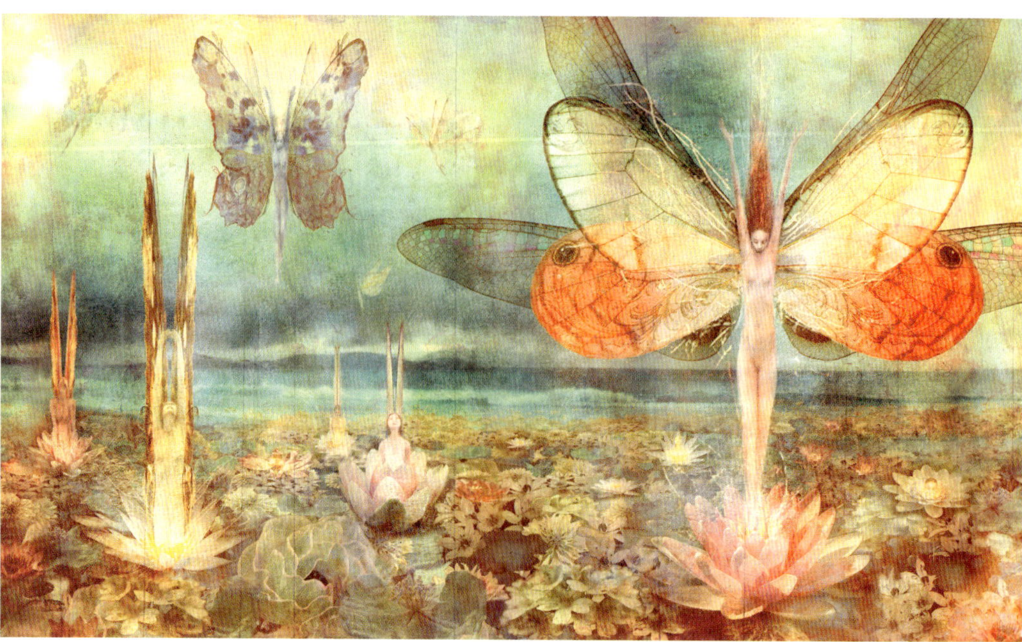
3

4

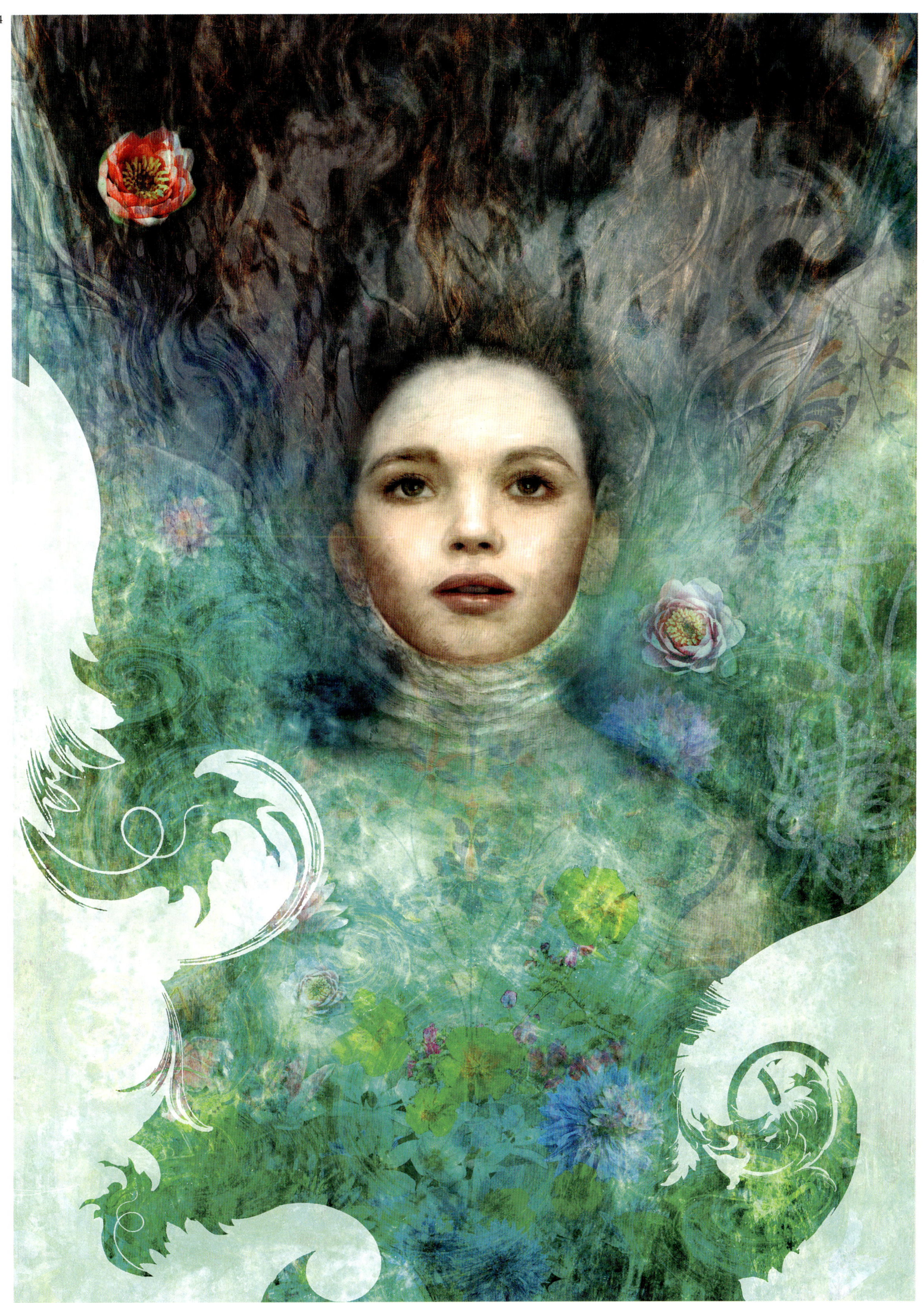

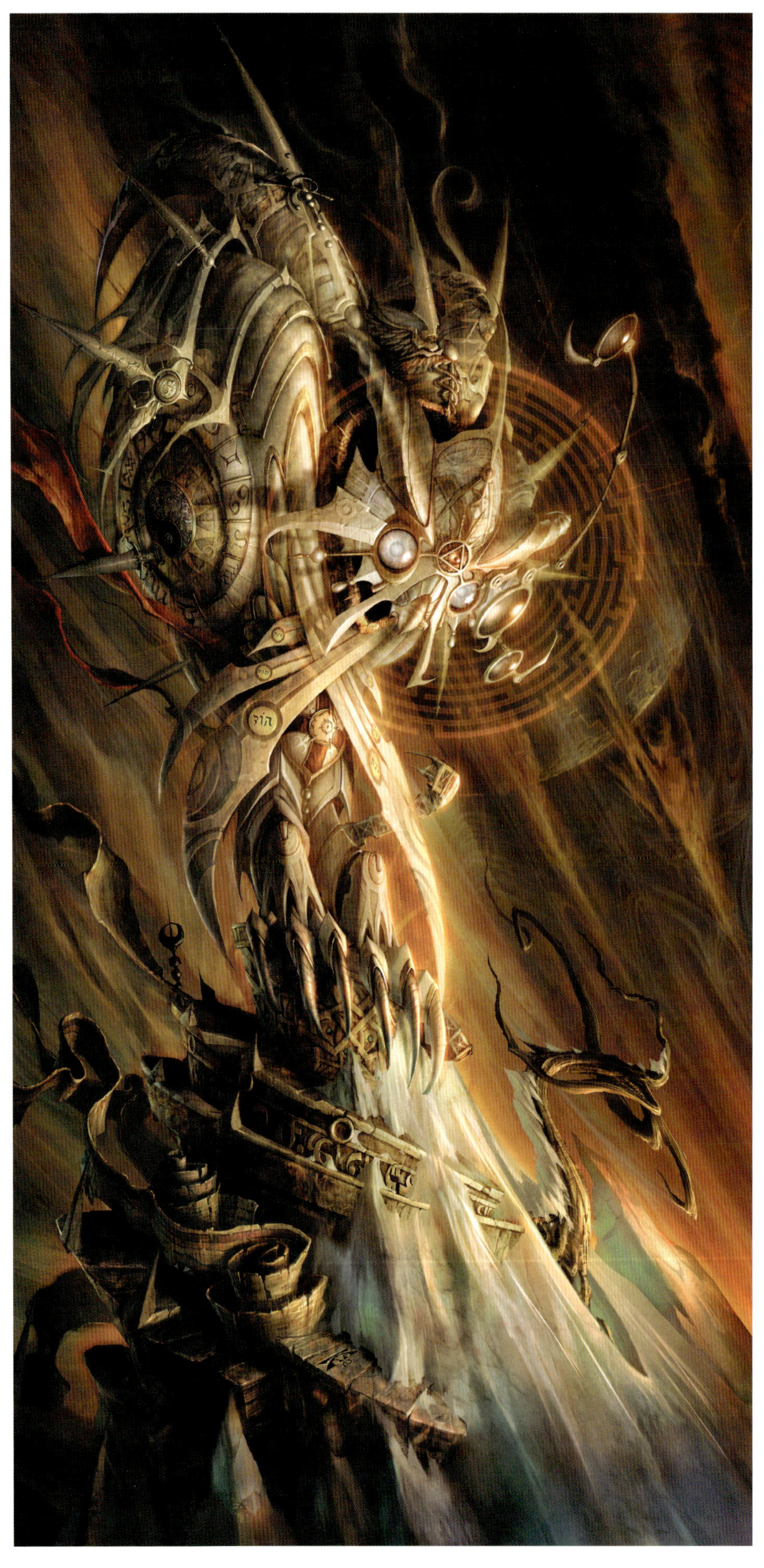

artist: **Raymond Swanland**
title: The Forgotten Mountain *medium:* Digital

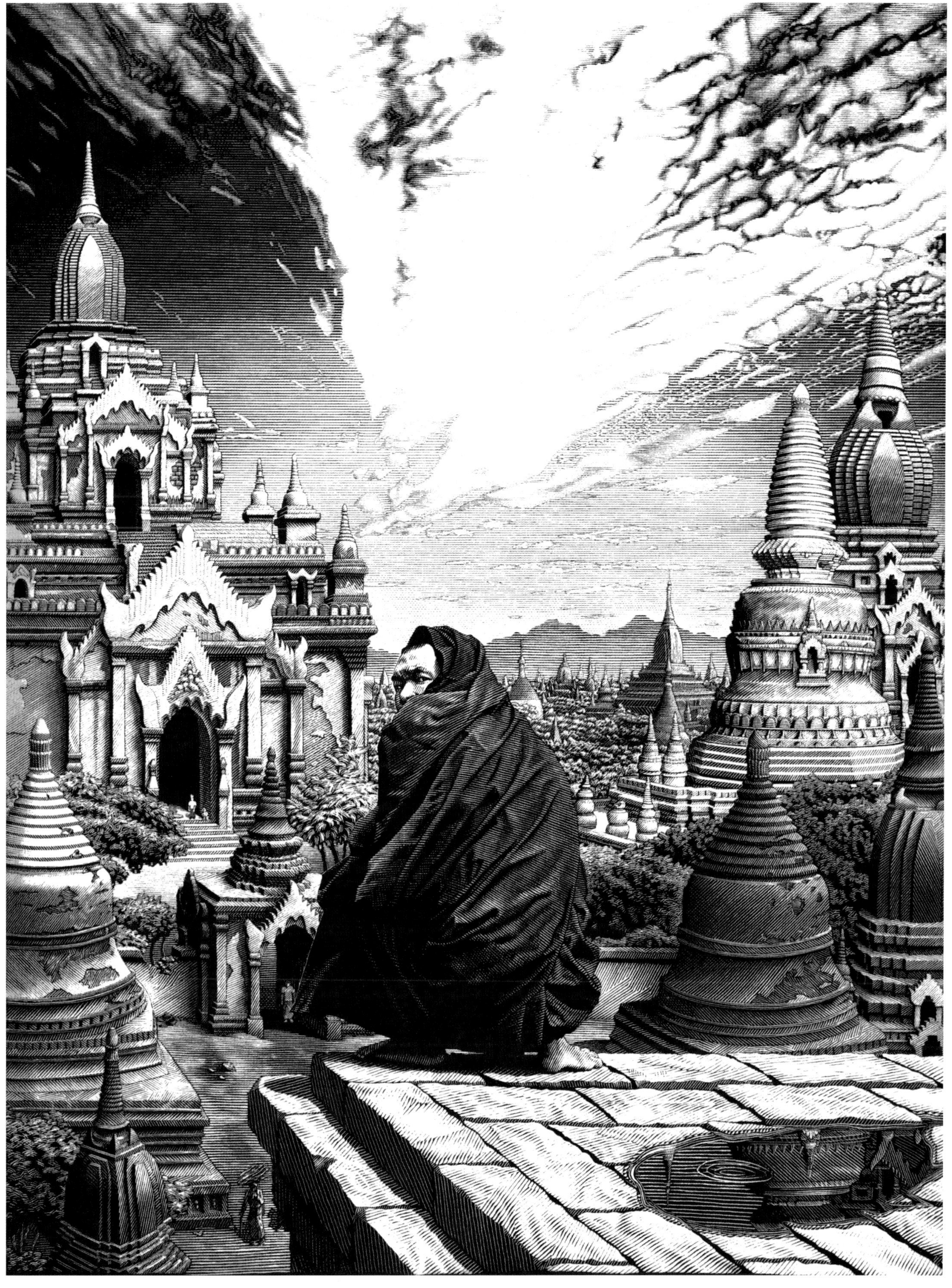

artist: **Patrick Arrasmith**
title: Bagan *medium:* Scratchboard *size:* 12″x17″

Unpublished

1
artist: **Anita Kunz**
title: Womb
medium: Watercolor
size: 11″x14″

2
artist: **Fabrice Lavollay**
title: F/02
medium: Mixed
size: 49 1/4″x68 3/4″

3
artist: **Fabrice Lavollay**
title: Magie 1
medium: Mixed
size: 11 7/8″x16 1/2″

4
artist: **Anita Kunz**
title: Triplets
medium: Watercolor
size: 11″x14″

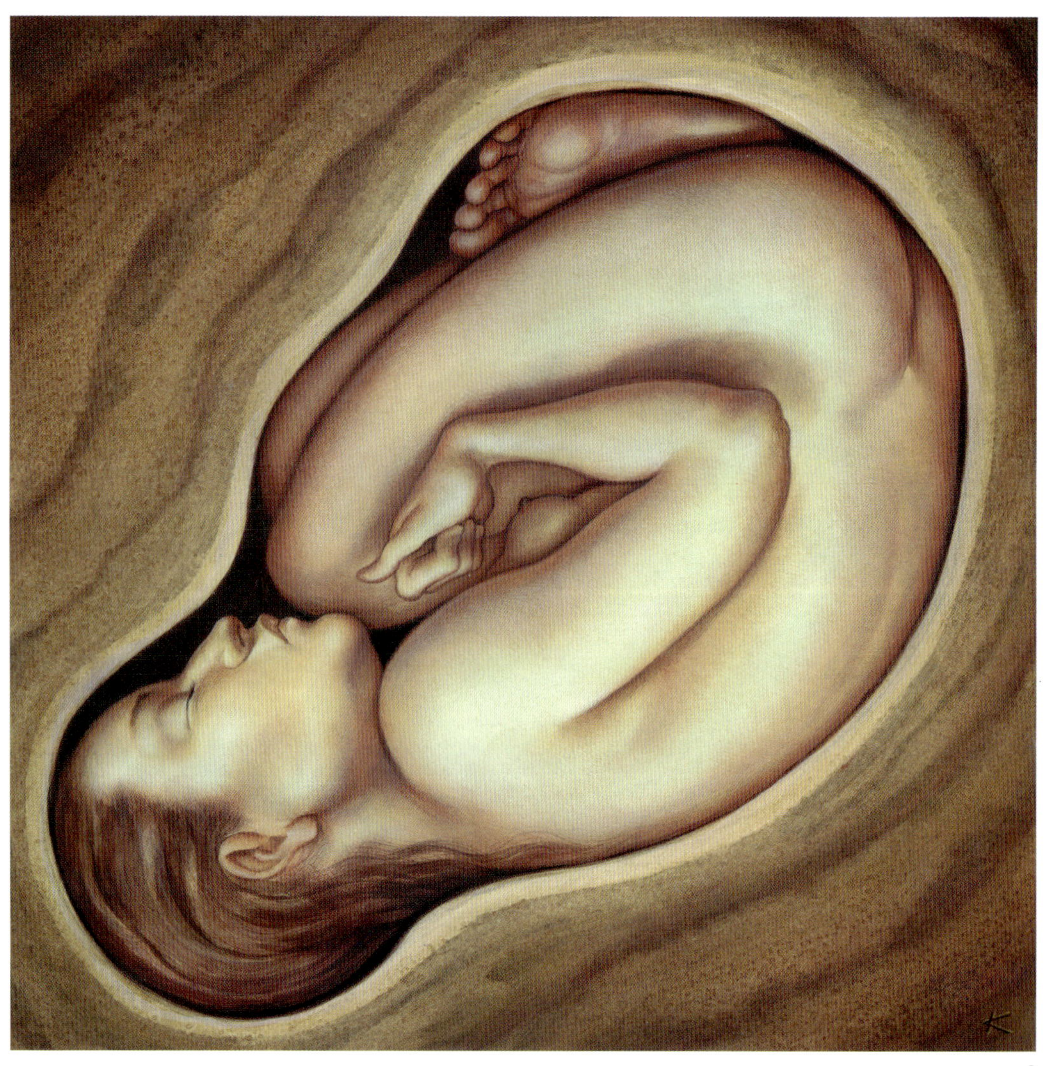

1

2

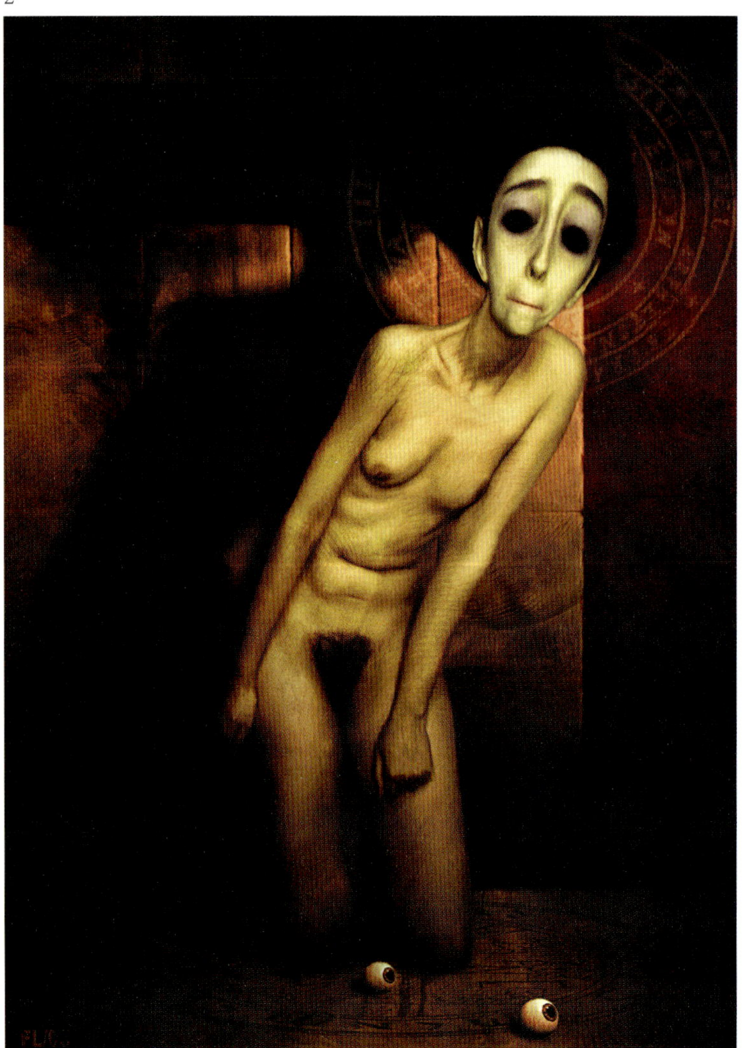

3

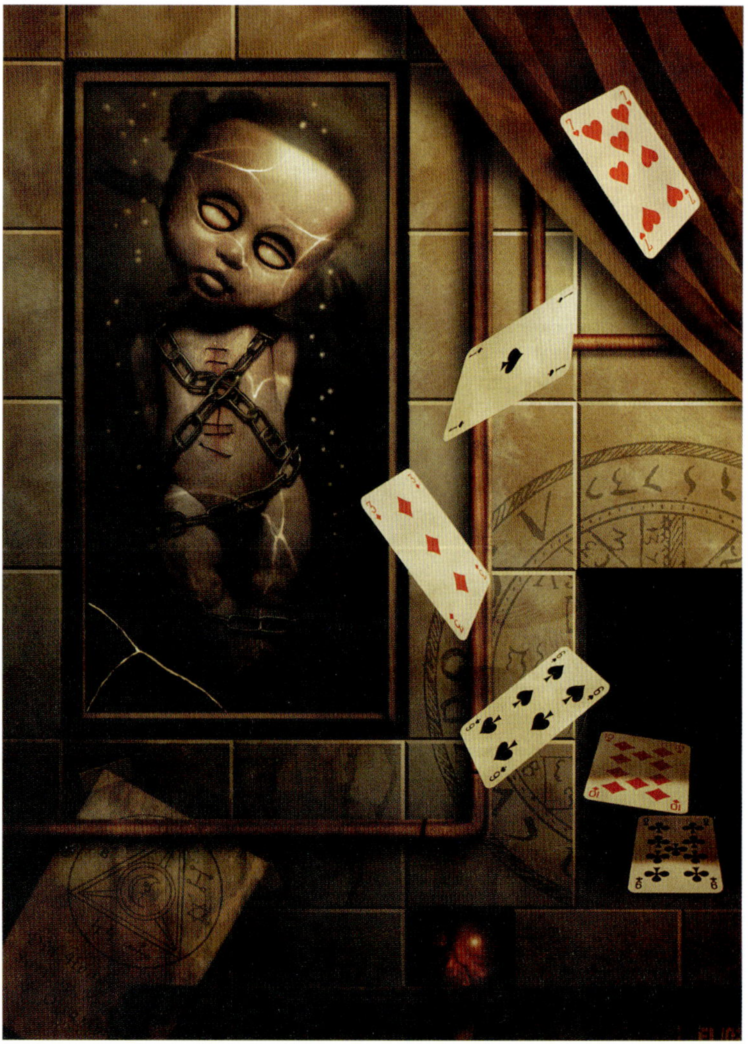

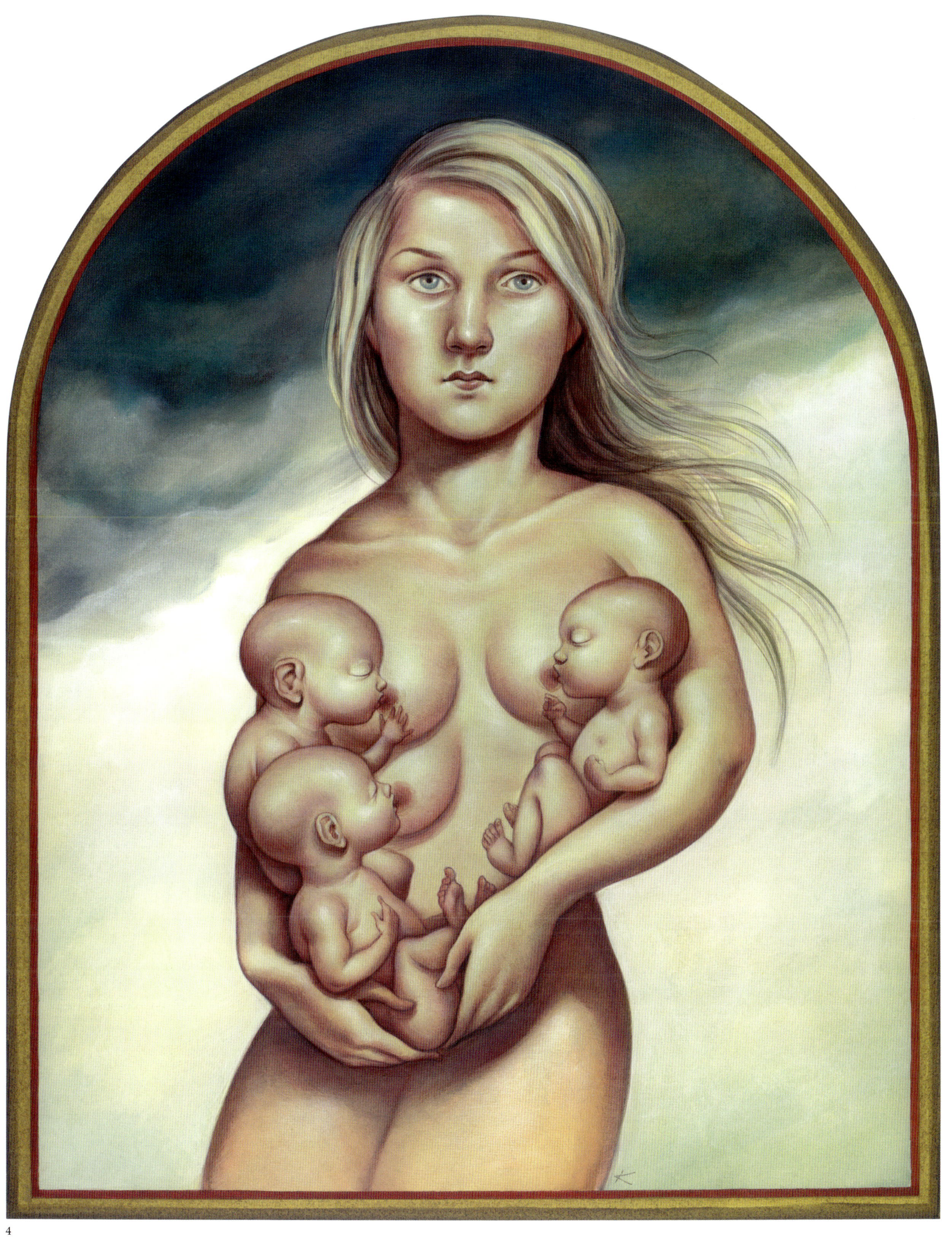

4

Unpublished

1
artist: **Kip Omolade**
title: Expecting
medium: Oils
size: 18″x24″

2
artist: **Richard Raney**
medium: Mixed
size: 18″x24″

3
artist: **Huey Nguyen**
medium: Acrylics
size: 9″x12″

4
artist: **Richard Raney**
title: The Amazing White Elephant
medium: Mixed
size: 18″x24″

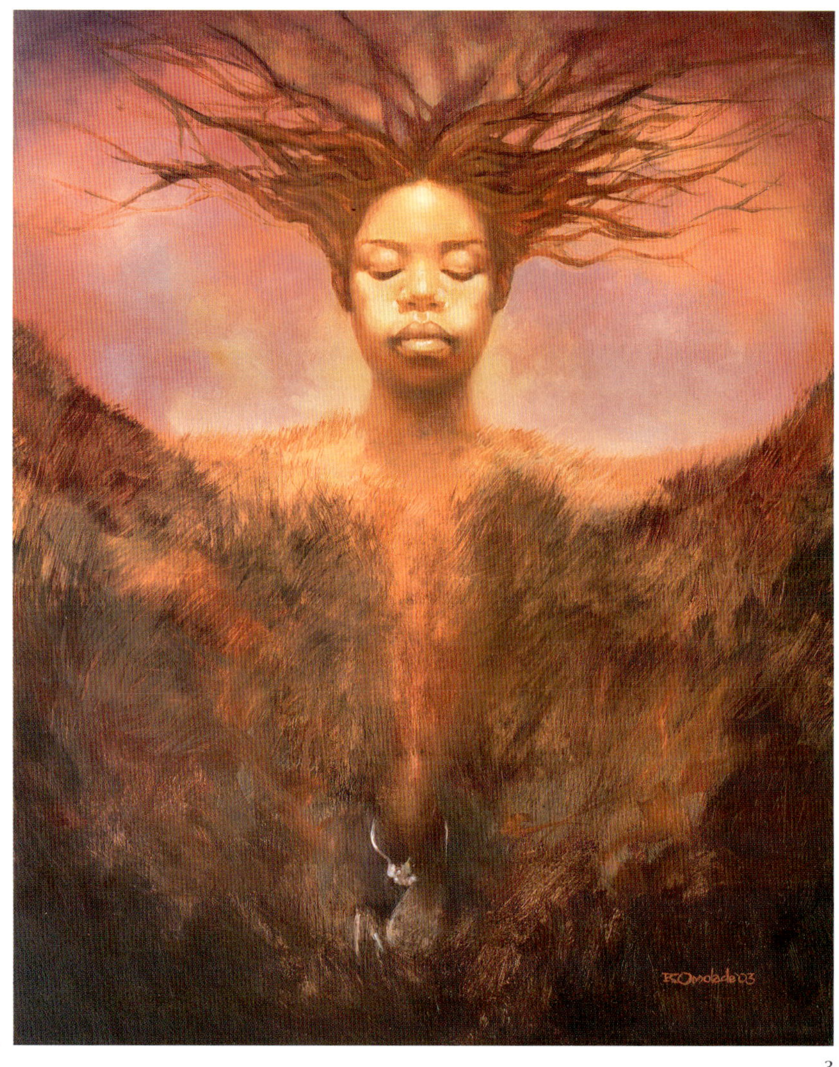

1

2
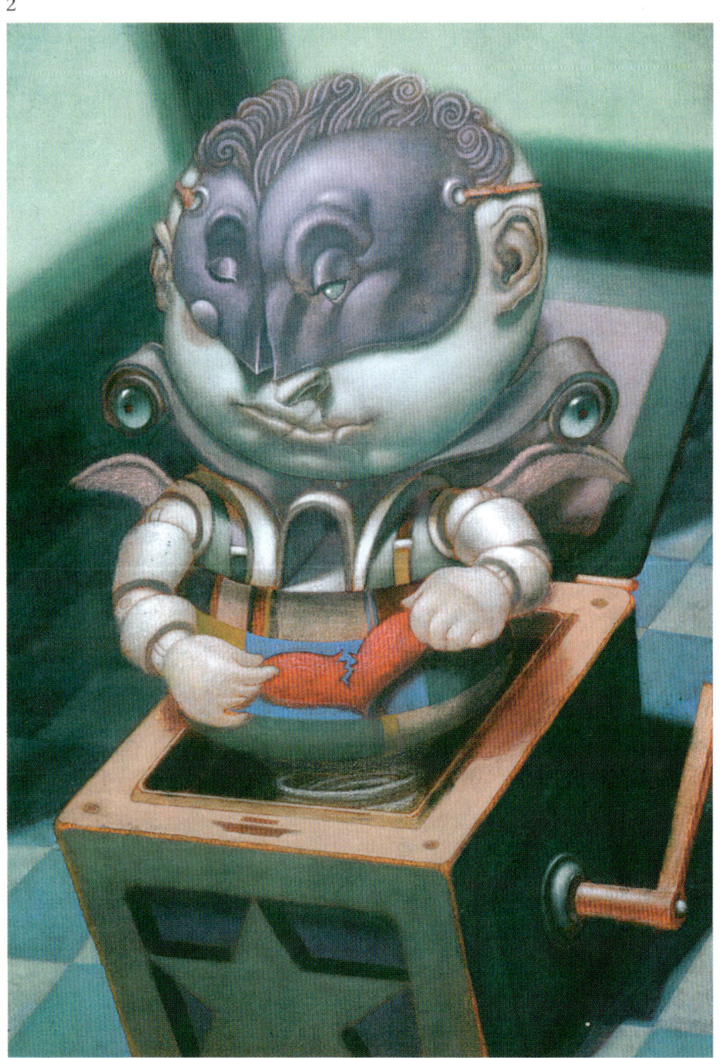

3
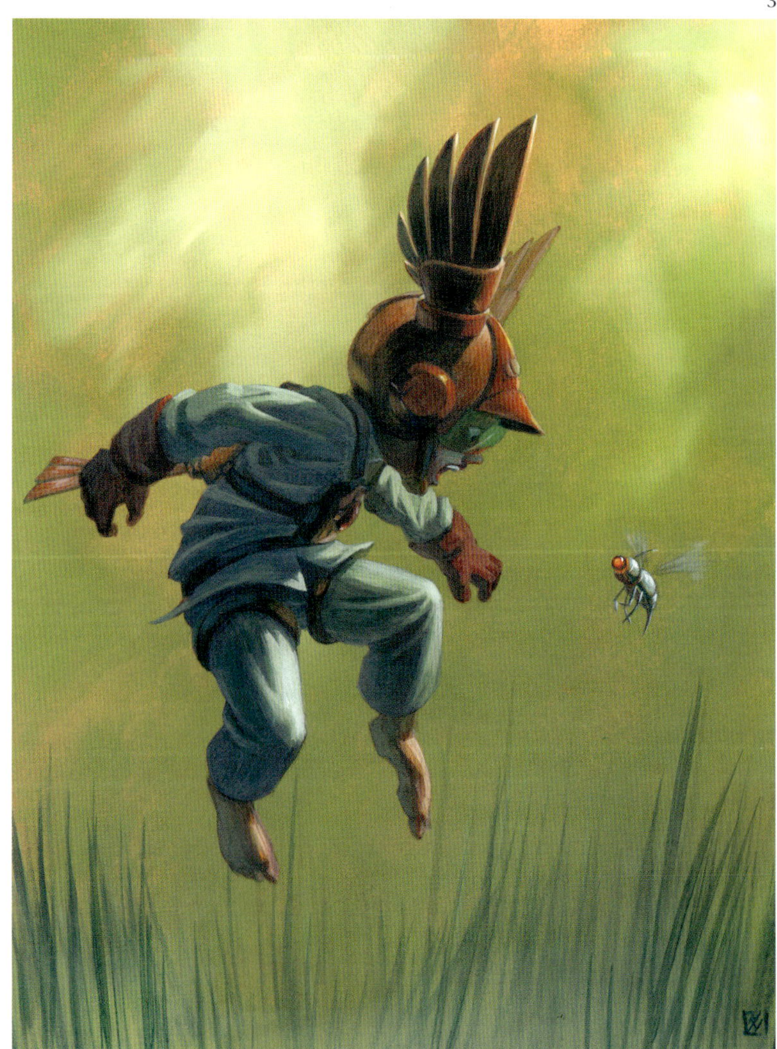

4

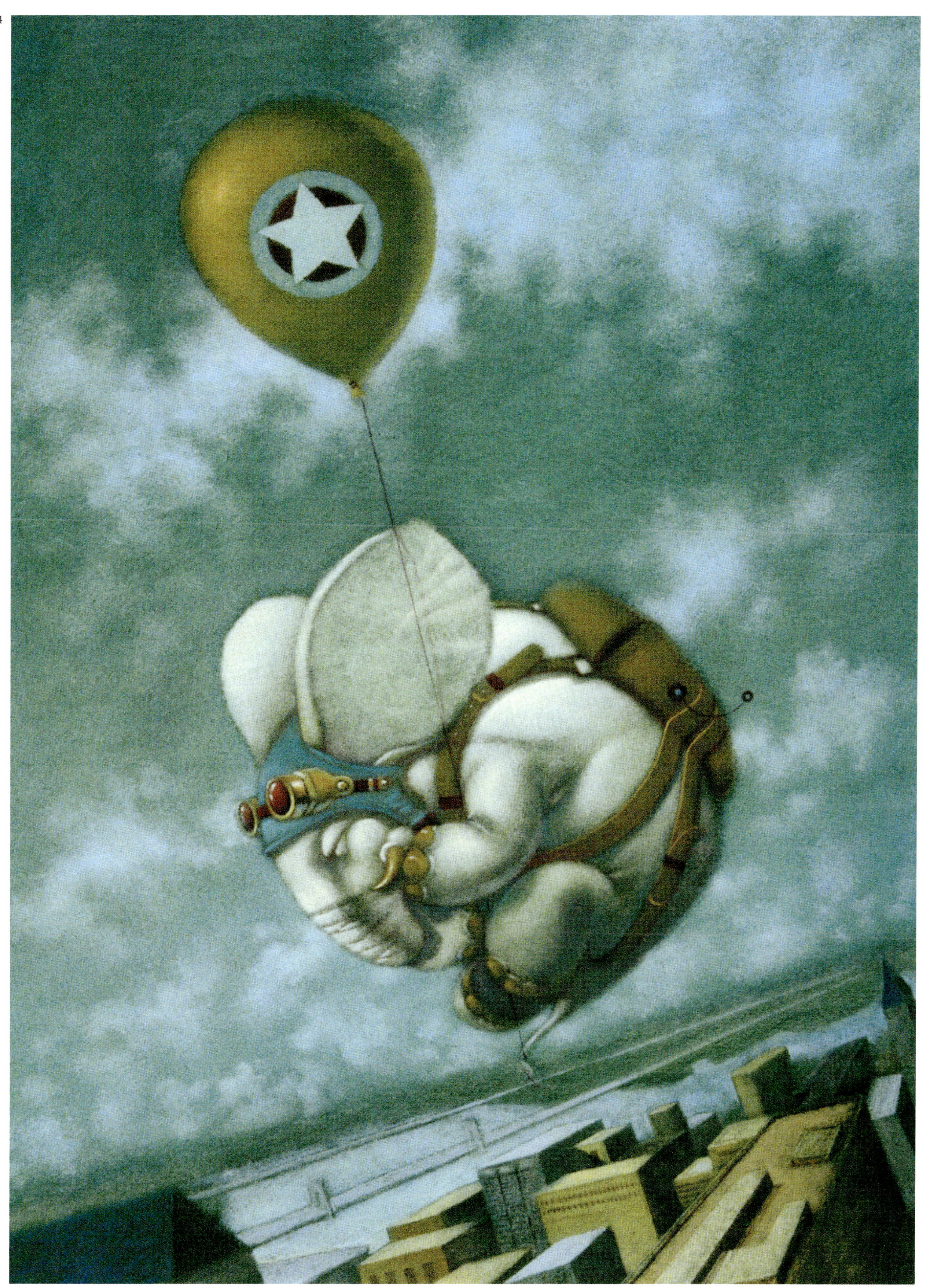

Unpublished

1
artist: **Dave Seeley**
title: Image Junkie
medium: Digital

2
artist: **Scala**
client: Le Bélial
title: Bifrost
medium: Mixed
size: 15 3/4"x23 9/16"

3
artist: **Raúl Cruz**
title: Mecasaurio
medium: Acrylics/watercolors
size: 20"x30"

4
artist: **John Berkey**
title: Trouble in Ortenville
medium: Casein acrylics
size: 22 1/2"x15 1/2"

5
artist: **John Berkey**
title: Moving Forward
medium: Casein acrylics
size: 28"x16"

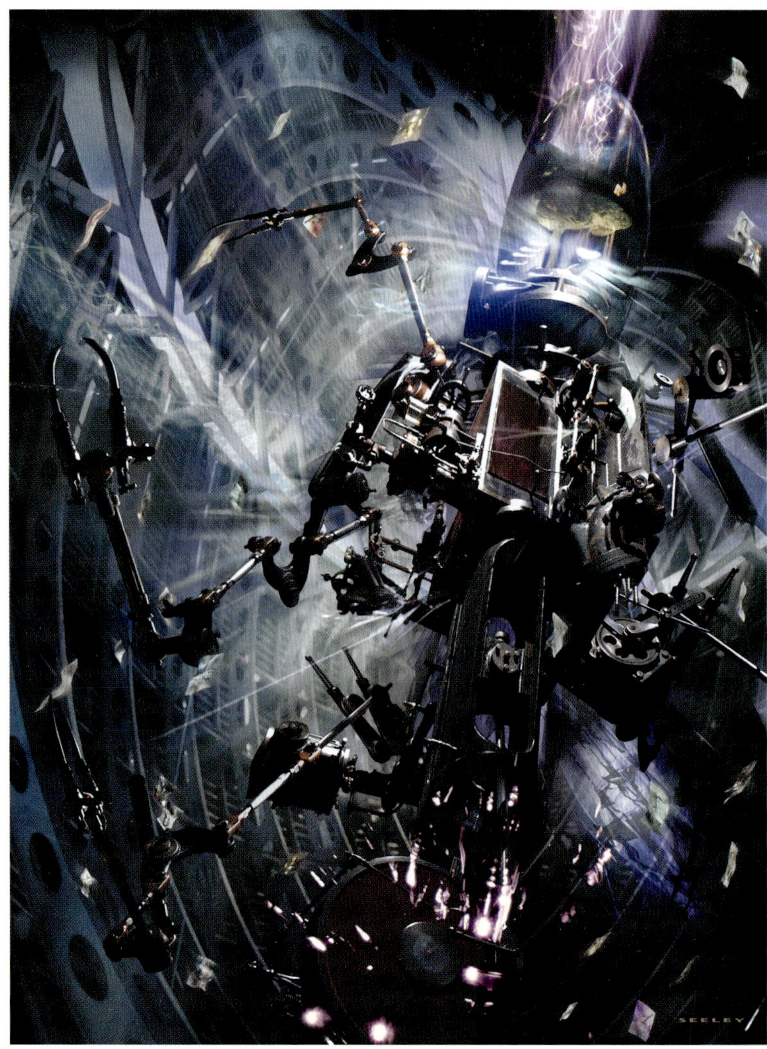

1

2

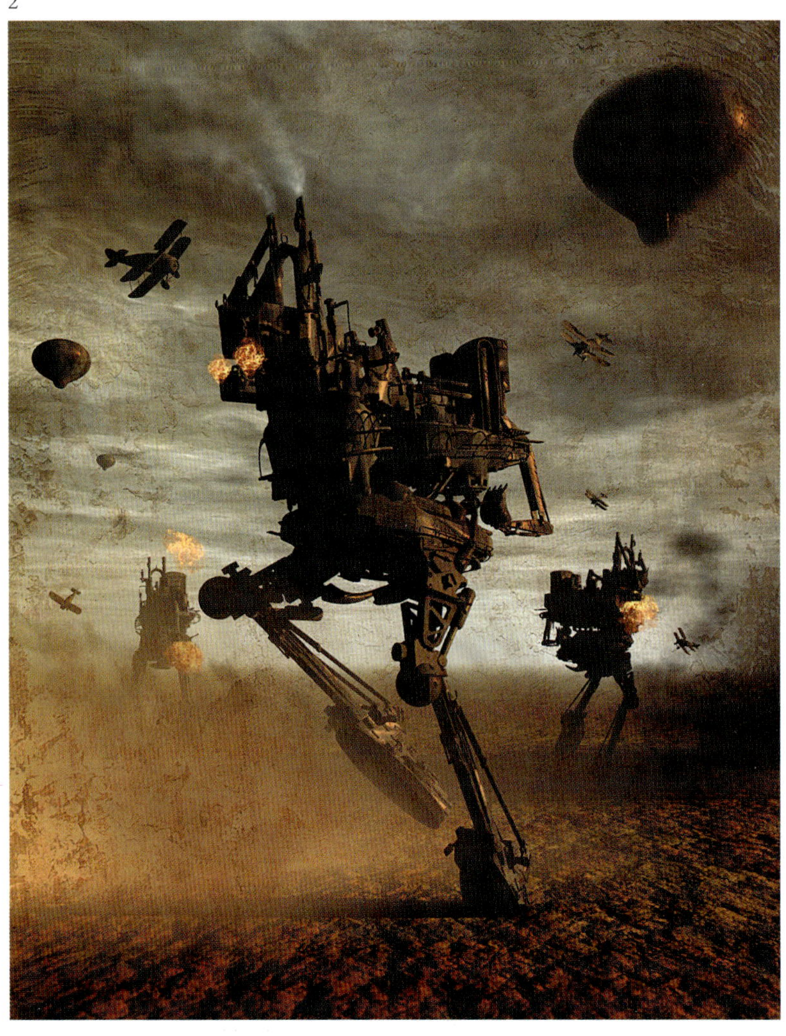

3

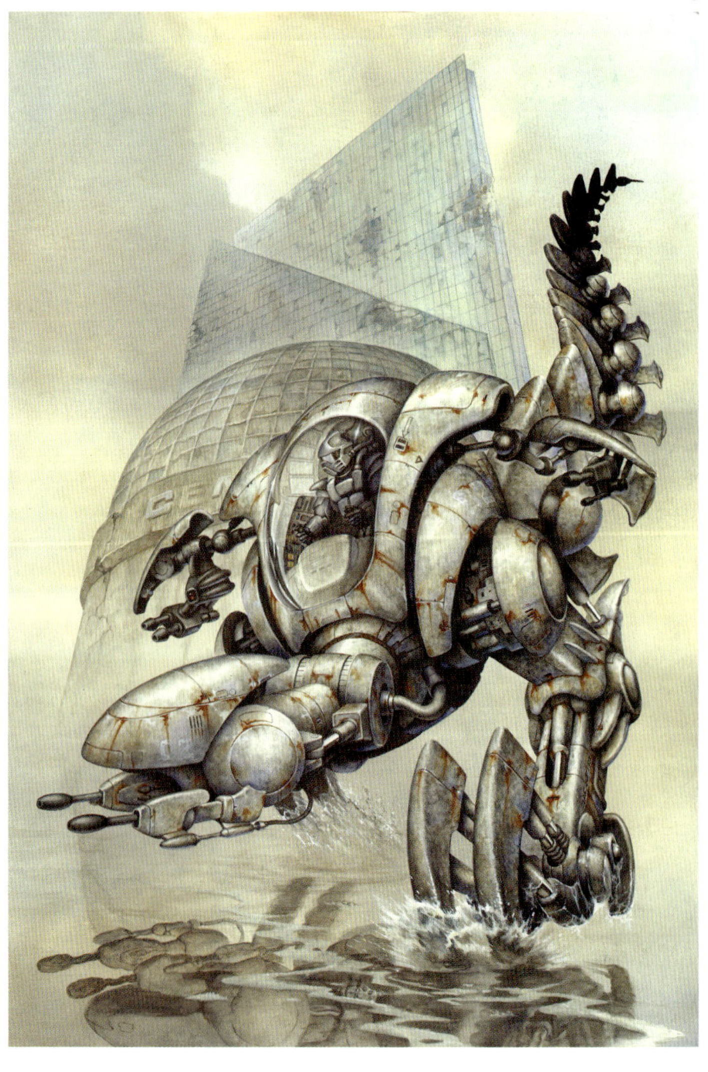

4

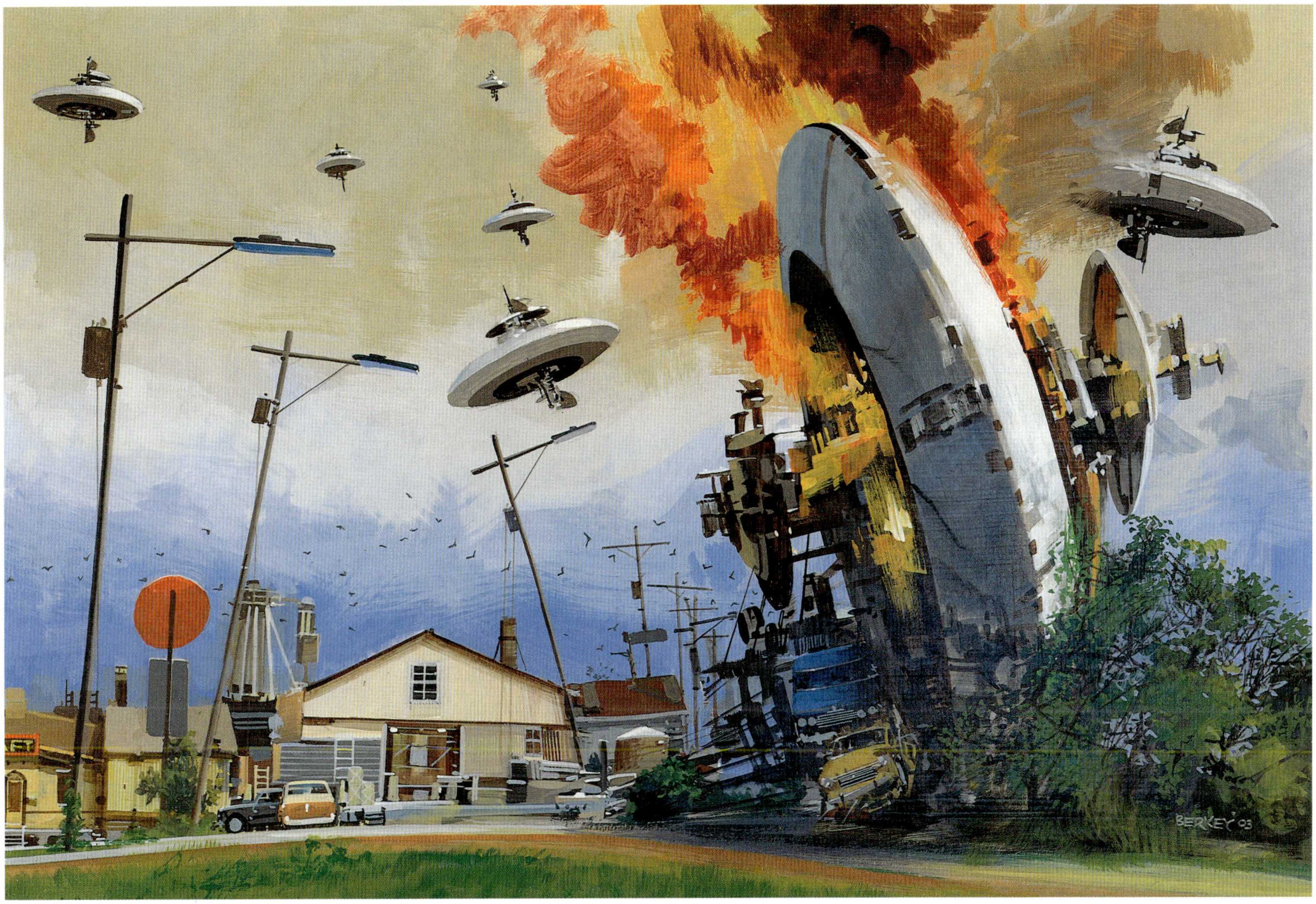

5

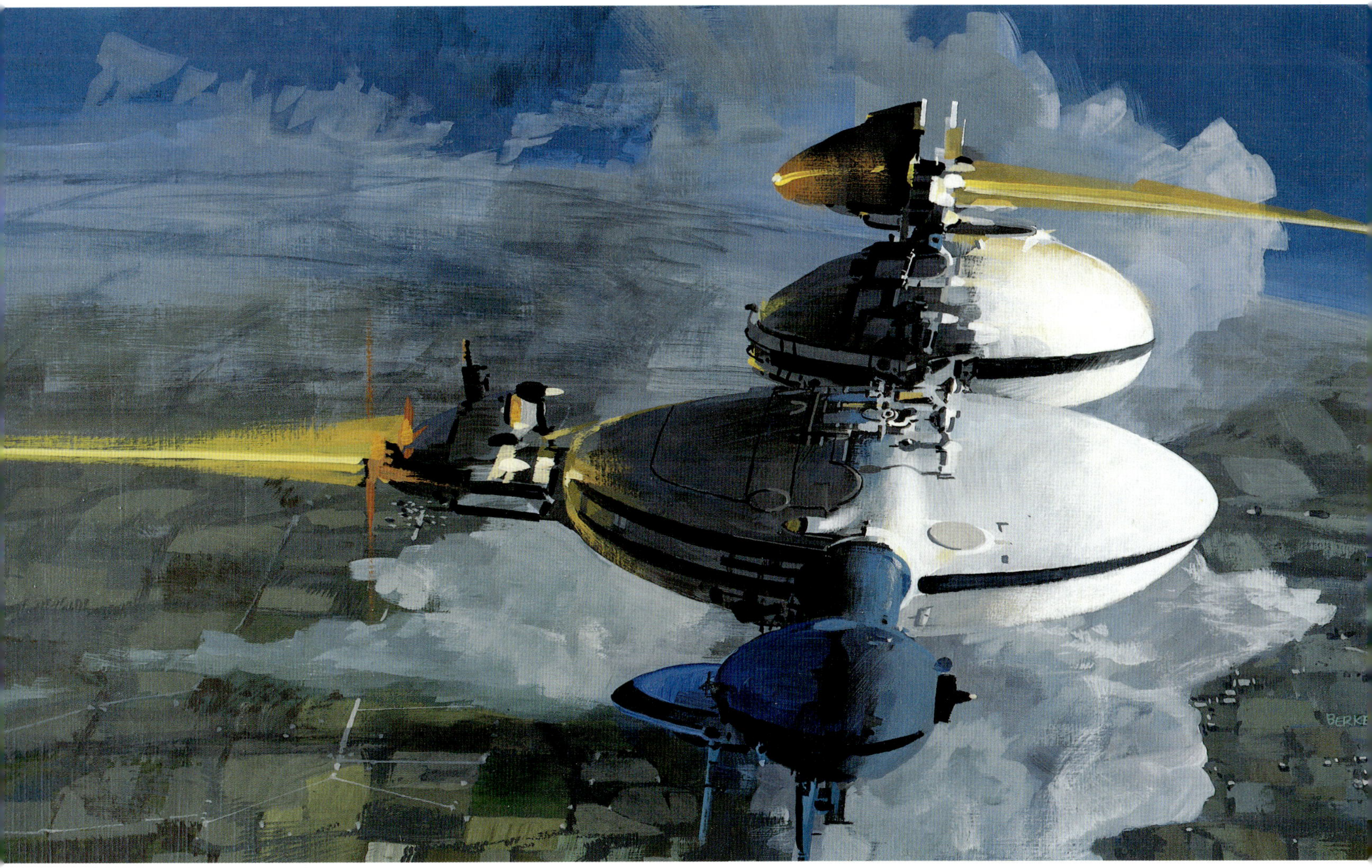

Unpublished

1
artist: **Omar Rayyan**
title: Fluffy
medium: Watercolors
size: 8"x10"

2
artist: **Robert E. Mankowski, Jr.**
title: Rune
medium: Acrylics
size: 15"x30"

3
artist: **Peter Sakievich**
title: Death
medium: Digital
size: 8½"x13½"

4
artist: **Omar Rayyan**
title: The Horny Duchess
medium: Oils on panel
size: 24"x28"

1

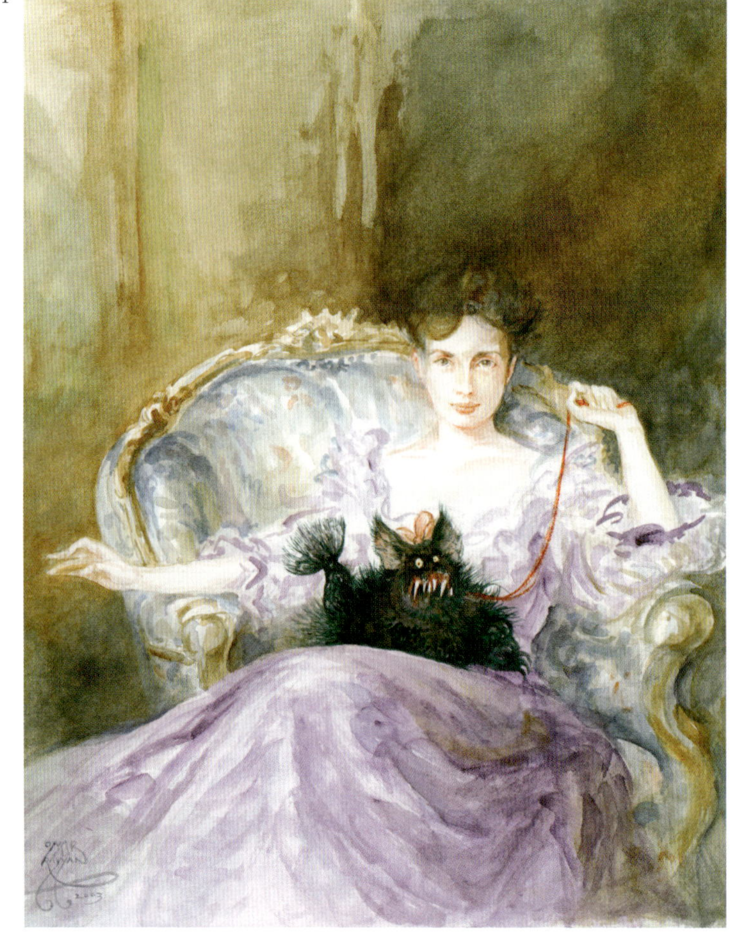

2

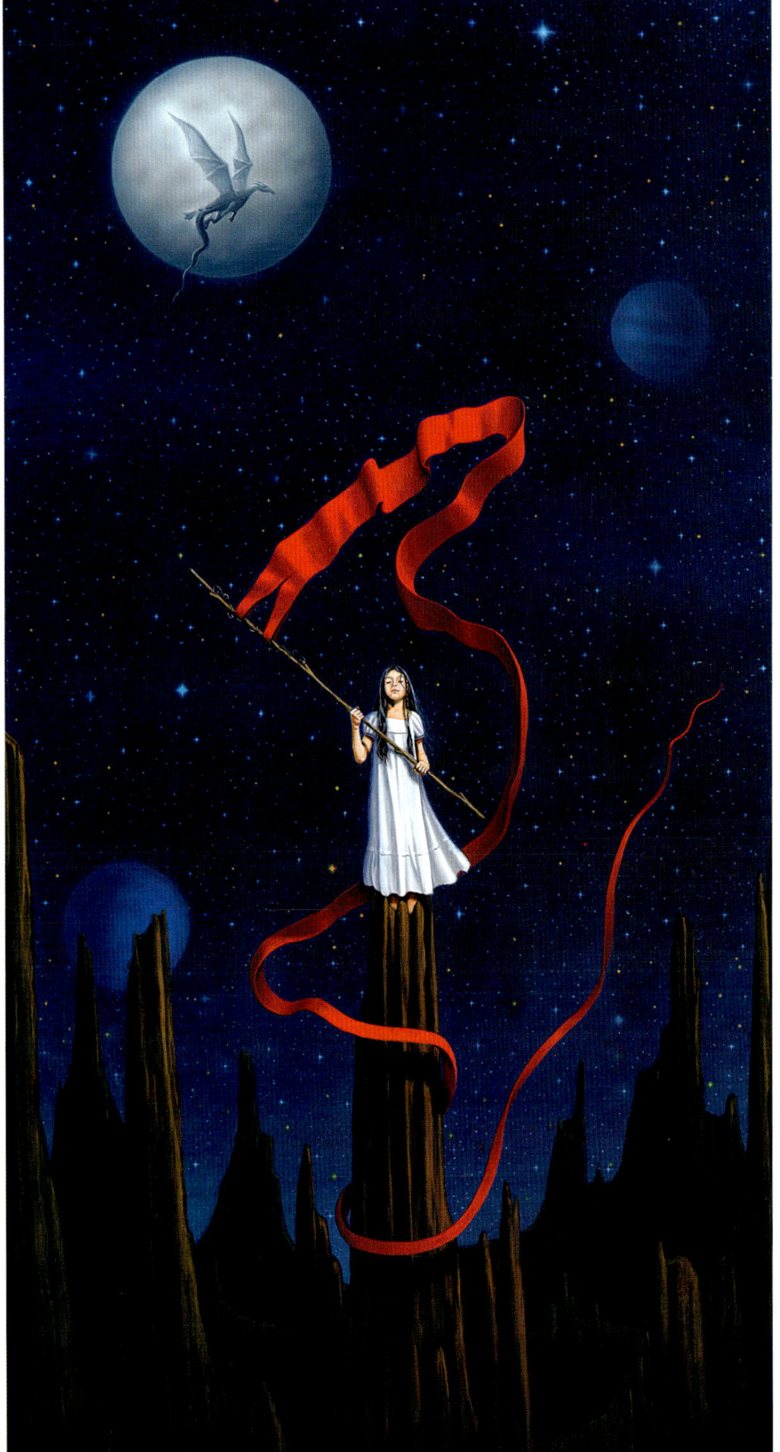

3

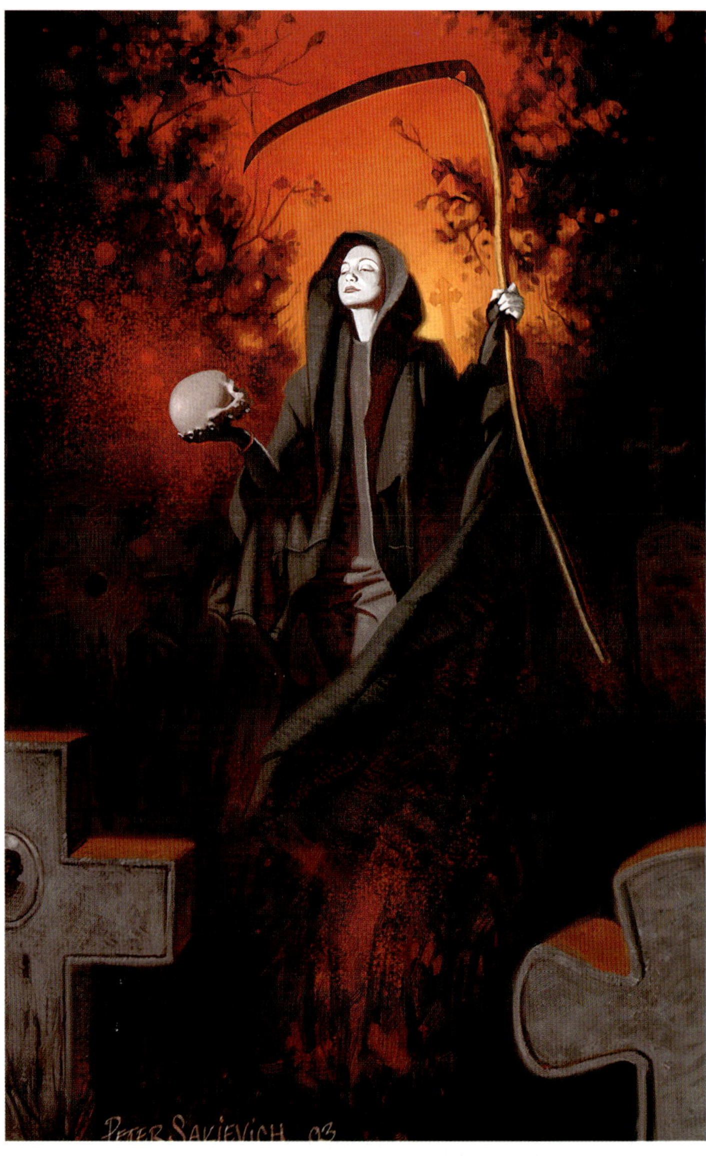

4

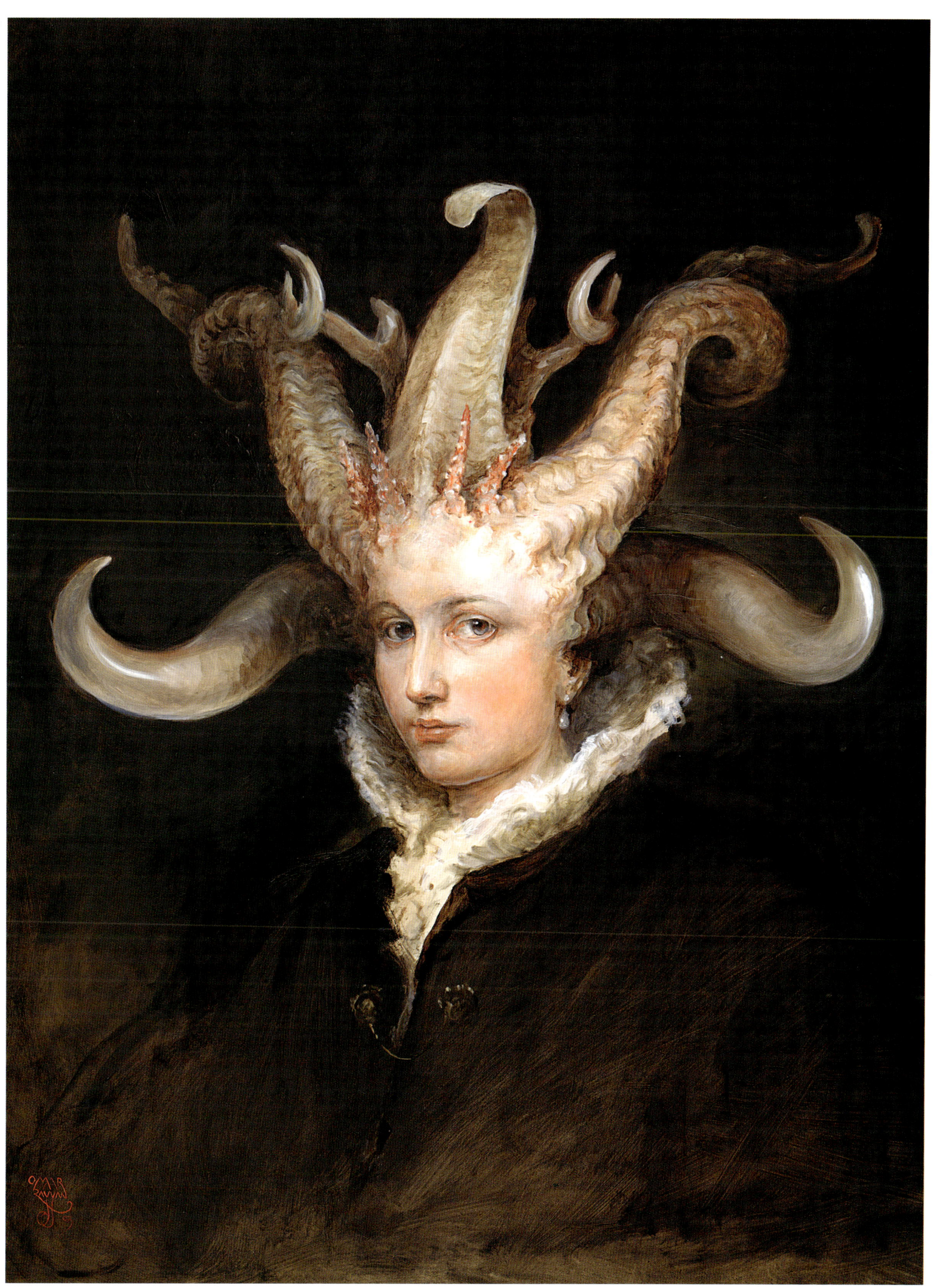

Unpublished

1
artist: **Jeremy Geddes**
title: Thwack-Thwack-Thwack
medium: Oils on board
size: 85cmx45cm

2
artist: **Steve Pilcher**
title: Chains
medium: Mixed
size: 30"x24"

3
artist: **Dennis Allain**
title: Tractor Jacking
medium: Digital
size: 17"x6"

4
artist: **Joe Kovach**
title: Not So Superman
medium: Acrylics
size: 10 3/4"x15"

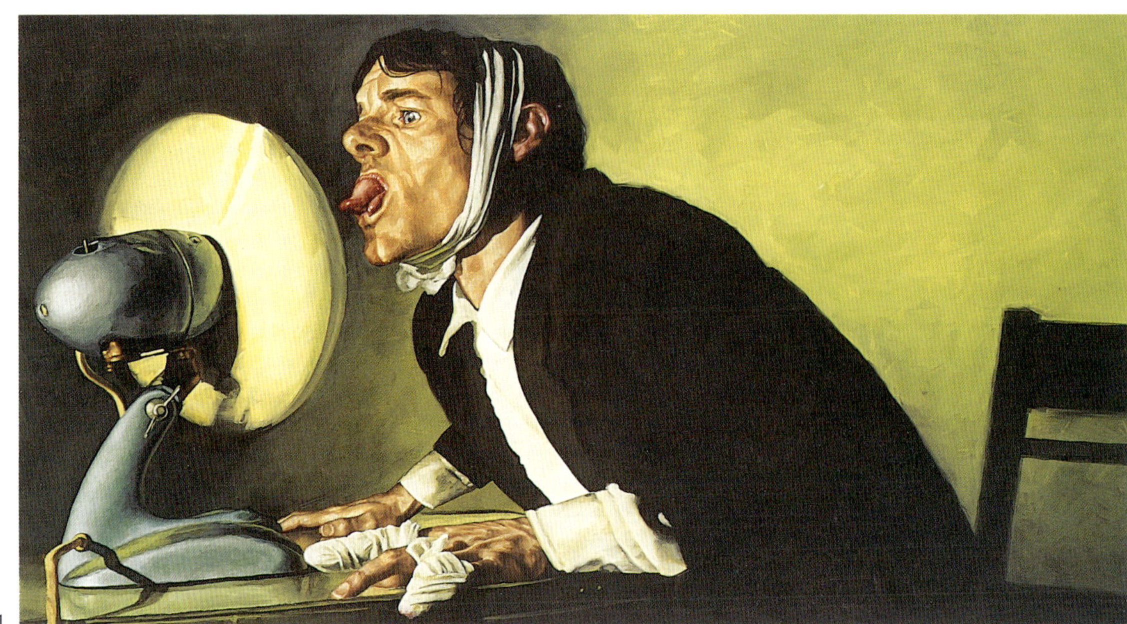

1

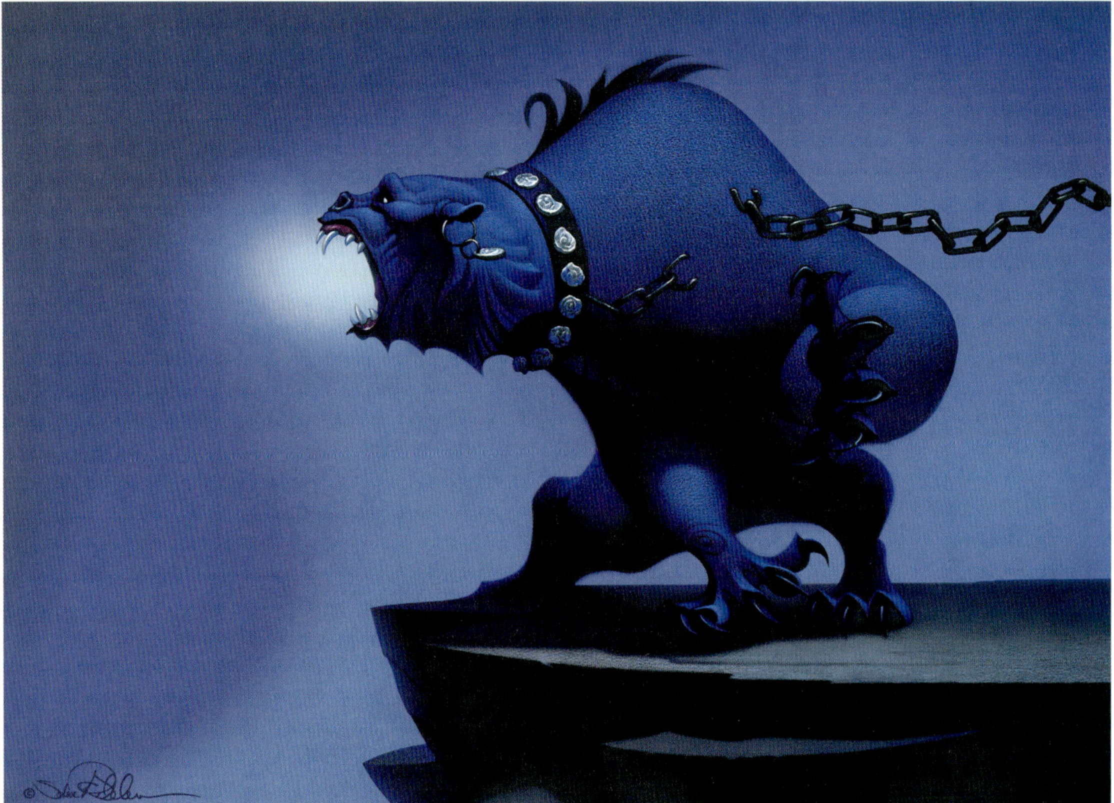

2

3

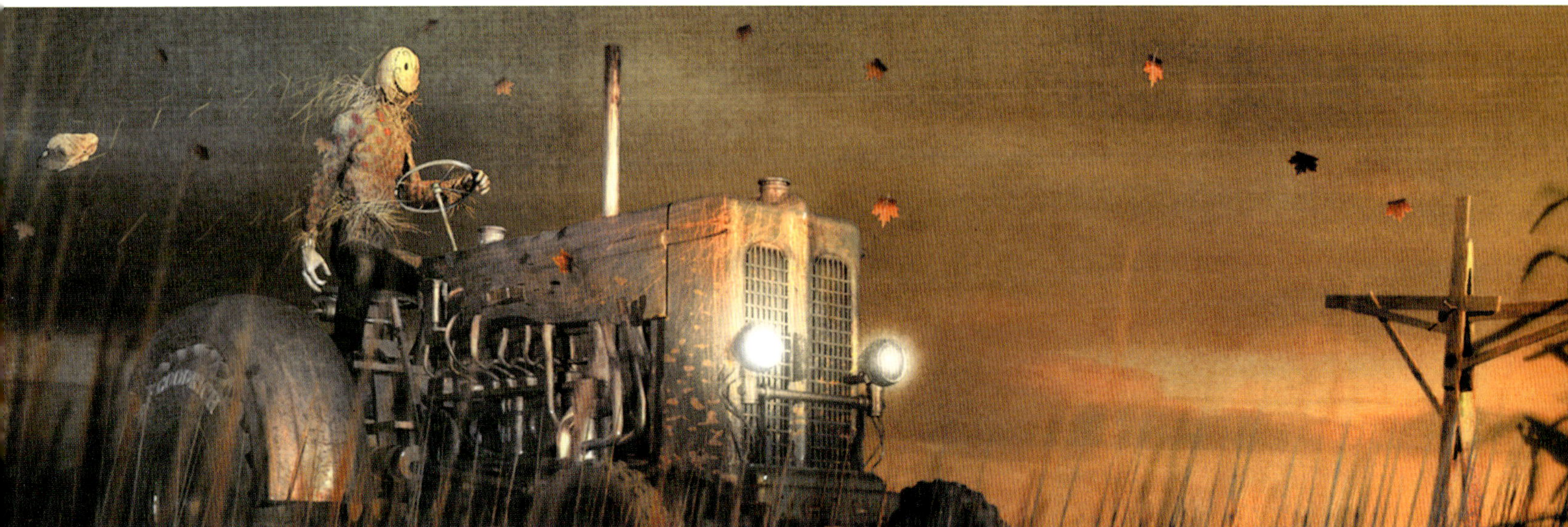

4

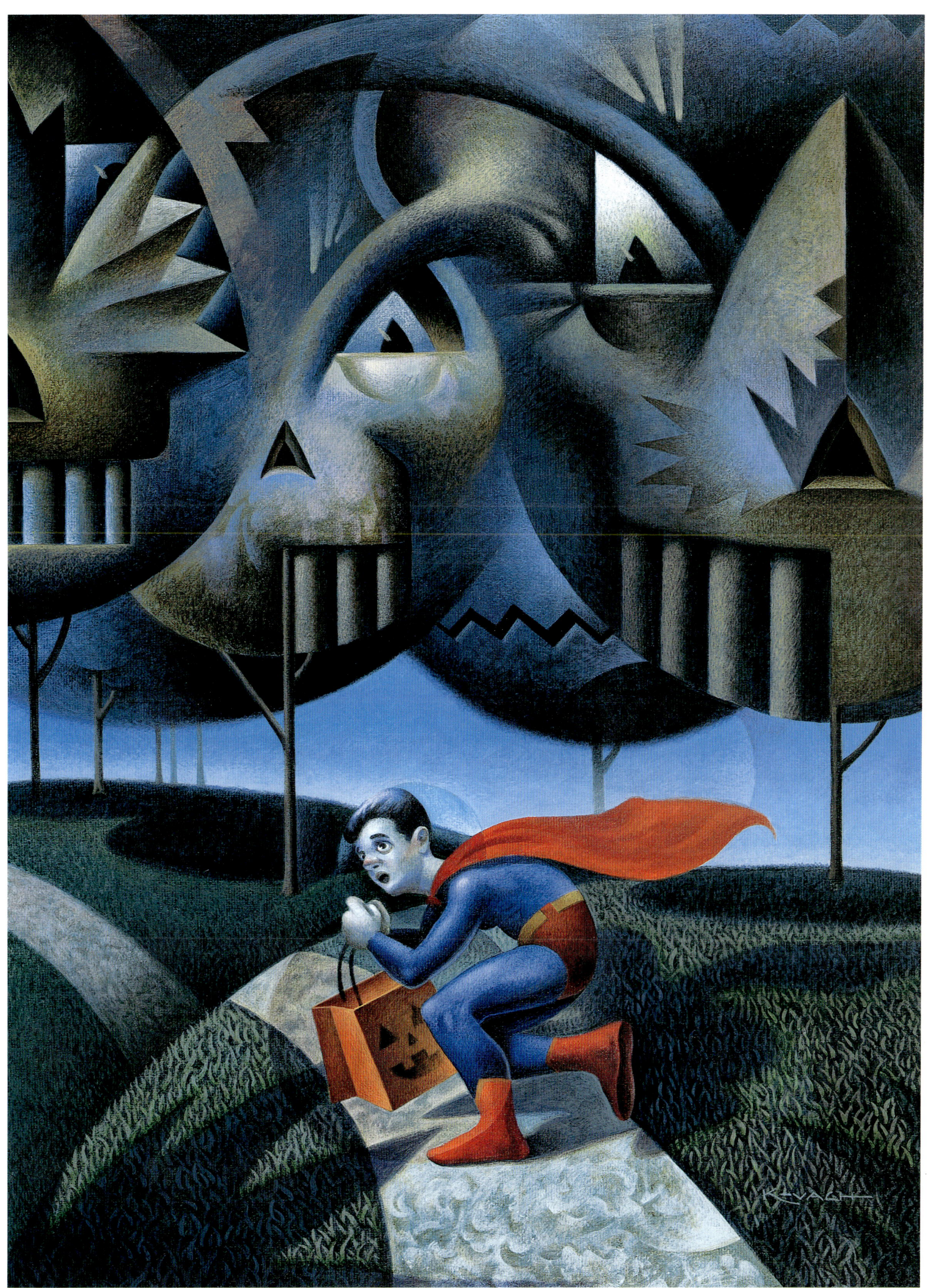

1
artist: **Marc A. Fishman**
title: Midsummer's Night
art director: Angi Sullins
client: Duirwaigh Publishing
medium: Oils on canvas
size: 4'x5'

2
artist: **Eric Boden**
title: Coming Home
medium: Digital
size: 12"x6"

3
artist: **E.M. Gist**
title: Late Nite Visitors
medium: Graphite
size: 20"x30"

4
artist: **Justin Gerard**
art director: Brannon McAllister
designer: Justin Gerard
title: To Chain the Beast
medium: Digital
size: 14"x21"

5
artist: **Christopher J. Anderson**
title: The Coldest Day
medium: Digital
size: 13"x11"

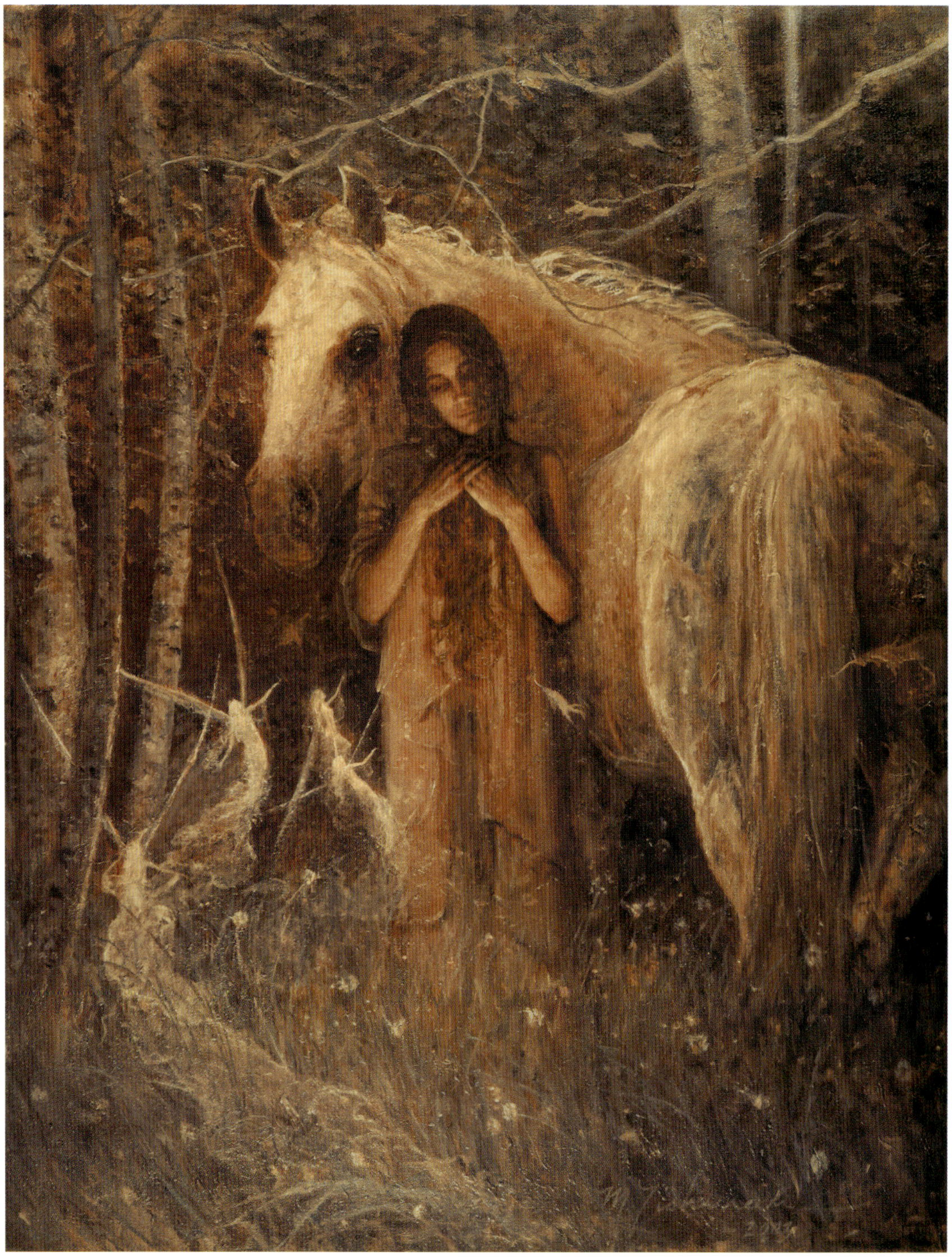

1

2

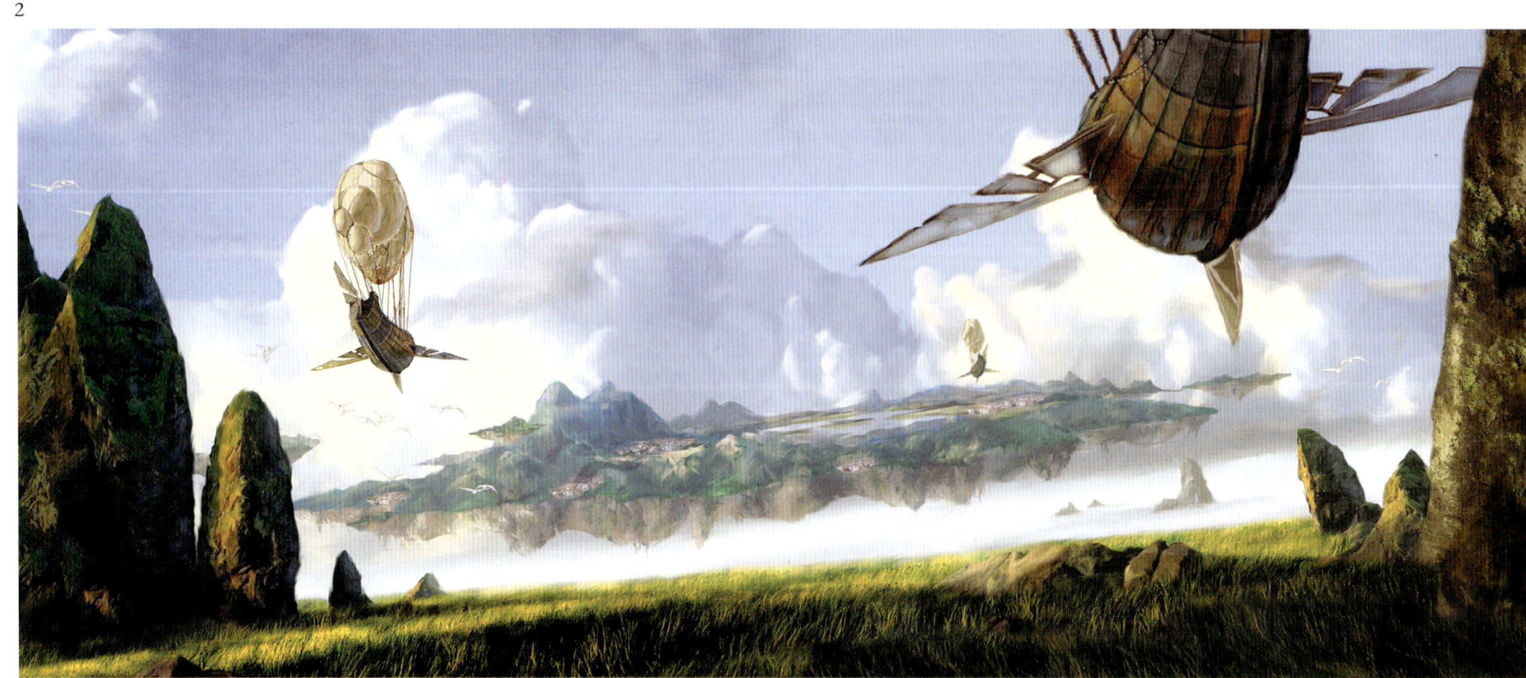

3

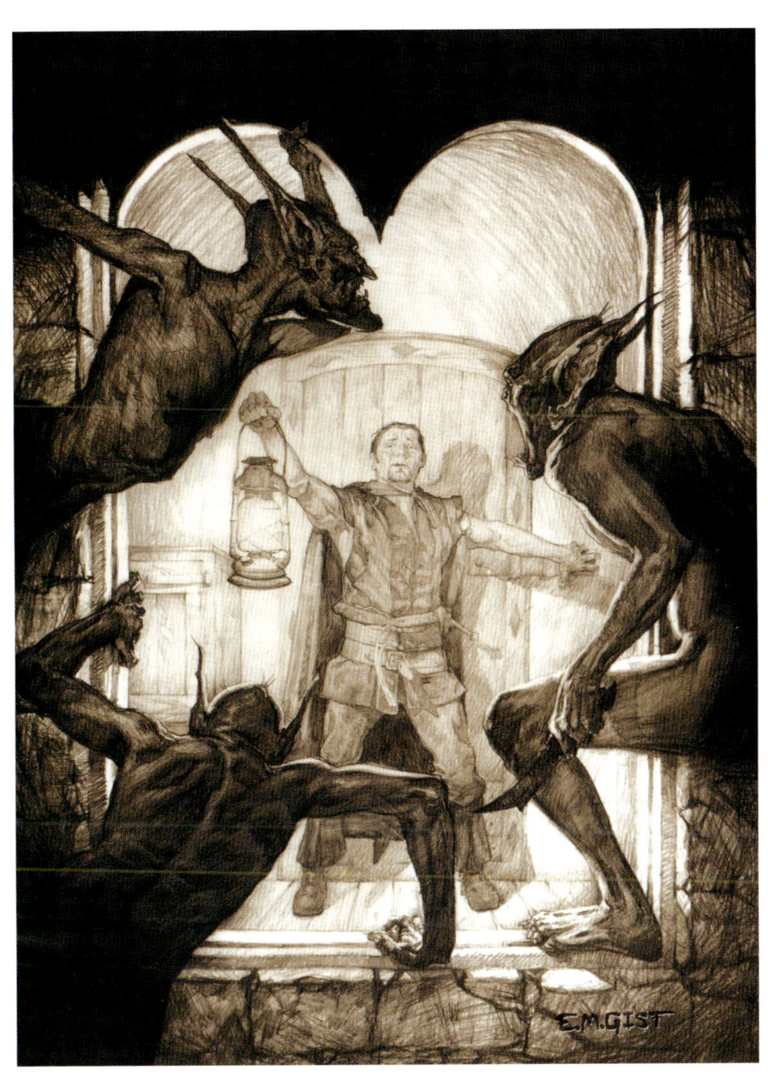

4

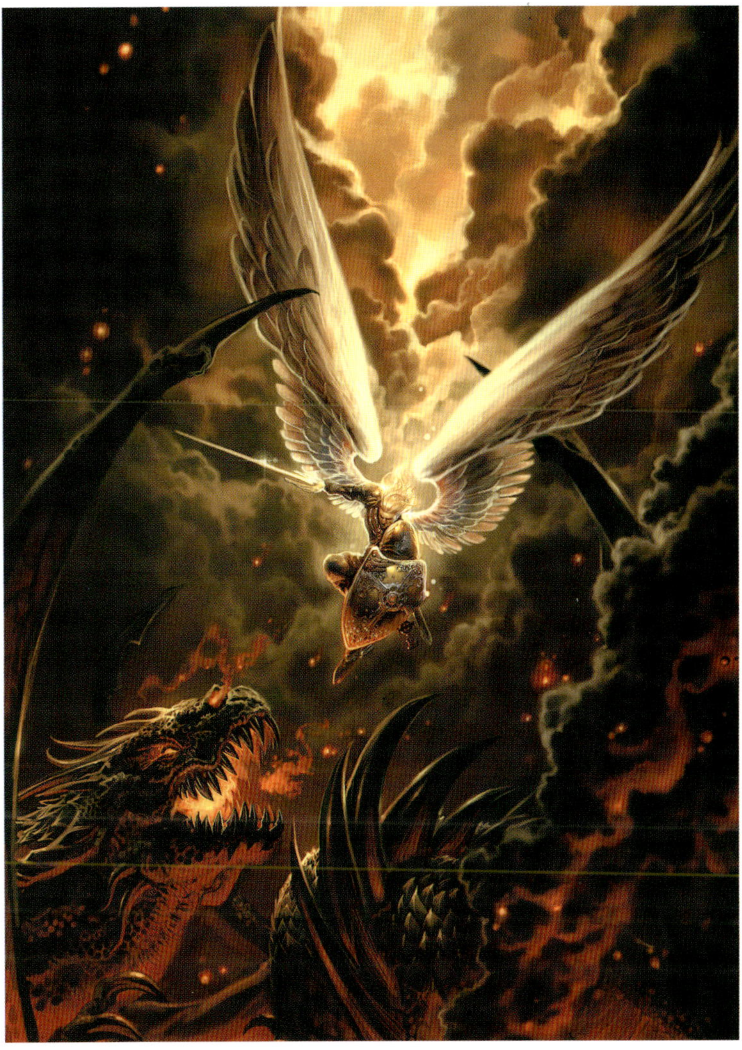

5

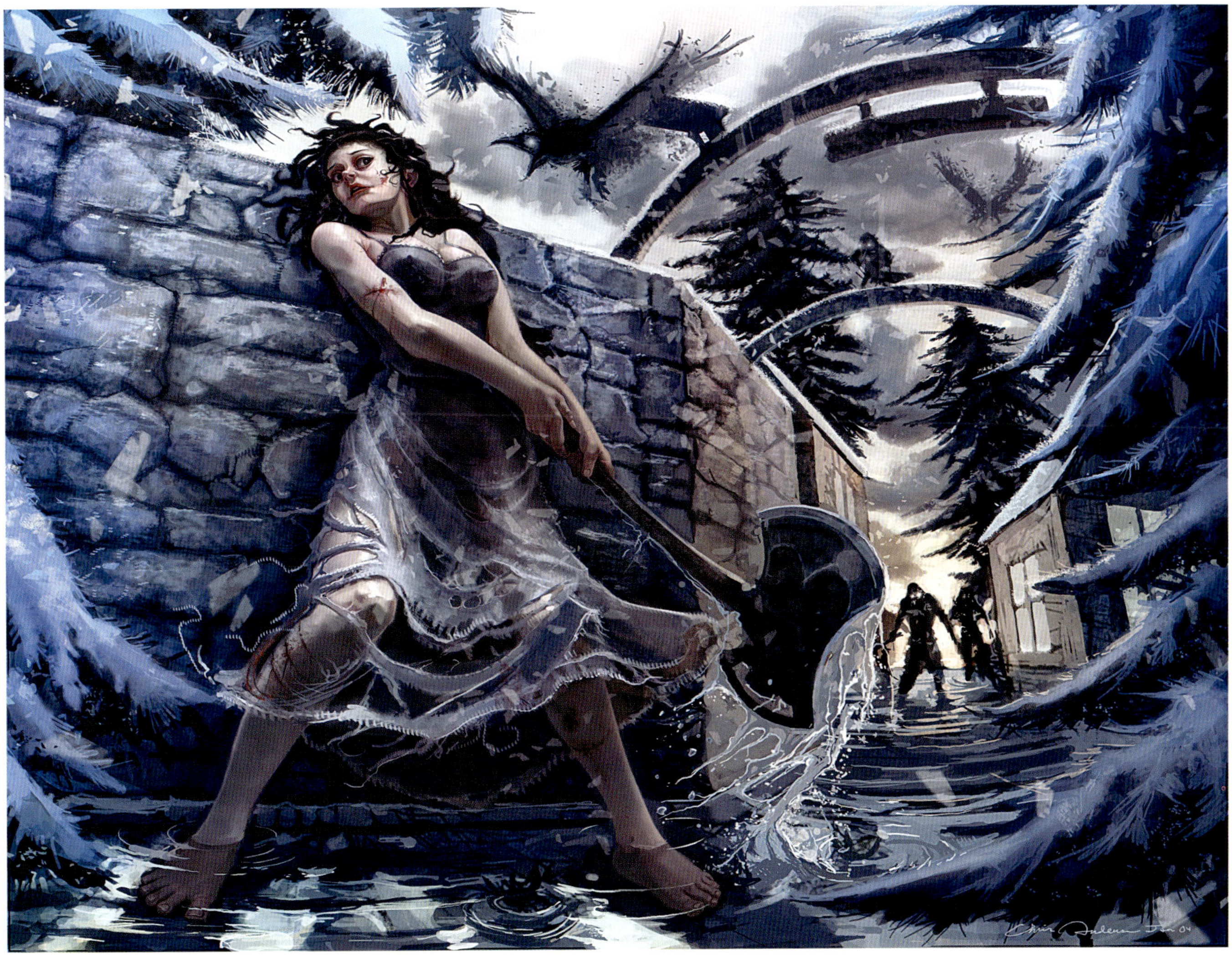

1
artist: **Christophe Vacher**
title: Spring
medium: Oils
size: 18″x24″

2
artist: **Petar Meseldžija**
client: ITPZMAJ/Novi Sad
title: A Legend Called Steel-Bashow 1
medium: Oils
size: 19 1/2″x27 1/2″

3
artist: **Kinuko Y. Craft**
client: Kai Larson
title: Portrait of Claire
medium: Oils over watercolor on board
size: 16″x20″

4
artist: **Petar Meseldžija**
title: Remembrance
medium: Oils
size: 19 1/2″x27 1/2″

1

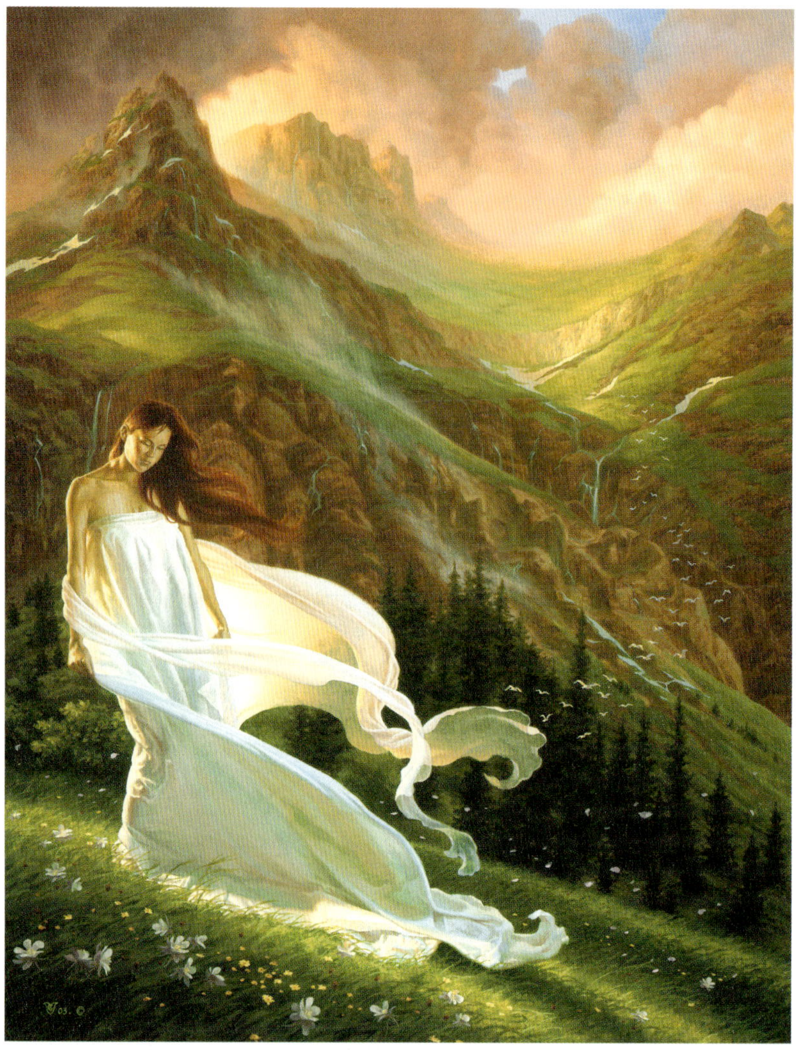

2

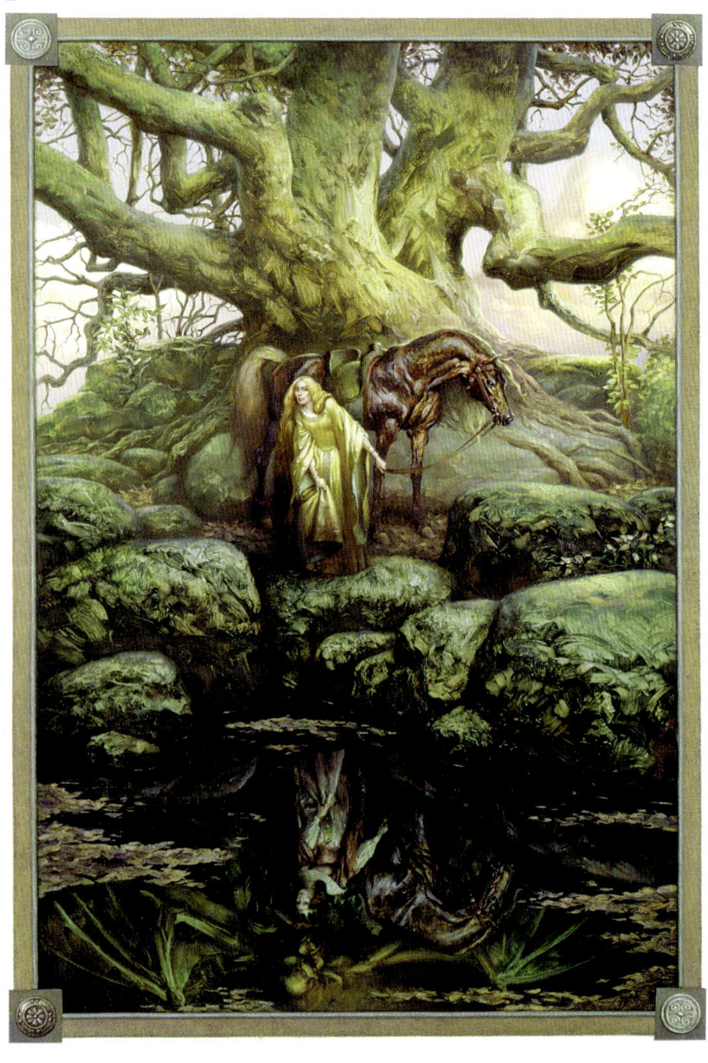

3

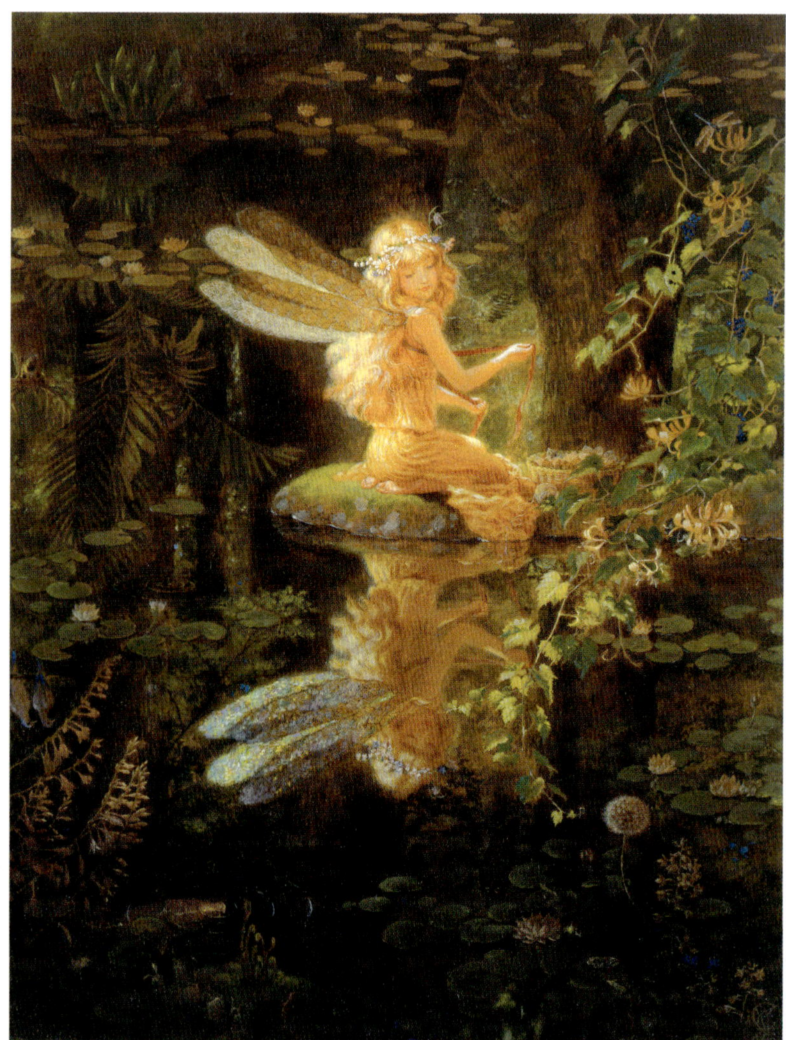

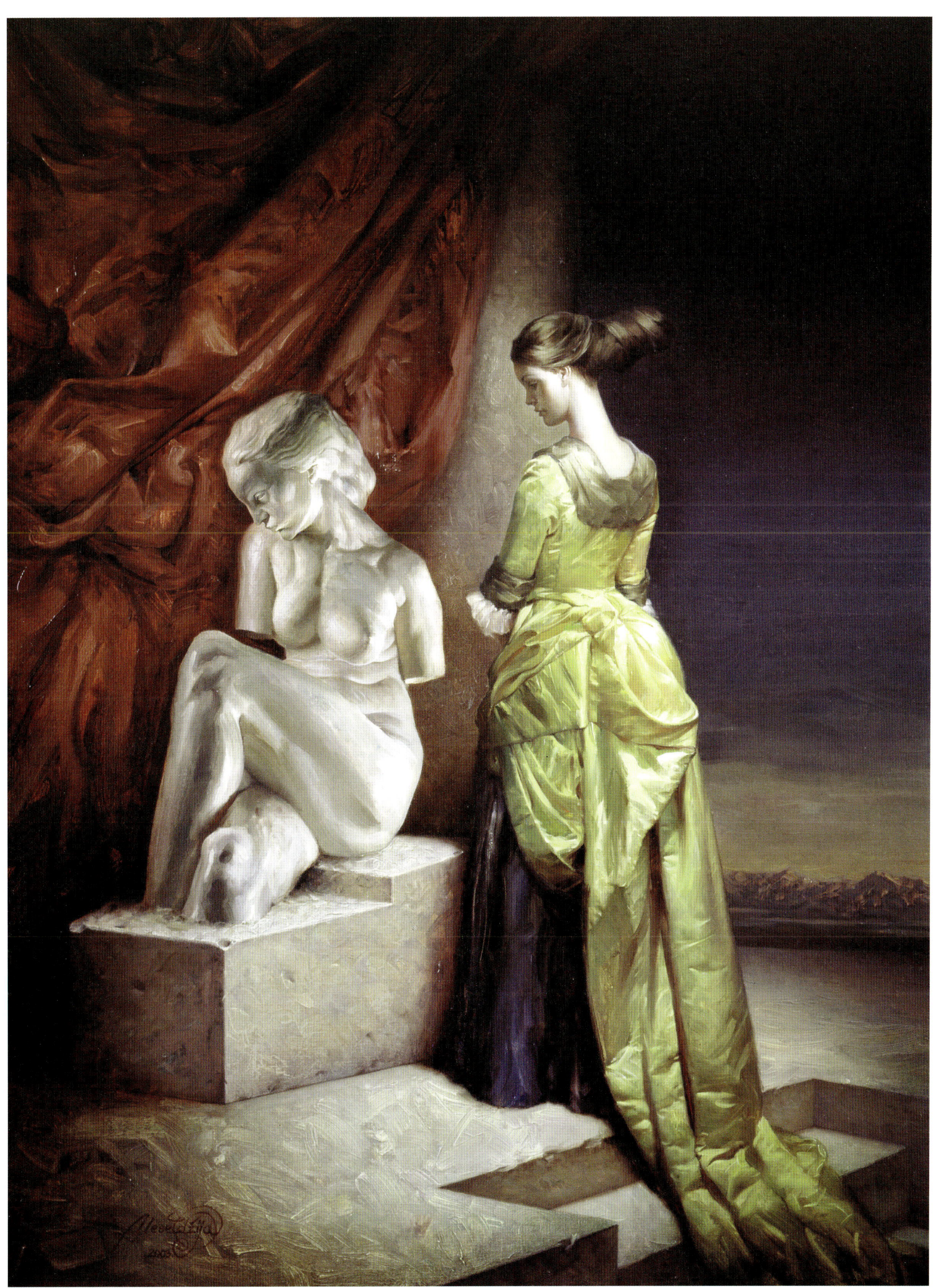

Unpublished

1
artist: **Christian Alzmann**
title: Bond
medium: Mixed/digital

2
artist: **Steven Kenny**
title: The Scaffold
medium: Oils on canvas
size: 21"x26"

3
artist: **Rob Johnson**
title: Bag of Tricks
medium: Mixed
size: 16"x29"

4
artist: **Christian Alzmann**
title: Stationed
medium: Mixed/digital

1

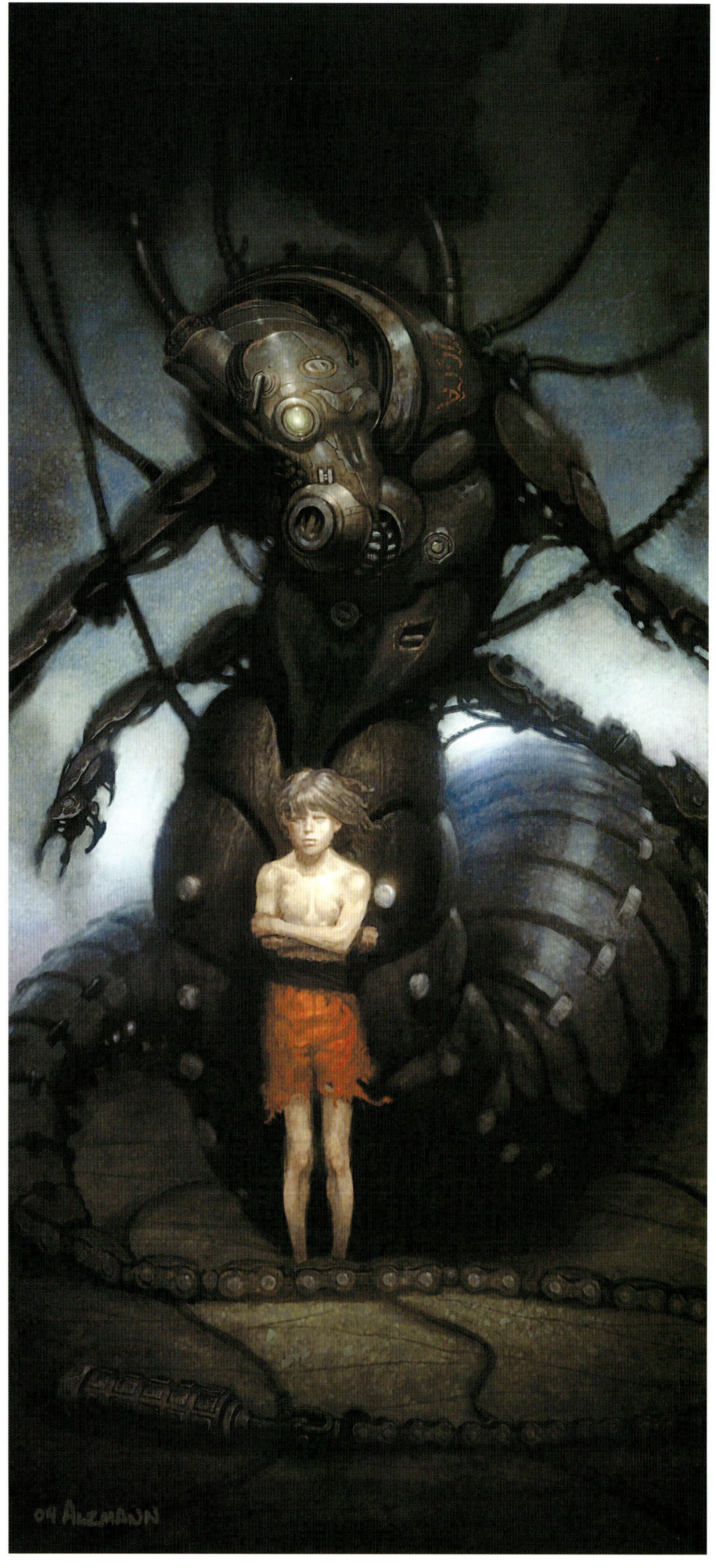

2

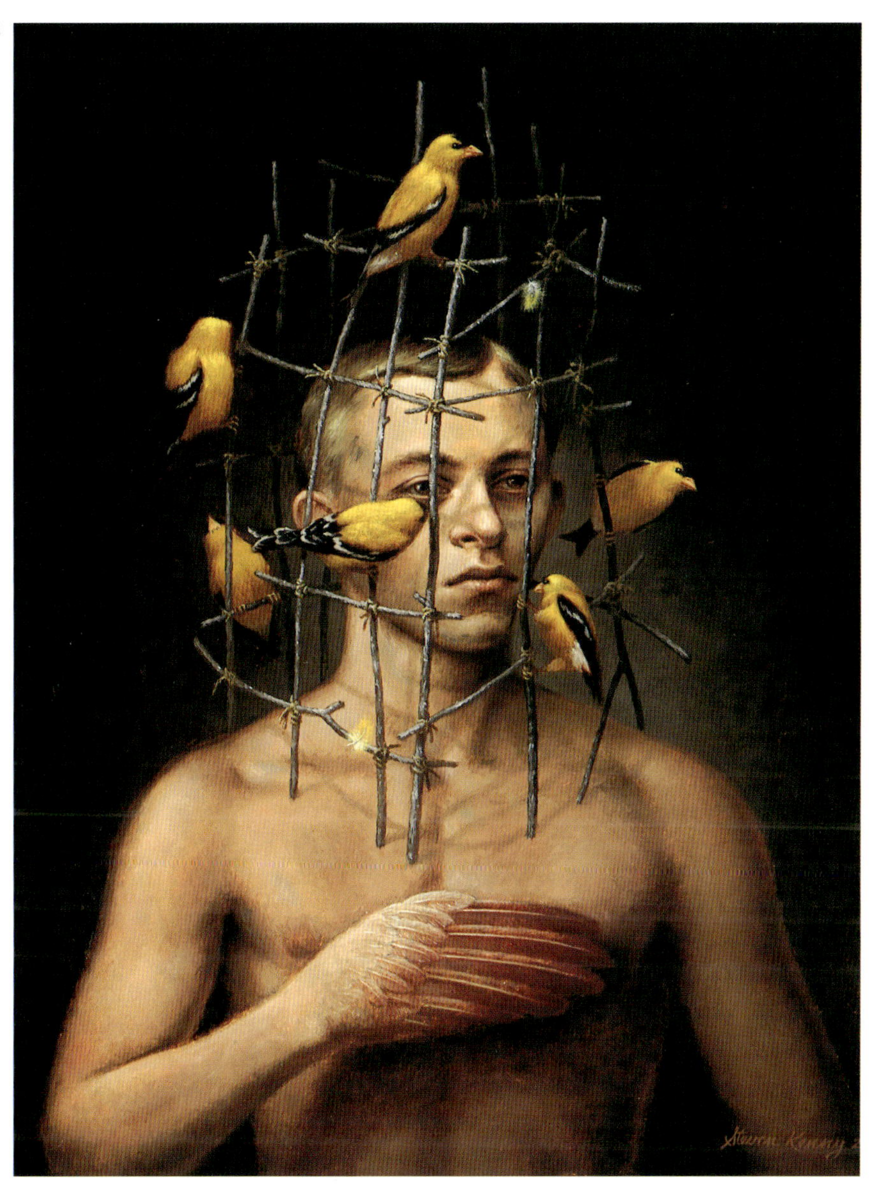

3

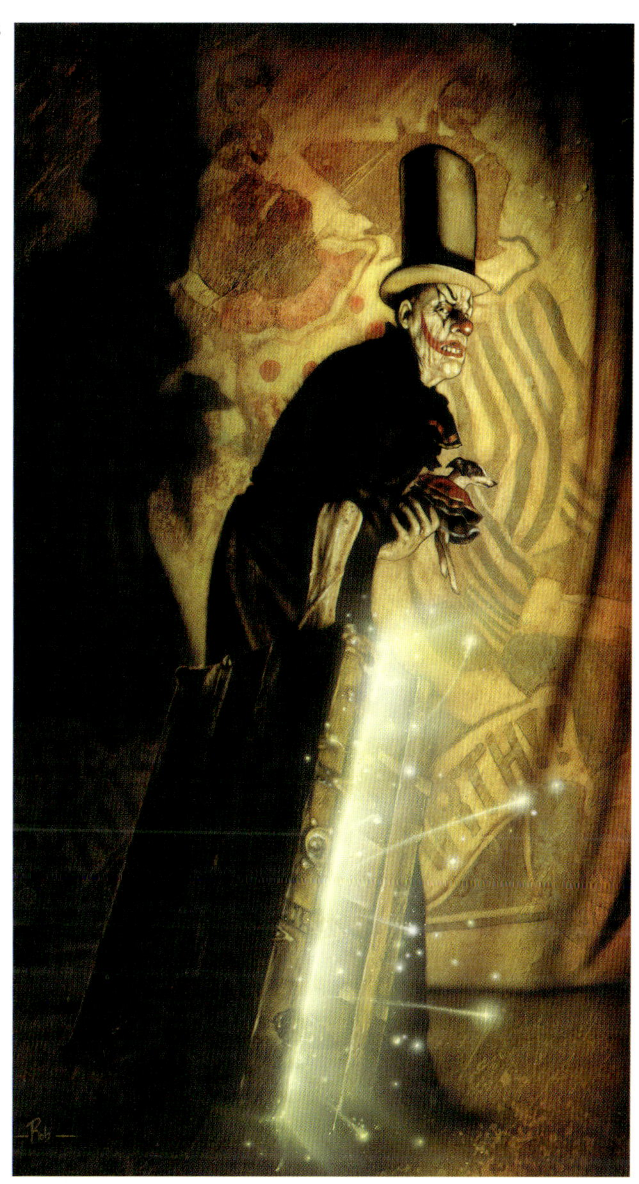

4

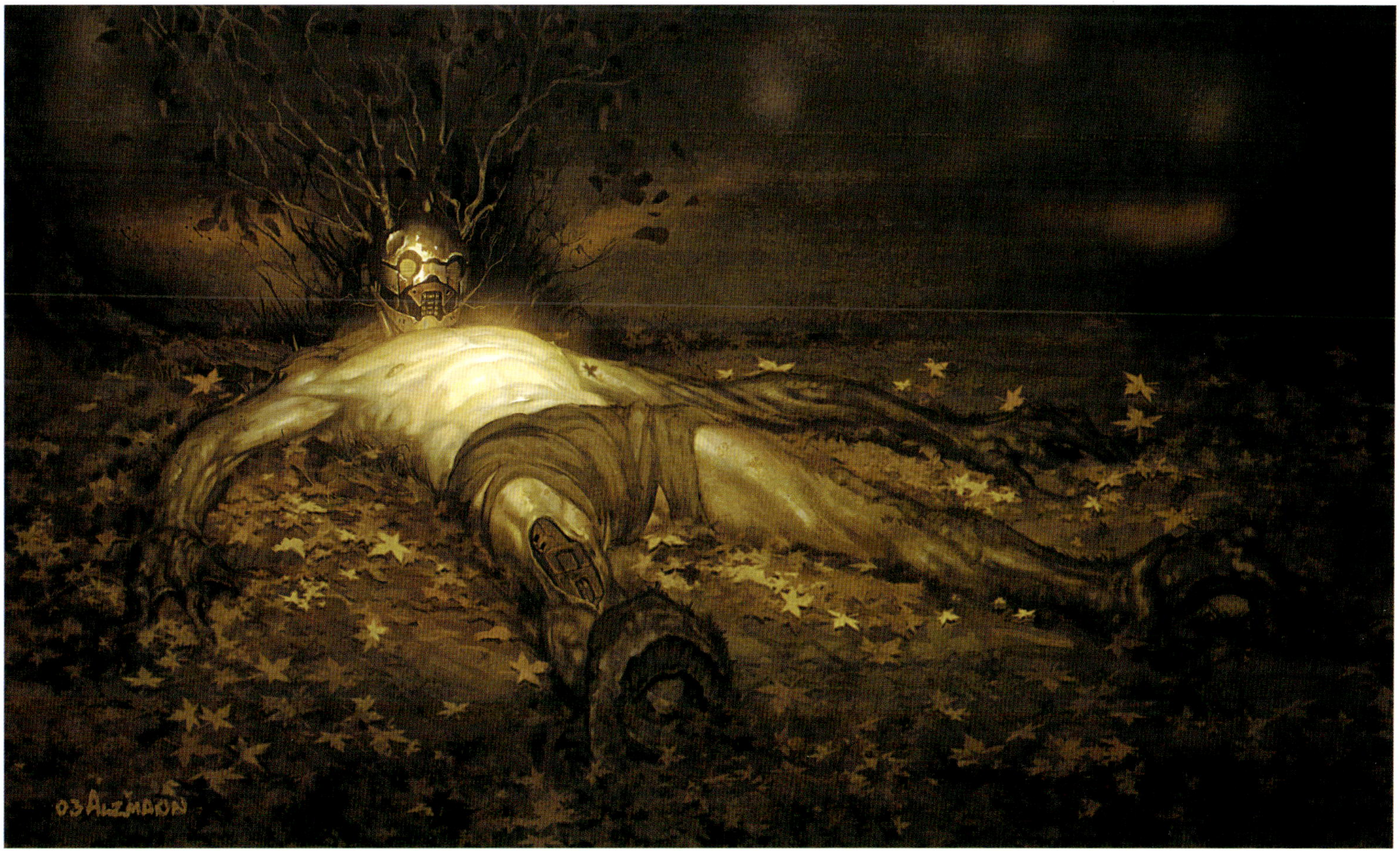

Unpublished

1
artist: **Jasmine Becket-Griffith**
title: Hunger Pains
medium: Acrylics
size: 16″x20″

2
artist: **Ilich Henriquez**
title: The Commander
medium: Digital
size: 24cmx26cm

3
artist: **Jun-ichi Fukushima**
title: Arrival
medium: Digital
size: 10″x13″

4
artist: **Michelle Spalding**
title: Phil the Mechanic
medium: Digital
size: 8″x11″

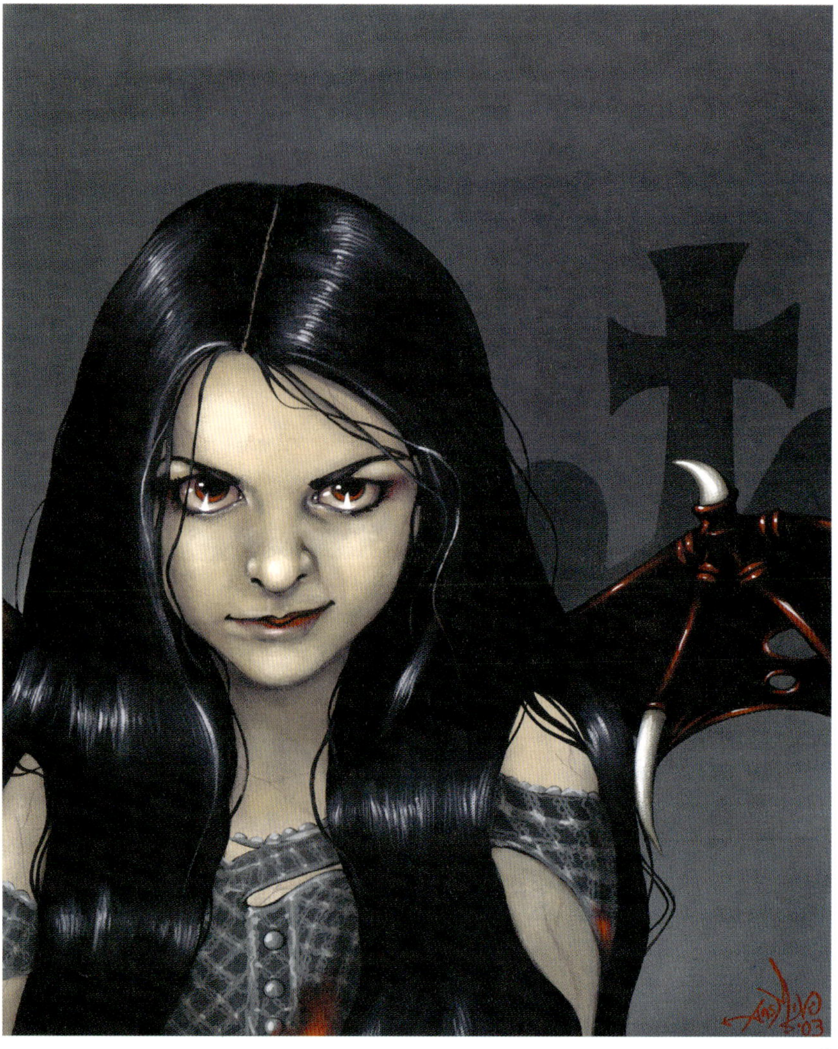

1

2

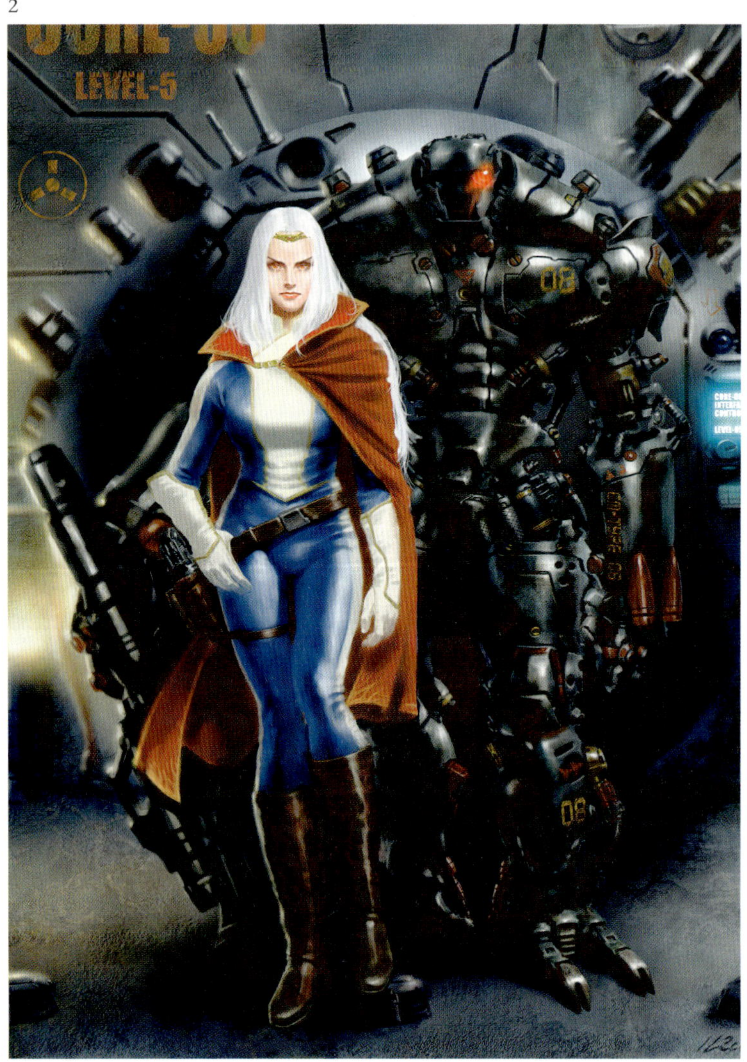

3

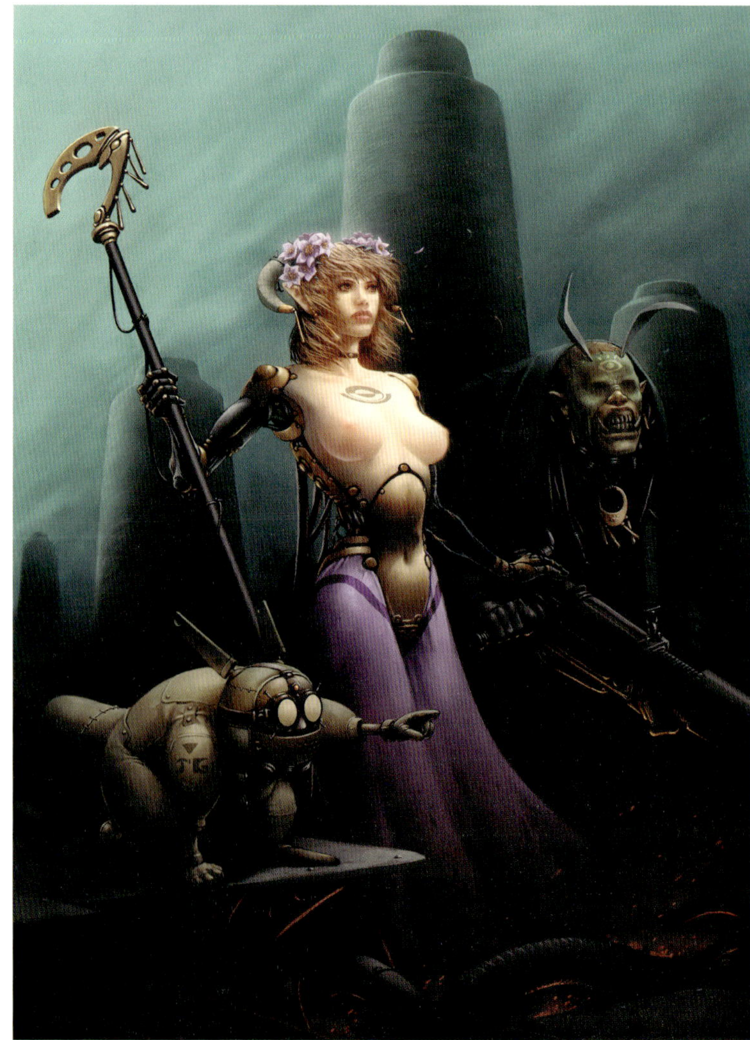

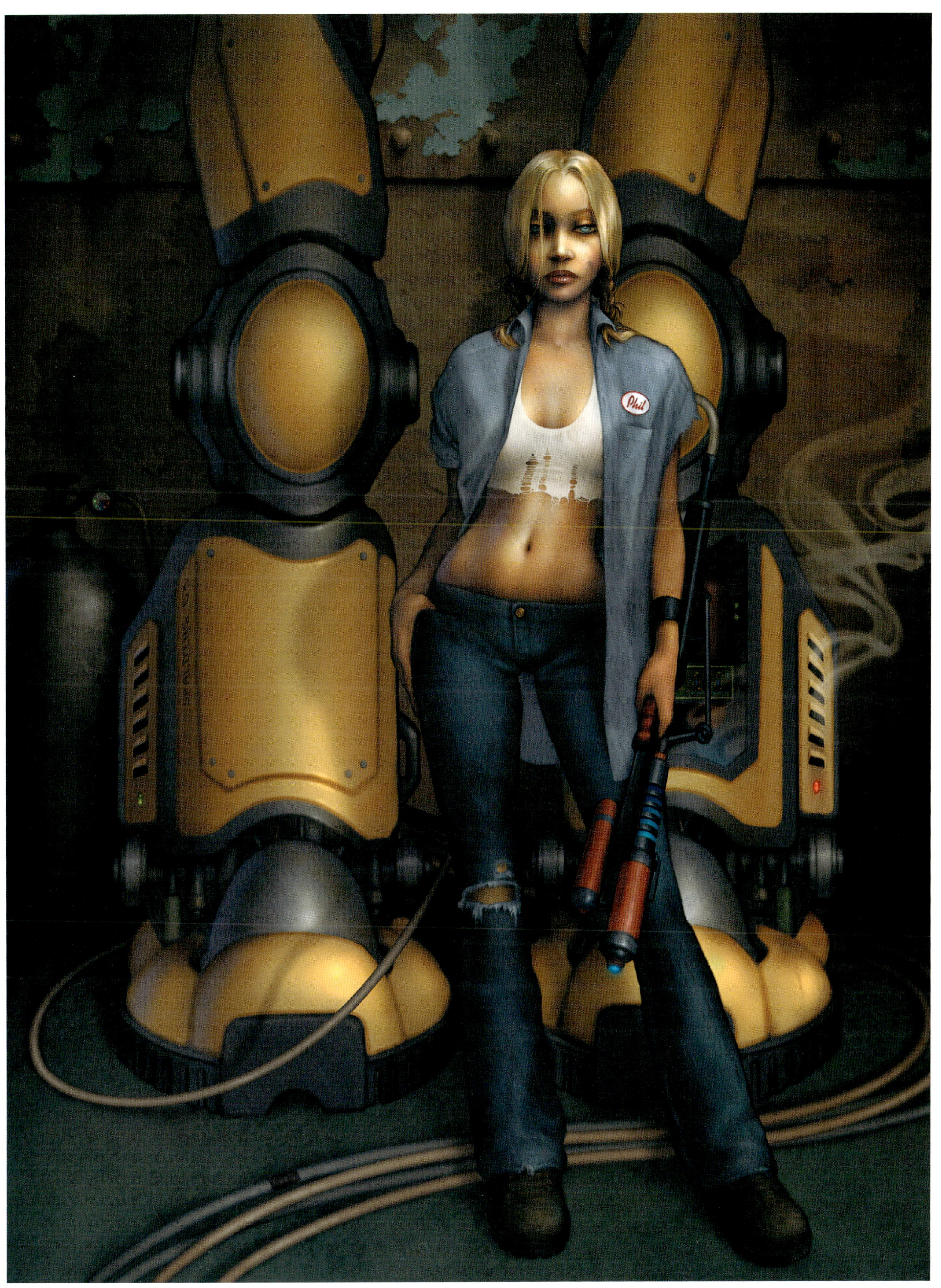
Phil

1
artist: **Gaetan & Paul Brizzi**
title: Orlando Furioso
Canto 6
medium: Penci
size: 25″x18″

2
artist: **Hunter Brown**
medium: Watercolor, gouache

3
artist: **Gaetan & Paul Brizzi**
title: Orlando Furioso
Canto 33
medium: Pencil
size: 25″x18″

4
artist: **Gaetan & Paul Brizzi**
title: Orlando Furioso
Canto 42
medium: Pencil
size: 25″x18″

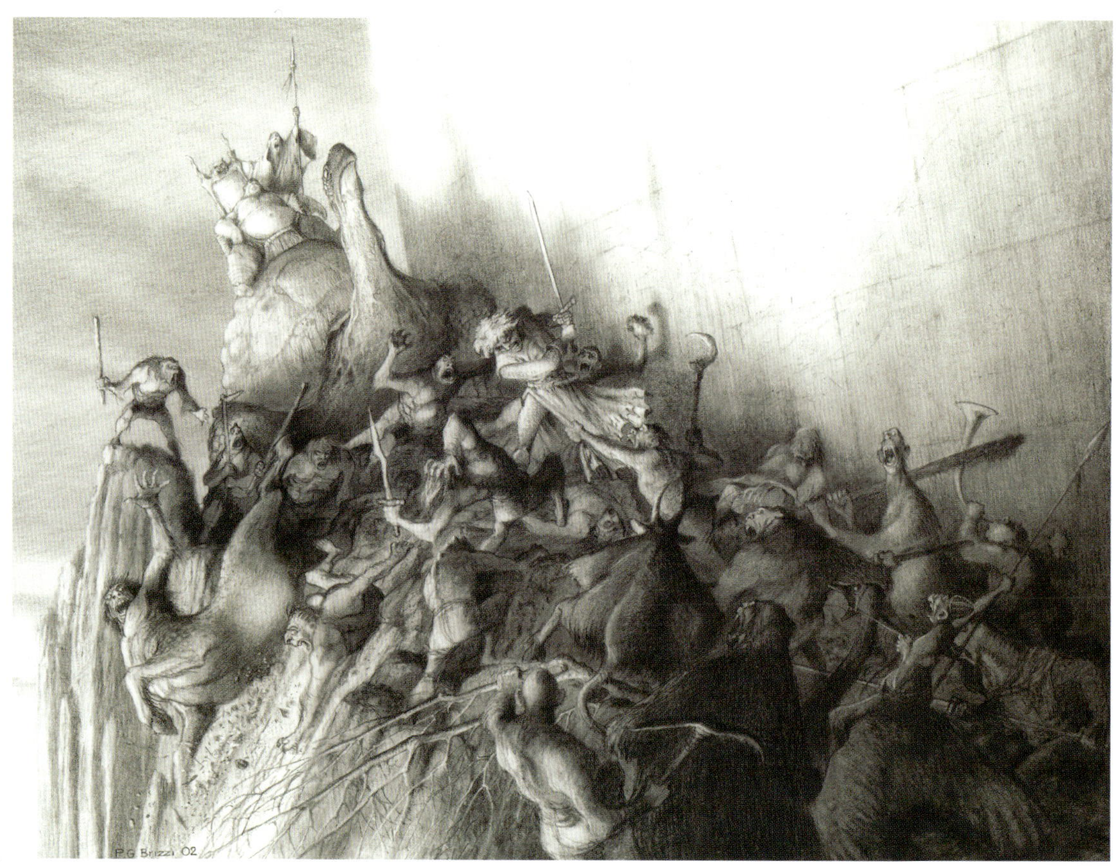

1

2

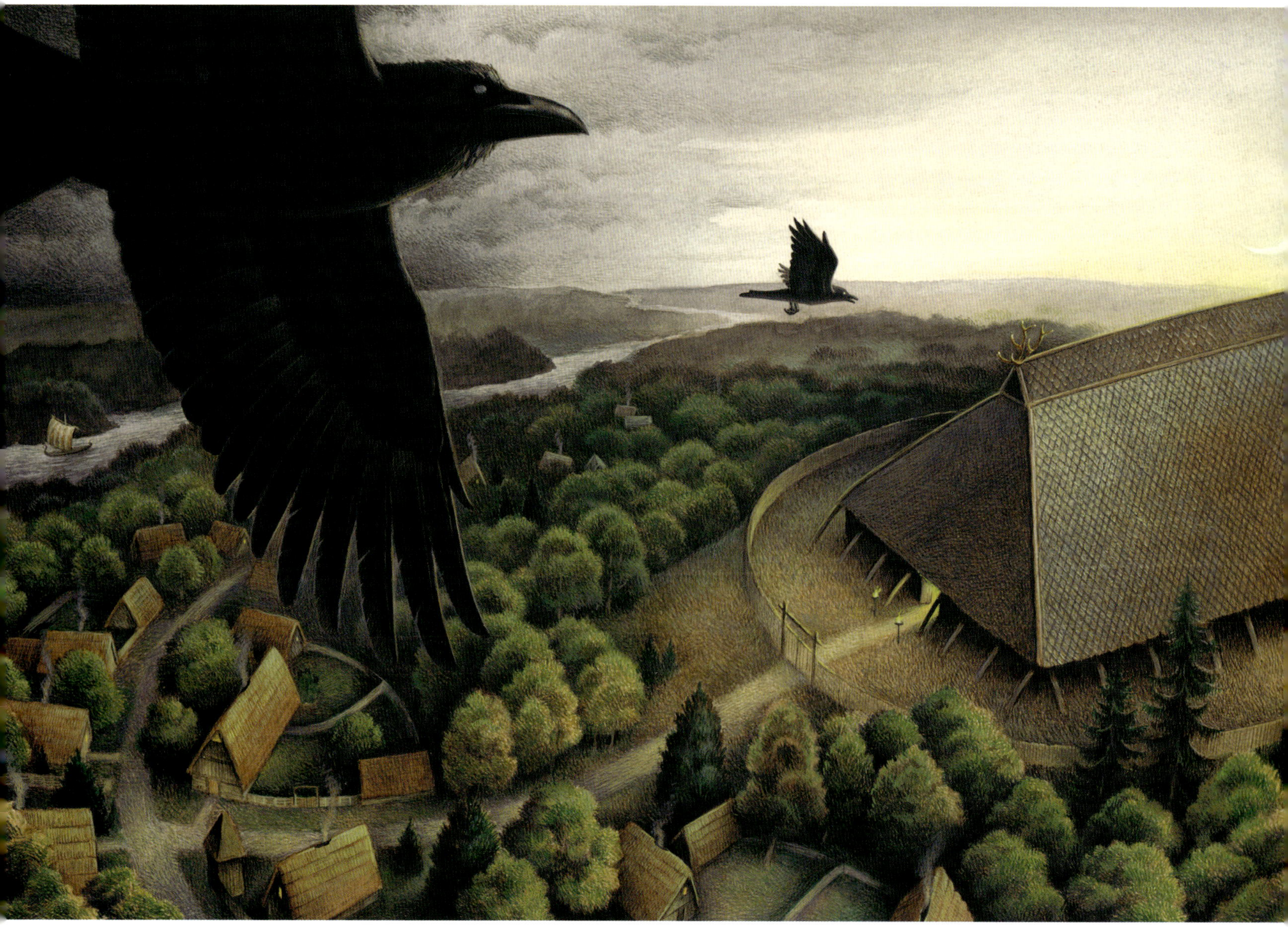

3

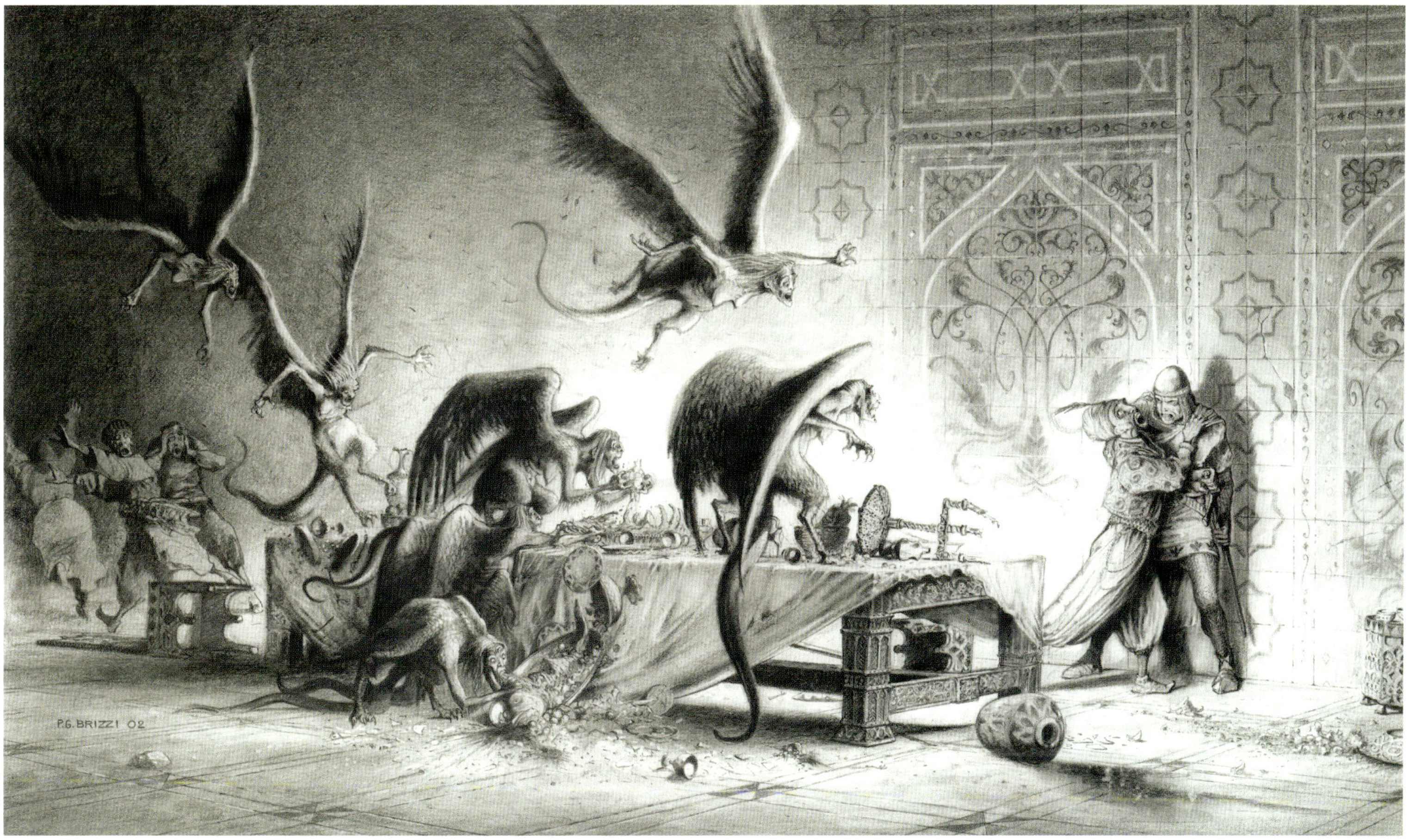

4

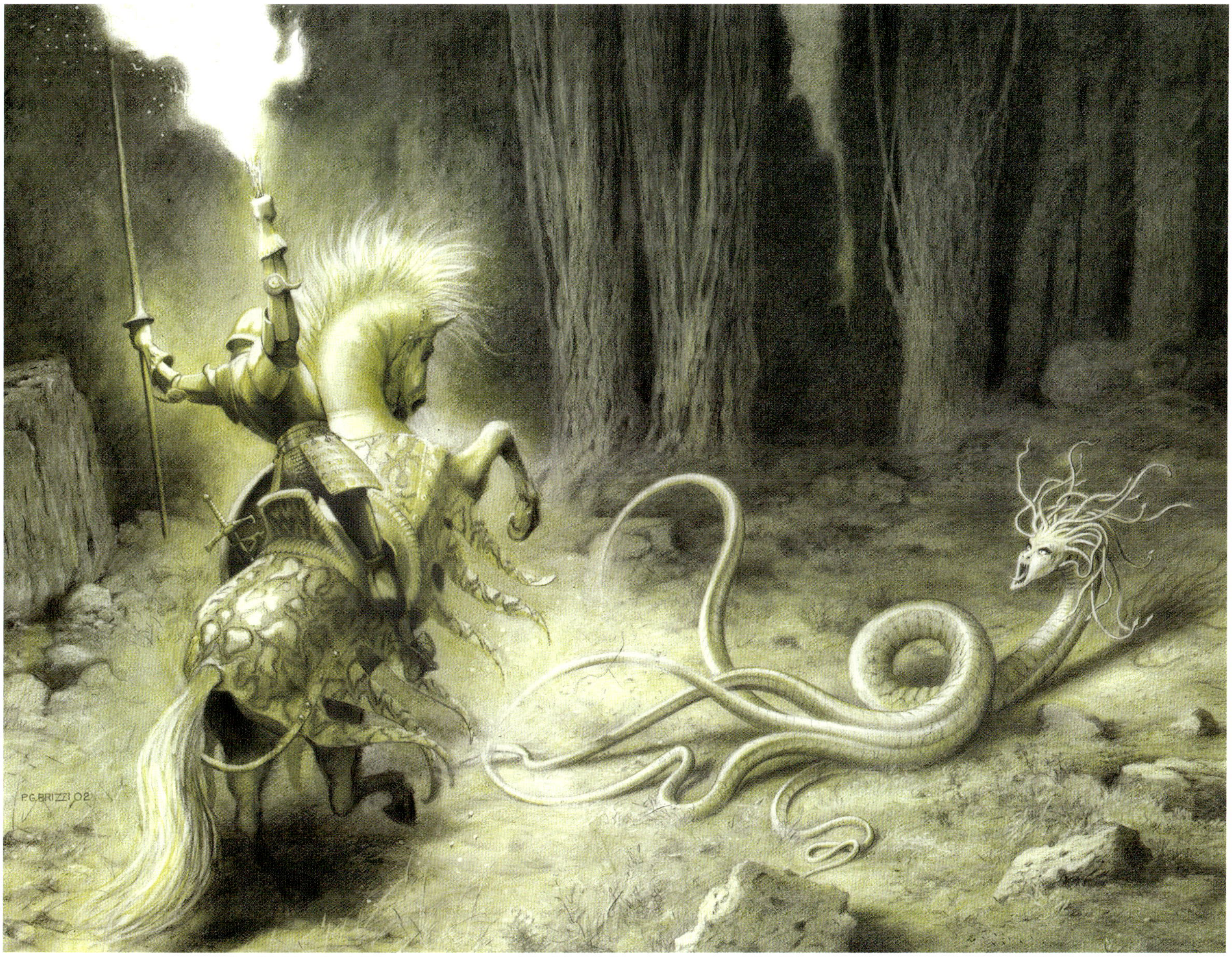

1
artist: **August Hall**
title: The Witches
medium: Acrylics
size: 10″x8″

2
artist: **August Hall**
title: The Dance
medium: Acrylics
size: 10″x8″

3
artist: **August Hall**
title: The River
medium: Acrylics
size: 10″x8″

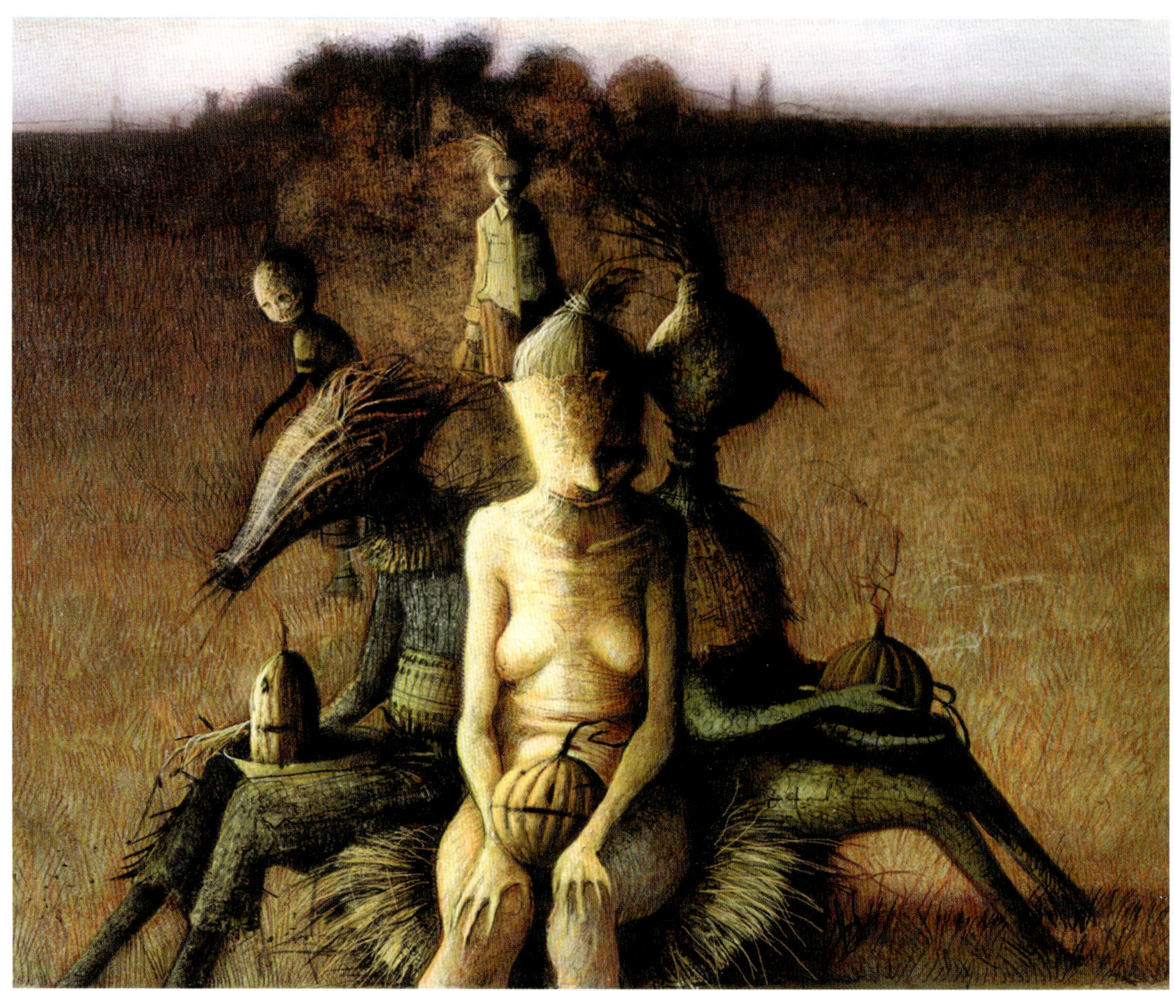

1

2

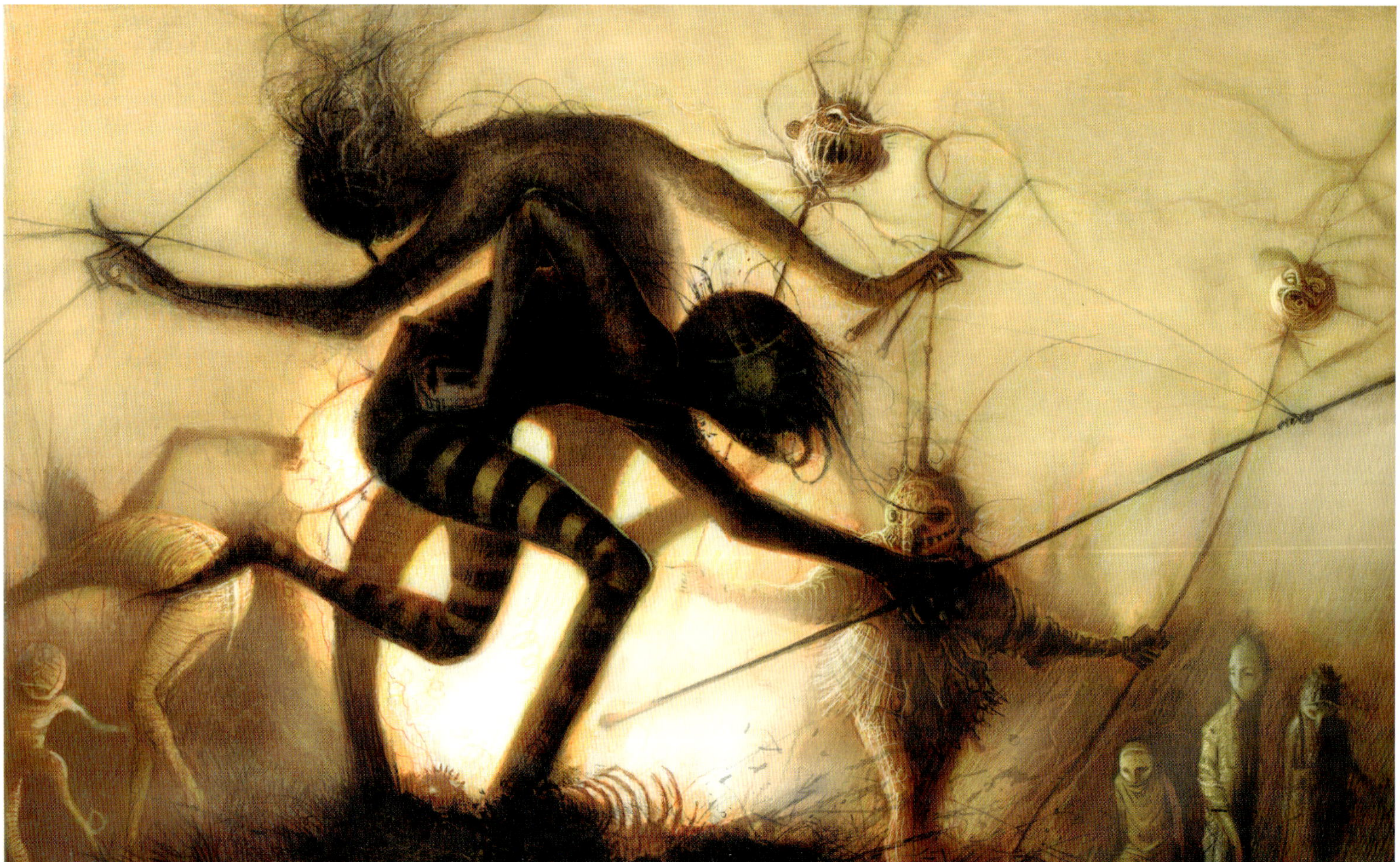

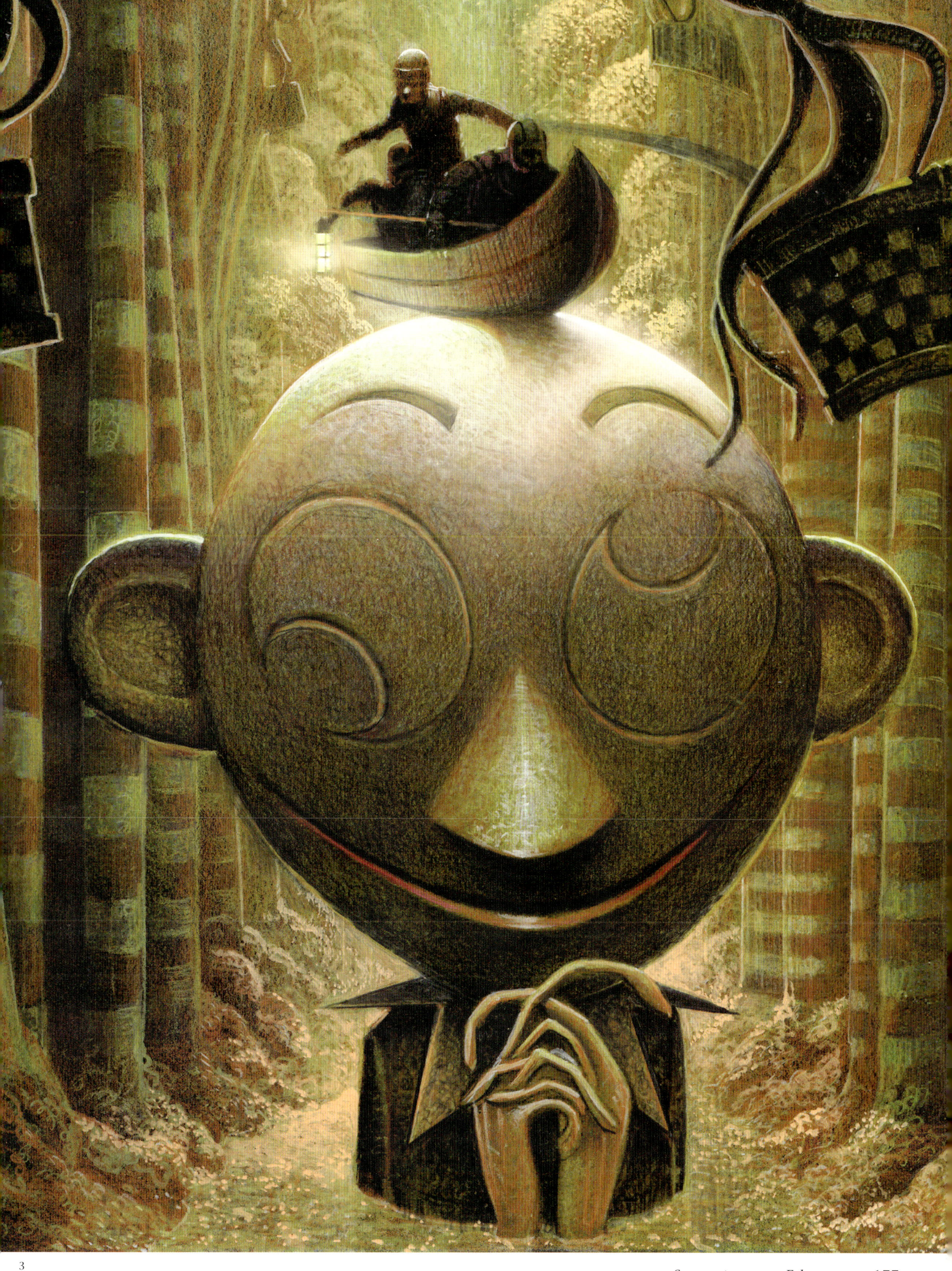

3

1
artist: **Travis A. Louie**
title: Chicken Noir: Counterfeit Cluckers
medium: Acrylics on board
size: 28″x17″

2
artist: **Seung Ho Henrik Holmberg**
title: Somnio 1
medium: Digital

3
artist: **Amanda M. Sartor**
title: Pin Up
medium: Watercolor/digital
size: $6^{5}/_{8}$″x$3^{1}/_{3}$″

4
artist: **Mike Sosnowski**
client: Soz Studios
title: To Live Forever Watching Cartoons
medium: Oils on canvas
size: 30″x24″

5
artist: **Vince Natale**
title: Falco Luciferus
medium: Oils
size: 9″x6″

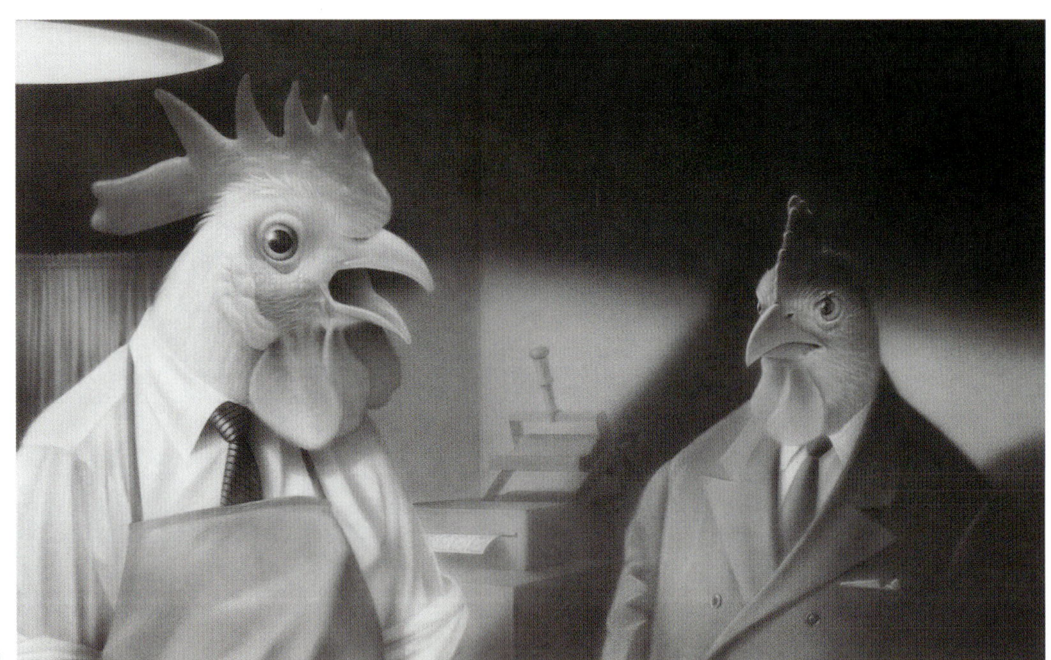
1

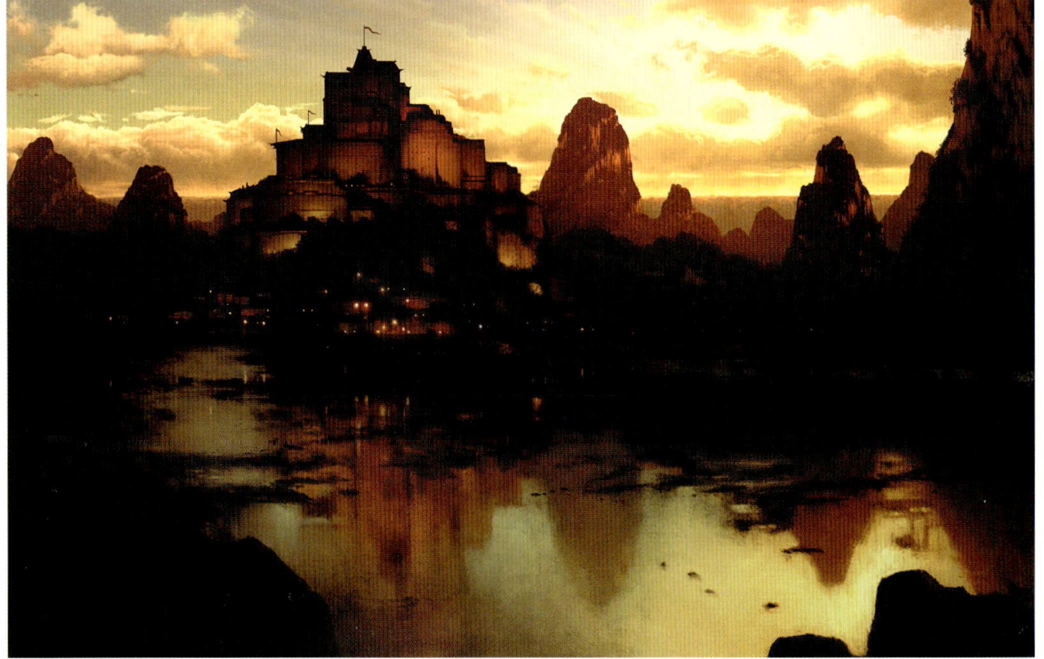
2

3
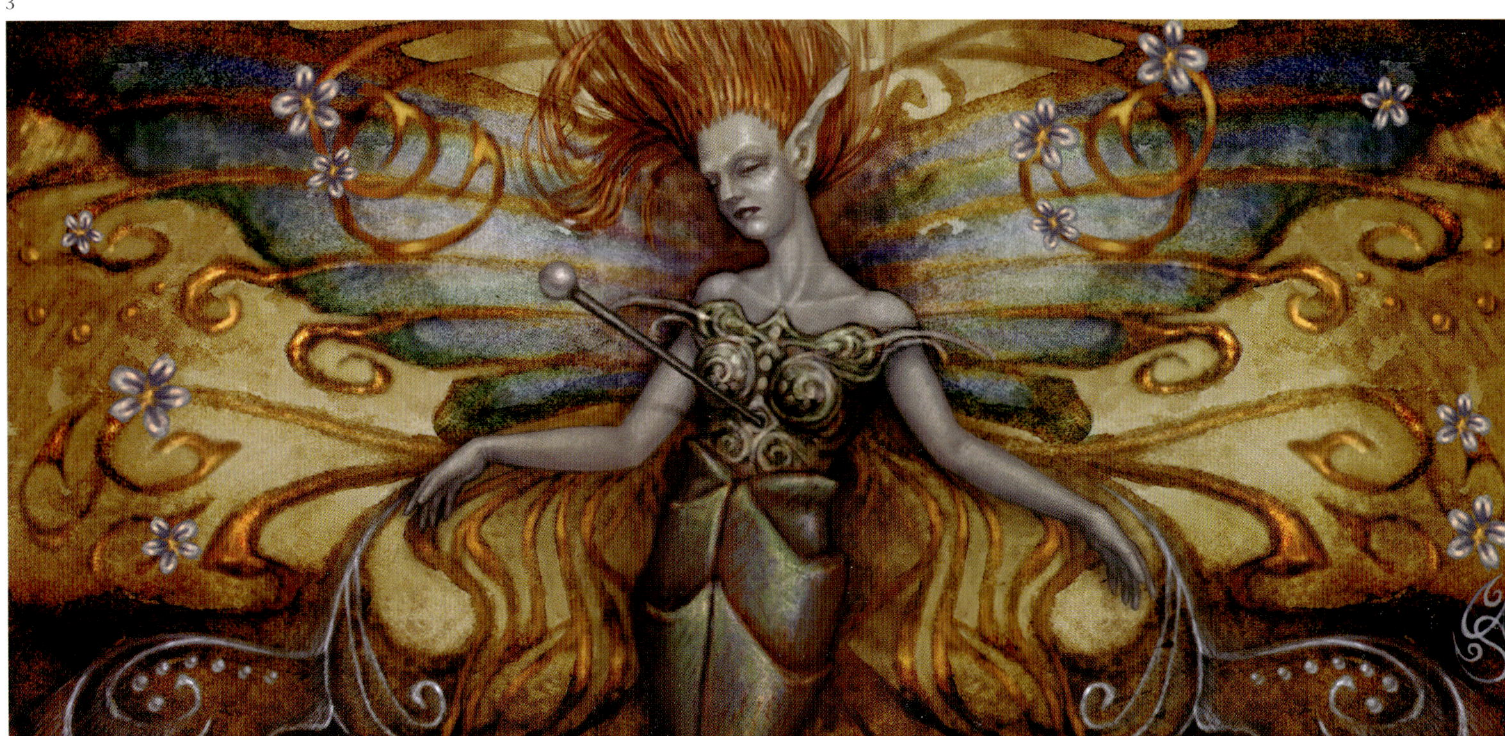

4

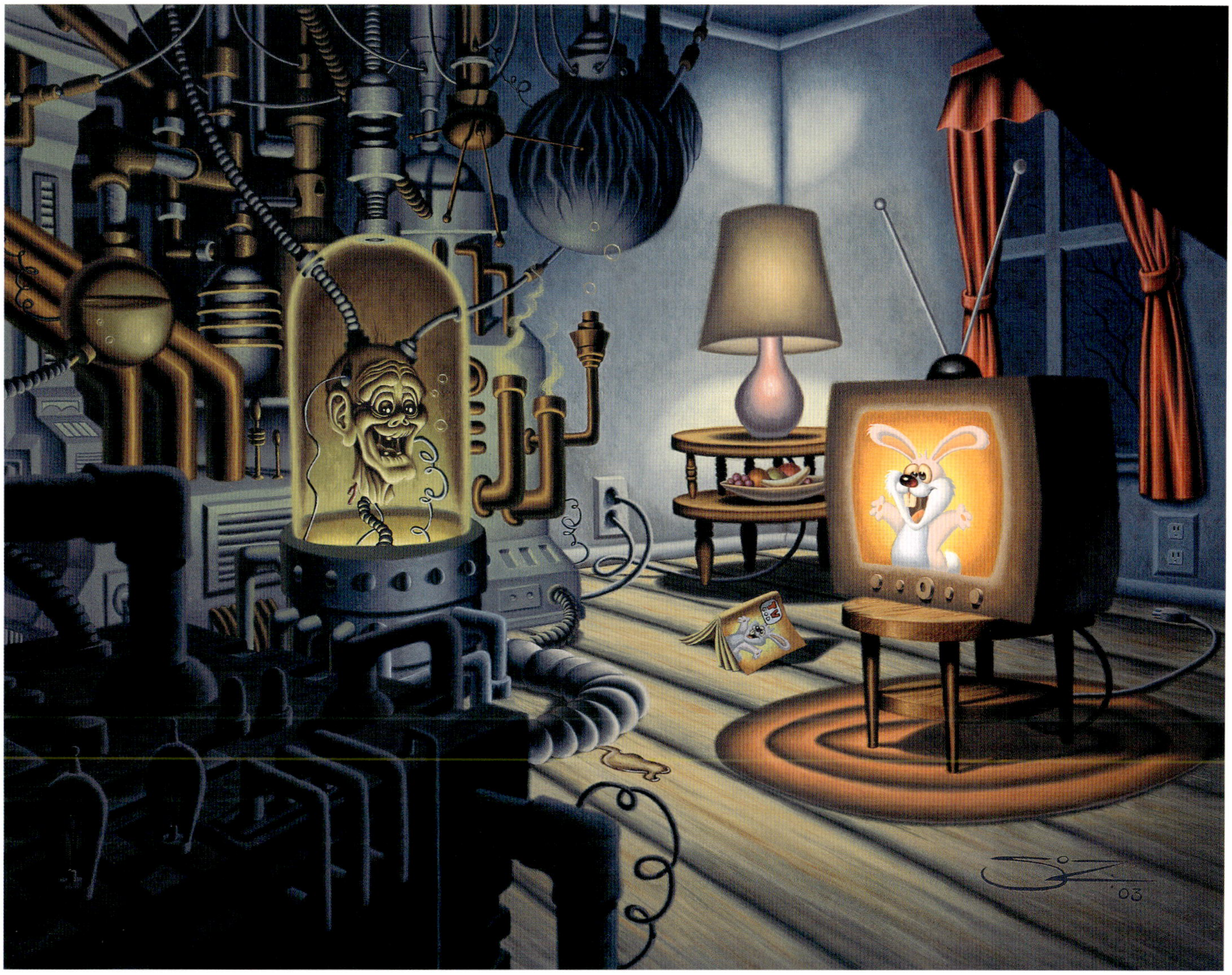

5

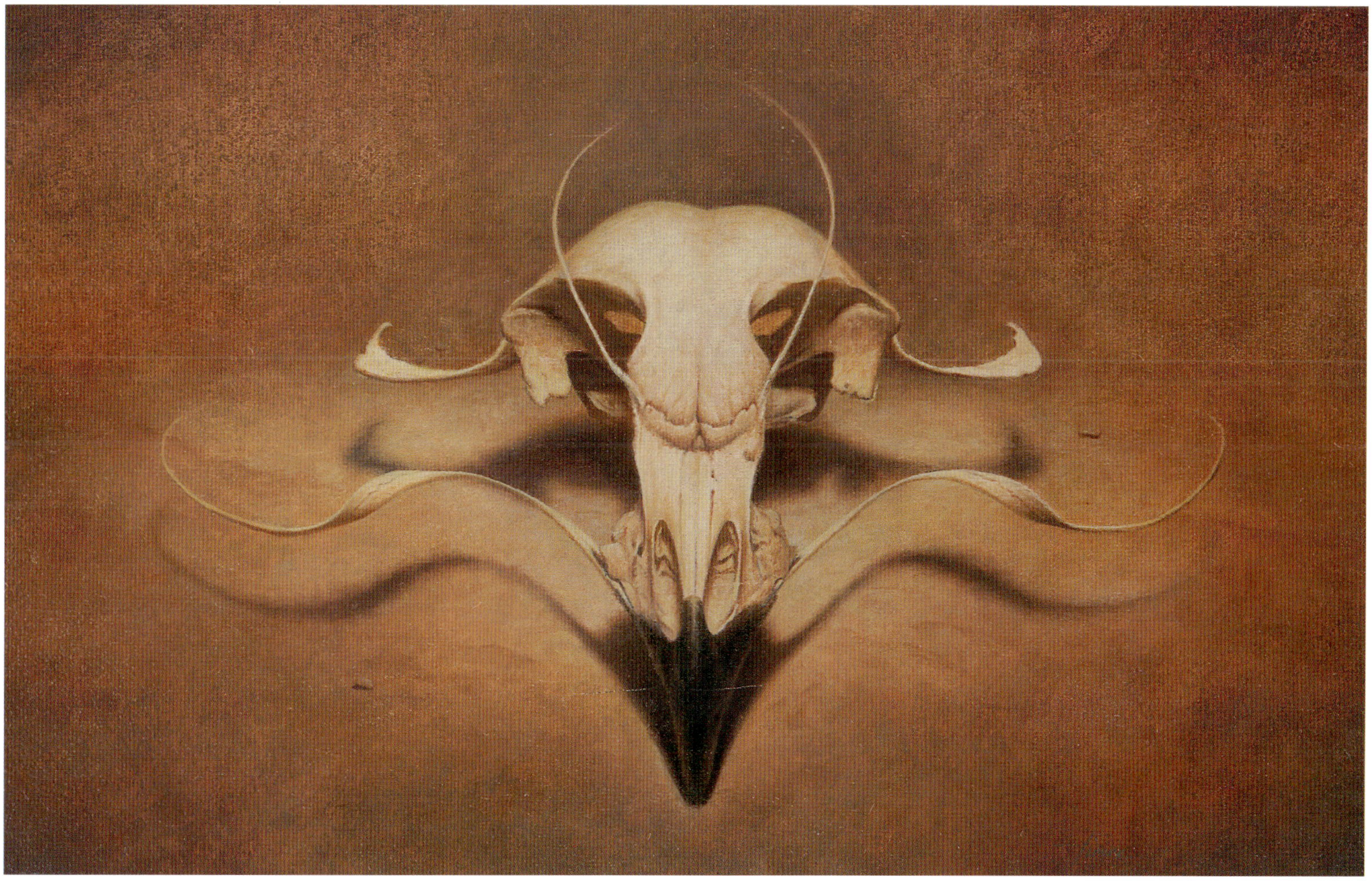

Unpublished

1
artist: **Scott Anderson**
title: Texas
medium: Oils & watercolor

2
artist: **Eric Deschamps**
title: Beasts of Burden
medium: Digital
size: 10″x6″

3
artist: **Jennifer Crampton**
title: Desert Queen
medium: Digital
size: 10″x5″

4
artist: **Ezra Tucker**
title: Beginner
medium: Acrylics
size: 15″x20″

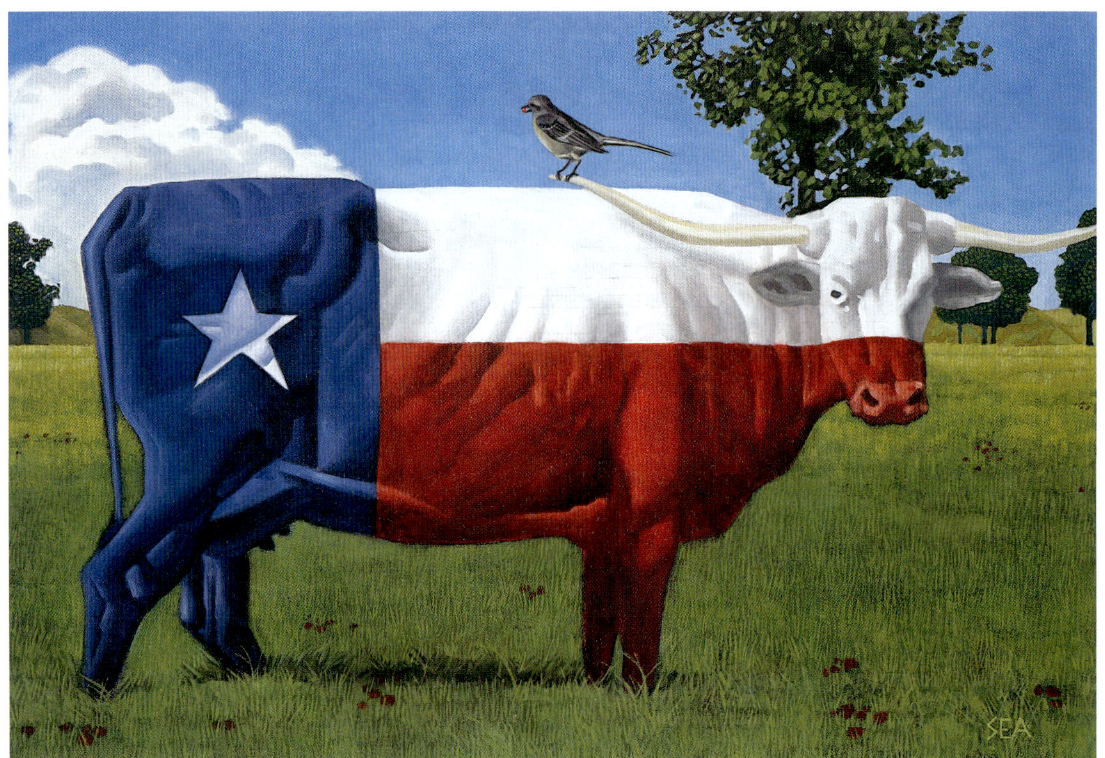

1

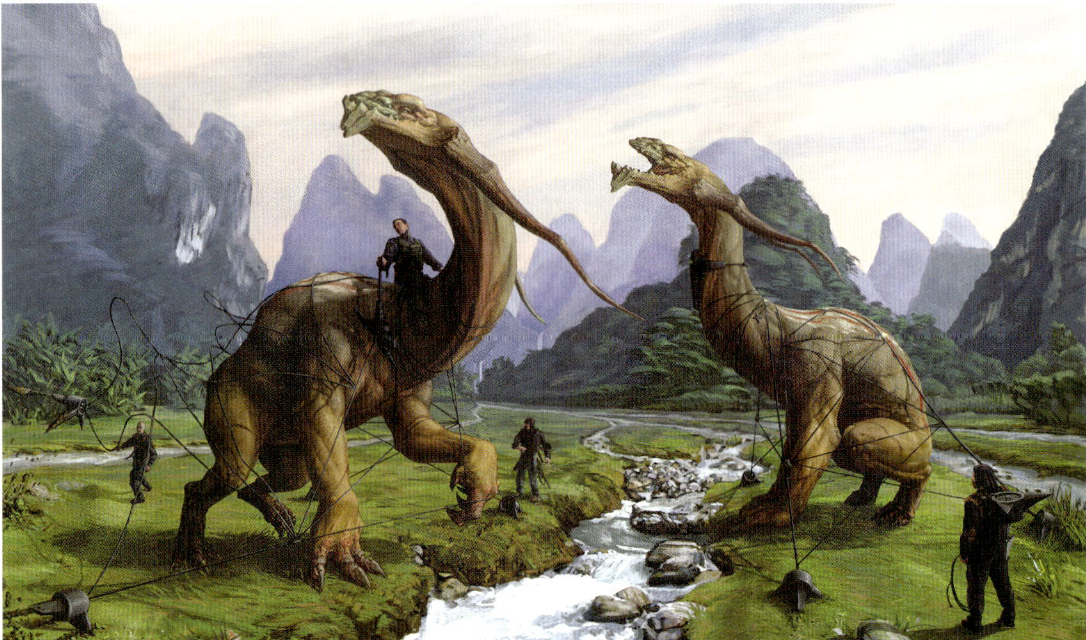

2

3

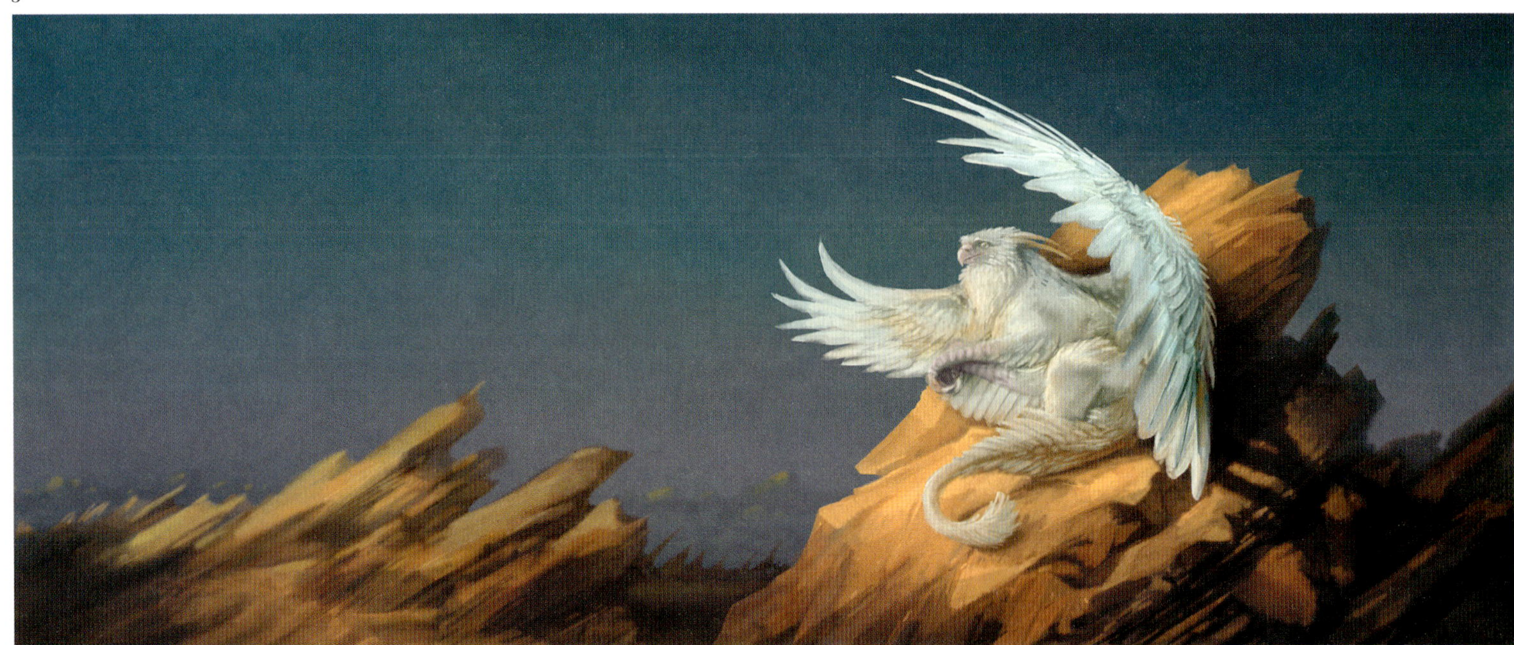

4

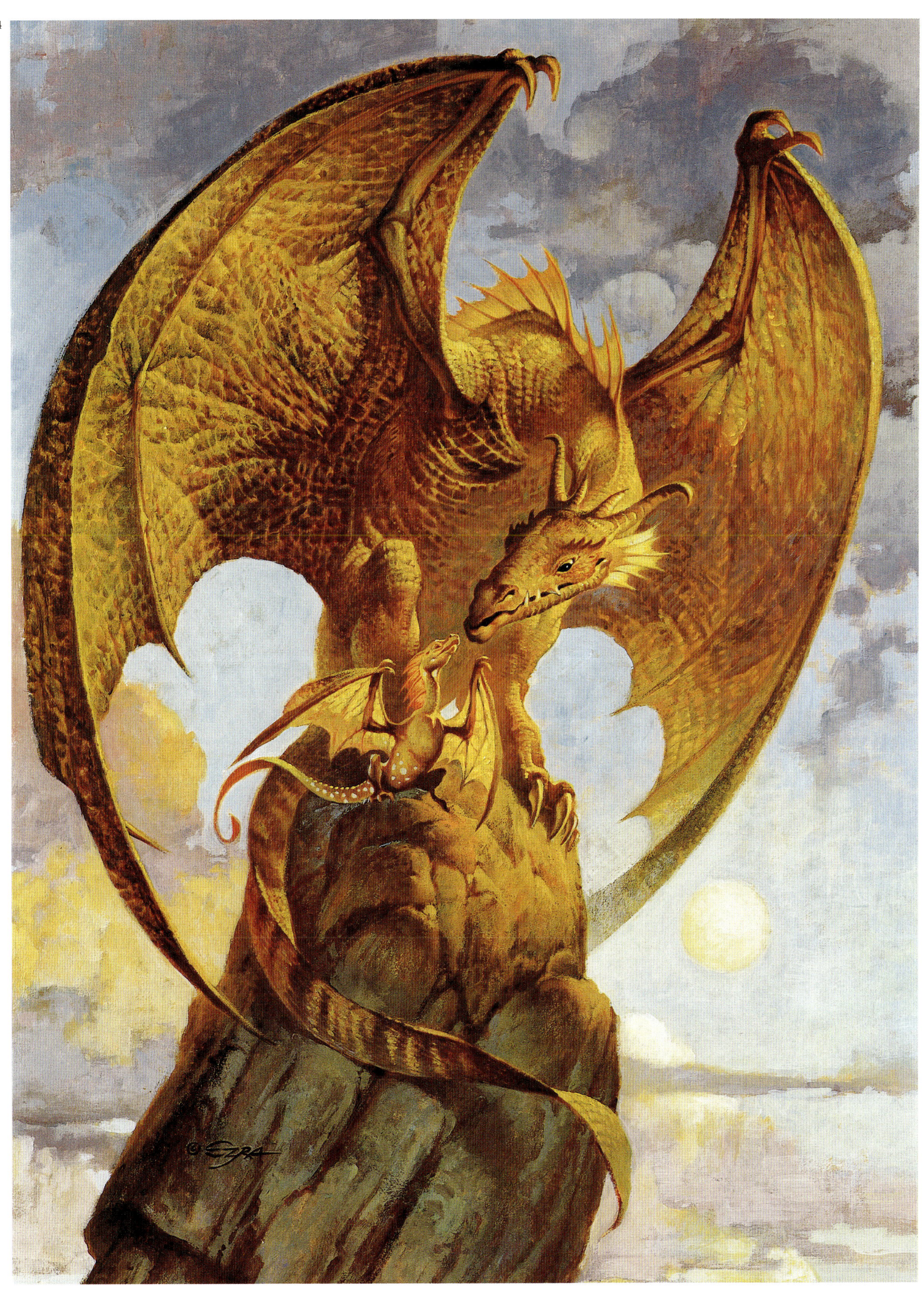

Unpublished

1
artist: **Dan Santat**
title: Excuse Me
medium: Acrylics & ink
size: 8″x16″

2
artist: **Ted Terranova**
client: www.terranovaart.com
title: Refueling
medium: Digital
size: 10″x8″

3
artist: **Aaron McBride**
title: Moto-Stride Ambush
medium: Digital
size: 17″x10$^{1}/_{2}$″

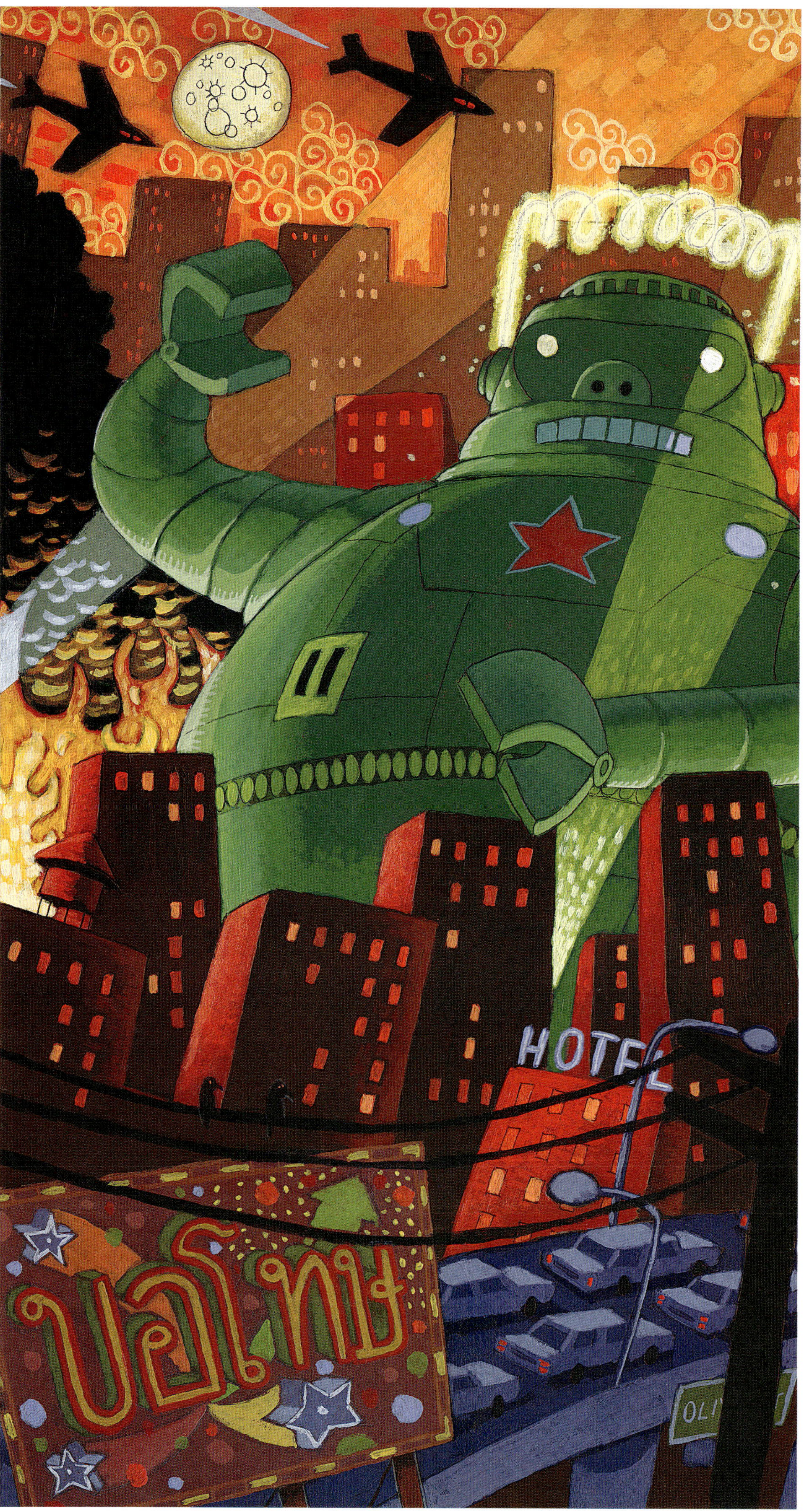

1

2

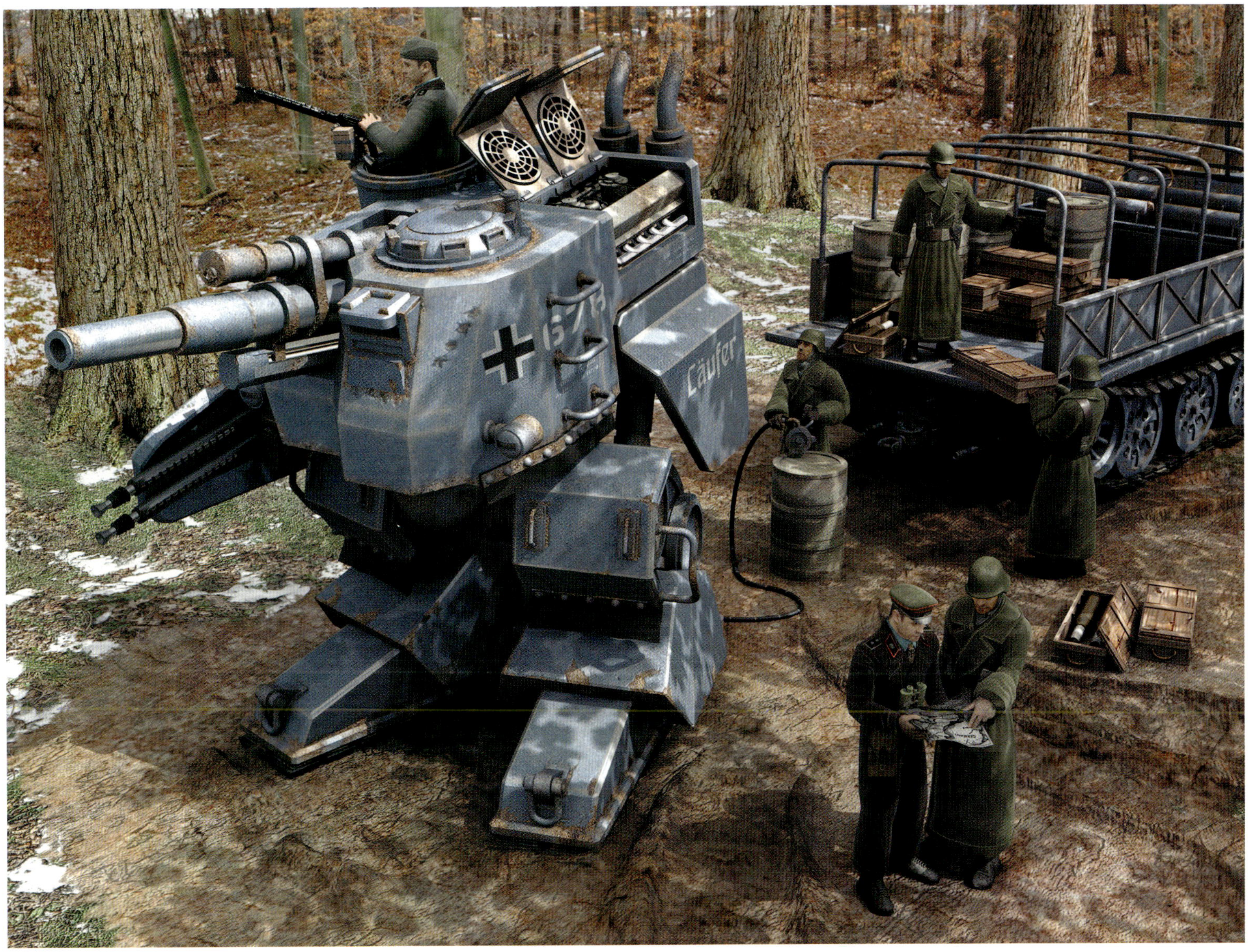

3

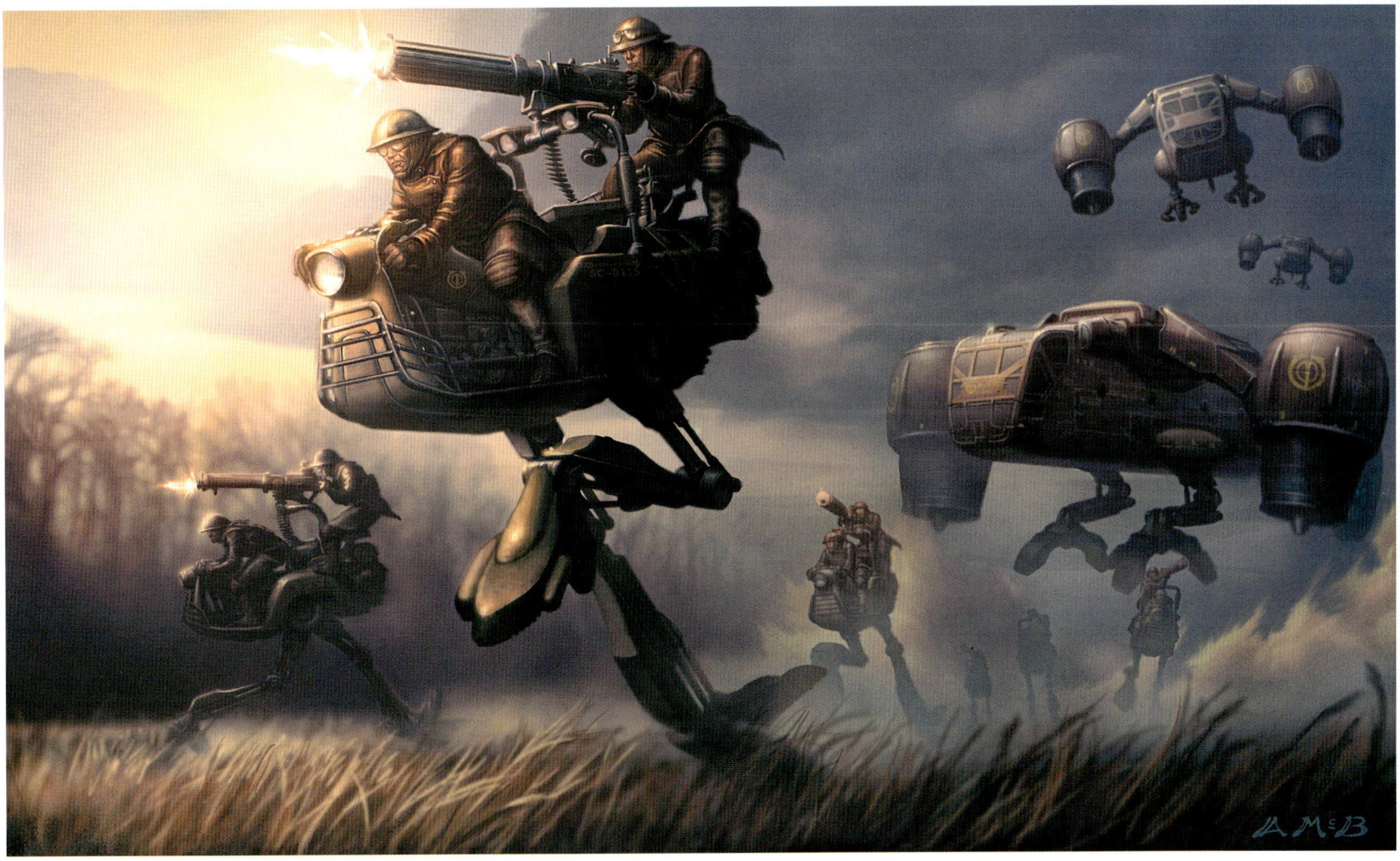

1
artist: **Miles Teves**
client: Teves Design Studio
title: Nocturna 2
medium: Acrylics
size: 29″x30″

2
artist: **Steve Pilcher**
title: Artemis
medium: Mixed

3
artist: **Stephen Hickman**
client: Richard Lee
title: Avonne
medium: Oils
size: 20″x34″

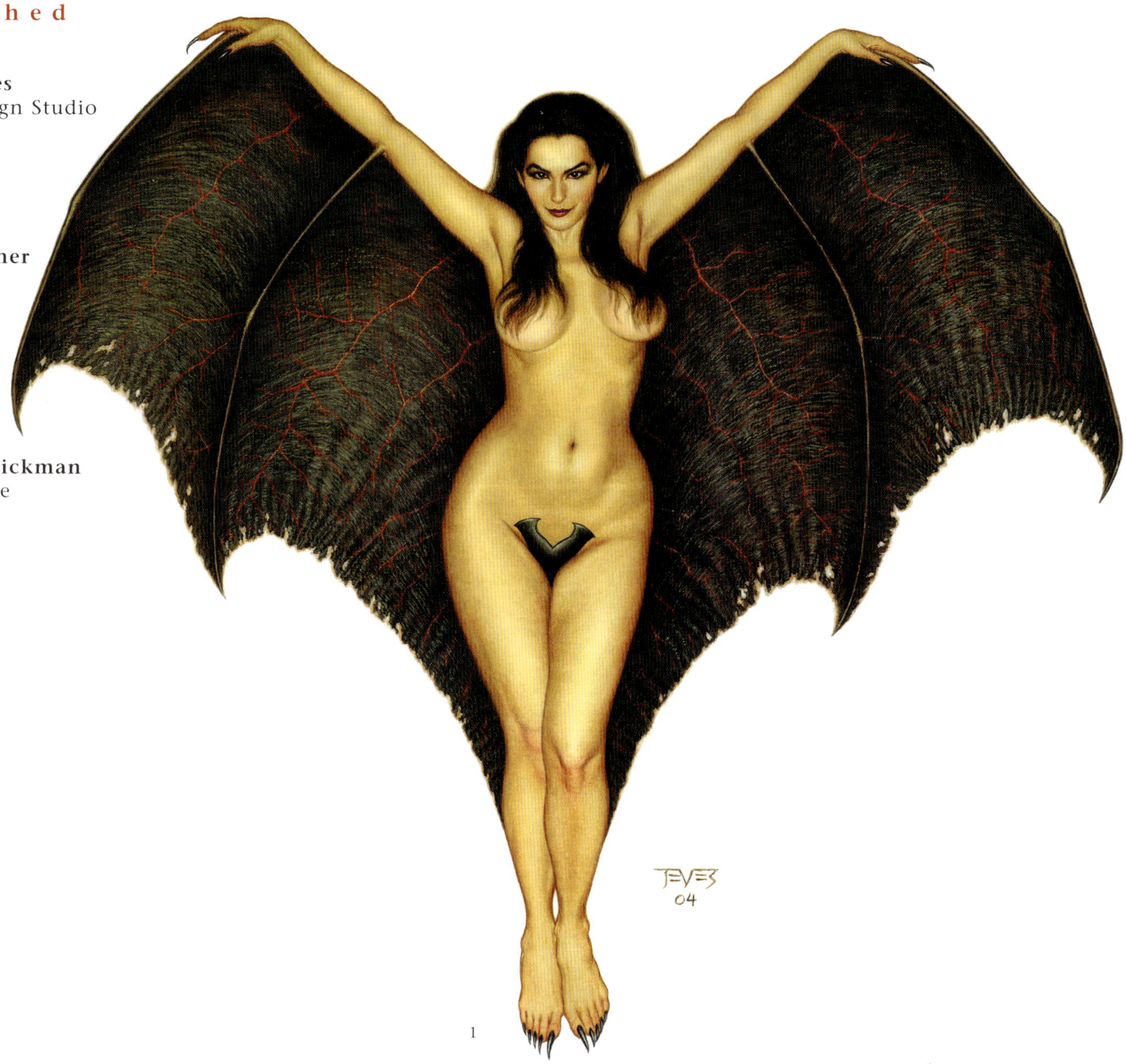

1

2

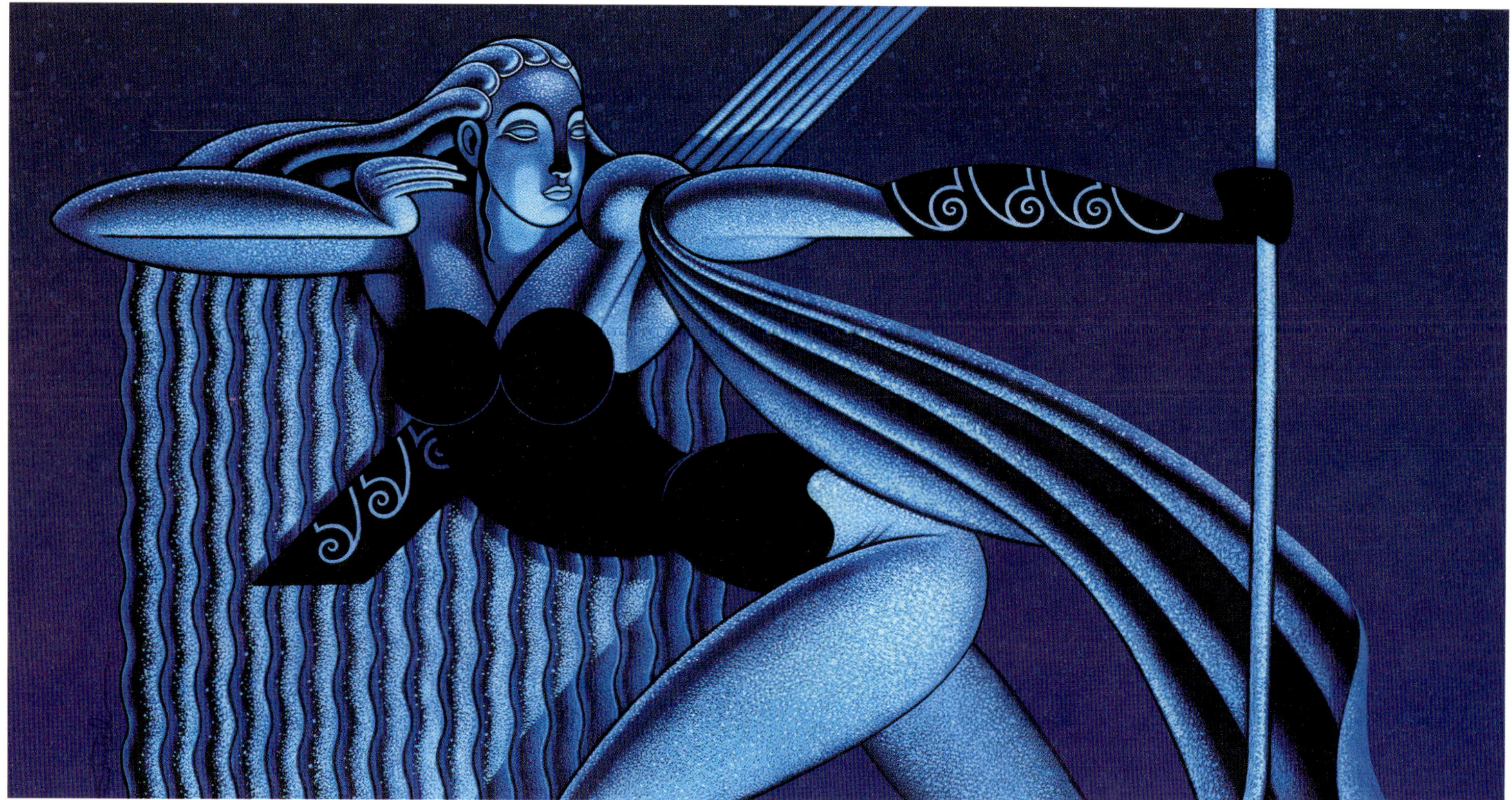

3

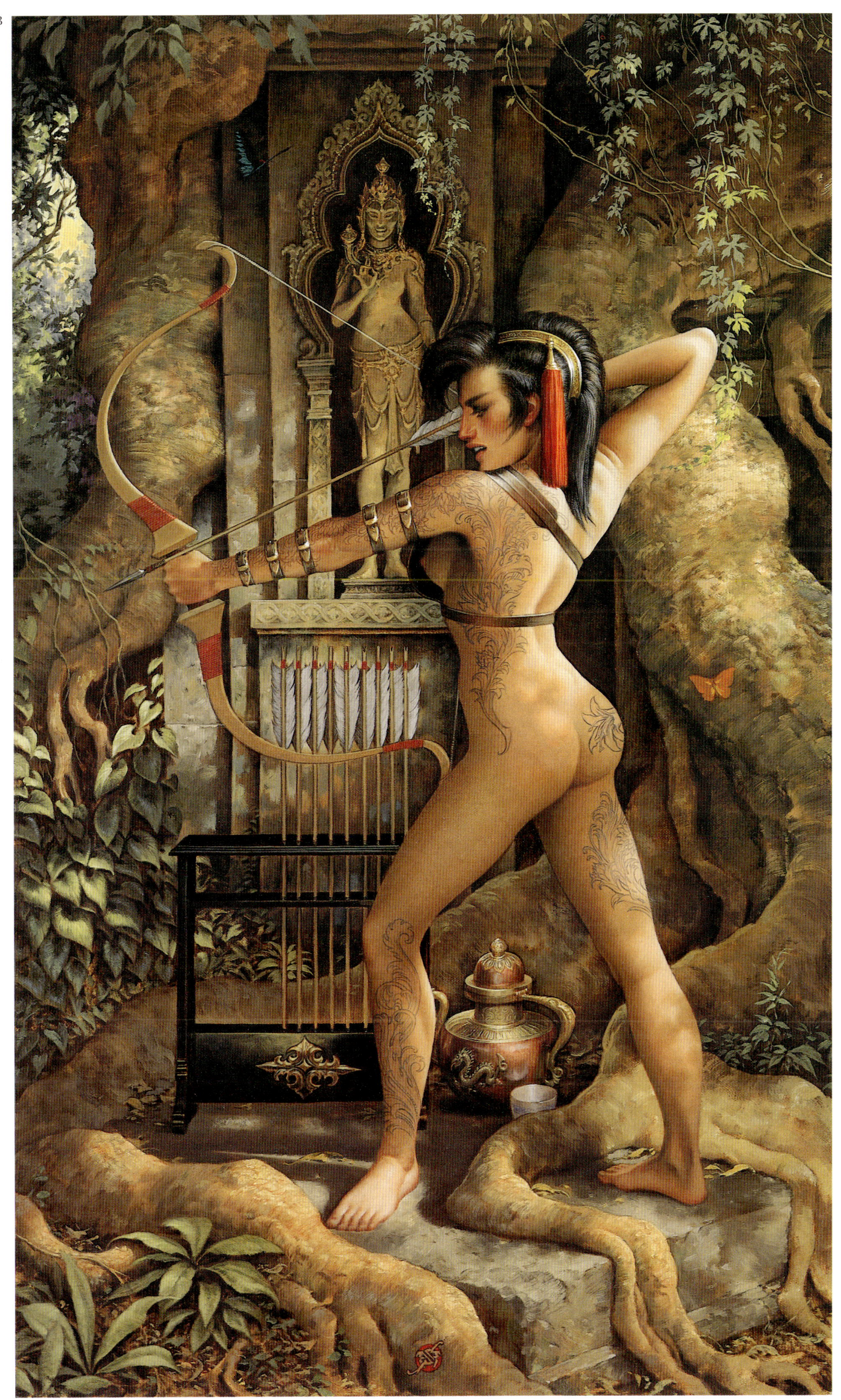

Unpublished

1
artist: **José Roosevelt**
title: Pandora
medium: Oils on canvas
size: 37½″x37½″

2
artist: **John Howe**
title: War in Middle-Earth
medium: Watercolor
size: 24″x12″

3
artist: **Richard Hescox**
title: Guardian of the Horizon
medium: Oils
size: 36″x28″

4
artist: **Raoul Vitale**
title: In My Father's House
medium: Oils
size: 29¼″x19″

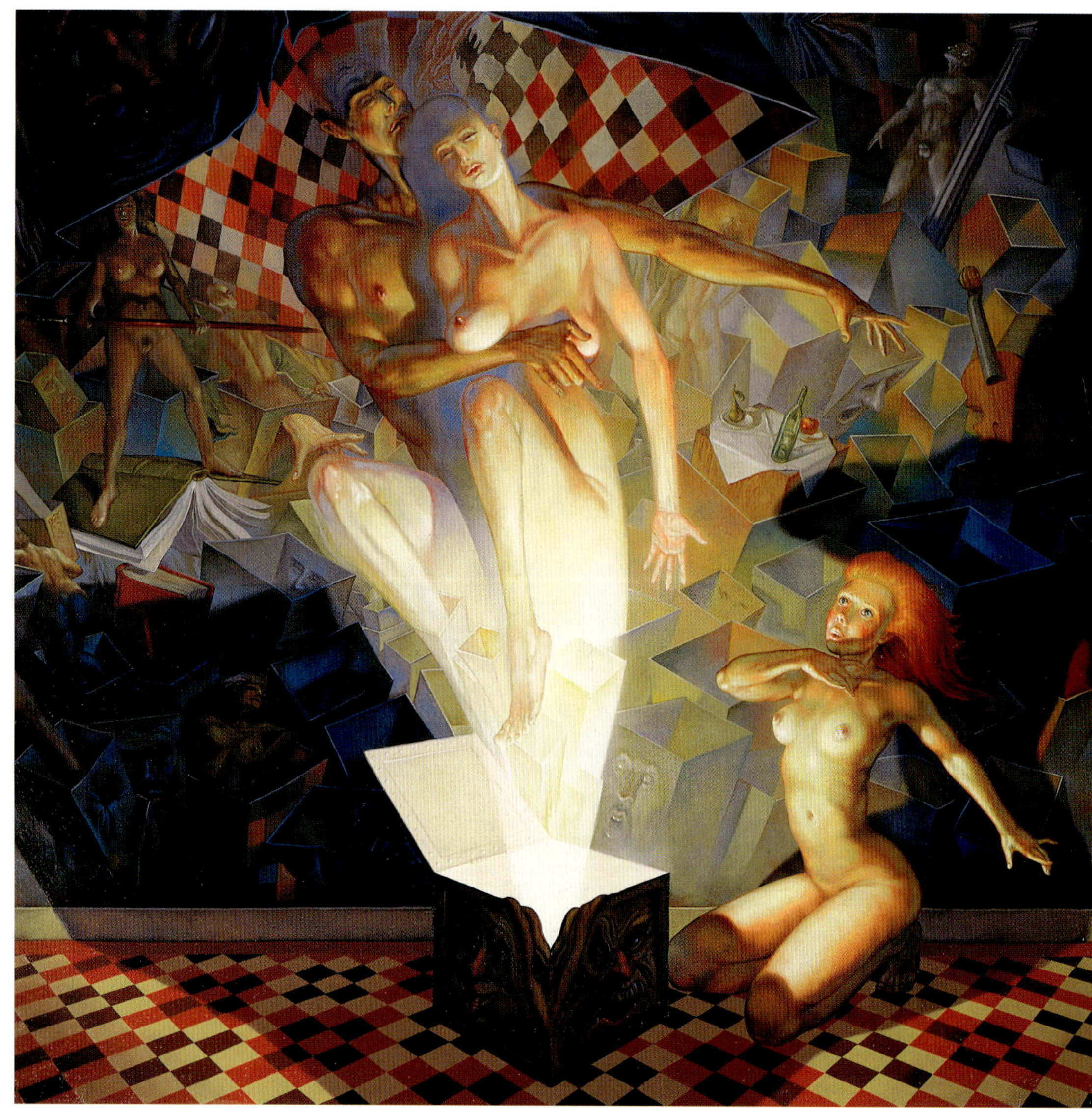

1

2

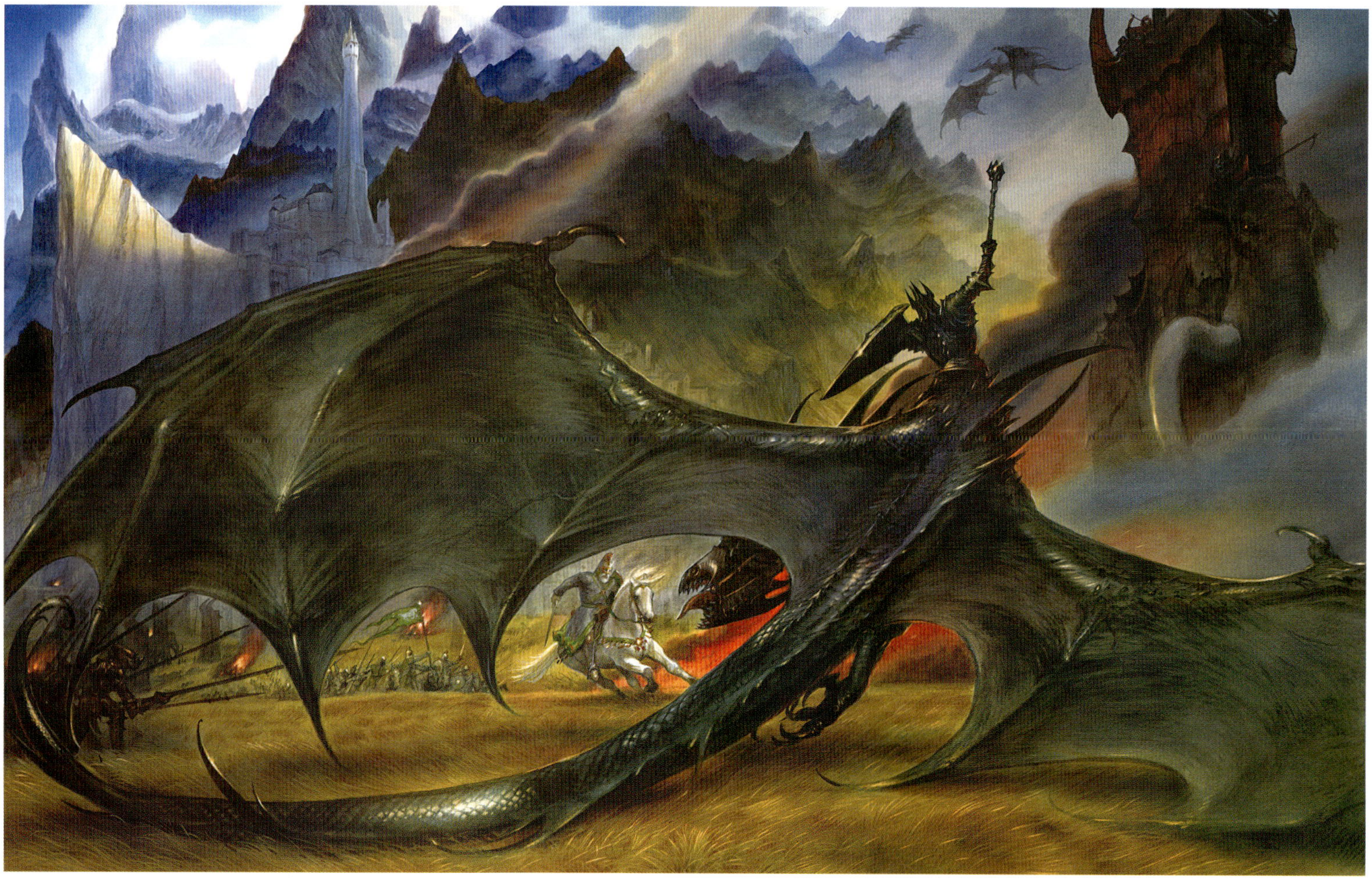

3

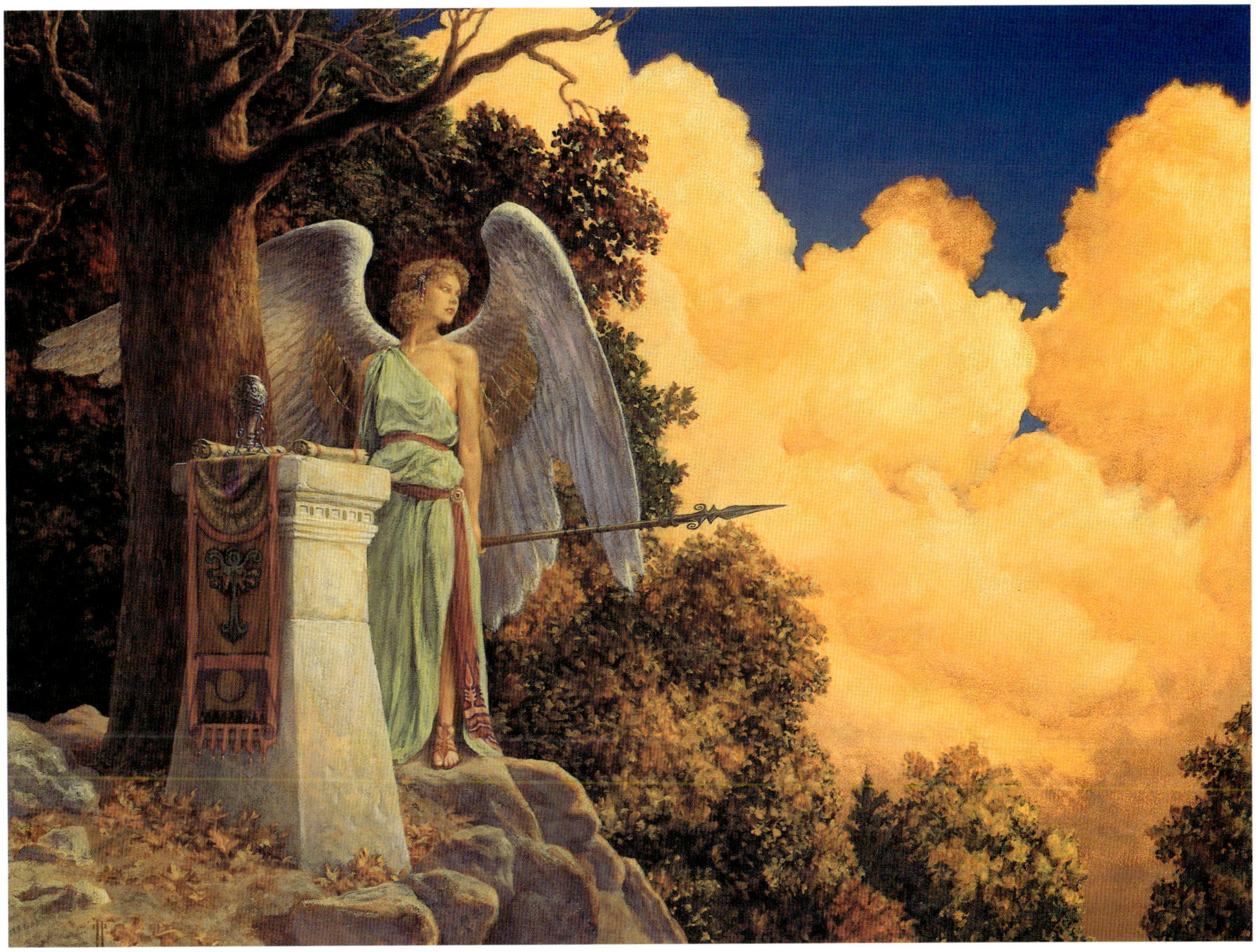

4

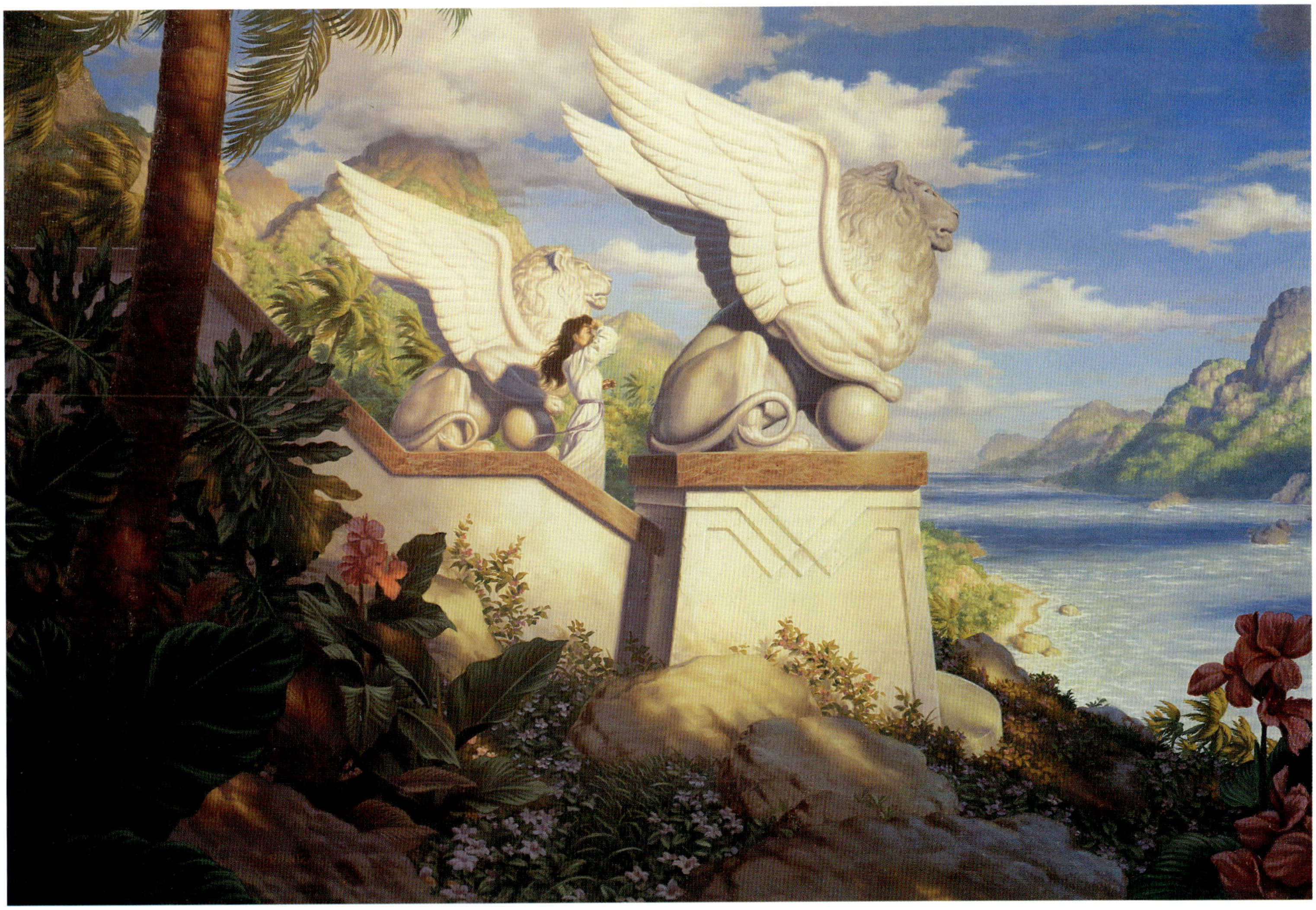

Unpublished

1
artist: **Coro**
title: The Offering
medium: Oils on Canvas
size: 54"x54"

2
artist: **David Bowers**
title: Fragmented Homemaker
medium: Oils
size: 21"x20"

3
artist: **Mark A. Nelson**
client: Grazing Dinosaur Press
title: KD: Lucky Sign
medium: Colored pencil
size: 14"x17"

4
artist: **Coro**
medium: Mixed/digital
size: $8^1/2$"x$11^1/2$"

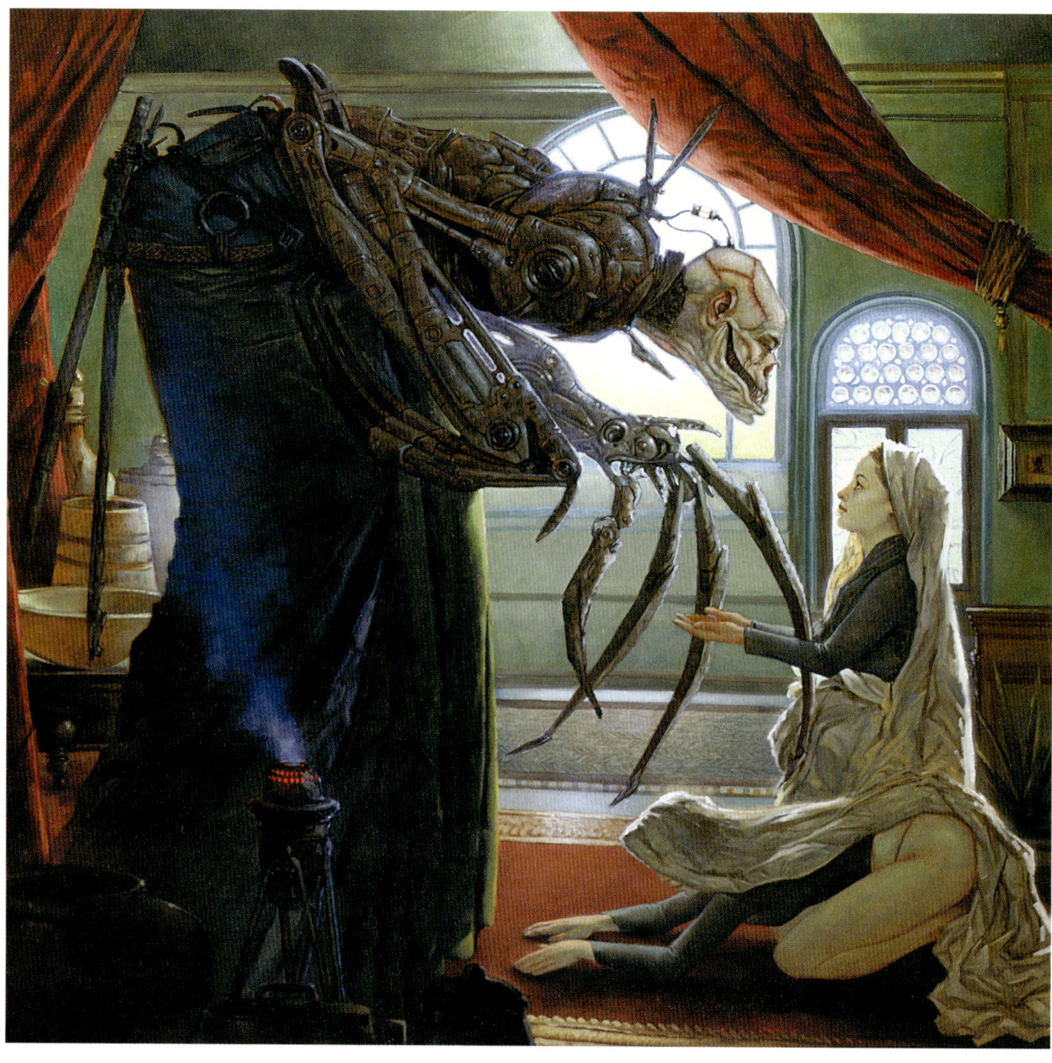

1

2

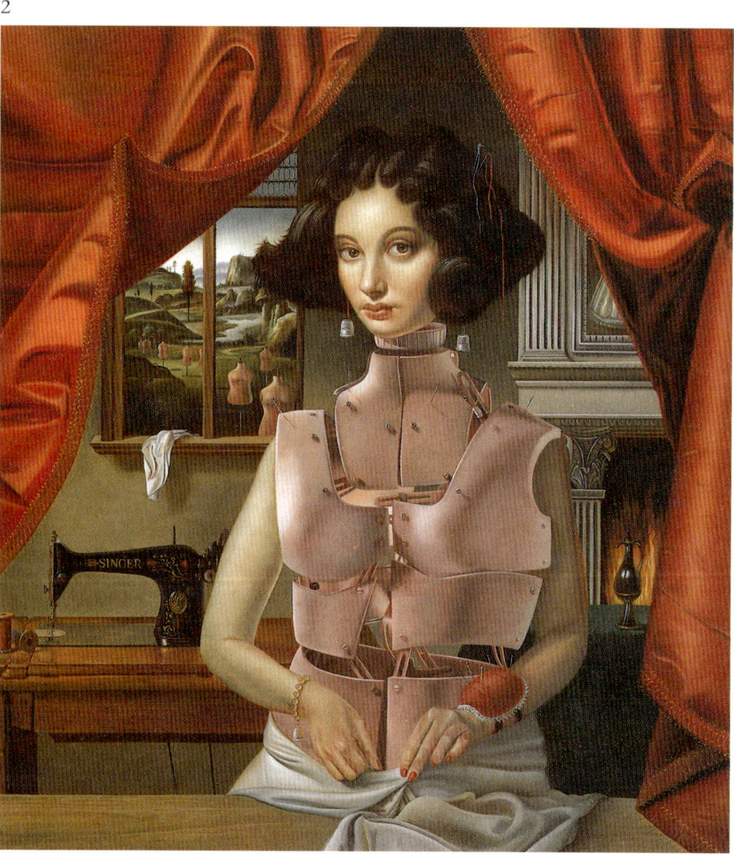

3

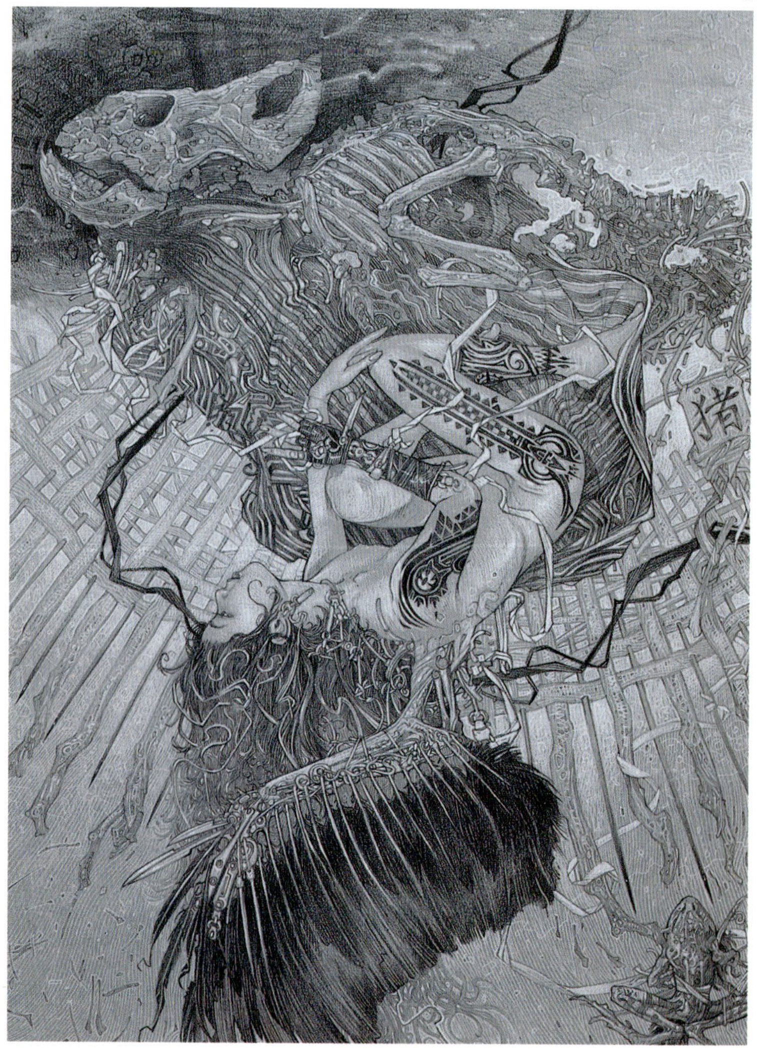

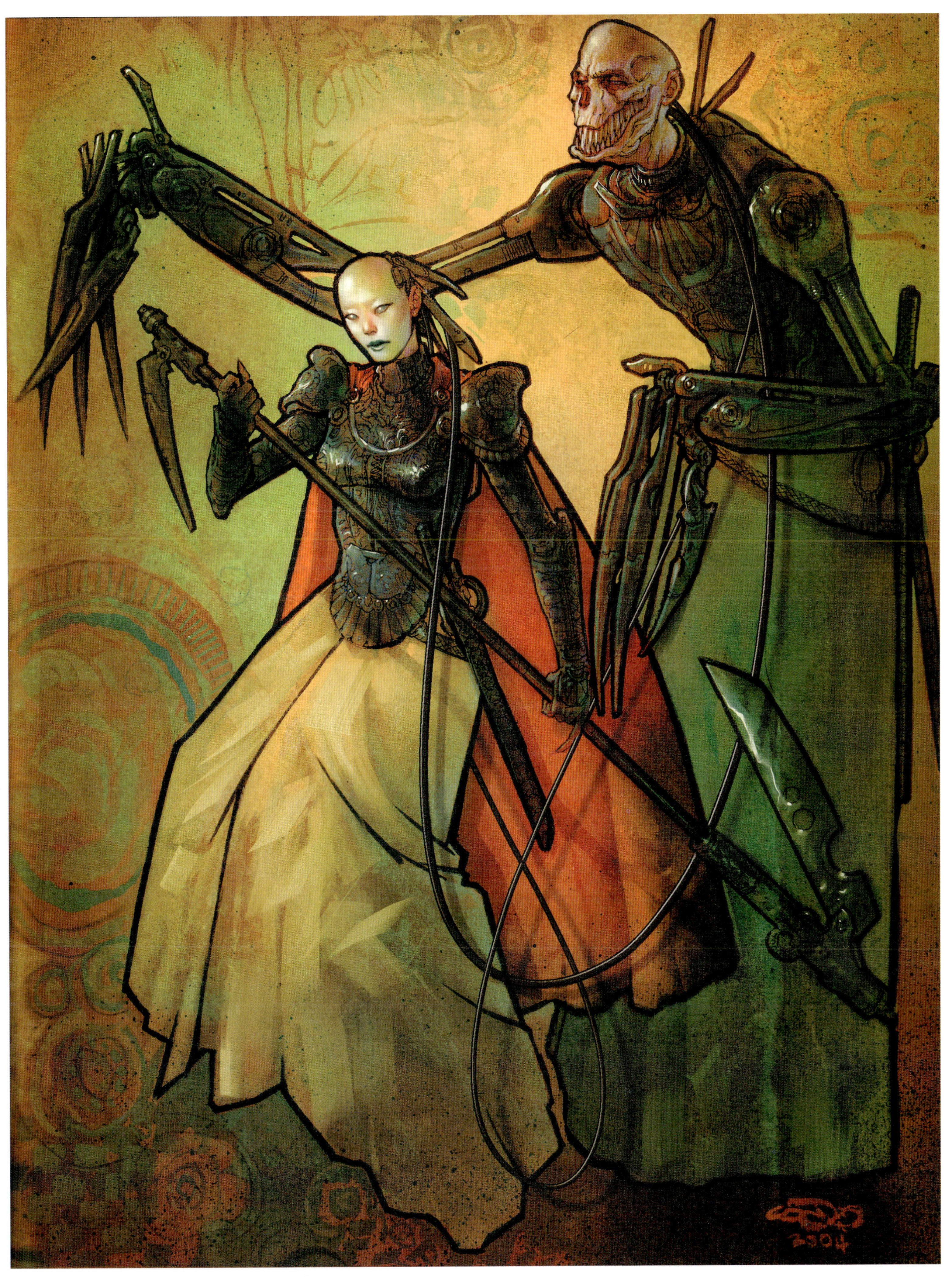

1
artist: **David Ho**
title: One Step Closer
medium: Digital
size: 11″x11″

2
artist: **David Ho**
title: World Order
medium: Digital
size: 11″x11″

3
artist: **Keith Thompson**
title: The Prophet
medium: Mixed
size: 5 1/4″x11″

4
artist: **Socar Myles**
title: The Revenant
medium: Blow
size: 8 1/4″x13 7/8″

5
artist: **Viktor Koen**
title: Vanitas No. 39
medium: Digital
size: 13″x19″

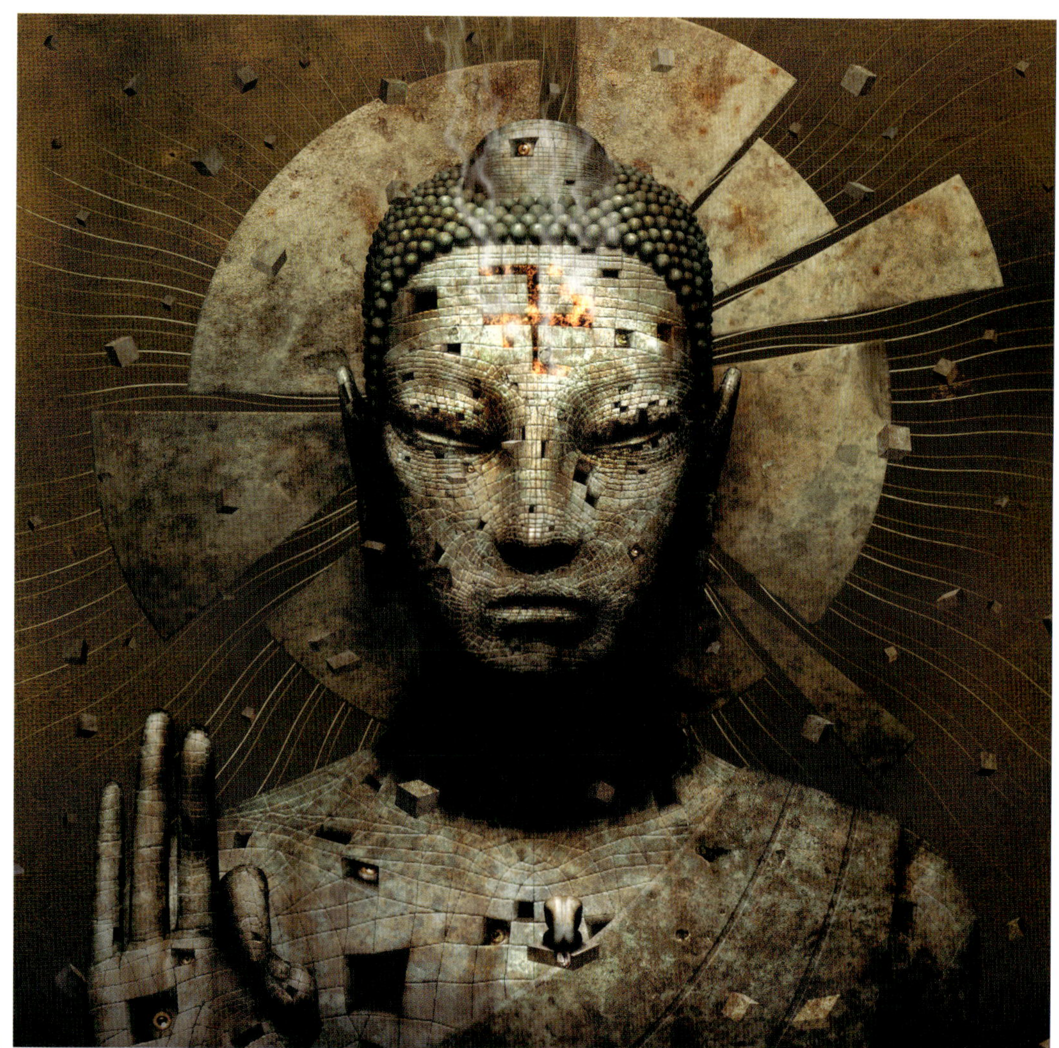

1

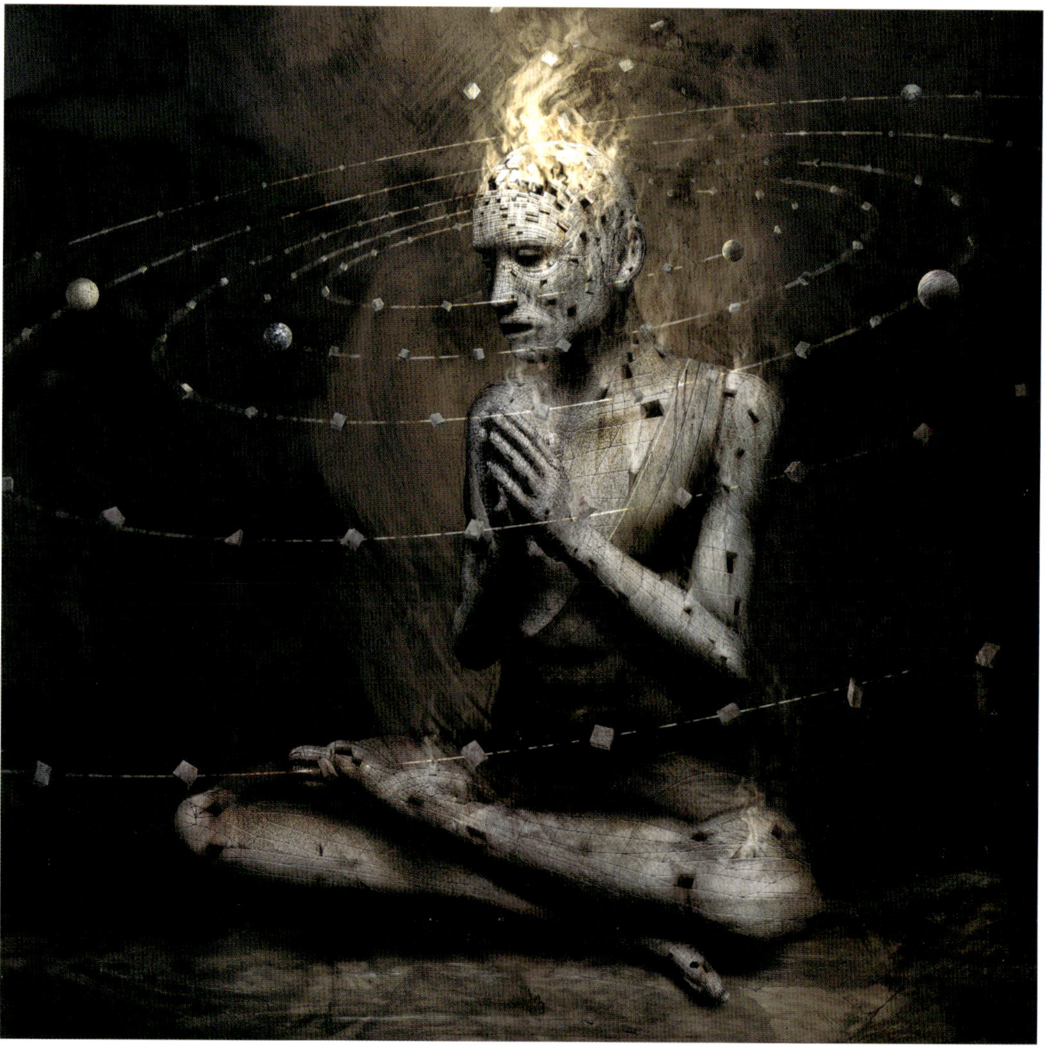

2

3

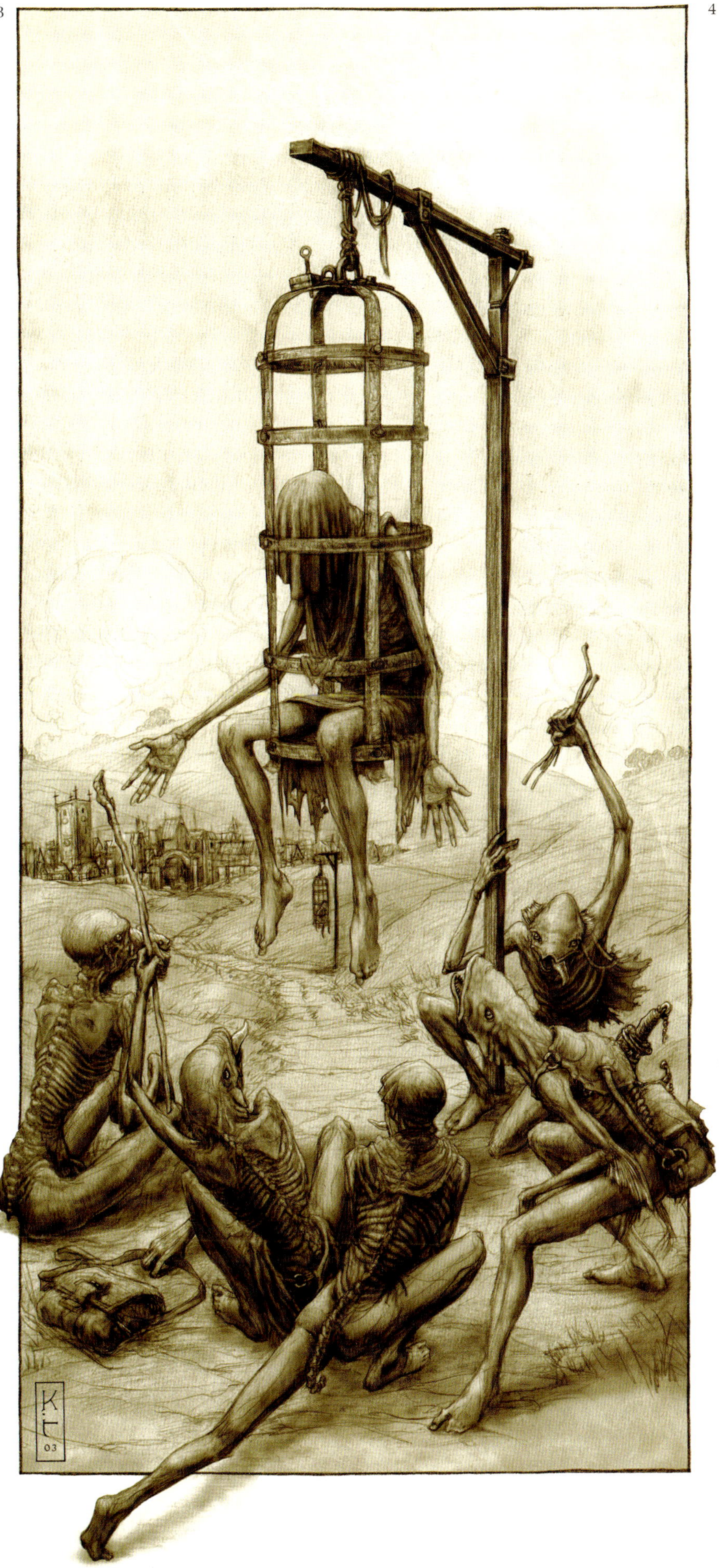

4

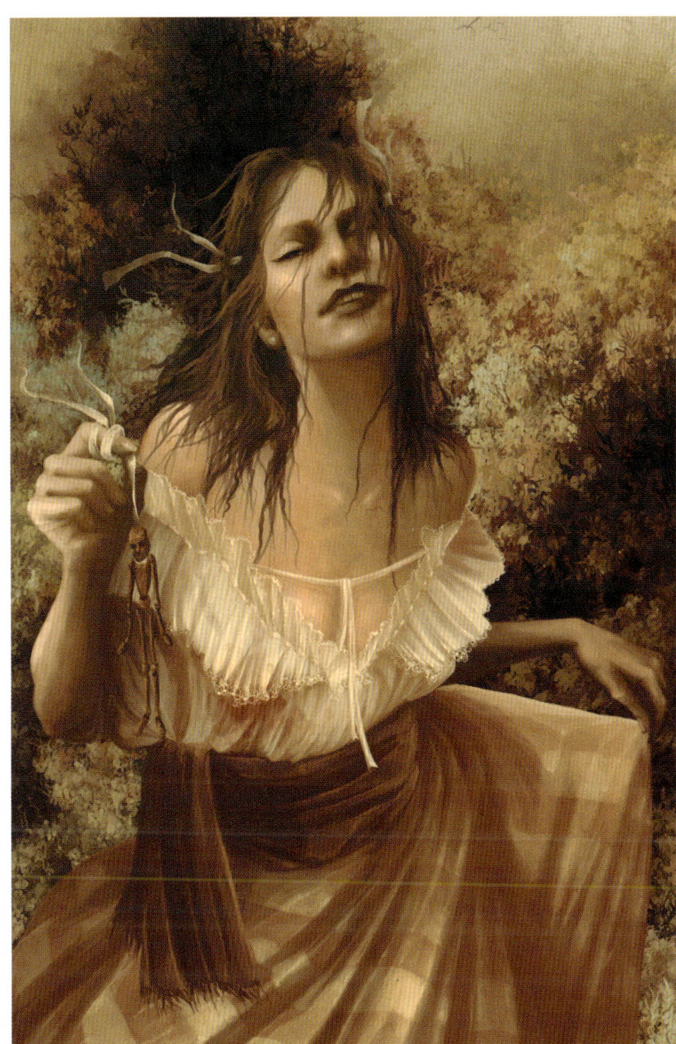

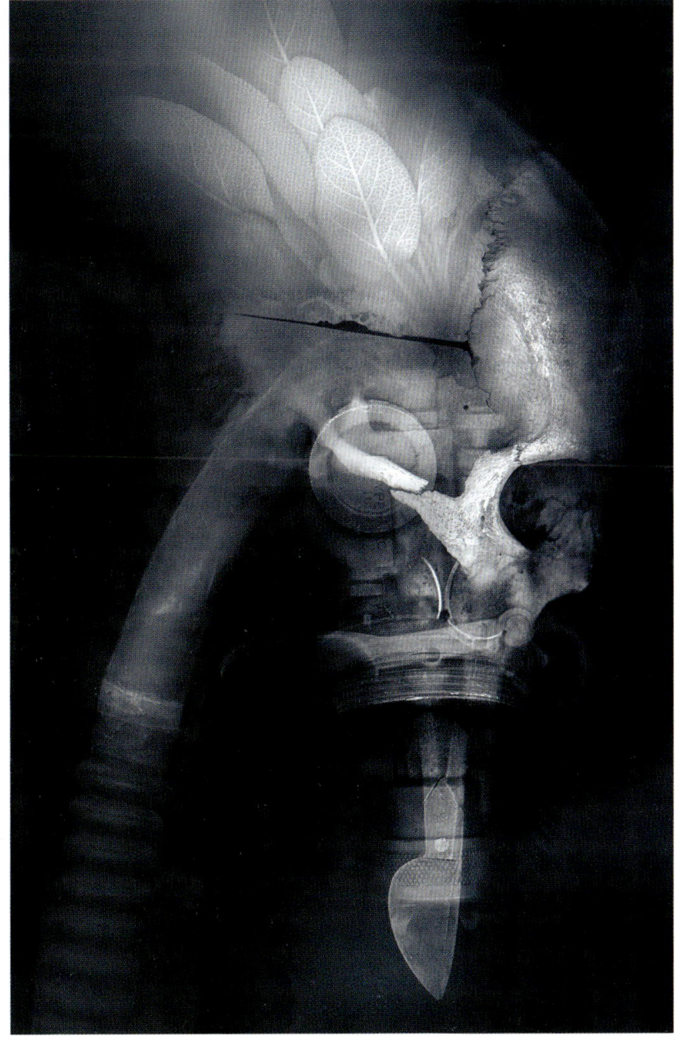

5

Unpublished

1
artist: **Naoto Hattori**
title: Chaosmos
medium: Acrylics on board
size: 14"x13"

2
artist: **Elio Guevara**
medium: Oils/mixed
size: 20"x25"

3
artist: **James S. Cole**
title: Chapel at the Dawn
medium: Digital

4
artist: **David Christiana**
title: The Third Body
medium: Oils on canvas
size: 22"x68"

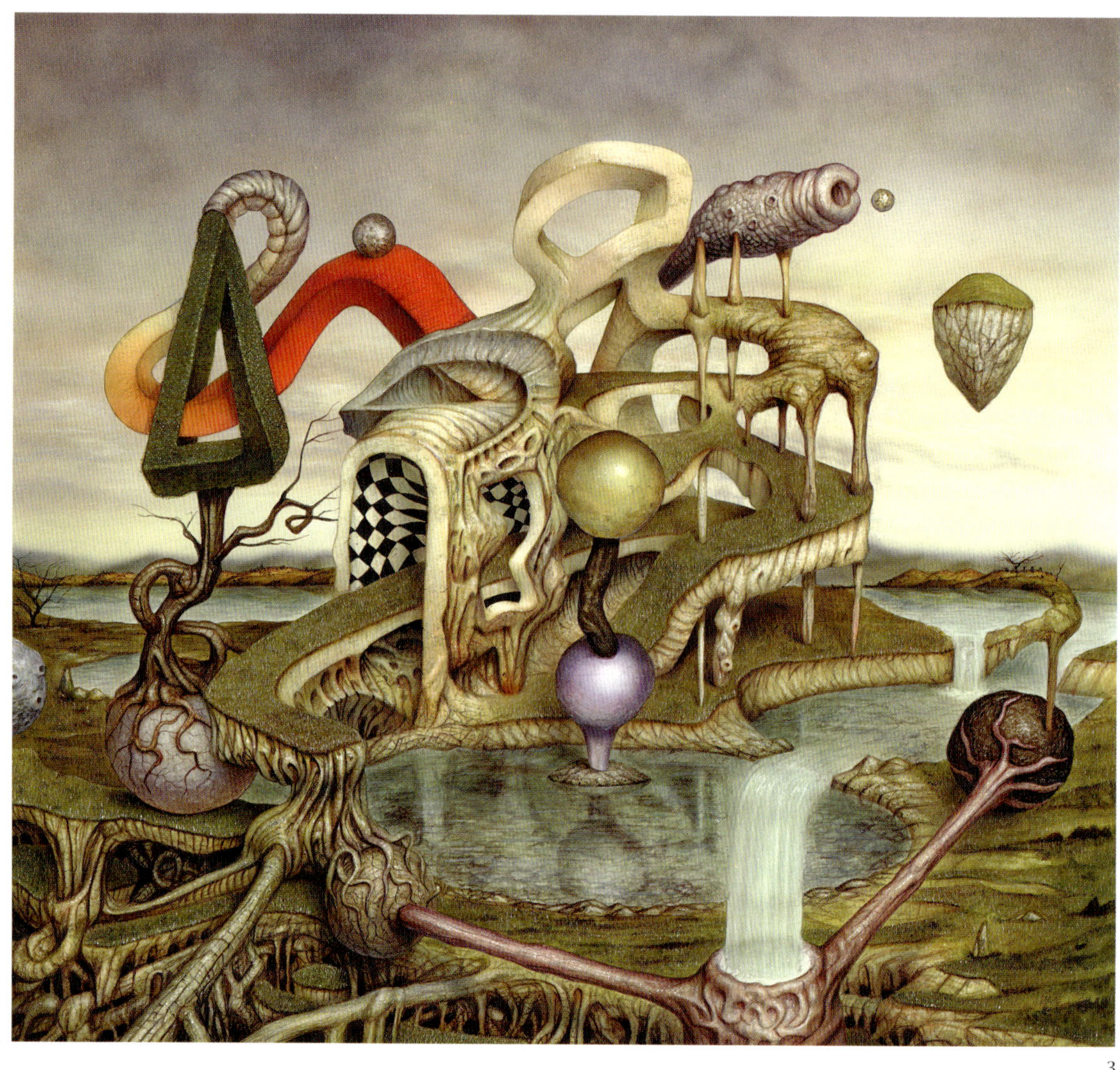

1

2

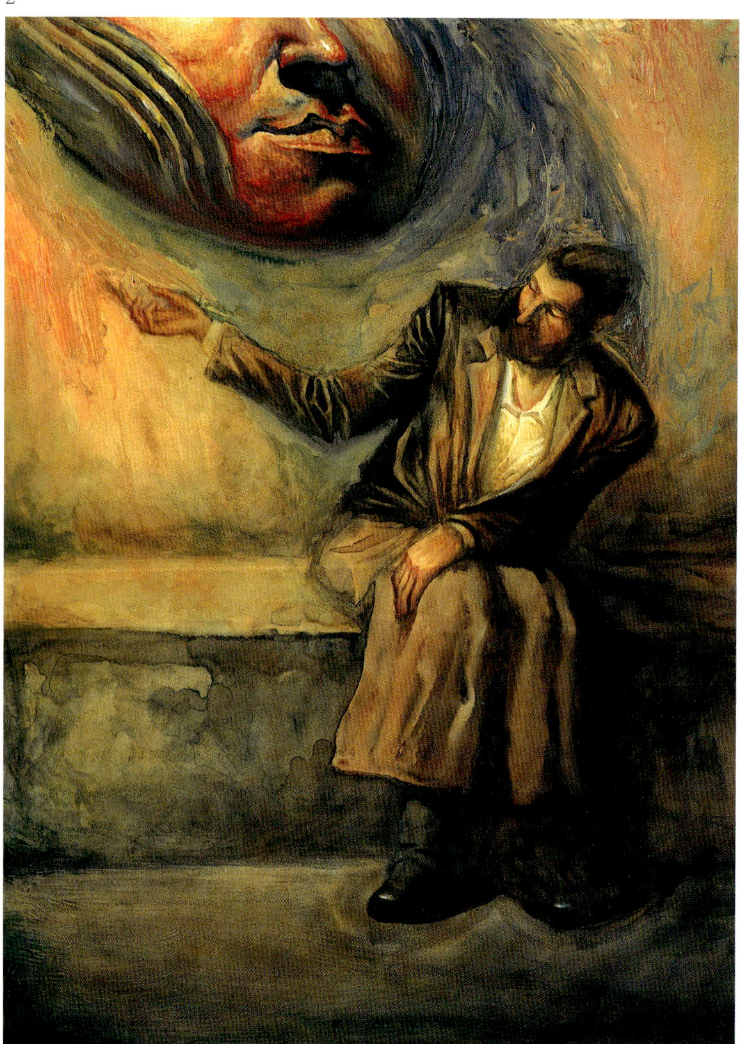

3

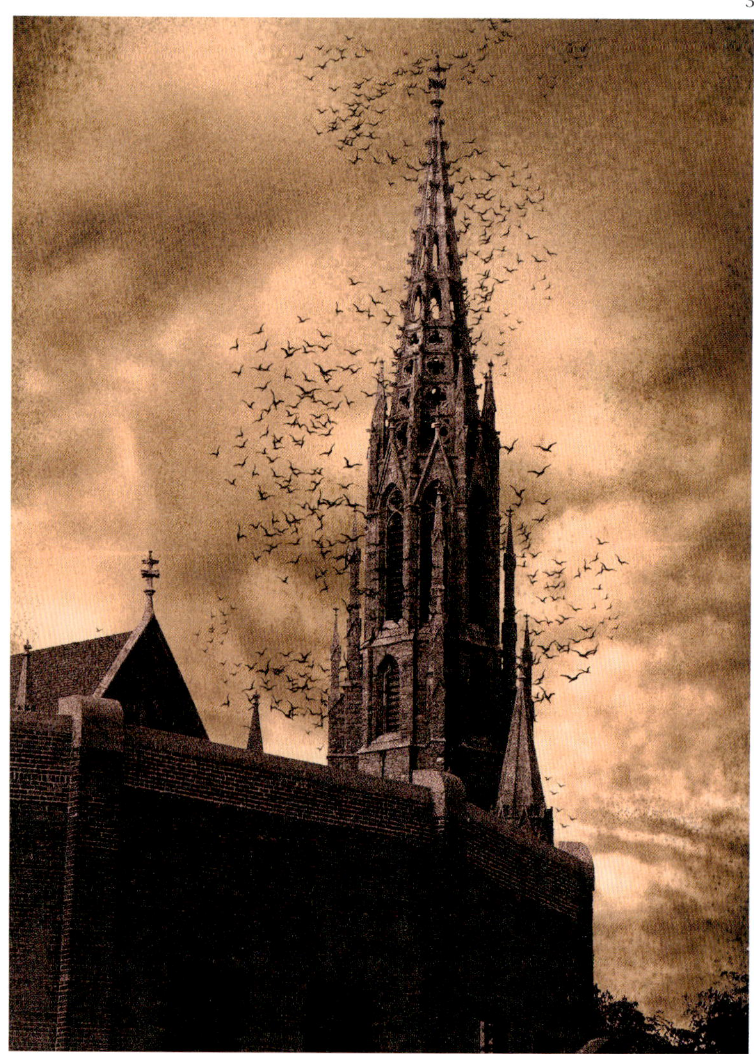

4

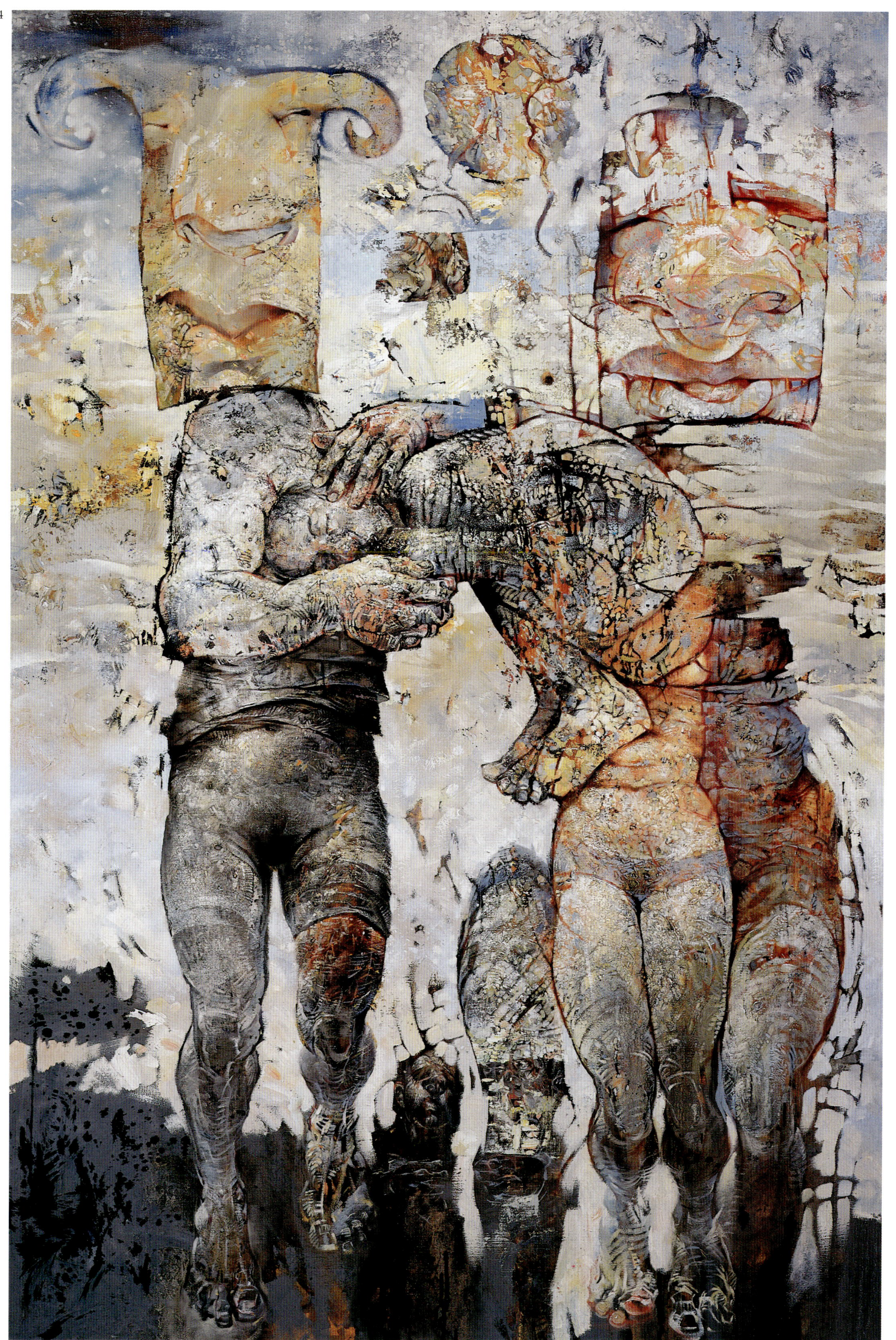

Unpublished

1
artist: **Richard Sardinha**
title: Awakening Leviathan
medium: Oils *size:* 36″x24″

2
artist: **Charles Frizzell**
client: Merlin's [Aspen]
title: Wizard's Vale
medium: Oils *size:* 54″x36″

3
artist: **Greg Horn**
client: Wizard
title: Spider-Man 2
medium: Digital

4
artist: **Bob Eggleton**
client: NESFA
title: Gun For a Dinosaur
medium: Gouache
size: 16″x20″

5
artist: **Jeff Spackman**
title: Egyptian Cats
medium: Acrylics
size: 17″x11″

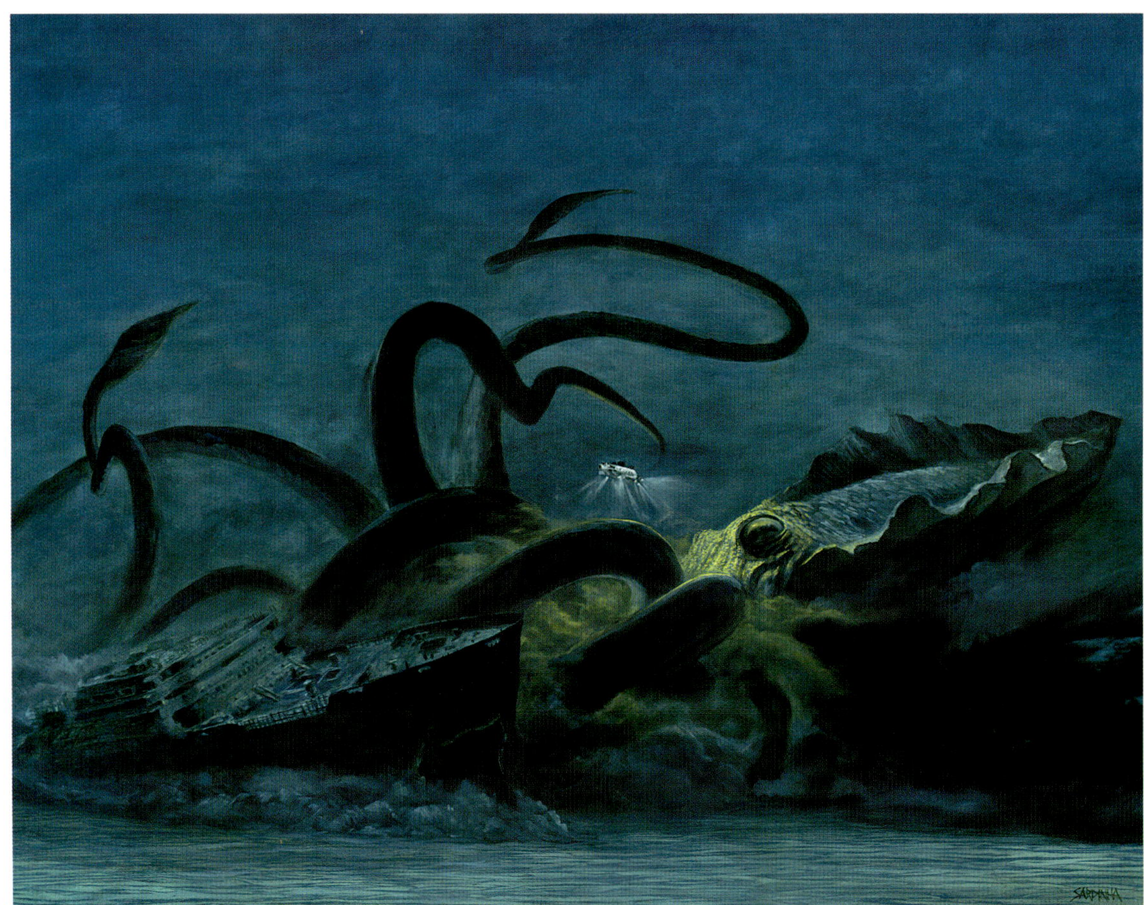

1

2

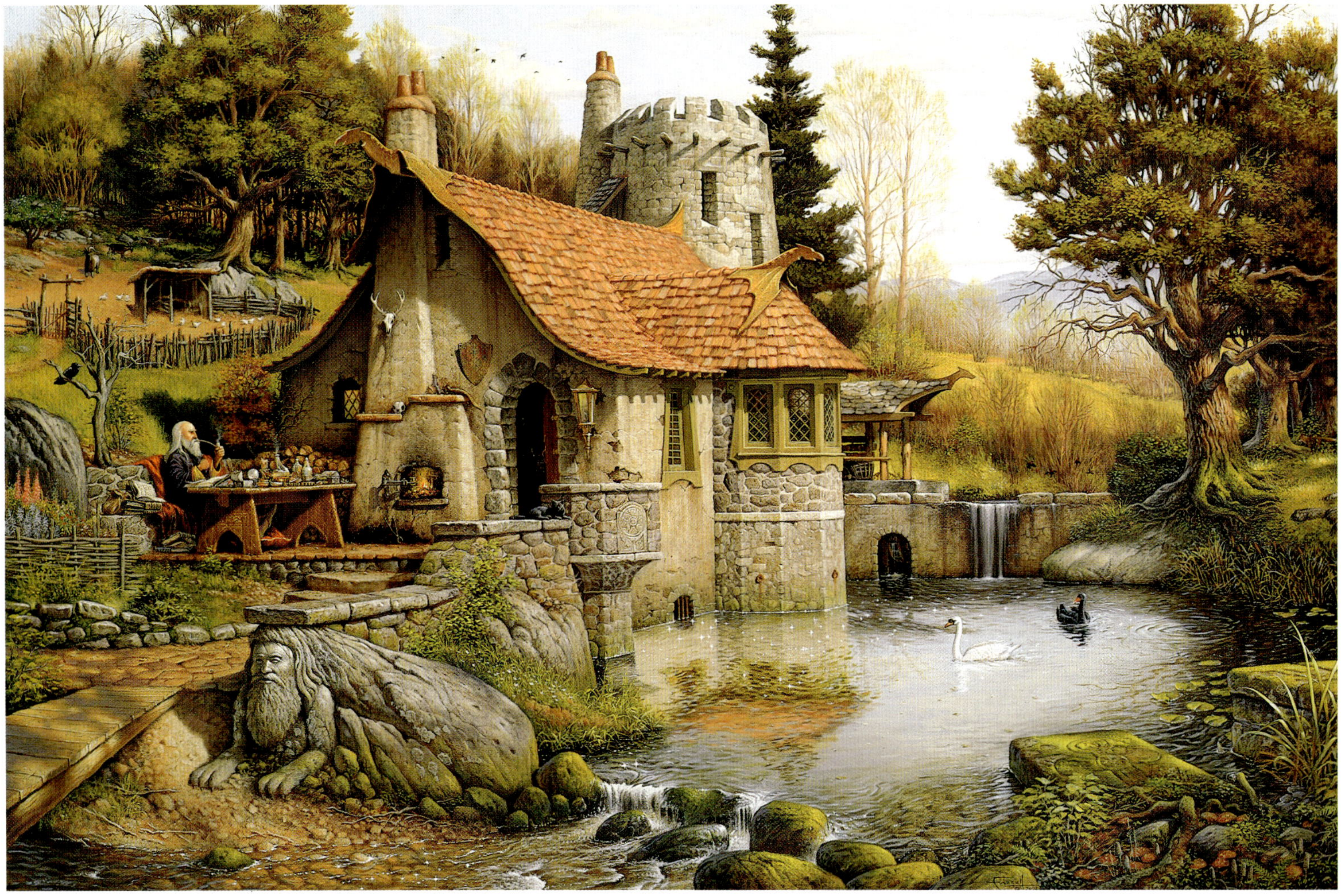

3

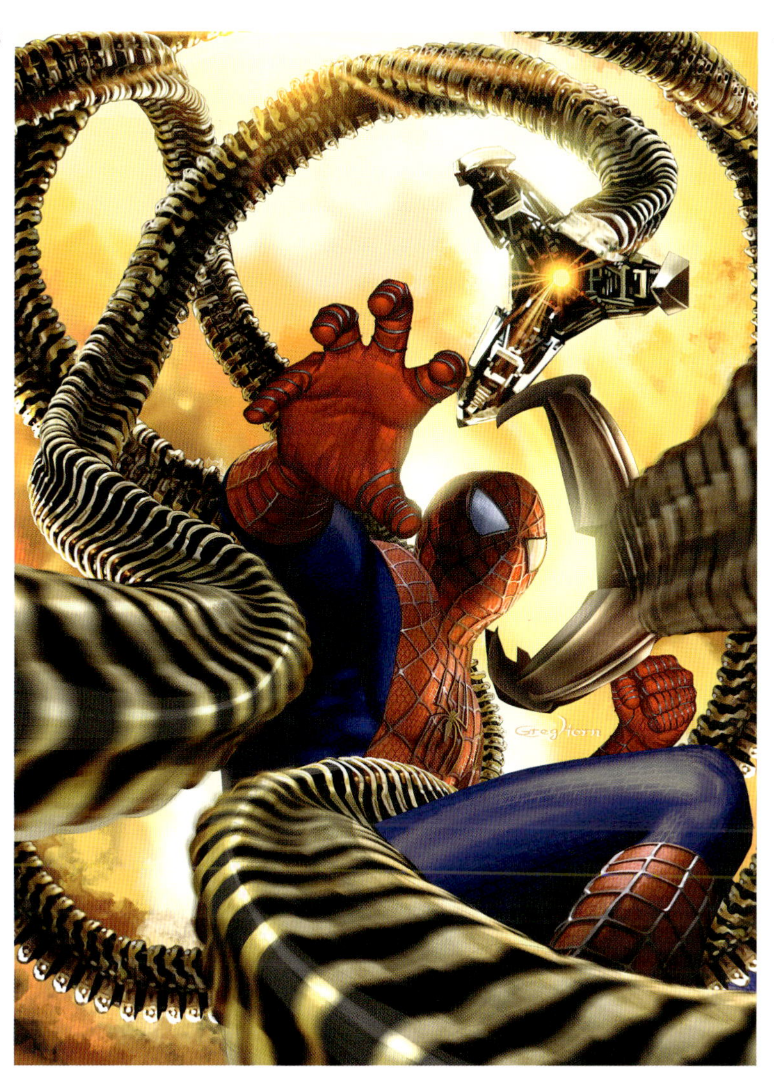

4

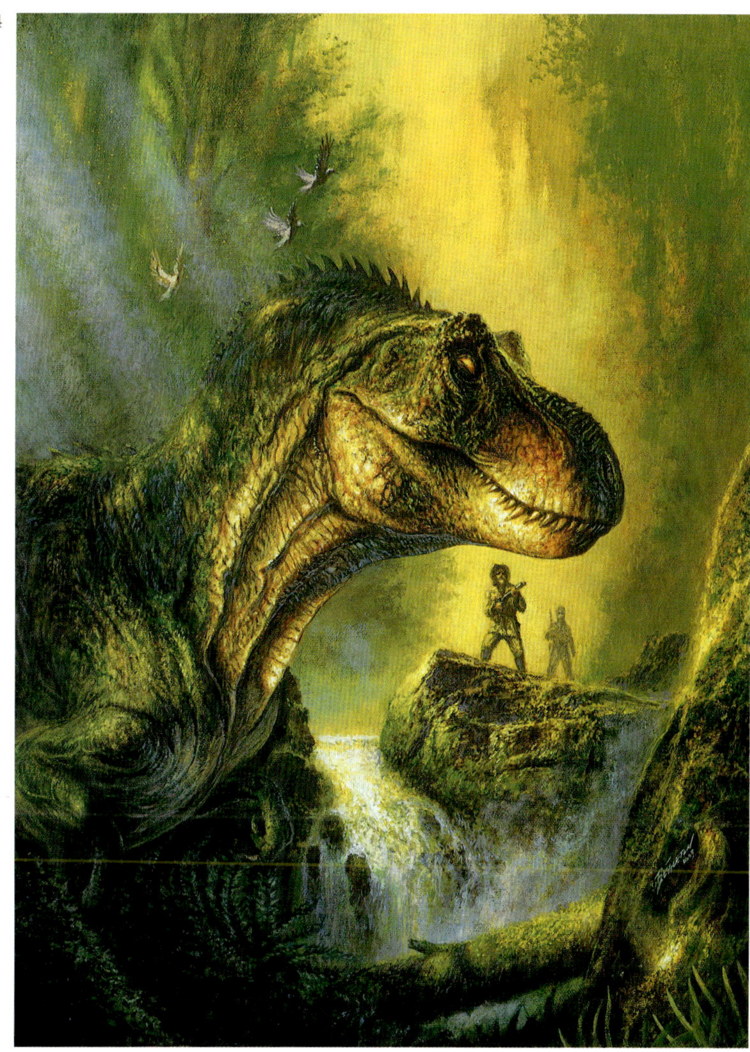

5

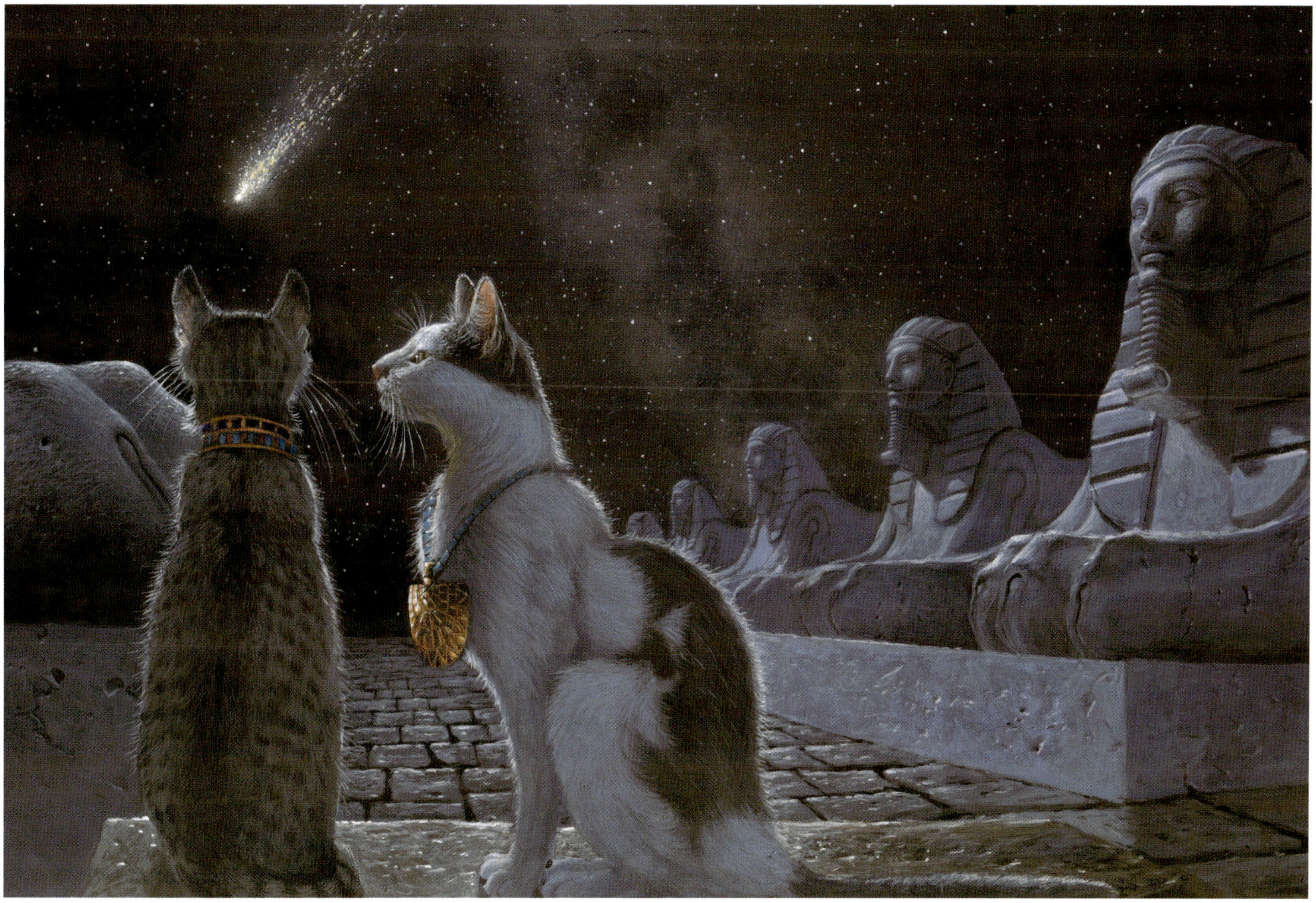

1
artist: **Raúl Colón**
title: Sleeping Woman
medium: Watercolor/colored pencil
size: 13″x17″

2
artist: **Jay Epperson**
title: Yoshiko San
medium: Oils
size: 16″x22″

3
artist: **Danielle Bedics**
medium: Digital
size: 8″x12″

4
artist: **Mark A. Nelson**
client: Grazing Dinosaur Press
title: E2: Ing-Yang
medium: Colored pencil
size: 22″x16 1/2″

5
artist: **David Bowers**
client: Halcyon Gallery [London]
title: Venus and the Rabbits
medium: Oils on linen
size: 24″x18″

1

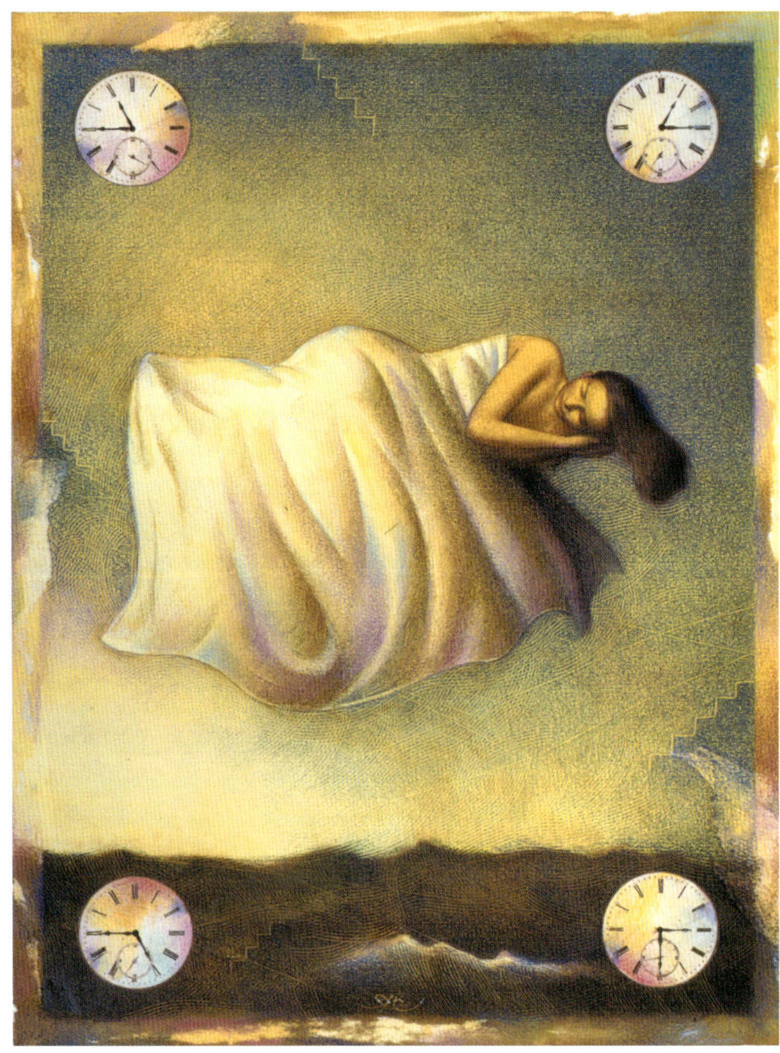

2

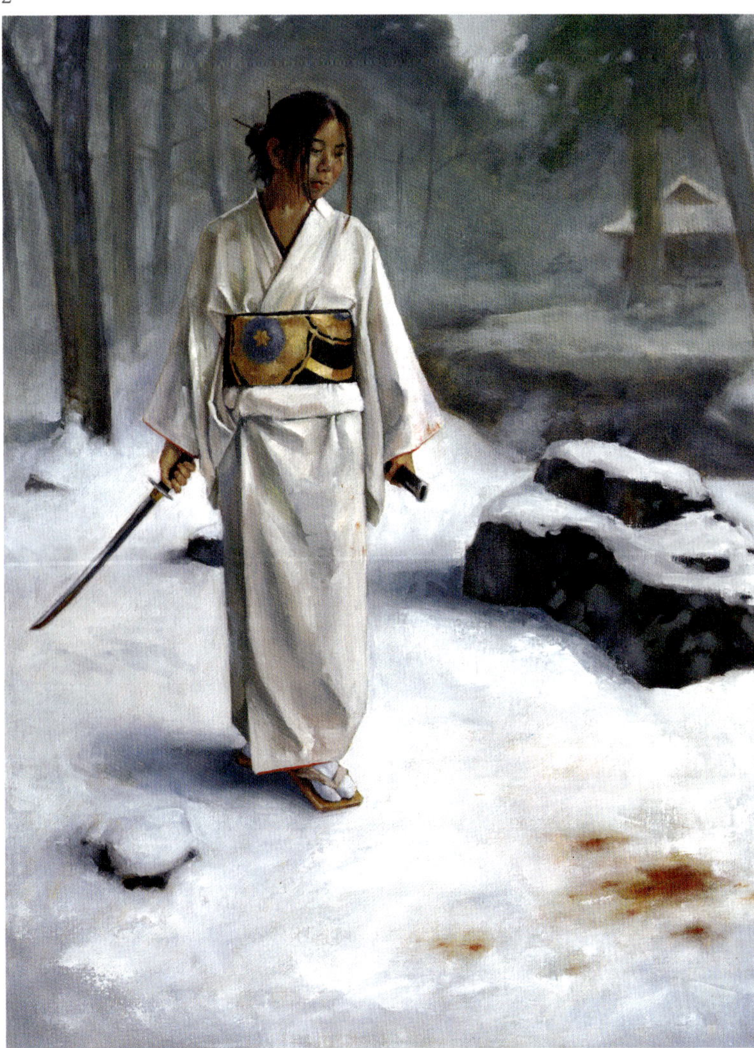

3

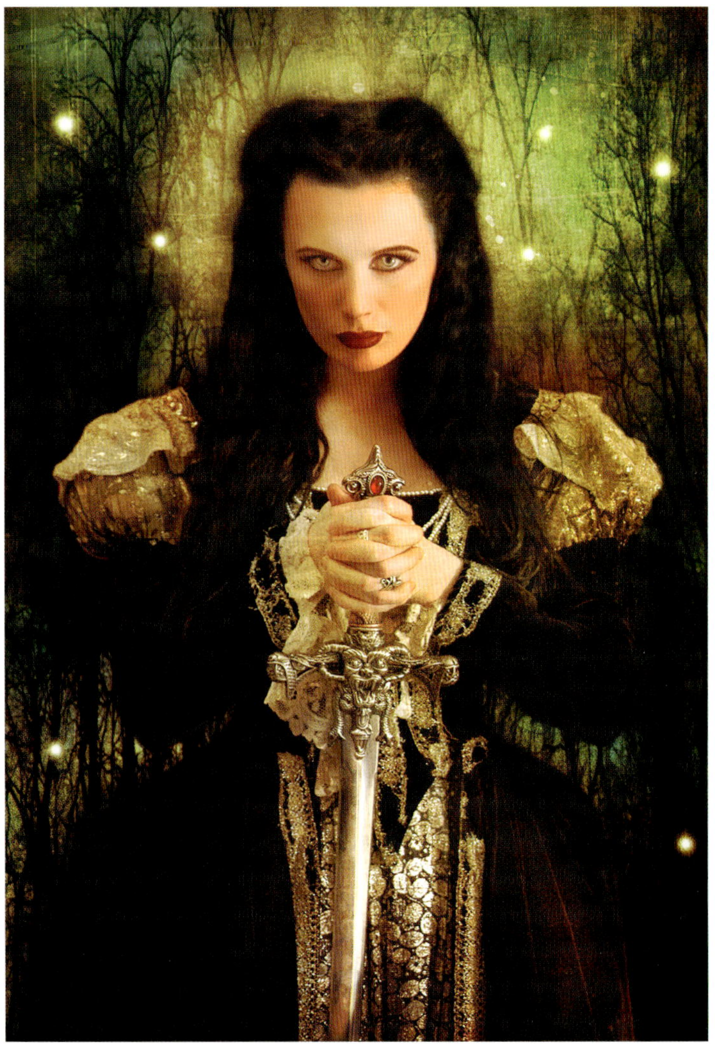

4

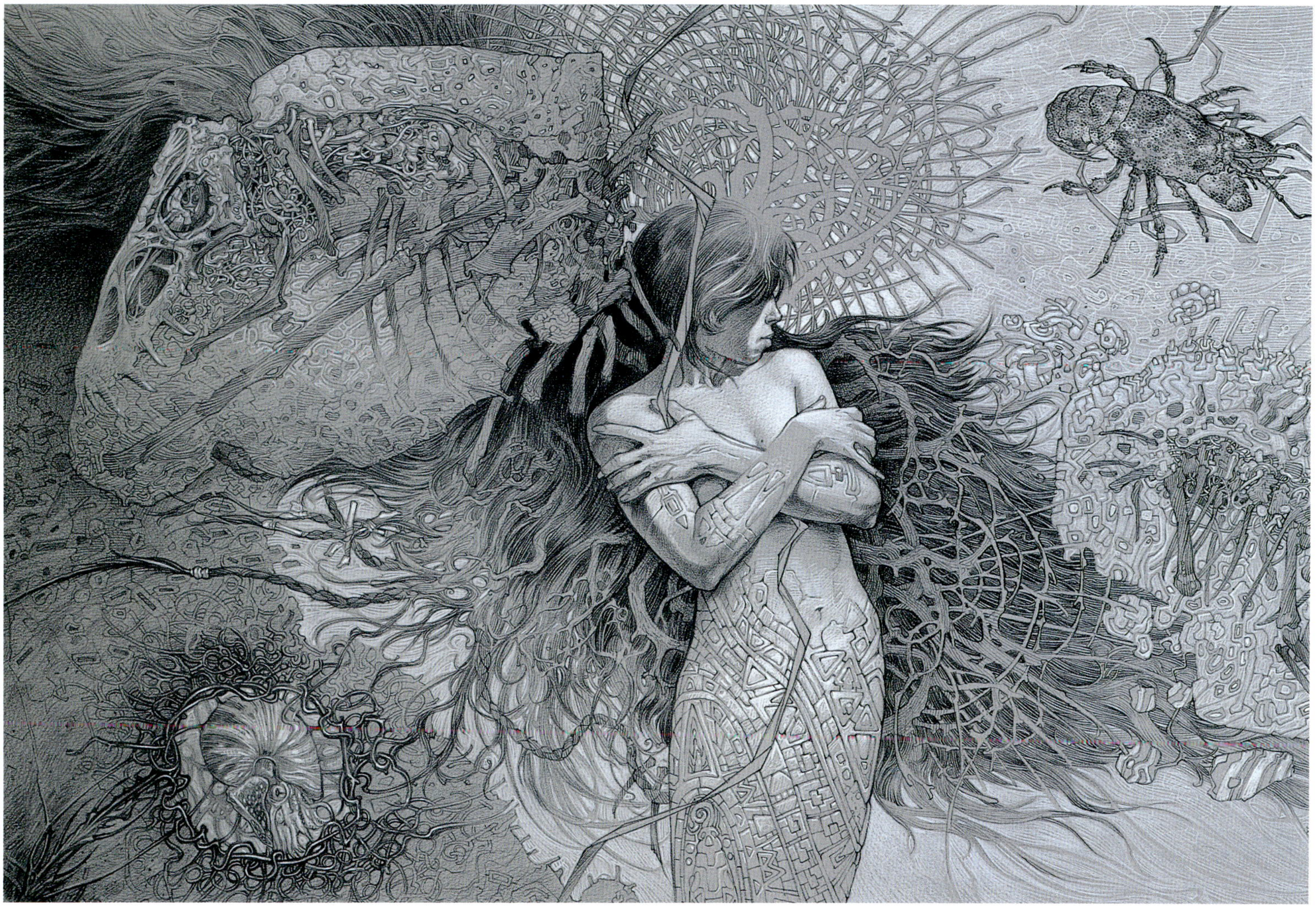

5

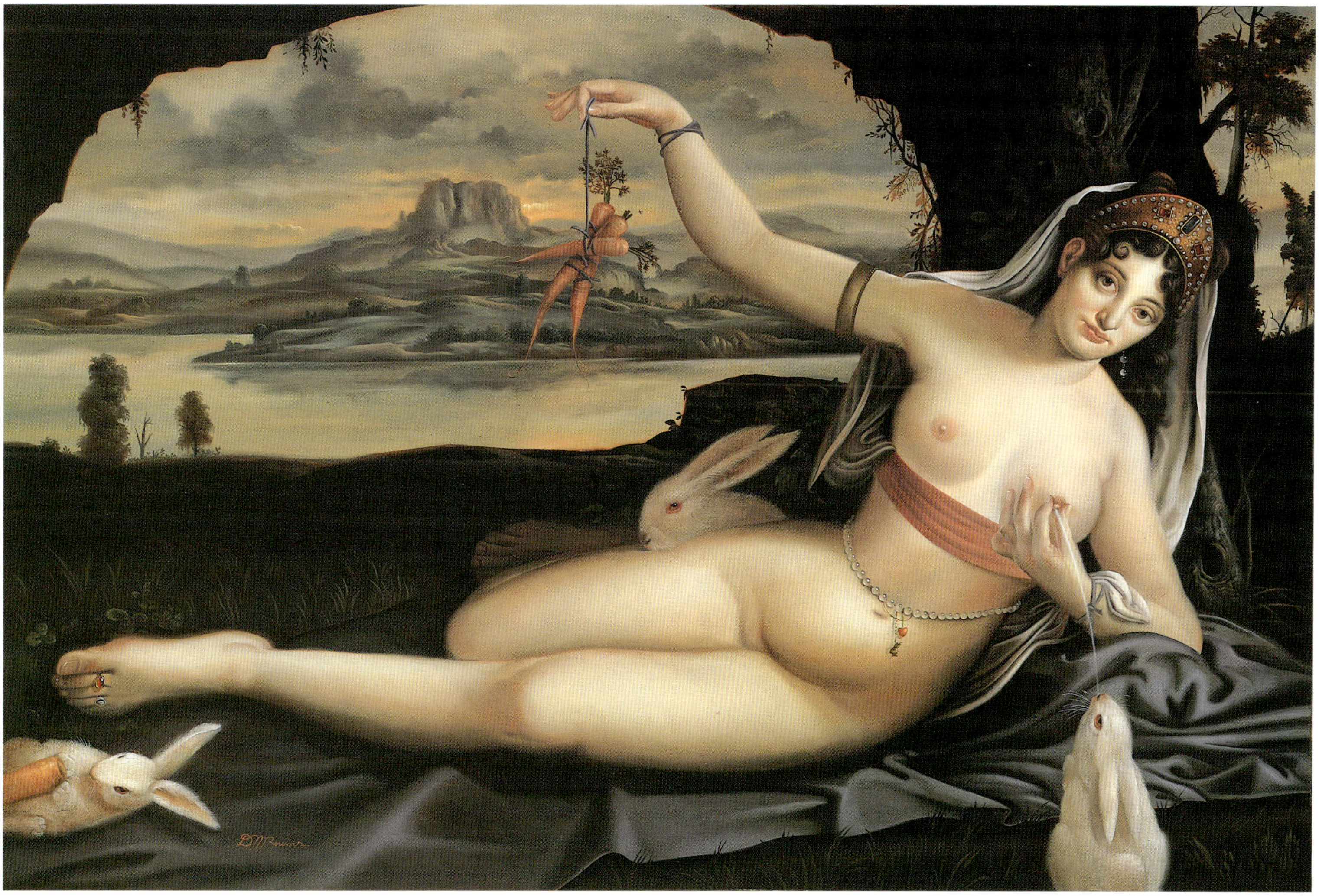

1
artist: **Steven Kenny**
title: The Glade
medium: Oils on canvas
size: 36″x32″

2
artist: **Richard Sardinha**
title: ACME Extermination
medium: Oils
size: 18″x24″

3
artist: **Ken Wong**
title: Fire Without Warmth
medium: Digital

4
artist: **Craig Elliott**
title: Jade
medium: Acrylics
size: 19″x25″

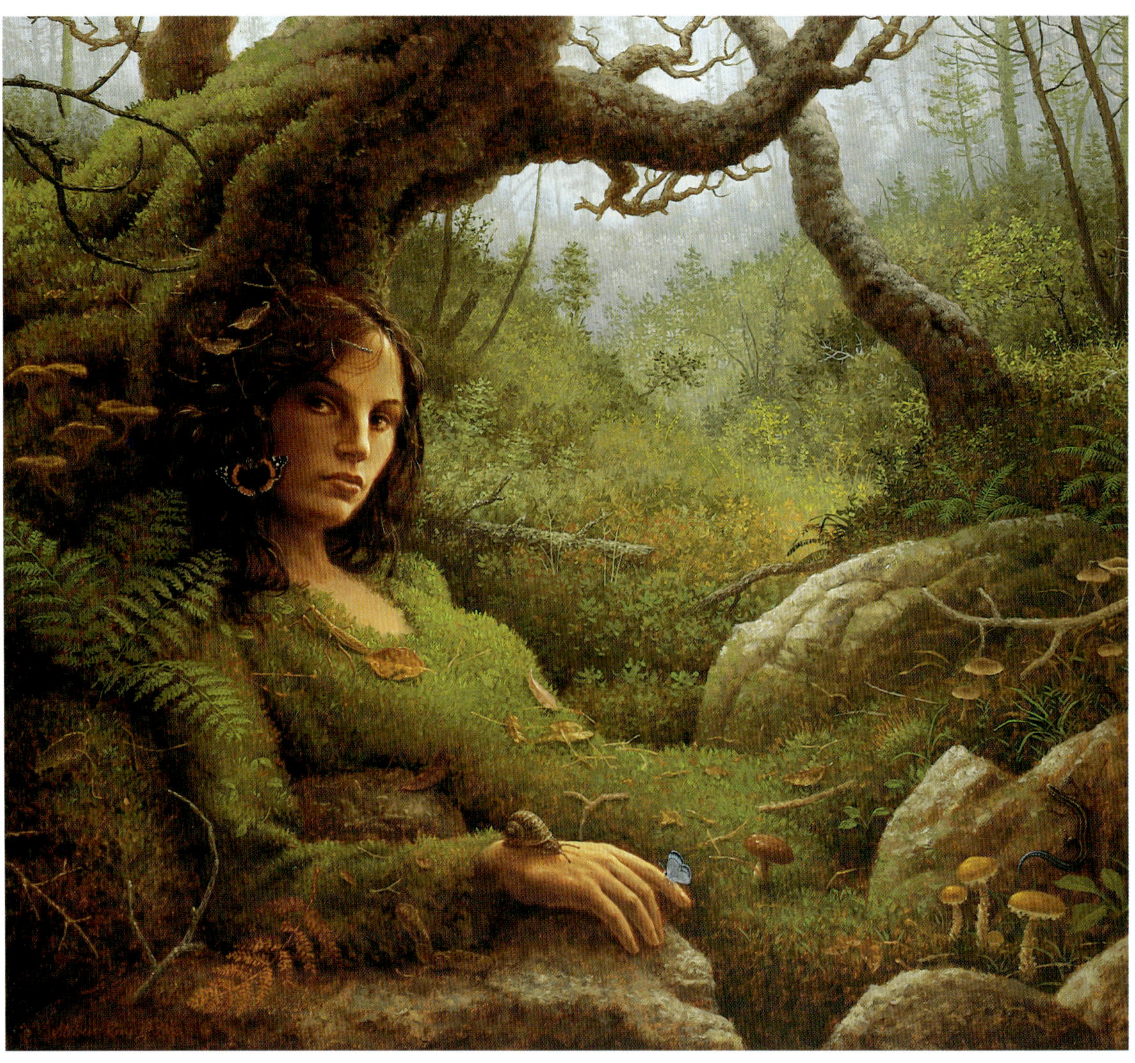
1

2
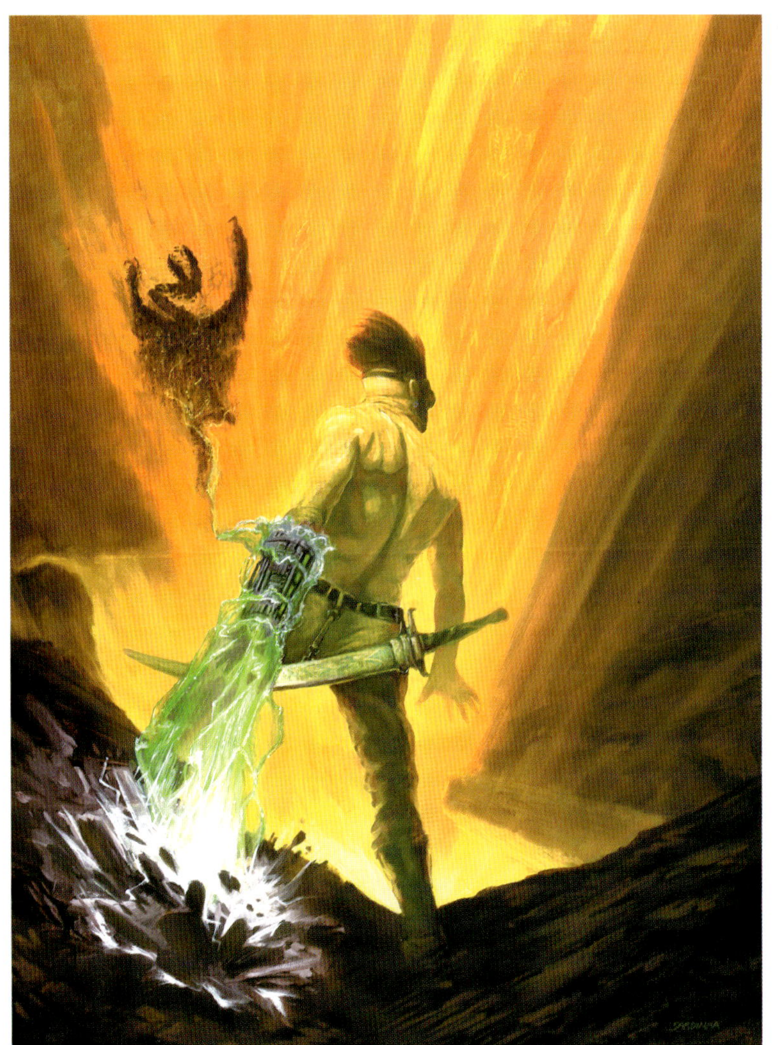

3
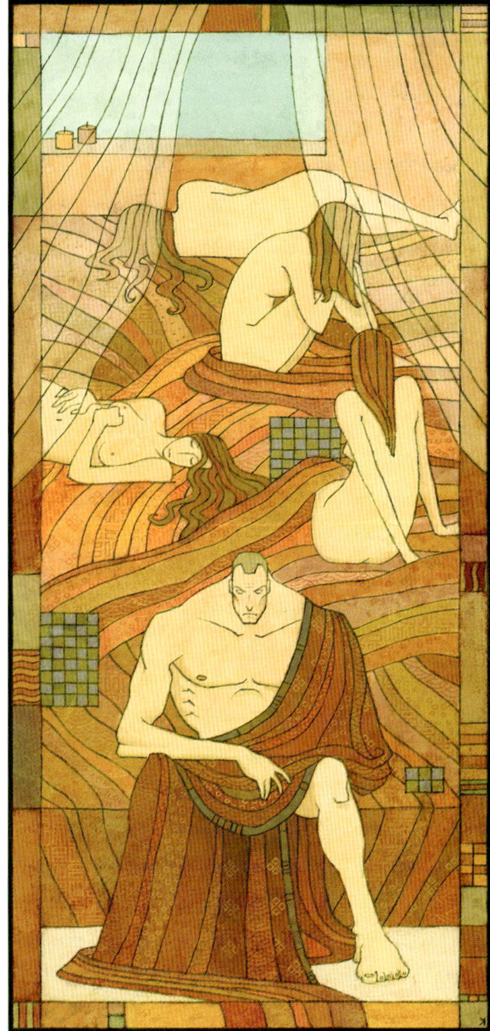

4

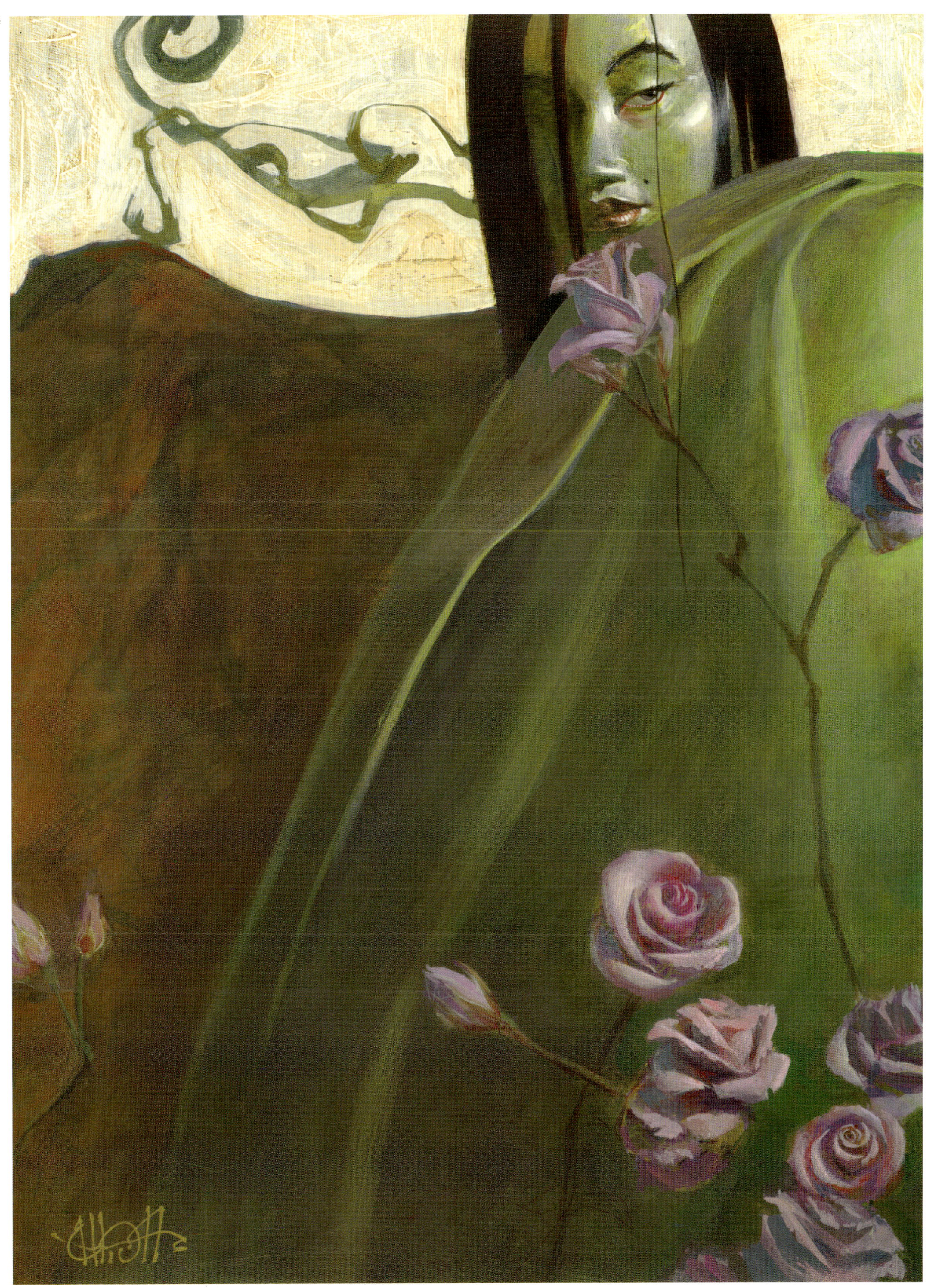

1
artist: **Hunter Brown**
title: Life & Death
medium: Watercolor, gouache
size: 12″x12″

2
artist: **Darrel Anderson**
title: The Three Bugs Berry
medium: Graphite/digital
size: 24″x11″

3
artist: **Beric Henderson**
title: Aeronauticus
medium: Acrylics
size: 60cmx20cm

4
artist: **Don Maitz**
title: Riding the Storm Out
medium: Oils on masonite
size: 18″x27″

5
artist: **Montgomery S. Kane**
title: Green Cloak
medium: Oils and acrylics
size: 36″x24″

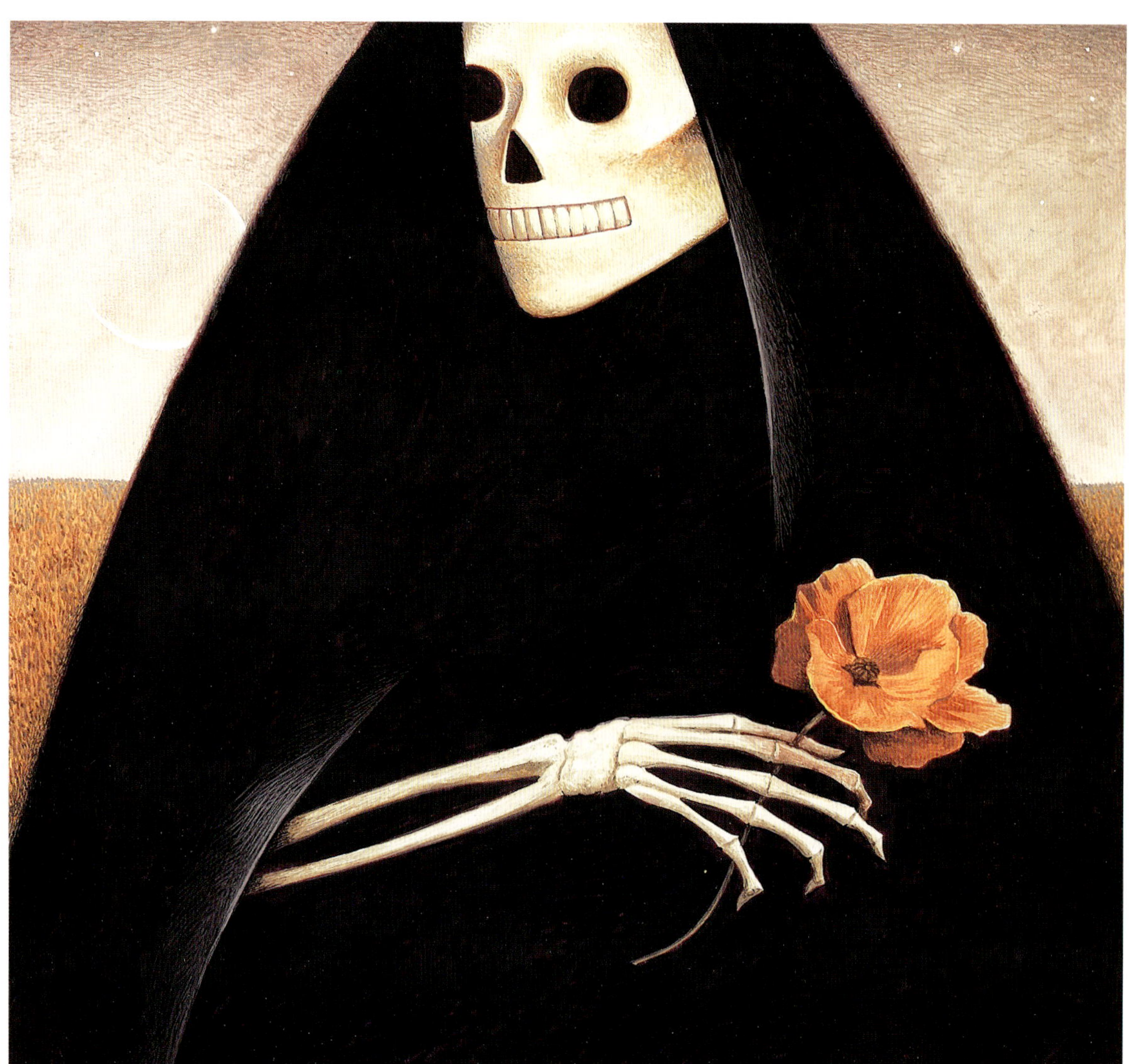

1

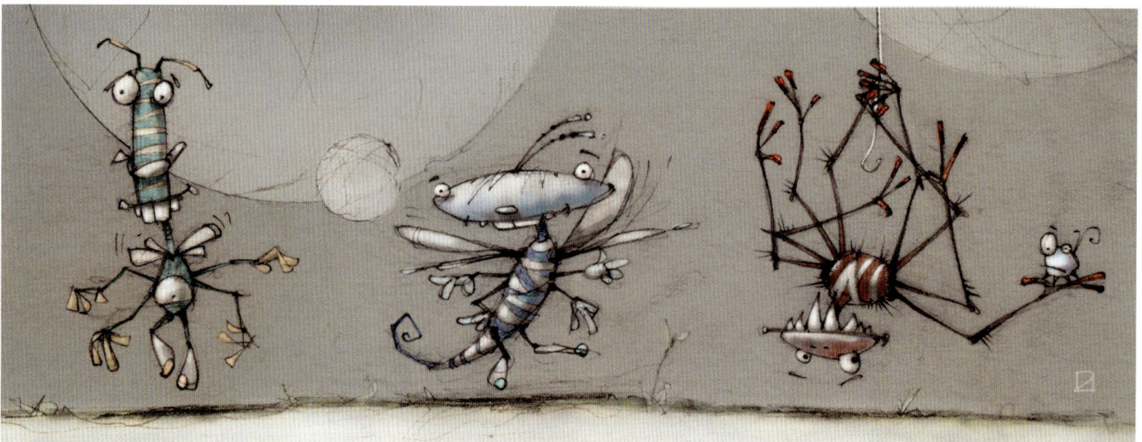

2

3

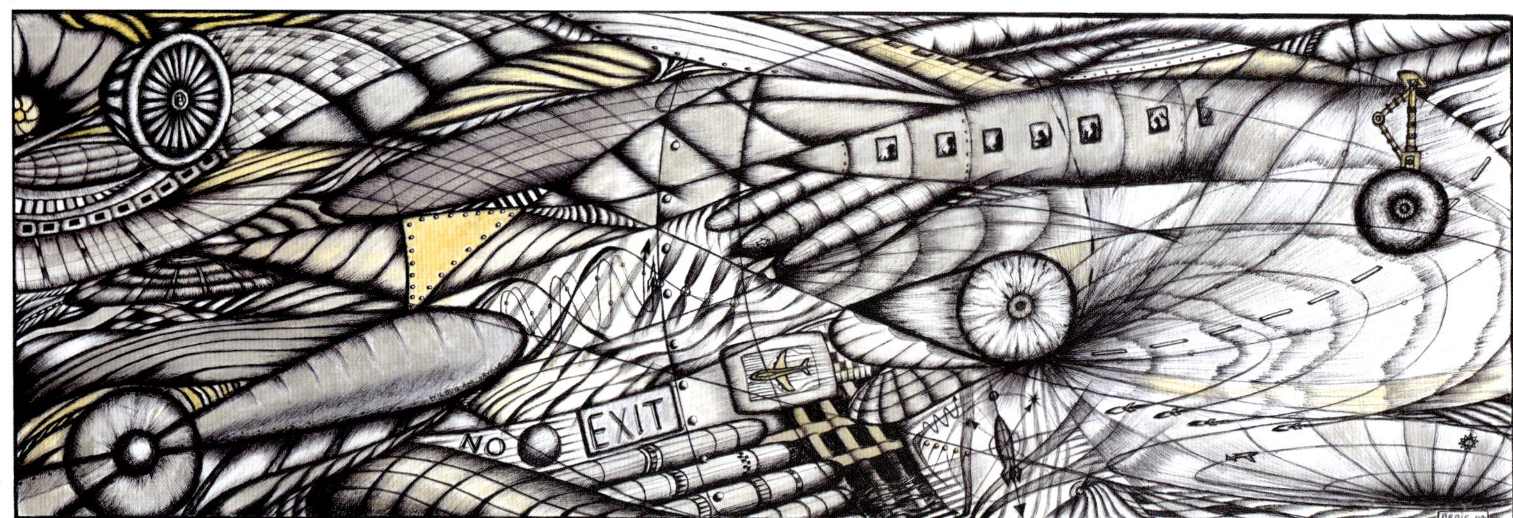

4

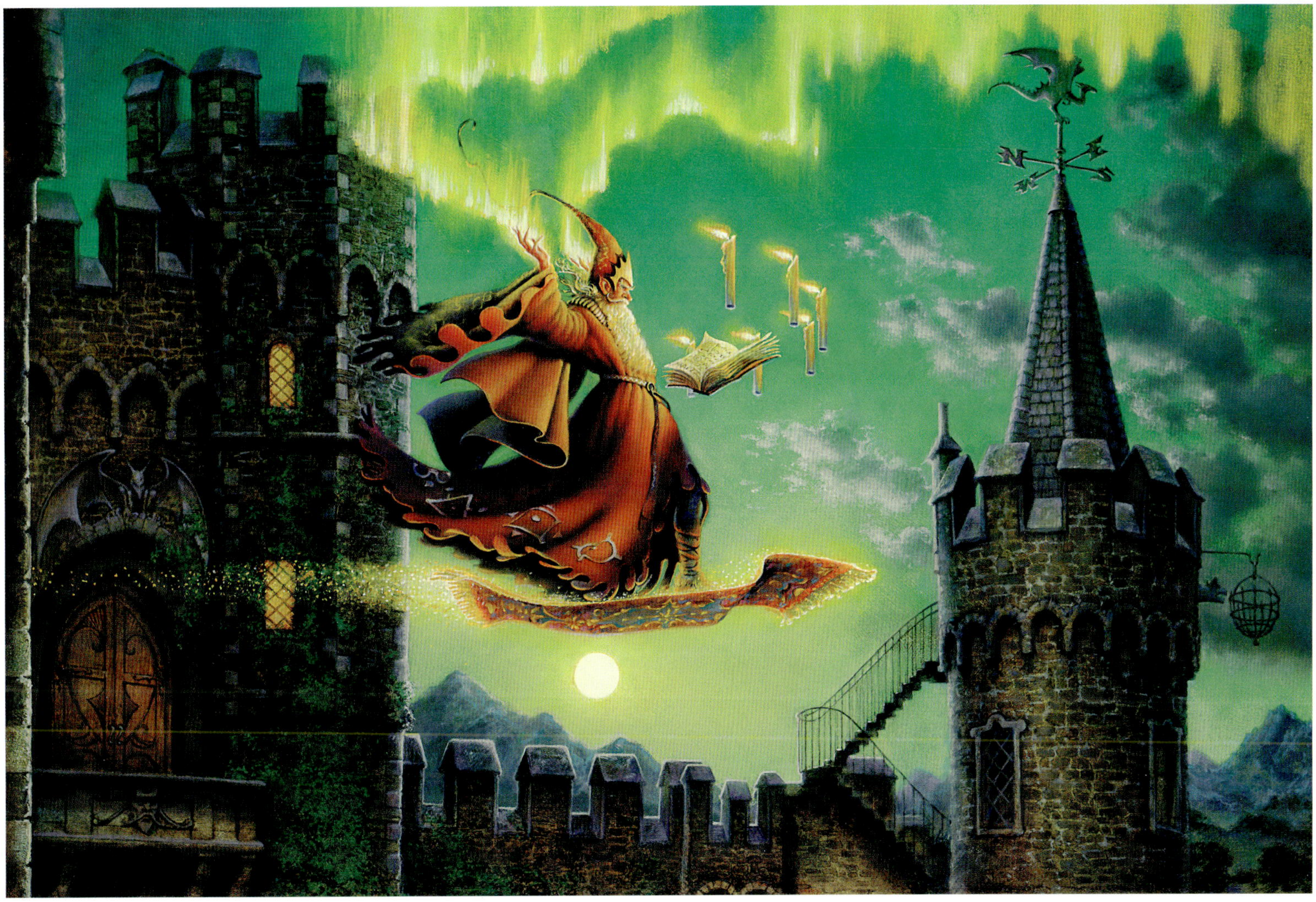

5

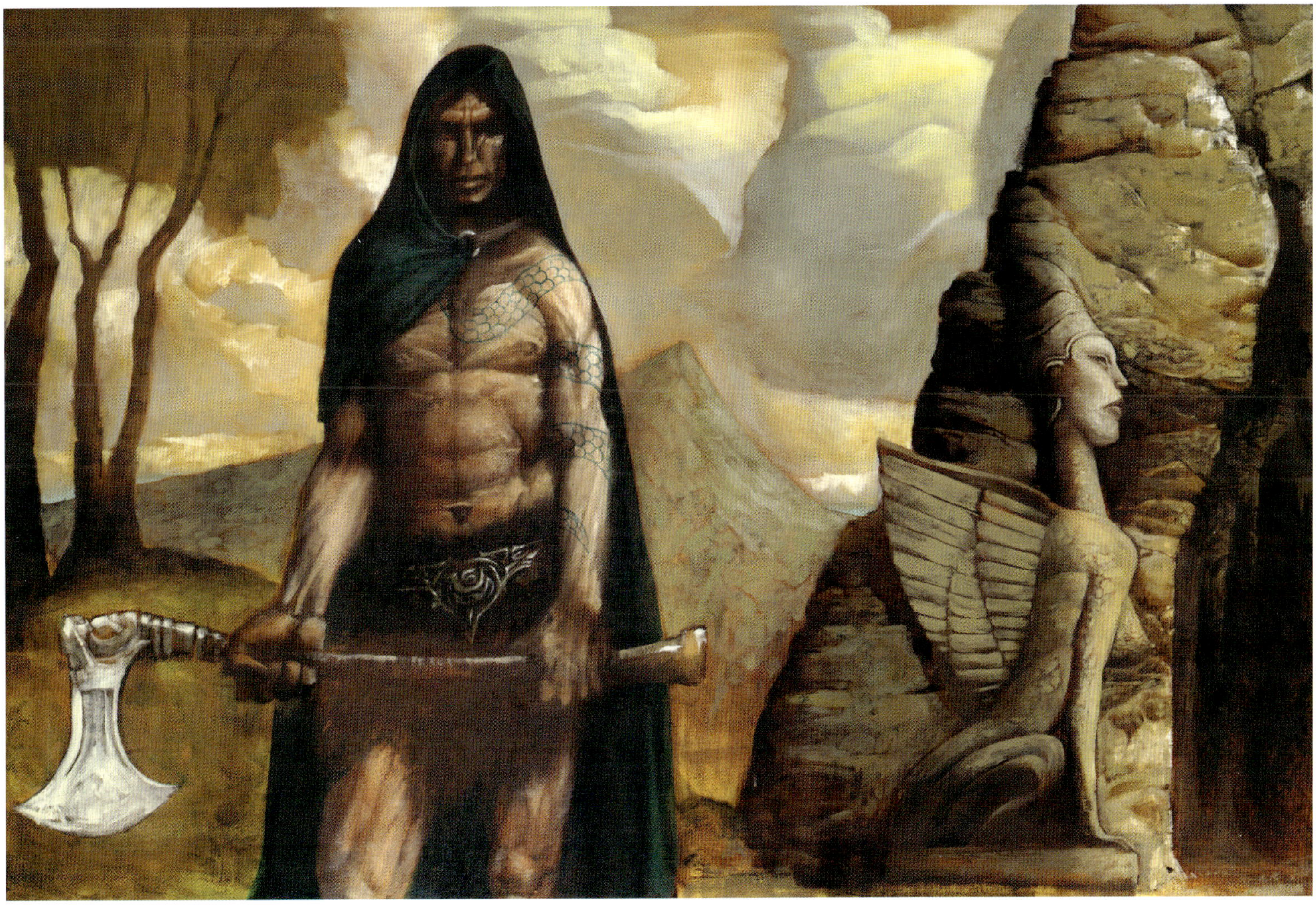

1
artist: **Angel Dominguez**
title: Akelarre
medium: Watercolor
size: 500mmx500mm

2
artist: **Dan L. Henderson**
title: Amblyopia
medium: Charcoal
size: 20″x26″

3
artist: **Scott Lewis**
title: Vampire
medium: Acrylics
size: 14″x19″

4
artist: **Arthur Adams**
title: The Queen
medium: Pen & ink
size: 11″x17″

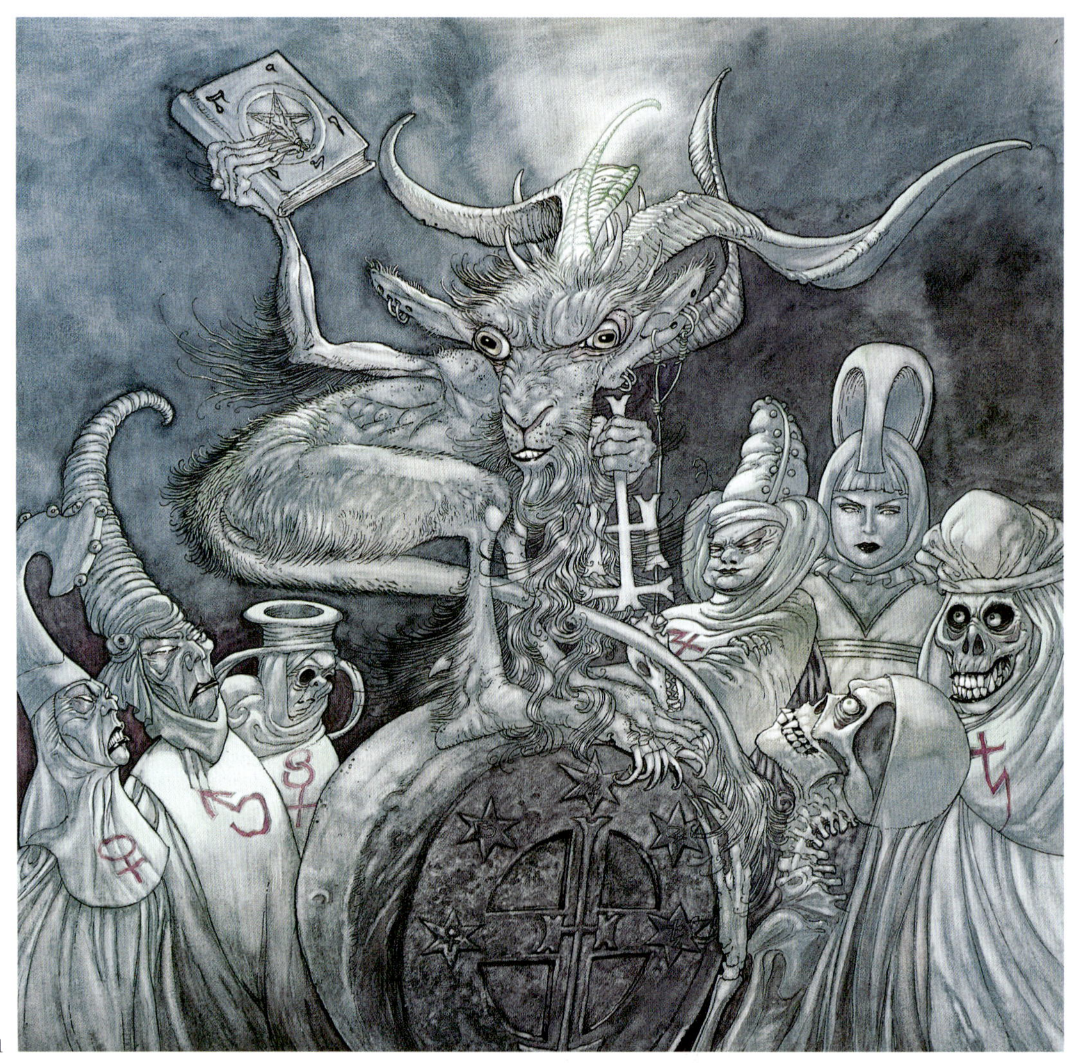

1

2

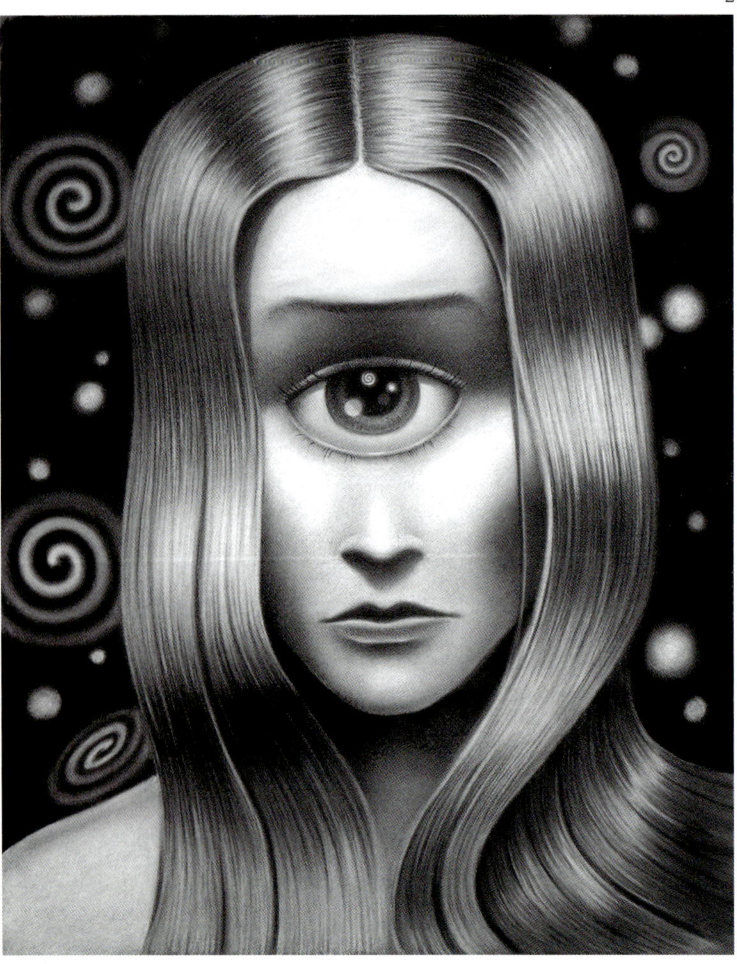

3

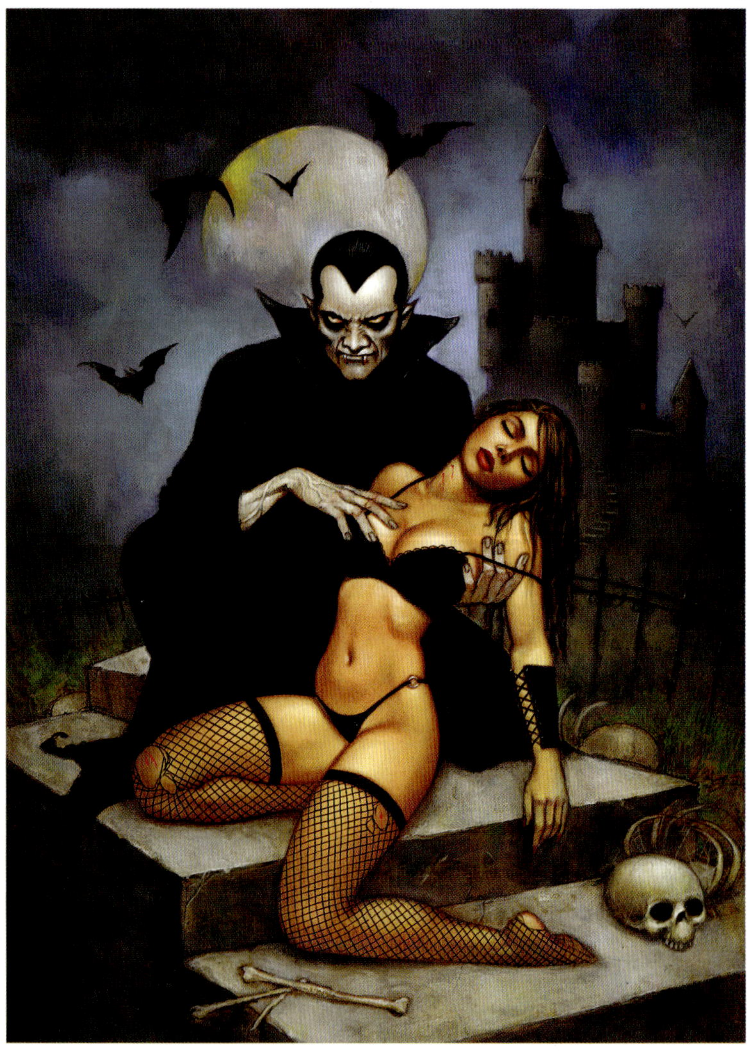

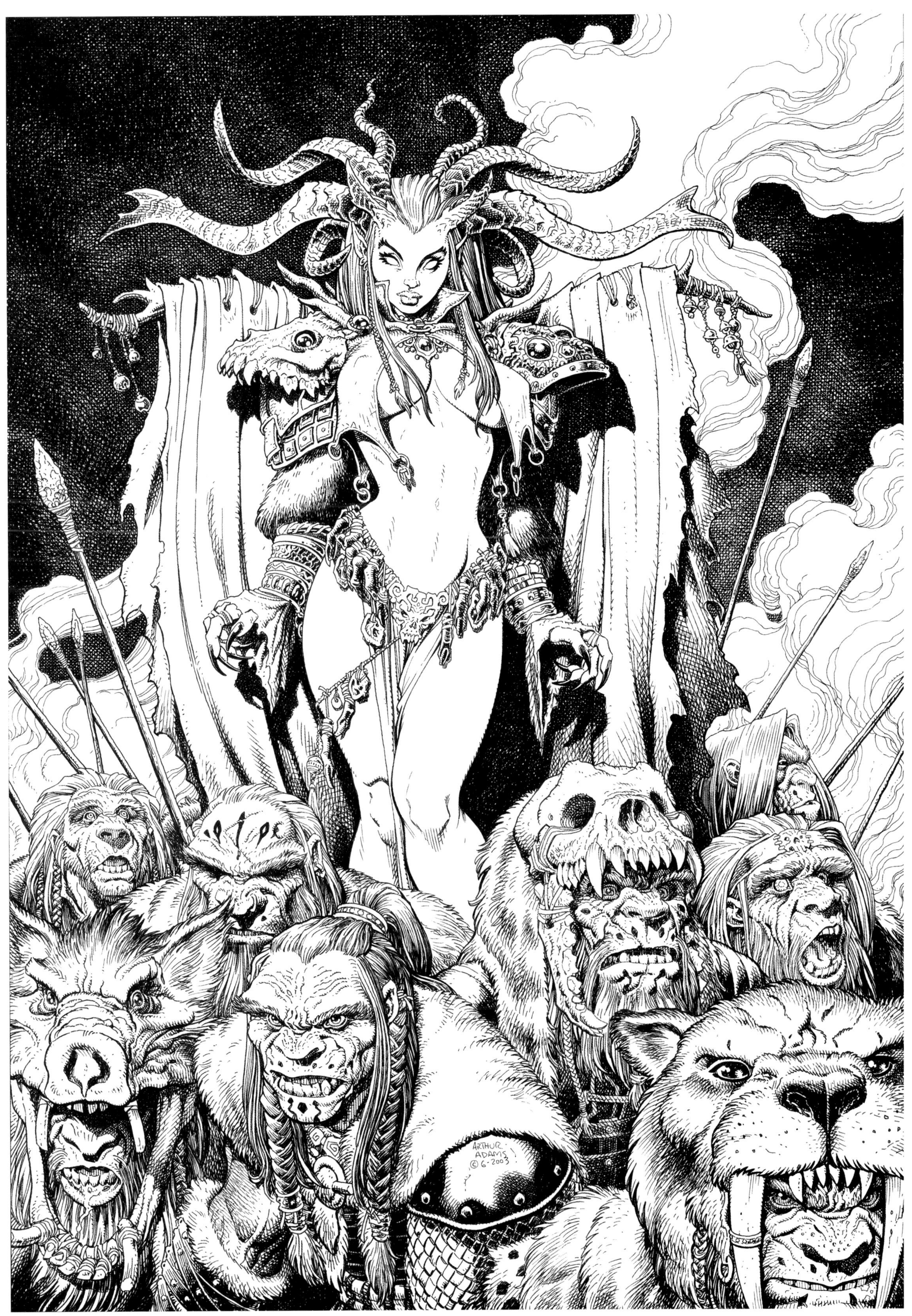
ARTHUR
ADAMS
©6-2003

Unpublished

1
artist: **Burton**
client: Gray Squad
title: Peppermint Lady
medium: Digital
size: 12″x12″

2
artist: **Ben Blatt**
title: Westward Salamandropold!
medium: Watercolor/gouache
size: 25¼″x17″

3
artist: **Melissa Ferreira**
title: Manihii
medium: Acrylics
size: 8″x11″

1

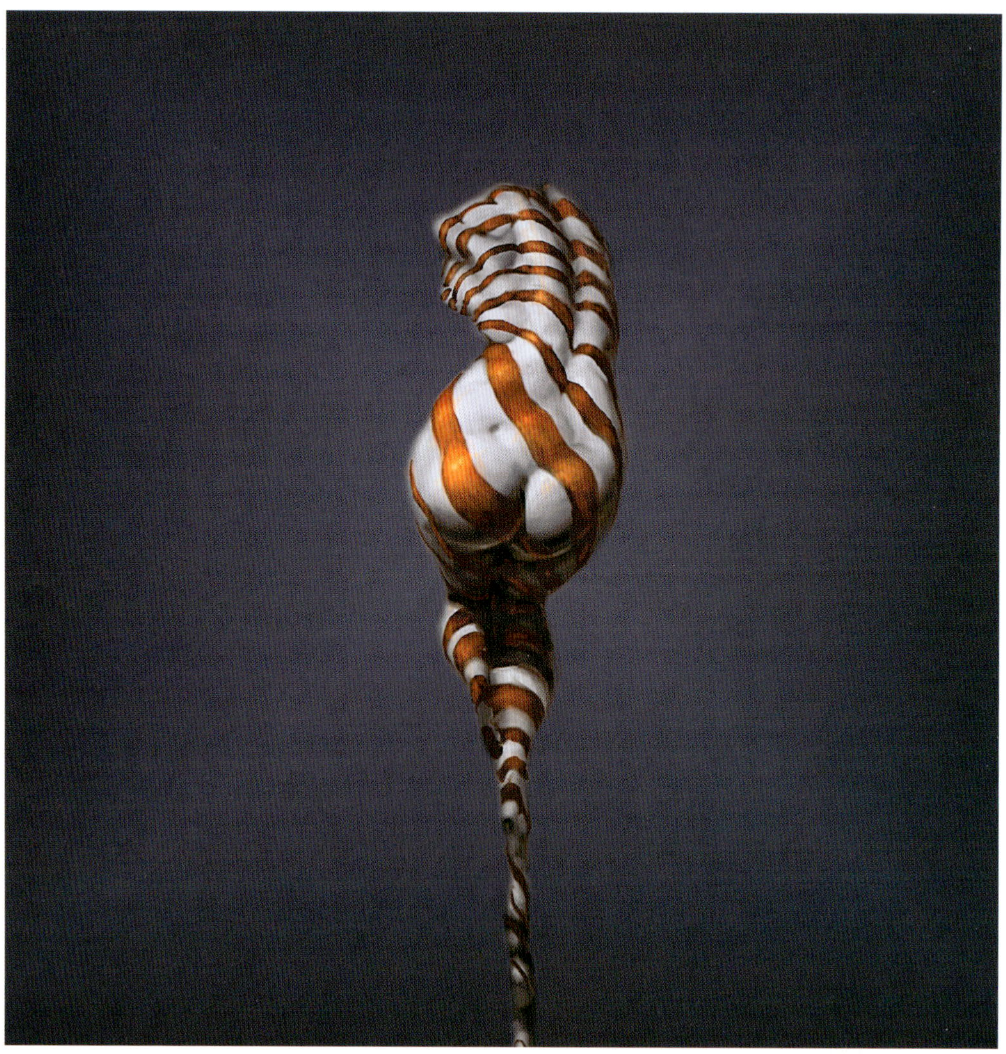

2

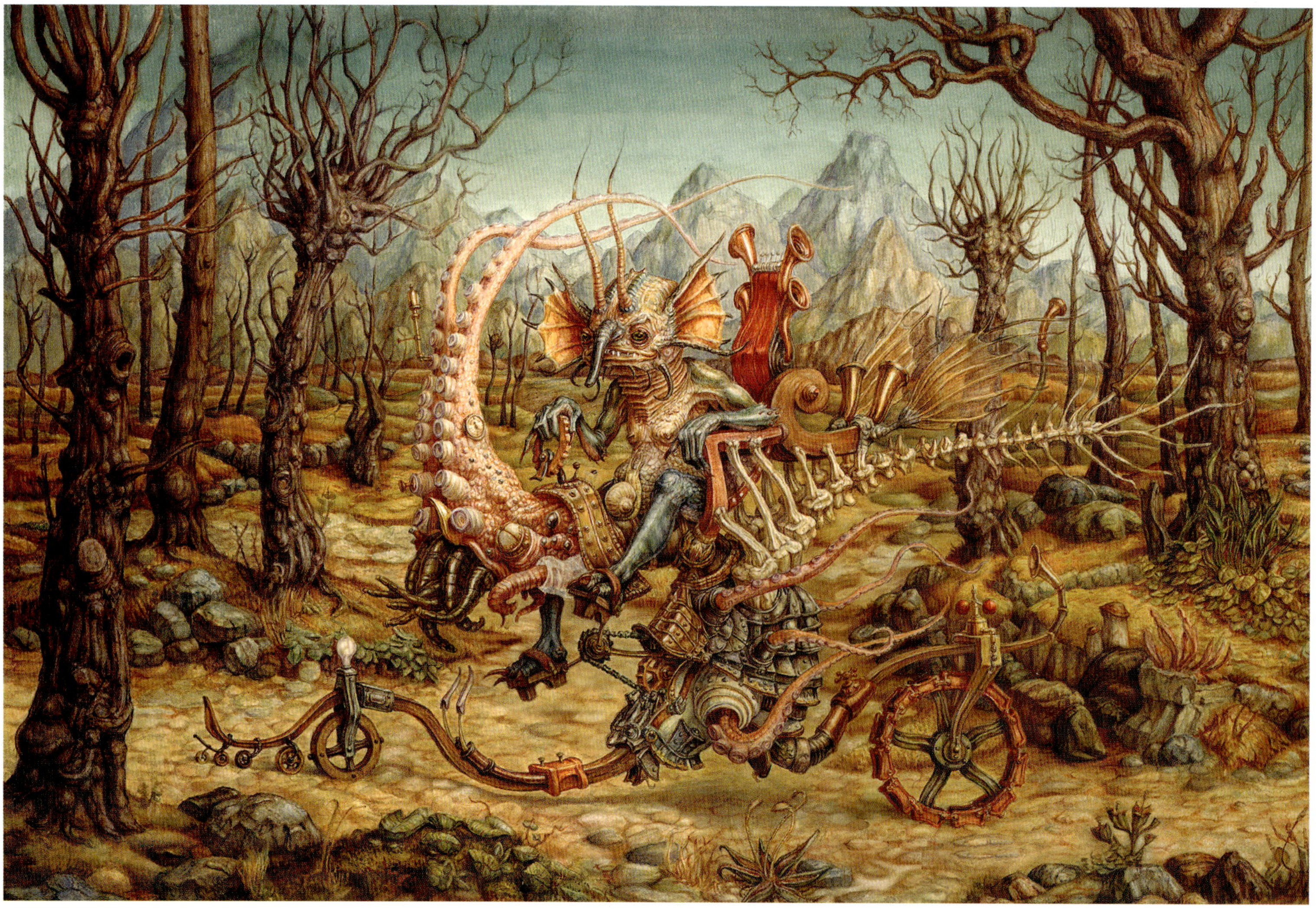

3

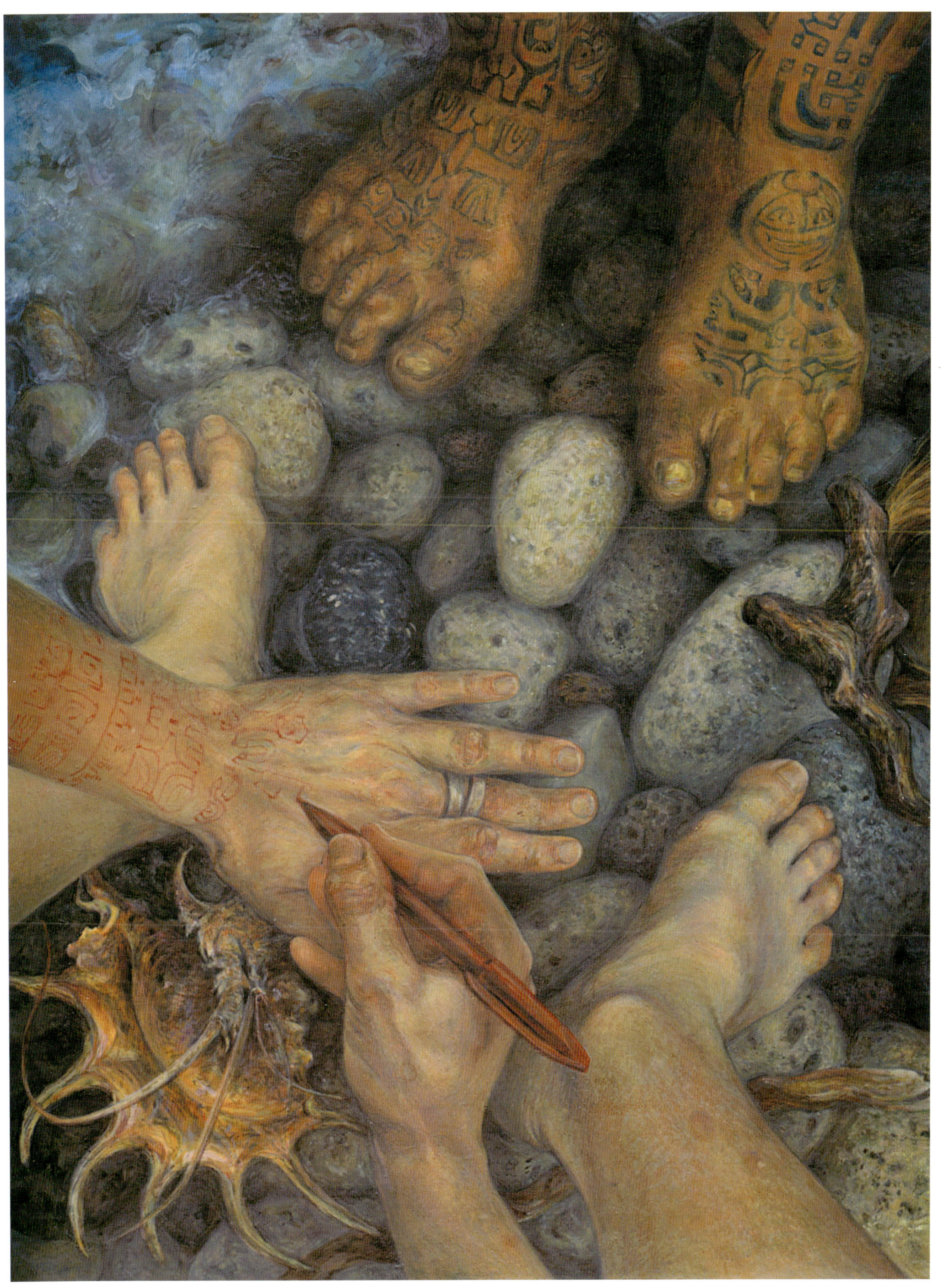

Elio Guevara **192**
100 Independence Way
Roswell, GA 30075
404-358-2037
calvorota@hotmail.com

James Gurney **108**
P.O. Box 693
Rhinebeck, NY 12572
845-876-7746
jgurneyart@yahoo.com

John Steven Gurney **51**
710 Western Ave.
Brattleboro, VT 05301
802-258-2654
jsgurney@adelphia.net

Scott Gustafson **52, 150**
4045 N Kostner
Chicago, IL 60641
773-725-8338
scott@scottgustafson.com

James Hakola **88**
P.O. Box 171
Los Alamitos, CA 90720
562-429-1009
james@mrdandy.com

Phil Hale **73, 118**
93 Mayola Rd.
London E5 0RF U.K.

August Hall **176, 177**
c/o Allen Spiegel Fine Arts
221 Lobos Ave.
Pacific Grove, CA 93950
831-372-4672
asfa@redshift.com

John Harris **43**
c/o Alan Lynch
116 Kelvin Pl.
Ithaca, NY 14850
607-257-0330
alartists@aol.com

Naoto Hattori **192**
naoto@wwwcomcom.com
www.wwwcomcom.com

Beric Henderson **200**
13 Russell Street Riverwood
Sydney, NSW 2210 Australia
beric_henderson@wmi.usyd.edu.au
www.berichenderson.com

Dan L. Henderson **202**
197 Chelsea Dr.
Decatur, GA 30030
hendall@mindspring.com
www.mindspring.com/~hendall

Ilich Henriquez **172**
Jahnstrasse 8
91099 Poxdorf, Germany
ilich.henriquez@web.de
www.ilich-digitalart.com

Richard Hescox **187**
P.O. Box 338
Hobart, WA 98025
triffid@comcast.net
www.richardhescox.com

Stephen Hickman **185**
10 Elm St.
Red Hook, NY 12571
845-758-3930
www.stephenhickman.com

David Ho **111, 190**
3586 Dickenson Common
Fremont, CA 94538
510-656-2468
ho@davidho.com

Seung Ho Henrik Holmberg **178**
Röskärsvägen 22
383 92 Mönsterås, Sweden
henrik.holmberg@spray.se
www.henrik.cgcommunity.com

Chris Hopkins **135**
425-347-5613
www.chrishopkinsart.com

Greg Horn **16, 106, 195**
P.O. Box 540-578
Greenacres, FL 33454-0578
561-967-5765
greghornart@yahoo.com

Brian Horton **74, 82, 107**
104 Sandcastle
Aliso Viejo, CA 92656
949-362-3170
bri_sue@cox.net

John Howe **186**
c/o Alan Lynch
116 Kelvin Pl.
Ithaca, NY 14850
607-257-0330
alartists@aol.com

David Hudnut **144**
1614 North Serrano Ave.
Los Angeles, CA 90027
david@hudnutart.com
www.hudnutart.com

Frazer Irving **74**
201 Balfour Rd.
Ilford, Essex 1G1 4HU U.K.
+44 208-478-8774
art@frazerirving.com

Jeremy Jarvis **120**
437 Moss Trail
Goodlettsville, TN 37072
info@jeremyjarvis.com
www.jeremyjarvis.com

Bruce Jensen **48**
3939 47th St.
Sunnyside, NY 11104
718-937-1887
bruce@brucejensen.com

Rob Johnson **171**
15515 184th Place NE
Wopdinville, WA 98072
silverbackrob@msn.com
www.silverbackworks.com

Stephen Johnson **100**

Katherine Jones **102**
7 (IFI) Murieston Crescent
Edinburgh, Scotland EH11 2LG
+44 (0)131-3133757
katyjonesillustrator@btopenworld.com

Alejandra Jorquera **88, 89**
Jujuy 1460
San Justo, Buenos Aires 1754
Argentina
54-011-44612070
hernanyale@sion.com

Eric Joyner **cover, 130, 131**
111 New Montgomery St. #402
San Francisco, CA 94105
415-305-3992
eric@ericjoyner.com

Michael Wm. Kaluta **81**
312 W 92nd St. #5A
New York, NY 10025
212-873-7573
rotvang@earthlink.net

Rainer Kalwitz **16, 18**
Ernst-Reuter-Str. 18
Recklinghausen, Germany 45665
+49 (0) 170-5921812
kalwitz@hotmail.com

Montgomery S. Kane **201**
P.O. Box 82654
Pittsburgh, PA 15218
m@montgomerystevenskane.com
www.montgomerystevenskane.com

Steven Kenny **171, 198**
130 Fodderstack Rd.
Washington, VA 22747
540-675-2355
www.stevenkenny.com

Tom Kidd [Gnemo] **42, 56**
59 Cross Brook Rd.
New Milford, CT 06776
860-355-1781
tkidd@snet.net

Douglas Klauba **100**
9741 S. Hamlin Ave.
Evergreen Park, IL 60805
708-229-2507
www.douglasklauba.com

Lori Koefoed **104**
913 Old Topanga Canyon
Topanga, CA 90290
310-455-2220
www.lorikoefoed.com

Viktor Koen **191**
310 E 23rd St. #10A
New York, NY 10010
212-254-3159
www.viktorkoen.com

Cos Koniotis **70**
102 Hewitt Rd.
London N8 0BN U.K.
07932-964-460
info@coskoniotis.com

Joe Kovach **165**
6733 Lower Brook Way
New Albany, OH 43054
800-355-1647
www.joekovach.com

Thomas S. Kuebler **84, 85, 92**
tskuebler@earthlink.net
www.tskuebler.com

Anita Kunz **156, 157**
218 Ontario St.
Toronto, ONT M5A 2V5 Canada
416-364-3846
akunz@anitakunz.com

Jean-Marc Laroche **94**
16, rue Alexandre Dumas
78160 Marly le Roi, France
33-1-39-16-16-58
www.jmlaroche.com

Richard Laurent **138**
531 S Plymouth Ct. #205
Chicago, IL 60605
312-939-7130
richard@ameritech.net

Fabrice Lavollay **156**
rue d'Ecosse, 92
1060 Brussels, Belgium
fabrice@fabricelavollay.com
www.fabricelavollay.com

Patricia Lewis **148**
38 Jenny Court
Stoney Creek, ONT L8G 4N8 Canada
905-662-7747
underhillstudio@cogeco.ca

Scott Lewis **202**
P.O. Box 480791
Kansas City, MO 64148
913-814-7581
www.lewisart.com

Gary A. Lippincott **95**
48 Bliss Hill Rd.
Royalston, MA 01368
978-249-9620
gary@garylippincott.com

Todd Lockwood **28, 38, 46, 47, 100**
20523 125th St. CT E
Bonney Lake, WA 98390
253-826-2265
todd.lockwood@comcast.net

Jerry Lofaro **23, 139**
58 Gulf Rd.
Henniker, NH 03242
603-428-6135
jerrylofaro@mcttelecom.com

Angela Giovanna Loroux **89**
2806 Valley View Dr.
Bath, PA 18014
610-837-0224
www.lorouxgallery.com

Travis Louie **178**
18 Echo Valley Rd.
Red Hook, NY 12571
845-758-9460
www.travislouie.artroof.com

David Cheng Lu **91**
c/o Monte Moore
5360 N Franklin St
Denver, CO 80216
303-294-0146
mavmktg@qadas.com

Howard Lyon **102**
3134 E McKellips #87
Mesa, AZ 85213
480-330-7728
me@howardlyon.com

Don Maitz **201**
5824 Bee Ridge Rd., MB #106
Sarasota, FL 34233
donmaitz@paravia.com
www.home.paravia.com/DonMaitz/

Gregory Manchess **66, 67**
15234 D SW Teal Blvd.
Beaverton, OR 97007
503-590-5447
503-590-6331 [fax]

Manchu **44**
6 Allee des Erables
Tours 37000 France
(33) 0247371603
philippe-bouchet7@wanadoo.fr

Robert E. Mankowski, Jr. **162**
397 Foxwood Rd.
Union, NJ 07083
908-358-4315

Maurizio Manzieri **105**
C.so Orbassano 191/28
Torino, 10137 Italy
studio@manzieri.com
www.manzieri.com

Stephan Martiniere **40, 41, 72, 104**
596 Morgan Ranch Dr.
Grass Valley, CA 95945
530-271-0904
martiniere@neteze.com

Jonathan Matthews **86, 95**
63 E. Selby Blvd.
Worthington, OH 43085
614-430-3486
jonlmatthews@columbus.rr.com

David Mattingly **33**
1112 Bloomfield St.
Hoboken, NJ 07030
201-659-7404
www.davidmattingly.com

Aaron McBride **183**
2420 Steiner St. #11
San Francisco, CA 94115
xexahylus@yahoo.com
www.sagania.com

Chris McGrath **42**
3526 Wayne Ave.
Bronx, NY 10467
chrismcgrath@mac.com

Petar Meseldzija **168, 169**
Kogerwatering 49
1541 XB Koog aan de Zaan
The Netherlands
petarmeseldzija@planet.nl
www.petarmeseldzijaart.com

Edward Miller c/o Les Edwards **60**
63 Mayfair Ave.
Ilford, Essex 1G1 3DQ UK
les.edwards7@btopenworld.com
www.lesedwards.com

Kurt Miller **30**
3503 Keene Ave.
Baltimore, MD 21214
410-319-9509
kurtj.miller@verizon.net

René Milot **14, 148**
49 Thorncliffe Park Dr. #1604
Toronto, ONT M4H 1J6 Canada
416-425-7726
renemilot@rogers.com

Christopher Moeller **79, 144**
210 Parkside Ave.
Pittsburgh, PA 15228
412-531-3629
moellerc@adelphia.net

Chris Moore **33**
Black Moss Barn, Black Moss Rd.
Blacko, Nelson, Lancashire BB9 6LE UK
044 (0) 1282 611555
chrismoore@illust.demon.co.uk

Larry Moore **35**
2440 Roxbury Rd.
Winter Park, FL 32789
407-222-8585

Robin Muller **66**
46 Wolfrey Ave.
Toronto, ONT M4K 1K8 Canada
416-461-1508
robinlmuller@hotmail.com

Duane O. Myers **53**
304 Cardinal Rd.
Lititz, PA 17543
717-626-5986
dmyersinc@dejazzd.com

Socar Myles **191**
rats@gorblimey.com
www.gorblimey.com

Vince Natale **50, 179**
36 John St.
West Hurley, NY 12491
845-679-0354
vnatale@hvc.rr.com

Mark A. Nelson **188, 197**
3738 Coachman Way
Cross Plains, WI 53528
608-798-3783
mnelson@ravensoft.com

Greg Newbold **47**
3724 S 2700 E
Salt Lake City, UT 84109
801-274-2407
www.gregnewbold.com

Huey Nguyen **158**
718 Marlin Ave. #1
Foster City, CA 94404
650-372-0491
superg42@hotmail.com

Terese Nielsen **43, 147**
9661 Las Tunas Dr. Suite C
Temple City, CA 91780
626-286-5200
hiddenkingdom@earthlink.net

Eric Nocella **89**
551 Observer Highway
Hoboken, NJ 07030
201-892-0981
goldmane2003@hotmail.com

Lawrence Northey **96**
145 Tyee Drive #197
Point Roberts, WA 98281
www.robotart.net

William O'Connor **61**
2072 Frand St.
Scotchplains, NJ 07076
908-322-3299
woc@earthlink.net

Oddworld Inhabitants **126**
869 Monterey St.
San Luis Obispo, CA 93401
805-503-3000

Rafal Olbinski **21, 22, 152**
142 E 35 St.
New York, NY 10016
212-532-4328
rafal.olbinski@mindspring.com

Sean Olmos **89**
P.O. Box 937
Cameria, CA 93428
805-909-1164
opifex10@hotmail.com

Kip Omolade **158**
284 Eastern Parkway #2L
Brooklyn, NY 11225
718-789-7790
kipomolade@yahoo.com

INDEX

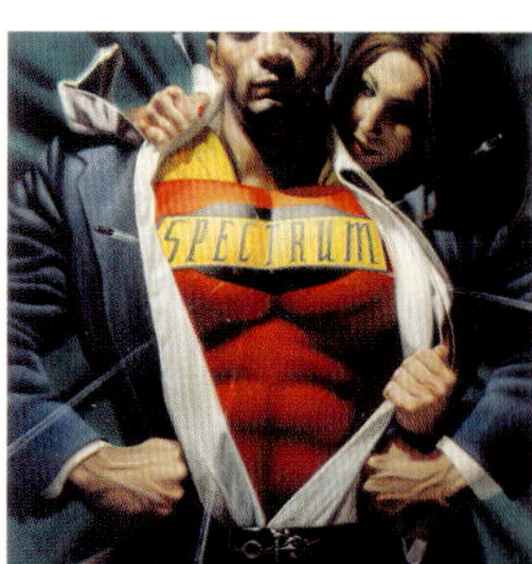

Artists, art directors, and publishers interested in receiving information for the SPECTRUM 12 competition should send their name and address to:

Spectrum Design, P.O. Box 4422, Overland Park, KS 66204

Or visit our website for information:
www.spectrumfantasticart.com

Call For Entries posters are mailed out every October.